Pro .NET 2.0 Windows Forms and Custom Controls in C#

Matthew MacDonald

Apress®

Pro .NET 2.0 Windows Forms and Custom Controls in C#

Copyright © 2006 by Matthew MacDonald

ISBN-13 (pbk): 978-1-59059-439-1
ISBN-13 (pbk): 1-59059-439-8

Printed and bound in the United States of America 9 8 7 6 5 4 3 2

Lead Editor: Dominic Shakeshaft
Technical Reviewer: Christophe Nasarre
Editorial Board: Steve Anglin, Dan Appleman, Ewan Buckingham, Gary Cornell, Tony Davis, Jason Gilmore, Jonathan Hassell, Chris Mills, Dominic Shakeshaft, Jim Sumser
Associate Publisher: Grace Wong
Project Manager: Beckie Brand
Copy Edit Manager: Nicole LeClerc
Copy Editor: Candace English
Assistant Production Director: Kari Brooks-Copony
Production Editor: Janet Vail
Compositor: Susan Glinert
Proofreader: Nancy Sixsmith
Indexer: Michael Brinkman
Artist: Kinetic Publishing Services, LLC
Interior Designer: Van Winkle Design Group
Cover Designer: Kurt Krames
Manufacturing Director: Tom Debolski

Distributed to the book trade worldwide by Springer-Verlag New York, Inc., 233 Spring Street, 6th Floor, New York, NY 10013. Phone 1-800-SPRINGER, fax 201-348-4505, e-mail orders-ny@springer-sbm.com, or visit http://www.springeronline.com.

For information on translations, please contact Apress directly at 2560 Ninth Street, Suite 219, Berkeley, CA 94710. Phone 510-549-5930, fax 510-549-5939, e-mail info@apress.com, or visit http://www.apress.com.

The information in this book is distributed on an "as is" basis, without warranty. Although every precaution has been taken in the preparation of this work, neither the author(s) nor Apress shall have any liability to any person or entity with respect to any loss or damage caused or alleged to be caused directly or indirectly by the information contained in this work.

The source code for this book is available to readers at http://www.apress.com in the Source Code section.

For Nora and Paul

Contents at a Glance

PART 1 ▪▪▪ Windows Forms Fundamentals

PART 2 ▪▪▪ Custom Controls

PART 3 ▪▪▪ Modern Controls

PART 4 ■■■ Windows Forms Techniques

PART 5 ■■■ Advanced Custom Controls

Contents

PART 1 ▄▄▄ Windows Forms Fundamentals

PART 2 ■■■ Custom Controls

PART 3 ■■■ Modern Controls

PART 4 ■■■ Windows Forms Techniques

PART 5 ■■■ Advanced Custom Controls

Foreword

The late 1990s brought us the revolution of the Internet. After 15 years of moving from a server-based model of computing to a client/server-based model, the pendulum swung back heavily toward the server with the rapid growth of Web pages, HTML, and server-based applications.

There was much to like about Web applications. Designers liked them because they had lots of great ways to apply nice-looking style sheets and layouts. Companies liked them because they did away with all the expensive and risky aspects of deploying client applications. All that had to be done was to install the application on a Web server, and you were done. No risk of breaking other applications or need to physically install the software on every machine in the organization. And for document viewing, HTML was a relatively easy language to learn, so it allowed many people to do some manner of software development with no prior skills.

But not everything was perfect. Large-scale Web applications were difficult to write and manage. There were differences between browsers. There weren't very good tools for debugging and developments. The applications weren't taking advantage of all the power on the client machines—hard drives, video cards, and CPUs. And most importantly, the user interfaces generally were well-suited only to the most basic data entry. If you needed real-time display or advanced visualization, things got very difficult.

In early 2002, Windows Forms was released as part of the Microsoft .NET Framework, Version 1.0. This changed the landscape in two fundamental ways. First, it gave programmers a consistent, approachable API and toolset with which to build very sophisticated applications for Microsoft Windows without having to know the Win32 SDK forward and backward. And second, the .NET Framework and Common Language Runtime (CLR) allowed client applications to be deployed via a Web server. Once you got the .NET Framework installed on the client machines you could have true zero-cost or "no-touch" deployment.

In conjunction with this, organizations were beginning to recognize the aforementioned shortcomings of Web applications in certain scenarios, and started to once again deploy client applications.

With the release of Version 2.0 of the Microsoft .NET Framework, even more client momentum is building. Windows Forms now allows developers to build applications with the look and feel of not only Windows itself, but of Microsoft Office as well. And then they can deploy those applications using a much-improved deployment technology called ClickOnce that is integrated directly into the Microsoft Visual Studio 2005 design experience. Gone are the days when organizations had to default to writing Web applications. Now they can choose the technology that is appropriate for the task at hand, which means they can implement their vision without compromising the user experience. Version 1.0 of Windows Forms and the .NET Framework were a good start, but Version 2.0 takes smart client development to the next level!

Matthew MacDonald understands this and has built a great resource for developers using Windows Forms to create great, rich applications. Whether the goal is to write components for internal use or a full application, this book will help you get there and deliver great results. Welcome back to the client.

Before Windows Forms, there were application developers and there were control developers. Even with Visual Basic, controls were usually authored in another language like Visual C++ and required a specific set of skills. However, with an object-oriented framework like Windows Forms, customizing control behavior is done with the same techniques as other application development, which gives developers a powerful new tool to really make their client applications deliver a great user experience that just can't be matched anywhere else. *Pro .NET 2.0 Windows Forms and Custom Controls in C#* does an excellent job of highlighting those possibilities and equipping developers with the techniques to make them a reality. Whether it's creating an owner-drawn TreeView, using the new layout features to build dynamic interfaces, or creating skinned custom controls, this book shows you how.

The practical, task-based approach of *Pro .NET 2.0 Windows Forms and Custom Controls in C#* allows it to cover a wide range of Windows Forms topics, but still provide the technical depth to help developers deliver features. While many other resources read more like technical reference docs, *Pro .NET 2.0 Windows Forms and Custom Controls* does an excellent job of filtering the information down to what developers really need to harness the power and innovations of Windows Forms 2.0 to deliver truly world-class client applications.

Shawn Burke
Development Manager, Windows Forms Team
Microsoft Corporation

About the Author

MATTHEW MACDONALD is an author, educator, and MCSD developer. He's a regular contributor to programming journals, and the author of more than a dozen books about .NET programming, including *User Interfaces in C#: Windows Forms and Custom Controls* (Apress), *Pro ASP.NET 2.0* (Apress), and *Microsoft .NET Distributed Applications* (Microsoft Press). In a dimly remembered past life, he studied English literature and theoretical physics.

About the Technical Reviewer

 **CHRISTOPHE NASARRE** is a development architect for Business Objects, a company which develops desktop and Web-based business intelligence solutions. During his spare time, Christophe writes articles for *MSDN Magazine*, *MSDN/Longhorn*, and *ASPToday*, and he has reviewed books on Win32, COM, MFC, and .NET since 1996.

Acknowledgments

No author can complete a book without a small army of helpful individuals. I'm deeply indebted to the whole Apress team, including Grace Wong, Beckie Stones, and Janet Vail, who helped everything move swiftly and smoothly; Candace English, who performed the copy edit; and many other individuals who worked behind the scenes indexing pages, drawing figures, and proofreading the final copy.

I owe a special thanks to Gary Cornell, who always offers invaluable advice about projects and the publishing world.

I owe a sincere thanks to Christophe Nasarre, who provided unfailingly excellent and insightful tech-review comments—they've helped me to fill gaps and improve the overall quality of this book. I've worked with many technical reviewers, and Christophe is clearly one of the best. Just as useful were the readers who took time out to report problems and ask good questions about the first edition of this book.

This book was written with close support from the Microsoft Windows Forms team, who took time out to review individual chapters and answer many emails filled with obscure questions. Although I didn't always know where the answers were coming from, I can safely say that I owe thanks to Shawn Burke, Mike Harsh, Jessica Fosler, Joe Stegman, Miguel Lacouture-Amaya, Jeff Chrisope, Mark Boulter, Scott Berry, Mike Henderlight, Raghavendra Prabhu, Simon Muzio, Mark Rideout, and many others for their replies and tech-review comments. I'm especially indebted to Erick Ellis, who fielded all my questions and followed up to make sure I had timely information and review comments. It was a great experience to write this book with their feedback.

Finally, I'd never write *any* book without the support of my wife and these special individuals: Nora, Razia, Paul, and Hamid. Thanks, everyone!

Matthew MacDonald

Introduction

Four years after the .NET Framework first hit the programming scene, smart client applications still refuse to die.

This is significant because when .NET first appeared, all too many people assumed it was about to usher in a new world of Web-only programming. In fact, for a short time Microsoft's own Web site described the .NET Framework in a single sentence as a "platform for building Web services and Web applications"—ignoring the Windows technology that made the company famous.

Now that the dust has settled, it's clear that Web and Windows applications aren't locked in the final rounds of a life-or-death battle. Instead, both technologies are flourishing. And not only are both technologies gaining strength, but they're also stealing some of each other's best features. For example, the latest release of .NET gives Web developers rich controls like menus and trees that were previously the exclusive domain of Windows coders (or Web-heads who weren't afraid to write a mess of hardcore client-side JavaScript). On the other hand, Windows applications are gaining easy Web-based deployment, more-flexible layout options, and the ability to display HTML. All of these innovations point to many productive years ahead for Web and Windows developers alike.

If you've picked up this book, you've already decided to learn more about programming Windows smart clients with .NET. Although both Web and Windows applications have their strengths and weaknesses, only Windows applications allow you to break out of the confines of the browser and take full advantage of the client computer. With Windows Forms, you can play sound and video, display dynamic graphics, react to the user's actions instantaneously, and build sophisticated windowed interfaces.

In this book, you'll learn how to use all of these techniques to design state-of-the-art application interfaces. Best of all, you won't just learn how to use the existing controls of the .NET Framework—you'll also learn everything you need to extend, enhance, and customize them.

About This Book

This book focuses relentlessly on *Windows Forms*, the .NET toolkit for building modern Windows interfaces.

In this book you'll learn about several sides of user interface programming. Some of the key themes include the following:

- **Dissecting the .NET controls.** Although this book is not a reference, it contains an exhaustive tour of just about every .NET user interface element you'll ever want to use.

- **Best practices and design tips.** As a developer, you need to know more than how to add a control to a window. You also need to know how to create an entire user interface framework that's scalable, flexible, and reusable.

- **How to enhance .NET controls and build your own.** In this book, you'll learn key techniques to extend existing controls and create your own from scratch. You'll even learn how to draw controls from scratch with GDI+, the remarkable .NET drawing framework.

- **How to design elegant user interfaces for the average user.** This subject isn't the focus of the book, but you'll get a great overview from Appendix A. You'll also learn more from tips and notes throughout the book.

- **Advanced user interface techniques.** Features are neat, but how do you use them? In this book you'll see practical examples of common techniques like document-view architecture, validation, and hit testing. You'll also learn how to dynamically generate forms from a database, unshackle data binding, and build an integrated help system.

Of course, it's just as important to point out what this book *doesn't* contain. You won't find the following subjects in this book:

- **A description of core .NET concepts.** These key concepts, like namespaces, assemblies, exception handling, and metadata, are explained in countless books, including a number of excellent C# and VB .NET titles from Apress.

- **A primer on object-oriented design.** No .NET programmer can progress very far without a solid understanding of classes, interfaces, and other .NET types. In this book, many examples rely on these basics, using objects to encapsulate, organize, and transfer information.

- **A reference for Visual Studio 2005.** The new integrated design environment provides powerful customization, automation, and productivity features that deserve a book of their own. Though this book assumes you're using Visual Studio, and occasionally points out an often-overlooked feature, it assumes that you already know your way around the development environment.

You'll get the most out of this book if you've already read another, more general .NET book. If you haven't learned the .NET fundamentals yet, you'll still be able to work through this book, but you'll need to travel at a slower pace and you may need to refer to the MSDN Help files to clear up issues you'll encounter along the way.

▪Note This book is targeted at experienced developers who want to get the most out of .NET. If you have never programmed with a language like Visual Basic, C++/C#, or Java before, this isn't the place to start. Instead, start with an introductory book on object-oriented design or programming fundamentals. On the other hand, if you already have some experience with .NET 1.0 or 1.1, welcome—you'll find yourself right at home!

Chapter Overview

The following overview describes what each chapter covers. If you already have some experience with Windows Forms, feel free to skip from chapter to chapter. If you're relatively new to Windows Forms development, it's probably best to read through the book to make sure you learn the basics before tackling more-advanced topics.

Part 1: Windows Forms Fundamentals

In this part you'll consider the core topics you need to understand to design smart clients. In Chapter 1 you'll start out by exploring the class model that underpins Windows Forms user interfaces. In Chapters 2 and 3 you'll explore the fundamental Control and Form classes. Chapter 4 describes the most common Windows controls. Chapter 5 shows how you can embed images and other binary resources into your compiled applications. Chapter 6 considers trees and lists, a hallmark of modern Windows applications. Finally, Chapters 7 and 8 consider two impressive higher-level features that are built into the Windows Forms model—GDI+ (for hand-drawing controls) and data binding (for displaying and updating data without writing tedious code).

Part 2: Custom Controls

In this part, you'll tackle one of the most important areas of Windows Forms design—creating customized controls that add new features, use fine-tuned graphics, and encompass low-level details with higher-level object models. In Chapter 9 you'll learn about the basic types of custom controls you can create and see how to set up a custom control project. You'll then continue to create user controls, which combine other controls into reusable groups (Chapter 10); derived controls, which enhance existing .NET control classes (Chapter 11); and owner-drawn controls, which use GDI+ to render UI from scratch (Chapter 12). Chapter 13 shows how you can add design-time support so your custom controls behave properly at design time.

Part 3: Modern Controls

In this part, you'll branch out to some of the most powerful Windows Forms controls. In Chapter 14, you'll explore the new ToolStrip, which provides a thoroughly customizable and flexible model for toolbars, menus, and status bars. In Chapter 15 you'll consider the DataGridView—an all-in-one grid control for displaying data. In Chapter 16 you'll look at the still woefully weak support for sound and video in the .NET Framework, and learn how to improve the picture with interop. Finally, in Chapter 17 you'll learn how the WebBrowser lets you show HTML pages in a Windows application, and you'll learn some remarkable tricks for integrating the two (with Windows code that manipulates the page and JavaScript Web code that triggers actions in your application).

Part 4: Windows Forms Techniques

In this part, you'll considerable indispensable techniques for serious Windows Forms programmers. In Chapter 18 you'll consider a host of approaches to validation, from masked edit controls to custom validation components that mimic ASP.NET, and perform their work automatically. Chapter 19 tackles MDI and SDI interfaces and shows you how to build a document-view framework. Chapter 20 explores the world of multithreading, and provides practical advice on how to write safe, performance-asynchronous code in a Windows application. Chapter 21 shows how you can build a new breed of Windows application with the highly adaptable, Web-like layout engines. Chapter 22 considers how you can build Help and integrate it into your application.

Part 5: Advanced Custom Controls

The final part considers some advanced topics that illustrate interesting subjects and help you extend your expertise. In Chapter 23 you'll see how to build slick applications with shaped forms, skinned controls, and custom buttons. In Chapter 24 you'll see a complete vector-drawing application that contrasts custom controls against a more powerful drawing model. Chapter 25 considers how you can extend existing controls with custom extender providers, and Chapter 26 picks up where Chapter 13 left off, by exploring more features and frills of design-time support for custom controls.

Appendixes

In the appendixes, you'll take a look at principles for user interface design in any language (Appendix A) and the new ClickOnce deployment technology (Appendix B).

Moving from .NET 1.x to .NET 2.0

If you've programmed with .NET 1.x, you'll find that a great deal remains the same in .NET 2.0. The underlying model for creating Windows Forms applications and custom controls remains unchanged. However, there are some significant new feature areas.

For the most part, this book doesn't emphasize the difference between features that have existed since .NET 1.x and those that are new in .NET 2.0, chiefly because some significant features and programming techniques have remained the same since .NET 1.0, but are still misunderstood by many developers. However, if you have extensive .NET 1.x programming experience, you may want to begin by exploring some of the feature areas that have changed the most.

The following list of the 14 most important changes points you to the right chapters:

1. **The SplitContainer control (Chapter 3).** Finally, there's an easier way to design complex windows with multiple split panes. It's a small addition, but it's a major convenience.

2. **AutoComplete (Chapter 4).** You see it in lists and text boxes throughout the Windows world. Now there's an easy way to get AutoComplete behavior without coding it by hand.

3. **Design-time support for resources (Chapter 5).** Deploying image files with your application is too fragile. But in the past, the alternative (embedding them in an assembly) has been awkward. Visual Studio 2005 solves the problem with new features for embedding and managing resources.

4. **Visual styles (Chapter 7).** Not only does .NET 2.0 make it easy to take advantage of Windows XP visual styles (for all controls), it also includes a new set of classes that lets you paint custom controls using the Windows XP theming API.

5. **Automatic data binding (Chapter 8).** Some love it; some hate it. Either way, you'll need to understand quite a bit about the new support for code-free data binding if you want to have any chance of creating a practical, scalable application.

6. **The ToolStrip control (Chapter 14).** Microsoft solves the problems of the out-of-date menu, status bar, and toolbar in one step with a new model revolving around the ToolStrip class. Best of all, the ToolStrip is endlessly customizable.

7. **The DataGridView control (Chapter 15).** The underpowered and inflexible DataGrid of .NET 1.x fame is replaced with a completely new grid control. Highlights include a fine-grained style model and support for extremely large sets of data through virtualization.

8. **The SoundPlayer control (Chapter 16).** This new control gives basic WAV playback features, but it still comes up far short, with no support for more-modern standards like MP3 audio or video. (Chapter 16 also shows you how to get around these problems with the Quartz library.)

9. **The WebBrowser control (Chapter 17).** Finally, a clean, easy way to show a Web page in a window. Use it with local or remote data. Best of all, you have the ability to explore the DOM model of your page, and react to JavaScript events in your Windows code.

10. **Masked editing (Chapter 18).** A new MaskedEdit control gives you a text box with masked editing features. You can also use lower-level classes to integrate masked editing into any control.

11. **The BackgroundWorker component (Chapter 20).** Use this class to perform an asynchronous task without worrying about marshalling your code to the user-interface thread. (However, though the BackgroundWorker fits certain scenarios, you'll still need to take control of multithreading on your own for many tasks.)

12. **Dynamic interfaces (Chapter 21).** It just might be the most underreported yet most significant shift in Windows applications. The new layout managers allow you to build flowing, Web-like applications that lay out different modules in a variety of flexible ways. They also make it easier to deal with expanding and contracting text in localization scenarios.

13. **Smart tags (Chapter 26).** Smart tags provide a helpful panel through which you perform a variety of tasks with a control at design time. Why not build your own for custom controls?

14. **ClickOnce (Appendix B).** ClickOnce doesn't really change the existing .NET deployment model—instead, it adds a higher-level set of features you can use to easily support self-updating applications, particularly over the Web or an intranet.

This list doesn't include all the minor features and tune-ups you'll discover as you explore Windows Forms and read through this book.

What's Still Missing in .NET 2.0

Even though .NET 2.0 is more than a minor upgrade to .NET 1.x, there is still a host of features that longtime Windows developers may find lacking.

Here are some examples of what you still *won't* find:

- Window management, including tabbed and dockable windows

- Charting and other controls for data visualization

- A commanding architecture (so that multiple actions in a user interface trigger the same operation)

- Markup-based layout features

- Support for MS Help 2.0, the (unsupported) standard that's used for the Visual Studio help files

- A document-view framework for building applications

- More high-level controls (like an Outlook bar, task panes, a wizard framework, and so on)

Some of these features are easy to develop on your own, while others are extremely difficult to do properly. In all these cases, third-party components have already emerged to fill the gaps (with varying levels of success). However, it's unlikely that a native Framework solution will emerge for any of these features, because the focus in rich client development is shifting to the new Avalon framework, which is a part of the upcoming Windows Vista operating system.

■**Note** Some third-party-component developers that you might want to check out are www.dotnetmagic.com, www.divil.co.uk, and www.actiprosoftware.com.

Conventions Used in this Book

You know the drill. This book uses *italics* to emphasize new terms and concepts. Blocks of code use constant width formatting. Note and tip boxes are scattered throughout the book to identify special considerations and useful tricks you might want to use.

Code Samples

It's a good idea to download the most recent, up-to-date code samples. You'll need to do this to test most of the more-sophisticated code examples described in this book, because the less-important details are usually left out. Instead, this book focuses on the most important sections so that you don't need to wade through needless extra pages to understand an important concept. To download the source code, navigate to www.prosetech.com. The source code for this book is also available to readers at http://www.apress.com in the Source Code section. On the Apress Web site, you can also check for errata and find related titles from Apress.

Variable Naming

Hungarian notation, which names variables according to their data type (like strFirstName instead of FirstName), was the preferred standard for C++ and Visual Basic 6. These days, Hungarian notation is showing its age. In the world of .NET, where memory management is handled automatically, it seems a little backward to refer to a variable by its data type, especially when the data type may change without any serious consequences, and the majority of variables are storing references to full-fledged objects. Microsoft now steers clear of variable prefixes, and recommends using simple names.

In this book, data-type prefixes aren't used for variables. The only significant exception is with control variables, where it is still a useful trick to distinguish between types of controls (like txtUserName and lstUserCountry), and with some data objects. Of course, when you create your own programs you're free to follow whatever variable naming convention you prefer, provided you make the effort to adopt complete consistency across all your projects (and ideally across all the projects in your organization).

■**Note** Microsoft provides detailed information about recommended coding and naming standards in the MSDN (see `http://msdn.microsoft.com/library/en-us/cpgenref/html/cpconNETFrameworkDesignGuidelines.asp`). If you plan to release a component for use by third-party developers, you'll need to read these documents carefully.

Feedback

This book has the ambitious goal of being the best tutorial and reference for programming Windows Forms. Toward that end, your comments and suggestions are extremely helpful. You can send complaints, adulation, and everything in between directly to `apress@prosetech.com`. I can't solve your .NET problems or critique your code, but I will benefit from information about what this book did right and wrong (and what it may have done in an utterly confusing way).

PART 1

Windows Forms Fundamentals

CHAPTER 1

■ ■ ■

User Interface Architecture

Some developers hate the headaches of user-interface programming. They assume it's all about painting icons, rewording text, and endlessly tweaking dialog boxes until an entire company agrees that an application looks attractive. However, developers who are involved in creating and maintaining sophisticated applications realize that there is another set of design considerations for user-interface programming. These are considerations about application architecture.

Every day, first-rate programming frameworks are used to build terrible applications. In Windows applications, developers often insert blocks of code wherever it's convenient, which is rarely where it makes most sense. To make the jump from this type of scattered user interface coding to a more elegant approach, you need to stop thinking in terms of windows and controls and start looking at a user interface as an entire interrelated framework.

In this chapter, you'll start on this journey by learning about a few key concepts that you'll return to throughout this book. They include the following:

- A quick review of how .NET defines types, including structures, classes, delegates, enumerations, and interfaces.

- How user interfaces are modeled with objects in a Windows Forms application. You'll learn about several key types of .NET classes, including controls, forms, components, and applications.

- Why inheritance is more important for user interfaces than for business logic. (The short answer is that it's the best way to customize almost any .NET control.)

- How Visual Studio generates the code for your user interface and how that code works.

- The best practices for building a well-encapsulated user interface that's easy to enhance, extend, and debug.

- What three-tier design promises, and why it's so hard to achieve.

The emphasis in this chapter is on general concepts. You'll see some code, but you won't learn about the intricate details like the properties and methods that each control provides. Instead, you'll explore these details as you travel deeper into user interface coding in the following chapters.

Classes and Objects

Today, it's generally accepted that the best way to design applications is by using discrete, reusable components called *objects*.

A typical .NET program is little more than a large collection of class definitions. When you start the program, your code creates the objects it needs using these classes. Of course, your code can also make use of the classes that are defined in other referenced assemblies and in the .NET class library (which is itself just a collection of assemblies with useful classes).

The Roles of Classes

It's important to remember that although all classes are created in more or less the same way in your code, they can serve different logical roles. Here are the three most common examples:

- **Classes can model real-world entities.** For example, many introductory books teach object-oriented programming using a Customer object or an Invoice object. These objects allow you to manipulate data, and they directly correspond to an actual *thing* in the real world.

- **Classes can serve as useful programming abstractions.** For example, you might use a Rectangle class to store width and height information, a FileBuffer class to represent a segment of binary information from a file, or a WinMessage class to hold information about a Windows message. These classes don't need to correspond to tangible objects; they are just a useful way to shuffle around related bits of information and functionality in your code. Arguably, this is the most common type of class.

- **Classes can collect related functions.** Some classes are just a collection of static methods that you can use without needing to create an object instance. These helper classes are the equivalent of a library of related functions, and might have names like GraphicsManipulator or FileManagement. In some cases, a helper class is just a sloppy way to organize code and represents a problem that should really be broken down into related objects. In other cases, it's a useful way to create a repository of simple routines that can be used in a variety of ways.

Understanding the different roles of classes is crucial to being able to master object-oriented development. When you create a class, you should decide how it fits into your grand development plan, and make sure that you aren't giving it more than one type of role. The more vague a class is, the more it resembles a traditional block of code from a non-object-oriented program.

Classes and Types

The discussion so far has reviewed object-oriented development using two words: classes and objects. *Classes* are the definitions, or object templates. *Objects* are classes in action. The basic principle of object-oriented design is that you can use any class to create as many objects as you need.

In the .NET world, there's another concept—*types*. Types is a catchall term that includes the following ingredients:

- Structures

- Classes

- Delegates

- Enumerations

- Interfaces

To get the most out of this book, you should already know the basics about .NET types and how they can be used. If you need to refresh your memory and get reacquainted with the .NET object family, browse through the following sections. Otherwise, you can skip ahead to the "User Interface Classes in .NET" section.

Structures

Structures are like classes, but are generally simpler and more lightweight. They tend to have only a few properties (and even fewer important methods). A more important distinction is that structures are *value types*, whereas classes are *reference types*. As a result, these two types of objects are allocated differently and have different lifetimes (structures must be released explicitly, while classes exist in memory until they're tracked down by the garbage collector).

Another side effect of the differences between the two is the fact that structures act differently in comparison and assignment operations. If you assign one structure variable to another, .NET copies the contents of the entire structure, not just the reference. Similarly, when you compare structures, you are comparing their contents, not the reference.

The following code snippet demonstrates how a structure works:

```
structureA = structureB; // structureA has a copy of the contents of structureB.
                         // There are two duplicate structures in memory.

if (structureA == structureB)
{
    // This is true as long as the structures have the same content.
    // This type of comparison can be slow if the structure is large.
}
```

Some of the structures in the class library include Int32, DateTime, and graphics ingredients like Point, Size, and Rectangle.

Classes

This is the most common type in the .NET class library. All .NET controls are full-fledged classes.

Note The word "class" is sometimes used interchangeably with "type" (or even "object") because classes are the central ingredients of any object-oriented framework like .NET. Many traditional programming constructs (like collections and arrays) are classes in .NET.

Unlike structures, classes are reference types. That means that when you manipulate an instance of a class in code, you are actually working with a reference that points to the full-fledged object, which exists somewhere else in memory. Usually, this low-level reality is completely hidden from you, but it does show up when you perform comparison or assignment operations.

The following code snippet shows how classes behave:

```
objectA = objectB;    // objectA and objectB now both point to the same thing.
                      // There is one object, and two ways to access it.

if (objectA == objectB)
{
    // This is true if both objectA and objectB point to the same thing.
    // This is false if they are separate, yet identical objects.
}
```

Occasionally, a class can override its default reference type behavior. For example, the String class is a full-featured class in every way, but it overrides equality and assignment operations to work like a value type. When dealing with text, this tends to be more useful (and more intuitive) for programmers. For example, if the String class acted like a reference type it would be harder to validate a password. You would need a special method to iterate through all the characters in the user-supplied text, and compare each one separately.

Arrays, on the other hand, are classes that behave like traditional classes. That means copy and comparison operations work on the reference, not the content of the array. If you want to perform a sophisticated comparison or copy operation on an array, you need to iterate through every item in the array and copy or compare it separately.

Delegates

Delegates define the signature of a method. For example, they might indicate that a function has a string return value, and accepts two integer parameters. Using a delegate, you can create a variable that points to specific method. You can then invoke the method through the delegate whenever you want.

Here's a sample delegate definition:

```
// A delegate definition specifies a method's parameters and return type.
public delegate string StringProcessFunction(string input);
```

Once you define a delegate, you can create a delegate variable based on this definition, and use it to hold a reference to a method. Here's the code that does exactly that:

```
StringProcessFunction stringProcessor;
// This variable can hold a reference to any method with the right signature.
// It can be a static method or an instance method. You can then invoke it later.

// Here we assume that the code contains a function named CapitalizeString.
stringProcessor = new StringProcessFunction(CapitalizeString);

// This invokes the CapitalizeString function.
string returnValue = stringProcessor("input text");
```

Besides being a way to implement type-safe function pointers, delegates are also the foundation of .NET's event handling. For every event that a .NET control provides, there is a corresponding delegate that defines the event signature (although this isn't a one-to-one relationship, as many events share the same delegate). If you want to handle the event, you need to create an event handler with the same signature.

In other words, when you use controls, you'll often use delegates. And when you create controls, you'll probably define your own custom delegate types. You'll see many examples of custom delegates in this book.

Enumerations

Enumerations are simple value types that allow developers to choose from a list of constants. Behind the scenes, an enumeration is just an ordinary integral number where every value has a special meaning as a constant. However, because you refer to enumeration values using their names, you don't need to worry about forgetting a hard-coded number, or using an invalid value.

To define an enumeration, you use the block structure shown here:

```
public enum FavoriteColors
{
    Red,
    Blue,
    Yellow,
    White
}
```

This example creates an enumeration named FavoriteColors with three possible values: Red, Blue, and Yellow.

Once you've defined an enumeration, you can assign and manipulate enumeration values like any other variable. When you assign a value to an enumeration, you use one of the predefined named constants. Here's how it works:

```
// You create an enumeration like an ordinary variable.
FavoriteColors buttonColor;

// You assign and inspect enumerations using a property-like syntax.
buttonColor = FavoriteColors.Red;
```

In some cases, you need to combine more than one value from an enumeration at once. To allow this, you need to decorate your enumeration with the Flags attribute, as shown here:

```
[Flags]
public enum AccessRights
{
    Read = 0x01,
    Write = 0x02,
    Shared = 0x04,
}
```

This allows code like this, which combines values using a bitwise or operator:

```
AccessRights rights = AccessRights.Read | AccessRights.Write | AccessRights.Shared;
```

You can test to see if a single value is present using bitwise arithmetic with the & operator to filter out what you're interested in:

```
if ((rights & AccessRights.Write) == AccessRights.Write)
{
    // Write is one of the values.
}
```

Enumerations are particularly important in user-interface programming, which often has specific constants and other information you need to use but shouldn't hard-code. For example, when you set the color, alignment, or border style of a button, you use a value from the appropriate enumeration.

Interfaces

Interfaces are contracts that define properties, methods, and events that a class must implement. Interfaces have two main uses:

- **Interfaces are useful in versioning situations.** That's because they allow you to enhance a component without breaking existing clients. You simply need to add a new interface.[1]

- **Interfaces allow polymorphism.** This means many different classes that use the same interface can be treated the same way. In a very real sense, an interface acts like a "control panel" that you can use to access a standardized set of features in a class.

With user-interface programming, the second consideration is the most interesting. For example, imagine you create your own button control with a unique stylized look. You want this control to have all the features of the standard .NET button, including the ability to be used as the default button in a window (the button that is activated when the user presses Enter). To give your button this capability, all you need to do is implement the IButtonControl interface in your custom button control code. Even though the .NET infrastructure doesn't know the specific details about how your control works, it knows enough about how to use an IButtonControl class to programmatically "click" your button when the user presses Enter.

■**Tip** If you haven't had much experience with object-oriented or interface-based programming, I encourage you to start with a book about .NET fundamentals. Two good starting points are *A Programmer's Introduction to C#* by Eric Gunnerson, or *C# and the .NET Platform* by Andrew Troelsen, both published by Apress. Classes and other types are the basic tools of the trade, and you need to become comfortable with them before you can start to weave them into full-fledged object models and Windows applications.

---

1. Technically speaking, you don't need to use interfaces for versioning in .NET (unlike previous component systems, such as COM). That's because .NET stores *metadata*—information about your types and their members—in your compiled code. This metadata allows the .NET runtime to make sure that classes are compatible, even after they've been updated. However, many object-oriented gurus still like defining interfaces to encourage proper design.

User Interface Classes in .NET

The first step when considering class design is to examine what rules are hard-wired into the .NET Framework. Your goal should be to understand how the assumptions and conventions of .NET shape user-interface programming. Once you understand the extent of these rules, you will have a better idea about where the rules begin and end and your object designs take over.

In the following sections, you'll take a look at a number of examples that show how classes plug into the Windows Forms architecture.

Controls Are Classes

In the .NET Framework, every control is a class. Windows controls are clustered in the System.Windows.Forms namespace. Web controls are divided into three core namespaces: System.Web.UI, System.Web.UI.HtmlControls, and System.Web.UI.WebControls. (Web controls use a superficially similar but substantively different model than Windows controls, and they won't be covered in this book.)

In your code, a control class acts the same as any other class. You can create an instance of it, set its properties, and use its methods. The difference is in the lineage. Every Windows control inherits from System.Windows.Forms.Control, and acquires some basic functionality that allows it to paint itself on a window. In fact, even the window that hosts the control inherits from the Control base class.

On its own, a control object doesn't do much. The magic happens when it interacts with the Windows Forms engine. The Windows Forms engine handles the Windows operating system messages that change focus or activate a window, and tells controls to paint themselves by calling their methods and setting their properties. The interesting thing is that although these tasks are performed automatically, they aren't really hidden from you. If you want, you can override methods and fiddle with the low-level details of the controls. You can even tell them to output entirely different content.

To use a control, all you need to do is create an instance of a control class, just like you would with any other object. For example, here's how you might create a text box:

```
System.Windows.Forms.TextBox txtUserName = new System.Windows.Forms.TextBox();
```

Once you create the control object, you can set its properties to configure how it behaves and what it looks like:

```
txtUserName.Name = "txtUserName";
txtUserName.Location = new System.Drawing.Point(64, 88);
txtUserName.Size = new System.Drawing.Size(200, 20);
txtUserName.TabIndex = 0;
txtUserName.Text = "Enter text here!";
```

This code positions the text box in a specific location, sets its size and its position in the tab order, and then fills in some basic text. But none of this actually creates a visible control in a window. So how does the .NET runtime know whether you are just creating a control object to use internally (perhaps to pass to another method) or if you want it to be painted on a specific form and able to receive input from the user? The answer is in *class relations*, as you'll see in the next section.

Controls Can Contain Other Controls

The System.Windows.Forms.Control class provides a property called Controls, which exposes a collection of child controls. For example, a Windows Form uses this Controls property to store the first level of contained controls that appear in the window. If you have other container controls on the form, like group boxes, they might also have their own child controls.

In other words, controls are linked together by containment using the Controls collection. Because every control is a class that derives from System.Windows.Forms.Control, every control supports the ability to contain other controls. The topmost object for an application is always a Form object, which represents the window you see on your screen.

■**Tip** To be technically accurate, this collection is actually an instance of the System.Windows.Forms. Control.ControlCollection class. This collection is customized to make sure that it can contain only controls, not other types of objects. However, you don't really need to know that to use the Controls collection, because it implements the IList, ICollection, and IEnumerable interfaces that allow you to treat it like any other collection class.

Figure 1-1 shows a sample form, and Figure 1-2 diagrams the relationship of the controls it contains.

Figure 1-1. *A sample form*

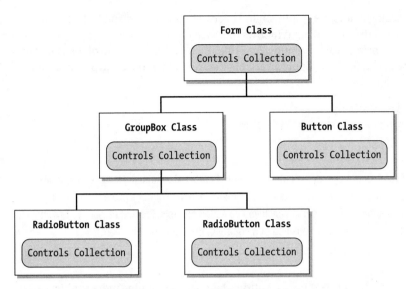

Figure 1-2. *Control containment for a sample form*

To place a control in a window, you just need to add it to the form's Controls collection. Like most collection classes, the Controls collection provides some standard methods like Add() and Remove().

For example, the following line of code takes the TextBox control object and places it inside a form. The text box immediately appears in the frmMain window:

```
frmMain.Controls.Add(txtUserName);
```

If you want the TextBox to be located inside a group box or panel, you would use this code instead:

```
// Add the panel to the form.
frmMain.Controls.Add(pnlUserInfo);

// Add the text box to the panel.
pnlUserInfo.Controls.Add(txtUserName);
```

The control's location property is automatically interpreted in terms of the parent control. For example, (0, 0) is the top-left corner of the container, and (100, 100) is 100 pixels from both the top and left edges. Chapter 2 talks about control size and positioning in more detail.

If you add a control to a form window that already exists, it appears immediately. If, however, the form hasn't been displayed yet, you need to use the form's Show() or ShowDialog() method to display the form:

```
frmMain.Show();
```

Forms automatically handle the responsibility of coordinating the display of all their contained controls using the underlying Windows message infrastructure.

A control can be removed from a window by using the Remove() method of the Controls collection. In this case, you need to supply a variable that references the control you want to remove, as shown here:

```
// Remove the textbox control.
frmMain.pnlUserInfo.Controls.Remove(txtUserName);
```

■**Note** You can remove a control by index number using the RemoveAt() method. However, the index number doesn't have any concrete meaning—it doesn't correspond to the control's place in the window, and it doesn't necessarily correspond to the order in which you've added controls. For that reason, you're unlikely to pay much attention to the index-number position of a control in the Controls collection.

All controls, whether they are text boxes, buttons, labels, or something more sophisticated, are added to (and removed from) container controls in the same way. In the next section you'll see how you can use this to your advantage by defining and displaying your custom controls.

Controls Can Extend Other Controls

In a popular book introducing the .NET Framework, Dan Appleman suggests that inheritance is an overhyped feature with a few specific uses, but a host of potential problems and considerations. In his words, inheritance is the "coolest feature you'll never use." Object-oriented gurus who have seen the havoc that can be caused by a poorly thought-out class hierarchy will be quick to agree. Though inheritance can be useful when creating your business and data objects, it's generally not the best approach, and it's never the only one.

In the world of controls, however, inheritance just might be the single most useful feature you'll ever find. Essentially, inheritance allows you to acquire a set of specific functionality *for free*. You don't need to worry about how to handle the messy infrastructure code for what you want to do. Instead, you simply inherit from a class in the .NET class library, add a few features that are specific to your needs, and throw it into your program.

This approach can be used to create customized controls quickly and easily. Following is the definition for a custom text box. It has all the powerful features of a text box, manages its appearance automatically, provides sophisticated user editing capability, and takes care of basic details like painting itself and managing focus. In addition, the custom text box adds two new features that make it more useful for dealing with mostly numeric data (like phone numbers). It has a property that returns the total number of numeric characters in the text string (NumberOfDigits), and a method that quickly trims out any non-numeric characters (TrimToDigits). To provide this functionality, it uses some standard .NET tricks to iterate through a string and the System.Text.StringBuilder class, which provides efficient string manipulation.

```
public class NumericTextBox : System.Windows.Forms.TextBox
{
    public int NumberOfDigits
    {
        get
        {
            int digits = 0;
            foreach (char c in Text)
            {
                if (Char.IsDigit(c)) digits++;
            }
            return digits;
        }
    }

    public void TrimToDigits()
    {
        StringBuilder newText = new StringBuilder();
        foreach (char c in Text)
        {
            if (Char.IsDigit(c)) newText.Append(c);
        }
        Text = newText.ToString();
    }
}
```

Arguably, this custom text box doesn't provide much more than the ordinary text box control. But the remarkable part of this example is the fact that you can use this class in exactly the same way that you use a control class from the .NET class library.

Here's the code you might use to display the custom text box in a window:

```
CustomControlProject.NumericTextBox txtCustom;
txtCustom = new CustomControlProject.NumericTextBox();
txtCustom.Name = "txtCustom";
txtCustom.Location = new System.Drawing.Point(64, 88);
txtCustom.Size = new System.Drawing.Size(200, 20);
txtCustom.TabIndex = 0;
txtCustom.Text = "Enter text in the custom textbox here!";
frmMain.Controls.Add(txtCustom);
```

The interesting part of this example is not what's in the code, but what is left out. Clearly, there are a lot of Windows-specific details that you don't need to worry about when using inheritance to create a custom control. Custom controls in .NET are painless and powerful.

■**Note** If you were really planning to create numeric text boxes, you'd have a host of more powerful options than the NumericTextBox control in this example. You can handle key presses to reject invalid characters, or you can use the new MaskedTextBox (see Chapter 18).

Throughout this book you'll see a variety of custom-control programming techniques, and you'll learn how to license, distribute, and manage custom controls in the development environment. Custom control examples appear throughout the book. You'll use them to do the following:

- Automate control validation

- Build in common usage patterns or helper routines

- Rigorously organize code

- Preinitialize complex controls

- Tailor controls to specific types of data, even replacing basic members with more-useful, higher-level events and properties

Creating custom controls is a key way of playing with Windows Forms, and one of the most important themes of this book.

Inheritance and the Form Class

Inheritance isn't just used when you want to extend an existing class with additional features. It's also used to organize code. One of the best examples is the System.Windows.Forms.Form class.

In a Windows application, you could create an instance of a System.Windows.Forms.Form and manually go about adding controls and attaching events. For example, the following code creates a new generic form and adds a single text box to it:

```
// Create the form.
System.Windows.Forms.Form frmGenericForm = new System.Windows.Forms.Form();

// Create and configure the text box.
System.Windows.Forms.TextBox txtUserName = new System.Windows.Forms.TextBox();
txtUserName.Name = "txtUserName";
txtUserName.Location = new System.Drawing.Point(64, 88);
txtUserName.Size = new System.Drawing.Size(200, 20);
txtUserName.TabIndex = 0;
txtUserName.Text = "Enter text here!";

// Add the text box to the form.
frmGenericForm.Controls.Add(txtUserName);

// Show the form.
frmGenericForm.Show();
```

The problem with this approach is that the code that creates the form also needs to go to all the work of configuring it. If you're not careful, you'll wind up mingling your user interface code with the rest of your application logic, causing endless headaches.

Visual Studio enforces a more structured approach. When you create a new form in, it automatically creates a customized class that inherits from the Form class. This derived class encapsulates all the logic for adding child controls, setting their properties, and responding to their events in one neat package. It also provides you with an easy way to create identical copies of a form, which is particularly useful in document-based applications.

The following is a simplified example of a custom form class that contains a simple constructor method. When the form class is instantiated, it automatically creates and configures a text box, and then adds the text box to its Controls collection.

```
public class MainForm : System.Windows.Forms.Form
{
    private System.Windows.Forms.TextBox txtUserName;

    public MainForm()
    {
        txtUserName = new System.Windows.Forms.TextBox();
        txtUserName.Name = "txtUserName";
        txtUserName.Location = new System.Drawing.Point(64, 88);
        txtUserName.Size = new System.Drawing.Size(200, 20);
        txtUserName.TabIndex = 0;
        txtUserName.Text = "Enter text here!";
        Controls.Add(txtUserName);
    }
}
```

The custom form class automatically gains all the features of a standard System.Windows. Forms.Form object, including the ability to display itself with the Show() and ShowDialog() methods. That means that you can quickly create and show your customized form using the two lines of code shown here:

```
// Create the form (at this point, its constructor code will run and add
// the textbox control).
MainForm frmCustomForm = new MainForm();

// Show the form.
frmCustomForm.Show();
```

■**Note** The Form.Show() method shows a form modelessly, which means it doesn't interrupt your code. Your code can continue to run more logic and show additional windows. The Form.ShowDialog() method shows a form modally, which means your code is put on hold and doesn't continue until the form is closed. You'll see how this plays a role in determining your application lifetime in the "Application Lifetime" section of this chapter.

Accessing Controls

Once a custom form object has been instantiated, there are two different ways to access the controls it contains: through the Controls collection or, more simply, using form-level member variables.

In the previous example, the only control MainForm contains (a text box) is referenced with the member variable txtUserName. This means you can easily access it in other methods in your custom form class using code like this:

```
txtUserName.Text = "John";
```

It's up to you whether you want to make a control variable accessible to other classes in your program. By default, all control variables in C# are private, so they aren't available to other classes. (In Visual Basic .NET projects, all controls are declared with the Friend keyword, and any other class can access them as long as it exists in the current project. This is similar to the way that previous versions of VB worked, and matches the accessibility of the internal keyword in C#.) Either way, the difference is minor. Generally, you should avoid breaking encapsulation by fiddling with the user interface of a form from another class. However, there is *always* one open back door. No matter what the language, you can access any control through the form's Controls collection, which is always public.

■Tip If you want to add a control but you don't want Visual Studio to create a member variable for it, set the GenerateMember property of the control to false. In addition, if you want to change the accessibility of a control to be something other than private, you can change the Modifiers property. Both of these properties are design-time properties that aren't a part of the Control class. Instead, they're added to the Properties window by Visual Studio and used to control the automatically generated code.

The member variables allow access to all the controls on a form. Assuming you've built your form in Visual Studio, each control will have its own member variable. On the other hand, only the first level of controls will appear in the Controls collection. Controls that are inside container controls like group boxes, tab controls, or panels will appear in the Controls collection of the control that contains them (as diagrammed in Figure 1-2).

Unfortunately, controls are indexed only by number in the Controls collection, not by name. That means that if you want to find a control using the Controls collection, you need to iterate through the entire collection and examine each control one by one until you find a match. You can look for a specific type of control or a specifically named control. For example, when a control is created in Visual Studio, the Name property is automatically set to match the name used for the member variable, as shown here:

```
txtUserName.Name = "txtUserName";
```

This is just a convenience—you are not forced to set the Name property. However, it allows you to easily look up the control by iterating through the Control collection:

```
// Search for and remove a control with a specific name.
foreach (Control ctrl in Controls)
{
    if (ctrl.Name == "txtUserName")
    {
        Controls.Remove(ctrl);
    }
}
```

Usually, you'll avoid the hassle of digging up your controls in the Control collection, and just rely on the member variables. But there are exceptions to this rule, such as when you are creating highly dynamic interfaces or generic code. For example, you might want to clear every text box on an input form by examining each control, checking if it's a text box, and then resetting the text property. Here's a simple method that handles this task:

```
private void ClearControls(Control topControl)
{
    // Ignore the control unless it is a textbox.
    if (topControl.GetType() == typeof(TextBox))
    {
        topControl.Text = "";
    }
    else
    {
        // Process controls recursively.
        // This is required if controls contain other controls
        // (for example, if you use panels, group boxes, or other
        // container controls).
        foreach (Control childControl in topControl.Controls)
        {
            ClearControls(childControl);
        }
    }
}
```

Now you can recursively search through all the controls on a form and clear all text boxes with a single line of code:

```
ClearControls(this);
```

Note The Controls collection is always accessible to other forms. However, you shouldn't use this as a back door to allow one form to modify another. For one thing, using a string to identify the name of a control is extremely fragile—if the original form is changed, the code may stop working, but it won't raise a helpful compile-time error.

Components

Controls aren't the only ingredient you can put on a form. There are also *components*, or "invisible controls." Unlike controls, components don't take up any piece of form real estate. Some components display something, but only in specific circumstances and not necessarily on the form itself. For example, .NET includes components that can show a help window, an error message, a system tray icon, or a standard dialog box when needed. Other components have no visual appearance at all, and just represent a unit of useful functionality. (Examples of this sort of component include Timer and SqlConnection.) However, components share one important feature with controls—they can be attached to a form and configured at design time.

For example, imagine you want to show an animation on your form by reacting to a timer every few milliseconds and refreshing the display. You could create the timer by hand, and write the code that initializes it, configures it, and attaches its event to the appropriate event handler. However, it's much asier to drag a Timer component onto a form at design time and tweak it to your heart's content using the Properties window.

Components have two key responsibilities:

- **They must support design-time use.** In technical terms, that means components can be *sited* on a design surface.

- **They must provide a way to release resources.** All components provide a Dispose() method that, when called, causes the component to release all its unmanaged resources immediately.

Programmers often assume that components are a special type of control, but the reality is the other way around—controls are actually a special type of component. In fact, the base Control class, which all forms derive from, itself derives from the Component class, as shown in Figure 1-3.

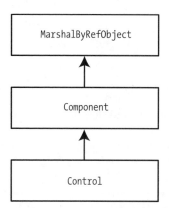

Figure 1-3. *Control and component inheritance*

Component classes are fairly straightforward. They simply need to implement the IComponent interface (from the System.ComponentModel namespace).

The IComponent interface is quite simple (if a little unintuitive):

```
public interface IComponent : IDisposable
{
    event EventHandler Disposed;
    ISite Site { get; set; }
}
```

Essentially, IComponent extends IDisposable (which forces objects to implement a Dispose() method that releases resources). On top of that, IComponent adds an event that fires when it's been disposed, and a Site property. The Site property binds the component to its container. This is the starting point that allows a container (like a form) to manage a collection of components.

Most components don't implement IComponent directly. Instead, they take a simpler shortcut, and derive from the System.ComponentModel.Component class, which provides a standard implementation of IComponent.

One awkward difference between controls and components is the way that they're tracked in a form. As you've already seen, the Form class includes a Controls collection that tracks every control on the form. Unfortunately, components don't use a similar model of containment. Instead, components are given the *option* of adding themselves to a private component container called components. The component container isn't a part of the basic Form class. However, Visual Studio automatically defines it and adds it to every form class you create.

The component container is intended only to help make sure components are cleaned up properly. It's not meant to help you keep track of what components a form uses. The general rule of thumb is that if a component holds on to unmanaged resources, it should add itself to the component container. This way, when the form is destroyed it can dispose of any components that need to be released. However, if a component doesn't use unmanaged resources and doesn't need any special cleanup, it probably won't add itself to the component container at all.

Note The component container is one of the messier workarounds in .NET. One problem is that because the component must add itself to the container, there's no way for you to tell just by looking at your form code whether or not a given component will be added. For a hands-on look at components, be sure to read Chapter 18, which develops a set of validation components and considers how you can track them in a form.

Interacting with a Control

In a typical Windows application, your code sits idly by, doing very little. When the user takes a certain action, like clicking a button, typing in text, or moving the mouse, your code springs into action. Usually, your code completes in a matter of seconds, and goes back to waiting for the next move from the user.

One interesting and often overlooked fact about .NET controls is that they provide two different ways that you can respond to user actions—you can create a custom class and override its methods, or you can react to events. These approaches are discussed in the next two sections.

Overriding Methods

In order to override a method, you need to create a custom inherited control. For example, imagine you have a text box that's designed for numeric entry, and you want to examine every key press to make sure that it corresponds to a number, and not a letter. To perform this type of task, you can create a customized text box, and override the OnKeyPress() method to add this extra verification logic.

```
public class NumericTextBox : System.Windows.Forms.TextBox
{
    protected override void OnKeyPress(KeyPressEventArgs e)
    {
        base.OnKeyPress(e);
        if (!char.IsControl(e.KeyChar) && !char.IsDigit(e.KeyChar))
        {
            e.Handled = true;
        }
    }
}
```

The OnKeyPress() method is invoked automatically by the Windows Forms engine when a key is pressed in a TextBox control. The overridden method in the preceding example checks to see if the entered character is a number. If it isn't, the Handled flag is set to true, which cancels all further processing, effectively making sure that the character will never end up in the text box.

Note When overriding a method, it's a good practice to call the base class implementation, which may have some required functionality. More commonly, the base class implementation simply raises the associated event (in this case, KeyPress), allowing other objects to handle it. You'll learn more about overriding methods when you build derived controls in Chapter 11.

This design pattern is useful if you use a number of controls with extremely similar behavior. It allows you to create a custom control that you can use whenever you need this set of features. If, on the other hand, you need to fine-tune behavior for distinct, even unique tasks, this approach is much less useful. For example, consider a button control. You could react to a button click by creating a special class for every button on your application, and giving each button its own overridden OnClick() method. Although your program would still work well, it would quickly become completely disorganized, swamped by layers of button classes that have little to do with one another. To circumvent this problem, .NET uses the view-mediator pattern, as described in the next section.

The View-Mediator Pattern

When you create a new form with Visual Studio, it generates a custom form class. It *doesn't* generate any other custom control classes. Instead, Visual Studio relies on events to manage the interaction between controls and your form. Each event you want to handle is added as a separate method in your form class.

In other words, every form acts as a giant switchboard for all the controls it contains. This type of design pattern, which is so natural to .NET and most Windows development that you might not have even noticed it, is called the *view-mediator* pattern. It dictates that one central class organizes each individual window.

Using events and the view-mediator pattern, you can rewrite the text box example you saw earlier. In this example, a form-level event handler reacts to the TextBox.KeyPress event. In this example, the event handler is hooked up using a delegate in the constructor for the form.

```
public class MainForm : System.Windows.Forms.Form
{
    System.Windows.Forms.TextBox txtUserName;

    public MainForm()
    {
        txtUserName = new System.Windows.Forms.TextBox();
        txtUserName.Name = "txtUserName";
        txtUserName.Location = new System.Drawing.Point(64, 88);
        txtUserName.Size = new System.Drawing.Size(200, 20);
        txtUserName.TabIndex = 1;
        txtUserName.Text = "Enter text here!";
        Controls.Add(txtUserName);

        // Connect the event handler using the KeyPressEventHandler delegate.
        txtUserName.KeyPress += new
          System.Windows.Forms.KeyPressEventHandler(this.txtUserName.KeyPress);
    }

    private void txtUserName_KeyPress(object sender,
     System.Windows.Forms.KeyPressEventArgs e)
    {
        if (!char.IsControl(e.KeyChar) && !char.IsDigit(e.KeyChar))
        {
            e.Handled = true;
        }
    }

}
```

Notice that the actual logic for processing the key press is identical, but the way it's integrated into the application is completely different. The form is now responsible for the validation, *not* the control itself. This is an ideal approach if the form needs to handle the complex validation of multiple different controls using the same event handler. It's a less suitable approach if you need to perform the same type of validation for the same control in different windows, because you'll probably need to copy the code into multiple form-level event handlers. Neither approach is automatically better than the other—it all depends on how complex your code is, and how you want to reuse it.

Smart Controls

So far you have seen two distinct ways to use controls from the .NET class library:

- Create an instance of a generic control class "as is." Then configure its properties.

- Define a new class that inherits from a generic control class, and customize this class for your needs. Then create an object based on this specialized class.

The difference is shown in Figure 1-4.

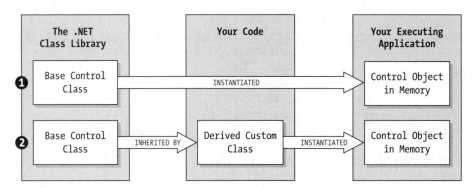

Figure 1-4. *Two ways to interact with controls*

Visual Studio uses inheritance (the first method) when you create forms. When you configure controls, however, it inserts them as is, and adds the appropriate logic for modifying their properties (the second method). This is the default approach in .NET, but it's not the only approach.

When Visual Studio adds controls and derives a custom form class, it's making a design decision for you. This decision helps clear out the clutter that would result from creating dozens of custom control classes. However, like all design decisions, it's not always right for all people and in all situations. For example, if you use numerous similar controls (like text boxes that refuse numeric input), you may find yourself duplicating the same code in event handlers all over your program. In this case, you might be better off to step beyond Visual Studio's default behavior, and create customized controls with some additional intelligence.

When you are creating a new application and planning how to program its user interface, one of the most important tasks is deciding where to draw the line between smart controls (custom control classes) and smart switchboards (custom forms with event-handling logic). A good decision can save a lot of repetitive work. As you'll see in this book, custom controls are not just for redistributing neat user interface elements, but also for building intelligence into parts of a large application, and helping to reduce repetition and enforce consistency.

Smart Forms

As explained earlier, every form class in your application is a custom class that inherits from System.Windows.Forms.Form. However, you don't need to derive directly from the Form class. Instead, you can derive from *another* custom form class. Figure 1-5 diagrams this relationship.

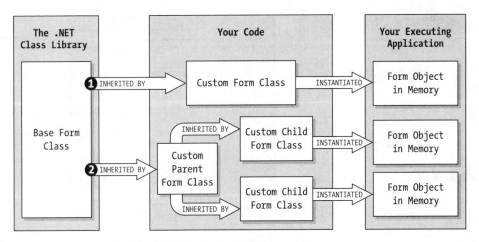

Figure 1-5. *Ordinary forms and visual inheritance*

This technique is commonly referred to as *visual inheritance*, although it's no different from any other type of control-class inheritance. It allows you to standardize related windows (like the steps of a wizard), and it can help you centralize and reuse specific form functionality. You'll take a close look at visual inheritance in Chapter 11.

Visual Studio

Very few developers will ever attempt to write their user interface code by hand. Doing so is a recipe for endless headaches and a lot of tedium. Instead, integrated design tools like Visual Studio make it much easier to design forms and tweak controls.

Visual Studio includes two project types designed for Windows applications:

- Windows Application creates the standard stand-alone EXE application.

- Windows Control Library creates a DLL that you can use in other EXE applications. You'll use this type of project to build custom controls and other components that you want to reuse in multiple Windows applications.

If you're new to Visual Studio, you might want to refer to one of the many useful books that dissect the IDE in detail. However, most developers don't take any time to get used to the Visual Studio development environment. You can do a lot just by dragging controls from the Toolbox and arranging them on a form.

Visual Studio gives you two ways to configure a typical control. Usually, the most flexible approach is to use the Properties window. Once you select the control you want to work with on the form, you can change its properties or click the lightning bolt icon to switch to event view, where you can create and hook up event handlers. (To switch back to properties view, click the grid icon.) Figure 1-6 shows an example with a basic TextBox control.

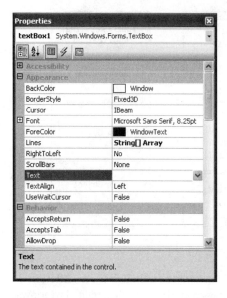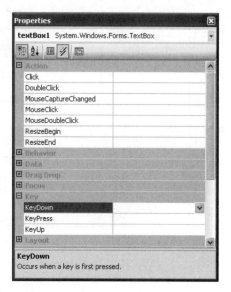

Figure 1-6. *Configuring control properties (left) and events (right)*

■**Note** When you select a property in the Properties window, you'll see explanatory text that describes it. To build your own controls that provide this type of information, you need to apply specific attributes. Chapter 13 describes how you can tackle this job.

If you already have a method that matches the signature of the event (in other words, it has the correct parameters), you can choose it from a drop-down list. This is particularly convenient if you want to connect one event handler to many different events. On the other hand, if you want to add a new event handler, just double-click in the text box next to one of the events in the list. Visual Studio will switch to code view, insert an event handler method, and quietly add the delegate code that connects your event handler to the control event.

For example, if you want to add a new event handler for the TextBox.TextChanged event, simply find the event name in the list, and double-click in the empty box. Assuming the control is named textBox1, Visual Studio will create and display the following event handler:

```
private void textBox1_TextChanged(object sender, EventArgs e)
{
}
```

It will also wire up this event handler in the designer-generated code (which is discussed in the next section):

```
textBox1.TextChanged += new System.EventHandler(textBox1_TextChanged);
```

Caution If you change the name of your event handler or remove it, you'll get a compile error the next time you build your project, and you'll need to remove the offending line by hand.

Another way to configure a control is to use its designer smart tag. Not all controls provide a smart tag, and the abilities of a smart tag vary depending on how much functionality the control developer decided to give it. However, for many of .NET's more-sophisticated controls, smart tags automate tasks that might require several steps. To see how smart tags work, drop a DataGridView control onto a form. The smart tag appears to the right of a control as soon as you add it, but you can hide or display it at any time by clicking the small arrow icon that's displayed in the top-right corner of a control when you select it. (If you don't see any arrow icon when you select a control, it doesn't provide a smart tag for you to use.) Figure 1-7 shows an example.

Figure 1-7. *The smart tag for the DataGridView*

Using the smart tag, you can quickly set certain properties via check boxes and drop-down lists. You can click one of the links in the smart tag to perform various all-in-one tasks (like adding a batch of standard items to a menu) or call up additional dialog boxes with more editing options.

Generating User-Interface Code in Visual Studio

So far you've looked at code that can create control objects dynamically. When you use Visual Studio to create a form at design-time, the story is a little different—or is it?

In fact, when you build a form in the IDE, Visual Studio generates the same code that you would need to write by hand. First of all, when you add a form to a Windows application, Visual Studio creates a customized form class. As you add, position, and configure controls in the design-time environment, Visual Studio adds the corresponding code to the Form class, inside a method called InitializeComponent(). The form's constructor calls the InitializeComponent() method—meaning that the generated code is automatically executed every time you create an instance of your Form class (even before the form is displayed). A sample (commented and slightly shortened) Form class with an InitializeComponent() method is shown below. It configures the window shown in Figure 1-1.

```
public class TestForm : System.Windows.Forms.Form
{
    // Form level control variables.
    // They provide the easiest way to access a control on the window.
    System.Windows.Forms.GroupBox groupBox1;
    System.Windows.Forms.Button button1;
    System.Windows.Forms.RadioButton radioButton1;
    System.Windows.Forms.RadioButton radioButton2;

    public TestForm()
    {
        // Add and configure the controls.
        InitializeComponent();
    }

    private void InitializeComponent()
    {
        // Create all the controls.
        groupBox1 = new System.Windows.Forms.GroupBox();
        button1 = new System.Windows.Forms.Button();
        radioButton1 = new System.Windows.Forms.RadioButton();
        radioButton2 = new System.Windows.Forms.RadioButton();

        // This is our way of telling the controls not to update their layout
        // because a batch of changes are being made at once.
        this.groupBox1.SuspendLayout();
        this.SuspendLayout();

        // (Set all the properties for all our controls here.)
        // (Configure the form properties here.)

        // Add the radio buttons to the GroupBox.
        this.groupBox1.Controls.Add(this.radioButton1);
        this.groupBox1.Controls.Add(this.radioButton2);

        // Add the button and group box controls to the form.
        this.Controls.Add(this.button1);
        this.Controls.Add(this.groupBox1);
```

```
        // Now it's back to life as usual.
        this.groupBox1.ResumeLayout(false);
        this.ResumeLayout(false);
    }

}
```

The key point here is that a form and its controls are always created and configured through code, even when you design it with the IDE. The only real difference between the code examples earlier in this chapter and the code Visual Studio generates is that the latter includes a dedicated InitializeComponent() method for better organization.

Note You may notice that the code Visual Studio generates uses the this keyword when referring to properties of the base Form class (like the Controls collection) or the control member variables (like button1). This is simply a convention adopted by Visual Studio that underscores the fact that these properties are members of the class, not local variables. However, if the this keyword is omitted, the code will still function in the same way. Visual Studio takes this precaution because there is no way to assure that one of the controls it serializes won't generate code for a local variable with the same name (although this is extremely unlikely).

The Component Tray

There's still one minor detail the form code omits. Remember, a form can host two types of objects: controls, which occupy a distinct piece of screen real estate, and non-control components, which don't have any visual representation on the form at all.

When you drag a component onto the form surface, an icon appears for it in the component tray (see Figure 1-8). You can configure the component's properties and handle its events by selecting this icon.

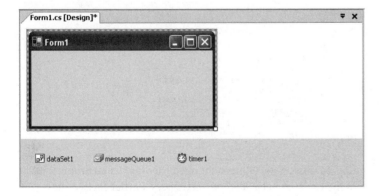

Figure 1-8. *The component tray*

If you look at the automatically generated code for the form, you'll see that the code for creating and configuring the component is added to the InitializeComponent() method, just like it is for controls. However, the component is *not* added to the form's Controls collection. What you will find is this generic block of code that Visual Studio uses to clean up any components that hold unmanaged resources:

```
private System.ComponentModel.IContainer components = null;

protected override void Dispose(bool disposing)
{
    if (disposing && (components != null))
    {
        components.Dispose();
    }
    base.Dispose(disposing);
}
```

The Hidden Designer Code

The only problem with automatically generated code is that it can be fragile. For example, if you try to edit the code that Visual Studio has generated, you may inadvertently end up removing something fundamental. If the problem is severe enough, Visual Studio will refuse to design the form at all—instead, when you switch to design mode, you'll see an unhelpful error message, as shown in Figure 1-9.

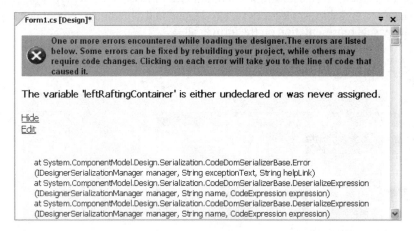

Figure 1-9. *A form that's been tampered with*

To stop this from happening, Microsoft developers changed the way Visual Studio 2005 works by using a new feature of the C# language called *partial classes*. Partial classes allow you to split a class definition into more than one file. When the code is compiled, the C# compiler tracks down all the separate pieces and assembles them into one class. You know that partial classes are at work when a class definition includes the word partial as shown here:

```
public partial class TestForm : System.Windows.Forms.Form
{ ... }
```

Visual Studio uses this technique to separate every form into two pieces: the piece that contains the code you write, and the piece that contains all the code that Visual Studio generates when you build the form by adding controls at design time. For example, if you add a form named TestForm to your project, Visual Studio actually adds two files: TestForm.cs with your code, and TestForm.Designer.cs with the automatically generated code.

To find the designer code, click the plus (+) symbol next to your form, as shown in Figure 1-10.

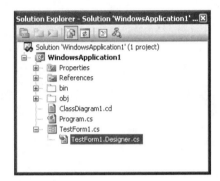

Figure 1-10. *Finding a form's designer code*

There are two reasons you might want to look at the designer code for a form.

- **You want to see how things work.** For example, you might decide you need to write some code to add a control dynamically at runtime. If you're not quite sure what code you need, you could add the code at design time, and then just cut and paste from the designer file to a new location, with only minor modifications needed.

- **You want to modify your controls without using the designer.** Despite Visual Studio's strong design-time support, some changes are still easier to perform with a search-and-replace operation. One example is if you have multiple controls with text that includes your company name, and you want to change all of these instances to use a different name. Making these changes in the Properties window would be much more time-consuming.

■**Tip** As a rule of thumb, it's safe to make changes in the designer region, but you should never add code—even comments. That's because Visual Studio will most likely throw out whatever you've added the next time it re-creates the serialized code based on the objects on the design surface.

Here's the skeletal structure that shows the two pieces that comprise any form in Visual Studio 2005:

Testform.cs

```
public partial class TestForm : System.Windows.Forms.Form
{
    public TestForm
    {
        InitializeComponent();
    }

    // (Any event-handling code you write goes here.)
}
```

Testform.Designer.cs

```
public partial class TestForm
{
    // (Form level control variables go here).

    private void InitializeComponent()
    {
        // (Code for creating and configuring the controls goes here.)
    }

    // Code for cleaning up components follows.
    private System.ComponentModel.IContainer components = null;
    protected override void Dispose(bool disposing)
    {
        if (disposing && (components != null))
        {
            components.Dispose();
        }
        base.Dispose(disposing);
    }
}
```

No self-respecting .NET programmer should be afraid to take a look at the designer code. In fact, it just might reveal a few new tricks.

■Tip If you look at the designer code for a form you've created in Visual Studio, you'll notice a few more changes from the code listing shown earlier. Here's why. First, controls are defined and then created in two separate steps (and the creation takes place in the InitializeComponent() method). Second, controls are added all at once using the Controls.AddRange() method, which accepts an array of control objects, and saves a few lines of code at the expense of readability.

Application Lifetime

You are probably already keenly aware that your application needs an *entry point*—a code routine that shows the first window and gets everything started. In C#, that entry point always takes the form of a static Main() method.

You can place the entry point inside a form (as was the default in earlier versions of Visual Studio .NET), or you can create a separate class, which is usually clearer. Visual Studio 2005 always creates a file named Program.cs when you create a new Windows application. Inside that file is a Program class with a Main() method that looks like this:

```
public static class Program
{
    [STAThread]
    private static void Main()
    {
        Application.EnableVisualStyles();
        Application.Run(new Form1());
    }
}
```

This example begins by enabling Windows XP visual styles, which ensures that common controls use a slightly more up-to-date rendering style on Windows XP operating systems. (On non-XP operating systems, the EnableVisualStyles() method has no effect.) Next, the example creates a new instance of Form1, and then passes it to the Application.Run() method. The Run() method starts a message loop, ensuring that your application stays alive until the window is closed.

▓**Note** Keen eyes will notice the STAThread attribute that's attached to the Main() method in every application. This attribute is one of the ugly leftovers of .NET and COM interoperability. Essentially, it signifies that your application is to be treated as though it uses the single-threaded apartment model for the purpose of inter-acting with COM components. For the most part, this won't interest you, but occasionally it is important because you may wind up using a COM component without realizing it. (Examples include when you interact with the clipboard, use drag-and-drop, or host an ActiveX component.) In some situations, you may need to replace the STAThread attribute with the MTAThread attribute to signal that you are able to use the multi-threaded apartment model when interacting with COM components. You need one or the other—without either of these attributes, your application is treated as though its threading model is "unknown," potentially disabling features that require COM interoperability.

You might wonder why you don't just use the Form.Show() method rather than rely on the Application class. The problem is that as soon as the Main() method finishes executing, the application terminates, and any open windows are automatically closed. Because the Show() method shows a modeless form and doesn't halt your code, the following sample application will start and end immediately:

```
private static void Main()
{
    Form1 frm = new Form1();

    // Show() shows a modeless window, which does not interrupt the code.
    // The Main() method code continues, the application terminates
    // prematurely, and the window is closed automatically.
    frm.Show();
}
```

On the other hand, you don't *need* to use the Application.Run() method if you use the Form.ShowDialog() method, which shows a modal form. Your code isn't resumed until the form is closed. The following example shows two forms (one after the other), and ends only when the second form is closed.

```
private static void Main()
{
    LoginForm frmLogin = new LoginForm();

    // ShowDialog() shows a modal window
    // The Main() method does not continue until the window is closed.
    frmLogin.ShowDialog();

    MainForm frmMain = new MainForm();
    // Now the code does not continue until the main form is closed.
    frmMain.ShowDialog();
}
```

Finally, if you want complete unrestricted freedom, you can call Application.Run() without supplying a window name. This starts a message loop that continues until you explicitly terminate it by calling Application.Exit(). (For example, you might do this when a form closes by handling the Form.Closed event.)

```
private static void Main()
{
    MainForm frmMain = new MainForm();
    SecondaryForm frmSecondary = new SecondaryForm();

    // Show both Windows modelessly at the same time.
    // The user can use both of them.
    frmMain.Show();
    frmSecondary.Show();

    // Keep the application running until your code decides to end it.
    Application.Run();
}
```

In this case, you need to make sure that you end the application somewhere. Otherwise, if you leave the code like that, the user could close both your forms, leaving your application alive even though there isn't any of your code running. You can use Task Manager to confirm that your application process is running.

You'll learn much more about modeless and modal windows in Chapter 3, along with techniques for interacting between forms. Until then, it's worth noting that the Program class is a great place to track forms so that they are available when you need to access them later.

■**Note** The entry point is a basic piece of form infrastructure. The code examples in this book rarely include the entry point or the Windows designer code, both of which would only clutter up the book and add extra pages.

Designing Windows Forms Applications

Now you've learned all the fundamentals about the object underpinnings of Windows Forms applications. To dive into Windows Forms programming, you can skip straight to the next chapter.

However, there's still another set of considerations that are keenly important for user-interface programmers—those that deal with application architecture. Application architecture determines how a user interface "plugs in" to the rest of an application. Development platforms like .NET make this interaction fairly straightforward and, as a result, developers usually spend little or no time thinking about it. User interface code is often inserted wherever it's most convenient for the developer when the code is written. This approach almost always leads to interface code that's tightly bound to a particular problem, scenario, or data source, and heavily interwoven with the rest of the application logic. The interface might look good on the outside, but the code is almost impossible to enhance, reuse, or alter with anything more than trivial changes.

To avoid these disasters, you need to look at user interface as an entire interrelated framework, and consider the best ways to organize your code, separate your user interface details, and shuffle data from one place to another. These are the topics that I'll touch on in the remainder of this chapter.

Encapsulation

Encapsulation is the principle that suggests classes should have separate, carefully outlined responsibilities. Everything that a class needs to fulfill these responsibilities should be wrapped up, hidden from view, and accomplished automatically wherever possible. Encapsulation is often identified as a pillar of object-oriented programming, but it's played a part in good program design since the invention of software. A properly encapsulated function, for example, performs a discrete well-identified task, and has a much better chance of being reused in another application (or even the same program).

The best way to start separating your user-interface code is to think more consciously about encapsulation. The custom form class, with its "switchboard" design, is an excellent example of encapsulation at work. However, it also presents a danger. It potentially encourages you to embed a great amount of additional logic in the form event handlers. A large part of good user-interface programming is simply a matter of resisting this urge.

The following sections lay out some guidelines that can help you keep encapsulation in mind.

Use a Central Switchboard

The form acts as a switchboard for all the controls it contains. Always remember that the real goal of a switchboard is to route calls to a new destination. In other words, when you create the event handler for a button's Click event, this event handler usually has two purposes:

- To forward the command to another object that can handle the task.

- To update the display based on any feedback that's returned.

Depending on the button, only one of these tasks may be necessary. But the important concept is that an event handler is almost always part of a user-interface class—the form switchboard. (After all, this is the design that Visual Studio uses.) As a result, it's a terrible place to put business logic. The form is meant to handle user-interface tasks and delegate more-complicated operations to other classes. That way, your interface won't become tightly bound to the rest of your application logic, and you'll be able to revise and enhance it at a later point without running into trouble.

Ideally, you should be able to remove a form, add a new one, or even combine forms without having to rewrite much code. To accomplish this goal, forms should always hand off their work to another switchboard. For example, it might be easy to update a record according to a user's selections by creating a new object in the form code and calling a single method. However, if you add another layer of indirection by forcing the form to call a more generic update method in a central application switchboard, which *then* accesses your business objects, your user interface will become more independent and more manageable.

Figure 1-11 shows how this process might work when updating a customer record. The update is triggered in response to a control event. The event handler calls a DoCustomerUpdate() switchboard method, which then calls the required methods in the CustomerDb business object. This way, the form contains user-interface only code, the CustomerDb contains business-only logic, and the application switchboard acts as an interface between the two.

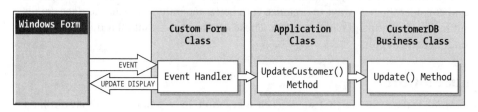

Figure 1-11. *Using form and application switchboards*

■**Tip** Here's another way to look at Windows Forms design. Start by building a multilayered application object model that supplies all the features of your application. Then you can "drive" these features by calling methods on these objects. This way, you can make your calls from any event handler, whether it's in response to a menu command, a toolbar button click, or an automated testing tool that you've developed to help you debug your code.

Use Enumerations and Helper Classes

User-interface controls often require sets of constants, and trying to hard-code them is a tempting trap. Instead, you should create enumerations with meaningful names, and place them in dedicated helper classes. For example, you can define enumerations that help you manage and identify different levels of nodes in a TreeView control (see Chapter 6), distinguish different types of items in a ListView, or just pass information to other methods in your program. Similarly, extraneous details like SQL stored procedure names should be strictly confined to helper classes.

Don't Share Control References

It's easy to pass control references to helper methods. For example, you can create utility classes that automatically fill common list controls. However, this type of design, where you rely on extraneous classes to perform user-interface tasks, can make it extremely difficult to make even simple modifications to the user interface. As a rule of thumb, business code should never rely on the existence of a specific type of user-interface control.

Use Collections

Objects are only as good as the way you can access them. On its own, a data object is a group of related information. By using a collection or other classes that contain collections, you can represent the underlying structure of an entire set of complex data, making it easier to share with other parts of your program.

Create Data-Driven User Interfaces

One good technique is to design your user interface around the data it manages. This may sound like a slightly old-fashioned concept in today's object-oriented way, but it's actually a good habit to prevent yourself from subconsciously combining user interface and business-processing logic.

The single greatest challenge when creating a reusable object framework is deciding how to retrieve data and insert it into the corresponding controls without mingling the business and the presentation logic. Think of your user interface as having one "in" and one "out" connection. All the information that flows into your user interface needs to use a single consistent standard. All forms should be able to recognize and process this data. To achieve this, you might want to use data objects that rely on a common interface for providing data. Or you might want to standardize on the DataSet object, which provides a nearly universal solution for transferring information. Chapter 8 explores the ways you can tame data in a user interface, and Chapter 21 shows an example of an application that builds its interface dynamically using the information in a data source.

■**Note** When is a data-driven interface just another bit of jargon? Probably when you aren't creating an application based on processing, displaying, and managing data. In the business world, the majority of applications deal with databases, and the majority of their work is processing and formatting complex information. For that reason, a great deal of emphasis is placed on how this information is managed and transferred. If, on the other hand, you plan to create the next three-dimensional action game, the rules may change.

Developing in Tiers

An object-oriented application framework sets out rules that determine how objects will interact and communicate. When creating a user interface, you have to develop your application framework at the same time that you plan your individual classes. One overall guideline that can help you shape an application is *three-tier design*.

The basic principle of three-tier design is simple. An application is divided into three distinct subsystems. Every class belongs to only one of these three partitions, and performs just one kind of task. The three tiers are usually identified as the following:

- **The presentation tier.** This tier converts a user's actions into tasks and outputs data using the appropriate controls.

- **The business tier.** This is the tier where all the calculations and processing specific to the individual business are carried out.

- **The data tier.** This is the tier that shuttles information back and forth from the database to the business objects.

An object in one tier can interact only with the adjacent tiers, as shown in Figure 1-12.

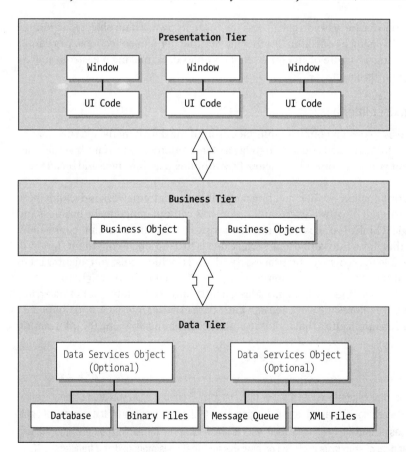

Figure 1-12. *Three-tier design*

Almost everyone agrees that this sort of structure is the best way to organize an application, but it's not always easy to implement this design. Though the plan looks simple, modern user interfaces are usually quite complicated, and sometimes make assumptions or have expectations about the way they will receive information. The result is that everyone recommends this model, but very few developers follow it successfully. The problems, although not insurmountable, are found in every tier. The next three sections explain some of the challenges you'll face.

The Presentation Tier

Though it doesn't explicitly state it, three-tier design requires a fair degree of consistency among user-interface controls. In the real world, this consistency doesn't exist. For example, making what is conceptually a minor change—like substituting a ListView control for a Data-GridView—requires a totally different access model. The DataGridView is filled exclusively by data binding. The ListView, on the other hand, acts like a collection of items. To get information into other ListView columns, you need to add a collection of fields to each individual item. These quirks are easy enough to master, but they don't make it possible to create business objects that can quickly and efficiently fill common controls.

For example, consider an application that reads customer information from a database and displays it in an attractive list control. At first glance, it seems like a straightforward task. But consider the number of different ways it could be modeled with objects:

- A CustomerDb class fetches information from the database, and returns it as a DataSet. Your form code then manually reads the DataSet and adds the information to a list control.

- A CustomerDb class fetches information from the database. You also create a custom CustomerList control class that knows how to fill itself using the DataSet it receives from CustomerDb.

- A CustomerDb class fetches information from the database. However, the CustomerDb class also receives a reference to the list control that needs to be filled. The CustomerDb class has the built-in smarts to know how to fill the list control's collection of items.

- A CustomerDb class fetches information from the database. A helper class, FillListFromDataSet, handles the conversion of the information in the DataSet to information in the generic list control.

Which approach is the best one? It's difficult to say. The first approach does the trick, but probably isn't generic enough, which will limit your ability to reuse your solution. The second approach also works, but is probably too much effort because you'll need to create a dedicated custom control. The third option is suspicious, because it seems that the CustomerDb class is being given additional responsibilities beyond the scope it was designed for. Overall, some variation on the final option will probably give you the best tradeoff between simplicity and reusability. By dividing the solution up into an extra piece (FillListFromDataSet), it makes the user interface more loosely coupled. But the greatest problem with all of these examples is that there is no guarantee that the other classes in the application will follow this pattern. And it should come as no surprise that when you read the vast quantity of .NET articles and books, you'll see examples of all of these techniques.

> **■Tip** The single most important decision you can make is to define how your user interface classes should interact. This is the simplest way to improve your designs without adopting a single specific type of architecture.

The Business Tier

In three-tier design, it's assumed that the user interface is isolated from the underlying data source. Information for a control is requested through a layer of business objects. These business objects handle all the application-specific tasks, including enforcement of *business rules*. In other words, the business objects validate data to make sure it's consistent with the rules of the systems. The key benefit of this is that you can change the rules of your application by modifying the business components, rather than by creating and deploying a new client application, which makes it much easier to put up with the ever-changing requests of some fickle management types.

Unfortunately, this ideal introduces as many problems as it solves. The key problem is that the error checking happens after the process is started, which is too late for the validation to be useful in the user interface. As a result, you're more likely to waste time, confuse users, and (at worst) lose information. To make a productive user interface, you need to act on an error as soon as it happens and give immediate feedback, or better yet, forbid it entirely. That means that your user interface always needs to be designed with some built-in business rules (for example, forbidding letters in a text box that represents an invoice amount).

> **■Tip** Chapter 18 discusses the best ways to integrate validation into your applications, and gives many more practical tips about how you can deal with validation in an elegant, componentized way.

The Data Tier

Keeping the data tier separate from the business tier is another battle. To optimize performance, databases in enterprise applications usually rely on stored procedures, views, and other optimized ways to retrieve and update data. However, the user-interface tier can't be built in a database-friendly way, because it is designed to be completely generic. It also can't rely on tricks that programmers love, like dynamically generated SQL statements, because it is supposed to be completely isolated from the data tier. The result is a tradeoff, where you can favor any one of the following approaches:

- Create a "thin" business layer that uses methods that correspond very closely to stored procedures and other database-specific parameters. Unfortunately, this business layer requires significant reworking if the database changes.

- Create an average business layer that lets the user interface retrieve whatever data it wants. The business tier relies on accessing the database using generic SQL statements. It's very expandable and generic, but database performance will be terrible.

- Create a "thick" business layer that tries to match requests from the user interface with an optimized execution path for a specific database. With a little luck and careful coding, performance could be as good as in the first option, and the layer could be nearly as generic as in the second. However, writing this tier is a major programming undertaking that takes exponentially more time.

So which approach is the best compromise? Usually developers decide based on the scalability needs of their application. In an application that needs to serve a large number of simultaneous users, the first approach is almost always preferred. In a smaller-scale application, developers are more likely to choose flexibility over optimization and go with the second choice. If you have a lot of extra time on your hands, you could attempt the third approach, but it's an academic ideal that's rarely achieved in practice.

Three-Tier Design in .NET

It's important to remember that three-tier design is an abstraction. No successful application will implement it exactly. However, it's a powerful guideline that helps you shape how classes interact in your application.

.NET 2.0 provides a set of tools to manage data and the way it's displayed in a Windows application. Some of these tools are indispensable for dealing with data in a business application. Others make it far too easy to break the rules of encapsulation and create tightly bound interfaces with data access code embedded in your application's user interface. In Chapter 8 you'll take your first look at these features, and you'll consider some common, practical approaches to make sure you keep a well-designed application.

The theme of separating user-interface code from other types of application code will recur throughout this book, even when you aren't using data binding. (For example, you'll use it in Chapter 19 with the document-view model, which rigidly separates user interface code from the documents an application creates.) You'll also learn when to break through simplifications of three-tier design, such as when building systems for validation and dynamic help—and how to do it in a well-encapsulated, componentized way.

It may seem strange to discuss tiers and business objects in a book on user-interface design. (In fact, there are other excellent .NET books written entirely about architecture and design patterns.) But as you'll see, when you set specific rules about how the user interface tier can communicate with other parts of your program, you start to make the transition from a simple collection of objects to a true user-interface framework.

The Last Word

This chapter introduced you to the broad picture of user interfaces in the .NET world, and the basic design assumptions that Visual Studio makes automatically. You can make different design decisions, and .NET allows you a considerable amount of freedom to create the exact framework that you want. In later chapters you'll learn how to exploit this freedom to create all types of custom controls.

Finally, this chapter provided an introduction to the concepts of application architecture, which will crop up from time to time throughout this book as you design the user-interface layer of your application.

■■■

CHAPTER 2

Control Basics

In Windows Forms, everything begins with the Control class—the fundamental class from which every other control derives. The Control class defines the bare minimum functionality that every control needs, from the properties that let you position it in a window to the events that let you react to key presses and mouse clicks.

This chapter introduces the Windows Forms toolkit, and then explores the Control class in detail. You'll learn about the following basics:

- How controls are positioned in a window and layered on top of each other.

- How to configure the appearance of a control with fonts and colors.

- How controls handle focus and the tab sequence.

- How you can get keyboard and mouse information by reacting to events or at any time.

You won't look at specific control classes in this chapter. Instead, you'll concentrate on the fundamentals that apply to all controls.

The Windows Forms Package

.NET provides two toolkits for application design: one for Web applications (called ASP.NET), and one for Windows development (called Windows Forms, or WinForms). Windows Forms allows you to create the traditional rich graphical interfaces found in everything from office productivity software to arcade games. The one detail that all Windows Forms applications have in common is the fact that they are built out of windows—tiny pieces of screen real estate that can present information and receive user input.

It's easy to imagine that the term "Windows Forms" refers to a special part of the .NET class library, where fundamental classes like Form and Control are stored. This is true, but it isn't the whole story. More accurately, Windows Forms is the technology that allows the common language runtime to interact with control objects and translate them into the low-level reality of the Windows operating system. In other words, you create objects that represent controls and windows, and the common language runtime handles the details like routing messages, keeping track of window handles, and calling functions from the Windows API.

This idea isn't new. In the past, developers have used the MFC framework in C++, WFC in J++, and Visual Basic's own "Ruby" forms engine to insulate themselves from some of the low-level details of Windows programming. These frameworks all provide an object-oriented wrapper around the Windows API (which, on its own, is a disorganized collection with hundreds of miscellaneous C routines). These frameworks were well-intentioned, but they have all suffered from a few problems.

- **Lack of consistency.** If you learn how to use MFC, you still won't know anything about creating Visual Basic user interfaces. Even though every framework ultimately interacts with the Windows API, they have dramatically different object models and philosophies.

- **Thin layer/thick layer problems.** Frameworks tend to be either easy to use or powerful, but not both. MFC is really only a couple of steps away from Windows messages and low-level grunt work. On the other hand, Visual Basic developers have the benefit of a simple framework, but face the lingering dread that they will need to delve into the raw Windows API for complex or unusual tasks that are beyond Visual Basic's bounds.

- **Limitations of the Windows API.** The Windows API dictates certain harsh realities. For example, once you create a fixed-border window, you can't make its border resizable. These limitations make sense based on how the Windows API is organized, but they often lead to confusing inconsistencies in a framework's object model.

The result of these limitations is that there are essentially two types of frameworks: those that are complicated to use for simple tasks (like MFC), and those that are easy to use for simple tasks but difficult or impossible to use for complex tasks (like VB). These object models provide a modern way to code user interfaces, but many programmers wonder why they should abstract the Windows API when its restrictions remain.

The .NET Solution

.NET addresses these problems by being more ambitious. The result is a user-interface framework that uses some innovative sleight of hand to perform tasks that are difficult or seemingly impossible with the Windows API. Here are some examples:

- Change fixed style properties like the selection type of a list box or the border type of a window after its creation.

- Change a form's owner.

- Move an MDI child window from one MDI parent window to another.

- Transform an MDI child window into an MDI parent and vice versa.

- Move controls from one container to another.

Clearly this list includes a couple of tricks that a self-respecting application will probably never need to use. Still, they illustrate an important fact: .NET doesn't just provide an easier object model to access the Windows API—it also provides capabilities that *extend* it. The result is a framework that works the way you would intuitively expect it to work based on its objects.

■**Note** The online samples for this chapter (in the Source Code area of www.apress.com) include a project named ImpossibleAPI, which shows one of these "broken rules"—a child window that can jump between different MDI parents whenever the user clicks a button.

All of this raises an interesting question. How can a programming model built on the Windows API actually perform feats that the Windows API can't? Truthfully, there's nothing in the preceding list that couldn't be simulated with the Windows API after a fair bit of effort. For example, you could appear to change the border style of a window by destroying and re-creating an identical window. To do so you would have to rigorously track and restore all the information from the previous window.

In fact, this is more or less what takes place in .NET. If you examine the control or window handle (the numeric value that identifies the window to the operating system), you'll see that it changes when you perform these unusual operations. This signifies that, on an operating-system level, .NET actually provides you with a new window or control. The difference is that .NET handles this destruction and re-creation automatically. The illusion is so perfect that it's hardly an illusion at all (any more than the illusion that ASP.NET Web controls can maintain state, or that television shows continuous movement rather than just a series of still images).

The cost of this functionality is a runtime that requires a fair bit of intelligence. However, .NET programs already need an intelligent runtime to provide modern features like improved code access security and managed memory. Windows Forms are just another part of the ambitious .NET Framework.

Some programmers may nonetheless feel they need to resort to the Windows API. You can still use API calls in your .NET applications without much trouble (and in a rare cases, you might need to in order to get certain functionality). However, the best overall approach is to abandon these habits and use the new .NET abstractions. Not only is it easier but it also provides a short path to some remarkable features.

■**Tip** One of the best pieces of advice for beginning programmers in traditional development was to master the Windows API. However, in .NET the story changes. In .NET, you'll get the most benefit by studying the low-level details of the .NET object libraries, not the API. Believe it or not, the operating system details will not be as important in the next generation of software development. Instead, you'll need to know the full range of properties, methods, and types that are at your fingertips to unlock the secrets of becoming a .NET guru.

The Control Class

Chapter 1 introduced the .NET Control class, and examined its place in the overall architecture of an application. Here's a quick review:

- You create and manipulate controls and forms using .NET classes. The common language runtime recognizes these classes, and handles the low-level Windows details for you.

- You use a control from the .NET class library by creating an instance of the appropriate class, and adding it to the Controls collection of a container control, like a panel or form. Whether you add the control at design time or runtime, the code is the same.

- You configure controls by setting properties. In addition, you can react to control events in two ways: by creating an event handler (typically in a custom form class), or by deriving a custom version of the control and overriding the corresponding method.

Every .NET control derives from the base class System.Windows.Forms.Control. Depending on the complexity of the control, it may pass through a few more stages in its evolution.

The Control class is interesting mainly for the basic functionality that it defines. Sorting through the functionality is no easy task. The 200-plus members include countless properties, events that fire to notify you when certain common properties are changed (like VisibleChanged, TextChanged, SizeChanged, and so on), and methods that reset values to their defaults, along with some more useful and unusual members. The sections in this chapter sort through the most important Control properties by topic. But before you begin your exploration, you may want to check out some of the basic and system-related members in Table 2-1.

Table 2-1. *Basic Control Members*

Member	Description
Name	Provides a short string of descriptive text that identifies your control. Usually (and by default, if you're using Visual Studio), the form-level member variable that refers to the control is given the same name. However, there's no direct relation; the Name property is provided just to help you when iterating through a control collection looking for a specific item.
Tag	Provides a convenient place to store any type of object. The Tag property is not used by the .NET Framework. Instead, you use it to store associated data (like a data object or a string with a unique ID).
Controls	The Controls collection stores references to all the child controls.
Invoke(), InvokeRequired, and CheckForIllegalCrossThreadCalls	These members are used in multithreaded programming. InvokeRequired returns true if the current thread is not the one in which the control has been created. In this case, you should not attempt to call directly any other method or property of the control. Chapter 20 shows how you can create and manage multithreaded forms.
DesignMode	Returns true if the control is in design mode. This property is used when you are creating a custom control, so you don't perform time-consuming operations when the program is not running (like an automatic refresh).
Dispose()	This method releases the resources held by a control (like the operating system window handle). You can call this method manually to clean up, or you can let the common language runtime perform its lazy garbage collection. When you call Dispose() on a container control, Dispose() is automatically called on all child controls. This also means that if you call Dispose() on a form, all the controls on that form are disposed.

Because every control is derived from the Control class, you can always use it as a lowest common denominator for dealing with some basic Control properties in your application. For example, consider the form in Figure 2-1, which provides a text box, label, and button control.

You'll find this example (called the ControlMedley project) in the Downloads area of the Apress Web site, www.apress.com.

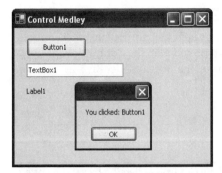

Figure 2-1. *A medley of different controls*

The Click event for all these controls (and the underlying form) is handled by one event handler: a method named ctrlClick(). Here's the event handler:

```
private void ctrlClick(System.Object sender, EventArgs e)
{
    Control ctrl = (Control)sender;
    MessageBox.Show("You clicked: " + ctrl.Name);
}
```

The code in the ctrlClick() event handler is completely generic. It converts the object reference of the sender into the control type, and then displays a message with the name of the clicked control.

Once you've created this event handler, you can easily attach it to the Click event of each of the three controls on the form using Visual Studio. To add an event handler, select the appropriate control on the form. Then click the lightning bolt in the Properties window to see the list of its events. Find the event you want (in this case the Click event), and attach it to the existing ctrlClick() method using the drop-down list.

Once you complete this step, Visual Studio adds the following designer code:

```
Button1.Click += new System.EventHandler(this.ctrlClick);
TextBox1.Click += new System.EventHandler(this.ctrlClick);
Label1.Click += new System.EventHandler(this.ctrlClick);
```

Remember, this code is hidden out of site in the designer code file. However, you can see this file and browse its code (as described in Chapter 1) by right-clicking the project name in the Solution Explorer and choosing Show All Files.

This technique of creating a generic event handler is quite useful. It allows you to handle similar events from any type of control, rather than limiting you to one type of control (e.g., a Button) and one type of event (e.g., Button.Click). For example, you could use this approach to dynamically highlight different controls as the user moves the mouse cursor over them. When the appropriate event fires, you just need to retrieve the control reference from the sender parameter and set that control's foreground and background colors accordingly. In later chapters, you'll see examples that use this technique to simplify drag-and-drop code and show a control's linked context menu.

Control Relations

Chapter 1 described how controls like forms, panels, and group boxes can contain other controls. To add or remove a child control, you use the collection provided in the Controls property. Control objects also provide other properties that help you manage and identify their relationships (see Table 2-2).

Table 2-2. *Members for Control Relationships*

Member	Description
HasChildren	Returns true if the Controls collection has at least one child control.
Controls	A collection of contained controls. You can use this collection to examine the existing child controls, remove them, or add new ones.
ControlAdded and ControlRemoved events	These events fire when controls are added to or removed from the Controls collection. You can use these events to automate layout logic. Chapter 21 deals with this issue in more detail.
Parent	A reference to the parent control (the control that contains this control). This could be a form or a container control like a group box. You can set this property to swap a control into a new container.
TopLevelControl and FindForm()	The TopLevelControl property returns a reference to the control at the top of the hierarchy. Typically, this is the containing form. The FindForm() method is similar, but it returns null if the control is not situated on a form.
Contains()	This method accepts a control, and returns true if this control is a child of the current control. This method works with children of children, so you can test if a given control is contained anywhere in the control tree of another container.
GetChildAtPoint()	This method accepts a Point structure that corresponds to a location inside the current control. If a child control is located at this point, it is returned. This method is often used when hit-testing to see if the mouse pointer is over a child control. This method finds only immediate children (not children of children).
ContextMenuStrip and MenuStrip	These properties return the associated ContextMenuStrip object (for a basic control) or MenuStrip object (for a form). Chapter 14 has much more information about menus and toolbars.

Windows XP Styles

Windows XP introduced a revamped look for Windows applications that refreshes the way common graphical elements like buttons and boxes are drawn. Figure 2-2 shows the difference.

 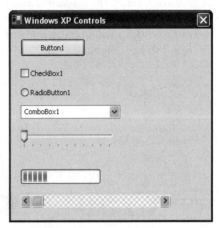

Figure 2-2. *Normal (left) and Windows XP (right) visual styles*

In .NET 1.0, you needed to do the tedious work of creating an additional XML file (known as a manifest) to support the Windows XP look. In .NET 2.0, life is a whole lot easier. You simply need to remember to call the Application.EnableVisualStyles() method when your application starts, before showing any forms. This line is a basic ingredient that Visual Studio adds to the Program class whenever you create a new project. If you forget to call EnableVisualStyles(), you'll still see the Windows XP look for nonclient portions of your form (such as the border and minimize/maximize buttons). However, the Windows XP look won't be used for the form surface, which means that basic user-interface elements, like buttons, check boxes, and radio buttons, will still have the antiquated look that they've used since Windows 95.

In either case, the way your application works with earlier operating systems is unchanged. The EnableVisualStyles() call is harmlessly ignored on non-XP versions of Windows. There's one more quirk—the Visual Studio design environment doesn't pay attention to whether or not your application uses visual styles, because it has no way to determine whether you will call the EnableVisualStyles() method before showing a given form. As a result, Visual Studio always uses the Windows XP styles if you're designing your application on a Windows XP computer.

■**Note** Many button-style (like Button, CheckBox, and RadioButton) controls provide a FlatStyle property. If you set FlatStyle to a value other than System or Standard, the Windows XP styles won't be used. However, the default setting for all controls is Standard, which ensures that you get the appearance you expect as long as you call EnableVisualStyles().

Position and Size

A control's position is defined by the distance between its top-left corner and the top-left corner of its container. Often, the container is a form, but it could also be a container control, like a panel or group box. Similarly, the size of a control is measured as the width and height of the control from its top-left corner (not including the space occupied by the form border and caption). By convention, the position measurement is positive in the downward and rightward directions. Figure 2-3 shows the relationship.

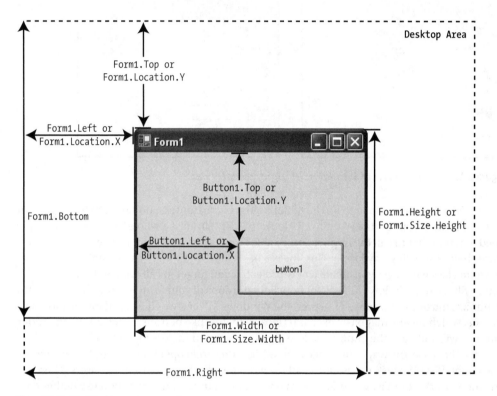

Figure 2-3. *Control measurements*

All coordinates and dimensions are represented by integer values that are measured in pixels. They are provided through several properties, including Top, Left, Right, and Bottom for position, and Width and Height for size. Out of these, only Top, Left, Width, and Height can be adjusted (the Right and Bottom properties are calculated based on these values and are read-only).

■**Note** Pixels, of course, are the smallest physical measurement of screen resolution. A typical consumer computer monitor uses a display resolution of 1024 x 768 or 800 x 600 pixels. Because the current generation of the Windows operating systems is based on pixels, application windows can look quite different (cramped and small or spacious and expansive) depending on the hardware on your computer. Future versions of Windows, like Vista, promise to change this system by adding a truly scalable rendering engine.

Although you can change the Top and Left properties, the preferred way to set position is by setting the Control.Location property using a Point object. A Point object is a simple structure that represents a coordinate. It consists of just two properties—X and Y.

Here's an example that uses a Point object:

```
System.Drawing.Point pt = new System.Drawing.Point();
pt.X = 300;              // The control will be 300 pixels from the left
pt.Y = 500;             // The control will be 500 pixels from the top.
ctrl.Location = pt;    // Now ctrl.Left = 300 and ctrl.Top = 500
```

Similarly, the preferred way to define a control's size is to set the Control.Size property with a Size object, which represents a rectangle. The Size structure consists of a Width and Height property.

```
System.Drawing.Size sz = new System.Drawing.Size();
sz.Width = 50;
sz.Height = 60;
ctrl.Size = sz;

// Just for fun, set another control to have the same size.
ctrl2.Size = ctrl.Size;
```

■**Note** All standard controls are treated as rectangles. In Chapter 23, you'll see how it's possible to create specialized controls and forms that have irregular boundaries by using the Region property.

These basic structures originate from the System.Drawing namespace. By importing the System.Drawing namespace and using some handy constructors, you can simplify these examples considerably, as shown here:

```
ctrl.Location = new Point(300, 500);  // Order is (X, Y)
ctrl.Size = new Size(50, 60);         // Order is (Width, Height)
```

Visual Studio takes this approach when it creates code for your controls at design time. One other useful shortcut is the SetBounds() method, which is handy if you want to set location and size in a single step:

```
ctrl.SetBounds(300, 500, 50, 60);     // Order is (X, Y, Width, Height)
```

Along with the basic Size property, controls and forms also provide a ClientSize property. Essentially, Size is the full measure of the screen real estate taken by a control. ClientSize is the size of the control, ignoring elements that the control isn't directly responsible for drawing. This may include the borders of the control, and the scroll bar. Figure 2-4 shows the difference between Size and ClientSize.

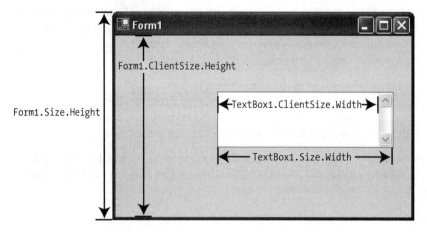

Figure 2-4. *The Size property compared to the ClientSize property*

Typically, the ClientSize property is most useful when you're performing coordinate calculations with a form and you want to ignore the title bar region. Here's an example:

```
// This code attempts to center a label vertically.
// It's a little too low because the title bar is not accounted for.
label1.Location.Y = (this.Size.Height - label1.Height) / 2;

// This code centers a label vertically.
// It succeeds because it uses the client region for its calculations.
label1.Location.Y = (this.ClientSize.Height - label1.Height) / 2;
```

There are still other size- and position-related properties, such as those used for anchoring and docking when creating automatically resizable forms. These properties are described in detail in Chapter 3.

■**Tip** There are actually two ways to measure the position of a control. Typically, you'll use the Location property, which measures the distance between the control borders and the bounds of the container. However, you can also use absolute screen coordinates, which measure the distance between the control borders and the edges of the screen. If you have one type of measurement and you need another, don't worry—you can use the Control.PointToClient() and Control.PointToScreen() methods to convert the coordinate. Chapter 4 shows an example with a drag-and-drop operation that spans two forms.

Overlapping Controls

When you place more than one control in the same place, one will end up on top, and the other will end up underneath. Usually this is the result of a minor mistake, such as incorrectly using the anchoring and docking features (described in Chapter 3) to create resizable forms. In some cases, however, you might want to overlap controls for a specific effect.

When controls overlap, it's the *z-index* that determines which control ends up on top. Essentially, every control exists in its own distinct numbered layer. A control that has the z-index layer 1 will appear above a control in z-index layer 2 if they overlap. Usually, the z-index of a group of controls is determined by the order in which you add the controls, so that the last control you add is always in the topmost layer (with a z-index of 0). However, you can change these options.

To determine or set the z-index of a control, you can use the GetChildIndex() and SetChildIndex() methods of the Controls collection. Here's an example that moves a control to the third layer in the z-index:

```
Controls.SetChildIndex(ctrl, 2);
```

Usually, you won't need this kind of fine-grained control. Instead, you'll just want to drop a control to the back of the z-index (the bottom-most layer) or bring it to the top. You can accomplish this feat at design time by right-clicking on a control and choosing Bring to Front or Send to Back. You can also perform the same task programmatically using the Control.BringToFront() or Control.SendToBack() methods.

```
ctrl.BringToFront();    // This is equivalent to Controls.SetChildIndex(ctrl, 0)
```

Every container control tracks z-index separately. As a result, you need to worry about control overlap only if two controls exist at the same level. You don't need to worry about it when one control is contained *inside* another. For example, if you put a button inside a group box, the group box won't obscure the button.

■**Tip** Usually, overlapping controls are more frustration than they're worth. That's because .NET doesn't support real background transparency. If you want to overlap content for a specific graphical effect, you'll probably want to develop your own owner-drawn controls, as described in Chapter 12.

ALIGNING CONTROLS IN VISUAL STUDIO

The Visual Studio designer provides a slew of tools that make it easier to lay out controls. Here are some useful starting points:

- Select a Control, and set its Locked property to true in the Properties window. This locks it in place, ensuring that it won't accidentally be moved while you create and manipulate other controls.

- As you move or resize a control, look for blue snap lines, which automatically align an edge of your control with another control. Snap lines are new in Visual Studio 2005, and they make it much easier to arrange a column of text boxes or buttons.

- Look under the Format menu for options that let you automatically align, space, and center controls. For example, select several existing controls and choose Format ➤ Align ➤ Left to align their left edges. Or, choose Format ➤ Make Same Size ➤ Width to expand both controls to have the same width, or Format ➤ Vertical Spacing ➤ Make Equal to space them out evenly from top to bottom.

- To quickly place a control in the middle of a form, select the control and use one of the options in the Format ➤ Center in Form menu.

Color

Every control defines a ForeColor and BackColor property. For different controls, these properties have slightly different meanings. In a simple control like a label or text box, the foreground color is the color of the text, while the background color is the area behind it. These values default to the Windows system-configured settings.

Colors are specified as Color structures from the System.Drawing namespace. It's extremely easy to create a color object, because you have several different options. You can create a color using any of the following:

- **An ARGB (alpha, red, green, blue) color value.** You specify each value as an integer from 0 to 255.

- **A predefined .NET color name.** You choose the correspondingly named property from the Color class.

- **An HTML color name.** You specify this value as a string using the ColorTranslator class.

- **An OLE color code.** You specify this value as an integer (representing a hexadecimal value) using the ColorTranslator class.

- **A Win32 color code.** You specify this value as an integer (representing a hexadecimal value) using the ColorTranslator class.

- **An environment setting from the current color scheme.** You choose the correspondingly named property from the SystemColors class.

■Note To change the currently defined system colors, right-click the desktop, choose Properties, and then click the Advanced button in the Appearance tab. Keep in mind that if you're using Windows XP themes, these colors are effectively ignored.

The code listing that follows shows several ways to specify a color using the Color, ColorTranslator, and SystemColors types. To use this code as written, you must import the System.Drawing namespace.

```
// Create a color from an ARGB value.
int alpha = 255, red = 0;
int green = 255, blue = 0;
ctrl.ForeColor = Color.FromArgb(alpha, red, green, blue);

// Create a color from an environment setting.
ctrl.ForeColor = SystemColors.HighlightText;

// Create a color using a .NET name.
ctrl.ForeColor = Color.Crimson;

// Create a color from an HTML color name.
ctrl.ForeColor = ColorTranslator.FromHtml("Blue");
```

```
// Create a color from an OLE color code.
ctrl.ForeColor = ColorTranslator.FromOle(0xFF00);

// Create a color from a Win32 color code.
ctrl.ForeColor = ColorTranslator.FromWin32(0xA000);
```

The next code snippet shows how you can transform the KnownColors enumeration into an array of strings that represent color names. This can be useful if you need to display a list of valid colors by name in an application.

```
string[] colorNames;
colorNames = System.Enum.GetNames(typeof(KnownColor));
```

Changing a color-name string back to the appropriate enumerated value is just as easy using the special static Enum.Parse() method. This method compares the string against all the available values in an enumeration, and chooses the matching one.

```
KnownColor myColor;
myColor = (KnownColor)Enum.Parse(typeOf(KnownColor), colorName);

// For example, if colorName is "Azure" then MyColor will be set
// to the enumerated value KnownColor.Azure (which is also the integer value 32).
```

Incidentally, you can use a few useful methods on any Color structure to retrieve additional color information. For example, you can use GetBrightness(), GetHue(), and GetSaturation().

Here's a complete program that puts all of these techniques to work. When it loads, it fills a list control with all the known colors. When the user selects an item, the background of the form is adjusted accordingly (see Figure 2-5). The only exception is the Transparent color, which generates an exception. (See Chapter 3 to learn how to create a truly transparent form.)

```
public partial class ColorChange : System.Windows.Forms.Form
{
    // (Windows designer code omitted.)

    private void ColorChange_Load(object sender, System.EventArgs e)
    {
        string[] colorNames;
        colorNames = System.Enum.GetNames(typeof(KnownColor));
        lstColors.Items.AddRange(colorNames);
    }

    private void lstColors_SelectedIndexChanged(object sender,
      System.EventArgs e)
    {
        KnownColor selectedColor;
        selectedColor = (KnownColor)System.Enum.Parse(
          typeof(KnownColor), lstColors.Text);
        this.BackColor = System.Drawing.Color.FromKnownColor(selectedColor);
```

```
        // Display color information.
        lblBrightness.Text = "Brightness = " +
          this.BackColor.GetBrightness().ToString();
        lblHue.Text = "Hue = " + this.BackColor.GetHue().ToString();
        lblSaturation.Text = "Saturation = " +
          this.BackColor.GetSaturation().ToString();
    }
}
```

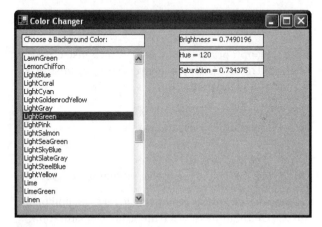

Figure 2-5. *A color-changing form*

■Note ForeColor and BackColor are *ambient properties*—properties that, if not set, are retrieved from the parent. For example, if you add a Label to a Form and don't set the BackColor, the Label uses the BackColor of the Form. If you add a Label to a Panel and don't set the BackColor, the Label uses the BackColor or the Panel (and if that isn't set, the Panel uses the BackColor of the Form). Other ambient properties include Font and Cursor.

Alpha Blending

The most flexible way to set colors for a .NET control is to use an ARGB value, which consists of four separate numbers representing an alpha, red, green, and blue component. The red, green, and blue components are easy to understand (for example, a color with a red component of 255 is much redder than one with a red component of 0). The alpha value is a little trickier—it represents the transparency of a color from 0 (completely transparent) to 255 (opaque). If you set a background color with an alpha value other than 255, you are electing to make the control's background partially transparent.

You can use this code to set the alpha component of any color to 0, making it transparent:

```
// Make a label transparent.
label1.BackColor = Color.FromArgb(0, label1.BackColor);
```

You can also use the system-defined color Color.Transparent. If you want to set this through the Properties window, you'll find the Transparent color in the Web tab of the drop-down color picker.

Unfortunately, the standard .NET controls don't handle transparent backgrounds very well. In fact, they only pretend to be transparent with a rather ugly workaround. When you set a control to have a transparent background, it simply looks at the background of the parent control, and uses that (if the alpha value is 255) or blends it with the specified color (if the alpha value is somewhere between 0 and 255). As a result, when you overlap one "transparent" control with another, the topmost control will still overlap any content in the bottom control. Figure 2-6 demonstrates the problem with two supposedly transparent controls.

Figure 2-6. *A not-quite-transparent label*

There is no way to solve this problem, except to use GDI+ to create custom owner-drawn controls that don't suffer from the same limitations.

Fonts and Text

The Control object defines a Text property that is used by derived controls for a variety of purposes. For a text box, the Text property corresponds to the information displayed in the text box, which can be modified by the user. For controls like labels, command buttons, or forms, the Text property refers to static descriptive text displayed as a title or caption.

The font of a control's text is defined by the Font property, which uses an instance of the System.Drawing.Font class. Note that a Font object does not just represent a typeface (such as Tahoma). Instead, it encapsulates all details about the font family, point size, and styles (like bold and italic).

```
// You can create a font with one of the 13 constructors.
ctrl.Font = new Font("Tahoma", 8, FontStyle.Bold);
```

The Font class also provides a Height property, which returns the line spacing of your chosen font in pixels. This setting allows you to perform calculations when you are drawing special graphics or text on a control manually. For example, you could manually space lines the appropriate amount when drawing text directly onto a form background.

■**Tip** A traditional default font for Windows programs is Microsoft Sans Serif. However, applications since Windows 98 consistently use the more attractive Tahoma font (which is also better for input, as it distinguishes between characters like a lowercase *L* and uppercase *I*). You should use the Tahoma font in your applications.

Note that font families are set using a string rather than a type-safe enumerated property. If you try to create an object using a name that does not correspond to an installed font, .NET automatically (and unhelpfully) defaults to the Microsoft Sans Serif font. An error does not occur. You may want to explicitly check the Font.Name property to check if this automatic substitution has been made.

To determine what fonts are installed on the system, you can enumerate through them with the System.Drawing.Text.InstalledFontCollection class. The following example adds the name of every installed font to a list box.

```
InstalledFontCollection fonts = new InstalledFontCollection();
foreach (FontFamily family in fonts.Families)
{
    lstAvailableFonts.Items.Add(family.Name);
}
```

The online samples for this chapter (in the Downloads area at www.apress.com) include a FontViewer utility that uses this technique to create a list of fonts. The user can choose a font from a drop-down list control, and a sample line of text will be painted directly on the window (see Figure 2-7). To perform the font painting, the application uses some of the GDI+ methods you'll see in Chapter 7.

Figure 2-7. *A simple font viewer*

System Fonts

Windows has a lot of font conventions. Different fonts are used for different screen elements. You can retrieve the correct default font using the System.Drawing.SystemFonts class, which includes handy properties like CaptionFont, DefaultFont, DialogFont, IconTitleFont, MenuFont, MessageBoxFont, SmallCaptionFont, and StatusFont. Using these font objects ensures your application blends in with the scenery. Here's how you assign the caption font to a control:

```
ctrl.Font = SystemFonts.CaptionFont;
```

The SystemFont class differs from other classes dedicated to system settings, like SystemColors, SystemBrushes, and SystemPens. The difference is that when you retrieve one of the properties from SystemFont, a new Font object is created. That means if you're using a font for dynamic drawing (a topic explored in Chapter 7), you should release the font when you're finished by calling its Dispose() method. Very few applications are brought to their knees by wasting a few extra font handles, but it's good to get in the habit of cleaning up every resource you use before a problem develops.

Large Fonts

The Windows operating system has a rather kludgey feature called "large fonts" that allows you to bump up the default text size on your computer. This feature is designed to let you use higher resolutions for increased quality without sacrificing readability. However, most users steer away from the large fonts feature because it works unpredictably with many applications. Some become unusable (important content may be bumped right off a form) while most show no change at all.

■**Tip** To change the font DPI on your computer, select Display from the Control Panel, choose the Settings tab, and click Advanced. In the General tab, there's a drop-down list of DPI options, including normal-size and large-size fonts.

By default, your .NET applications won't change when large fonts are used. However, you can choose to support this feature by setting the Font property of your form to SystemFonts. IconTitleFont. As odd as it seems, this is the correct font to support default text—it's the font that Visual Studio uses for its dialogs. Additionally, you should handle the UserPreferenceChanged event to refresh the font immediately when the user changes the font DPI setting (no reboot is required).

Here's what your code should look like:

```
public partial class SmallOrLargeForm : Form
{
    public SmallOrLargeForm ()
    {
        this.Font = SystemFonts.IconTitleFont;
        InitializeComponent();
        SystemEvents.UserPreferenceChanged += new
            UserPreferenceChangedEventHandler(SystemEvents_UserPreferenceChanged);
    }

    private void SystemEvents_UserPreferenceChanged(object sender,
        UserPreferenceChangedEventArgs e)
    {
        if (e.Category == UserPreferenceCategory.Window)
        {
            this.Font = SystemFonts.IconTitleFont;
        }
    }

    protected override void Dispose(bool disposing)
    {
        if (disposing)
        {
            SystemEvents.UserPreferenceChanged -=
                new UserPreferenceChangedEventHandler(
                SystemEvents_UserPreferenceChanged);
            if (components != null) components.Dispose();
        }
        base.Dispose(disposing);
    }
}
```

Assuming the Form.AutoScaleMode is set to AutoScaleMode.Font (the default), your form and all its controls will resize to fit the new fonts. However, the result still isn't perfect, and you may find that your alignment goes slightly out of whack with some controls. A better solution to dealing with on-screen elements that may change in size is to use the layout controls described in Chapter 21.

Access Keys

Some controls (namely buttons, labels, and menu items) allow a character in their caption to be highlighted and used as an access key. For example, button controls often underline one character in the caption. If the user presses the Alt key and that character, the button is "clicked" automatically. To configure these shortcut keys just add an ampersand (&) before the special letter, as in "Sa&ve" to make v the access key. (If you actually want to use an ampersand, you'll need to include two ampersands: &&.)

Focus and the Tab Sequence

In the Windows operating system, a user can work with only one control at a time. The control that is currently receiving the user's key presses is the control that has focus. Sometimes this control is drawn slightly differently. For example, the button control uses a dotted line around its caption to show that it has the focus. Figure 2-8 shows focused and unfocused buttons with both the Windows XP visual styles and the classic Windows look.

Figure 2-8. *Focused buttons*

To move the focus, the user can click the mouse or use the Tab and arrow keys. The developer has to take some care to make sure that the Tab key moves focus in a logical manner (generally from left to right and then down the form). The developer also has to choose the control that should receive the focus when the window is first presented.

All controls that support focusing provide a Boolean TabStop property. When set to true, the control can receive focus through the Tab key. When set to false, the control is left out of the tab sequence and can be reached only using a mouse click.

■**Tip** You should set the TabStop property to false for controls that can accept key presses but are not directly accessed by the user in your application. For example, you might provide a DataGridView control, but use it to display static information. Of course, the disadvantage to this approach is that setting the TabStop to false also means the user will need to use the mouse to scroll the control if its contents extend beyond the bounds of its display region.

To set the tab order, you configure a control's TabIndex property. The control with a TabIndex of 0 gets the focus first. When the user presses the Tab key, the focus moves to the next control in the tab order, as long as it can accept focus. Visual Studio provides a special tool, shown in Figure 2-9, that allows you to quickly set tab order. Just select View ► Tab Order from the menu. You can then assign TabIndex values by clicking controls in the desired order.

Label controls have a TabIndex setting even though they cannot receive focus. This allows you to use a label with an access key. When the user triggers the label's access key, the focus is automatically forwarded to the next control in the tab order. For that reason, you should give your labels an appropriate place in the tab order, especially if they use access keys. (You create an access key by placing an ampersand character before a letter in the label's text.)

Controls that are invisible or disabled ("grayed out") are generally skipped in the tab order, and are not activated regardless of the TabIndex and TabStop settings. To hide or disable a control, you set the Visible and Enabled properties, respectively. Note that if you hide or disable a control at design time, the appearance is not modified. This is a deliberate idiosyncrasy designed to make it easier to work with controls at design time, and it is recommended that you follow this design when creating your own custom controls.

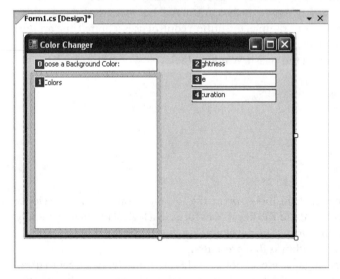

Figure 2-9. *The Visual Studio tab order tool*

Some other properties and methods for managing the focus programmatically are described in Table 2-3.

Table 2-3. *Members for Dealing with Focus at Runtime*

Member	Description
Focused	Returns true if the control currently has the focus.
ContainsFocus	Returns true if the control or one of its children currently has the focus.
Focus()	Sets the focus to the control. Note that this won't work if the control isn't visible. That means that you can't use it in an event handler for the Form.Load event, because the form isn't displayed until it is finished loading. To get around this problem, just set the TabIndex property of the control to 0 so that it will get the focus first.
SelectNextControl()	Sets the focus to a child control. For example, you can use Panel1.SelectNextControl() to set focus to a control inside the Panel1 container and Form1.SelectNextControl() to set focus to a control that's directly contained by the form. When you call SelectNextControl(), you supply a reference to one of the controls in the container, and the one that immediately follows in the tab order gets the focus.

Table 2-3. *Members for Dealing with Focus at Runtime*

Member	Description
GetNextControl()	Similar to SelectNextControl(), except this method returns the corresponding control object to your code instead of selecting it.
LostFocus and GotFocus events	These fire after the focus has moved. They do not give you the chance to stop the focus change, and are thus poor choices for validation routines. If you insist on programmatically resetting the focus in an event handler for one of these events, you may trigger a neverending loop of focus events. Instead, use the validation events or the ErrorProvider control, which are described in Chapter 18.

■**Tip** The GetNextControl() and SelectNextControl() methods are particularly useful when you are combining some type of interactive wizard or application help, as they can direct the user to an important control or part of the screen.

Responding to the Mouse and Keyboard

Controls also provide some built-in intelligence for dealing with the keyboard and mouse. These include low-level events that react to key presses and mouse movement, and methods that return key and mouse button state information. The next few sections describe all of these key ingredients.

Handling the Keyboard

Table 2-4 lists the events a typical control fires if it has focus when the user presses a key. These controls unfold in this order:

- KeyDown

- KeyPress

- KeyUp

Generally you will react to the KeyDown and KeyUp events when you need to react to special characters like the arrow keys, which do not trigger KeyPress events. The KeyPress event is used when you need to restrict input and perform character validation.

Table 2-4. *Events for Reacting to the Keyboard*

Event	Description
KeyDown	Occurs when a key is pressed while the current control has focus. The event provides additional information (through KeyEventArgs) about the state of the Alt and Ctrl keys and the key code.
KeyPress	This is a higher-level event that occurs once the key press is complete (but before the character appears, if the control is an input control). The event provides a KeyPressEventArgs object with information about the key character. The KeyPressEventArgs object also provides a Handled property, which you can set to true to cancel further processing, effectively canceling the character and suppressing its display in an input control.
KeyUp	This occurs when a key is released, just after the KeyPress event. It provides information through a KeyEventArgs object.

KeyPress and KeyDown

To understand the difference between KeyPress and KeyDown, consider what happens if the user holds down the Shift key and then presses the D key. In this scenario, the KeyPress event will fire once, and provide the exact character that was submitted (for example, the letter *D)*.

```
private void txt_KeyPress(object sender, KeyPressEventArgs e)
{
    // Show the key that was pressed.
    lbl.Text = "Key Press: " + e.KeyChar.ToString();
}
```

On the other hand, the KeyDown event will fire twice, once for the Shift key, and once for the D key.

```
private void txt_KeyDown(object sender, System.Windows.Forms.KeyEventArgs e)
{
    // Show the key letter that was pressed. For example, if the user presses
    // the D key, the key value will always be "D" regardless of whether Shift
    // was held down or not).
    lbl.Text = "Key Code: " + e.KeyCode.ToString();

    // Show the integer value for the key that was pressed
    // (like 16 for Shift or 68 for D).
    lbl.Text += "\nKey Value: " + e.KeyValue.ToString();

    // The KeyData contains information about every key that was held down,
    // as a combination of values from the Keys enumeration.
    // You can enumerate over these values, or just call ToString()
    // to a get a comma-separated list.
    lbl.Text += "\nKey Data: " + e.KeyData.ToString();
}
```

It's up to you to check the state of the Shift key the second time to determine that the user is trying to type a capital letter.

A number of keys (some of which are listed here) will trigger KeyDown and KeyUp events, but no KeyPress event:

- The function keys (F1, F2, etc.)

- The arrow (cursor) keys

- Shift, Ctrl, and Alt

- Caps Lock, Scroll Lock, and Num Lock

- Delete and Insert

- Pause and Break

- Home and End

- Page Up and Page Down

- Print Screen

If you want to update the display or react to a changed text value in an input control, you should probably not use any of these events. Instead, you should react to the higher-level Changed event, which fires when any modifications are made. The Changed event will fire if you modify the text programmatically or the user deletes the text via the right-click menu.

Key Modifiers

When a key event fires, you can test to see if a modifier key (like Ctrl, Alt, or Shift) is being held down. Here's the code you need:

```
private void txt_KeyDown(object sender, System.Windows.Forms.KeyEventArgs e)
{
    // You can use Modifiers to check for Alt, Control, and Shift.
    if ((e.Modifiers & Keys.Shift) == Keys.Shift)
    {
        lbl.Text += "\n" + "Shift was held down.";
    }

    // There is also an easier approach through the Alt, Control,
    // and Shift properties.
    if (e.Alt)
    {
        lbl.Text += "\n" + "Alt was held down.";
    }
}
```

To test the state of the Caps Lock, Scroll Lock, and Num Lock keys, you can use the static Control.IsKeyLocked method, which is new in .NET 2.0. Here's an example:

```
if (Control.IsKeyLocked(Keys.CapsLock))
{
    // Caps lock is enabled.
}
```

The Control.IsKeyLocked method accepts a member from the Keys enumeration. However, you can't test for any key other than Caps Lock, Scroll Lock, and Num Lock. Otherwise, a NotSupportedException will be thrown.

Tip You don't need to wait for an event to fire—you can use the Control.IsKeyLocked property at any time. If you want to check the state of a modifier key like Shift, Ctrl, or Alt outside of an event handler, just check the Control.ModifierKeys property in the same way that you would check the KeyEventArgs.Modifiers property. This is particularly useful when dealing with controls that don't provide a KeyDown event.

Unfortunately, the Control.IsKeyLocked method won't help you determine if the Insert key is pressed. If you want to make this determination (which is common if you're building a text input control like a text box), you need to make an unmanaged call to the GetKeyState() function. Here's how you define it:

```
[DllImport("User32.dll")]
private static extern short GetKeyState(System.Windows.Forms.Keys key);
```

And here's how you can check for the current state of the Insert key:

```
if (GetKeyState(Keys.Insert) == 1)
{
    // Overwrite mode is on.
}
else
{
    // Insert mode is on.
}
```

Intercepting Key Presses in a Form

Forms provide a Boolean KeyPreview property. If you set this to true, your form receives keypress events when any of its controls have focus, and it receives these events before the control does.

If, when handling the KeyPress event in the form, you set the KeyPressEventArgs.Handled property to true, the control that has focus won't receive the corresponding KeyPress event at all. (If you don't set the property to true, the control that has focus will still receive the event, but it will do so after the form.) The Handled property works for a single event, which means if you set Handled to true when dealing with the KeyPress event, the current control will still receive other events like KeyDown and KeyUp. If you want to stop any more events from firing for this keystroke (for both the form and the control), just set the KeyPressEventArgs.SuppressKeyPress property to true.

Handling keystrokes at the form level is useful if you need to take complete control of the keyboard. It's also useful if you want to capture a keystroke that occurs in any control. For example, you might listen for the F1 key and pop up a help window.

GetAsyncKeyState()

When you use the methods described so far, your code gets the *virtual key state*. This means it gets the state of the keyboard based on the messages you have retrieved from your input queue. This is not necessarily the same as the physical keyboard state.

For example, consider what happens if the user types faster than your code executes. Each time your KeyPress event fires, you'll have access to the keystroke that fired the event, not the typed-ahead characters. This is almost always the behavior you want.

Longtime Windows programmers know that the Win32 API also allows you to get the current state of the keyboard, which might be important if you're building some sort of keyboard logger or macro tool. Although this functionality isn't exposed through .NET, you can get in through an unmanaged call to the Win32 API (known as a Platform Invoke, or *PInvoke*). The method you need to use is called GetAsyncKeyState(). (By contrast, the .NET behavior matches the unmanaged GetKeyState() function.)

GetAsyncKeyState() takes a key value, and returns a value that tells you whether this key is currently pressed, and whether it has been pressed at all since the last GetAsyncKeyState() call.

Here's how you make the GetAsyncKeyState() function available in an application:

```
[DllImport("User32.dll")]
private static extern short GetAsyncKeyState(System.Windows.Forms.Keys key);
```

Now you can call GetAsyncKeyState() to check the state of any key. There are three possible values that can be returned, as illustrated in this example:

```
// Test for the letter D.
short state = GetAsyncKeyState(Keys.D);
switch (state)
{
    case 0:
        lbl.Text = "D has not been pressed since the last call.";
    case 1:
        lbl.Text =
 "D is not currently pressed, but has been pressed since the last call.";
    case -32767:
        lbl.Text = "D is currently pressed.";
}
```

Handling the Mouse

.NET includes a rich complement of methods for mouse handling (see Table 2-5). Using these events, you can react to clicks and mouse movements.

Table 2-5. *Events for Reacting to the Mouse*

Event	Description
MouseEnter	Occurs when the mouse moves into a control's region.
MouseMove*	Occurs when the mouse is moved over a control by a single pixel and also after a MouseUp event. Event handlers are provided with additional information about the current coordinates of the mouse pointer. Be warned that a typical mouse movement can generate dozens of MouseMove events. Event handlers that react to this event can be used to update the display, but not for more time-consuming tasks.
MouseHover	Occurs only once when the mouse lingers, without moving, over the control for a system-specified amount of time (typically a couple of seconds). Usually, you react to this event to highlight the control that is being hovered over, or update the display with some dynamic information.
MouseDown*	Occurs when a mouse button is clicked.
MouseUp*	Occurs when a mouse button is released. For many controls, this is where the logic for right-button mouse clicks is coded, although MouseDown is also sometimes used.
Click	Occurs when a control is clicked. Generally, this event occurs after the MouseDown event but before the MouseUp event. For basic controls, a Click event is triggered for left-button and right-button mouse clicks. Some controls have a special meaning for this event. One example is the button control. You can raise the Button.Click event by tabbing to the button and pressing the Enter key, or clicking with the left mouse button. Right-button clicks button trigger MouseDown and MouseUp events, but not Click events.
DoubleClick	Occurs when a control is clicked twice in succession. A Click event is still generated for the first click, but the second click generates the DoubleClick event.
MouseWheel	Occurs when the mouse wheel moves while the control has focus. The mouse pointer is not necessarily positioned over the control. This event does not work on unfocusable controls.
MouseLeave	Occurs when the mouse leaves a control's region.

* Indicates that the event handler uses the MouseEvent delegate, and provides additional information about the location of the mouse pointer (and the X and Y properties), the mouse wheel movement (Delta), and the state of the mouse buttons (Button).

The MouseMove, MouseDown, and MouseUp events provide additional information about the state of the mouse buttons. Separate MouseDown and MouseUp events are triggered for every mouse button. In this case, the MouseEventArgs.Button property indicates the button the caused the event.

```
private void lbl_MouseUp(Object sender, System.Windows.Forms.MouseEventArgs e)
{
    if (e.Button == MouseButtons.Right)
    {
        // This event was caused by a right-click.
        // Here is a good place to show a context menu.
    }
}
```

In the MouseMove event, however, the Button property indicates *all* the buttons that are currently depressed. That means that this property could take on more than one value from the MouseButtons enumeration. To test for a button, you need to use bitwise arithmetic.

```
private void lbl_MouseMove(Object sender, System.Windows.Forms.MouseEventArgs e)
{
    if ((e.Button & MouseButtons.Right) == MouseButtons.Right)
    {
        // The right mouse button is currently being held down.
        if ((e.Button & MouseButtons.Left) == MouseButtons.Left)
        {
            // You can get here only if both the left and the right mouse buttons
            // are currently held down.
        }
    }
}
```

Every control also provides a MousePosition, MouseButtons, and ModifierKeys property for information about the mouse and keyboard. The MouseButtons and ModifierKeys properties return information related to the last received message. The MousePosition property returns information about the *current* location of the mouse pointer, not the position where it was when the event was triggered. Additionally, the MousePosition property uses screen coordinates, not control coordinates, although you can translate between the two with the Form.PointToClient() and Form.ClientToPoint() methods.

There's one other detail to be aware of with mouse events. When a control receives a MouseDown event, it *captures* the mouse. That means it will continue to receive other mouse events (like MouseMove), even if the mouse pointer is moved off the bounds of the control. This continues until the user releases the mouse button and the MouseUp event fires. Intuitively, this behavior makes sense, but it's worth noting.

A Mouse/Keyboard Example

The mouse and keyboard events have some subtleties, and it's always best to get a solid and intuitive understanding by watching the events in action. The online code for this chapter provides an ideal example that creates a list of common mouse and keyboard events as they take place. Each entry also includes some event information, giving you an accurate idea of the order in which these events occur and the information they provide.

MouseMove events are not included in the list (because they would quickly swamp it with entries), but a separate label control reports on the current position of the mouse (see Figure 2-10).

Figure 2-10. *An event tracker*

For example, here's the code that adds an entry in response to the pic.MouseLeave event:

```
private void pic_MouseLeave(object sender, System.EventArgs e)
{
    Log("Mouse Leave");
}
```

The private Log() method adds the string of information, and scrolls the list control to the bottom to ensure that it is visible.

```
private void Log(String data)
{
    lstLog.Items.Add(data);
    int itemsPerPage = (int)(lstLog.Height / lstLog.ItemHeight);
    lstLog.TopIndex = lstLog.Items.Count - itemsPerPage;
}
```

Mouse Cursors

One other useful mouse-related property is Cursor. It sets the type of mouse cursor that is displayed when the mouse is moved over a control, and it applies to all child controls. If your application is about to perform a potentially time-consuming operation, you might want to set the Form.Cursor property to an hourglass. You can access standard system-defined cursors using the static properties of the Cursors class.

```
myForm.Cursor = Cursors.WaitCursor;
// (Perform long task.)
myForm.Cursor = Cursors.Default;
```

You can also create a custom cursor using the Cursor class, load a custom cursor graphic, and assign it to a control.

```
Cursor myCursor = new Cursor(Application.StartupPath + "\\mycursor.cur");
myCustomControl.Cursor = myCursor;
```

Cursor files are similar to icons, but they are stored in a .cur file format. Currently, animated cursors (.ani files) are not supported. However, you can support them through the unmanaged LoadCursorFromFile() function. Here's a class that provides this functionality:

```
public class AdvancedCursors
{
    [DllImport("User32.dll")]
    private static extern IntPtr LoadCursorFromFile(String str);

    public static Cursor Create(string filename)
    {
        // Get handle to cursor.
        IntPtr hCursor = LoadCursorFromFile(filename);

        // Check if it succeeded.
        if (!IntPtr.Zero.Equals(hCursor))
        {
            return new Cursor(hCursor);
        }
        else
        {
            throw new ApplicationException("Could not create cursor from file " +
                filename);
        }
    }
}
```

Now you can load an animated cursor with code like this:

```
try
{
    this.Cursor = AdvancedCursors.Create(
      Path.Combine(Application.StartupPath, "blob.ani"));
}
catch (ApplicationException err)
{
    MessageBox.Show(err.Message);
}
```

Low-Level Members

The .NET Framework hides the low-level messiness of the Windows API, but it doesn't render it inaccessible. This is a major advantage of .NET over other frameworks—it adds features without removing any capabilities.

For example, if you want to use a Windows API function that requires a window handle (a number that the operating system uses to identify every control uniquely), you can just read the Control.Handle property. The only special consideration is that you should retrieve the handle immediately before you use it. Changing some properties can cause a control to be re-created automatically, in which case it will receive a new handle. Already you've seen examples that use unmanaged calls to gain access to otherwise unsupported features like animated cursors and the live keyboard state.

You've probably also realized by now that low-level Windows messages are abstracted away in .NET controls, and replaced with more-useful events that bundle additional information. If, however, you need to react to a message that doesn't have a corresponding event, you can handle it directly by overriding the PreProcessMessage() or WndProc() method. (You can also attach global message filters for your entire application by using the Application.AddMessageFilter() method.) Table 2-6 gives an overview of all these members.

Table 2-6. *Low-Level Members*

Member	Description
Handle	Provides an IntPtr structure (a 32-bit integer on 32-bit operating systems) that represents the current control's window handle.
RecreatingHandle	Set to true while the control is being re-created with a new handle. There's no visible indication that allows the user to see this change is taking place, and it happens almost instantaneously.
GetStyle() and SetStyle()	Sets or gets a control style bit. Generally you will use higher-level properties to accomplish the same thing.
PreProcessMessage()and WndProc()	These methods allow you to receive a Windows message before it's handled by the Windows Forms infrastructure and turned into the corresponding event. In these methods, the message is represented as a Message structure, which you need to identify by ID number. Usually, you'll override one of these method to receive a message that would otherwise be ignored, or block a message you don't want the control to receive.
ProcessKeyPreview() and ProcessKeyMessage()	These methods allow you to receive Windows messages related to keyboard handling for a control. Typically you'll handle these messages if the control you're using doesn't provide KeyPress and KeyDown events and you want to intercept key presses. (One instance in which this is sometimes required is with the DataGrid control.)

This book focuses on pure .NET programming, and doesn't encourage the use of unmanaged calls unless necessary. Occasionally, a control will omit certain functionality, forcing you to intercept messages at a lower level to create the workaround you need. One example is the DataGrid control, which doesn't give developers the ability to control certain operations (like deleting records or handling errors). Another example is the TextBox, which doesn't allow the type of fine-grained keystroke handling you need to apply input masks. Happily, .NET remedies these shortcomings with a completely new DataGridView control (as described in Chapter 15) and a MaskedTextBox (as described in Chapter 18). However, there are still many cases in which you'll need to use a lower level. Some examples include video playback with the unmanaged Quartz library (see Chapter 16) and the GetWindowPlacementAPI() for saving and restoring form positions (shown in Chapter 3).

The Last Word

This chapter provided a sweeping tour through the basics of .NET controls, including how they interact, receive messages, process keystrokes and mouse movements, and handle focus. It also detailed the basic ingredients from the System.Drawing namespace for creating and managing colors, fonts, images, and more. The next chapter continues with another core topic for Windows user-interface programming—forms.

The Last Word

CHAPTER 3

■■■

Forms

Windows are the basic ingredients in any desktop application—so basic that the operating system itself is named after them. However, there's a fair deal of subtlety in exactly how you use a window, not to mention how you resize its content. This subtlety is what makes windows (or *forms*, to use .NET terminology) one of the most intriguing user-interface topics.

This chapter explores the Form class, and considers how forms interact and take ownership of one another. Along the way, you'll look at different types of containers, like the Panel, TabPage, and SplitContainer. You'll also explore the far-from-trivial problem of resizable windows, and learn how to design split-window interfaces.

The Form Class

The Form class is a special type of control that represents a complete window. It almost always contains other controls. The Form class does not derive directly from Control; instead, it acquires additional functionality through two extra layers, as shown in Figure 3-1.

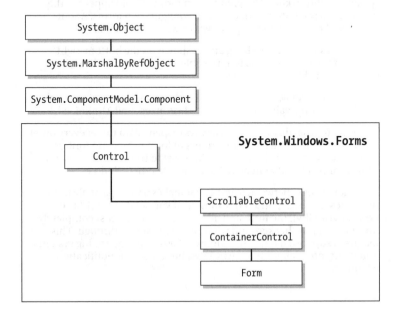

Figure 3-1. *The Form class lineage*

The Form class provides a number of basic properties that determine appearance and window style. Many of these properties (listed in Table 3-1) will be familiar if you are a seasoned Windows programmer because they map to styles defined by the Windows API.

Table 3-1. *Basic Style Properties*

Member	Description
FormBorderStyle	Specifies a value from the FormBorderStyle enumeration that identifies the type of window border. The form border you choose determines the border's appearance and whether it can be resized by the user.
ControlBox	Boolean property that determines whether the window has the system menu icon at the top-left corner. When clicked, this shows the system menu for moving, resizing, or closing the form.
MaximizeBox	Boolean property that determines whether the window has the maximize box at the top-right corner.
MinimizeBox	Boolean property that determines if the window has the minimize box at the top-right corner.
HelpButton	Boolean property that determines whether the window has the Help question-mark icon at the top-right corner. This button, previously used to trigger context-sensitive help, has fallen into disuse in most modern applications (and isn't supported in Windows XP).
Icon	References a System.Drawing.Icon object that is used to draw the window icon in the top-left corner. The visibility of this icon is determined by the ControlBox property.
ShowInTaskBar	Boolean property that determines whether a button appears for the window in the taskbar. Generally, main forms should appear in the taskbar, but secondary windows (like configuration forms, About boxes, and modal dialog boxes or windows? don't need to.
SizeGripStyle	Determines whether the sizing grip is shown on the bottom-right corner of the window. This is applicable only if FormBorderStyle is Sizable or SizableToolWindow.
WindowState	Identifies (and allows you to configure) the current state of a resizable window. Possible values are Normal, Maximized, and Minimized.
TopMost	When set to true, this window is always displayed on top of every other window in your application, regardless of form ownership (unless these other windows also have TopMost set to true). This is a useful setting for palettes that need to "float" above other windows.
Opacity	A fractional value between 0 and 1 that makes a form partially transparent if set to less than 1. For example, if you set this to 0.1 (a 10 percent visibility), the form and all its controls are almost completely invisible, and the background window clearly shows through. This feature is supported only on Windows 2000 or later operating systems, and is not intended for main windows, but for tool or notification windows.

Table 3-1. *Basic Style Properties*

Member	Description
TransparencyKey	Identifies a color that becomes transparent. Any occurrence of this color becomes invisible whether it is in the form background, another control, or even a picture contained inside a control. These transparent settings act like "holes" in your window. You can even click to activate another window if you see it through a transparent region. This feature is supported only on Windows 2000 or later. This is one of the techniques that allow you to create shaped, "skinnable" forms (the other property is Region, which lets you define a nonrectangular border). Both of these techniques are described in Chapter 23.

The Form class defines references to two special buttons, as shown in Table 3-2. These properties add automatic support for the Enter and Esc keys. If you don't set these properties, the Enter and Esc keys will have no effect.

Table 3-2. *Special Form Buttons*

Member	Description
AcceptButton	The button referenced by this property is automatically "clicked" when the user presses the Enter key. (In other words, its Click event fires.) This button is also sometimes known as the default button. On a form, the default button should always be the least-threatening button. Typically, this is a form's OK or Close button, unless that button could accidentally commit irreversible changes or discard work in progress.
CancelButton	The button referenced by this property is automatically "clicked" when the user presses the Esc key. (In other words, its Click event fires.) This is usually a Cancel button.

As you saw in Chapter 1, the preferred way to use .NET forms is to derive a custom class from the Form class. .NET forms also serve as switchboards that contain the event-handling code for all their child controls.

The Form class also defines some events of its own. These events (shown in Table 3-3) allow you to react when the form acquires focus, is about to be closed, or is first loaded into memory.

Table 3-3. *Form Events*

Event	Description
Activate and Deactivate	These events are the form equivalent of the LostFocus and GotFocus events for a control. Deactivate occurs when the user clicks a different form in the application or moves to another application. Activated occurs when the user switches to the window. You can also set the active form programmatically by callings its Activate() method, and you can retrieve the active form by inspecting the static ActiveForm property.

Table 3-3. *Form Events (Continued)*

Event	Description
Load	Occurs when the form first loads. It gives you the chance to perform additional control initialization (like filling a list control).
FormClosing	Occurs when the form is about to close. The CancelEventArgs object provides a Cancel property that you can set to true to force the form to remain open. Event handlers for this event often provide a message box prompting the user to save the document. This message box typically provides Yes, No, and Cancel buttons. If Cancel is selected, the operation should be canceled and the form should remain open.
FormClosed	Occurs when the form has closed.

The Closed and Closing events can be triggered for a variety of reasons. It's important to distinguish between some of these reasons so you know whether to prompt the user (for example, if the user initiated the shutdown) or just blindly save the current work (if the entire computer is shutting down).

In .NET 1.x, this information wasn't readily available because the Closed and Closing events don't provide it. However, in .NET 2.0 the FormClosing and FormClosed events replace these, and add a new EventArgs object that provides a CloseReason property. This can take one of several values from the CloseReason enumeration:

- ApplicationExitCall

- FormOwnerClosing

- MdiFormClosing

- TaskManagerClosing

- UserClosing

- WindowsShutDown

Finally, every form you create in Visual Studio has automatically generated designer code, which resides in a separate file named [FormName].Designer.cs. This code includes an InitializeComponent() method that is executed immediately when the form object is created but before it is displayed. The code in the designer region creates all the control objects and sets all the properties that you have configured at design time. Even for a simple window, this code is quite lengthy, and shouldn't be modified directly (as Visual Studio may become confused, or simply overwrite your changes). However, the hidden designer region is a great place to learn how to dynamically create and configure a control. For example, you can create a control at design time, set all its properties, and then simply copy the relevant code, almost unchanged, into another part of your code to create the control dynamically at runtime.

In the next few sections, you'll examine more advanced properties of the Form class and the classes it inherits from. You'll also learn the basic approaches for showing and interacting with forms.

Form Size and Position

The Form class provides the same Location and Size properties that every control does, but with a twist. The Location property determines the distance of the top-left corner of the window from the top-left corner of the screen (or desktop area). Furthermore, the Location property is ignored unless the StartPosition property is set to Manual. The possible values from the FormStartPosition enumeration are shown in Table 3-4.

Table 3-4. *StartPosition Values*

Value (from the FormStartPosition enumeration)	Description
CenterParent	If the form is displayed modally, the form is centered relative to the form that displayed it. If this form doesn't have a parent form (for example, if it's displayed modelessly), this setting is the same as WindowsDefaultLocation. However, there's a workaround—if you want to emulate the modal behavior, you can call Form.CenterToParent() in the event handler for the Load event, thereby centering a form whether it's modal or modeless.
CenterScreen	The form is centered in the middle of the screen.
Manual	The form is displayed in the location specified by the Location property, relative to the top-left corner of the desktop area.
WindowsDefaultLocation	The form is displayed in the Windows default location. In other words, there's no way to be sure exactly where it will end up.
WindowsDefaultBound	The form is displayed in the Windows default location, and with a default size (the Size property is ignored). This setting is rarely used, because you usually want exact control over a form's size.

The Screen Class

Sometimes you need to take a little care in choosing an appropriate location and size for your form. For example, you could accidentally create a window that is too large to be accommodated on a low-resolution display. If you are working with a single-form application, the best solution is to create a resizable form. If you are using an application with several floating windows, the answer is not as simple.

You could just restrict your window positions to locations that are supported on even the smallest monitors, but that's likely to frustrate higher-end users (who have purchased better monitors for the express purpose of fitting more information on the screen at a time). In this case, you usually want to make a runtime decision about the best window location. To do this, you need to retrieve some basic information about the available screen real estate using the Screen class.

Consider the following example that uses the Screen class to manually center the form when it first loads. It retrieves information about the resolution of the screen using the Screen.

PrimaryScreen property. Although this code is equivalent to calling Form.CenterToScreen(), the Screen class gives you the flexibility to implement different positioning logic.

```
private void dynamicSizeForm_Load(System.Object sender,
  System.EventArgse)
{
    Screen scr = Screen.PrimaryScreen;
    this.Left = (scr.WorkingArea.Width - this.Width) / 2;
    this.Top = (scr.WorkingArea.Height - this.Height) / 2;
}
```

The members of the Screen class are listed in Table 3-5.

Table 3-5. *Screen Members*

Member	Description
AllScreens (static)	Returns an array of Screen objects, with one for each display on the system. This method is useful for systems that use multiple monitors to provide more than one desktop (otherwise, it returns an array with one Screen object).
Primary (static)	Returns the Screen object that represents the primary display on the system.
Bounds	Returns a Rectangle structure that represents the bounds of the display area for the current screen.
GetBounds() (static)	Accepts a reference to a control, and returns a Rectangle representing the size of the screen that contains the control (or the largest portion of the control if it is split over more than one screen).
WorkingArea	Returns a Rectangle structure that represents the bounds of the display area for the current screen, minus the space taken for the taskbar and any other docked windows.
GetWorkingArea() (static)	Accepts a reference to a control, and returns a Rectangle representing the working area of the screen that contains the control (or the largest portion of the control, if it is split over more than one screen).
DeviceName	Returns the device name associated with a screen as a string.

Saving and Restoring Form Location

A common requirement for a form is to remember its last location. Usually, this information is stored in the registry. The code that follows shows a helper class that automatically stores information about a form's size and position using a key based on the name of a form.

```
public class FormPositionHelper
{
    public static string RegPath = @"Software\App\";
```

```
    public static void SaveSize(System.Windows.Forms.Form frm)
    {
        // Create or retrieve a reference to a key where the settings
        // will be stored.
        RegistryKey key;
        key = Registry.LocalMachine.CreateSubKey(RegPath + frm.Name);

        key.SetValue("Height", frm.Height);
        key.SetValue("Width", frm.Width);
        key.SetValue("Left", frm.Left);
        key.SetValue("Top", frm.Top);
    }

    public static void SetSize(System.Windows.Forms.Form frm)
    {
        RegistryKey key;
        key = Registry.LocalMachine.OpenSubKey(RegPath + frm.Name);

        if (key != null)
        {
            frm.Height = (int)key.GetValue("Height");
            frm.Width = (int)key.GetValue("Width");
            frm.Left = (int)key.GetValue("Left";
            frm.Top = (int)key.GetValue("Top");
        }
    }
}
```

■**Note** This example uses the HKEY_LOCAL_MACHINE branch of the registry, which means that changes are global for the current computer. You might want to use HKEY_CURRENT_USER instead to allow user-specific window settings. This is also a requirement if your user does not have administrator rights, in which case the application will encounter a SecurityException. In this case, just use the Registry.CurrentUser value instead of Registry.LocalMachine in the code.

To use this class in a form, you call the SaveSize() method when the form is closing:

```
private void MyForm_Closing(object sender,
 System.ComponentModel.CancelEventArgs e)
{
    FormPositionHelper.SaveSize(this);
}
```

and call the SetSize() method when the form is first opened:

```
private void MyForm_Load(object sender, System.EventArgs e)
{
    FormPositionHelper.SetSize(this);
}
```

In each case, you pass a reference to the form you want the helper class to inspect.

GetWindowPlacement()

The previous example has a serious limitation. If you save the window state while the window is maximized or minimized, you'll end up saving the maximized or minimized size coordinates. This is exactly what you *don't* want. The next time you restore the size information, your window will have lost its standard size, and may appear unnaturally small or large.

You could defend against this by refusing to save the window coordinates if its WindowState is anything other than Normal. This partly solves the problem, but it still means that if you resize a window, maximize it, and then close it, you won't get the benefit of storing the previous size information. Unfortunately, this is one of the more glaring omissions in the Windows Forms toolkit.

The proper workaround is to use the Win32 functions GetWindowPlacement() and SetWindowPlacement(), shown here:

```
[DllImport("user32.dll")]
private static extern bool GetWindowPlacement(IntPtr handle,
[In, Out] ManagedWindowPlacement placement);

[DllImport("user32.dll")]
private static extern bool SetWindowPlacement(IntPtr handle,
ManagedWindowPlacement placement);
```

Using these methods isn't completely straightforward, because they work with structures that combine several pieces of window information (like coordinates and size). To use these methods, you need to add the correct definition for these structures to your application. Although they aren't shown in the next example, you can see the full ManagedPt, ManagedRect, and ManagedWindowPlacement classes with the downloadable code for this chapter (available in the Source Code area of the Apress Web site, www.apress.com).

Once you've added these structures, you can call GetWindowPlacement() to retrieve a ManagedWindowPlacement object that represents a specific window (which is identified by its handle). The easiest way to store this information in the registry is to use serialization, which lets you boil down the complete object into one long byte array.

Here's the code you need:

```
public static void SaveSize(System.Windows.Forms.Form frm)
{
    RegistryKey key;
    key = Registry.LocalMachine.CreateSubKey(RegPath + frm.Name);
```

```
    // Get the window placement.
    ManagedWindowPlacement placement = new ManagedWindowPlacement();
    GetWindowPlacement(frm.Handle, ref placement);

    // Serialize it.
    MemoryStream ms = new MemoryStream();
    BinaryFormatter f = new BinaryFormatter();
    f.Serialize(ms, placement);

    // Store it as a byte array.
    key.SetValue("Placement", ms.ToArray());
}
```

It's easy to retrieve this information and reapply it with SetWindowPlacement():

```
public static void SetSize(System.Windows.Forms.Form frm)
{
    RegistryKey key;
    key = Registry.LocalMachine.OpenSubKey(RegPath + frm.Name);

    if (key != null)
    {
        MemoryStream ms = new MemoryStream((byte[])key.GetValue("Placement"));
        BinaryFormatter f = new BinaryFormatter();
        ManagedWindowPlacement placement = (ManagedWindowPlacement)
          f.Deserialize(ms);
        SetWindowPlacement(frm.Handle, ref placement);
    }
}
```

Now the FormPositionHelper correctly handles maximized and minimized windows. When you reapply the ManagedWindowPlacement you set the form's normal size and its current window state in one step.

Scrollable Forms

The Form class inherits some built-in scrolling support from the ScrollableControl class. Generally, forms do not use these features directly. Instead, you will probably use scrollable controls like rich text boxes to display scrollable document windows. However, these features are still available, rather interesting, and effortless to use.

Figure 3-2 shows a form that has its AutoScroll property set to true. This means that as soon as a control is added to the form that does not fit in its visible area, the required scroll bars will be displayed. The scrolling process takes place automatically.

Figure 3-2. *A scrollable form*

■**Tip** All controls that derive from ScrollableControl also offer the useful ScrollControlIntoView() method. As long as AutoScroll is true, you can use ScrollControlIntoView() with the reference of a child control you want to show. If this control isn't already visible, ScrollControlIntoView() will automatically scroll through the window until it is.

If Figure 3-2 looks a little strange, that's because it is. Scrollable forms make a few appearances in Windows applications (Microsoft Access is one example) but are relatively rare. They should be discouraged as unconventional. Instead, it probably makes more sense to use another class that derives from ScrollableControl, like Panel (see Figure 3-3).

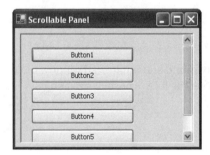

Figure 3-3. *A scrollable panel*

By default, scroll bars aren't shown unless a control is off the edge of the form, or you explicitly set the Boolean HScroll and VScroll properties. However, you can configure an AutoScrollMinSize, which specifies the required space, in pixels, between each control and the window border. If this minimum space is not provided, scroll bars are shown.

The Form class doesn't derive directly from ScrollableControl. Instead, it derives from the ContainerControl (which does derive from ScrollableControl). Like the ScrollableControl class, the ContainerControl class doesn't provide many members that you are likely use. It includes a ProcessTabKey() method that the .NET Framework uses transparently to manage focus, a ParentForm property that identifies the form that contains this control, and an ActiveControl property that identifies or sets the control that currently has focus.

Showing a Form

To display a form, you need to create an instance of the Form class and use the Show() or ShowDialog() method.

The Show() method creates a modeless window, which doesn't stop code from executing in the rest of your application. That means you can create and show several modeless windows, and the user can interact with them all at once. When using modeless windows, synchronization code is sometimes required to make sure that changes in one window update the information in another window to prevent a user from working with invalid information.

Here's an example that uses the Show() method:

```
MainForm frmMain = new MainForm();
frmMain.Show();
```

The ShowDialog() method, on the other hand, interrupts your code. Nothing happens on the user interface thread of your application until the user closes the window (or the window closes in response to a user action). The controls for all other windows are "frozen," and attempting to click a button or interact with a control has no effect (other than an error chime, depending on Windows settings). This makes the window ideal for presenting the user with a choice that needs to be made before an operation can continue. For example, consider Microsoft Word, which shows its Options and Print windows modally, forcing you to make a decision before continuing. On the other hand, the windows used to search for text or check the spelling in a document are shown modelessly, allowing the user to edit text in the main document window while performing the task.

Custom Dialog Windows

Often when you show a dialog window, you are offering the user a choice. The code that displays the window waits for the result of that choice, and then acts on it.

You can easily accommodate this design pattern by creating some sort of public property on the dialog form. When the user makes a selection in the dialog window, this special property is set, and the form is closed. Your calling code can then check for this property and determine what to do next based on its value. (Remember, even when a form is closed, the form object and all its control information still exists until the variable referencing it goes out of scope.)

For example, consider the form shown in Figure 3-4, which provides two buttons: OK and Cancel.

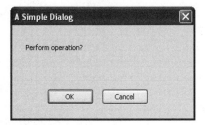

Figure 3-4. *A simple dialog form*

The form class provides a UserSelection property, which uses a custom enumeration to identify the action that was used to close the window:

```
public partial class DialogForm : System.Windows.Forms.Form
{
    // (Constructor code omitted.)

    public enum SelectionTypes
    { OK, Cancel }

    // This property must be public so the caller can access it.
    public SelectionTypes UserSelection;

    private void cmdOK_Click(object sender, EventArgs e)
    {
        UserSelection = SelectionTypes.OK;
        this.Close();
    }

    private void cmdCancel_Click(object sender, EventArgs e)
    {
        UserSelection = SelectionTypes.Cancel;
        this.Close();
    }

}
```

The code that creates the form shows it modally. It then checks the UserSelection property after the window is closed to determine what action the user selected:

```
DialogForm frmDialog = new DialogForm();
frmDialog.ShowDialog();

// The code uses a custom enumeration to make the code readable and less
// error-prone.
switch (frmDialog.UserSelection)
{
    case DialogForm.SelectionTypes.OK:
        // (Do something here.)
        break;
    case DialogForm.SelectionTypes.Cancel:
        // (Do something else here.)
        break;
}

// Release the form and all its resources.
frmDialog.Dispose();
```

Note When you show a window with ShowDialog(), the window and control resources aren't released after the window is closed. That's because you may still need these objects (for example, to determine what values the user entered in a set of input controls). However, once you've retrieved the information you need, you should explicitly call the Dispose() method to release all your control handlers immediately rather than waiting for the garbage collector to do the work later on.

This is an effective, flexible design. In some cases, it gets even better: You can save code by using .NET's built-in support for dialog forms. This technique works best if your dialog needs only to return a simple value like Yes, No, OK, or Cancel. It works like this: In your dialog form, you set the DialogResult of the appropriate button control to one of the values from the DialogResult enumeration (found, like all user-interface types, in the System.Windows.Forms namespace). For example, you can set the Cancel button's result to DialogResult.Cancel, and the OK button's result to DialogResult.OK. When the user clicks the appropriate button, the dialog form is immediately closed, and the corresponding DialogResult is returned to the calling code. Best of all, you don't need to write any event-handling code to make it happen.

Your calling code would interact with a .NET dialog window like this:

```
DialogForm frmDialog = new DialogForm();
DialogResult result;
result = frmDialog.ShowDialog();

switch (result)
{
    case DialogResult.OK:
        // The window was closed with the OK button.
        break;
    case DialogResult.Cancel:
        // The window was closed with the Cancel button.
        break;
}
```

The code is cleaner and the result is more standardized. The only drawback is that you are limited to the DialogResult values shown in the following list (although you could supplement this technique with additional public form variables that would be read only if needed):

- OK

- Cancel

- Yes

- No

- Abort

- Retry

- Ignore

Form Interaction

You should minimize the need for form interactions, as they complicate code unnecessarily. If you do need to modify a control in one form based on an action in another form, create a dedicated method in the target form. That makes sure that the dependency is well-identified, and adds another layer of indirection, making it easier to accommodate changes to the form's interface. Figures 3-5 and 3-6 show two examples for implementing this pattern. Figure 3-5 shows a form that triggers a second form to refresh its data in response to a button click. This form does not directly attempt to modify the second form's user interface; instead, it relies on a custom intermediate method called DoUpdate().

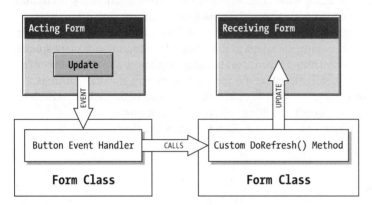

Figure 3-5. *A single-form interaction*

The second example, Figure 3-6, shows a case in which more than one form needs to be updated. The acting form relies on a higher-level application method, which calls the required form update methods (perhaps by iterating through a collection of forms). This approach is better because it works at a higher level. In the approach shown in Figure 3-5, the acting form doesn't need to know anything specific about the controls in the receiving form. The approach in Figure 3-6 goes one step further—the acting form doesn't need to know anything at all about the receiving form class.

You can go even one step further in decoupling this example. Rather than having the Application class trigger a method in the various forms, it could simply fire an event and allow the forms to choose how to respond to that event.

■**Note** These rules don't apply for MDI applications, which have built-in features that help you track child and parent windows. Chapter 19 presents a few detailed examples of how MDI forms can interact with one another.

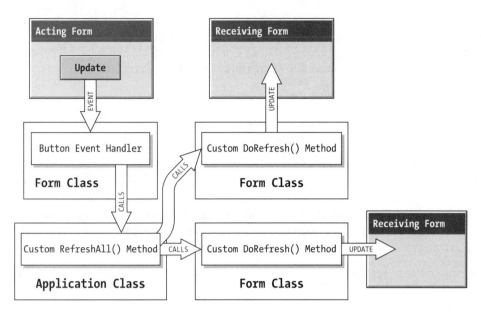

Figure 3-6. *A one-to-many form interaction*

Tracking Forms

Once you create a form, it exists until you end your application or explicitly call the Form.Close() method. As with all controls, even when a form variable goes out of scope, the actual window continues to exist. However, without the form variable, your code has no way to access the form.

This isn't a problem if you code your forms independently and place all the code that uses the form inside the appropriate form class. This way, your code can simply use the reference to access the form (as this always points to the current instance of a class). However, things become a little trickier if you need to allow interaction between forms. For example, if you want to trigger an action in another form, you need to make sure you track the form variable so it's available when you need it.

All this raises a good question: where should you store the references to a form that you might need later? Two common choices are to use the Program class that Visual Studio creates in all new Windows projects, or to create a dedicated class. Either way, you can track the forms in your application using static member variables. The following code presents one such example class that keeps static references for two forms:

```
public static class AppForms
{
    public static MainForm Main;
    public static SecondaryForm Secondary;
}
```

Using this class, you can refer to the forms you need anywhere in your application with syntax like this:

```
AppForms.MainForm.Show();
```

Static members are always available, so you won't need to create an instance of the AppForms class to access the two forms. Also, keep in mind that the AppForms class doesn't actually set the form references. You'll need to do that when you create and display the form. One easy way to automate this process is to insert a little code into the Form.Load event handler:

```
private void MainForm_Load(object sender, EventArgs e)
{
    // Register the newly created form instance.
    AppForms.Main = this;
}
```

This approach works well if every form class is created only once. If you want to track multiple instances of the same form, you probably want to use a collection object in your AppForms class. The following example uses the generic List<T> collection, although you can also use the generic Dictionary<TKey, TValue> collection if you want to index every form with a key. Both collection types are found in the System.Collections.Generic namespace.

```
public static class AppForms
{
    public static MainForm Main;
    public static List<Form> SecondaryForms = new List<Form>();
}
```

Forms can add themselves to this collection as needed:

```
private void SecondaryForm_Load(object sender, EventArgs e)
{
    // Register the newly created form instance.
    AppForms.SecondaryForms.Add(this);
}
```

When trying to read one of the form variables, you should also explicitly check if the value is null (in other words, it hasn't yet been created) before attempting to access the form object.

.NET 2.0 introduces another solution for tracking forms: the Application.OpenForms property. Every time you show a form, it's automatically added to this collection. When the form is closed, it's removed from the collection. Forms aren't indexed in any way, so you'll need to loop through the collection to find what you're interested in. One commonly used approach is to check the form caption (the Text property) or the form name (the Name property), although both of these approaches are fragile. A better solution is to check if a form is an instance of a given class by using the is or as keyword, as shown here:

```
foreach (Form frm in Application.OpenForms)
{
    if (frm is SecondaryForm)
    {
        // The SecondaryForm class provides a custom DoRefresh() method.
        // You need to cast this form reference to access it.
        ((SecondaryForm)frm).DoRefresh();
    }
}
```

The OpenForms collection provides a set of generic Form objects. It's up to you to cast the reference to the correct custom form class if you need to access additional properties or methods that you've added.

Note You can also get the currently active form in your application by checking the static Form.ActiveForm property. However, if you use this object be aware of a few idiosyncrasies. The ActiveForm reflects the active form in the current application. If a window in another application is active, you'll get a null reference. Oddly enough, you'll also get a null reference if your application is in the process of showing a message box. These quirks typically appear when you're creating a multithreaded application that has some code that runs perpetually, outside of any specific form.

Form Ownership

.NET allows a form to "own" other forms. Owned forms are useful for floating toolbox and command windows. One example of an owned form is the Find and Replace window in Microsoft Word. When an owner window is minimized, the owned forms are also minimized automatically. When an owned form overlaps its owner, it is always displayed on top. Table 3-6 lists the Form class properties that support owned forms.

Table 3-6. *Ownership Members of the Form Class*

Member	Description
Owner	Identifies a form's owner. You can set this property to change a form's ownership or release an owned form.
OwnedForms	Provides an array of all the forms owned by the current form. This array is read-only.
AddOwnedForm() and RemovedOwnedForm()	You can use these methods to add or release forms from an owner. It has the same result as setting the Owner property.

The following example (shown in Figure 3-7) loads two forms, and provides buttons on the owner that acquire or release the owned form. You can try this sample (included under the project name FormOwnership in the downloadable code for this chapter—visit the Source Code area of www.apress.com) to observe the behavior of owned forms.

```
public partial class OwnerForm : System.Windows.Forms.Form
{
    // (Constructor code omitted.)

    private OwnedForm frmOwned = new OwnedForm();
```

```
private void Owner_Load(object sender, System.EventArgs e)
{
    this.Show();
    frmOwned.Show();
}

private void cmdAddOwnership_Click(object sender, System.EventArgs e)
{
    this.AddOwnedForm(frmOwned);
    frmOwned.lblState.Text = "I'm Owned";
}

private void cmdReleaseOwnership_Click(object sender, System.EventArgs e)
{
    this.RemoveOwnedForm(frmOwned);
    frmOwned.lblState.Text = "I'm Free!";
}
}
```

Note that for this demonstration, the lblState control in the owned form has been modified to be publicly accessible (by changing the access modifier from internal to public). As described in the "Form Interaction" section of this chapter, this violates encapsulation and wouldn't be a good choice for a full-scale application. A much better idea would be to wrap the label text in a custom property.

Figure 3-7. *An owned-form tester*

Prebuilt Dialogs

.NET provides some custom dialog types that you can use to show standard operating-system windows. The most common of these is the MessageBox class, which exposes a static Show() method. You can use this code to display a standard Windows message box (see Figure 3-8):

```
MessageBox.Show("You must enter a name.", "Name Entry Error",
                MessageBoxButtons.OK, MessageBoxIcon.Exclamation) ;
```

Figure 3-8. *A simple message box*

The message-box icon types are listed in Table 3-7. The button types you can use Show() method with a message box are as follows:

- AbortRetryIgnore

- OK

- OKCancel

- RetryCancel

- YesNo

- YesNoCancel

Table 3-7. *MessageBoxIcon Values*

MessageBoxIcon	Displays
Asterisk or Information	A lowercase letter *i* in a circle
Error, Hand, or Stop	A white *X* in a circle with a red background
Exclamation or Warning	An exclamation point in a triangle with a yellow background
None	No icon
Question	A question mark in a circle

In addition, .NET provides useful dialogs that allow you to show standard windows for opening and saving files, choosing a font or color, and configuring the printer. These classes all inherit from System.Windows.Forms.CommonDialog. For the most part, you show these dialogs like an ordinary window, and then inspect the appropriate property to find the user selection.

For example, the code for retrieving a color selection is as follows:

```
ColorDialog colorDialog = new ColorDialog();

// Sets the initial color select to the current color,
// so that if the user cancels, the original color is restored.
if (colorDialog.ShowDialog() == DialogResult.OK)
    shape.ForeColor = colorDialog.Color;
```

The dialogs often provide a few other properties. For example, with a ColorDialog you can set AllowFullOpen to false to prevent users from choosing a custom color, and ShowHelp to true to allow them to invoke Help by pressing F1. (In this case, you need to handle the HelpRequest event.)

OpenFileDialog and SaveFileDialog acquire some additional features (some of which are inherited from the FileDialog class). Both support a filter string, which sets the allowed file extensions. The OpenFileDialog also provides properties that let you validate the user's selection (CheckFileExists) and allow multiple files to be selected (Multiselect). Here's an example:

```
OpenFileDialog myDialog = new OpenFileDialog();

myDialog.Filter = "Image Files(*.BMP;*.JPG;*.GIF)|*.BMP;*.JPG;*.GIF" +
                  "|All files (*.*)|*.*";
myDialog.CheckFileExists = true;
myDialog.Multiselect = true;

if (myDialog.ShowDialog() == DialogResult.OK)
{
    string selectedFiles = "";
    foreach (string file in myDialog.FileNames)
    {
        selectedFiles += file + " ";
    }
    lblDisplay.Text = "You chose: " + selectedFiles;
}
```

Table 3-8 provides an overview of the prebuilt dialog classes. Figure 3-9 shows a small image of each window type.

Table 3-8. *Common Prebuilt Dialog Classes*

Class	Description
ColorDialog	Displays the system colors and controls that allow the user to define custom colors. The selected color can be found in the Color property.
OpenFileDialog	Allows the user to select a file, which is returned in the FileName property (or the FileNames collection, if you have enabled multiple file select). Additionally, you can use the Filter property to set the file format choices, and use CheckFileExists to enforce validation.
SaveFileDialog	Allows the user to select a file, which is returned in the FileName property. You can also use the Filter property to set the file format choices, and set the CreatePrompt and OverwritePrompt Boolean properties to instruct .NET to display a confirmation if the user selects a new file or an existing file, respectively.
FontDialog	Allows the user to choose a font face and size, which is provided in the Font property (and its color through the Color property). You can limit the size selection with properties like MinSize and MaxSize, and you can set ShowColor and ShowEffects to configure whether the user changes the font color and uses special styles like underlining and strikeout.
PageSetupDialog	Allows the user to configure page layout, page format, margins, and the printer.
PrintDialog	Allows the user to select a printer, choose which portions of the document to print, and invoke printing. To use this dialog, simply place the PrintDocument object for the document you want to print in the PrintDialog.Document property.
PrintPreviewDialog	This is the only dialog that is not a part of standard Windows architecture. It provides a painless way to show a print preview—just assign the PrintDocument to the Document property and display the form. The same logic you write for handling the actual printing is used automatically to construct the preview. Alternatively, you can use the PrintPreviewControl to show the same preview inside one of your custom windows.

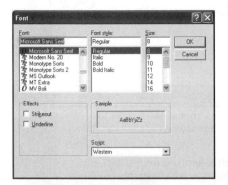

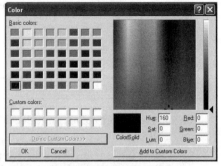

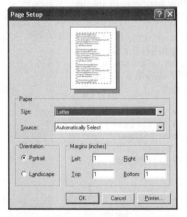

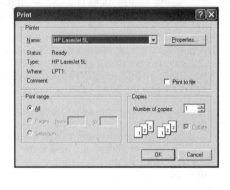

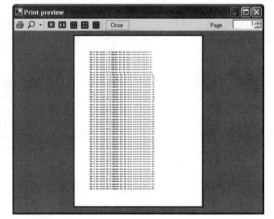

Figure 3-9. *Common dialogs*

Resizable Forms

Each week, Windows developers from every programming language spend countless hours trying to solve the problem of resizable windows that smoothly and nicely rearrange their contained controls. Some purchase third-party ActiveX controls designed to transform static forms into resizable wonders automatically. These components are easy to use, but generally provide mediocre results that aren't suitable for professional applications. Other developers ignore the problem, and stubbornly lock interfaces into fixed-size dialog boxes, making them seem unmistakably primitive. Many developers eventually give in and write lengthy code routines to resize their forms by hand.

.NET adds two features—anchoring and docking—that provide built-in support for resizable forms. These features allow you to configure a few properties, and end up with intelligent controls that adjust themselves automatically. The catch? It's extremely easy to end up with a window that resizes its controls in an embarrassingly unprofessional way with far less effort than was needed before.

Matching a good resizing approach with a sophisticated interface is possible, but it requires a little more subtlety and a few tricks. The next few sections describe these tricks, such as adding container controls and using the DockPadding property. Along the way, you learn how to create scrollable windows and controls, and see a full-fledged Explorer-style application that uses automatic resizing the right way.

The Problem of Size

The resizable-forms dilemma stems from the fact that the Windows operating system supports a variety of monitors at several different resolutions. A window that looks decently sized on one computer may shrink to a toylike box on another, or even stretch beyond the bounds of the desktop, obscuring important controls.

For many simple applications, these types of problems are not serious because programmers usually design their applications for a set minimum standard resolution (such as 800 × 600 or, more commonly today, 1024 ×768). It's generally accepted that users with much larger viewable areas expect to run several programs at once, and purchased larger screens so that they can put different programs side by side. They don't expect to use up the extra viewable area with larger fonts or extra white space in a dialog box.

A document-based application can't afford to ignore these considerations. Users with more available space expect to be able to use it to see more information at a time. Programs that ignore this consideration are irredeemably frustrating.

One common solution is to write procedures that dynamically resize the window by responding to a resize event or message. For example, you could store the distance between a control and the form edges using code like this when the form loads:

```
private int buttonMargin = 0;

private void Form_Load(object sender, System.EventArgs e)
{
    // Store the offset of the button1 control.
    // Use ClientSize rather than Size to ignore details like
    // scroll bars and the form border.
    buttonMargin = ClientSize.Width - button1.Width;
}
```

Now you simply need to react to the Form.SizeChanged event to resize the button1 control, keeping it at the same distance from both the left and right edges:

```
private void Form_SizeChanged(object sender, System.EventArgs e)
{
    button1.Width = ClientSize.Width - buttonMargin;
}
```

Unfortunately, if your window has more than a few controls, this code becomes long, repetitive, and ugly. It's also hard to alter or debug when the form changes even slightly. In .NET, the picture improves considerably with built-in support for resizing.

Minimum and Maximum Form Size

The first useful feature the Form class introduces for managing size is the MaximumSize and MinimumSize properties, which stop users abruptly when they try to resize a form beyond its set limits.

If you have the Show Window Contents While Dragging environment setting enabled, the border suddenly becomes fixed when you hit the minimum size, as though it's glued in place. Similarly, you can set a maximum size, although this is less conventional. In this case, even when you try to maximize a window, it won't go beyond the set size, which can confuse the user.

The Visual Studio IDE also stops you from resizing your form to an invalid size at design time when you have these properties set. If you set the form size to an invalid value in code, no error will occur. Instead, your window just automatically shrinks or expands to a valid size if it's outside the bounds of the MinimumSize or MaximumSize properties.

One final caveat: both of these settings are ignored if you make your window an MDI child inside another window. In that case, your window will be freely resizable.

Anchoring

Anchoring allows you to latch a control on to one of the form's corners. Anchored controls always stay a fixed distance from the point they are bound to. By default, every control is anchored to the top-left corner. That means if you resize the form, the controls stay fixed in place.

On the other hand, you can use .NET to anchor a control to a different corner or edge. For example, if you chose the top-right corner, the control moves as you expand the window width-wise to stay within a fixed distance of the top-right corner. If you expand the form heightwise, the control stays in place because it's anchored to the top. It doesn't need to follow the bottom edge.

Figure 3-10 shows a window with two controls that use anchoring. The button is anchored to the bottom-right, and the text box is anchored to all sides.

To anchor a button in .NET, you set the Anchor property using one of the values from the AnchorStyles enumeration. It's almost always easiest to set anchoring at design time using the Properties window. A special editor (technically, a UITypeEditor) lets you select the edges you are anchoring to by clicking them in a miniature picture, as shown in Figure 3-11. You don't need to run your program to test your anchoring settings; the Visual Studio IDE provides the same behavior when you resize the form.

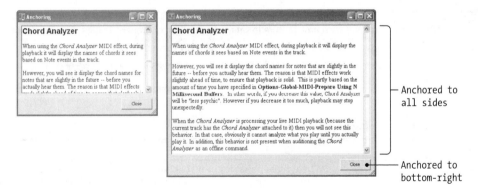

Figure 3-10. *Reiszing a window that uses anchoring*

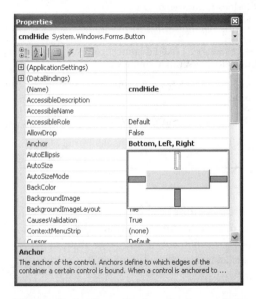

Figure 3-11. *Setting control anchoring at design time*

Resizing Controls with Anchoring

Anchoring to one corner works best with controls that don't need to change size but should remain in a consistent position. This typically includes buttons (for example, OK and Cancel should always remain at the bottom of the window) and simple controls like labels and text boxes. If you use this type of anchoring on every control, you create a window that gradually spreads out as it enlarges (which is almost never the effect you want).

Instead, you can anchor a control to more than one side at once. Then, as you expand the window, the control needs to expand to keep a fixed distance from all the anchored sides. Table 3-9 lists some of the ways that you can combine anchor settings for different effects.

■**Tip** When using a resizable ListBox control, be sure to set the IntegralHeight property to false. This ensures that the ListBox can grow evenly. Otherwise, the ListBox is automatically resized to ensure that no list item is partially displayed. This causes it to "jump" awkwardly between valid sizes as its height grows or shrinks.

Table 3-9. *Common Anchoring Choices*

Anchoring	Description
Top + Left	The typical behavior controls have on pre-.NET platforms. Controls remain a fixed distance from the top-left corner, but they don't move or expand as the form changes size.
Top + Right	The control moves to stay a fixed distance from the right of the form, but it does not move down.
Right + Left	The control's width expands as the form widens.
Bottom + Left	The control moves to stay a fixed distance from the bottom of the form, but it does not move to the side.
Bottom + Right	The control moves to keep a fixed distance from the bottom-right corner.
Top + Bottom	The control's height expands as the form lengthens.
Top + Bottom + Right + Left	The control's width and height expand as the form is enlarged.

The controls that benefit the most from anchoring to more than one side are those that contain more information than they can display at once. For example, a DataGridView, a RichTextBox, or even a ListBox control may present a scrolled view into a large amount of information. It makes sense for these controls to resize to use available screen area. On the other hand, a button usually shouldn't be set to resize itself.

Minimum and Maximum Control Size

Forms aren't the only classes to provide the MaximumSize and MinimumSize properties. In fact, these properties are defined in the base Control class, and are available to all controls. Using them, you can create a resizable control that stops expanding or shrinking when it reaches a predefined point. The user can still continue to expand or shrink the form (subject to its MaximumSize and MinimumSize properties), but the size of the control won't change.

The MaximumSize and MinimumSize properties come into effect only when you have a control anchored to opposite sides of a form. One limitation of these settings is that once the control reaches its maximum size, it essentially behaves like a Top + Left anchored control. In other words, there's no easy way to create a control that expands to a maximum size as the form is resized, and then continues to move with the bottom or right edge of the form.

Containers and Anchoring

Rather than try to anchor every control in a window, you should use one or more container controls to save some work. Containers also make it easier to rearrange portions of user interface simultaneously, or even transplant them from one form to another.

To use anchoring with container controls, you need to understand that anchoring is always relative to the container. That means that if you place a button inside a group box and you anchor it to the bottom right, it will be anchored to the bottom-right corner of the group box. It won't move when the size of the form changes; it will move only when the size of the container changes. For example, consider the button shown in Figure 3-12. The form is resized, but the group box doesn't change, and so the button also remains in place.

Figure 3-12. *Anchored controls follow a corner in the container.*

Nothing happens in the previous example because there's no change in the container. To get around this, you could anchor the group box to all sides of the window. Then, as the group box grows, the button will move to keep a consistent distance from the bottom-right corner. This version is shown in Figure 3-13.

Figure 3-13. *Anchoring the control and its container*

Container controls become particularly important when you start to add docking and split windows to your designs.

Docking

Docking allows a control to bind itself to an edge in the form or container control. When you resize the container, the control resizes itself to fit the entire edge. A control can be bound to any one edge, or it can be set to fill the entire available area. The only limitation is that you can't dock and anchor the same control (if you think about it for a moment, you'll realize that it wouldn't make sense anyway).

For example, you can solve the problem you saw with the button in the container control in the preceding examples by docking the group box to the right edge of your form. Now, when you resize the window, the group box expands to fit the edge. Because the button inside is anchored to the bottom-right corner of the group box, it also moves to the right side as the form is enlarged. Similarly, you could set the group box docking to fill so that it would automatically resize itself to occupy the entire available area. Figure 3-14 shows an example of this behavior.

Figure 3-14. *A docked group box*

To configure docking, you set the control's Dock property to a value from the DockStyle enumeration. Typically, you use the Property window to choose a setting at design time.

If you experiment with docking, your initial enthusiasm quickly drains away as you discover the following:

- Docked controls insist on sitting flush against the docked edge. This results in excessive crowding, and doesn't leave a nice border where you need it.

- Docked controls always dock to the entire edge. There's no way to tell a docked control to bind to the first half (or 50 percent) of an edge. It automatically takes the full available width, which makes it difficult to design a real interface.

Every control that derives from the ScrollableControl class has an additional feature called *dock padding*. Dock padding allows you to insert a buffer of empty space between a container and its docked controls. Some containers that derive from ScrollableControl include Panel,

Form, UserControl, SplitContainer, and ToolStrip. The GroupBox control does not derive from ScrollableControl and does not provide any padding.

Figure 3-15 shows another example with a group box and a contained button. Because the Form is the container for the group box, you need to modify the form's padding property by finding DockPadding in the properties window, expanding it, and setting All to 10 (pixels). Now the group box will still bind to all sides, but it will have some breathing room around it.

Figure 3-15. *A docked group box with padding*

At this point you may wonder why you need docking at all. It seems like a slightly more awkward way to accomplish what anchoring can achieve easily. However, in many cases anchoring alone is not enough. There are two common scenarios:

- You are using an advanced window design that hides and shows various window elements. In this scenario, docking forces other controls to resize and make room, while anchoring leads to overlapping controls.

- You want to create a window that the user can resize, like a split window design. In this case, you need to use docking because it allows controls to resize to fit the available space.

You examine both of these designs later in this chapter, in the "Splitting Windows" section.

■**Note** The sample code for this chapter (in the Source Code area of the Apress Web site, www.apress.com) includes a program that lets you play with a number of different combinations of anchoring and docking so you can see how they do or don't solve a problem.

Autosizing

In .NET 2.0, the Control class adds a new AutoSize property, which allows you to create controls that expand or shrink as their content changes.

All .NET controls provide the AutoSize property, although some interpret it differently from others (and some, like TextBox, ignore it completely). If you set AutoSize to true for controls like the Label, LinkLabel, Button, CheckBox, and RadioButton, the control automatically expands to fit the displayed text. This is useful in two key scenarios:

- You are displaying highly dynamic content. For example, you want to read text from a file or database and show it in a label.

- You are displaying localizable content. For example, depending on the current language, the captions on your button need to change.

By default, all of the controls listed earlier have AutoSize set to true by default, except for the Button control. Autosizing takes place every time the control content is changed (or another size-related property, such as the control's font, is modified).

The exact behavior of autosizing depends on another property, called AutoSizeMode. If this property is set to GrowAndShrink, autosizing is used only to expand the width. If you reduce the amount of content, the control will shrink back to its original size, but it will never become smaller than the original size you set. On the other hand, if you use an AutoSizeMode of GrowOnly, you won't be able to set the size of the control at all. Instead, the control will take the exact size of its content.

■**Note** Autosizing also respects the MaximumSize and MinimumSize properties of each control. Controls will never be resized beyond the defined limits.

Text-based controls aren't the only ones to automatically size themselves. For example, if you set AutoSize to true for the PictureBox control, it resizes itself to accommodate the current image. Even more interesting is the way that container controls support autosizing. For example, a Panel or GroupBox will expand itself to fit the widest and highest contained control if AutoSize is true (by default, it's false). Container controls follow the same behavior as buttons—they expand as needed, but never shrink to be smaller than the originally defined size.

■**Note** Although all controls inherit the AutoSize and AutoSizeMode properties, not all support them. For example, a scrollable control like the TextBox or ListBox doesn't need to resize itself automatically because you can scroll to see all of its content. Similarly, some controls (namely the Label) support autosizing but don't give you a choice of mode. In the case of the Label, you're locked into GrowAndShrink.

Finally, even the greatest container of them all—the form—supports autosizing. If AutoSizeMode is GrowOnly, the form expands to fit enlarged content. If AutoSizeMode is GrowAndShrink, the form is sized just large enough to fit every control (and the extra space dictated by the Form.Padding property and the Control.Margin property of the outlying controls).

Figure 3-16 shows an example with an autosizing label that's contained in an autosizing group box, which is situated on an autosizing form.

Figure 3-16. *Autosizing controls in their initial state*

By specifying new label text and clicking the button, the label, the group box, and the form all grow, as shown in Figure 3-17. To ensure that there's a sufficient amount of space left between the form border and the group box, you need to set the Form.Padding property. (You can also set the GroupBox.Padding property to keep some minimum space between the label and its container.)

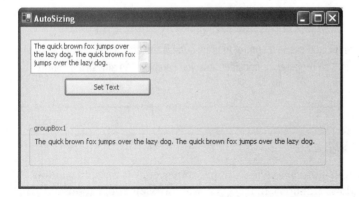

Figure 3-17. *Autosizing controls that have been expanded*

As shown in Figure 3-17, autosized controls tend to grow wider rather than taller. However, you can change this behavior using the MaximumSize property. For example, if you set a label to have a MaximumSize.Width of 200 (rather than the default 0, which allows it to be as wide as it wants), the label will autosize itself to a maximum of 200 pixels. If it can't fit all the content into that line, it will enlarge its height and add additional lines (until it reaches Maximum-Size.Height, if you've set a limit). The only caveat is that as a control grows wider and taller, it risks overlapping with other nearby controls. To prevent this, you need to use a more dynamic approach to layout. The layout controls (demonstrated in Chapter 21) address this problem.

■**Tip** If you need to display a large amount of scrollable static text, don't forget the old standby of using a TextBox instead of a label, but set ReadOnly to true so it can't be modified.

Autosizing raises an interesting question—how does it interact with anchoring? Essentially, it doesn't. When using autosizing, you should always use the default Top-Left anchor settings. Other anchor settings may be ignored or have unpredictable results.

Behind the scenes, autosizing works through the Control.GetPreferredSize() method. Essentially, every container (including the Panel and Form) has its own layout engine. The layout engine iterates over all the contained controls and calls the GetPreferredSize() method to find their ideal dimensions. The GetPreferredSize() method takes width and height arguments, which allows the layout engine to constrain the size. In other words, the layout engine can ask for the required width based on a constrained height, or vice versa. Each control is free to implement GetPreferredSize() in whatever way is most appropriate for its content. Similarly, every layout engine is free to either use or ignore the preferred size of a control. As you've seen, in ordinary grid layout, autosized controls are given their preferred size unless this conflicts with anchor settings. However, .NET also includes some container controls that use different types of layouts, and you can design your own layout managers. You'll learn about both topics in Chapter 21.

■**Tip** If you're not careful, autosizing could cause a control to grow outside the bounds of a nonautosizing form. To avoid this, use the MaximumSize property, or consider how you can place an autosizing control inside a scrollable control.

Splitting Windows

One of the most recognizable user-interface styles in applications today is the split window (arguably popularized by Windows Explorer). In fact, split-window-view applications are beginning to replace the former dominant paradigm of MDI, and Microsoft has led the charge (although many developers still favor MDI design for many large-scale applications).

In .NET 1.0, split windows were built out of two Panel controls separated by a Splitter control. This worked perfectly well, but it could be a little awkward because the two Panel controls and the Splitter had to be docked in the correct order. In .NET 2.0, the Splitter control is tucked out of sight. (It no longer appears in the toolbox, although you can add it by right-clicking on the toolbox and selecting Choose Items.) Instead, .NET introduces a new higher-level control: the SplitContainer. The SplitContainer wraps two panels and a splitter bar that separates them.

The splitter bar can be horizontal or vertical, depending on the Orientation property. Table 3-10 lists the key SplitContainer members.

Table 3-10. *Key SplitContainer Members*

Member	Description
Orientation	You can set the orientation to one of two values: Vertical (to create a splitter bar that runs from top to bottom) or Horizontal (to create a splitter bar that runs from left to right).
IsSplitterFixed	When set to true, this prevents the user from moving the splitter bar. However, you can still change its position programmatically by setting the SplitterDistance property.
SplitterIncrement	The number of pixels that represents a single increment of movement for the splitter bar. For example, if this is 5, when the user drags the splitter bar it moves in increments of 5 pixels. By default, this is 1.
SplitterDistance	Gets or sets the location of the splitter, in pixels, from the left edge (for a vertical split bar) or top edge (for a horizontal split bar).
Panel1 and Panel2	Panel1 provides a reference to the left or top panel of the SplitContainer (depending on the orientation). Panel2 provides a reference to the right or bottom panel. Using these references, you can set other Panel properties. For example, you may want to set the padding for all the controls docked in this panel, or enable automatic scrolling with the AutoScroll property.
Panel1Collapsed and Panel2Collapsed	When set to true, the corresponding panel is temporarily hidden, along with the splitter bar.
Panel1MinSize and Panel2MinSize	Sets the minimum width (for a vertical splitter) or height (for a horizontal splitter) of the appropriate panel. The user will not be able to drag the splitter to shrink the panel beyond this minimum.
FixedPanel	Takes one of three values: None, Panel1, or Panel2. If you set FixedPanel to Panel1 or Panel2, this panel will remain the same size when the SplitContainer is resized. If you use the value None, both panels will be sized proportionately when the SplitContainer is resized. Usually, the SplitContainer is resized because it's docked or anchored to the form or another panel that is being resized.
SplitterMoved and SplitterMoving events	SplitterMoving occurs while the user is in the process of moving the splitter bar. SplitterMoved fires when it's released in its new position.

Figure 3-18 shows a SplitContainer that contains a TreeView and a ListView. By moving the position of the splitter bar at runtime, the user can change the relative size of these two controls.

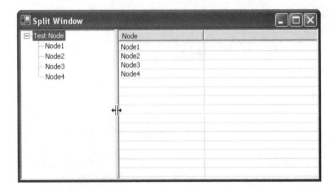

Figure 3-18. *A basic split window*

Creating this example is easy. Begin by dragging the SplitContainer onto the form. By default, the SplitContainer.Dock property will be set to DockStyle.Fill so that it fills the entire form. Next, you can drag the TreeView into the left panel, and a ListView into the right panel. For each of these controls, you also need to set the Dock property to DockStyle.Fill so they fill their respective panels. You can do this through the Properties window or by choosing the Dock in Parent Container link from the control's smart tag.

In this case, the window is somewhat claustrophobic. To improve the spacing, you can set a buffer using the form's Padding property. However, this won't add any extra spacing between the controls and the splitter bar—to add that, you need to modify the Padding property of the two panels, which you can access as SplitContainer.Panel1.Padding and SplitContainer.Panel2.Padding. (You can set both of these through the Properties window in Visual Studio by expanding the Panel1 and Panel2 properties.)

Building Split Windows with Panels

Usually you won't dock a SplitContainer to fill an entire form. Instead, you'll use a combination of panels. For example, you might dock a panel to a side of the form, and then use the SplitContainer to fill the remaining space. For Figure 3-19 shows an example (taken from Chapter 8) that uses a customized TreeView/ListView explorer.

The panel on the left includes a single TreeView, but the panel on the right includes two label controls spaced inside a panel to give a pleasing border around the label text. (If the same window simply used a single label control with a border, the text in the label would sit flush against the border.) The horizontal rule and the Close button at the bottom of the window aren't included in the resizable portion of the window. Instead, they are anchored in a separately docked panel, which is attached to the bottom of the form.

To implement this design, a panel control is first docked to the bottom to hold the Close button. Then, a SplitContainer control is docked to fill the remainder of the window. The other controls can then be anchored or docked to fill their respective areas. Figure 3-20 shows the overall design.

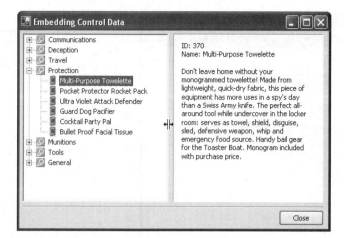

Figure 3-19. *A split window*

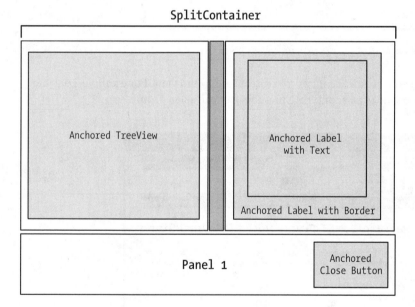

Figure 3-20. *A docking strategy*

Other Split Windows

Another reason to split a window is to provide two different views of the same data. Consider the example shown in Figure 3-21, which shows an HTML page using the WebBrowser control and an ordinary text box. In this case, the SplitContainer uses a horizontal splitter.

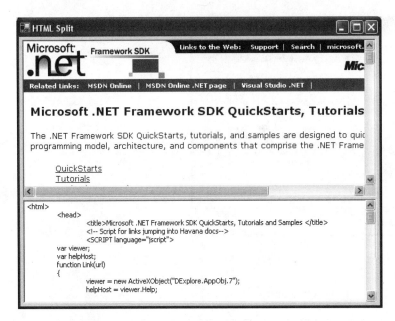

Figure 3-21. *A split view of a single document*

You could also add a vertical splitter to create a compound view. For example, consider Figure 3-22, which provides a list of HTML files the user can select from.

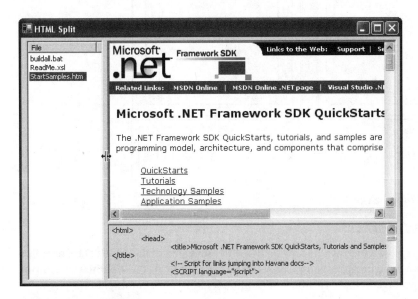

Figure 3-22. *Multiple splits*

One of the best characteristics of docked designs is that they easily accommodate hidden or modified controls. Figure 3-23 shows an alternate design that allows the file-selection panel to be collapsed and then restored to its original size with the click of the button. To implement this design, two panels are placed in the left region of the SplitContainer, one named pnlFileList and the other named pnlShow. However, only one of these panels is shown at a time. The contents of the rest of the window automatically resize themselves to accommodate the additional view when it is displayed.

The code for this operation is trivial:

```
private void cmdHide_Click(object sender, System.EventArgs e)
{
    splitContainer1.Panel1Collapsed = true;
    pnlShow.Visible = true;
}

private void cmdShow_Click(object sender, System.EventArgs e)
{
    pnlShow.Visible = false;
    splitContainer1.Panel1Collapsed = false;
}
```

This sample, called SplitWindow, is included in the online code for this chapter.

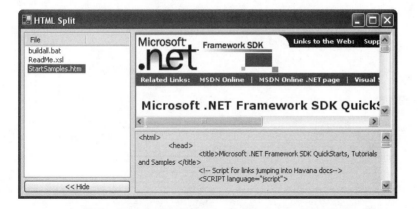

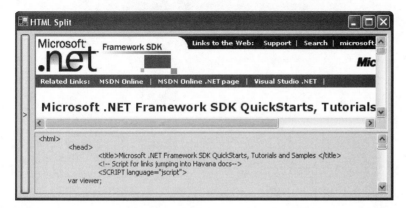

Figure 3-23. *A collapsible split window*

The Last Word

In this chapter you've toured through the basics of Windows forms—creating them, displaying them, and handling their interactions. You've also learned how to build resizable forms and split windows. However, there are still more techniques to study. In Chapter 23 you'll learn how to create shaped forms, and in Chapter 11 you'll see how to use visual inheritance to build specialized forms based on more-general templates. Chapter 21 will teach you to create flexible, highly dynamic user interfaces using layout managers. All these techniques build on the basics you've learned so far.

In the next chapter you'll continue with the basics of Windows forms by considering the basic set of Windows controls.

CHAPTER 4

■■■

The Classic Controls

This chapter considers some of the most common types of controls, such as labels, text boxes, and buttons. Many of these controls have existed since the dawn of Windows programming and don't need much description. To keep things interesting, this chapter also presents some related .NET variants. For example, at the same time you look at the label, list box, and domain controls, you will learn about the hyperlink label, checked list box, and rich date controls.

In addition, you'll see a few features that are supported by a wide variety of controls: drag and drop, automatic completion, and tooltips. You'll also learn how to create wrappers that let you use legacy ActiveX controls, and you'll see how to create a system tray application with the NotifyIcon control.

The Classic Control Gallery

Over the past three chapters, you've learned about the basic fundamentals of controls and forms. Now it's time to look at some of the familiar controls every programmer knows and loves.

■**Note** Many common controls also support images. For example, you can display an image alongside text in a label control. You'll learn about this in Chapter 5.

Labels

Label controls place static text on a form. The text is contained in the Text property and aligned according the TextAlign property. Table 4-1 lists a few less familiar (but useful) label properties.

Table 4-1. *Label Properties*

Property	Description
AutoEllipsis	If set to true and the label text doesn't fit in the current bounds of the label, the label will show an ellipsis (…) at the end of the displayed text. This property has no effect if you have set AutoSize to true. Note that the ellipsis may occur in the middle of a word.
BorderStyle	Gives you a quick way to add a flat or sunken border around some text (consider container controls such as the Panel for a more powerful and configurable approach). Be sure to use this in conjunction with the Padding property so there is some breathing room between the text and the border.
UseMnemonic	When set to true, ampersands in the label's Text property are automatically interpreted as Alt access keys. The user can press this access key, and the focus switches to the next control in the tab order (for example, a labeled text box).

LinkLabel

This specialty label inherits from the Label class, but adds some properties that make it particularly well suited to representing links. For example, many applications provide a clickable link to a company Web site in an About window.

The LinkLabel handles the details of displaying a portion of its text as a hyperlink. You specify this portion in the LinkArea property using a LinkArea structure that identifies the first character of the link and the number of characters in the link. Depending on the LinkBehavior property, this linked text may always be underlined, it may be displayed as normal, or it may become underlined when the mouse hovers over it.

Here's the basic code that creates a link on the Web site address:

```
lnkWebSite.Text = "See www.prosetech.com for more information.";

// Starts at position 4 and is 17 characters long.
lnkWebSite.LinkArea = new LinkArea(4, 17);
lnkWebSite.LinkBehavior = LinkBehavior.HoverUnderline;
```

■**Tip** You can also set the LinkArea property using a designer in Visual Studio. Just click the ellipsis (…) next to the LinkArea property, and select the area you want to make clickable so it becomes highlighted.

You need to handle the actual LinkClicked event to make the link functional. In this event handler, you should set the LinkVisited property to true so that the color is updated properly and then perform the required action. For example, you might start Internet Explorer with the following code:

```
private void lnkWebSite_LinkClicked(Object sender,
 LinkLabelLinkClickedEventArgs e)
{
    // Change the color if needed.
    e.LinkVisited = true;

    // Use the Process.Start method to open the default browser with a URL.
    System.Diagnostics.Process.Start("http://www.prosetech.com");
}
```

If you need to have more than one link, you can use the Links property, which exposes a special collection of Link objects. Each Link object stores its own Enabled and Visited properties, as well as information about the start and length of the link (Start and Length). You can also use the LinkData object property to associate some additional data with a link. This is useful if the link text does not identify the URL (for example, a "click here" link).

```
lnkBuy.Text = "Buy it at Amazon.com or Barnes and Noble.";
lnkBuy.Links.Add(10, 10, "http://www.amazon.com");
lnkBuy.Links.Add(24, 16, "http://www.bn.com");
```

You can also access LinkArea objects after you create them and modify the Start, Length, or LinkData property dynamically.

```
lnkBuy.Links[0].LinkData = "http://www.amazon.co.uk";
```

The LinkClicked event provides you with a reference to the Link object that was clicked. You can then retrieve the LinkData and use it to decide what Web page should be shown.

```
private void lnkBuy_LinkClicked(Object sender, LinkLabelLinkClickedEventArgs e)
{
    e.Link.Visited = true;
    System.Diagnostics.Process.Start((string)e.Link.LinkData);
}
```

Figure 4-1 shows both of these LinkLabel examples. Table 4-2 lists the LinkLabel properties, and Table 4-3 provides the LinkLabel.Link properties.

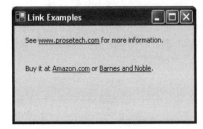

Figure 4-1. *Two LinkLabel examples*

Table 4-2. *LinkLabel Properties*

Property	Description
ActiveLinkColor, DisabledLinkColor, LinkColor, and VisitedLinkColor	Sets colors for the links in the LinkLabel (the rest of the text has its color determined by the standard ForeColor property). Links can be visited, disabled, enabled (normal), or active (while they are in the process of being clicked).
LinkArea and Links	LinkArea specifies the position of the link in the text. If you have more than one link, you can use the Links property instead, which exposes a collection of LinkArea objects. Links cannot overlap.
LinkBehavior	Specifies the underlining behavior of the link using the LinkBehavior enumeration.
LinkVisited	When set to true, the link appears with the visited link color.

Table 4-3. *LinkLabel.Link Properties*

Property	Description
Enabled	Allows you to enable or disable a link. Disabled links do not fire the LinkClicked event when clicked.
Length and Start	Identifies the position of the link in the LinkLabel.
LinkData	Provides an object property that can hold additional data, such as the corresponding URL. You can retrieve this data in the LinkClicked event handler.
Visited	When set to true, the link appears with the visited link color.

Button

Quite simply, buttons "make things happen." The most important point to remember about buttons is that their Click events have a special meaning: it occurs when you trigger the button in any way, including with the keyboard, and it is not triggered by right-clicks. Buttons are old hat to most developers, but Table 4-4 lists a few interesting members that may have escaped your attention.

Table 4-4. *Special Button Members*

Member	Description
PerformClick()	"Clicks" the button programmatically. In other words, it causes the button to fire the Click event. This method is useful for wizards and other feature where code "drives" the program. It also allows you to set up relationships between controls. For example, if you set a default button for a form (by setting the Form.AcceptButton property to point to your button), the form can programmatically "click" your button by calling PerformClick() when the user presses the Enter key.
DialogResult	If set, indicates that this button will close the form automatically and return the indicated result to the calling code, provided the window is shown modally. This technique is explained in Chapter 3, which discusses dialog forms.
FlatStyle and FlatAppearance	FlatStyle allows you to choose between standard button rendering and two more unusual modes. If FlatStyle is set to FlatStyle.Popup, the button is given a thin etched border that appears to become raised when the mouse moves over the button. If FlatStyle is set to FlatStyle.Flat, the FlatAppearance settings take over. They specify the width of the border, its color, and the background color that should be employed when the user moves the mouse over the button and presses it. Overall, the results are far from impressive, and a better choice is to use the custom button-drawing techniques covered in Chapter 23.

TextBox

Another staple of Windows development, the text box allows the user to enter textual information. The previous chapter explained how you can react to and modify key presses in the text box. Interestingly, text boxes provide a basic set of built-in functionality that the user can access through a context menu (see Figure 4-2).

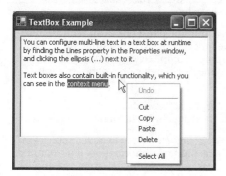

Figure 4-2. *The built-in TextBox menu*

Much of this functionality is also exposed through TextBox class members, and some of it is implemented by the base class TextBoxBase (which is shared with the MaskedTextBox and RichTextBox classes). See Table 4-5 for a complete rundown.

Table 4-5. *TextBox Members*

Member	Description
AcceptsReturn and Multiline	If you set Multiline to true, the text box can wrap text over the number of available lines (depending on the size of the control). You can also set AcceptsReturn to true so that a new line is inserted in the text box whenever the user hits the Enter key. (Otherwise, pressing the Enter key will probably trigger the form's default button.) When adding multiple lines of text into a text box, you must separate each line with the character sequence \r\n (as in "Line1\r\nLine2"). On its own, the \n character sequence will simply appear as a nondisplayable character (a box).
AcceptsTab	If true, when the user presses the Tab key, it inserts a hard tab in the text box (rather than causing the focus to move to the next control in the tab order).
AutoCompleteMode, AutoCompleteCustomSource, AutoCompleteSource	These properties support the autocompletion feature, which is also supported by the ComboBox. It's discussed later in this chapter, in the section "AutoComplete."
CanUndo	Determines whether the text box can undo the last action. An undo operation can be triggered using the Undo() method or when the user right-clicks the control and chooses Undo from the context menu.
Cut(), Copy(), Paste(), Clear(), Undo(), Select(), and SelectAll()	These methods allow you to select text and trigger operations such as copy and cut, which work with the clipboard. The user can also access this built-in functionality through the context menu for the text box.
CharacterCasing	Forces all entered characters to become lowercase or uppercase, depending on the value you use from the CharacterCasing enumeration. When you set this property, any existing characters are also modified. It's important to realize that CharacterCasing doesn't simply change the way text is displayed; it actually replaces the TextBox.Text string with a capitalized or lowercased value.
Lines	Gets or sets the text in a multilined text box as an array of strings, with one string for each line. When setting this property, you must supply a completely new array (you can't simply modify a single line by changing one of the strings in the array).
MaxLength	The maximum number of characters or spaces that can be entered in the text box. The default value of 0 indicates no limit.
PasswordChar and UseSystemPasswordChar	If PasswordChar is set to a character, that character appears in place of the text box value, hiding its information. For example, if you set this to an asterisk, the password "sesame" will appear as a series of asterisks (******). In recent versions of Windows, the usual password character is not an asterisk but a bullet (•). You can set the UseSystemPasswordChart property to true to use the system-defined password character.
SelectedText, SelectionLength, and SelectionStart	The SelectionStart and SelectionLength properties allow you to set the text that is currently selected in the text box.

Table 4-5. *TextBox Members*

Member	Description
ReadOnly	If true, the contents of a read-only text box can be modified in your code, but not by the user. Making a text box read-only instead of disabling it allows the text to remain clearly visible (instead of "grayed out"), and it allows the user to scroll through if it does not fit in the display area, and select and copy the content to the clipboard.
ShortcutsEnabled	When false, the user won't be able to use the shortcut keys for copying and pasting text or be able to use the right-click context menu with the same commands.
WordWrap	In a multiline text box, this property indicates whether text should automatically wrap to the next line (the default, true), or extend indefinitely until a line break is reached (false). If you set this property to false, you'll probably also set AcceptReturn to false to allow the user to insert hard returns.
ScrollToCaret()	In a multiline text box, this method moves to the location of the cursor.
GetPositionFromCharIndex(), GetLineFromCharIndex(), GetFirstCharIndexFromLine(), GetCharFromPosition(), and GetCharIndexFromPosition()	These methods (new in .NET 2.0) allow you to get detailed information about the current position of the cursor in the text box, either as an offset into the text string (char index) or as the screen location (point). This is handy if you need to show a pop-up menu next to the current insertion point in a large text box. These methods are also available (and generally more useful) for the RichTextBox control.

■**Tip** .NET 2.0 also adds a masked text box control that automatically formats data as the user enters text. For more information about this useful addition, and how to extend it, refer to Chapter 18.

RichTextBox

If you're looking for a text box control with more formatting muscle, consider the RichTextBox. Although it won't help you build the next Microsoft Word (for that, you'd need much more fine-grained control to intercept key presses and control painting), it does allow you to format arbitrary sections of text in the font, color, and alignment you choose.

The RichTextBox control derives from TextBoxBase, as does the TextBox, so it shares most of its properties and methods (as listed in Table 4-5). Along with these features, the RichTextBox adds the ability to handle rich formatting, images, and links. It also provides a LoadFile() and a SaveFile() method for saving RTF documents painlessly.

One of the key enhancements the RichTextBox adds is a set of selection properties that allow you to manipulate the formatting of the currently selected text. The RichTextBox supports the familiar SelectedText, SelectionLength, and SelectionStart properties, but it also adds a much more impressive set of properties including SelectionColor, SelectionBackColor, SelectionFont, and SelectionAlignment, which allow you to adjust the formatting of the selected text. Table 4-6 has the lowdown.

Table 4-6. *RichTextBox Added Members*

Member	Description
AutoWordSelection	If true, the nearest word is automatically selected when the user double-clicks inside the text box.
BulletIndent	Sets the number of pixels to indent text that's styled as bulleted. You use the SelectionBullet property to turn this style on or off.
DetectUrls and LinkClicked event	If the DetectUrls property is true (the default), the text box will detect URLs in the text and convert them to clickable hyperlinks. You can handle the LinkClicked event handler to examine what text was clicked, and handle the click (for example, by showing a new document or launching an external process like Internet Explorer).
EnableAutoDragDrop	If true, the user can rearrange selected text and images by dragging them to a new position. The default is false.
Rtf and SelectedRtf	Whereas the Text property gets the plain, unformatted text content, the Rtf property gets or sets the formatted text, including all rich text format (RTF) codes. This is useful primarily when interacting with another program that understands RTF (like Microsoft Word). For more information about RTF codes, see the rich text format (RTF) specification at http://msdn.microsoft.com/library/en-us/dnrtfspec/html/rtfspec.asp.
SelectionAlignment	The type of horizontal alignment (left, right, or center) to use to align the selected text.
SelectionBackColor	The background color for the selected text. If this is equal to Color.Empty, it indicates that the selection includes more than one background color.
SelectionBullet	True if the selected text should be formatted with the bullet style (meaning each paragraph is preceded by a bullet).
SelectionCharOffset	Determines whether the selected text appears on the baseline, as a superscript, or as a subscript below the baseline.
SelectionColor	The foreground color for the selected text. If this is equal to Color.Empty, it indicates that the selection includes more than one color.
SelectionFont	The font used for the selected text. A null reference indicates that the selection includes more than one typeface.
SelectionHangingIndent	The spacing (in pixels) between the left edge of the first line of text in the selected paragraph and the left edge of subsequent lines in the same paragraph.
SelectionIndent	The spacing (in pixels) between the left edge of the text box and the left edge of the text selection.
SelectionRightIndent	The distance (in pixels) between the right edge of the text box and the right edge of the text selection.
SelectionProtected and Protected event	If set to true, the user will be prevented from modifying this text. Initially, no text is protected. If the user attempts to change protected text, the Protected event is raised.

Table 4-6. *RichTextBox Added Members*

Member	Description
ShowSelectionMargin	Shows a margin on the left where the user can click to quickly select a line of text (or double-click to select an entire paragraph).
ZoomFactor	Adjusts the scaling of the text to make it larger or smaller. A ZoomFactor of 1 (the default) is equivalent to 100%, which means each font appears at its normal size. A ZoomFactor of .75 is 75%, 2 is 200%, and so on.
LoadFile() and SaveFile()	Allows you to save (or load) the content for the text box. You can use a string with a file path, or supply a stream. You also have the choice of saving (or loading) plain text files or formatted RTF files.
SelectionChanged event	Fires when the SelectionStart of SelectionLength properties change.

Unless you want to master the complexities of RTF codes (which are not for the faint of heart), steer away from the Rtf and SelectedRtf properties. Instead, perform all your formatting by manipulating the selection properties. First set the SelectionStart and SelectionLength properties to define the range of text you want to format. Then apply the formatting by assigning a new selection color, font, or alignment through properties like SelectionColor and SelectionFont. Use the SelectedText property to set or change the content of the selected text.

Here's an example that formats the text in the entire control with bold formatting:

```
richTextBox1.SelectionStart = 0;
richTextBox1.SelectionLength = richTextBox1.Text.Length-1;
richTextBox1.SelectionFont = new Font(richTextBox1.SelectionFont, FontStyle.Bold);
```

Notice that you can't modify the properties of the SelectionFont. Instead, you need to assign a new font, although you can use the current font as a starting point, and simply change the style or size as needed.

You can set the selection formatting properties even if there's currently no selected text (in other words, SelectionLength is 0). In this case, the formatting options apply to the current insertion point (wherever SelectionStart is positioned). In other words, if you use the following line of code, when the user starts to type, the text will appear in blue. However, if the user first moves to a new location, this formatting selection will be lost.

```
richTextBox1.SelectionColor = Colors.Blue;
```

You can also use this technique to add formatted text. For example, here's the code that adds some text to the end of the text box, using a large font:

```
richTextBox1.SelectionStart = richTextBox1.Text.Length-1;
richTextBox1.SelectionFont = new Font("Tahoma", 20);
richTextBox1.SelectedText = "Hi";
```

Note that if you swapped the first and second line so that you applied the selection formatting before you set the selection position, the formatting would be lost and the new text would have the default formatting (the formatting of the character immediately to the left of the cursor).

Figure 4-3 shows a simple test program (available with the downloadable examples), that allows the user to style selected section of text using toolbar buttons.

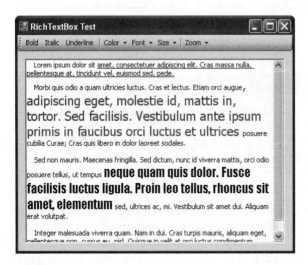

Figure 4-3. *Formatting text in the RichTextBox*

The code for this example is fairly straightforward. When a button is clicked, you simply need to modify the corresponding selection property. However, there are a few considerations you need to take into account.

When applying font styles (like underlining, bold, and italics), you need to be a little more careful. First, you need to check if the style is already present. If so, it makes sense to remove the style flag. (For example, if the underline button is clicked twice in succession, the text should revert to normal.) Second, you need to make sure that you don't wipe out any of the other existing formatting. (For example, the user should be able to bold and underline text.) Thus, you need to use bitwise arithmetic with the FontStyle enumeration to add or remove the appropriate style option without changing the others. Third, you need to test the SelectionFont property for a null reference, which occurs if there is more than one font family in the selected text.

Note .NET follows some slightly unusual rules for setting selection properties when the selection includes varied formatting. For example, the SelectionFont will always indicate false for underlining, bold, italics, and strikeout unless it's applied to the whole selection. If there is more than one size, the Font.Size property reflects the smallest size. However, if there's more than one font face, the Font object can't be created and the SelectionFont property returns null. Similar sleight of hand happens with other selection properties—for example, expect a SelectionColor or Color.Empty if the selection includes multiple colors (as SelectionColor can't return a null reference because it's a value type).

Here's the complete code that allows any text to be underlined:

```
private void cmdUnderline_Click(object sender, EventArgs e)
{
    if (richTextBox1.SelectionFont == null)
    {
        // The selection includes multiple fonts. Sadly, there's
        // no way to get information about any of them.
        // You could fall back on the RichTextBox.Font property,
        // but if you make any change to the SelectionFont you will
        // override the current fonts, so it's safer to do nothing.
        return;
    }

    // Get the current style.
    FontStyle style = richTextBox1.SelectionFont.Style;

    // Adjust as required.
    if (richTextBox1.SelectionFont.Underline)
    {
        style &= ~FontStyle.Underline;
    }
    else
    {
        style |= FontStyle.Underline;
    }

    // Assign font with new style.
    richTextBox1.SelectionFont = new Font(richTextBox1.SelectionFont, style);
}
```

You can also react to SelectionChanged to update the status of controls. For example, you could set a toolbar button like Bold to have an indented (pressed) appearance when the user moves through a section of bold text. To do so, you need to react to the SelectionChanged event, as shown here:

```
private void richTextBox1_SelectionChanged(object sender, EventArgs e)
{
    if (richTextBox1.SelectionFont != null)
    {
        cmdBold.Checked = richTextBox1.SelectionFont.Bold;
        cmdItalic.Checked = richTextBox1.SelectionFont.Italic;
        cmdUnderline.Checked = richTextBox1.SelectionFont.Underline;
    }
}
```

To place an image in the RichTextBox, you need to use the copy-and-paste features of the clipboard. The basic strategy is to copy an image object to the clipboard, move to the desired position in the text box, and then paste it into place. Here's an example:

```
// Get the image.
Image img = Image.FromFile(Path.Combine(Application.StartupPath, "planet.jpg"));

// Place it on the clipboard.
Clipboard.SetImage(img);

// Move to the start of the text box.
richTextBox1.SelectionStart = 0;

// Paste the image.
richTextBox1.Paste();

// Optionally, remove the data from the clipboard.
Clipboard.Clear();
```

This is not an ideal solution, because it modifies the clipboard without notifying the user, which is a problem if the user already has some data there. Unfortunately, there's no other solution possible without mastering the intricacies of RTF codes. For more information and a more complex workaround, you may want to check out an article on the subject at http:// www.codeproject.com/cs/miscctrl/csexrichtextbox.asp.

CheckBox and RadioButton

The CheckBox and RadioButton controls provide a Checked property that indicates whether the control is checked or "filled in." After the state is changed, a CheckedChanged event occurs.

You can create a special three-state check box by setting the ThreeState property to true. You need to check the CheckState property to examine whether it is Checked, Unchecked, or Indeterminate (shaded but not checked).

By default, the control is checked and unchecked automatically when the user clicks it. You can prevent this by setting AutoCheck to false and handling the Click event. This allows you to programmatically prevent a check box or radio button from being checked (without trying to "switch it back" after the user has made a change).

PictureBox

A picture box is one of the simplest controls .NET offers. You can set a valid image using the Image property and configure a SizeMode from the PictureBoxSizeMode enumeration. For example, you can set the picture to automatically stretch to fit the picture box.

```
pic.Image = System.Drawing.Image.FromFile("mypic.bmp");
pic.SizeMode = PictureBoxSizeMode.StretchImage;
```

You'll learn more about how to manipulate images in .NET in Chapter 5 and Chapter 7.

List Controls

.NET provides three basic list controls: ListBox, CheckedListBox, and ComboBox. They all inherit (directly or indirectly) from the abstract ListControl class, which defines basic function-ality that allows you to use a list control with data binding. Controls can be bound to objects such as the DataSet, arrays, and ArrayList collections, regardless of the underlying data source (as you'll see in Chapter 8).

```
// Bind a list control to an array of city names.
String[] cityChoices = {"Seattle", "New York", "Singapore", "Montreal"};
lstCity.DataSource = cityChoices;
```

You can access the currently selected item in several ways. You can use the SelectedIndex property to retrieve the zero-based index number identifying the item, or you can use the Text property to retrieve the displayed text. You can also set both of these properties to change the selection.

```
// Search for the item with "New York" as its text, and select it.
lstCity.Text = "New York";

// Select the first item in the list.
lstCity.SelectedIndex = 0;
```

If you are using a multiselect ListBox, you can also use the SelectedIndices or SelectedItems collection. Multiselect list boxes are set based on the SelectionMode property. You have two multiselect choices: SelectionMode.MultiExtended, which requires the user to hold down Ctrl or Shift while clicking the list to select additional items, and SelectionMode.MultiSimple, which selects and deselects items with a simple mouse click or press of the space bar. The CheckedListBox does not support multiple selection, but it does allow multiple items to be checked. It provides similar CheckedIndices and CheckedItems properties that provide infor-mation about checked items.

Here's an example that iterates through all the checked items in a list and displays a message box identifying each one:

```
foreach (string item in chkList.CheckedItems)
{
    // Do something with checked item here.
    MessageBox.Show("You checked " + item);
}
```

You can also access all the items in a list control through the Items collection. This collec-tion allows you to count, add, and remove items. Note that this collection is read-only if you are using a data-bound list.

```
lstFood.Items.Add("Macaroni");        // Added to bottom of list.
lstFood.Items.Add("Baguette");        // Added to bottom of list.

lstFood.Items.Remove("Macaroni");     // The list is searched for this entry.
lstFood.Items.RemoveAt(0);            // The first item is removed.
```

Table 4-7 dissects some of the properties offered by the list controls. It doesn't include the properties used for data binding, which are discussed in Chapter 8.

Table 4-7. *List Control Properties*

Property	Description
IntegralHeight	If set to true, the height is automatically adjusted to the nearest multiple-row height, ensuring no half-visible rows are shown in the list. Not supported by the CheckedListBox.
ItemHeight	The height of a row with the current font, in pixels.
Items	The full collection of items in the list control. List items can be strings or arbitrary objects that supply an appropriate string representation when their ToString() method is called.
MultiColumn and HorizontalScrollbar	A multicolumn list control automatically divides the list into columns, with no column longer than the available screen area. Vertical scrolling is thus never required, but you may need to enable the horizontal scroll bar to see all the columns easily. These properties are supported only by the ListBox.
SelectedIndex, SelectedIndices, SelectedItem, SelectedItems, and Text	Provides ways to access the currently selected item (as an object), its zero-based index number, or its text. Not supported by the CheckedListBox.
SelectionMode	Allows you to configure a multiselect list control using one of the SelectionMode values. Multiple selection is not supported for CheckListBox controls.
Sorted	If set to true, items are automatically sorted alphabetically. This generally means you should not use index-based methods, as item indices change as items are added and removed. Not supported by the CheckedListBox.
TopIndex	The index number representing the topmost visible item. You can set this property to scroll the list. Supported only by the ListBox.
UseTabStops	If set to true, embedded tab characters are expanded into spaces. This, in conjunction with properties such as MultiColumn and ColumnWidth, allows you to line up multiple columns of text in a ListBox. However, it's almost always preferable to use a more sophisticated control such as the ListView (see Chapter 6) if you need multiple columns. Supported only by the ListBox.

The CheckedListBox has no concept of selected items. Instead, it recognizes items that are either checked or not checked. Table 4-8 shows the properties it adds.

Table 4-8. *CheckedListBox-Specific Properties*

Property	Description
CheckedItems and CheckedIndices	Provides a collection of currently checked items (as objects) or their index numbers. Supported only by the CheckedListBox.
CheckOnClick	If set to true, the check box for an item is toggled with every click. Otherwise, you need to click first to select the item and then click again to change the checked state. Supported only by the CheckedListBox.
ThreeDCheckBoxes	Configures the appearance of check boxes for a CheckedListBox. Has no effect if Windows XP styles are used.

The ComboBox supports the same selection properties and Items collection as a standard ListBox. It also adds the properties shown in Table 4-9. The ComboBox can work in one of three modes, as specified by the DropDownStyle property. In ComBoxStyle.DropDown mode, the combo box acts as a nonlimiting list where the user can type custom information. In ComboBoxStyle.DropDownList, pressing a key selects the first matching entry. The user cannot enter items that are not in the list.

■**Tip** You should always make sure to choose the right kind of combo box. The DropDown style is ideal for selected choices that are not comprehensive (such as a field where users can type the name of their operating system). The available list items aren't mandatory, but they will encourage consistency. The DropDownList style is ideal for a database application where a user is specifying a piece of search criteria by using the values in another table. In this case, if the value doesn't exist in the database, it's not valid and can't be entered by the user.

Table 4-9. *ComboBox-Specific Properties*

Property	Description
AutoCompleteMode, AutoCompleteCustomSource, AutoCompleteSource	These properties support the autocompletion feature, which is also supported by the TextBox. It's discussed later in this chapter, in the section "AutoComplete."
DropDownStyle	This specifies the type of drop-down list box. It can be a restrictive or nonrestrictive list.
DropDownHeight	This specifies the height (in pixels) of the drop-down portion of the list.
DropDownWidth	This specifies the width (in pixels) of the drop-down portion of the list.

Table 4-9. *ComboBox-Specific Properties (Continued)*

Property	Description
DroppedDown	This Boolean property indicates whether the list is currently dropped down. You can also set it programmatically.
FlatStyle	Allows you to change the rendering of the ComboBox to a flat look that was considered more modern before the introduction of Windows XP styling.
MaxDropDownItems	This specifies how many items will be shown in the drop-down portion of the list.
MaxLength	For an unrestricted list, this limits the amount of text the user can enter.
DropDown and DropDownClosed events	These events occur when the drop-down portion of the combo box is shown and when it is hidden, respectively.

List Controls with Objects

In the preceding examples, the Items property was treated like a collection of strings. In reality, it's a collection of objects. To display an item in the list, the list control automatically calls the object's ToString() method. In other words, you could create a custom data object and add instances to a list control. Just make sure to override the ToString() method, or you will end up with a series of identical items that show the fully qualified class name.

For example, consider the following Customer class:

```
public class Customer
{
    public string FirstName;
    public string LastName;
    public DateTime BirthDate;

    public Customer() {}

    public Customer(string firstName, string lastName, DateTime    birthDate)
    {
        FirstName = firstName;
        LastName = lastName;
        BirthDate = birthDate;
    }

    public override string ToString()
    {
        return FirstName + " " + LastName;
    }
}
```

You can add customer objects to the list control natively. Figure 4-4 shows how these Customer objects appear in the list.

```
lstCustomers.Items.Add(new Customer("Maurice", "Respighi", DateTime.Now));
lstCustomers.Items.Add(new Customer("Sam", "Digweed", DateTime.Now));
lstCustomers.Items.Add(new Customer("Faria", "Khan", DateTime.Now));
```

It's just as easy to retrieve the currently selected Customer.

```
Customer cust = (Customer)lstCustomers.SelectedItem;
MessageBox.Show("Birth Date: " + cust.BirthDate.ToShortDateString());
```

Figure 4-4. *Filling a list box with objects*

Other Domain Controls

Domain controls restrict user input to a finite set of valid values. The standard ListBox is
an example of a domain control, because a user can choose only one of the items in the list.
Figure 4-5 shows an overview of the other domain controls provided in .NET.

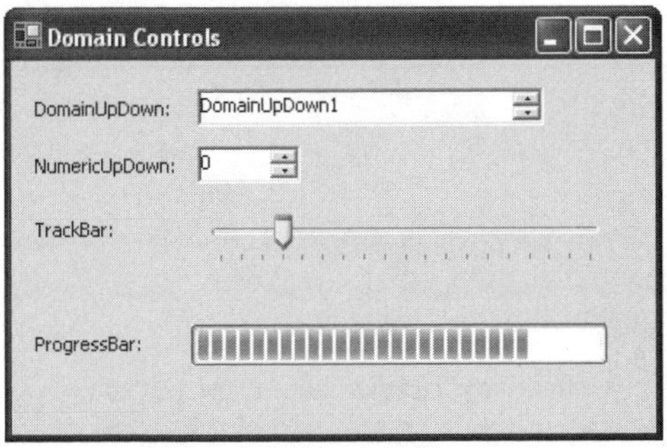

Figure 4-5. *The domain controls*

DomainUpDown

DomainUpDown is similar to a list control in that it provides a list of options. The difference is
that the user can navigate through this list using only the up/down arrow buttons, moving to
either the previous item or the following item. List controls are generally more useful, because
they allow multiple items to be shown at once.

To use the DomainUpDown control, add a string for each option to the Items collection.
The Text or SelectedIndex property returns the user's choice.

```
// Add Items.
udCity.Items.Add("Tokyo");
udCity.Items.Add("Montreal");
udCity.Items.Add("New York");

// Select the first one.
udCity.SelectedIndex = 0;
```

NumericUpDown

The NumericUpDown list allows a user to choose a number value by using the up/down arrow buttons (or typing it in directly). You can set the allowed range using the Maximum, Minimum, and DecimalPlaces properties. The current number in the control is set or returned through the Value property.

```
// Configure a NumericUpDown control.
udAge.Maximum = 120;
udAge.Minimum = 18;
udAge.Value = 21;
```

TrackBar

The track bar allows the user to choose a value graphically by moving a tab across a vertical or horizontal strip (use the Orientation property to specify it). You set the range of values through the Maximum and Minimum properties, and the Value property returns the current number. However, the user sees a series of "ticks," not the exact number. This makes the track bar suitable for a setting that doesn't have an obvious numeric significance or where the units may be arbitrary, such as when setting volume levels or pitch in an audio program.

```
// Configure a TrackBar.
barVolume.Minimum = 0;
barVolume.Maximum = 100;
barVolume.Value = 50;

// Show a tick every 5 units.
barVolume.TickFrequency = 5;

// The SmallChange is the amount incremented if the user clicks an arrow button
// (or presses an arrow key).
// The LargeChange is the amount incremented if the user clicks the barVolume
// (or presses PageDown or PageUp).
barVolume.SmallChange = 5;
barVolume.LargeChange = 25;
```

ProgressBar

The progress bar is quite different from the other domain controls because it doesn't allow any user selection. Instead, you can use it to provide feedback about the progress of a long-running task. As with all the number-based domain controls, the current position of the progress bar is identified by the Value property, which is significant only as it compares to the Maximum and Minimum properties that set the bounds of the progress bar. You can also set a number for the Step property. Calling the Step() method then increments the value of the progress bar by that number.

```
// Configure the progress bar.
// In this case we hard-code a maximum, but it would be more likely that this
// would correspond to something else (such as the number of files in a directory).
progress.Maximum = 100;
progress.Minimum = 0;
progress.Value = 0;
progress.Step = 5;

// Start a task.
for (int i = progress.Minimum; i < progress.Maximum; i += progress.Step)
{
    // (Do work here.)

    // Increment the progress bar.
    progress.PerformStep();
}
```

The Date Controls

Retrieving date information is a common task. For example, requiring a date range is a good way to limit database searches. In the past, programmers have used a variety of controls to retrieve date information, including text boxes that required a specific format of month, date, and year values.

The date controls make life easier. For one thing, they allow dates to be chosen from a graphical calendar view that's easy to use and prevents users from choosing invalid dates (such as the 31st day in February, for example). They also allow dates to be displayed in a range of formats.

Two date controls exist: DateTimePicker and MonthCalendar. DateTimePicker is ideal for choosing a single date value and requires the same amount of space as an ordinary drop-down list box. When the user clicks the drop-down button, a full month calendar page appears. The user can page from month to month (and even from year to year) looking for a specific date with the built-in navigational controls. The control handles these details automatically.

The MonthCalendar shows a similar expanded display, with a single month at a time. Unlike the DateTimePicker, it allows the user to choose a range of dates. Figure 4-6 shows both controls.

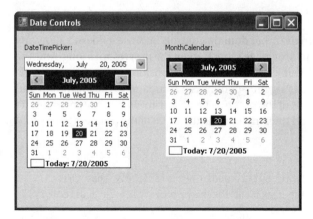

Figure 4-6. *The date controls*

The DateTimePicker

The DateTimePicker allows a user to choose a single date. One nice feature the DateTimePicker has is that it automatically considers the computer's regional settings. That means you can specify Short for the DateTimePicker.Format property, and the date might be rendered as yyyy/mm/dd format or dd/mm/yyyy depending on the date settings. Alternatively, you can specify a custom format by assigning a format string to the CustomFormat property and make sure the date is always presented in the same way on all computers. Figure 4-7 shows the date formats.

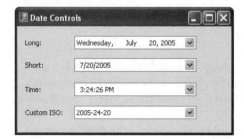

Figure 4-7. *Common date formats*

The Value property provides the selected date. One important detail about date controls is that they always use the System.DateTime date type, which represents a date *and* time. Depending on your needs, you might configure a date control to show only the day or time portion. In this case, you may need to be careful to retrieve just the appropriate part.

For example, imagine you are using a DateTimePicker control, which allows the user to choose the start date for a database search. The date control is configured to show dates in the long format, which doesn't include time information.

When the form loads, you configure the date control.

```
dtStart.Value = DateTime.Now;    // Sets dtStart to the current date and time.
```

The user might then click a different date. However, choosing a different date updates only the month, year, and day components of the date. The time component remains, even though it is not displayed!

```
// The next line performs a search based on the date and the original time.
// This artificially limits the returned results.
string SQLSelect = "SELECT * FROM Orders WHERE Date >'" +
 dtStart.Value.ToString() + "'";
```

If you initialized the DateTimePicker at lunchtime, you could lose the first half of the day from your search.

You can avoid this problem in a number of ways. For example, you can use the DateTime.Date property, which returns another DateTime object that has its time portion set to 0 (midnight).

```
// This gets the full day.
string SQLSelect = "SELECT * FROM Orders WHERE Date >'" +
 dtStart.Value.Date.ToString() + "'";
```

You could also use the DateTime.Today property to set the initial value instead of DateTime.Now. This is a good technique for the MonthCalendar control as well. The MonthCalendar automatically sets the time component for the current value to 0 when the user selects a date, but if the user leaves the default date unchanged, and you've assigned a date with information, the time portion remains.

But the best approach is to use a format string to control exactly what comes out when you convert a date to a string. Here's an example that ensures you're using the ISO-standard year-month-day format, which is understood by almost every relational database product:

```
// This ensures the correct date format (and ignores the time component).
string SQLSelect = "SELECT * FROM Orders WHERE Date >'" +
 dtStart.Value.Date.ToString("yyyy-mm-dd") + "'";
```

You can also use a DateTimePicker to represent a time value with no date component. To do so, set the Format property to Time. You also need to set the UseUpDown property to true. This prevents the drop-down month display from being shown. Use the up/down scroll buttons instead to increment the highlighted time component (hours, minutes, or seconds).

Table 4-10 lists the important properties of the DateTimePicker control.

Table 4-10. *DateTimePicker Properties*

Properties	Description
CalendarFont, CalendarForeColor, CalendarMonthBackground, CalendarTitleBackColor, CalendarTitleForeColor, and CalendarTrailingForeColor	These properties configure the calendar's font and the color used for parts of its interface. The default colors are provided as static read-only fields for this class (such as DefaultTitleForeColor). However, they are protected, which means you can change them by deriving a custom control from DateTimePicker. Note that the CalendarTrailingForeColor changes the color of the "trailing" dates. These are the dates that appear on a month page from the previous month (at the beginning) or from the next month (at the end). They are used to fill in the grid.
ShowCheckBox and Checked	ShowCheckBox displays a small check box inside the drop-down list box. Unless it is checked, the date cannot be modified.
Format and CustomFormat	The Format property specifies a value from the DateTimePickerFormat enumeration. These options map to date and time formats defined in the Regional and Language Options section of the Control Panel. Alternatively, you can manually specify an exact form by assigning a format string to the CustomFormat property (such as "yyyy/MM/DD hh:mm:ss").
DropDownAlign	Determines whether the drop-down month page lines up with the left or right edge of the combo box.
MaxDate and MinDate	Sets a maximum and minimum date, beyond which the user cannot select. This is a great tool for preventing error messages by making invalid selections impossible.
ShowUpDown	When set to true, disables the drop-down month pages and uses up/down scroll buttons for incrementing part of the date. This is ideal for time-only values.
Text and Value	Text returns the formatted date as a string, according to how it is currently displayed. Value returns the represented DateTime object.

MonthCalendar

The MonthCalendar control looks like the DateTimePicker, except that it always shows the month page display, and it doesn't allow the user to enter a date by typing it into a text box. That makes the MonthCalendar slightly less useful, except for situations when you need to let the user select a range of contiguous dates.

You set the maximum number of dates that the user can select in the MaxSelectionCount property. The user selects a group of dates by dragging and clicking. Selected dates must always be next to each other. The first and last selected dates are returned as DateTime objects in the SelectionStart and SelectionEnd properties. Figure 4-8 shows a range of four days.

```
// Set a range of four days.
dt.SelectionStart = new DateTime(2006, 01, 17);
dt.SelectionEnd = new DateTime(2006, 01, 20);
```

Figure 4-8. *Selecting multiple dates*

■**Caution** The MonthCalendar control doesn't properly support Windows XP styles. If you try to use this control with a project that uses Windows XP styles, the display does not appear correctly when the user selects more than one date at a time. There is no workaround, so this control is not recommended with a MaxSelectionCount other than 1 or 0.

Depending on your needs, you may still need to perform a significant amount of validation with selected dates to make sure they fit your business rules. Unfortunately, you can't easily use the DateChanged and DateSelected events for this purpose. They fire only after an invalid date has been selected, and you have no way to remove the selection unless you choose a different date range. Information about the original (valid) date range is already lost.

Though the MonthCalendar control looks similar to the DateTimePicker, it provides a different set of properties, adding some features while omitting others. Table 4-11 lists the most important properties.

Table 4-11. *MonthCalendar Properties*

Property	Description
AnnuallyBoldedDates, MonthlyBoldedDates, and BoldedDates	These properties accept arrays of DateTime objects, which are then shown in bold in the calendar. MonthlyBoldedDates can be set for one month and are repeated for every month, while AnuallyBoldedDates are set for one year and repeated for every year.
FirstDayOfWeek	Sets the day that will be shown in the leftmost column of the calendar.
MaxDate, MinDate, and MaxSelectionCount	Sets the maximum and minimum selectable date in the calendar and the maximum number of contiguous dates that can be selected at once.
ScrollChange	The number of months that the calendar "scrolls through" every time the user clicks a scroll button.
SelectionEnd, SelectionStart, and SelectionRange	Identifies the selected dates. The SelectionRange property returns a special structure that contains a SelectionEnd date and a SelectionStart date.

Table 4-11. *MonthCalendar Properties (Continued)*

Property	Description
ShowToday and ShowTodayCircle	These properties, when true, show the current day in a special line at the bottom of the control and highlight it in the calendar.
ShowWeekNumbers	If true, displays a number next to each week in the year from 1 to 52.
TodayDate and TodayDateSet	TodayDate indicates what date is shown as "today" in the MonthCalendar. If you set this value manually in code, TodayDateSet is true.
TitleBackColor, TitleForeColor, and TrailingForeColor	Sets colors associated with the MonthCalendar. Note that the TrailingForeColor changes the color of the "trailing" dates. These are the dates that appear on a month page from the previous month (at the beginning) or from the next month (at the end). They are used to fill in the grid.

Container Controls

The .NET Framework defines a few controls that are designed explicitly for grouping other controls:

- **GroupBox.** This control is drawn as a titled box and is commonly used for visually isolating related groups of controls.

- **Panel.** This control has no default appearance but supports scrolling and padding.

- **SplitContainer.** This control combines two Panel controls, separated by a splitter bar.

- **TabControl.** This control hosts one or more TabPage controls (only one of which can be shown at a time). The TabPage controls are the containers that hold your controls.

- **FlowLayoutPanel and TableLayoutPanel.** These controls are designed for automating highly dynamic or configurable interfaces and are discussed in Chapter 21.

The Panel and GroupBox are the simplest of the five. The Panel control is similar to the GroupBox control; however, only the Panel control can have scroll bars (when the AutoScroll property is set to true), and only the GroupBox control displays a caption (set in the Text property). Also, the Panel control supports DockPadding, which makes it a necessary ingredient in the complex resizable forms you'll learn about later in this chapter). The GroupBox control does not provide this ability.

You will probably group controls using one of these container controls for two reasons. The first reason occurs when you have more than one group of radio buttons. To associate these as a group (so that only one option in the group can be selected at a time), you must place them into separate containers. The other reason is to manage the layout of the controls. Some controls do little in this regard (such as the GroupBox), while others add support for resizing dynamically (the SplitContainer), hiding individual groups (the TabControl), scrolling (the Panel), and producing complex layouts (the FlowLayoutPanel and TableLayoutPanel).

You've already learned about the GroupBox, Panel, and SplitContainer in the previous chapter. The next section describes the TabControl.

The TabControl

The TabControl is another staple of Windows development—it groups controls into multiple "pages." The technique has become remarkably successful because it allows a large amount of information to be compacted into a small, organized space. It's also easy to use because it recalls the tabbed pages of a binder or notebook. Over the years, the tab control has evolved into today's forms, which are sometimes called *property pages*.

In .NET, you create a TabControl object, which contains a collection of TabPage objects in the TabPages property. Individual controls are then added to each TabPage object. The example that follows shows the basic approach, assuming your form contains a TabControl called tabProperties:

```
TabPage pageFile = new TabPage("File Locations");
TabPage pageUser = new TabPage("User Information");

// Add controls to the tab pages.
// The code for creating and configuring the child controls is omitted.
pageUser.Controls.Add(txtFirstName);
pageUser.Controls.Add(txtLastName);
pageUser.Controls.Add(lblFirstName);
pageUser.Controls.Add(lblLastName);
tabProperties.TabPages.Add(pageFile);
tabProperties.TabPages.Add(pageUser);
```

Figure 4-9 shows the output for this code.

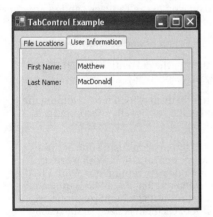

Figure 4-9. *Using the TabPage control*

Of course, most of the time you won't create a tab page and add controls by hand. Instead, you'll drag and drop controls at design time, and Visual Studio will add the necessary code to your form.

Table 4-12 lists some of the most important TabControl properties. Table 4-13 lists the TabPage properties.

Table 4-12. *TabControl Members*

Member	Description
Alignment	Sets the location of the tabs. With few exceptions, this should always be TabAlignment.Top, which is the standard adopted by almost all applications.
Appearance	Allows you to configure tabs to look like buttons that stay depressed to select a page. This is another unconventional approach.
DrawMode and the DrawItem event	Allow you to perform custom drawing with GDI+ to render the tabs. (This setting doesn't affect the content on the tab pages.) Chapter 7 has more about drawing with GDI+, and Chapter 12 covers owner-drawn controls.
HotTrack	When set to true, the text in a tab caption changes to a highlighted hyperlink style when the user positions the mouse over it.
ImageList	You can bind an ImageList to use for the caption of each tab page (see Chapter 5 for more).
Multiline	When set to true, allows you to create a tab control with more than one row of tab pages. This is always true if Alignment is set to Left or Right. If set to false and there are more tab pages than will fit in the display area, a tiny set of scroll buttons is added at the edge of the tab strip for scrolling through the list of tabs.
Padding	Configures a minimum border of white space around each tab caption. This does not affect the actual tab control, but it is useful if you need to add an icon to the TabPage caption and need to adjust the spacing to accommodate it properly.
RowCount and TabCount	Retrieves the number of rows of tabs and the number of tabs.
SelectedIndex and SelectedTab	Retrieves the index number for the currently selected tab or the tab as a TabPage object, respectively.
ShowToolTips	Enables or disables the tooltip display for a tab (assuming the corresponding TabPage.TooltipText is set). This property is usually set to false.
SizeMode	Allows you to set the size of tab captions using one of three values from the TabSizeMode enumeration. With Normal, each tab is sized to accommodate its caption text. With Fixed, all tabs are the same width (and text that doesn't fit is truncated). You define the width using the TabPage.ItemSize property. With FillToRight, the width of each tab is sized so that each row of tabs fills the entire width of the TabControl. This is applicable only to tab controls with more than one row, when Multiline is true.
TabPages	A collection of TabPage objects representing the tabs in the TabControl.
SelectedIndexChanged event	Occurs when the SelectedIndex property changes, usually as a result of the user clicking on a different tab.

Table 4-13. *TabPage Properties*

Property	Description
ImageIndex and ImageKey	The image shown in the tab (see Chapter 5).
Text	The text shown in the tab.
ToolTipText	The tooltip shown when the user hovers over the tab, if the TabControl.ShowToolTips property is true. No ToolTipProvider is used.

AutoComplete

Looking for a way to make text entry a little easier? A common solution in Windows applications is AutoComplete input controls. These controls store recent entries and offer them when the user starts to type something similar. You'll see autocompletion at work when you type a URL into Internet Explorer's address bar or when you enter a file name in the Run dialog box (choose Run from the Start menu). Other applications use them for a variety of purposes, such as tracking recent help searches in Microsoft Word and tracking recent cell entries in Microsoft Excel.

In .NET 1.0 and 1.1, developers who wanted autocompletion functionality had to code it themselves. And though the process is conceptually simple, the low-level quirks in how different controls handle keystrokes and selection often caused problems or unusual behavior. In .NET 2.0, the TextBox and ComboBox controls provide built-in support for autocompletion through three properties: AutoCompleteSource, AutoCompleteMode, and (optionally) AutoCompleteCustomSource. When using autocompletion, you can use your own list of suggestions or one of the lists maintained by the operating system (such as the list of recently visited URLs).

First, you need to specify what list of values will be used for suggestions. You do this by setting the AutoCompleteSource property to one of the values listed in Table 4-14.

Table 4-14. *AutoCompleteSource Values*

Value	Description
FileSystem	Includes recently entered file paths.
HistoryList	Includes URLs from Internet Explorer's history list.
RecentlyUsedList	Includes all the documents in the current user's list of recently used applications, which appears in the Start menu (depending on system settings).
AllUrl	Represents the combination of the HistoryLisy and RecentlyUsedList (with duplicates omitted).
AllSystemSources	Represents the combination of the FileSystem and AllUrl options (with duplicates omitted).
ListItems	This option applies only to a ComboBox (it isn't supported for TextBox controls). If you use this option, this list of items is taken from the ComboBox.Items collection.
CustomSource	Uses the collection of strings you've specified in the control's AutoCompleteCustomSource collection. You need to add these items at design time using the Properties window or add them programmatically.

■Tip When using autocompletion with a combo box, the AutoCompleteSource.ListItems option makes the most sense. Otherwise, you'll have two different lists of items that the user can choose from—a list of items that appears in the control and a list of autocompletion suggestions that appears as the user types.

Next, you need to set the control's AutoCompleteMode mode to one of the options in Table 4-15. This determines how the autocompletion behavior will work with the control.

Table 4-15. *AutoCompleteMode Values*

Value	Description
Append	With this mode, the AutoComplete suggestion is automatically inserted into the control as the user types. For example, if you start by pressing the E key within a text box, the first item that starts with *E* appears in the control. However, the added portion is selected so that if the user continues to type, the new portion will be replaced. This is the autocompletion behavior used in Excel and older versions of Internet Explorer.
Suggest	With this mode, a drop-down list of matching AutoComplete values appears underneath the control. If one of these entries matches what you want, you can select it and it will be inserted in the control automatically. This is usually the preferred autocompletion option, because it allows the user to see multiple suggestions at once. It's the same as the behavior provided in modern versions of Internet Explorer.
SuggestAppend	This mode combines Append and Suggest. As with Suggest, a list of matches appears in a drop-down list under the control. However, the first match is also added inserted in the control and selected.

Figure 4-10 shows an AutoComplete combo box that uses AutoCompleteMode. SuggestAppend and AutoCompleteSource.ListItems. The items are added to the list with this line of code:

```
string[] colorNames = Enum.GetNames(typeof(KnownColor));
lstColors.Items.AddRange(colorNames);
```

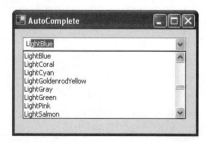

Figure 4-10. *An AutoComplete combo box*

Drag-and-Drop

Drag-and-drop operations aren't quite as common today as they were a few years ago, because programmers have gradually settled on other methods of copying information that don't require holding down the mouse button (a technique that many users find difficult to master). For example, a drawing program is likely to use a two-step operation (select an object, and then draw it) rather than a single drag-and-drop operation. Programs that do support drag-and-drop often use it as a shortcut for advanced users, rather than a standard way of working.

Drag-and-drop is also sometimes confused with the ability to "drag" a picture or piece of user interface around a window. This "fake" drag-and-drop is useful in drawing and diagramming applications (including the drawing application developed in Chapter 24), but it needs to be coded manually. In the following sections, you will learn about both types of dragging operations.

"Fake" Drag-and-Drop

True drag-and-drop is a user-initiated way to exchange information between two controls. You don't need to use drag-and-drop events to create objects that the user can move around the form. For example, consider the program shown in Figure 4-11, which allows a user to click a picture box, drag it, and release it somewhere else on the form.

Figure 4-11. *Dragging a control around a form*

Conceptually, a control is being dragged and dropped, but all the logic takes place in the appropriate mouse-handling events of the draggable control. In this case, you need to handle MouseDown (to start the dragging operation), MouseUp (to end it), and MouseMove (to move the control if the drag is in progress). A Form-level isDragging variable keeps track of when fake drag-and-drop mode is currently switched on.

```
// Keep track of when fake "drag-and-drop" mode is enabled.
private bool isDragging = false;

// Store the location where the user clicked the control.
private int clickOffsetX, clickOffsetY;
```

```
// Start dragging.
private void picDragger_MouseDown(System.Object sender,
 System.Windows.Forms.MouseEventArgs e)
{
    isDragging = true;
    clickOffsetX = e.X;
    clickOffsetY = e.Y;
}

// End dragging.
private void picDragger_MouseUp(System.Object sender,
 System.Windows.Forms.MouseEventArgs e)
{
    isDragging = false;
}

// Move the control (during dragging).
private void picDragger_MouseMove(System.Object sender,
 System.Windows.Forms.MouseEventArgs e)
{
    if (isDragging)
    {
        // The control coordinates are converted into form coordinates
        // by adding the label position offset.
        // The offset where the user clicked in the control is also
        // accounted for. Otherwise, it looks like the top-left corner
        // of the label is attached to the mouse.
        lblDragger.Left = e.X + lblDragger.Left - clickOffsetX;
        lblDragger.Top = e.Y + lblDragger.Top - clickOffsetY;
    }
}
```

Three components factor into the position calculation:

- The e.X and e.Y parameters provide the position of the mouse over the control, where (0,0) is the top-left corner of the control.

- The lblDragger.Left and lblDragger.Top properties give the distance between the top-left corner of the control and the top-left corner of the form.

- The ClickOffsetX and ClickOffsetY variables give the position between the control's top-left corner and where the user actually clicked to start dragging. By taking this into account, the label acts as though it is "glued" to the mouse at that point.

Authentic Drag-and-Drop

Real drag-and-drop operations are quite a bit different from fake ones. Essentially, they work like this:

1. The user clicks a control (or a specific region inside a control) and holds down the mouse button. At this point, some information is set aside, and a drag-and-drop operation begins.

2. The user moves the mouse over another control. If this control can accept the current type of content (for example, a picture or text), the mouse cursor changes to a special drag-and-drop icon. Otherwise, the mouse cursor becomes a circle with a line drawn through it.

3. When the user releases the mouse button, the control receives the information and decides what to do with it. The operation should also be cancelable by pressing the Esc key (without releasing the mouse button).

Unlike the fake drag-and-drop example, a real drag-and-drop operation can easily take place between controls, or even two different applications, as long as the drag-and-drop contract is followed.

The example program shown in Figure 4-12 uses drag-and-drop to take a picture from a label control and draw it onto a picture box control. You'll find the complete code with the samples for this chapter under the project name AuthenticDragAndDrop.

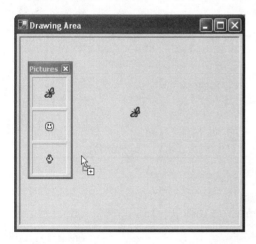

Figure 4-12. *A sample drag-and-drop application*

The first step is to configure the picture box control to accept dropped information.

```
picDrawingArea.AllowDrop = true;
```

To start the drag-and-drop, you can use the DoDragDrop() method of the source control. In this case, it is one of three labels. Dragging is initiated in the MouseDown event for the label.

```
private void lbl_MouseDown(object sender, System.Windows.Forms.MouseEventArgs e)
{
    Label lbl = (Label)sender;
    lbl.DoDragDrop(lbl.Image, DragDropEffects.Copy);
}
```

The same event handler takes care of the MouseDown event for each label. In the event handler, the generic sender reference (which points to the object that sent the event) is converted into a label. Then, a drag-and-drop copy operation starts. The information associated with this operation is the image from the label control.

To allow the drop target picture box to receive information, you need to verify that the information is the correct type in the DragEnter event and then set a special event argument (e.Effect). DragEnter occurs once when the mouse moves into the bounds of the control.

```
private void picDrawingArea_DragEnter(object sender,
 System.Windows.Forms.DragEventArgs e)
{
    if (e.Data.GetDataPresent(DataFormats.Bitmap))
        e.Effect = DragDropEffects.Copy;
    else
        e.Effect = DragDropEffects.None;
}
```

The last step is to respond to the information once it is dropped by handling the DragDrop event. You can do anything you want with the dropped information. In the current example, a GDI+ drawing operation starts (although it could make just as much sense to set its Image property).

```
private void picDrawingArea_DragDrop(object sender,
 System.Windows.Forms.DragEventArgs e)
{
    // Use this offset to center the 30x30-pixel images.
    int offset = 15;

    // Convert the coordinates from screen-based to form-based.
    Point p = this.PointToClient(new Point(e.X - offset, e.Y - offset));

    // Paint a temporary picture at this location.
    Graphics g = picDrawingArea.CreateGraphics();
    g.DrawImage((Image)e.Data.GetData(DataFormats.Bitmap), p);
    g.Dispose();
}
```

Note that the event handler provides screen coordinates, which must be converted into the appropriate coordinates for the picture box.

Practically, you can exchange any type of object through a drag-and-drop operation. However, while this free-spirited approach is perfect for your applications, it isn't wise if you need to communicate with other applications. If you want to drag and drop into other applications, you should use data from a managed base class (such as String or Image) or an object that implements ISerializable or IDataObject (which allows .NET to transfer your object into a stream of bytes and reconstruct the object in another application domain).

Extender Providers

Extender providers are a specialized type of component that can add properties to other controls on the same form. They're useful because they allow you to add a feature to a number of controls at the same time. The possible alternatives—writing code for each individual control or deriving custom controls—require much more work. Of course, because of the way provider components are implemented, they work only for certain types of extensions. Because providers are separate classes, they don't have the ability to reach into a control and tweak its inner workings. However, they do have the ability to react to events, display information elsewhere on the form, and perform any other action.

The easiest way to understand the role of extender providers is to consider an example. .NET provides three extender provider components:

- **ToolTip.** This provider lets you show a pop-up tooltip window with descriptive information next to any control. The ToolTip provider is discussed in this section.

- **ErrorProvider.** This provider lets you show a flashing error icon (with a tooltip error message) when invalid data is entered. It's described in Chapter 18.

- **HelpProvider.** This provider lets you show help messages or launch a context-sensitive help topic in another window. You'll use it in Chapter 22.

■**Note** Three other .NET types implement the IExtenderProvider interface but aren't considered to be dedicated extender providers. The FlowLayoutPanel and TableLayoutPanel use it to add features to the child controls they contain (see Chapter 21). The PropertyTab uses it as part of the infrastructure for the Visual Studio Properties window.

Some providers derive from Component and appear in the component tray under the design surface of the form. Other providers derive from Control, which allows them to be placed on the form. It all depends on how the extender provider works and whether it needs a piece of dedicated screen real estate. For example, the ToolTip provider appears in the component tray. It displays a tooltip on any control when the mouse hovers over it.

Once you've added a ToolTip provider to a form, you can set a tooltip on any control in one of two ways:

- At design time, select the appropriate control, and look in the Properties window for the property ToolTip on tipProvider (where tipProvider is the name of the ToolTip component).

- At runtime, call tipProvider.SetToolTip() with a reference to the control. You can also use the GetToolTip() method to retrieve a control's tooltip.

Tip There really isn't any difference between using the SetToolTip() method and the extended ToolTip property provided by the Form designer. With providers, Visual Studio simply translates what you type in the Properties window into the appropriate method call and adds the code to the form class. So, when you visually set the ToolTip property, you are still in fact using the SetToolTip() method. Take a look at InitializeComponent() to see what is generated by Visual Studio.

Here's an example of how you can (and can't) use a ToolTip provider programmatically:

```
// This code works. It uses the SetToolTip() method to attach a tooltip
// to the txtName control.
tips.SetToolTip(txtName, "Enter Your Name Here");

// This code doesn't work! It attempts to set the tooltip of the txtName control
// directly, even though the TextBox class does not provide a ToolTip property.
txtName.ToolTip = "Enter Your Name Here";
```

Figure 4-13 shows a titled tooltip at runtime.

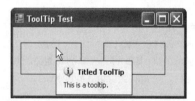

Figure 4-13. *A tooltip with an icon and a title*

You can also configure some generic tooltip settings by adjusting the properties of the ToolTip provider, as detailed in Table 4-16. If you've programmed with earlier versions of .NET, you'll notice that .NET 2.0 adds quite a few graphical niceties to the ToolTip provider for displaying more than the generic yellow box.

Table 4-16. *ToolTipProvider Members*

Member	Purpose
Active	When set to false, no tooltips are shown for any controls.
AutomaticDelay, AutoPopDelay, InitialDelay, and ReshowDelay	These settings specify the number of milliseconds before the tooltip appears, the time that it remains visible if the mouse is stationary, and the time required to make it reappear. Generally, you should use the default values.
ShowAlways	If set to true, tooltips appear when the mouse hovers over a control even if the window containing the control does not currently have focus.

Table 4-16. *ToolTipProvider Members*

Member	Purpose
SetToolTip(), GetToolTip(), and RemoveAll()	These methods allow you to attach a descriptive string to a control and retrieve it. To remove a tooltip, either attach an empty string or use RemoveAll() to clear all tooltips at once. (To temporarily disable tooltips without removing the tooltip information, use the Active property.)
ForeColor and BackColor	Adjusts the colors of the tooltip text and background.
ToolTipTitle	Sets a title that appears, in boldface, above the tooltip text in the tooltip window. Note that this title isn't control-specific—you set it once, and it applies to all the tooltips you show.
ToolTipIcon	Takes one of four values: None, Info, Warning, or Error. If you don't use None, the corresponding icon will appear in the tooltip window.
IsBalloon	Draws the tooltip as a balloon. This will fail without an error if you've disabled balloon tips. Balloon tips are disabled when there's an EnableBalloonTips registry setting with a value of 0 in the HKEY_CURRENT_USER\Software\Microsoft\Windows\CurrentVersion\Explorer\Advanced section.
UseAnimation and UseFading	Sets whether the tooltip uses animated effects and when they appear and fade away, if the system settings allow them.
OwnerDraw and Draw events	If set to true, your code has the chance to draw the tooltip. To do so, you need to respond to the Draw event and use GDI+ drawing code, as described in Chapter 7.

Note For a lower-level look at how providers work, see Chapter 25, where you'll learn how to create your own.

The NotifyIcon

In many other programming frameworks, it's difficult to use a system tray icon. In .NET it's as easy as adding the straightforward NotifyIcon component, which is described in Table 4-17.

Table 4-17. *NotifyIcon Members*

Member	Description
ContextMenuStrip	The ContextMenuStrip object defines a menu for your system tray icon. It is displayed automatically when the user right-clicks the icon. For more information about creating and fine-tuning menus, see Chapter 14.
Icon	The graphical icon that appears in the system tray (as an Icon object). You can get a few commonly used icons from the properties of the SystemIcons class, or use the image library included with Visual Studio (see Chapter 5 for details).
Text	The tooltip text that appears above the system tray icon.

Table 4-17. *NotifyIcon Members (Continued)*

Member	Description
Visible	Set this to true to show the icon. It defaults to false, giving you a chance to set up the rest of the required functionality.
Click, DoubleClick, MouseDown, MouseMove, and MouseUp events	These events work the same as the Control-class events with the same names. They allow you to respond to the mouse actions.
BalloonTipText, BalloonTipTitle, BalloonTipIcon	Define the text, title, and icon for a balloon-style tooltip. This tooltip won't appear until you call the ShowBalloonTip() method in your code.
ShowBalloonTip()	Shows the balloon tooltip defined by the BalloonTipText, BalloonTipTitle, and BalloonTipIcon properties. You specify the delay (in milliseconds) before the tooltip is cleared. An overloaded version of this method allows you to specify a new BalloonTipText, BalloonTipTitle, and BalloonTipIcon.
BalloonTipShown, BalloonTipClicked, and BalloonTipClosed events	Allow you to react when the tip is first shown, subsequently clicked, and closed by the user.

Technically, the NotifyIcon is a component (not a control), that displays an icon in the system tray at runtime. In many cases, it's more useful to create the NotifyIcon dynamically at runtime. For example, you might create a utility application that loads into the system tray and waits quietly, monitoring for some system event or waiting for user actions. In this case, you need to be able to create the system tray icon without displaying a form.

The next example demonstrates exactly such an application. When it first loads, it creates a system tray icon (see Figure 4-14), attaches two menu items to it, and begins monitoring the file system for changes (using the System.IO.FileSystemWatcher class). No windows are displayed.

Figure 4-14. *A system tray icon*

In this example, it's important that the NotifyIcon is displayed even though no forms have been loaded. This is a fairly easy task to accomplish. All you need to do is create the form that contains the NotifyIcon component, without calling the Show() or ShowDialog() method to display that form. The NotifyIcon appears immediately when its Visible property is set to true.

For a lightweight option, you can host the NotifyIcon on a component class instead of a form. To create the component, just select Project ➤ Add Component in Visual Studio. Every component has the ability to host design-time controls—just drag and drop the control onto the design-time view of the class, and Visual Studio will create the code in the special hidden designer region, just as it does with a form. And for an even lighter option, you could create the NotifyIcon object yourself in the Main() method, and set its Visible property to true to make it appear in the system tray. However, you'll surrender some notable design-time conveniences.

For example, if you want to create a linked menu for the icon, you'll need to write the code by hand. If you've placed your NotifyIcon on a form or component, you can simply add a ContextMenuStrip in the same place, and customize it in the Properties window.

Here's an example of a component that includes a NotifyIcon, ContextMenuStrip, and FileSystemWatcher:

```
public partial class FileSystemTray : Component
{
    // Constructors omitted.

    // Track newly created files here.
    private List<string> newFiles = new List<string>();

    // Fires when a new file is added.
    private void fileSystemWatcher1_Changed(object sender,
      System.IO.FileSystemEventArgs e)
    {
        newFiles.Add(e.Name);
    }

    // Fires when the Exit menu command is clicked.
    private void cmdExit_Click(object sender, System.EventArgs e)
    {
        Application.Exit();
    }

    // Fires when the Show Files menu command is clicked.
    private void cmdShowFiles_Click(object sender, System.EventArgs e)
    {
        FileList frmFileList = new FileList();
        frmFileList.FillList(newFiles);
        frmFileList.Show();
    }
}
```

And here's the Main() method code that gets it all started:

```
static void Main()
{
    Application.EnableVisualStyles();

    // Show the system tray icon.
    FileSystemTray cmp = new FileSystemTray();

    // Start a message loop and don't exit.
    Application.Run();
}
```

■**Tip** One example of this type of program is a batch file processor. It might scan a directory for files that correspond to work orders or invoices, and immediately add database records, send e-mails, or perform some other task.

ActiveX Controls

.NET includes excellent interoperability features that allow you to continue using COM components and ActiveX controls in your current applications. If you're using Visual Studio, the process is even automated for you.

To add an ActiveX control to one of your projects in Visual Studio, right-click the toolbox and select Choose Items. Select the COM Components tab, find the appropriate control on the list, and put a check mark next to it.

Nothing happens until you add an instance of this control to a form. The first time you do this, Visual Studio automatically creates an interop assembly for you. For example, if you add the MSChart control, which has no direct .NET equivalent, it creates a file with a name like AxInterop.MSChart20Lib_2_0.dll.

The "Ax" at the beginning of the name identifies that this interop assembly derives from System.Windows.Forms.AxHost. This class creates any .NET wrapper for an ActiveX control. It works "between" your .NET code and the ActiveX component, as shown in Figure 4-15.

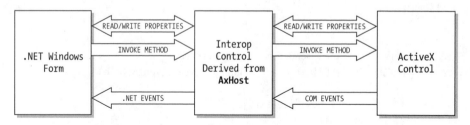

Figure 4-15. *AxHost interaction*

The control on your form is a legitimate .NET control, as you can see by examining the automatically generated designer code that defines and instantiates it. For example, consider an automatically generated interop class that supports the MSChart control:

```
AxMSChart20Lib.AxMSChart AxMSChart1;
```

Here's the code used to configure the control, in true .NET fashion:

```
this.AxMSChart1 = new AxMSChart20Lib.AxMSChart();
this.AxMSChart1.Location = new System.Drawing.Point(36, 24);
this.AxMSChart1.Name = "AxMSChart1";
this.axMSChart1.OcxState =
  ((System.Windows.Forms.AxHost.State)(resources.GetObject("axMSChart1.OcxState")));
this.AxMSChart1.Size = new System.Drawing.Size(216, 72);
this.AxMSChart1.TabIndex = 4;
```

You can see that this control supports basic .NET properties such as Size and Location. It also uses a special OcxState property (inherited from the AxHost class) that retrieves the persisted state of an ActiveX control. From your program's point of view, you can communicate with a normal .NET control that supports .NET event handling and the basic set of features in the Control class. The AxHost-based control quietly communicates with the original ActiveX control and mimics its behavior on the form. You can even dynamically resize the control and modify its properties using the built-in property pages, and it will respond exactly as it should.

In some cases, the new class may introduce changes. For example, when the MSFlexGrid control is imported, it changes the syntax used to set some properties into method calls:

```
grid.set_ColWidth(1, 3000);        // This was grid.ColWidth(1) = 3000;
grid.set_ColAlignment(0, 1);       // This was grid.ColAlightment(0) = 1;
```

Fortunately, you can always use the Object Browser to get to the bottom of any new changes.

If you are a war-hardened COM veteran, you can create interop controls by hand. However, this process is time-consuming and error-prone, and it generally won't produce a better result than Visual Studio's automatic support. Instead, you might want to subclass the interop control that Visual Studio creates. In other words, you could create a custom control that inherits from the interop control. This extra layer gives you the chance to add .NET features and won't hamper performance.

Should You Import ActiveX Controls?

Importing controls is easy, and it most cases it works without a hitch. However, it introduces an ugly legacy of problems:

- **ActiveX registration issues are back.** .NET controls demonstrate the amazing xcopy installation capability of the .NET platform. ActiveX controls, however, need to be registered and reregistered whenever a change occurs. This isn't a new problem, but the return of an ugly one.

- **Security issues appear.** The .NET Framework uses a fine-grained approach to security, which allows controls to be used in semitrusted environments with most of their functionality intact. ActiveX controls require full unmanaged code permission, which makes them more difficult to use in some scenarios.

- **Performance could be affected.** Generally, this is the least likely concern. ActiveX emulation is extremely fast in .NET. In some cases, certain controls may exhibit problems, but that will be the exception.

.NET controls will always be the best solution, and many third-party .NET controls surpass most of the legacy ActiveX controls still around today. Well-known component vendors with cutting-edge .NET offerings include Infragistics (www.componentsource.com), ComponentOne (www.componentone.com), and Developer Express (www.devexpress.com).

The Last Word

This chapter has toured the most common Windows controls and demonstrated a few .NET twists. You've also learned about the basic types of controls and the techniques you can use for AutoComplete edit boxes, drag-and-drop support, and tooltips. In the next chapter, you'll learn how controls work with images and other types of resources.

■■■

CHAPTER 5

Images and Resources

In Chapter 1 you took your first look at code serialization, which is the process Visual Studio uses to generate the code for your form as you configure your controls in the design environment. Code serialization captures all the properties of your controls and components, from the position of a button to the text of a label.

However, there are certain types of data that can't be conveniently stored in code, like large binary images and media files. There are also cases in which you want the flexibility to draw text data from different files so that you can substitute content in different languages when your application is running in different locales. In .NET, both of these scenarios are dealt with using embedded *resources*.

In this chapter you'll take a look at how resources work, and how you can use them to embed data into your assemblies and create localized forms. But first, you'll look at .NET's support for pictures with the Image class.

■**Tip** Visual Studio provides a ready-made image library that includes standard icons used in Microsoft Office and Windows. You can find this image library in a directory like c:\Program Files\ Microsoft Visual Studio 8\Common7\VS2005ImageLibrary (assuming you've installed to the default location on C:).

The Image Class

To manipulate picture data in .NET, you use the System.Drawing.Image class. Other classes, like System.Drawing.Bitmap and System.Drawing.Imaging.Metafile, derive from the Image class and represent data of a specific format. However, it's usually easiest to work directly with the more generic Image class.

You can't create an Image object directly, because it is an abstract class. However, you can use the static Image.FromFile() method to read data from a file and create the corresponding Image. The FromFile() method supports standard bitmap formats (like BMP, GIF without support of animation, JPEG, and PNG files).

Here's an example:

```
Image myImage = Image.FromFile(Path.Combine(Application.StartupPath, "mypic.bmp"));
```

The Image also includes the static FromStream() method for retrieving image data from any stream (which might wrap a database field, a file being downloaded from the Internet, or in-memory data). You can also use the static FromHbitmap() method to convert an unmanaged Windows handle for a GDI bitmap to an Image object. This is useful if you need to use the unmanaged GDI library to get access to a feature that GDI+ (discussed in Chapter 7) doesn't provide.

The Image class provides its own set of properties and methods. Some of the most interesting include RotateFlip(), which changes the picture orientation by rotating or inverting it, and GetThumbnailImage(), which returns an image object of the specified size that condenses the information from the original Image.

```
Image myImage = Image.FromFile(Path.Combine(Application.StartupPath,
 "mypic.bmp"));

// Rotate by 270 degrees and flip about the Y-axis.
myImage.RotateFlip(RotateFlipType.Rotate270FlipY);

// Create a 100 x 100 pixel thumbnail.
Image myThumbnail = myImage.GetThumbnailImage(100, 100, null, IntPtr.Zero);
```

Tip .NET also includes a System.Drawing.Icon class for loading and manipulating icon resources.

Common Controls and Images

Many controls support showing an image. In fact, all controls inherit the BackgroundImage and BackgroundImageLayout properties, although only some actually support it. Supporting controls include the Button, RadioButton, CheckBox, PictureBox, and container controls like the GroupBox, Panel, and Form. A background image is always painted at the back of the control (underneath any child controls), and is positioned at the top-left corner and stretched, zoomed, centered, or tiled to fit (depending on the BackgroundImageLayout property).

Note Zooming is similar to stretching—it shrinks or expands the image to fit the control dimensions. However, unlike stretching, zooming doesn't change the aspect ratio, which means the image won't be distorted.

Many controls also support foreground images with the Image and ImageAlign properties. A foreground image appears alongside any text content, and if the two overlap, the text is always displayed on top of the image. Figure 5-1 shows common controls with embedded pictures.

■**Note** You'll need to turn off AutoSize for controls that support it, like the Label. This allows you to resize the control to accommodate its text and picture content. Auto sizing is based only on the control's text, except in the case of the PictureBox.

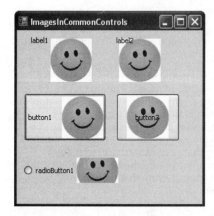

Figure 5-1. *Common control picture support*

For even more flexibility, you can render your own image content and paint it on a form or control using GDI+. You'll learn more about this technique in Chapter 7.

■**Tip** Many controls, like the Button, support both a background and a foreground image. If you use both, the foreground image appears in front of the background image.

Table 5-1 lists the image-related properties you'll find in .NET controls.

Table 5-1. *Control Properties for Images*

Property	Description
BackgroundImage	Allows you to show a picture in the background of a control. If this control contains other child controls, the background image is always shown underneath these controls.
BackgroundImageLayout	Sets how the background image should be laid out. You can choose None, Tile, Center, Stretch, or Zoom. The difference between Stretch and Zoom is that zooming an image preserves its aspect ratio, while stretching an image adjusts the image to fit the control bounds exactly.

Table 5-1. *Control Properties for Images (Continued)*

Property	Description
Image*	This property isn't a part of the base Control class, but it does appear in several common controls, including Label, PictureBox, Button, CheckBox, and RadioButton. The Image property allows you to insert a picture alongside or instead of text, as a foreground image (see Figure 5-1).
ImageAlign*	Sets how the foreground image should be laid out. You can align a picture to any side or corner of the control. Note that the PictureBox does not provide this property.
ImageList*, ImageIndex*, and ImageKey*	These properties serve the same purpose as the Image property, and allow you to specify a foreground image. The ImageList is a reference to an ImageList component, which contains a collection of images. Once you set the ImageList property, you can set the ImageIndex (a numeric index based on the position) or ImageKey (a descriptive keyword that you assigned to the image previously) to indicate the specific image that you want to use from the ImageList. If you use these properties *and* the Image property, the one you apply last takes precedence. Note that the PictureBox does not provide these properties.
ImageLocation**	Specifies a URL (in the form http://...) or a file path (like c:\...) that points to an image file. The PictureBox will download the image immediately when the property is set, or asynchronously, depending on the WaitOnLoad property.
WaitOnLoad**	Used in conjunction with ImageLocation. If true, the PictureBox will download the image immediately when the ImageLocation property is set. If false (the default), the PictureBox will behave somewhat like a Web browser, and download the picture asynchronously. The InitialImage will not be shown until the operation is completed. During the download, the LoadProgressChanged and LoadCompleted events will fire.
InitialImage** and ErrorImage**	Used in conjunction with ImageLocation. InitialImage specifies which image should be shown before the image is downloaded, if WaitOnLoad is false. ErrorImage specifies the image that will be shown if the image can't be downloaded. By default, this is a small error-page icon, like that shown in a Web browser.

* Not provided by all controls

** Provided only by the PictureBox

The ImageList

The ImageList component is a collection that holds images of a preset size and color depth. Other controls access pictures in the ImageList using the appropriate index numbers or string key names. In this way, an ImageList acts as a resource for other controls, providing icons for controls like the ToolStrip and TreeView.

To create an ImageList at design time, drag it onto your form (it will appear in the component tray). The basic members of the ImageList are described in Table 5-2.

Table 5-2. *ImageList Members*

Member	Description
ColorDepth	A value from the ColorDepth enumeration that identifies the color resolution of the images in the control. Some common choices are 5-bit (256-color mode), 16-bit (high color), and 24-bit (true color).
Images	The collection of Image objects that are provided to other controls.
ImageSize	A Size structure that defines the size of the contained images (with a maximum of 256 x 256 pixels). ImageList controls should contain only images that share the same size and color depth. Images are converted to the specified format when they are added.
TransparentColor	Some image types, like icons and GIFs, define a transparent color that allows the background to show through. By setting the TransparentColor property, you can define a new transparent color that will be used when this image is displayed. This is useful for graphic formats that don't directly support transparency, like bitmaps.
Draw()	This overloaded method provides a quick and easy way to take an image and output it to a GDI+ drawing surface.

■**Tip** Transparent regions are a must when mixing custom images and standard controls. If you simply use an icon with a gray background, your interface becomes garish and ugly on a computer where the default color scheme is not used, as a gray box appears around the image. You also run into problems if the icon can be selected, at which point it is highlighted with a blue background.

You can add, remove, and rearrange images using the ImageList designer. Just click the ellipsis (...) next to the Images property in the Properties window. Images can be drawn from almost any common bitmap file, including bitmaps, GIFs, JPEGs, and icons. When you add a picture, some related read-only properties about its size and format appear in the window (see Figure 5-2).

Figure 5-2. *The ImageList designer*

Once you have images in an ImageList control, you can use them to provide pictures to another control. Many modern controls provide an ImageList property, which stores a reference to an ImageList control. Individual items in the control (like tree nodes or list rows) then use an ImageIndex property, which identifies a single picture in the ImageList by index number (starting at 0) or an ImageKey property, which identifies a single picture by its string name.

ImageList Serialization

If you look at the automatically generated code for your form, you'll see that the image files you add are stored in a resource file in your project. When the form is created, the images are deserialized into Image objects and placed in the collection. This takes place in the InitializeComponent() helper method that's hidden in the designer file for your form. A special class, the ImageListStreamer, makes this process a simple one-line affair, regardless of how many images are in your ImageList:

```
this.imagesLarge.ImageStream = ((System.Windows.Forms.ImageListStreamer)
  (resources.GetObject("imagesLarge.ImageStream")));
```

Initially, the name is set to match the file name of the original image. However, at no point will your application use the original file. Instead, it uses the embedded binary resource. If you change the picture, you need to remove the image and add it back again (or use resources, which are discussed later in this chapter).

The image key isn't actually stored in the resource file that contains the pictures. Instead, they are applied in the InitializeComponent() method using the SetKeyName() method. Here's an example that shows what takes place:

```
this.imagesLarge.ImageStream = ((System.Windows.Forms.ImageListStreamer)
  (resources.GetObject("imagesLarge.ImageStream")));
this.imagesLarge.Images.SetKeyName(0, "Zapotec.bmp");
```

Although this might seem to be a fragile approach at first glance, it doesn't cause any problems in practice. If you remove an image or change the order of images using the ImageList designer, Visual Studio updates this code region. You aren't able to change the image content any other way, because the ImageList uses a proprietary serialization format. If you browse the resource file for your form (like Form1.resx for a form named Form1) you'll find the ImageList data is shown as a single opaque binary blob of information.

Manipulating the ImageList in Code

If you want to have an ImageList object around for a longer period (for example, to use in different forms), you can create it directly in code. You might also want to create Image objects out of graphic files rather than use a project resource.

First, you need a variable to reference the ImageList:

```
private ImageList iconImages = new ImageList();
```

Then, you can create a method that fills the ImageList:

```
// Configure the ImageList.
iconImages.ColorDepth = System.Windows.Forms.ColorDepth.Depth8Bit;
iconImages.ImageSize = new System.Drawing.Size(16, 16);

// Get all the icon files in the current directory.
string[] iconFiles = Directory.GetFiles(Application.StartupPath, "*.ico");

// Create an Image object for each file and add it to the ImageList.
// You can also use an Image subclass (like Icon).
foreach (string iconFile in iconFiles)
{
    Icon newIcon = new Icon(iconFile);
    iconImages.Images.Add(newIcon);
}
```

Notice that when you use this approach, you no longer have the benefit of the ImageKey property. Although you could set the key names for individual images, it doesn't make much sense to hard-code strings for this purpose if you already need to load the files by hand.

The example that follows loops through an ImageList and draws its images directly onto the surface of a form. The result is shown in Figure 5-3.

```
// Get the graphics device context for the form.
Graphics g = this.CreateGraphics();

// Draw each image using the ImageList.Draw() method.
for (int i = 0; i < iconImages.Images.Count; i++)
{
    iconImages.Draw(g, 30 + i * 30, 30, i);
}

// Release the graphics device context.
g.Dispose();
```

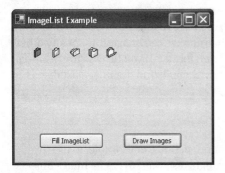

Figure 5-3. *Outputting an ImageList directly*

As with all manual drawing, these icons are erased as soon as the form is repainted (for example, if you minimize and then maximize it). You'll tackle this issue in Chapter 7.

Limitations of the ImageList

The ImageList may seem like a good all-purpose repository for image data, but it does have a few limitations:

- If you fill the ImageList at design time, you'll need to place it on a single form or on a custom component. That can make it difficult to reuse the same images across multiple windows.

- There's no support for updating the source graphics in the ImageList. When you add the figures to the ImageList, they're copied and no link is maintained to the original files. If you want to change them, you need to delete the image and read it. If you're relying on the ImageIndex property to find images in the ImageList, you'll also need to make sure the order remains the same.

- There's no way to store different sizes and formats of images in the same ImageList. Similarly, the ImageList isn't any help if you want to store other types of content, like audio files.

To tackle these problems, .NET introduces a more powerful alternative—resources.

Resources

It's easy to load the content for an Image object from an external file. However, it's not the most robust approach. Not only will you need to worry about deploying all the image files with your application and making sure they remain in the expected directory, but you're also at the risk of users who carelessly or deliberately delete them. To avoid these sorts of problems, it's common to embed external files like images and sounds directly into your compiled assembly file. These embedded files are known as *resources*.

.NET has supported resources since version 1.0. However, Visual Studio 2005 is the first version of the IDE that adds strong design-time support that allows you to add and manage resources at design time. Best of all, Visual Studio uses automatic code generation to create *strongly typed* resources, which means you can use them in your code without worrying about misspelling the resource name (and thereby creating an unexpected runtime error) or attempting to cast the resource to a data type that's not supported.

Adding a Type-Safe Resource

To add a resource, start by expanding the Properties folder in the Solution Explorer. The Properties node contains three items:

- **AssemblyInfo.cs.** This code file includes attributes that set various bits of metadata that are compiled into your assembly, including qthe publisher information and the version number. You can edit this information directly by modifying this file, or by using the project properties dialog box.

- **Resources.resx.** This XML file identifies the resources that you've added to your project. These resources are made available to your application through the automatically generated code in Resources.Designer.cs.

- **Settings.settings.** This XML file is hidden by default. It identifies the settings that you've configured for your application, and stores the values for application-scoped settings. These settings are made available to your application through the automatically generated code in Settings.Designer.cs.

There are two ways to modify the resource information in the Resources.resx file. You can double-click directly on the file in the Solution Explorer, or you can double-click the Properties folder and then click the Resources tab in the application properties sheet. Either way, you'll see the resource browser shown in Figure 5-4.

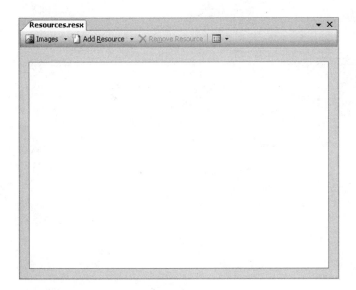

Figure 5-4. *The resource browser*

The resources in your application are subdivided into categories (strings, images, icons, audio, and files). Depending on the category, you'll see a different visualization of the resource.

For example, pictures are shown as thumbnails, while sound files are shown with a media icon that plays the sound when double-clicked. The string view shows a list of text values.

To add an image, click the Add button and select Existing File. Browse to an image file, select it, and click OK. If you don't have an image file handy, try using one from the Windows directory. If the file is not in the current project, Visual Studio copies the image file into a Resources subfolder in your project (see Figure 5-5). If the Resources folder doesn't exist yet, it's created automatically.

Figure 5-5. *The Resources folder*

Next, Visual Studio adds an entry for that resource into the resource browser (see Figure 5-6).

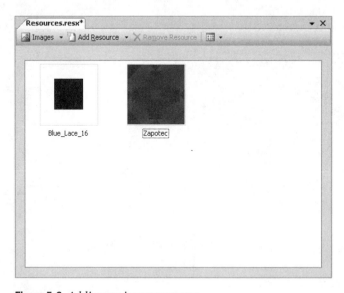

Figure 5-6. *Adding an image resource*

By default, the resource is given the same name as the file, but you can rename it once you've added it. It's best to make sure the resource name is a valid variable name (no spaces or extended characters, begins with a letter, and so on). Otherwise, the property name you use to retrieve the resource won't match exactly. For example, a resource named Blue Lace 16 is exposed through a property named Blue_Lace_16.

Once you've added a resource, it's easy to use in your code. You can access all resources through an automatically generated Resources class. The Resources class is created in the Properties namespace, which is nested inside the default namespace for your application. For example, if you create an application named ResourceTest, you could use code like this to retrieve an image and show it in a picture box:

```
pictureBox1.Image = ResourceTest.Properties.Resources.Zapotec;
```

Notice that the Zapotec property is strongly typed as an image. That means there's no need to cast or convert it when you retrieve it. Similarly, text files are returned as strings, but binary files are returned using a byte array, and audio content is returned as a memory stream (which you can pass to the SoundPlayer component described in Chapter 16).

It's important to realize that when you execute this code, you are actually retrieving the Zapotec resource from the compiled assembly, not the stand-alone image file. (To verify this, you can delete the image file from the Resources folder after you compiled the application, and it will still run without a problem.) Based on this fact, you might wonder why Visual Studio uses the Resources folder at all. The reason is because it allows you to easily update your resources.

For example, if you want to replace the Zapotec image with a newer version, you simply need to overwrite the file in the Resources folder. The next time you compile your application, the newer version will be embedded into the assembly. You don't need to modify any of your code.

To remove a resource, delete the file from the Resources folder and recompile. Alternatively, you can delete the entry in the resource browser. However, this only removes the resource information—it doesn't actually delete the corresponding file in the Resources folder.

How Type-Safe Resources Work

Now that you've seen how easy it is to use resources in your application, you're probably wondering about the underpinnings that make it all work. Essentially, the Resources.resx file is an XML document that lists the resources you've added (using a <data> tag for each one), and indicates where to find the associated file in the Resources subfolder. Each entry also indicates the corresponding .NET data type.

Here's a heavily reduced version of the Resources.resx file that leaves out the comment text and schema information, which describes the structure of the file. In this example, there are two image resources.

```
<?xml version="1.0" encoding="utf-8"?>
<root>
  <!-- Schema information omitted. -->
  <data name="Blue Lace 16" type="System.Resources.ResXFileRef,
 System.Windows.Forms">
    <value>..\Resources\Blue Lace 16.bmp;System.Drawing.Bitmap,
 System.Drawing, Version=2.0.3600.0, Culture=neutral,
```

```
PublicKeyToken=b03f5f7f11d50a3a</value>
  </data>
  <data name="Zapotec" type="System.Resources.ResXFileRef, System.Windows.Forms">
    <value>..\Resources\Zapotec.bmp;System.Drawing.Bitmap, System.Drawing,
Version=2.0.3600.0, Culture=neutral, PublicKeyToken=b03f5f7f11d50a3a</value>
  </data>
</root>
```

This type of file is a *linked* resource file, because it links to other files that contain the actual picture data. Technically, the .resx format also supports creating *embedded* resource files, in which case the data for each resource is merged into the .resx file as a Base64-encoded string. However, Visual Studio doesn't use this approach, because it risks creating extremely large unwieldy files, and it makes it more difficult to individually update different resources. It also requires more space, because Base64 encoding is larger than the original raw binary data.

■Note The term "embedded resources" is used in two ways, which can potentially cause confusion. There is a difference between two types of .resx files, which contain their data directly (embedded) or simply link to it (linked). However, no matter which .resx format you use, when you compile your application the .resx is always compiled into an embedded *.resources* file that is inserted into your assembly, data and all.

No matter what type of resource file you use, when you compile the application the .resx file is converted into a binary .resource file, which is embedded into your assembly. To take a closer look, you need to use the IL Disassembler (ildasm.exe) tool included with .NET (or Lutz Roeder's Reflector, which is available at www.aisto.com/roeder/dotnet).

Resources are placed in a special noncode portion of the assembly called the *manifest*. The manifest includes metadata about the assembly (like versioning and publishing information) and all the resources. To check for the resource data, open the compiled application file in IL Disassembler and double-click the Manifest entry in the tree. Scroll down, and you'll see the following:

```
.mresource public ResourceTest.Properties.Resources.resources
{
}
```

This declares the compiled .resources file that contains the pictures. You'll notice that the binary picture data isn't actually shown, because the IL Disassembler can't decompile it. Instead, you'll simply see a set of empty braces.

This explains how embedded resources work, but it doesn't explain how you can retrieve them in your code through the static properties of the Resources class. The trick is that as you add resources, Visual Studio generates a class with the code for retrieving the information from the embedded resource. To see the file, expand the Resources.resx node and look for a file named Resources.Designer.cs (see Figure 5-7).

Figure 5-7. *The automatically generated Resources class*

The Resources class retrieves the embedded resource from the assembly, and casts it to the appropriate data type. For example, the BlueLace16 property shown below retrieves the resource named BlueLace16, and casts it to a Bitmap object:

```
internal static System.Drawing.Bitmap BlueLace16
{
    get
    {
        return ((System.Drawing.Bitmap)
          (ResourceManager.GetObject("BlueLace16", resourceCulture)));
    }
}
```

The ResourceManager is static property that's defined in the same class. The first time you access it, a new ResourceManager object is created and cached for later use. The ResourceManager does the work of extracting the resources from the embedded resource.

```
private static global::System.Resources.ResourceManager resourceMan;

internal static global::System.Resources.ResourceManager ResourceManager
{
    get
    {
        if (resourceMan == null)
        {
            global::System.Resources.ResourceManager temp =
              new global::System.Resources.ResourceManager(
              "ResourceTest.Properties.Resources",
              typeof(Resources).Assembly);
            resourceMan = temp;
        }
        return resourceMan;
    }
}
```

■**Tip** You don't have to stick with a single .resx file in your project. You can add more by choosing Project ➤ Add New Item and then choosing Assembly Resource File. When you double-click your .resx file, you'll see the same resource browser that allows you to set content and attach files (which will be copied to the Resources folder). However, Visual Studio won't generate a code file that wraps these resources, so it's up to you to create a ResourceManager, call GetObject() to retrieve the resource by name, and then cast the data to the appropriate type.

Form Resources

Under certain situations, Visual Studio also generates a .resx file for a form. Two examples include when you add an ImageList to your form, and when you use localization (described later in this chapter). In both situations, Visual Studio automatically adjusts the serialized form code to use the form resources for retrieving data.

The .resx file that's generated for a form always has the same name as the form, as in Form1.resx. However, you won't see the .resx file in the Solution Explorer unless you select Project ➤ Show All Files. Once you do, the .resx file appears under each form node in the Solution Explorer. For example, Figure 5-8 shows a form .resx file that contains the data for an ImageList.

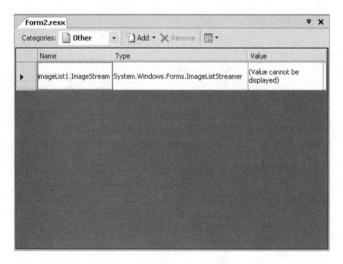

Figure 5-8. *An ImageList in a form .resx file*

Note that unlike image resources, the ImageList information is stored in a proprietary format that only the ImageListStreamer can interpret. If you were to crack open the .resx file, you'd find that it has the embedded information in a <value> tag that looks something like this:

```
<data name="imageList1.ImageStream"
 mimetype="application/x-microsoft.net.object.binary.base64">
  <value>AAEAAAD/////AQAAAAAAAAMAgAAFpTeXN0ZW0uV2luZG93cy5Gb3JtcywgVmVyc2lvb
jOyLjAuMzYwMC4wLCBDdWx0dXJlPW5ldXRyYWwsIFB1YmxpYY0tleVRva2VuPWI3N2E1YZU2MTkzNGU
wODkFAQAAACZTeXN0ZW0uV2luZG93cy5Gb3Jtcy5JbWFnZUxppc3RdHJlYW11cgEAAA...</value>
</data>
```

As with any other .resx file, when you compile your application it's compiled to a binary .resources file which is then embedded into the application assembly. That guarantees that the required information is always available, without needing to rely on an external file that could be moved or deleted.

In previous versions of Visual Studio, a .resx file is created for a form as soon as you add any binary data (for example, when you set the Image property of a PictureBox). However, Visual Studio 2005 gives you a choice.

To see how this works, click the ellipsis (…) in the Properties window next to the BackgroundImage or Image property for a control. (Try, for example, the PictureBox control.) A designer appears that lists all the global .resx files in the project, but not the resource files that are associated to individual forms. When you choose a file, it shows all the available images in the file, as shown in Figure 5-9.

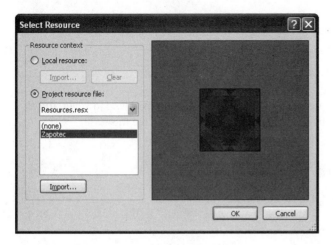

Figure 5-9. *Linking a control Image to a resource*

If you choose Local Resource and click Import, the image file is imported directly, in which case it's stored in the .resx file for the form (as in previous versions of Visual Studio). However, if you choose Project Resource File you can use any of the resources in the global Resources.resx file. You can even click Import to add the picture as a new global resource before you link it to the control. This has the same effect as using the Add Existing File command in the resource browser.

It's almost always better to use global resources. That way, you have the flexibility to easily update your images later by replacing the file, which isn't possible with form-specific resources or the ImageList.

Creating Additional Resource Files

There's no reason you need to stick with one global resources class. If you need to manage a wide range of resources, you might prefer to create several project-specific global .resx files. In fact, you might even choose to make separate resources for different forms.

To add a new global resource, simply right-click your project and select Add ➤ New Item. Choose Resources File, enter a file name, and click Add. This creates in your project folder a new .resx file with a .Designer.cs file that defines the corresponding class (see Figure 5-10).

Figure 5-10. *Adding a new global resource*

You can use the class in the same way that you use the Resources class. However, the namespace changes slightly. Instead of using Properties.Resources, like this

```
pictureBox1.Image = ResourceTest.Properties.Resources.Zapotec;
```

you access the resource class directly in your project namespace:

```
pictureBox1.Image = ResourceTest.CustomResources.Zapotec;
```

or just

```
pictureBox1.Image = CustomResources.Zapotec;
```

When you add resources to your file, they'll be copied into the Resources folder, exactly as they are with the Resources.resx file. If you use stricter organization (or you have different resource files with the same name), there is an easy workaround. First, add a subfolder for you new resources to your project. Then, add the resource files using the Add ➤ Existing Item command. Finally, link these items to the appropriate resource by opening the .resx file, choosing the appropriate category, and dragging the resource from the Solution Explorer onto the resource browser. This way, an entry is created for your resource, but the actual file is left in its original project subfolder.

Localization

Resource files aren't just for dealing with binary data. They also come in handy when you need to localize a form. Using resource files, you allow controls to change according to the current culture settings of the Windows operating system. This is particularly useful with text labels and images that need to be translated into different languages.

When using resources for localization, it isn't as convenient to embed the resource into your application assembly. That's because the localization-specific information might need to change after the project is compiled, or you might want to add support for additional locales after a program is deployed. To allow this, you need to use *satellite assemblies*—assemblies that work with your application, but are stored in separate subfolders. When you create a localized form in .NET, the information is compiled into satellite assemblies, and the directory structure you need is created automatically.

Creating a Localizable Form

The basic process for creating a localizable form is simple. First, you must set the Localizable property for the Form to true using the Properties window. This tells Visual Studio to start storing all settings in a resource file instead of directly in the form code.

Note Technically, there is no Form.Localizable property. Visual Studio adds this property at design time to allow you to configure how it serializes control properties.

Once you've set the Localizable property to true, it's time to start setting locale-specific settings. First, choose the locale that you want to add support for by setting the Language property of the form. You'll be provided with the full list of recognized locales (see Figure 5-11).

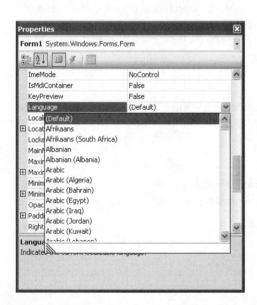

Figure 5-11. *Choosing a language when designing a form*

Technically, you aren't choosing a language but a *culture*, which consists of two identifiers separated by a hyphen. The first portion identifies the language. The second portion identifies the country. Thus, fr-CA is French as spoken in Canada, while fr-FR represents French in France. In the Language list in the Properties window, fr-CA is displayed as French (Canada), while fr-FR is displayed as French (France).

This presumes a fine-grained localization that might be more than you need. Fortunately, you can localize a form based just on a language. For example, if you select fr as your culture, you can apply settings that will be used for any French-language region. To use this option, just select French in the Language property list.

■**Note** For a full list of culture names and their two-part identifiers, refer to the System.Globalization.CultureInfo class in the MSDN help library.

Once you've chosen your language, you can configure the properties of various controls. The value you supply won't be serialized in the form code—instead, it will be stored in a dedicated resource file for this language, provided the property is localizable. In a typical control, most properties are localizable. For example, properties like Text, Font, Image, Location, Size, Enabled, and Visible are all localizable. (The control developer designates localizable properties by applying the Localizable(true) attribute to the property declaration.)

You can repeat these two steps to add information for multiple languages. As soon as you change the language, all the localizable properties of the controls on your form revert to the settings in the resource file for that language.

The final step is to test how your application works at runtime. As you'll learn in the next section, .NET automatically uses the property settings that match the current culture settings. However, you can override these settings to test how your application will work under different cultures by setting the Thread.CurrentUICulture property for the current thread. For example, this statement sets the culture to the fr-FR culture.

```
Thread.CurrentThread.CurrentUICulture = new CultureInfo("fr-FR");
```

Note that you need to run this line of code *before* the InitializeComponent() method of the form is executed in order for it to read the correct localized information.

How Localization Works

For every localizable form, you'll see multiple .resx files with different language identifiers. In fact, there will be one for each language you've configured in the design environment. Figure 5-12 shows an example with two additional languages.

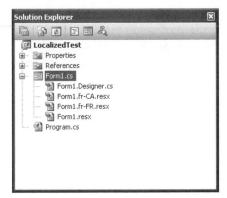

Figure 5-12. *Multiple .resx files for a form*

When you double-click one of these .resx files, you'll see a grid that lists all the localizable settings that you set, as shown in Figure 5-13.

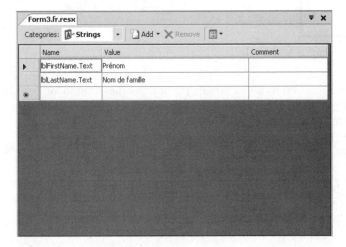

Figure 5-13. *Localizable settings for a form*

Tip In some cases, you might want to localize information that doesn't correspond directly to a control property. For example, you might want to localize error messages or the text that appears in a message box. In this case, the solution is to add the information to the appropriate .resx file by hand as a string. Unfortunately, there isn't any built-in support for localizing project-specific resource files.

When you compile this project, Visual Studio creates a separate directory using the language identifier, and uses it to store the satellite assembly with the localization settings. You can see these files in the Solution Explorer by choosing Project ➤ Show All Files (see Figure 5-14).

Figure 5-14. *Multiple satellite assemblies*

The greatest part about this is that you won't have to delete or move files around for different versions. Because of the way probing works with .NET assemblies, you can count on the common language runtime (CLR) to automatically inspect the right directory based on the computer's regional settings and load the correct localized text. For example, if you're running in the fr-FR culture, the CLR will look for a fr-FR subdirectory, and use the satellite assemblies it finds there. That means that if you want to add support for more cultures to a localized application, you simply need to add more subfolders and satellite assemblies without disturbing the original application executable.

When the CLR begins probing for a satellite assembly, it follows a few simple rules of precedence:

1. First, it checks for the most specific directory that's available. That means it looks for a satellite assembly that's targeted for the current language and region (like fr-FR).

2. If it can't find this directory, it looks for a satellite assembly that's targeted for the current language (like fr).

3. If it can't find this directory, it falls back on whatever defaults are stored in the application assembly. You can set these defaults by choosing (Default) for the Language property.

This list is slightly simplified. If you decide to use the global assembly cache (GAC) to share some components over the entire computer, you'll need to realize that .NET actually checks the GAC at the beginning of step 1 and step 2. In other words, in step 1 the CLR checks if the language- and region-specific version of the assembly is in the GAC, and uses it if it is. The same is true for step 2.

■**Note** As a rule of thumb, localization is never as easy as it appears, because of the subtleties involved with different languages and the way they are supported by the various versions of the Windows operating system. For more help, you can refer to another Apress book, *Internationalization and Localization Using Microsoft .NET* (2002), by Nick Symmonds, which is dedicated to this topic, or the globalization topics in the MSDN help library.

USING THE WINDOWS FORMS RESOURCE EDITOR

Visual Studio and the .NET SDK also include a utility called Winres.exe, which is extremely useful for localization. It allows another person to edit the information in a .resx resource file using a scaled-down form editor. This is useful because it allows translators and other nonprogramming professionals to create the locale-specific resource files without allowing them the chance to see sensitive code or inadvertently alter it. They also won't need to have Visual Studio installed—just the freely distributable Winres.exe tool.

The Last Word

In this chapter, you looked at the Image and ImageList classes, which allow you to manipulate picture data. You also considered how you can embed images and other types of data into an assembly using resources. This is a technique that's useful in any Windows application that needs to rely on binary content like audio snippets and images, or needs to protect string data like HTML pages or text files so it can't be tampered with.

The end of this chapter discussed how resources can provide localization. Visual Studio includes convenient support that makes localizing a Windows Form almost effortless, but unfortunately it doesn't have a comparable tool for localizing other project content. For example, if you need to use local-specific error messages, it's up to you to manage the localized strings. You can use the resource infrastructure to keep this information in localized satellite assemblies (and .NET has rich support for this approach in the class library), but there's still no integration in Visual Studio.

CHAPTER 6

■ ■ ■

Lists and Trees

The ListView and TreeView are two of the most widespread and distinctive controls in modern application design. As far as controls go, they have it all—an attractive appearance, a flexible set of features, and the ability to condense a significant amount of information in one place. And thanks to Windows Explorer, most computer users already know how to use the ListView and TreeView to browse through data.

These days, it's hard to find programs that *don't* use the ListView and TreeView. The Windows operating system makes heavy use of them in its administrative windows. You'll also see them at work in tools for SQL Server, Visual Studio, and the .NET Framework. In this chapter, you'll learn how to use the ListView and TreeView in your own .NET applications.

ListView Basics

The ListView control is often used to show a multicolumn list of items. In this way, the ListView provides a simple, attractive grid. Unlike the other .NET grid controls (namely, the DataGrid and DataGridView), the ListView lacks support for data binding, which means you always need to fill it by hand.

■**Tip** Nothing prevents you from deriving a custom ListView that supports data binding. You can find an implementation of this labor-intensive job at `http://msdn.microsoft.com/library/en-us/dnadvnet/html/vbnet08262002.asp`. However, because the DataGridView provides almost all the functionality of the ListView and many more features, it's usually the better route.

View Modes

While the ListView is most commonly used to create grids, it actually supports five distinct modes that you've probably already seen in Windows Explorer. You specify the mode by setting the ListView.View property to one of the values from the View enumeration, as listed in Table 6-1.

Table 6-1. *Values for ListView.View*

Value	Description
LargeIcon	Displays full-sized (usually 32×32 pixel) icons with a title beneath each one. Items are displayed from left to right and then on subsequent lines.
SmallIcon	Displays small (usually 16×16 pixel) icons with descriptive text at the right. Items are displayed from left to right and then on subsequent lines.
List	Displays small icons with descriptive text at the right. It's the same as SmallIcon, except it fills items from top to bottom and then in additional columns. The scroll bar (if needed) is horizontal.
Tile	Displays large icons with the item label and additional information to the right of it. This view is supported only on Windows XP and Windows Server 2003. On earlier operating systems, the ListView will revert to a LargeIcon view.
Details	Displays the familiar multicolumn layout. Each item appears on a separate line, and the leftmost column contains a small icon and label. Column headers identify each column and allow user resizing. Columns can also be rearranged if the ListView.AllowColumnReorder property is true. The Details view and the Tile view are the only views that support showing more than one piece of information per item.

To understand the different styles of ListView, it helps to create a simple example. First, create a ListView and two ImageList controls, one to hold any required small (16×16 pixel) icons and one to hold large (32×32 pixel) icons. Next, you can associate the ListView with the corresponding ImageList by setting the SmallImageList and LargeImageList properties.

```
listView.SmallImageList = imagesSmall;
listView.LargeImageList = imagesLarge;
```

Once the ImageList is associated, you can assign images to individual list items by setting the ImageIndex or ImageKey property (as you did in Chapter 5). You can change the ImageIndex at any time to indicate an item that has changed status.

The following code loads information into a ListView in response to a button click. This example relies on a GetProducts() method that returns a DataTable (either by querying a database or by constructing it manually).

```
private void cmdFillList_Click(object sender, System.EventArgs e)
{
    // Don't forget to clear the current content of the ListView.
    listView.Items.Clear();

    // Fill a DataTable using a helper class (not shown).
    DataTable dt = StoreDB.GetProducts();

    foreach (DataRow dr in dt.Rows)
    {
```

```
    // Create the item, with the text from the ModelName field.
    ListViewItem listItem = new ListViewItem(dr["ModelName"].ToString());

    // Give every item the same picture.
    listItem.ImageIndex = 0;

    // Add the item to the ListView.
    listView.Items.Add(listItem);
    }
}
```

■**Note** This book won't cover the ADO.NET code you might use to create this DataTable (as this is better served by a dedicated book about databases and .NET), although you can look at the online code for this chapter to see the details. As with many of the examples, the data is retrieved from an XML file, which guarantees that you can use the examples even if you don't have a relational database product handy.

This is ListView code at its simplest. ListViewItem objects are created and added to the list. The ListViewItem constructor allows you to specify the default item text (the Text property), and the ImageIndex points to the first picture in the collection. Note that the ImageIndex applies to both the SmallImageList and LargeImageList, meaning that your ImageList objects must use the same ordering. The appropriate picture is chosen based on the view style.

Finally, to make the code a little more interesting, a group of radio buttons allows the user to switch between the different view styles. Each option button is associated with a different view mode, using the handy Tag property:

```
optLargeIcon.Tag = View.LargeIcon;
optSmallIcon.Tag = View.SmallIcon;
optDetails.Tag = View.Details;
optList.Tag = View.List;
optTile.Tag = View.Tile;
```

Rather than scatter the code for this in multiple procedures, all the option button clicks are handled by a single method, which retrieves the appropriate view mode and applies it.

```
private void NewView(object sender, System.EventArgs e)
{
    // Set the current view mode based on the number in the tag value of the
    // selected radio button.
    listView.View = (View)(((Control)sender).Tag);

    // Display the current view style.
    this.Text = "Using View: " + listView.View.ToString();
}
```

Figure 6-1 shows the ListView in SmallIcon, LargeIcon, Details, and List view modes.

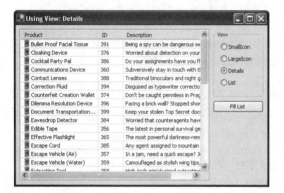

Figure 6-1. *Different view styles with the ListView control*

Table 6-2 lists the core set of ListView members.

Table 6-2. *Basic ListView Members*

Member	Description
Columns	Holds the collection of ColumnHeader objects used in Details view.
FocusedItem, SelectedItem, and SelectedIndices	Allows you to retrieve the item that currently has focus or the currently selected items (the user can select multiple icons by dragging a box around them or by holding down the Ctrl and Shift keys). You can also examine the Focused and Selected properties of each ListViewItem.
Items	Holds the collection ListViewItem objects displayed in the ListView.
LabelEdit	When set to true, ListViewItem text can be modified by the user or in code using the BeginEdit() method. If you are using the Details view, only the text in the first column can be changed. Subitems cannot be modified.

Table 6-2. *Basic ListView Members*

Member	Description
LargeImageList and SmallImageList	References the ImageList control that is used for large and small icons. The individual icons are identified by the ListViewItem.ImageIndex property, starting at 0 for the first icon.
MultiSelect	When set to false, prevents a user from selecting more than one item at a time.
Sorting	Allows you to specify an ascending or descending sort order, which considers the main text of the ListViewItem only (not any subitems).
View	Sets the ListView style using the View enumeration. Supported views are LargeIcon, SmallIcon, List, Tile, and Details.
AutoArrange and ArrangeIcons()	In SmallIcon and LargeIcon view, the AutoArrange property determines whether icons automatically snap to a grid or can be positioned anywhere by the user. If you allow the user to reposition icons (by setting AutoArrange to false), you can call ArrangeIcons() to put things back in order.
BeginUpdate() and EndUpdate()	Allows you to temporarily suspend the ListView drawing so that you can add or modify several items at once without flickering.
AfterLabelEdit and BeforeLabelEdit events	Events that fire before and after a label is modified. Both events provide the index to the appropriate ListViewItem and a property that allows you to cancel the edit.
ColumnClick event	Occurs when a user clicks a column. You can react to this event to perform column-specific sorting.
SelectedItemIndexChanged event	Occurs whenever the user selects an item, except when the same item is selected twice in a row.

If you try this application as it stands right now, you'll see that it doesn't work in Details view. The reason is that the ListView displays information in Details view only if you have added the appropriate column headers. If you add items without adding the column headers, you're left with a blank display. The next section corrects the problem.

Details Mode

When you set a ListView to Details mode, it behaves a little differently. Unless you correctly configure the column headers, the display remains blank, with no information at all.

The following example rewrites the ListView code to fill multiple columns of information. It uses three column headers. The first column is automatically filled with the ListViewItem text. To fill the other two columns, you need to add two subitems to the ListViewItem.SubItem collection of each item. Note that the extra information in these columns is ignored in LargeIcon, SmallIcon, and List view modes.

```
private void cmdFillList_Click(object sender, System.EventArgs e)
{
    listView.Items.Clear();

    DataTable dt = StoreDB.GetProducts();

    // Suspending automatic refreshes as items are added/removed.
    listView.BeginUpdate();

    // Add column headers for Details view (if they haven't been added before).
    if (listView.Columns.Count == 0)
    {
        listView.Columns.Add("Product", 100, HorizontalAlignment.Left);
        listView.Columns.Add("ID", 100, HorizontalAlignment.Left);
        listView.Columns.Add("Description", 100, HorizontalAlignment.Left);
    }

    foreach (DataRow dr in dt.Rows)
    {
        ListViewItem listItem = new ListViewItem(dr["ModelName"].ToString());
        listItem.ImageIndex = 0;

        // Add subitems for Details view.
        listItem.SubItems.Add(dr["ProductID"].ToString());
        listItem.SubItems.Add(dr["Description"].ToString());

        listView.Items.Add(listItem);
    }

    // Re-enable the display.
    listView.EndUpdate();
}
```

When adding a ColumnHeader, you have the chance to specify a width in pixels, a title, and the alignment for values in the column. Figure 6-2 shows the ListView in grid mode.

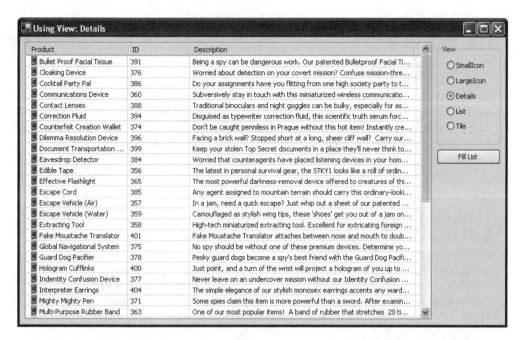

Figure 6-2. *A ListView grid*

You can also programmatically resize the columns using the AutoResizeColumns() method (or the AutoResizeColumn() method if you want to work with a single column). You supply a value from the ColumnHeaderAutoResizeStyle enumeration to indicate the type of resizing. Use ColumnContent if you want to fit the widest entry in a column or HeaderSize if you want to fit the caption text. The AutoResizeColumns() method will both enlarge and shrink columns as necessary.

The ListView is different from almost any other grid control in that it designates every column except the first one as a subitem. This idiosyncrasy shouldn't trouble you too much, but note that it causes the column header indices to differ from the subitem indices. For example, the first subitem is listItem.SubItems[0], while the corresponding column is listView.Columns[1].

■**Tip** The previous example uses a ListView for its most common task: representing items. However, ListView controls can also represent actions. For example, consider the Control Panel, which uses a ListView in LargeIcon view to provide access to a number of features. Remember, different view styles suggest different uses (and in the case of the Details view, show different information), so you should always choose the most suitable style when creating the control.

LINKING EXTRA INFORMATION TO A LISTVIEWITEM

A typical application often needs to store information about display items that isn't rendered in the user inter-
face. For example, you might want to keep track of unique identifier numbers that will allow you to look up a
given item in a database, but you won't show this information to the end user, because it's of no use to them.
Sometimes, programmers handle this in a control-specific way using hidden columns or other workarounds.
However, a more generic and elegant approach is to find some way to link the extra information to the control.
You can add information to a ListView control to represent custom data in two ways:

- Derive a custom ListViewItem, and add the properties you need for your particular type of data.

- Use the Tag property of the ListViewItem to store the related DataRow or custom data object.

The first option is the only approach directly explained in the MSDN reference. However, it's probably the
least convenient because it tightly integrates details about the structure of your data into the user interface
code. This means you need to modify these classes if the data changes or if you move to a different type of
control (such as the TreeView).

The second approach is more flexible, because it maintains the state separately, but it makes it easy to
find when you need it. The only disadvantage is that the Tag property isn't strongly typed, so you need to cast
it to the object you expect when you want to retrieve the linked information.

If you decide to use the ListView as a grid control, you can use a few useful properties to
fine-tune the display by adding gridlines and row selection (rather than single-column value
selection).

```
listView.GridLines = true;
listView.FullRowSelect = true;
```

Table 6-3 lists some more properties for fine-tuning the appearance of a ListView.

Table 6-3. *Appearance-Related ListView Members*

Member	Description
Activation and HoverSelection	Activation determines how items in the ListView are highlighted. If you select OneClick, the mouse cursor becomes a hand icon when it hovers over an item. The HoverSelection property, when set to true, auto-matically selects an item when the user hovers over it. This formerly cutting-edge feature is now discour-aged as being unintuitive (and somewhat "touchy").
Alignment	Sets the side of the ListView that items are aligned against.
AllowColumnReorder	When set to true, the user can drag column headers around to rearrange column order in Details view, without requiring any code.
BackgroundImage	Specifies a background image that will appear behind the items in the list and be tiled if appropriate.

Table 6-3. *Appearance-Related ListView Members*

Member	Description
FullRowSelect	When set to true, the entire row will be highlighted when you select an item in Details view, not just the first column. It's a useful setting for database applications that are using the ListView as a grid control.
GridLines	Displays attractive column and row gridlines in Details view. Useful if you are displaying many rows of complex or hard-to-read information.
HeaderStyle	Allows you to configure whether column headers respond to clicks (Clickable) or ignore them (Nonclickable).
LabelWrap	Allows the text label to wrap in one of the icon views.
OwnerDraw, DoubleBuffered, RedrawItems(), and the DrawItem and DrawSubItem events	You can set the OwnerDraw property to true to perform custom drawing. You must then handle the DrawItem event (and the DrawSubItem event, if you're using the grid view). In addition, you can use the RedrawItems() method to force a group of items be redrawn (perhaps because the underlying data has been modified) and set the DoubleBuffered property to true to optimize the drawing process. Chapter 12 has more information about owner-drawn controls.
ShowItemTooltips	If true, the text specified in the ListViewItem. ToolTipText property is displayed when the user hovers over an item with the mouse.
TileSize	In Tile view mode, this specifies (as a Size structure) the dimensions of the tile used for each item.

Tile Mode and Large Images

So far, you've seen examples of the ListView with relatively small images (16- or 32-pixel squares). However, many of the ListView modes can handle much larger images. In LargeIcon mode, the image can be arbitrarily large. The text is centered underneath. In Tile mode, the height of the row is automatically expanded to fit taller images (and you specify the width). The List and SmallIcon modes produce less helpful results, because the larger image usually crowds out any text.

Tile mode is particularly well suited to handling large images. When using Tile mode, the image is displayed on the left, and the content appears on the right. However, it's up to you to set a tile size that allows enough room for the image and text content. You do that by setting the ListView.TileSize property, as shown here:

```
// Create a tile that is 300 pixels wide and 50 pixels high.
listView.TileSize = new Size(300, 50);
```

Tiles are organized left to right (if the width allows) and then in subsequent rows. Interestingly, Tile mode is the only mode that can work equally well with or without subitems. If you've provided subitems, they appear on separate lines. Sadly, you can't control the formatting of individual lines—if you want that ability, you'll need to create an owner-drawn ListView.

Figure 6-3 shows the ListView with large images in Tile mode. Remember, on non–Windows XP computers, Tile mode is equivalent to LargeIcon, and the extra subitem information does not appear.

Figure 6-3. *Tiling with large images*

More Advanced ListViews

So far you've seen the basic bread-and-butter work of ListView and its five view styles. In the following sections, you'll dig into a few frills and more advanced features.

ListView Sorting

You'll often want a way to sort the information in your ListView. This is particularly the case if you're showing a multicolumned list, in which case you probably want the user to be able to trigger a sort by clicking the appropriate column.

If you need to sort using only the ListItem.Text property, you can use the Sorting property. Just set it to configure the sort order, as shown here:

```
listView.Sorting = SortOrder.Ascending;
```

If you want to sort based on more complex rules, or if you want to sort using the information in another column, you need to do a little more work. On its own, the ListView control has no intrinsic support for sorting by column. However, you can easily develop a custom IComparer sorting class to fill the gap.

An IComparer class has a single responsibility in life—to examine two instances of the same object and return a 1, 0, or –1 depending on which one is deemed "larger" than the other. It performs this work by implementing a public Compare() method that accepts two parameters. In the custom comparer you create, you need to create an implementation of Compare() that examines the column data that interests you. Here's an example:

```
public class MyComparer : IComparer
{
    public int Compare(object x, object y)
    {
        ListViewItem listX = (ListViewItem)x;
        ListViewItem listY = (ListViewItem)y;

        // Get the integer in the second column of each ListViewItem.
        int intX = Int32.Parse(listX.SubItems[0].Text);
        int intY = Int32.Parse(listX.SubItems[0].Text);

        // Compare this column.
        if (intX > intY)
            return 1;
        else if (intX < intY)
            return -1;
        else
            return 0;
    }
}
```

In most cases, you can simplify your work by farming the comparison out to the CompareTo() method in one of the base data types (such as string, int, decimal, and so on). Here's an example of this shortcut:

```
public int Compare(object x, object y)
{
    ListViewItem listX = (ListViewItem)x;
    ListViewItem listY = (ListViewItem)y;

    int intX = Int32.Parse(listX.SubItems[0].Text);
    int intY = Int32.Parse(listX.SubItems[0].Text);

    return intX.CompareTo(intY);
}
```

Of course, you have no good reason to create a new MyComparer for every different column you want to compare. Instead, the best option is to create a more generic IComparer class that can compare any column. To accomplish this, your IComparer should provide a column index property. When you create the IComparer, you can set the column index to the column you want to compare. To make your IComparer even more useful, you can create another property that allows you to switch between numeric and alphabetic comparisons (Numeric) and create a property that lets you implement descending sorts (Descending).

Here's the complete code you need:

```csharp
public class ListViewItemComparer : IComparer
{
    private int column;
    public int Column
    {
        get {return column;}
        set {column = value;}
    }

    private bool numeric = false;
    public bool Numeric
    {
        get {return numeric;}
        set {numeric = value;}
    }

    private bool descending = false;
    public bool Descending
    {
        get {return descending;}
        set {descending = value;}
    }

    public ListViewItemComparer(int columnIndex)
    {
        Column = columnIndex;
    }

    public int Compare(object x, object y)
    {
        ListViewItem listX, listY;
        if (descending)
        {
            listY = (ListViewItem)x;
            listX = (ListViewItem)y;
        }
        else
        {
            listX = (ListViewItem)x;
            listY = (ListViewItem)y;
        }
```

```
        if (Numeric)
        {
            // Convert column text to numbers before comparing.
            // If the conversion fails, the value defaults to 0.
            decimal valX, valY;
            Decimal.TryParse(listX.SubItems[Column].Text, out valX);
            Decimal.TryParse(listY.SubItems[Column].Text, out valY);

            // Perform a numeric comparison.
            return Decimal.Compare(valX, valY);
        }
        else
        {
            // Perform an alphabetic comparison.
            return String.Compare(
               listX.SubItems[Column].Text, listY.SubItems[Column].Text);
        }
    }
}
```

Now, you can easily create a ListView that re-sorts itself as a column header when it is clicked by handling the ColumnClicked event, generating a new ListViewItemComparer object, and calling the ListView.Sort() method.

```
private void listView_ColumnClick(object sender, ColumnClickEventArgs e)
{
    // Specify an alphabetic sort based on the column that was clicked.
    listView.ListViewItemSorter = new ListViewItemComparer(e.Column);

    // Perform the sort.
    listView.Sort();
}
```

With a little more creativity, you can implement a reversible sort so that clicking twice in a row on the same column uses a descending sort instead of an ascending sort.

```
private void listView_ColumnClick(object sender, ColumnClickEventArgs e)
{
    // Check the current sort.
    ListViewItemComparer sorter = listView.ListViewItemSorter as
      ListViewItemComparer;

    if (sorter == null)
    {
        sorter = new ListViewItemComparer(e.Column);
        listView.ListViewItemSorter = sorter;
    }
```

```
    else
    {
        if (sorter.Column == e.Column && !sorter.Descending)
        {
            // The list is already sorted on this column.
            // Time to flip the sort.
            sorter.Descending = true;

            // Keep the ListView.Sorting property
            // synchronized, just for tidiness.
            listView.Sorting = SortOrder.Descending;
        }
        else
        {
            listView.Sorting = SortOrder.Ascending;
            sorter.Descending = false;
            sorter.Column = e.Column;
        }
    }

    // Perform the sort.
    listView.Sort();
}
```

Note Another interesting trick is column reordering. This allows the user to rearrange columns by dragging the column header. This technique takes place automatically if you set the ListView.AllowColumnReorder property to true. Unfortunately, there is no easy way to save these view settings and apply them later. To manage this type of advanced data display, you may want to consider the DataGridView control described in Chapter 15.

Label Editing

The ListView includes an automatic label-editing feature that you have probably already witnessed in Windows Explorer. You trigger the label editing by clicking a selected item once or by pressing the F2 key. This automatic editing is confusing to many new users. If you use it, you should also provide another way for the user to edit the corresponding information.

To enable label editing, set the LabelEdit property to true. You can programmatically start label editing for a node using the node's BeginEdit() method.

```
private void cmdStartEdit_Click(object sender, System.EventArgs e)
```

```
{
    // The user clicked a dedicated Edit button.
    // Put the label of the first selected item into edit mode.
    if (listView.SelectedItems.Count > 0)
    {
        listView.SelectedItems[0].BeginEdit();
    }

    // (You might also want to disable other controls until the user completes
    // the edit and the AfterLabelEdit event fires.)
}
```

In addition, you can prevent certain nodes from being edited by handling the BeforeLabelEdit event and setting the Cancel flag to true. You can also fix any invalid changes by reacting to the AfterLabelEdit event.

■**Tip** If you want to use the BeginEdit() method but prevent users from being able to modify the label by clicking it, you must set the LabelEdit property to true. To prevent users from editing labels directly, set a special form-level property (such as AllowEdit) before you use the BeginEdit() method, and check for this property in the BeforeLabelEdit event. If it has not been set, this indicates that the user initiated the edit by double-clicking, and you should cancel it. If you forget to set LabelEdit to true, a call to BeginEdit() raises a System.InvalidOperationException.

ListView Grouping

The ListView examples you've seen so far gave you a "flat" look at your data. All the items have had equal precedence. And although the ListView lacks the muscle to represent complex hierarchies of information (an area where the TreeView excels), it can subgroup items into separate categories.

To use grouping, take these two steps:

1. Define the groups you want to use through the ListView.Groups collection.

2. Put each ListViewItem into the appropriate group when you create it by setting the ListViewItem.Group property.

In addition, you need to make sure the ListView.ShowGroups property is set to true (the default). Groups are respected in all view modes except List. Figure 6-4 shows an example in grid view.

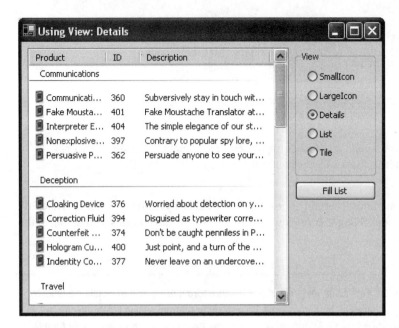

Figure 6-4. *Using ListView subgrouping*

To define the grouping, you need to add one ListViewGroup object for each group to the ListView.Groups property. The ListViewGroup class has two important properties—Header (the text title that appears above the group) and HeaderAlignment (how the text is aligned in the ListView).

Here's the code that creates category labels for the product ListView shown in Figure 6-4:

```
DataTable dt = StoreDB.GetCategories();
foreach (DataRow dr in dt.Rows)
{
    listView.Groups.Add(dr["CategoryID"].ToString(),
      dr["CategoryName"].ToString());
}
```

The CategoryName is used for the header text, and the CategoryID is used for the key in the collection. That means you can retrieve the group from the ListView.Groups collection later using the CategoryID.

And here's the code that attaches each product to the appropriate group based on the value of the CategoryID:

```
foreach (DataRow dr in dt.Rows)
{
    ListViewItem listItem = new ListViewItem(dr["ModelName"].ToString());
    listItem.Group = listView.Groups[dr["CategoryID"].ToString()];

    ...
    listView.Items.Add(listItem);
}
```

Searching and Hit Testing

The ListView has a number of methods that can help you find items. Using these methods (described in Table 6-4), you can find the ListViewItem at a specific mouse coordinate or with specific text. Once you've found an item, you can retrieve other ListViewItem properties or use EnsureVisible() to scroll it into view.

Table 6-4. *Searching the ListView*

Member	Description
FindItemWithText()	Finds the first ListView whose text begins with the string you supply. You can use an overload of this method that searches subitems as well (look for the Boolean includeSubItemsInSearch parameter) and starts at a specific position (look for the startIndex parameter). If no match is found, null is returned.
EnsureVisible()	Scrolls to make sure a specified ListViewItem is visible. You indicate the item by its zero-based row index. Alternatively, you can set the ListView.TopItem property to point to the ListViewItem you want to appear at the top of the list (the ListView is then scrolled so that this is the first visible item).
GetItemAt()	Retrieves the ListViewItem at the given X and Y coordinates. Useful for hit testing and drag-and-drop operations.
FindNearestItem()	Similar to GetItemAt() but finds items that are near (but not directly at) the given point. You provide a value from the SearchDirectionHint enumeration to indicate the direction to search in (Up, Down. Left, or Right). If no item is found and the border of the control is reached, this method returns null.
HitTest()	Similar to GetItemAt() but returns a ListViewHitTestInfo object instead of a ListViewItem. The ListViewHitTestInfo allows you to distinguish whether the clicked element was item text or subitem text (just check the Item and SubItem properties) and exactly what part of the ListViewItem was clicked (using the Location property). For example, you can distinguish between a click on an image in the ListViewItem, the text, the client area to the side, and so on.
InsertionMark	The insertion mark helps indicate (to the user) where the target of a drag-and-drop operation will be placed. The InsertionMark property returns a ListViewInsertionMark object. You can adjust the color of the insertion mark and set the ListViewInsertionMark,Index property to determine where it appears during a drag-and-drop operation.

ListView Virtualization

One limitation of the ListView is that, like all Windows controls, it stores all its ListView items in memory. That means if you want to create a ListView that shows tens of thousands of data-heavy records, you're left with an unavoidable footprint in memory.

In .NET 2.0, the ListView adds support for *virtualization*, which allows it to support large sets of data. With virtualization, the ListView loads only the data that's currently being displayed. As the user scrolls to a new place in the list, the appropriate items are requested and filled in as needed. This separates data storage that's associated with the ListView from the control itself, allowing you to implement a more efficient way of retrieving and caching data.

The following example demonstrates ListView virtualization with a list of order records stored in a SQL Server database. At any given time, 100 records are cached in the client's memory. As the client scrolls to new information, these records are discarded, and a new set of 100 are fetched. This design assumes that the records are extremely large, and the memory saving of storing only 100 at a time trumps the additional database work and latency that's involved in querying the database multiple times.

IS VIRTUALIZATION A GOOD IDEA?

It goes without saying that there's a lot of design and testing required to create a truly efficient virtualized ListView. You need to weight the memory requirements against the database latency (for a single user) and the database load (which affects the scalability for multiple users).

For example, if the cost of retrieving the records is high, you might choose to cache a much larger number of records but still retrieve them only in bite-sized chunks. It's also up to you to determine when to fetch new ones (asynchronously, on demand, and so on) and how to optimize the process of getting a subset of records. Depending on your approach, getting a single page of records may be just as intensive for the database as the cost of performing the whole query. If it is, your memory-friendly virtualization technique will lead to a database-intensive bottlenecked application.

Finally, you should always ask yourself whether you really need all that data. If nothing else, scrolling through pages of uninteresting information might annoy the user. A more straightforward option is to use (or force the user to choose) tight searching criteria so that only a few hundred records are shown at a time.

Selecting just the page of records you need isn't as easy as it seems at first. You might think you can select a range of records based on a unique identity field, but you have no easy way to know how many values fall in a specified range.

For example, imagine you want to get the rows in position 40 to 50. Even if you know the first row has a unique identity value of 1, you have no guarantee that row 40 will have an identity of 41. Unless all the records were inserted in one batch, it's likely that some identity values are skipped.

Unfortunately, SQL Server has no way to query an arbitrary page of records from a query (unlike Oracle, which provides the ROWNUM() function). To code around this limitation, you can use a stored procedure like the following one. It copies all the records from the Orders table into a new temporary table, numbering them with a new unique identifier. It then extracts the specified subset of rows by searching on the new unique identifier.

```
CREATE PROCEDURE GetOrdersByPage(@FromID int, @ToID int)
AS

-- Create a temporary table with the columns you are interested in.
CREATE TABLE #TempOrders
(
    ID int IDENTITY PRIMARY KEY,
    OrderID int,
```

```
    ShippedDate datetime
)

-- Fill the table with all the records.
INSERT INTO #TempOrders
(
    OrderID,
    ShippedDate
)
SELECT
    OrderID,
    ShippedDate
FROM
 Orders ORDER BY OrderID

-- Select the page of records.
SELECT * FROM #TempOrders WHERE ID >= @FromID AND ID <= @ToID
GO
```

Of course, if you want to make sure this performs well, you might want to consider keeping the temporary table around for a longer period of time and using a cluster index to make the range searching more efficient. (This example also assumes that no one else will insert new order records while a user is scrolling through the ListView.) However, this simple stored procedure is enough to create the virtual ListView test.

In the client, it makes sense to create a helper class that exposes the functionality you need. To create the ListView, you need a way to get the total number of available orders and a way to call the GetOrdersByPage stored procedure to extract just the information in which you're interested.

```
public class NorthwindDB
{
    private static string connectionString = "Data Source=localhost;" +
      "Initial Catalog=Northwind;Integrated Security=SSPI";

    public static int GetOrdersCount()
    {
        // Create the command and the connection.
        string sql = "SELECT COUNT(*) FROM Orders";
        SqlConnection con = new SqlConnection(connectionString);
        SqlCommand cmd = new SqlCommand(sql, con);

        // Get the number of records.
        using (con)
        {
            con.Open();
            return (int)cmd.ExecuteScalar();
        }
    }
```

```
public static DataTable GetOrders(int fromOrderID, int toOrderID)
{
    // Create the command and the connection.
    SqlConnection con = new SqlConnection(connectionString);
    SqlCommand cmd = new SqlCommand("GetOrdersByPage", con);
    cmd.CommandType = CommandType.StoredProcedure;
    cmd.Parameters.Add(new SqlParameter("@FromID", SqlDbType.Int, 4));
    cmd.Parameters["@FromID"].Value = fromOrderID;
    cmd.Parameters.Add(new SqlParameter("@ToID", SqlDbType.Int, 4));
    cmd.Parameters["@ToID"].Value = toOrderID;

    // Prepare to fill a new DataSet.
    SqlDataAdapter adapter = new SqlDataAdapter(cmd);
    DataSet ds = new DataSet();

    // Get the appropriate "page" of order records.
    adapter.Fill(ds);

    // Define the primary key (required for searching).
      ds.Tables[0].PrimaryKey = new DataColumn[] {ds.Tables[0].Columns["ID"]};

    return ds.Tables[0];
}
}
```

To designate a ListView as virtual, set the VirtualMode property to true, and set the VirtualListSize property to reflect the total number of rows. However, don't add anything to the ListView.Items collection.

```
listView.VirtualMode = true;
listView.VirtualListSize = NorthwindDB.GetOrdersCount();
```

When the ListView needs an item to display, it fires the RetrieveVirtualItem event. Your code must examine the requested index and then create the corresponding ListViewItem.

The RetrieveVirtualItem event fires for every item you want to display, so it's up to you to determine how you want to batch the retrieval process. In this example, the rows are cached in a DataTable. If the required row is found in the DataTable, it's used automatically. Otherwise, a new query is performed to find the nearest range of 100 rows. (For example, if row 50 is required, the code requeries rows 1 to 100.)

```csharp
private DataTable dtCachedItems;

private void listView_RetrieveVirtualItem(object sender,
  RetrieveVirtualItemEventArgs e)
{
    // Check whether the item is in the local cache.
    // Remember to add 1 to the index because SQL Server counts from 1 up,
    // while the ListView counts from 0.
    DataRow match = null;
    if (dtCachedItems != null)
      match = dtCachedItems.Rows.Find(e.ItemIndex + 1);

    if (match == null)
    {
        // The item isn't in memory.
        // Get a new range of 100 records.
        int from, to;
        if (e.ItemIndex < 50)
            from = 0;
        else
            from = (e.ItemIndex - 50);

        to = from + 100;
        dtCachedItems = NorthwindDB.GetOrders(from, to);
        match = dtCachedItems.Rows.Find(e.ItemIndex + 1);

        lblStatus.Text = String.Format(
          "Fetched rows from {0} to {1}.",
          from.ToString(), to.ToString());
    }

    // Create the ListViewItem for the matching record.
    e.Item = new ListViewItem(match["OrderID"].ToString());
    e.Item.SubItems.Add(match["ShippedDate"].ToString());
}
```

Figure 6-5 shows the result.

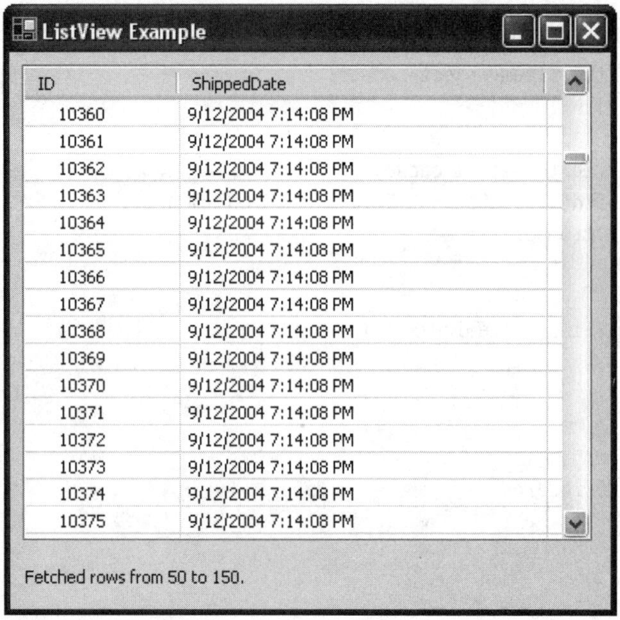

Figure 6-5. *A ListView that uses virtualization*

This approach is not the most efficient possible implementation, because it's likely that the DataTable being discarded has some of the information in the new DataTable. A more intelligent implementation would check what data is available and query only new records. (For example, if you have rows 50 to 150 and scroll to row 151, a new query is performed for rows 101 to 201. A better implementation would be to check the DataTable, discard rows 50 to 100, and just query rows from 151 to 201.)

■Tip The RetrieveVirtualItem even fires when an item is obscured and then displayed for any reason. This includes not only scrolling but also minimizing and maximizing the window and showing content over the top (such as a message box). For all these reasons, it's important to have the most efficient algorithm for caching and querying items.

Because all the items aren't available in the ListView at any one time, the methods for searching for an item won't work. If you want to supply this functionality, handle the SearchForVirtualItem event and supply your own logic to query the data source for the requested information.

TreeView Basics

The TreeView is a hierarchical collection of elements, which are called *nodes*. This collection is provided through the TreeView.Nodes property. With this collection, it's quite easy to add a few basic nodes.

```
treeFood.Nodes.Add("Apple");
treeFood.Nodes.Add("Peach");
treeFood.Nodes.Add("Tofu");
treeFood.Nodes.Add("Apple");
```

In this example, four nodes are added with descriptive text. The .NET implementation of the TreeView doesn't require a unique key for relating parent nodes to child nodes (which dodges a few headaches). This means it's easier to quickly insert a new node. It also means that unless you take specific steps to record a unique identifier with each item, you won't be able to distinguish duplicates. For example, the only difference between the two "Apple" entries in the example is their respective position in the list.

To specify more information about a node, you have to construct a TreeNode object separately and then add it to the list. In the example that follows, a unique identifier is stored in the Tag property:

```
TreeNode newNode = new TreeNode();
newNode.Text = "Apple";
newNode.Tag = 1;
treeFood.Nodes.Add(newNode);
```

In this case, a simple integer is used, but the Tag property can hold any type of object if needed, even a reference to a corresponding database record.

```
foreach (DataRow drFood in dtFoods.Rows)
{
    TreeNode newNode = new TreeNode();
    newNode.Text = drFoods["Name"].ToString();
    newNode.Tag = drFood;
    treeFood.Nodes.Add(newNode);
}
```

TreeView Structure

You can nest nodes in a complex structure with a virtually unlimited number of layers. Adding subnodes is similar to adding submenu items. First you find the parent node, and then you add the child node to the parent's Nodes collection.

```
TreeNode node;

node = treeFood.Nodes.Add("Fruits");
node.Nodes.Add("Apple");
node.Nodes.Add("Peach");
```

```
node = treeFood.Nodes.Add("Vegetables");
node.Nodes.Add("Tomato");
node.Nodes.Add("Eggplant");
```

The Add() method always returns the newly added node object. You can then use this node object to add child nodes. If you wanted to add child nodes to the Apple node, you would follow the same pattern and catch the node reference returned by the Add() method.

This code produces a hierarchical tree structure, as shown in Figure 6-6.

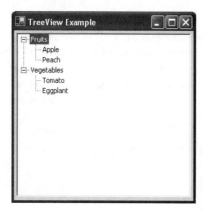

Figure 6-6. *A basic TreeView*

Microsoft suggests that the preferred way to add items to a TreeView is by using the AddRange() method to insert an entire block of nodes at once. It works similarly but requires an array of node objects.

```
TreeNode[] nodes = new TreeNode[2];

nodes[0] = new TreeNode("Fruits");
nodes[0].Nodes.Add("Apple");
nodes[0].Nodes.Add("Peach");

nodes[1] = new TreeNode("Vegetables");
nodes[1].Nodes.Add("Tomato");
nodes[1].Nodes.Add("Eggplant");

treeFood.Nodes.AddRange(nodes);
```

By using this technique, you ensure that the TreeView is updated all at once, improving performance dramatically. You can achieve a similar performance gain by using the BeginUpdate() and EndUpdate() methods, which suspends the graphical refresh of the TreeView control, allowing you to perform a series of operations at once.

```
// Suspend automatic refreshing.
treeFood.BeginUpdate();

// (Add or remove several nodes here.)

// Enable automatic refreshing.
treeFood.EndUpdate();
```

■**Note** If you use the AddRange() method, the BeginUpdate() and EndUpdate() methods are used behind the scenes, provided you are adding a large enough collection of nodes.

TreeView Navigation

The TreeView's multileveled structure can make it difficult to navigate through your tree structure to perform common tasks. For example, you might want to use a TreeView to provide a hierarchical list of check box settings (as Windows does for the View tab in its Folder Options dialog box, shown in Figure 6-7). You can configure the TreeView to display check boxes next to each node by setting a single property.

```
treeSettings.CheckBoxes = true;
```

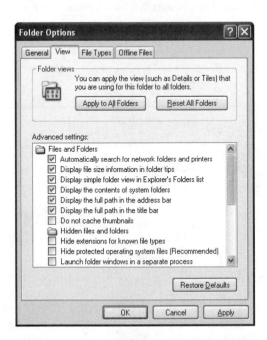

Figure 6-7. *Using a TreeView to configure settings*

When you click the OK or Apply button, you then search through the list of settings and make the corresponding changes.

The following section of code might seem like a reasonable attempt, but it won't work:

```
foreach (TreeNode node in treeSettings.Nodes)
{
    // (Process node here.)
}
```

The problem is that the TreeView.Nodes collection contains only the first level of the nodes hierarchy, which in this case corresponds to the main groupings (such as "Files and Folders.") The correct code would go another level deep.

```
foreach (TreeNode node in treeSettings.Nodes)
{
    // (Process first-level node here.)
    foreach (TreeNode nodeChild in node.Nodes)
    {
        // (Process second-level node here.)
    }
}
```

Alternatively, if you have a less structured organization where similar types of elements are held at various levels, you need to search through all the nodes recursively. The following code calls a ProcessNodes procedure recursively until it has walked through the entire tree structure:

```
private void cmdOK_Click(object sender, System.EventArgs e)
{
    // Start the update.
    ProcessNodes(treeSettings.Nodes);
}

private void ProcessNodes(TreeNodeCollection nodes)
{
    foreach (TreeNode node in nodes)
    {
        ProcessNode(node);
        ProcessNodes(node.Nodes);
    }
}

private void ProcessNode(TreeNode node)
{
    // Check whether the node interests us.
    // If it does, process it.
    // To verify that this routine works, display the node text.
    Debug.WriteLine(node.Text);
}
```

■**Tip** To count all the nodes in your tree, you don't need to enumerate through the collections and subcollections. Instead, you can use the TreeView.GetNodeCount() method. Make sure you specify true for the required parameter—this indicates you want to count the items in subtrees. Each TreeNode object also provides a GetNodeCount() method, allowing you to count the items in selected branches of a tree.

You can also use relative-based navigation. In this model, you don't iterate through the whole collection. Instead, you go from a current node to another node.

```
currentNode = currentNode.Parent.Parent.NextNode;
```

This example takes the current node, finds its parent (by moving one level up the hierarchy), then finds the parent's parent, and finally moves to the next sibling (the next node in the list that is at the same level). If there is no next node, a null reference is returned. If one of the parents is missing, an error occurs. Table 6-5 lists the relative-based navigation properties you can use.

Table 6-5. *Relative-Based Navigation Properties*

Node Property	Moves...
Parent	One level up the hierarchy, to the node that contains the current node
FirstNode	One level down the node hierarchy, to the first node in the current node's Nodes collection
LastNode	One level down the node hierarchy, to the last node in the current node's Nodes collection
PrevNode	To the node at the same level, but just above the current node
NextNode	To the node at the same level, but just below the current node

The next example shows how you could use the relative-based navigation to walk over every node in a tree:

```
private void cmdOK_Click(object sender, System.EventArgs e)
{
    // Start the update.
    ProcessNodes(treeUsers.Nodes [0]);
}

private void ProcessNodes(TreeNode nodeStart)
{
    do
    {
        ProcessNode(nodeStart);
```

```
        // Check for contained (child nodes).
        if (nodeStart.Nodes.Count > 0)
        {
            ProcessNodes(nodeStart.FirstNode);
        }

        // Move to the next (sibling) node.
        nodeStart = nodeStart.NextNode;
    }
    while (nodeStart != null);
}

private void ProcessNode(TreeNode node)
{
    // Check whether the node interests us.
    // If it does, process it.
    // To verify that this routine works, display the node text.
    Debug.WriteLine(node.Text);
}
```

This type of navigation is generally less common in .NET programs, because the collection-based syntax is more readable and easier to use.

Manipulating Nodes

Now that you have a good idea of how to add nodes and find them in the tree structure, it's time to consider how you can delete and rearrange nodes. Once again, you use the methods of the Nodes collection.

Generally, the best way to delete a node is by first obtaining a reference to the node. You could also remove a node using its index number, but index numbers can change as nodes are removed or if sorting is used, so they raise the potential for unexpected problems.

Once again, consider the example tree of food products:

```
TreeNode node = treeFood.Nodes.Add("Fruits");
node.Nodes.Add("Apple");
node.Nodes.Add("Peach");

node = treeFood.Nodes.Add("Vegetables");
node.Nodes.Add("Tomato");
node.Nodes.Add("Eggplant");
```

You can now search for the "Fruits" node in the collection and delete it. Note that when you use the Remove() method, all the child nodes are automatically deleted as well.

```
foreach (TreeNode searchNode in treeFood.Nodes)
{
    if (searchNode.Text.CompareTo("Fruits") == 0)
    {
```

```
        treeFood.Nodes.Remove(searchNode);
        break;
    }
}
```

You can use the Remove() method to delete a node that exists several layers down the hierarchy. In other words, if you obtain a reference to the "Apple" node, you can delete it directly from the treeFood.Nodes collection even though the collection doesn't really contain that node.

```
TreeNode nodeApple, nodeFruits;
nodeFruits = treeFood.Nodes.Add("Fruits");
nodeApple = nodeFruits.Nodes.Add("Apple");

// This works. It finds the nodeApple in the nodeFruits.Nodes subcollection.
treeFood.Nodes.Remove(nodeApple);

// This also works. It directly removes the apple from nodeFruits.Nodes.
nodeFruits.Nodes.Remove(nodeApple);
```

The Nodes property provides an instance of the Remove() method. Table 6-6 lists a few more of its node manipulation features. Some, such as the ability to use Clear() to wipe all child nodes and Insert() to add a node at a specific position, are particularly useful.

Table 6-6. *Useful TreeNodeCollection Methods*

Method	Description
Add()	Adds a new node at the bottom of the list.
AddRange()	Adds an array of node objects. You can use this technique to update a TreeView in a single batch operation and thereby optimize performance.
Clear()	Clears all the child nodes of the current node. Any sublevels are also deleted, meaning that if you call this method for the TreeView, the whole structure is cleared.
Contains()	Returns true or false, depending on whether a given node object is currently part of the Nodes collection. If you want to provide a search that is more than one level deep, you need write your own method and use recursion, as shown in the previous examples.
IndexOf()	Returns the current (zero-based) index number for a node. Remember, node indexes change as nodes are added and deleted. This method returns –1 if the node is not found.
Insert()	This method allows you to insert a node in a specific position. It's similar to the Add() method, but it takes an additional parameter specifying the index number where you want to add the node. The node that is currently there is shifted down. Unlike the Add() method, the Insert() method does not return the node reference.
Remove()	Accepts a node reference and removes the node from the collection. All children are removed, and all subsequent tree nodes are moved up one position.

.NET provides another way to manipulate nodes—using their own methods. For example, you can delete a node without worrying about what TreeView it belongs to by using the Node.Remove() method. This shortcut is extremely convenient.

```
nodeApple.Remove();
```

Nodes also provide a built-in clone method that copies the node *and* any child nodes. This can allow you to transfer a batch of nodes between TreeView controls without needing to iterate over every child node. (A node object cannot be assigned to more than one TreeView control.)

```
foreach (TreeNode node in treeView.Nodes)
{
    // Clone this node and all the sublevels.
    TreeNode nodeNew = (TreeNode)node.Clone();

    // Add the nodes to a new tree.
    treeDestination.Nodes.Add(nodeNew);
}
```

Selecting Nodes

On their own, TreeNode objects don't raise any events. The TreeView control, however, provides notification about important node actions such as selections and expansions. Each of these actions is composed of two events: a "Before" event that occurs before the TreeView display is updated and an "After" event that allows you to react to the event in the traditional way when it is completed. (You'll see in some of the advanced examples how the "Before" event can allow you to perform just-in-time node additions. This technique is used in Chapter 11 with a directory tree and in Chapter 8 with a database-browser application.) Table 6-7 lists the key TreeView events.

Table 6-7. *TreeView Node Events*

Event	Description
BeforeCheck and AfterCheck	Occurs when a user clicks to select or deselect a check box.
BeforeCollapse and AfterCollapse	Occurs when a user collapses a node, either by double-clicking it or by using the minus box.
BeforeExpand and AfterExpand	Occurs when a user expands a node, either by double-clicking it or by using the plus box.
BeforeSelect and AfterSelect	Occurs when a user clicks a node. This event can also be triggered for other reasons. For example, deleting the currently selected node causes another node to be selected.
BeforeLabelEdit and AfterLabelEdit	Occurs when a user edits a node label. This is possible only when TreeView.LabelEdit is true (in which case you can start an edit by calling BeginEdit(), or the user can initiate it by clicking once on the node text).

Every custom event in the TreeView is node-specific and provides a reference to the relevant node. The TreeView control also inherits some generic events that allow it to react to mouse clicks and other actions that occur to any part of the control, but these are generally not very useful. These TreeView node-based events provide a TreeViewEventArgs object (for AfterXxx() events) or TreeViewCancelEventArgs (for BeforeXxx () events). This object has a Node property that provides the affected node and an Action property that indicates how the action was triggered. The Action property uses the TreeViewAction enumeration and can indicate whether an event was caused by a key press, a mouse click, or a node expansion/collapse. The TreeViewCancelEventArgs also adds a Cancel property that you can use to cancel the attempted operation.

The next example reacts to the AfterSelect event and gives the user the chance to remove the selected node. You'll notice that when a node is deleted, the closest node is automatically selected.

```
private void treeUsers_AfterSelect(object sender,
 System.Windows.Forms.TreeViewEventArgs e)
{
    string message;
    message = "You selected " + e.Node.Text + " with this action: " +
              e.Action.ToString() + "\n\nDelete it?";

    DialogResult result;
    result = MessageBox.Show(message, "Delete", MessageBoxButtons.YesNo);
    if (result == DialogResult.Yes)
    {
        e.Node.Remove();
    }
}
```

Depending on your TreeView, just having a reference to the node object may not be enough. For example, you might add duplicate node entries to different subgroups. This technique isn't that unusual; for example, you might have a list of team members subgrouped by role (programmer, tester, documenter, and so on). A single team member might play more than one role. However, depending on what subgroup the selected node is in, you might want to perform a different action.

In this case, you need to determine where the node is positioned. You can use the node-relative properties (such as Parent) to move up the tree, or you can retrieve a string that represents the full path from the node's FullPath property. A few possible values for the FullPath property are as follows:

```
Fruits
Fruits\Peach
Country\State\City\Street
```

In these examples, a slash separates each tree level, but you can use a different delimiter by setting the TreeView.PathSeparator property.

More Advanced TreeViews

The TreeView is a sophisticated control, and it provides a great deal of customization possibilities. Table 6-8 describes some of the additional appearance-related properties.

Table 6-8. *TreeView Appearance Properties*

Property	Description
BackgroundImage	Specifies a background image that will appear behind the items in the list. This item may be stretched, stretched without distortion ("zoomed"), tiled, or centered according to the value of the BackgroundImageLayout property.
CheckBoxes	Set this to true to display a check box next to each node.
FullRowSelect	When set to true, selecting a node shows a highlight box that spans the full width of the tree. The FullRowSelect property is ignored if ShowLines is true.
HotTracking	When set to true, the text in a node changes to a high-lighted hyperlink style when the user positions the mouse over it.
Indent	Specifies the left-to-right distance between each level of items in the tree, in pixels.
ShowLines, ShowPlusMinus, and ShowRootLines	Boolean properties that configure the appearance of lines linking each node, the plus/minus box that allows users to easily expand a node, and the root lines that connect the first level of objects.
LineColor	Allows you to configure the color of the node lines.
DrawNode, DoubleBuffered, and the DrawNode event	You can set the DrawNode property to allow custom drawing. Use OwnerDrawAll if you want to draw all elements of a node or OwnerDrawText if you want the TreeView to handle details such as node lines, check boxes, icons, and the expand/collapse boxes. In either case, you need to handle the DrawItem event to perform the drawing. In addition, you can set the DoubleBuffered property to true to optimize the drawing process. Chapter 12 has more information about owner-drawn controls.
Sorted and TreeViewNodeSorter	When Sorted is set to true, nodes are sorted in each group alphabetically using their text names. If you want to specify a custom sort order, supply an IComparer object to the TreeViewNodeSorter property (as demonstrated earlier with the ListView).

The TreeNode also provides some useful properties that haven't been discussed yet (see Table 6-9). Mainly, these properties allow you to determine the state of node. Additional properties exist that let you modify a node's background and foreground color and determine its relatives, as you saw earlier.

Table 6-9. *TreeNode State Properties*

Property	Description
Checked	True if you are using a TreeView with check box nodes and the node is checked.
IsEditing	True if the user is currently editing this node's label. Label editing is explained later in this section.
IsExpanded	True if this node is expanded, meaning its child nodes are displayed.
IsSelected	True if this is the currently selected node. Only one node can be selected at a time, and you can control which one is using the TreeView.SelectedNode property.
IsVisible	True if the node is currently visible. A node is not visible if its parent is collapsed or if you need to scroll up or down to find it. To programmatically show a node, use its EnsureVisible() method.

■**Tip** In .NET 2.0, the TreeNode class adds a few useful formatting-related properties you can use to tweak the appearance of the TreeView on a node-by-node basis without resorting to full-out custom drawing. These include ForeColor, BackColor, and NodeFont.

Node Pictures

One frequently used feature is the ability to assign icons to each node. As with all modern controls, this works by using a paired ImageList control.

```
treeFood.ImageList = imagesFood;
```

You can assign a default picture index that will be used by any node that does not specifically override it.

```
treeFood.ImageIndex = 0;
```

You can set an image for each individual node through the properties of the TreeNode object. Each node can have two linked images: a default image and one that is used when the node is selected.

```
TreeNode node = new TreeNode("Apples");
node.ImageIndex = 1;
node.SelectedImageIndex = 2;
treeFood.Nodes.Add(node);
```

Unfortunately, it is not possible to have a different icon when the node is expanded from the one you use when it is collapsed (unless you handle the BeforeExpand and BeforeCollapse events to implement this behavior).

Expanding and Collapsing Levels

You've already learned how to react when the user expands and collapses levels. However, you can also programmatically expand and collapse nodes. This trick has many uses:

- Restoring a TreeView control to its "last viewed" state so users can continue right where they left off with the control in the same state.

- Ensuring that a particular node or set of nodes is visible to correspond with another activity. For example, the user might have made a selection in a different part of the window or might be using a wizard that is stepping through the process.

- Configuring the TreeView when the window is first loaded so that the user sees the most important (or most commonly used) nodes.

.NET provides a few ways to accomplish these tasks. First, every node provides four useful methods: Collapse(), Expand(), ExpandAll(), and Toggle(). The Expand() method acts on the immediate children, while ExpandAll() expands the node and all subnodes. To expand or collapse the entire tree, you can use one of the TreeView methods: ExpandAll() or CollapseAll().

```
node.Expand();      // Expand the node to display its immediate children.
node.Toggle();      // Switch the node: it was expanded, so now it is collapsed.
node.ExpandAll();   // Expand all nodes and subnodes.
tree.ExpandAll();   // Expand the entire tree.
```

Second, you can use a node's EnsureVisible() method. This extremely useful method expands whatever nodes are required to make a node visible and scrolls to the appropriate location. This is extremely useful if you are iterating through a tree looking for a node that matches certain criteria.

```
// Search the first level of a TreeView control.
foreach (TreeNode node in tree.Nodes)
{
    if ((int)(node.Tag) == 12)
    {
        // Collapse the whole tree to hide unimportant nodes.
        tree.CollapseAll();

        // Expand just the node that interests the user.
        node.EnsureVisible();
        break;
    }
}
```

The TreeView control also provides a TopNode property that references the first fully visible node at the top of the current display window. It also provides a VisibleCount property that identifies the maximum number of nodes that can be displayed at a time in the TreeView at its current height.

TreeView Drag-and-Drop

TreeView controls can support drag-and-drop operations just as easily as any other .NET control. However, when information is dragged onto a TreeView, you generally need to determine what node it was "dropped" on. To perform this magic, you need to perform your own hit testing, with a little help from the TreeView.GetNodeAt() method.

The following example presents a form with two TreeViews. The user can drag a node from one TreeView to the other TreeView or to another location in the same TreeView (see Figure 6-8). When a node is dropped, its content is copied, and the original branch is left untouched. Best of all, the code is generic, meaning that one set of event handlers responds to the events from both trees.

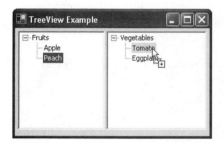

Figure 6-8. *Drag-and-drop operations with a TreeView*

To start, you need to make sure both TreeView controls can receive drag-and-drop events. At the same time, disable the HideSelection property so that you can highlight the node that will be the drop target, even if the TreeView doesn't have the focus.

```
treeOne.AllowDrop = true;
treeTwo.AllowDrop = true;
treeOne.HideSelection = false;
treeTwo.HideSelection = false;
```

The next step is to create the MouseDown event-handling logic that starts the drag-and-drop operation. This code needs to investigate whether there is a node under the mouse pointer. If there is, the node is copied (along with all subnodes), and a drag-and-drop operation is started.

```
private void tree_MouseDown(object sender, System.Windows.Forms.MouseEventArgs e)
{
    // Get the tree.
    TreeView tree = (TreeView)sender;

    // Get the node underneath the mouse.
    TreeNode node = tree.GetNodeAt(e.X, e.Y);
    tree.SelectedNode = node;
```

```
    // Start the drag-and-drop operation with a cloned copy of the node.
    if (node != null)
    {
        tree.DoDragDrop(node.Clone(), DragDropEffects.Copy);
    }
}
```

Note that all the TreeView event handlers handle events in *both* trees. For example, the MouseDown event handler is attached to treeOne.MouseDown and treeTwo.MouseDown. This provides the flexibility that allows the user to drag nodes back and forth between both trees. In addition, this means that the event handler must retrieve the TreeView reference from the sender parameter to determine which tree fired the event.

Next, both trees need to handle the DragOver event. Note that you use this event, instead of the DropEnter event, because the operation is permitted or allowed based on whether there is a node under the current mouse pointer.

```
private void tree_DragOver(object sender, System.Windows.Forms.DragEventArgs e)
{
    // Get the tree.
    TreeView tree = (TreeView)sender;

    // Drag and drop denied by default.
    e.Effect = DragDropEffects.None;

    // Is it a valid format?
    if (e.Data.GetData(typeof(TreeNode)) != null)
    {
        // Make sure it's not from the current tree.
        if (nodeSource.TreeView != tree)
        {
            // Get the screen point.
            Point pt = new Point(e.X, e.Y);

            // Convert to a point in the TreeView's coordinate system.
            pt = tree.PointToClient(pt);

            // Is the mouse over a valid node?
            TreeNode node = tree.GetNodeAt(pt);
            if (node != null)
            {
                // (You could also check the state of the Ctrl key to decide
                //  whether to copy or move nodes.)
                e.Effect = DragDropEffects.Copy;
                tree.SelectedNode = node;
            }
        }
    }
}
```

Note that the drag-and-drop events provide mouse coordinates in the screen's frame of reference (measuring from the top-left corner of the desktop). To perform the hit testing, you need to convert this point to a point in the TreeView control's coordinate system (which measures from the top left of the control).

Note GetNodeAt() returns a node as long as the mouse is positioned in a node row. It doesn't matter if you are a little bit to the left or right of the text; the GetNodeAt() method still treats it as though you are over the node.

Finally, the actual copied node is inserted by a DragDrop event handler. The node that contains the added node is expanded to ensure that the addition is visible.

```
private void tree_DragDrop(object sender, System.Windows.Forms.DragEventArgs e)
{
    // Get the tree.
    TreeView tree = (TreeView)sender;

    // Get the screen point.
    Point pt = new Point(e.X, e.Y);

    // Convert to a point in the TreeView's coordinate system.
    pt = tree.PointToClient(pt);

    // Get the node underneath the mouse.
    TreeNode node = tree.GetNodeAt(pt);

    // Add a child node.
    node.Nodes.Add((TreeNode)e.Data.GetData(typeof(TreeNode)));

    // Show the newly added node if it is not already visible.
    node.Expand();
}
```

You can try this example in the TreeViewDragAndDrop project. This example doesn't provide any restrictions—it allows you to copy nodes anywhere you want. Most programs probably add more restrictive logic in the DragOver event handler. In addition, you might want to create a tree where dragging and dropping moves items instead of copies them. In this case, the easiest approach is to store a reference to the original node object (without cloning it).

```
tree.DoDragDrop(node, DragDropEffects.Copy);
```

The DragDrop event handler would then remove the node from the source tree and add it to the target tree. However, you would typically need to perform some validation to ensure that the dragged node is an allowed child of the target node.

```
TreeNode nodeDragged = e.Data.GetData(typeof(TreeNode));

// Copy to new position.
node.Nodes.Add(nodeDragged.Clone());

// Remove from original position.
nodeDragged.Remove();
```

■Tip For even more advanced drag-and-drop possibilities, you can use the DoDragDrop() method with an instance of a custom class that encapsulates all the relevant information, instead of just the TreeNode object.

The Last Word

In this chapter, you looked at the ListView and TreeView, two staples of modern Windows programming. In the later chapters on custom control development, you'll see two ways to extend these controls. First, in Chapter 11, you'll learn how to derive a class from the TreeView to provide higher-level features and behavior tailored to your data. Next, in Chapter 12, you'll learn how to take complete control and paint a TreeView from scratch with owner drawing.

CHAPTER 7

■■■

Drawing with GDI+

If you've programmed rich graphics in the pre-.NET world, odds are you used the GDI (Graphics Device Interface) API. The key idea behind GDI is that your code can paint graphics to different devices (printers, monitors, and video cards) using the same set of functions, without needing to understand the underlying hardware. In turn, Windows ensures compatibility with a wide range of clients, and (to a certain extent) makes use of optimizations that the hardware might provide. Unfortunately, mastering the GDI functions requires coding wizardry and hard work.

.NET 1.x introduced a new toolkit of classes for two-dimensional drawing and rendering. These classes, most of which are found in the System.Drawing namespaces (and contained in the System.Drawing.dll assembly), constitute GDI+. Technically, GDI+ isn't built into .NET. Instead, .NET wraps the functions in unmanaged libraries (including gdiplus.dll and gdi32.dll). However, the .NET classes provide a higher level of abstraction, with prebuilt support for features like double buffering that are time consuming to implement on your own. All in all, GDI+ provides the most convenient and flexible drawing interface that Windows programmers have had to date.

You've already seen a sprinkling of GDI+ throughout this book. For example, in Chapter 3, you learned about some of the basic GDI+ ingredients in the System.Drawing namespace, including objects representing fonts, colors, position, and size. In the rest of this book, you'll see many more examples, including custom owner-drawn controls. This chapter gives you the basic principles of the underlying GDI+ model that makes it all possible. It also describes the new rendering support for Windows XP styles that's in .NET 2.0.

■**Note** .NET 2.0 has only minor changes for GDI+. Although there are areas where the model could be extended (and some where performance still lags), Microsoft no longer plans to refine GDI+. Instead, the focus has shifted to the creation of a next-generation drawing framework known as Avalon, which is planned for future versions of Windows. Avalon also may be made available for Windows XP and Windows Server 2003, but most probably with limitations or performance issues.

Understanding GDI+

GDI+ has three broad feature areas:

- **Two-dimensional vector graphics.** Using GDI+, you can draw lines, curves, and shapes on a drawing surface. Most of the examples you'll see in this chapter involve two-dimensional graphics.

- **Imaging.** GDI+ allows you to render bitmaps onto a drawing surface, and perform some operations on images (like stretching and skewing them). Images were introduced in Chapter 5.

- **Typography.** GDI+ allows you to render smooth, antialiased text in a variety of fonts, sizes, colors, and orientations. You learned about the basic Font class that makes this possible in Chapter 2.

You can use these features to render output on a window, or to the printer.

■**Note** GDI+ doesn't support rich multimedia like video or vector-based animation. For more information about how you can integrate these features into your applications, see Chapter 16.

There's another way of looking at GDI+—in terms of the namespaces you use to access its features. Table 7-1 has the lowdown.

Table 7-1. *GDI+ Namespaces*

Member	Description
System.Drawing	Provides the basic GDI+ graphics functionality, including the Graphics class you use to perform all your painting, and definitions for basic types like the Point, Rectangle, Color, Font, Pen, Brush, and Bitmap
System.Drawing.Drawing2D	Provides classes for more advanced two-dimensional painting, including types for blending, patterns, and gradients, the GraphicsPath, and enumerations that let you set the quality level of your rendering
System.Drawing.Imaging	Provides classes for manipulating bitmap and vector images
System.Drawing.Text	A small namespace that includes classes that let you access the currently installed fonts
System.Drawing.Printing	Provides types for rendering GDI+ content to the printer, including the PrintDocument class that represents an in-memory document you plan to print and the PrinterSettings class that exposes printer settings

GDI+ doesn't expose all the functionality of GDI, which means you need to fall back on unmanaged calls if you need to perform tasks like overwriting arbitrary areas of the screen (for example, in a custom screen saver). However, GDI+ fits the bill for the majority of cases in which you simply want to use custom drawing to create a snazzy interface, rather than build a custom drawing application.

Paint Sessions with GDI+

The heart of GDI+ programming is the System.Drawing.Graphics class. The Graphics class encapsulates a GDI+ drawing surface, whether it is a window or print document. You paint on the GDI+ drawing surface using a combination of the methods in the Graphics class.

Accessing the Graphics Object

There are essentially two ways to access a live instance of the Graphics class. The simplest and safest approach is to perform your painting inside a dedicated Paint event handler. In this case, the Graphics object is provided to your event handler through the PaintEventArgs parameter.

For example, the code that follows draws a curve onto a form using the Graphics.DrawArc() method (see Figure 7-1):

```
// This code handles the Form.Paint event.
private void Form_Paint(object sender, System.Windows.Forms.PaintEventArgs e)
{
    Pen drawingPen = new Pen(Color.Red, 15);
    e.Graphics.DrawArc(drawingPen, 50, 20, 100, 200, 40, 210);
    drawingPen.Dispose();
}
```

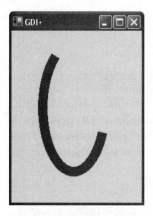

Figure 7-1. *Painting to a GDI+ surface*

You could perform the same task by overriding the OnPaint() method of a control. This is the approach you'll follow when creating an owner-drawn control, and it produces the same result.

```
// This code overrides the base Form.OnPaint() method.
protected override void OnPaint(System.Windows.Forms.PaintEventArgs e)
{
    Pen drawingPen = new Pen(Color.Red, 15);
    e.Graphics.DrawArc(drawingPen, 50, 20, 100, 200, 40, 210);
    drawingPen.Dispose();

    // Call the base class implementation (which raises the Paint event).
    this.OnPaint(e);
}
```

Of course, you don't have to wait for a Paint event to occur before you start drawing. Instead, you can directly obtain the Graphics object for a specific control or form using the Control.CreateGraphics() method. In this case, you should make sure to call the Graphics.Dispose() method when you're finished because the Graphics object uses unmanaged system resources. You don't take this step when handling the Paint event or overriding the OnPaint() method because the .NET Framework acquires and disposes of the Graphics object for you.

Here's an example that draws the same arc shown in Figure 7-1, but this time it does so by creating a Graphics object for the form in response to a button click.

```
private void button_Click(object sender, System.EventArgs e)
{
    Pen drawingPen = new Pen(Color.Red, 15);
    Graphics gdiSurface = this.CreateGraphics();
    gdiSurface.DrawArc(drawingPen, 50, 20, 100, 200, 40, 210);

    // Release your resources. You can also use the using statement
    // to take care of this task.
    drawingPen.Dispose();
    gdiSurface.Dispose();
}
```

Before you start using this approach, be warned—this code isn't equivalent to the earlier example! The problem is that as soon as you minimize or hide the window, the arc disappears. It won't be repainted until you click the button again. This odd behavior confuses just about everyone when they first tackle GDI+, and it's the source of the most common GDI+ questions on Microsoft newsgroups. To understand why this discrepancy exists, you need to take a closer look at how the Windows operating system handles paint operations, as described in the next section.

Painting and Repainting

Contrary to what you might expect, the Windows operating system doesn't store the graphical representation of a window in memory. This architecture stems from the early days of Windows programming when memory was scarce. Storing a bitmap image of every open Window could quickly consume tens of megabytes and cripple a computer.

Instead, Windows automatically discards the contents of a window as soon as it is minimized or hidden by another window. When the program window is restored, Windows sends a message to the application, asking it to repaint itself. In a .NET application, this means that the Control.OnPaint() method executes and the Control.Paint event fires. Similarly, if part of a window is obscured, only controls that are affected fire Paint events when they reappear on the screen.

Note These days, it makes sense to change the rules about how windows are painted. However, you can't revamp the architecture of the world's most popular operating system overnight. But don't be surprised to see that this approach changes when Windows Vista (Microsoft's long-awaited next-generation operating system) finally debuts with a whole new rendering model called Windows Presentation Foundation (codenamed Avalon), sometime in the future.

What this all boils down to is that it's the responsibility of the application (and hence the programmer) to repaint the window when needed. When you put your drawing logic in a Paint event handler, you can rest assured that it will be triggered automatically at the right time. However, if you perform painting inside another method, the result of your work will be lost unless you take specific steps to restore the window after it is hidden or minimized.

The best approach is to code around this limitation so that all painting is performed in the Paint event handler. The examples from Chapter 2 include a FontViewer application that draws text using the GDI+ Graphics class. When the user chooses a different font from the drop-down list box, the window is repainted with an example of the new font (see Figure 7-2). Although the repainting is triggered by the selection, the code still resides in the Paint event handler.

Figure 7-2. *Painting font text*

Here's how it works. The SelectedIndexChanged event for the ComboBox control uses the Control.Invalidate() method. This tells the Windows operating system that the form needs to be repainted. Windows then sends a message to the specific window, which the .NET Framework translates into a Paint event.

```
private void lstSize_SelectedIndexChanged(object sender, System.EventArgs e)
{
    this.Invalidate();
}
```

In the Paint event handler, the code reads the font selection and size from the appropriate controls and draws the text in the appropriate font.

```
private void FontForm_Paint(object sender, System.Windows.Forms.PaintEventArgs e)
{
    if (lstFonts.SelectedIndex != -1)
    {
        try
        {
            e.Graphics.DrawString(lstFonts.Text, new Font(lstFonts.Text,
                int.Parse(lstSize.Text)), Brushes.Black, 10, 50);
            StatusBar.Panels(0).Text = "";
        }
        catch (ArgumentException err)
        {
            // Can't create the font because it doesn't provide the selected
            // style (normal). It may exist in only a bold or italic version.
            statusBar.Panels[0].Text = err.Message;
        }
    }
}
```

Note that there is no way to erase content once you've drawn it. You can only paint over it or invalidate the window, at which point the entire window is repainted from scratch.

In a more complicated application, you could use form-level variables to track the drawing content. Then, an event handler can set these variables and invalidate the form, letting the Paint event handler take care of the rest. This technique is demonstrated later in this chapter.

■Tip You should never call the Paint event handler or OnPaint() method directly. This is especially true if your painting logic is complicated or potentially time consuming. If you call the Invalidate() method instead, Windows will queue the paint message if necessary and take care of other critical tasks first if the system is under a heavy load. Calling Invalidate() also allows Windows to save work. If the window is invalidated twice in quick succession, the window may just be repainted once. If you call the OnPaint() method twice, however, your painting code will always execute two times, resulting in a sluggish refresh time.

Refreshes and Updates

There's a potential stumbling block with the Invalidate() method. When you call it, you simply notify Windows that repainting is required. You won't actually know when the Paint event will fire (although it tends to be a matter of mere milliseconds). In the meantime, your code sails ahead.

This can present a problem if you perform multiple invalidations in quick succession. Usually, the best way to handle this model is to use a timer and invalidate the form each time the timer fires. This allows enough time between the timer ticks for Windows to dispatch the paint request. However, this isn't the case if you invalidate the form multiple times in a tight loop of code, like the one shown here:

```
private int size;
private void button_Click(object sender, EventArgs e)
{
    for (int i = 0; i < 500; i++ )
    {
        size = i;
        Invalidate();
    }
}

private void Form_Paint(object sender, PaintEventArgs e)
{
    Pen drawingPen = new Pen(Color.Red, 15);
    Rectangle rect = new Rectangle(new Point(0,0), new Size(size, size));
    e.Graphics.DrawRectangle(drawingPen, rect);
    drawingPen.Dispose();

    // Delay this code 10 milliseconds so you can see what was just painted.
    System.Threading.Thread.Sleep(10);
}
```

All this code does is paint a square that appears to grow on the form (by repainting a larger and larger square 500 times). Unfortunately, when you run this code the successive invalidate operations are so close together that only one repaint actually occurs, and all you end up seeing is the final 500-pixel-wide square.

To make this code respectable, you would use the timer approach, which solves the refresh problem and makes sure the square expanding happens at the same rate regardless of the speed of the computer's CPU. However, it's possible that you might see a variation of code like this that implements a small animation effect for a control without using a timer. You can fix the refresh problem using the Control.Update() method. Update() triggers a refresh and stalls your code until it's complete.

```
private void button_Click(object sender, EventArgs e)
{
    for (int i = 0; i < 500; i++ )
    {
        size = i;
        Invalidate();
        Update();
    }
}
```

The trick is that Update() causes the control or form to refresh only the areas that have been invalidated. If you haven't invalidated any part of the drawing surface, the Update() method does nothing.

The Invalidate() method also provides an overload that accepts a Boolean parameter. If you supply true, all child controls are also invalidated. The default is false.

If you want to invalidate the entire drawing surface, trigger a refresh, and wait, you can use the Control.Refresh() method instead of Invalidate() and Update(). However, the combination of Invalidate() and Update() gives you the most fine-grained control, especially if you're invalidating only certain regions (a technique you'll see later in this chapter). Internally, the Refresh() method simply executes these two lines of code:

```
Invalidate(true);
Update();
```

Painting and Resizing

One often overlooked fact about automatic repainting is that it only affects the portion of the window that is obscured. This is particularly important with window resizing. For example, consider the code that follows, which paints an ellipse that is the same size as the containing window.

```
private void FlawedResizing_Paint(object sender,

  System.Windows.Forms.PaintEventArgs e)
{
    Pen drawingPen = new Pen(Color.Red, 15);
    e.Graphics.DrawEllipse(DrawingPen, new Rectangle(new Point(0, 0),
      this.ClientSize));
    pen.Dispose();
}
```

When you resize this window, you'll discover that the painting code isn't working correctly. The newly exposed portions of the window are filled with the resized ellipse, but rest of the window is not updated, leading to a jumble of different ellipses that don't line up.

The problem is that Windows assumes that it only needs to repaint the portion of the window that has been hidden or restored. In this case, the *entire* content of the window depends on its dimensions, so the assumption is incorrect. Fortunately, there are several ways to solve this problem. You could use override the OnResize() method and manually invalidate the form every time it's resized. However, a better choice is to set the Form.ResizeRedraw property to true. This instructs .NET to invalidate the entire form automatically whenever the form size changes.

▓**Note** This phenomenon (incorrectly repainted forms) doesn't always appear when Form.ResizeRedraw is set to false. That's because a ResizeRedraw value of false simply indicates that you don't *require* a full repaint. However, under certain circumstances .NET will still decide to invalidate the entire form. One notable example is if you are showing a resizable form modally, and your form includes a sizing grip (as it does by default). In this case, the Windows Forms infrastructure invalidates the entire form after a resize so it can draw the sizing grip. (If you want to remove this quirk to more easily test the ResizeRedraw property or to eliminate unnecessary form refreshes, simply set the Form.SizeGripStyle property to SizeGripStyle.Hide. Now .NET won't draw the sizing grip, and the entire form won't be invalidated unless ResizeRedraw is true.)

The Graphics Class

Now that you've learned the basics of painting on a form, it's time to consider the different graphical elements that you can draw.

The majority of GDI+ drawing smarts is concentrated in the Graphics class. Table 7-2 describes the basic set of Graphics class members, many of which are explored in detail as the chapter progresses.

Table 7-2. *Basic Graphics Class Members*

Member	Description
CompositingMode and CompositingQuality	CompositingMode determines whether the drawing will overwrite the existing content or be blended with it. The CompositingQuality specifies the technique that will be used when blending, which determines the quality and speed of the operation.
InterpolationMode	Determines how properties are specified between the start point and end point of a shape (for example, when drawing a curve).
SmoothingMode and TextRenderingHint	These properties set the rendering quality (and optionally, the antialiasing) that will be used for drawing graphics or text on this GDI+ surface.
Clear()	Clears the entire drawing surface and fills it with the specified background color.
Dispose()	Releases all the resources held by the graphics object. The Graphics object can't be used after you call Dispose(). As a rule of thumb, never call Dispose() when handling a Paint event or when overriding OnPaint() because the Windows Forms infrastructure will take care of that task. However, always call it when you create the Graphics object yourself using a method like Control.CreateGraphics() or Graphics.FromImage().
FromHdc(), FromHwnd(), and FromImage()	These static methods create a Graphics object using either a handle to a device context, a window, or a .NET Image object.
GetHdc() and ReleaseHdc()	GetHdc() gets the Windows GDI handle that you can use with unmanaged code (for example, methods in the gdi32.dll library). You should use the ReleaseHdc() method to release the device context when you are finished, or call Dispose() to release the device context and dispose of the Graphics object.
IsVisible()	Accepts a point or a rectangle, and indicates whether it is in a visible portion of the graphics device (not outside the clipping region). This does not depend on whether the window is actually visible on the screen.
MeasureString()	Returns a Size structure that indicates the amount of space that is required for a given string of text in a given font. This method is useful when handling wrapped printing or drawing a multiline text display. However, if you're using the new text-rendering model, as all new applications do by default (thanks to the line of code `Application.SetCompatibleTextRenderingDefault(false);`), you'll get better results using the TextRenderer.MeasureText() method instead.
Save() and Restore()	Save() stores the state of the current Graphics object in a GraphicsState object. You can use this object with the Restore() method. This is typically used when you are changing the GDI+ surface coordinate systems.
SetClip()	Allows you to define the clipping region of this device context using a Rectangle, Region, or GraphicsPath. When you paint content on this surface, the only portions that appear are those that lie inside the clipping region.

The Graphics class also provides several methods for drawing specific shapes, images, or text. Most of these methods begin with the word "Draw." All shape-drawing methods draw outlines using a given pen; you need to use the corresponding "Fill" method to paint an interior fill region with a brush. Table 7-3 lists both types of methods. Keep in mind that many of these methods provide multiple overrides that accept different combinations of information.

Table 7-3. *Graphics Class Methods for Drawing*

Method	Description
DrawArc()	Draws an arc representing a portion of an ellipse in a rectangle specified by a pair of angles
DrawBezier() and DrawBeziers()	Draws the infamous and attractive Bezier curve, which is defined by four control points
DrawClosedCurve()	Draws a curve, and then closes it off by connecting the end points
DrawCurve()	Draws a curve (technically, a cardinal spline)
DrawEllipse()	Draws an ellipse defined by a bounding rectangle
DrawIcon() and DrawIconUnstretched()	Draws the icon represented by an Icon object and (optionally) stretches it to fit a given rectangle
DrawImage and DrawImageUnscaled()	Draws the image represented by an Image-derived object, and (optionally) stretches it to fit a given rectangle
DrawLine() and DrawLines()	Draws a line connecting the two or more points
DrawPath()	Draws a GraphicsPath object, which can represent a combination of curves and shapes
DrawPie()	Draws a "piece of pie" shape defined by an ellipse specified by a coordinate pair, a width, a height, and two radial lines
DrawPolygon()	Draws a multisided polygon defined by an array of points
DrawRectangle() and DrawRectangles()	Draws one or more ordinary rectangles
DrawString()	Draws a string of text in a given font (and using a given brush to fill the text)
FillClosedCurve()	Draws a curve, closes it off by connecting the end points, and fills it
FillEllipse()	Fills the interior of an ellipse
FillPath()	Fills the shape represented by a GraphicsPath object
FillPie()	Fills the interior of a "piece of pie" shape
FillPolygon()	Fills the interior of a polygon
FillRectangle() and FillRectangles()	Fills the interior of a rectangle
FillRegion()	Fills the interior of a Region object

As you've seen, GDI+ is stateless (unlike GDI), which means that every time you draw a shape, you need to supply the coordinates. When drawing a shape, you need a pen. When filling a shape, you need a brush. These objects aren't maintained for you—instead, you supply them to each call as method arguments.

Rendering Mode and Antialiasing

One factor that's hampered the ability of drawing tools in some programming frameworks is the lack of control over rendering quality. With GDI+, however, you can enhance the quality of your drawing with automatic antialiasing.

Antialiasing is a technique used to smooth out jagged edges in shapes and text. It works by adding shading at the border of an edge. For example, grey shading might be added to the edge of a black curve to make a corner look smoother. Technically, antialiasing blends a curve with its background. Figure 7-3 shows a close-up of an antialiased ellipse.

Figure 7-3. *Antialiasing with an ellipse*

To use smoothing on shapes in your applications, you set the SmoothingMode property of the Graphics object. You can choose between None (the default), HighSpeed, AntiAlias, and HighQuality (which is similar to AntiAlias but uses other, slower optimizations with LCD screens). The SmoothingMode property is one of the few stateful Graphics class members, which means that you set it before you begin drawing, and it applies to any shapes you draw in the rest of the paint session (until the Graphics object is disposed of). Here's an example:

```
e.Graphics.SmoothingMode = Drawing.Drawing2D.SmoothingMode.AntiAlias;
```

Figure 7-4 shows a form with several picture boxes. Each picture box handles its own paint event, sets a different smoothing mode, and then draws an ellipse. You can see the result of using higher quality, which is almost always the best way to go.

Antialiasing also can be used with fonts to soften jagged edges on text. The latest versions of the Windows operating system use antialiasing automatically with on-screen fonts. However, you can set the Graphics.TextRenderingHint property to ensure optimized text. Among your choices are SingleBitPerPixelGridFit (fastest performance and lowest quality), AntiAliasGridFit (better quality but slower performance), and ClearTypeGridFit (the best quality on an LCD display). Or, you can use the SystemDefault value to use whatever font smoothing settings the user has configured. Figure 7-5 compares different font smoothing modes.

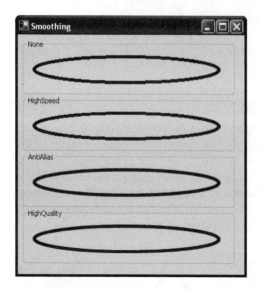

Figure 7-4. *Smoothing modes for shapes*

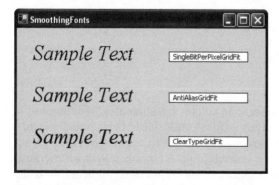

Figure 7-5. *Smoothing modes for fonts*

Pens

In Chapter 2, you learned about many of the GDI+ basics, including fonts, colors, points, and rectangles. However, GDI+ drawing code also uses other details like brushes and pens.

Pens are used to draw lines when you use the shape or curve drawing methods from the Graphics class. You can retrieve a standard pen using one of the static properties from the System.Drawing.Pens class, as shown below. These pens all have a width of 1; they differ only in their color.

```
Pen pen = Pens.Black;
```

You also can use the SystemPens class (which provides pens that correspond to various Windows color scheme settings, like the control background color or the highlight menu text color), or you can create a Pen object on your own, and configure all the properties described in Table 7-4.

```
Pen pen = new Pen(Color.Red);
pen.DashCap = DashCap.Triangle;
pen.DashStyle = DashStyle.DashDotDot;
e.Graphics.DrawLine(pen, 0, 0, 10, 0);
pen.Dispose();
```

Note When creating a new pen object, it's good practice to call Dispose() to release the pen when you no longer need it because it holds on to unmanaged resources. However, when using one of the ready-made pens from Pens or SystemPens, you must never dispose the object.

Table 7-4. *Basic Pen Properties*

Member	Description
Alignmentt	The alignment determines where the outline is drawn when you create a closed shape. By default, the alignment is PenAlignment.Center, which places the outline just outside the shape. PenAlignment.Inset draws the pen outline directly on the shape. (The difference is demonstrated with an example in this section.) Other PenAlignment values are not supported and are treated equivalently to PenAlignment.Center.
Color	Sets the color of the line that the pen draws.
DashPattern	Defines a dash style for broken lines using an array of dashes and spaces.
DashStyle	Defines a dash style for broken lines using the DashStyle enumeration.
LineJoin	Defines how overlapping lines in a shape will be joined together.
PenType	The type of fill that will be used for the line. Typically this will be SolidColor, but you also can use a gradient, bitmap texture, or hatch pattern by supplying a brush object when you create the pen. You cannot set the PenType through this property because it is read-only.
StartCap and EndCap	Determine how the beginning and ends of lines will be rendered. You can also define a custom line cap by creating a CustomLineCap object (typically by using a GraphicsPath), and then assigning it to the CustomStartCap or CustomEndCap property.
Width	The pixel width of lines drawn by this pen.

Pen Alignment

There is one notorious quirk with painting and drawing in GDI+. For unpleasant historical reasons, the DrawXxx() methods always extend an extra pixel below and to the right. For example, imagine you use this painting code:

```
Rectangle rect = new Rectangle(10, 10, 110, 110);
Pen pen = new Pen(Color.Red, 1);
e.Graphics.DrawRectangle(pen, rect);
e.Graphics.FillRectangle(Brushes.Blue, rect);
pen.Dispose();
```

Because both the DrawRectangle() and FillRectangle() methods use the same coordinates, you would expect that the fill operation completely overwrites the outline. (Usually, you'd reverse these two lines so that the outline is painted after the shape.) However, this isn't what happens. Instead, the originally red border still shows through, but only on the bottom and right edges (see Figure 7-6).

Figure 7-6. *An uneven border*

The DrawRectangle() method actually drew a larger rectangle than FillRectangle()—instead of 100 pixels, it used a height and width of 101 pixels.

It's important to understand this problem, because it doesn't necessarily disappear in real-world situations. For example, imagine you use a thicker pen:

```
Pen pen = new Pen(Color.Red, 11);
```

Now what's the result? It's not hard to figure out once you realize that the Pen.Alignment property is responsible for the slightly unusual behavior. By default, the alignment of any pen is PenAlignment.Center. In other words, the center of the line lies along the shape (taking one pixel), with five pixels of border visible outside the square, and five inside. Because the current code draws the shape and then fills it, you'll see only the outside of the border (meaning the border will appear to be 5 pixels wide in total). Of course, because the bottom edge is offset by that extra pixel, it is actually 6 pixels.

■**Note** If you use an even number for the pen width, like 10 or 12, all sides will appear equal. That's because the midline takes one pixel, leaving an uneven number of pixels (9 or 11) to be split over both sides. This uneven number of pixels leads to a fractional value on each side of the midline (4.5 or 5.5). This fraction is rounded up so that the width on both sides is the same (5 or 6). Strange but true.

You can change the alignment behavior so that lines are always drawn where you expect, right along the shape's edge. To do this, you need to make sure you're using a pen that's more than 1 pixel wide, and you need to set the alignment to PenAlignment.Inset:

```
Rectangle rect = new Rectangle(10, 10, 110, 110);
Pen pen = new Pen(Color.Red, 2);
pen.Alignment = PenAlignment.Inset;
```

```
e.Graphics.DrawRectangle(pen, rect);
e.Graphics.FillRectangle(Brushes.Blue, rect);
pen.Dispose();
```

Now the outline of the shape is drawn exactly where you would expect, and the fill operation overwrites it, leaving no visible border. If you create a thicker pen, it lies entirely inside the region of the square.

Figure 7-7 shows the difference between inset and centered alignment more clearly. In this example, the outline drawing is being performed *after* the shape filling, and an extra outline is used to indicate where the edge of the square fill falls. As you can see, the inset alignment paints a border inside this line, while the centered alignment splits the difference.

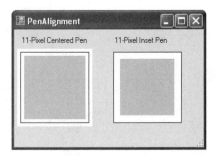

Figure 7-7. *Comparing pen alignment*

Pen Styling

There are a few other details you can use to style the borders you draw. Line caps determine the appearance of the start and end of a line (in an unclosed figure), and you can set them using the StartCap and EndCap properties of the Pen. Figure 7-8 shows your basic options (not including custom caps through the CustomStartCap or CustomEndCap properties).

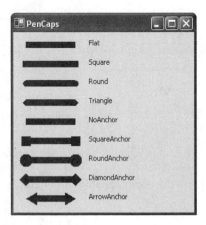

Figure 7-8. *Line caps*

You also can change the way the line itself is drawn using the DashStyle property. All of these options allow you to create broken lines according to a set pattern (see Figure 7-9).

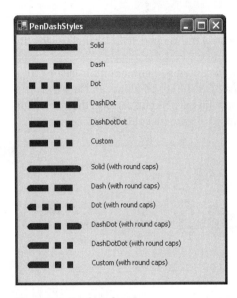

Figure 7-9. *Dash styles*

Finally, you can use the LineJoin property to change how the corners of a shape are rendered. For example, you can have a sharp edge (Mitered, the default), an angled edge (Bevel), or a rounded corner (Round). Figure 7-10 shows your options.

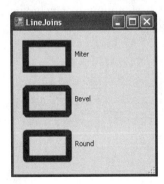

Figure 7-10. *Line joins*

To see the drawing code for all of these examples, refer to the downloadable content for this chapter.

Brushes

Brushes are used to fill the space between lines. Brushes are used when drawing text or when using any of the fill methods of the Graphics class for painting the inside of a shape.

You can quickly retrieve a predefined solid brush using a static property from the Brushes class, or the SystemBrushes class (which provides brushes that correspond to various Windows color scheme settings, like the control background color or the highlight menu text color).

```
Brush brush = SystemBrushes.Menu;
e.Graphics.FillRectangle(brush, 0, 0, 50, 50);
```

Finally, you can create a custom brush. You need to decide what type of brush you are creating. Solid brushes are created from the SolidBrush class, while other classes (HatchBrush, LinearGradientBrush, PathGradientBrush, and TextureBrush) allow fancier options. The next four sections consider these different types of brushes.

It's also worth noting that you can create a pen that draws using the fill style of a brush. This technique allows you to draw lines that are filled with gradients and textures. To do so, begin by creating the appropriate brush, and then create a new pen. One of the overloaded pen constructor methods accepts a reference to a brush—that's the one you need to use for a brush-based pen.

Here's an example:

```
Brush brush = new HatchBrush(HatchStyle.DiagonalCross,
  Color.Blue, Color.LightYellow);

// Create a pen that uses this hatch pattern (use a large enough width
// to see the fill pattern).
Pen pen = new Pen(brush, 10);
...
// Release both objects.
brush.Dispose();
pen.Dispose();
```

■**Tip** When you use DrawString() to render some text, you need to supply a brush, not a pen. That gives you some interesting possibilities—for example, you can create outline text or text filled with a texture or gradient by using more exotic brush types.

The HatchBrush

A HatchBrush has a foreground color, a background color, and a hatch style that determines how these colors are combined. Typically, colors are interspersed using stripes, grids, or dots, but you can even select unusual pattern styles like bricks, confetti, weave, and shingles.

Following is the code for a simple brush demonstration program that displays the available hatch brush styles. Figure 7-11 shows the result.

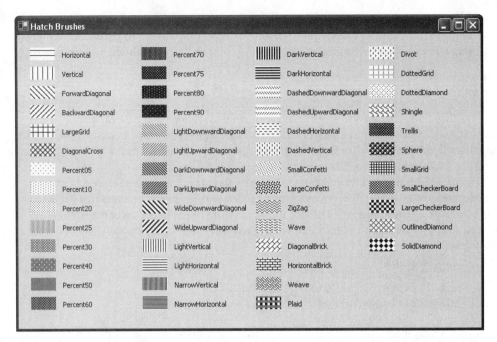

Figure 7-11. *HatchBrush styles*

Here's the code that creates this form:

```
private void HatchBrushes_Paint(object sender,
 System.Windows.Forms.PaintEventArgs e)
{
    int y = 20;
    int x = 20;
    Font font = new Font("Tahoma", 8);

    // Enumerate over all the styles.
    foreach (HatchStyle brushStyle in Enum.GetValues(typeof(HatchStyle)))
    {
        HatchBrush brush =
          new HatchBrush(brushStyle, Color.Blue, Color.LightYellow);

        // Fill a rectangle with the brush.
        e.Graphics.FillRectangle(brush, x, y, 40, 20);

        // Display the brush name.
        e.Graphics.DrawString(brushStyle.ToString(), font,
          Brushes.Black, 50 + x, y + 5);
```

```
        y += 30;
        if ((y + 30) > ClientSize.Height)
        {
            y = 20;
            x += 180;
        }
        brush.Dispose();
    }
    font.Dispose();
}
```

The LinearGradientBrush

The LinearGradientBrush allows you to blend two colors in a gradient pattern. You can choose any two colors (as with the hatch brush) and then choose to blend horizontally (from left to right), vertically (from top to bottom), diagonally (from the top-left corner to the bottom-right corner), or diagonally backward (from the top-right to the bottom-left corner). You also can specify the origin point for either side of the gradient.

Here's an example that fills a rectangle with a gradient:

```
int y = 20;
int x = 20;
int size = 100;
Rectangle rect = new Rectangle(x, y, size, size);
LinearGradientBrush brush = new LinearGradientBrush(rect,
  Color.Violet, Color.White, LinearGradientMode.BackwardDiagonal);
e.Graphics.FillRectangle(brush, x, y, size, size);
brush.Dispose();
```

Figure 7-12 shows the different gradient styles.

Figure 7-12. *The LinearGradientBrush*

The PathGradientBrush

For a truly unique effect, you can create a gradient that follows the path of a closed shape. In order to pull off this trick, you need to use the GraphicsPath class, which is discussed later in this chapter. Essentially, the GraphicsPath allows you to combine any combination of lines and shapes into a single figure.

Here's an example that creates a path that simply wraps a single ellipse, and then uses that path to create a PathGradientBrush.

```
// Create the path (which determines the shape of the gradient).
GraphicsPath path = new GraphicsPath();
int size = 150;
path.AddEllipse(10, 10, size, size);

// Create the brush, and set its colors.
PathGradientBrush brush = new PathGradientBrush(path);
brush.SurroundColors = new Color[] { Color.White };
brush.CenterColor = Color.Violet;

// Paint the gradient.
e.Graphics.FillRectangle(brush, 10, 10, size, size);

path.Dispose();
brush.Dispose();
```

Figure 7-13 shows the result.

Figure 7-13. *The PathGradientBrush*

The PathGradientBrush can take a bit of getting used to. In this example, it works because the region the code is painting and the region used for the brush match—they are both a 150 × 150 area starting at the point (10, 10). As a result, you see the full shape defined by the PathGradientBrush.

However, you'll get a less-intuitive result if you paint only a portion of the region defined by the brush. In this example, if you paint a smaller square or a square at a different location, you'll see only the part of the gradient circle that it overlaps.

The TextureBrush

Finally, the TextureBrush attaches a bitmap to a brush. The image is tiled in the painted portion of the brush, whether it is text or a simple rectangle. Here's an example that fills a form with a tiled bitmap. The result is shown in Figure 7-14.

```
private void TextureBrushExample_Paint(object sender,
 System.Windows.Forms.PaintEventArgs e)
{
    TextureBrush myBrush = new TextureBrush(Image.FromFile("tile.bmp"));
    e.Graphics.FillRectangle(myBrush, e.Graphics.ClipBounds);
}
```

Tip This example reads the image from a file, but a better approach is to embed the picture into your assembly and use the strongly typed resources feature described in Chapter 5. The online example uses this approach.

Figure 7-14. *The TextureBrush*

Drawing Text

As you've seen already, rendering graphics to a GDI+ drawing surface is as easy—you simply use the Graphics.DrawString() method and specify the text, a font, a brush, and the location:

```
e.Graphics.DrawString("Sample Text", font, brush, point);
```

However, there are several overloaded versions of the DrawString() method that give you some added features. One of the most interesting is the overload that replaces the Point object with a Rectangle object, as shown here:

```
e.Graphics.DrawString("Sample Text", font, brush, rectangle);
```

When you use this overload, .NET automatically wraps the text over multiple lines to fit inside the rectangle you've supplied. If the text doesn't completely fit in the rectangle, the remaining content is truncated. Although this technique is used only occasionally in a Windows interface, it's particularly handy when sending content to the printer. It saves you from needing to call methods like Font.GetHeight() and Graphics.MeasureString() to calculate word wrapping and line breaks manually. Of course, you'll need to fall back on the manual approach if you need to mix text with different colors or fonts, or if you want to have greater control over line alignment and (in the case of printing) spread text over multiple pages.

There are also several overloads of the DrawString() method that take a StringFormat parameter. A StringFormat object encapsulates a handful of layout and display details. One useful way to use StringFormat is to create blocks of wrapped text that are aligned differently than usual (for example, right-aligned or centered). To do this, you simply set the Alignment property (to center each line of text horizontally) and the LineAlignment property (to center the block of text), as shown here:

```
StringFormat stringFormat = new StringFormat();

// Center each line of text.
stringFormat.Alignment = StringAlignment.Center;

// Center the block of text (top to bottom) in the rectangle.
stringFormat.LineAlignment = StringAlignment.Center;

// Draw the text.
e.Graphics.DrawString(text, font, brush, rectangle, stringFormat);
```

You also can use the StringFormat object to configure what happens with text that extends beyond the bounds of the rectangle by setting the Trimming property. You can choose to chop it off at the letter (Character), to leave the last full word (Word), and to add an ellipsis (...) at the end to signify missing text (EllipsisCharacter or EllipsisWord). For a more unusual result, try EllipsisPath, which always removes the middle of the string to fit, and substitutes an ellipsis (similar to the way a path like c:\MyFiles\MyDocuments\MyDoc.doc can be replaced with c:\MyFiles\...\MyDoc.doc).

Figure 7-15 shows a text application that lets you manipulate these three settings.

Finally, there's one more trick hidden in the StringFormat object. You can use it to create perfectly rotated vertical text by adjusting the FormatFlags property:

```
StringFormat stringFormat = new StringFormat();
stringFormat.FormatFlags = StringFormatFlags.DirectionVertical;
```

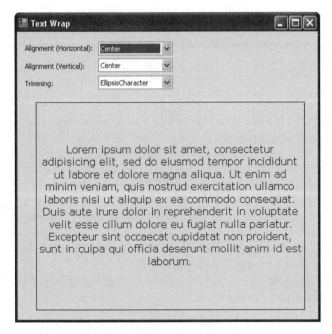

Figure 7-15. *Wrapping text*

The TextRenderer

.NET 2.0 adds a new TextRenderer class (in the System.Windows.Forms namespace), which implements a slightly different model for text rendering. Essentially, the TextRenderer draws text using GDI (or Uniscribe for non-Western characters) rather than GDI+. There are a few reasons why you might prefer to use the TextRenderer instead of the standard Graphics.DrawString() method:

- The rendering quality for international text has been improved regularly. As a result, GDI draws better quality text than GDI+ when using these complex scripts. Similarly, if the Windows operating system is updated to support new languages, the GDI drawing methods will draw these scripts correctly while GDI+ likely will not, even with the correct font.

- The Windows Forms controls often use GDI. In some cases (possibly when extending one of these controls), you might want to draw text that matches *exactly*. If you use GDI+, the alignment and smoothing may differ subtly but noticeably.

- GDI+ locks font files for the duration of the application's lifetime, making it difficult to update fonts.

Using the TextRenderer class is easy, as it exposes only two methods: MeasureText() and DrawText(), although there are multiple overloads of both.

Here's an example that draws text using the TextRenderer when a Paint event fires:

```
private void Form1_Paint(PaintEventArgs e)
{
    TextFormatFlags flags = TextFormatFlags.Bottom | TextFormatFlags.EndEllipsis;
    TextRenderer.DrawText(e.Graphics, "This text drawn with GDI.", this.Font,
        new Rectangle(10, 10, 100, 50), SystemColors.ControlText, flags);
}
```

The Windows Forms team faced a bit of a dilemma when they created the TextRenderer—namely, whether they should use it for better rendering in the standard .NET controls, even though it could alter existing applications (due to subtly different measuring and wrapping conventions). They settled on allowing controls to decide what rendering behavior to use based on a new Control.UseCompatibleTextRendering property. This property defaults to true, which means that the control should use the same rendering as it did in .NET 1.x. If you set this property to false, however, the control should switch to the TextRenderer. Of course, it's up to the control itself to check this property in its painting code and use the TextRenderer—simply setting the property on a control that doesn't use it has no effect. However, you'll notice that the .NET controls do respect the UseCompatibleTextRendering property.

To have the least effect on existing applications, UseCompatibleTextRendering defaults to true. Rather than set this property for each control in your application, you can call the Application. SetCompatibleTextRenderingDefault() method. In fact, every new Windows application created with Visual Studio 2005 automatically inserts a call to this method that passes an argument of false, thereby upgrading all standard controls to the TextRenderer.

The GraphicsPath

As you've learned, the Graphics class allows you to draw all the basic ingredients—lines, rectangles, ellipses, arcs, polygons, curves, and strings of text. The GraphicsPath allows you to combine a group of these elements into a single unit. You can then draw them all at once, or perform other tasks like hit testing.

To build a GraphicsPath object, you simply create a new instance, and use the methods in Table 7-5 to add all the required elements. Here's an example that creates a GraphicsPath made up of an ellipse and a rectangle:

```
GraphicsPath path = new GraphicsPath();
path.AddEllipse(0, 0, 100, 50);
path.AddRectangle(new Rectangle(100, 50, 100, 50));
```

These two shapes can overlap, but they don't need to. Either way, both shapes are merged into one logical entity for future manipulation. Once you've created the GraphicsPath object, you can copy it onto the drawing surface using the DrawPath() and FillPath() methods of the Graphics object:

```
e.Graphics.DrawPath(pen, path);
```

When you're finished, remember to clean up by disposing the path:

```
path.Dispose();
```

Using the GraphicsPath, you also can create a solid-filled figure out of line segments. To do this, you first call the StartFigure() method. Then you add the required curves and lines using the appropriate methods. When finished, you call the CloseFigure() method to close off the shape by drawing a line from the endpoint to the starting point. You can use the StartFigure() and CloseFigure() methods multiple times to add several closed figures to a single GraphicsPath object.

Here's an example:

```
GraphicsPath path = new GraphicsPath();
path.StartFigure();
path.AddArc(10, 10, 100, 100, 20, 50);
path.AddLine(20, 100, 70, 230);
path.CloseFigure();
```

Table 7-5. *GraphicsPath Methods*

Method	Description
AddArc()	Adds an arc representing a portion of an ellipse specified by a rectangle and two angles.
AddBezier() and AddBeziers()	Adds the infamous and attractive Bezier curve, which is defined by four control points.
AddClosedCurve()	Adds a curve, and then closes it off by connecting the end points.
AddCurve()	Adds a curve (technically, a cardinal spline).
AddEllipse()	Adds an ellipse defined by a bounding rectangle.
AddLine() and AddLines()	Adds a line (or a series of lines) connecting two points.
AddPath()	Adds another GraphicsPath object to this GraphicsPath object.
AddPie()	Adds a "piece of pie" shape defined by an ellipse and two angles.
AddPolygon()	Adds a multisided polygon defined by an array of points.
AddRectangle() and AddRectangles()	Adds one and more ordinary rectangles.
AddString()	Adds a string of text in a given font.
StartFigure() and CloseFigure()	StartFigure() defines the start of a new closed figure. When you use CloseFigure(), the starting point will be joined to the end point by an additional line.
Flatten()	Converts existing curves into a series of connected line segments.
Transform(), Warp(), and Widen()	Applies a matrix transform, a warp transform (defined by a rectangle and a parallelogram), or an expansion, respectively.

More-Advanced GDI+

Now that you've learned the basic techniques for drawing with pens, brushes, and the rendering smarts of the Graphics class, it's worth considering some of the more-powerful features of GDI+. In this section, you'll take a look at alpha blending, clipping, and coordinate transformations.

Alpha Blending

Sophisticated graphics often incorporate some level of semitransparency. For example, you may draw transparent text or shapes that allow the background to show through. This technique is called *alpha blending*, because the alpha value indicates the transparency of any color. Alpha values range from 0 to 255, where 255 represents a fully opaque color and 0 represents a completely transparent color.

As you learned in Chapter 2, every color in .NET is represented by the Color structure, and has a separate alpha, red, green, and blue component. Technically, when you use an alpha color that's anything other than 255, the following formula is used to blend the color with the background color:

```
displayColor = sourceColor × alpha / 255 + backgroundColor × (255 - alpha) / 255
```

The important detail is that alpha blending is performed on individual pixels. For example, if you draw a semitransparent rectangle, each pixel in the rectangle is blended with the pixel immediately underneath. This allows the obscured content to show through. (Depending on the Graphics.CompositingQuality setting, the values of nearby pixels also may be taken into account when calculating the background color.)

To try this out, you can use the following painting code. It paints three rectangles, with different levels of transparency, and then renders some semitransparent text for variety.

```
// Fill the background with a tile.
Bitmap bitmap = Properties.Resources.Pic;
TextureBrush brush = new TextureBrush(bitmap);
e.Graphics.FillRectangle(brush, ClientRectangle);
brush.Dispose();
bitmap.Dispose();

// Draw some solid content.
Color color = Color.Yellow;
int penWidth = 80;
Pen opaquePen = new Pen(color, penWidth);
e.Graphics.DrawLine(opaquePen, 0, 50, 200, 20);
opaquePen.Dispose();

// Make the color partly transparent (50%).
Color semiTransparentColor = Color.FromArgb(128, color.R, color.G, color.B);
Pen semiTransparentPen = new Pen(semiTransparentColor, penWidth);
e.Graphics.DrawLine(semiTransparentPen, 0, 200, 200, 140);
semiTransparentPen.Dispose();

// Make the color very transparent (70% transparent).
Color veryTransparentColor = Color.FromArgb(77, color.R, color.G, color.B);
Pen veryTransparentPen = new Pen(veryTransparentColor, penWidth);
e.Graphics.DrawLine(veryTransparentPen, 0, 350, 200, 260);
veryTransparentPen.Dispose();
```

```
// Draw some transparent text.
Brush transparentBrush = new SolidBrush(semiTransparentColor);
e.Graphics.DrawString("TRANSPARENT", new Font("Verdana", 36, FontStyle.Bold),
  transparentBrush, 80, 150);
transparentBrush.Dispose();
```

Figure 7-16 shows the result.

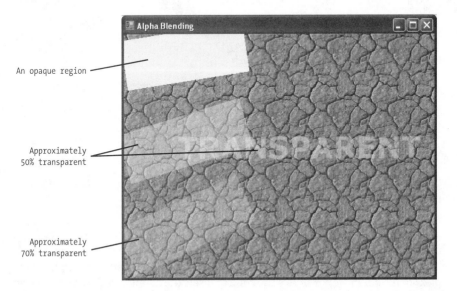

Figure 7-16. *Alpha blending*

Keen eyes will notice that the text doesn't appear to be equally transparent. The portions of the text that are over the semitransparent region (the letters "TRA") are more opaque. To understand why, you need to remember the order in which the drawing was performed. The text was added last, at which point it was blended with the current background. The current background includes the semitransparent region that is already shaded more yellow, and thus the blended text over this portion also becomes more yellow.

Clipping

Clipping is a technique that restricts drawing to a specific region. By default, your clipping region is the entire graphics surface. That means when you paint to a form, you have free range over the entire client area. When you paint to a picture box or panel, you can draw content anywhere in the client region of that control.

Although it's not immediately obvious, you can restrict the painting region even further. Usually, you'll do this to produce interesting effects. For example, you could set the clipping region to allow drawing only within a specific rectangular region. You can then paint content over the entire graphics surface, but only the content that overlaps with the rectangular region will appear.

To use clipping in this way, you need to set the Graphics.Clipping property before you paint. The Clipping property accepts a Region object representing the area where drawing is allowed. (Region objects represent the interior or closed figure, and are used primarily for clipping and hit testing, which you'll see later.)

Here's an example that creates a region based on a rectangle, sets the clipping, and then draws some content:

```
// Draw the rectangle.
Rectangle rectangle = new Rectangle(10, 10, 250, 50);
e.Graphics.DrawRectangle(Pens.Black, rectangle);

// Set the clipping so that any additional content will appear only when it
// overlaps with tis rectangle.
Region clippingRegion = new Region(rectangle);
e.Graphics.Clip = clippingRegion;

// Draw in the clipped region.
e.Graphics.DrawString("Clipped",
  new Font("Verdana", 36, FontStyle.Bold), Brushes.Black, 10, 10);
clippingRegion.Dispose();
```

When you're ready to return to normal drawing (and get access to the entire drawing surface), call ResetClip():

```
e.Graphics.ResetClip();
```

There are two ways to create a Region—from a rectangle (as shown in this example), and from a GraphicsPath. You'll need to use the GraphicsPath if you want to perform clipping with a more complex shape. For example, here's the code that sets the clipping region to an ellipse:

```
// Create the GraphicsPath with an ellipse.
GraphicsPath path = new GraphicsPath();
Rectangle rectangle = new Rectangle(10, 10, 250, 50);
path.AddEllipse(rectangle);

// Render the ellipse on the drawing surface.
e.Graphics.DrawPath(Pens.Red, path);

// Set the clipping.
Region clippingRegion = new Region(path);
e.Graphics.Clip = clippingRegion;

// Draw inside the ellipse.
e.Graphics.DrawString("Clipped",
  new Font("Verdana", 36, FontStyle.Bold), Brushes.Black, 10, 10);
clippingRegion.Dispose();
path.Dispose();
```

Figure 7-17 shows this example with and without clipping.

 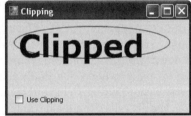

Figure 7-17. *Clipping to an ellipse (left), and not clipping (right)*

This technique allows for some truly interesting effects. For example, you can create a path out of a complex object like a string, and then create a region based on this path. If you do, the region where drawing is allowed is inside the outline of the letters. Here's the code you need:

```
// Clip to path (which represents text).
GraphicsPath path = new GraphicsPath();
path.AddString("Clipped", new FontFamily("Verdana"), 0, 70, new Point(10, 130),
  new StringFormat());
e.Graphics.DrawPath(Pens.Blue, path);

// Set the clipping.
Region clippingRegion = new Region(path);
e.Graphics.Clip = clippingRegion;

// Draw a series of ellipses in the clipped region.
for (int i = 0; i < 40; i++)
{
    e.Graphics.DrawEllipse(Pens.Red, 180 - i*3, 180 - i*3, i*6, i*6);
}
clippingRegion.Dispose();
path.Dispose();
```

Figure 7-18 shows this example with and without clipping.

 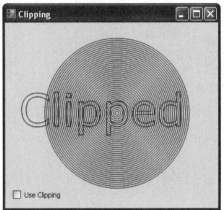

Figure 7-18. *Clipping to the outline of a text string (left), and not clipping (right)*

Coordinate Systems and Transformations

By default, when you draw GDI+ shapes, you use a coordinate system that designates the top-left corner as (0, 0). The *x*-axis value increases as you move to the right, and the *y*-axis value increases as you move down. The point (Form.ClientSize.Width - 1, Form.ClientSize.Height - 1) corresponds to the bottom-right corner of a form. Each unit corresponds to one pixel. This is nothing new—it's the same coordinate system you examined with control basics in Chapter 2. However, the Graphics class also gives you the flexibility to change the unit of measurement, point of origin, and rotation.

To change the unit of measurement, you simply set the PageUnit property of the Graphics class. You can use one of several values from the GraphicsUnit enumeration, including Pixel (the default), Display (the same as pixels when drawing to the screen or 1/100 inch for printers), Document (1/300 inch), Inch, Millimeter, and Point (1/72 of an inch).

```
e.Graphics.PageUnit = Graphics.Inch;
```

The ability to change the point of origin is more useful. It uses the Graphics. TranslateTranform() method, which accepts the coordinates of the new point that should become (0,0). Using the code below, the point at (50, 50) will become the new (0,0) origin. Points to the left or right of this origin must be specified using negative values.

```
e.Graphics.TranslateTransform(50, 50);
```

This trick is fairly handy. For example, it can allow you to perform simpler calculations by assuming the top-left point of your drawing is (0, 0). You also can use several transforms in a row and repeat the same drawing code. The figure you are drawing would then appear at several different points in the window, as shown in Figure 7-19.

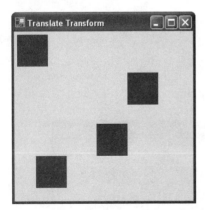

Figure 7-19. *Using translate transforms*

Here's the code that creates this effect:

```
private void Transform_Paint(object sender,
 System.Windows.Forms.PaintEventArgs e)
{
    // Draw several squares in different places.
    DrawRectangle(e.Graphics);
    e.Graphics.TranslateTransform(180, 60);
    DrawRectangle(e.Graphics);
    e.Graphics.TranslateTransform(-50, 80);
    DrawRectangle(e.Graphics);
    e.Graphics.TranslateTransform(-100, 50);
    DrawRectangle(e.Graphics);
}

private void DrawRectangle(Graphics g)
{
    Pen drawingPen = new Pen(Color.Red, 30);

    // Draw a rectangle at a fixed position.
    g.DrawRectangle(drawingPen, new Rectangle(20, 20, 20, 20));

    drawingPen.Dispose();
}
```

■**Note** Transforms are cumulative, so transforming by (50, 50) and then (20,10) is equivalent to a single (70, 60) transform.

The final transformation considered here is a rotational one. It uses the Graphics.RotateTransform() method, which rotates the coordinate system using an angle or matrix. It's important to remember that rotations are performed around the point of origin. If you haven't performed any translation transformations, this point will be in the top-right corner of the form.

The next example uses a translation transform to move the center point to the middle of the form, and then rotates text around that point with successive rotational transforms. The result is shown in Figure 7-20.

```
private void RotateTransform_Paint(object sender,
 System.Windows.Forms.PaintEventArgs e)
{
    // Optimize text quality.
    e.Graphics.TextRenderingHint = TextRenderingHint.AntiAliasGridFit;

    // Move origin to center of form so we can rotate around that.
    e.Graphics.TranslateTransform(this.Width / 2 - 30, this.Height / 2 - 30);
```

```
        DrawText(e.Graphics);
        e.Graphics.RotateTransform(45);
        DrawText(e.Graphics);
        e.Graphics.RotateTransform(75);
        DrawText(e.Graphics);
        e.Graphics.RotateTransform(160);
        DrawText(e.Graphics);
    }

    private void DrawText(Graphics g)
    {
        g.DrawString("Text", new Font("Verdana", 30, FontStyle.Bold),
            Brushes.Black, 0, 10);
    }
```

Figure 7-20. *Using rotational transforms*

There's much more that you can do with coordinate systems. To tackle advanced issues, check out the topics in the MSDN Help or look for a dedicated GDI+ book, such as *Pro .NET Graphics Programming* (Apress).

Performing a Screen Capture

Some specialized programs need to take a snapshot of the current display, with the Windows background and any visible applications. In the past, developers were forced to rely on GDI to get this functionality. However, .NET 2.0 adds a new Graphics.CopyFromScreen() method that simplifies life dramatically.

To use CopyFromScreen(), you need to first create an in-memory Bitmap object that has the same dimensions as the current screen.

```
Bitmap bmp = new Bitmap(Screen.PrimaryScreen.Bounds.Width,
    Screen.PrimaryScreen.Bounds.Height);
```

Now you can get a Graphics object for this Bitmap, and use the CopyFromScreen() method to capture the current screen. You need to supply coordinates that specify the top-left point of the screen where you want to start your capture, the top-left point in the Bitmap where you want to place the screen capture, and the size of the image you want to capture. The following code gets the entire screen.

```
Graphics g = Graphics.FromImage(bmp);
  g.CopyFromScreen(0, 0, 0, 0, bmp.Size);
```

Once you've captured the screen, you can continue by saving it (use the Bitmap.Save() method) or displaying it. Figure 7-21 shows a program that copies the captured screen to a picture box, which is placed inside a scrollable panel.

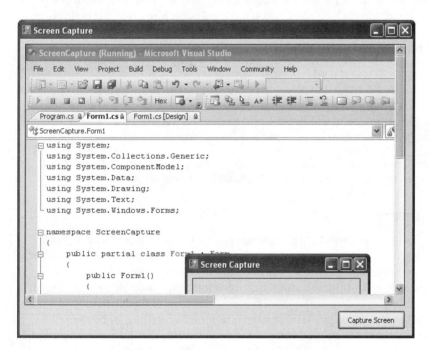

Figure 7-21. *Capturing the current screen*

Here's the code that captures the screen:

```
private void cmdCapture_Click(object sender, EventArgs e)
{
    if (pictureBox1.Image != null) pictureBox1.Image.Dispose();

    Bitmap bmp = new Bitmap(Screen.PrimaryScreen.Bounds.Width,
        Screen.PrimaryScreen.Bounds.Height);
    Graphics g = Graphics.FromImage(bmp);
    g.CopyFromScreen(0, 0, 0, 0, bmp.Size);
    g.Dispose();
    pictureBox1.Image = bmp;
    pictureBox1.Size = bmp.Size;
}
```

Optimizing GDI+ Painting

Painting is a performance-sensitive area for any application. Slow refresh rates and screen flicker may not stop your application from performing its work, but it will make it seem old, unprofessional, and underpowered. This section considers some techniques that optimize drawing with GDI+ surfaces.

Painting and Debugging

Debugging drawing code can be frustrating. For example, consider what happens if you set a breakpoint in the painting code for a form. When the breakpoint is reached, the code enters break mode, the IDE appears, and the application window is hidden. When you run the next line of code, the program is redisplayed, which triggers a second Paint event.

To escape this endless sequence of repainting, you can use a couple of tricks:

- If you have a high-resolution monitor, you can run your application alongside the program you are testing. Then, when your program enters break mode, the IDE window does not appear on top of your program window, and a repaint is not triggered. (Alternatively, you can use two monitors at once.)

- Alternatively, you can set the TopMost property of your form to true, which keeps it superimposed on your IDE window at all times. This should also avoid a repaint.

Double Buffering

You may notice that when you repaint a window frequently it flickers madly. The flicker is caused because, with each paint event, the image is erased and then redrawn object by object. The flash you see is the blank background that precedes the redrawn content.

You can reduce flickering by preventing a control or form from drawing its background. If you do, your code must begin by painting a background using one of the fill methods from the Graphics class. Otherwise, the original content remains underneath the new content.

To disable background painting, all you need to do is override the OnPaintBackground() method for the form or control and do nothing. In other words, you *won't* call the base OnPaintBackground() method.

```
protected override void OnPaintBackground(
   System.Windows.Forms.PaintEventArgs pevent)
{
   // Do nothing.
}
```

If you are filling a form or control with a custom background color, you should always follow this step, as it can improve performance dramatically. Otherwise, your window will flicker noticeably between the default background color and the color you paint every time you redraw the form.

Instead of overriding the OnPaintBackground() method, you can use the SetStyle() method and set the AllPaintingInWmPaint style to true. This tells the form to ignore messages asking it to repaint its background.

```
this.SetStyle(ControlStyles.AllPaintingInWmPaint, true);
```

Disabling the automatic background painting reduces flicker, but the flicker remains. To remove it completely, you can use a technique known as *double buffering*. With double buffering, an image is built in memory instead of on the surface of a form or control. When the image is completed, it's drawn in one shot to the form. The process of drawing takes just as long, but the refresh is faster because it is delayed until the image is completely rendered. Hence, there is very little flicker.

Although you could perform double buffering manually by drawing on an in-memory Image object, there's no need to. In .NET 2.0 all forms provide a DoubleBuffered property. If you set this property to true, GDI+ performs automatic double buffering. Even though your code appears to paint directly on the form surface, it really paints to an in-memory bitmap that has the same bounds as the client area of the form. When the painting code ends, the bitmap is copied onto the form in a single operation.

To try this out, consider an example that uses a simple animation, shrinking and growing an ellipse automatically (see Figure 7-22).

Figure 7-22. *Using double buffering*

The form is redrawn in response to the tick of a Timer control:

```
private bool isShrinking = false;
private int extraSize = 0;

// This code is triggered in response to the timer tick.
private void tmrRefresh_Tick(object sender,
 System.EventArgs e)
{
    // Change the circle dimensions.
    if (isShrinking)
        extraSize--;
    else
        extraSize++;

    // Change the sizing direction if needed.
    if (extraSize > (this.Width - 150))
        isShrinking = true;
    else if (extraSize < 1)
        isShrinking = false;

    // Repaint the form.
    this.Invalidate();
}
```

The paint code examines the state of a check box and decides whether or not it will implement double buffering.

```
private void DoubleBuffering_Paint(object sender,
  System.Windows.Forms.PaintEventArgs e)
{
    // Check if double buffering is needed.
    this.DoubleBuffered = chkDoubleBuffer.Checked;

    Graphics g = e.Graphics;
    g.SmoothingMode = System.Drawing.Drawing2D.SmoothingMode.HighQuality;

    // Draw a rectangle.
    Pen drawingPen = new Pen(Color.Black, 10);
    g.FillRectangle(Brushes.White, new Rectangle(new Point(0, 0),
                    this.ClientSize));
    g.DrawEllipse(drawingPen, 50, 50, 50 + extraSize, 50 + extraSize);
    drawingPen.Dispose();
}
```

When you test this application, you'll see that there is absolutely no flicker in double-buffered mode. There is significant flicker without it.

▪**Tip** The DoubleBuffered property always caches the graphic content of the entire form. If you're animating only a small portion, you'll probably opt to implement double buffering on your own. That way, you can cache just the region you need to repaint, reducing the memory overhead of your application. The following section describes custom double buffering.

Double-Buffered Controls

There's one limitation with automatic double buffering—it works only if you can set the DoubleBuffered property, which is protected. That means the control itself has the ability to control how it uses double buffering for its painting logic, but the application consuming the control can't.

For forms, this isn't a problem, because you always derive a new form class when you create a custom form. But for other controls, this isn't the case. When you add a control to your form, you aren't deriving a new class—you're simply using the existing class. As a result, you won't be able to access the DoubleBuffered property for the individual controls on your form.

In most cases, this distinction makes perfect sense. The core .NET controls rely on the Windows API, not GDI+, so double buffering would have no effect. However, there are some cases where this limitation does have an effect—namely, when you're handling the Paint event in a control to perform custom drawing. In this case, you don't have the ability to switch on double buffering.

The most typical example is a container control like the Panel. Assume you want to paint some custom content just inside a specific panel, while the rest of the form contains ordinary .NET controls. To implement this logic, you respond to the Panel.Paint event. However, if you want to optimize the painting process using double buffering, you need to use one of two techniques:

- **Perform manual double buffering.** To do so, you perform all your drawing using an in-memory Bitmap object, and then you copy that bitmap to the drawing surface when you're finished using the Graphics.DrawImageUnscaled() method.

- **Create a custom control that derives from Panel.** Override the constructor and set the protected Control.DoubleBuffered property to true. Use this panel when you want a double-buffered painting surface.

Both of these options are reasonable solutions. Manual double buffering requires more work because you are essentially reimplementing a feature that exists in .NET. However, it can be useful if you're using it inside a custom control to buffer just part of the visible region, which allows you to reduce the amount of memory that's used. Here's the basic model:

```
// Create an in-memory graphic that matches the dimensions of the drawing
// surface.
bitmap = new Bitmap(ctrl.ClientRectangle.Width, ctrl.ClientRectangle.Height);
g = Graphics.FromImage(bitmap);
```

```
// Paint on this in-memory graphics surface in the same way that you paint
// with an ordinary Graphics object.
...

// Copy the final image to the drawing surface and dispose of it.
e.Graphics.DrawImageUnscaled(bitmap, 0, 0);
g.Dispose();
bitmap.Dispose();
```

Creating a custom control neatly solves the problem and keeps the programming model simple and well encapsulated, but it forces you to generate additional classes. Here's an example:

```
public partial class BufferedPanel : Panel
{
    public BufferedPanel()
    {
        this.DoubleBuffered = true;
    }
}
```

Note Setting the DoubleBuffered property to true is equivalent to setting the AllPaintingInWmPaint and OptimizedDoubleBuffer control styles to true. If you perform painting in OnPaintBackground() as well as OnPaint(), you should set the OptimizedDoubleBuffer property to true but not set the DoubleBuffered property. (One control that does this is the ToolStrip.) If you do set the DoubleBuffered property to true and you perform painting in OnPaintBackground(), your background may not be repainted correctly when you Alt+Tab from one program to another.

Figure 7-23 shows an example that compares different approaches to double buffering. On the left is a custom double-buffered panel, in the middle is an ordinary panel, and on the right is a panel with manual double buffering. Each panel has the same task—to draw a graphic using time-consuming rendering code over a form that shows a custom graphic. All three panels are transparent.

In this example, the custom control performs the best, because it's the only one that's able to combine the background painting (using the form graphic) and the foreground painting in one operation, resulting in no flicker. The ordinary panel performs by far the worst—there's noticeable flicker as it re-creates the arcs individually. The manually buffered example paints the graphic in one operation, but it still requires two operations to refresh itself. The first paints the background, and the second paints the buffered graphic. This adds some flicker. To get a better feel for the difference, try out this example in the downloadable code.

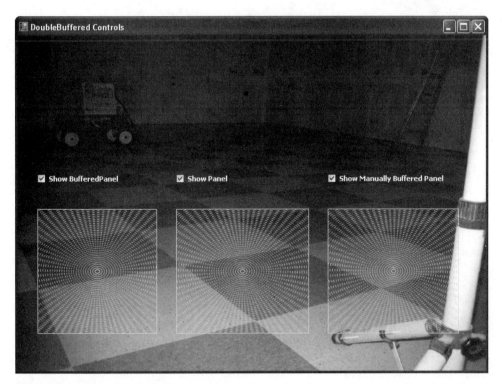

Figure 7-23. *Optimizing double buffering in a panel*

Painting Portions of a Window

In some cases, it just doesn't make sense to repaint the entire window when you need to update only a portion of the display. One example is a drawing program.

Consider a simple example program that allows the user to draw squares. Every time the user clicks on an area of the form, a new square is inserted (see Figure 7-24).

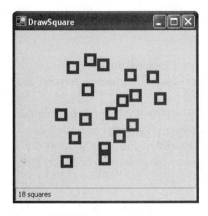

Figure 7-24. *A square-painting program*

To make sure this painting program keeps working even if the form is resized or minimized, all the painting is performed in the Paint event handler. When the user clicks with the mouse, a new square is created but not drawn. Instead, a rectangle object is added to a form-level collection so it can be tracked, and the form is invalidated. Not only does this offer better performance, it's also a conceptually solid design because you're separating your data (the square objects) from their visual representation (the drawing code).

```
// Store the squares that are painted on the form.
List<Rectangle> squares = new List<Rectangle>();

private void DrawSquare_MouseDown(object sender,
 System.Windows.Forms.MouseEventArgs e)
{
    // Define a new square based on where the user clicked.
    Rectangle square = new Rectangle(e.X, e.Y, 20, 20);
    squares.Add(square);

    // Request a repaint.
    Invalidate();
}
```

The painting logic then takes over, iterating through the collection, and drawing each rectangle. The number of squares that are currently being displayed is also written to a status bar at the end of this operation.

```
private void DrawSquare_Paint(object sender,
 System.Windows.Forms.PaintEventArgs e)
{
    Pen pen = new Pen(Color.Red, 10);
    foreach (Rectangle square in squares)
    {
        e.Graphics.DrawRectangle(pen, square);
    }
    pen.Dispose();
    lblCount.Text = " " + squares.Count.ToString() + " squares";
}
```

The problem with this code is that every time a rectangle is created, the entire form is redrawn. This causes noticeable screen flicker as the number of squares advances beyond 100. You can try this out using the sample code for this chapter.

There are two ways that you can remedy this problem. The fastest solution is to draw the square in two places: in the Paint logic *and* the MouseDown event handling code. With this approach, the MouseDown event handler does not need to invalidate the form. It draws the square directly, and stores enough information about the new rectangle for it to be successfully repainted if the window is minimized and restored. The potential drawback is that the code becomes significantly more tangled, especially if the drawing logic is complicated. To avoid writing the same code twice, you should separate the drawing logic into a separate subroutine that accepts a Graphics object and the item to draw. The following code snippet shows how this technique would work with the simple square painting program.

```
// Paint a square in response to a mouse click.
private void DrawSquare_MouseDown(object sender,
 System.Windows.Forms.MouseEventArgs e)
{
    Rectangle square = new Rectangle(e.X, e.Y, 20, 20);
    squares.Add(square);

    Graphics g = this.CreateGraphics();
    DrawRectangle(square, g);
    g.Dispose();
}

// Paint all the squares when the form needs to be refreshed
// in response to the Paint event.
private void DrawSquare_Paint(object sender,
 System.Windows.Forms.PaintEventArgs e)
{
    foreach (Rectangle square in squares)
    {
        DrawRectangle(square, e.Graphics);
    }
}

// This procedure performs the actual drawing, and is called by
// DrawSquare_MouseDown and DrawSquare_Paint.
private void DrawRectangle(Rectangle rect, Graphics g)
{
    Pen pen = new Pen(Color.Red, 10);
    g.DrawRectangle(drawingPen, rect);
    pen.Dispose();
    lblCount.Text = " " + squares.Count.ToString() + " squares";
}
```

A simpler solution is to use one of the overloaded versions on the Invalidate() method. This instructs Windows to repaint only a small portion of the window. The full painting code still runs (which could slow your application if the painting is complex), but only the specified region is repainted, thereby improving performance and drastically reducing screen flicker.

```
private void DrawSquare_MouseDown(object sender,
 System.Windows.Forms.MouseEventArgs e)
{
    Rectangle square = new Rectangle(e.X, e.Y, 20, 20);
    squares.Add(square);

    // Get a region that includes the square and its border.
    // Because the pen width is 10 pixels (and the center line is in
    // the middle), you'll need an extra 5 pixels on each side.
    square.Inflate(5, 5);
    Invalidate(square);
}
```

Finally, the last enhancement you can make is to modify the painting code to perform the repainting only if it falls in the invalidated region. You can determine the invalidated region by checking the PaintEventArgs.ClipRectangle property. For example, you could use conditional logic that paints the rectangle only if it falls into this region. In this situation, there isn't much performance benefit to be had because the step of painting the rectangle doesn't take much time (and the output isn't copied to the drawing surface anyway). However, if you need to perform a computationally intensive drawing task (for example, one that involves a gradient or a series of coordinate calculations), you can use this approach to avoid the work when it's not necessary.

■**Note** Another way to paint just a portion of a window is to develop owner-drawn controls that override their own OnPaint() methods. In Chapter 24, you'll see an example of a custom drawing program that demonstrates both the control-based approach and a pure GDI+ approach to drawing shape elements.

Hit Testing

The square painting program shown earlier presents some interesting possibilities. For example, you could use this code as the basis for a simple GDI+ drawing application. You probably would add controls that allow the user to draw more than one type of object. You would need to add a special class (perhaps called Shape) that encapsulates all the details about the drawn object, such as size, color, pen width, and so on. Your Paint event handler would then iterate through a collection of Shape objects and render all of them to the form using the appropriate information.

All these details are easy to implement, but what if you want to go another step and give the user the ability to select and manipulate shapes after they've been created? You'll need a way to respond to mouse actions and determine what shape the user is trying to select. Unfortunately, squares, ellipses, curves, and other shapes have no ability to capture mouse actions and raise the typical MouseDown and Click events. Instead, you need to intercept these events using the containing object (typically a form), and then manually determine whether a shape was clicked. This process is known as *hit testing*.

Hit Testing with Rectangles

.NET provides basic hit testing support through a Contains() method that's built into the Rectangle structure. It examines a supplied *x* and *y* coordinate, Point object, or Rectangle object, and returns true if it is located inside the Rectangle.

However, there are a couple of quirks that take some getting used to with Rectangle hit testing:

- A Rectangle is a combination of points (defined by a top-left corner, width, and height). It doesn't necessarily correspond to a region on the screen—that depends on whether you've drawn some sort of shape based on the Rectangle with one of the GDI+ drawing methods.

- The Rectangle is the only simple drawing structure that supports hit testing. That means that if you create another shape (like an ellipse), you need to convert its coordinates into a Rectangle object or use the GraphicsPath approach (described in the next section).

■Tip The Rectangle also provides methods that aren't considered here. For example, you can use Intersect() to return a Rectangle representing where two Rectangles intersect, Offset() to move it, and Inflate() to enlarge or reduce it.

The next example uses hit testing with the square-drawing program developed earlier. When the user right-clicks the form, the code loops through the collection of squares, and displays a message box for each one that contains the clicked point.

```
// Reacts to the Form.MouseDown event.
private void DrawSquare_MouseDown(object sender,
 System.Windows.Forms.MouseEventArgs e)
{
    if (e.Button == MouseButtons.Left)
    {
        // Add a square and update the screen.
        Rectangle square = new Rectangle(e.X, e.Y, 20, 20);
        squares.Add(square);
        square.Inflate(5, 5);
        Invalidate(square);
    }
    else if (e.Button == MouseButtons.Right)
    {
        // Search  for the clicked square.
        int squareNumber = 0;
        foreach (Rectangle square in squares)
        {
            squareNumber++;
```

```
        if (square.Contains(e.X, e.Y))
        {
            MessageBox.Show("Point inside square #" +
              squareNumber.ToString());
        }
      }
   }
}
```

Figure 7-25 shows what happens when the user clicks a square. Once you have determined which square was clicked, you could modify it and then invalidate the form, or allow drag-and-drop. Chapter 24 uses a similar, but more sophisticated, technique to create a vector-based drawing tool that allows users to draw, move, and resize shapes.

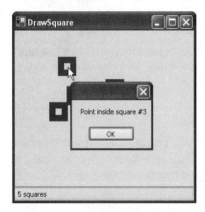

Figure 7-25. *Hit testing with squares*

Hit-Testing Nonrectangular Shapes

.NET does provide some help if you need to perform hit testing with a nonrectangular object. If you use the GraphicsPath object to create a shape (or combination of shapes), you can rely on the indispensable IsVisible() method, which accepts a point and returns true if this point is contained inside a closed figure in the GraphicsPath. This method works equally well, whether you click inside a prebuilt closed figure (like a square, ellipse, polygon, etc.), or if you click inside a figure you created with line segments using the StartFigure() and CloseFigure() methods of the GraphicsPath object.

```
private GraphicsPath path;

private void GraphicsPathExample_Paint(object sender,
 System.Windows.Forms.PaintEventArgs e)
{
    e.Graphics.SmoothingMode = SmoothingMode.AntiAlias;
    path = new GraphicsPath();
    path.StartFigure();
    path.AddArc(10, 10, 100, 100, 20, 50);
```

```
    path.AddLine(20, 50, 70, 230);
    path.CloseFigure();
    path.AddEllipse(120, 50, 80, 80);
    e.Graphics.FillPath(Brushes.White, path);
    e.Graphics.DrawPath(Pens.Black, path);
}

// Reacts to the Form.MouseDown event.
private void GraphicsPathExample_MouseDown(object sender,
 System.Windows.Forms.MouseEventArgs e)
{
    if (path.IsVisible(e.X, e.Y))
    {
        MessageBox.Show("You clicked inside the figure.");
    }
}
```

Figure 7-26 shows a successful use of hit testing with a nonrectangular shape.

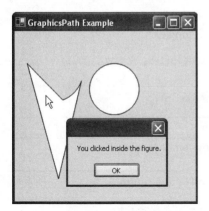

Figure 7-26. *Hit-testing a nonrectangular path*

Painting Windows Controls

The GDI+ classes allow you to build a drawing out of shapes, curves, and text. Using these drawing primitives, you can create more sophisticated elements. However, using GDI+ to draw a typical Windows control, like a check box or button, takes a significant amount of code.

Of course, Windows controls aren't rendered using GDI+. Instead, they're rendered by the system based on calls to the Windows API. You can get access to some of this functionality in .NET in two ways:

- The ControlPaint class, which allows you to draw standard (unthemed) Windows interface elements.

- The VisualStyleRenderer class, which allows you to draw themed Windows XP-style controls. The VisualStyleRenderer is new in .NET 2.0.

Although neither of these elements is technically a part of GDI+, both are useful in custom drawing scenarios. You'll examine them in the following sections.

The ControlPaint Class

The ControlPaint class offers methods for drawing standard Windows interface elements, like scroll buttons, borders, focus rectangles, and check boxes.

For example, if you want to create a special control that contains a list of items with check boxes, you have limited options. You can use control composition (and create contained check-box controls), but this limits the ways that you can use the check boxes and tailor the interface. Alternatively, you could attempt to draw your own and probably end up with a rather crude-looking square. With the ControlPaint class, however, you can use the DrawCheckBox() method, and end up with the perfectly shaded Windows standard for free. You can even create a check box of any size you like. Similarly, if you want to create a scroll button, or a button that displays a focus rectangle, you also can turn to the ControlPaint class.

The ControlPaint class consists entirely of static methods, as described in Table 7-6. Here's a line of code that uses it draw a check box:

```
ControlPaint.DrawCheckBox(e.Graphics, new Rectangle(10, 10, 50, 50),
   ButtonState.Checked);
```

And here's one that draws the familiar dotted focus rectangle:

```
ControlPaint.DrawFocusRectangle(e.Graphics, new Rectangle(130, 80, 20, 20));
```

Table 7-6. *Basic ControlPaint Methods*

Method	Description
DrawBorder() and DrawBorder3D()	Draws a border like on a button-style control
DrawButton() and DrawCaptionButton()	Draws a standard command button control
DrawCheckBox()	Draws a check-box control
DrawComboButton()	Draws the drop-down button for a combo box control
DrawFocusRectangle	Draws a dotted rectangular outline for a focus rectangle
DrawGrid()	Draws a grid of one-pixel dots with the specified spacing, within the specified bounds, and in the specified color
DrawImageDisabled() and DrawStringDisabled()	Draw an image or string of text in a disabled ("greyed-out") state
DrawLockedFrame() and DrawSelectionFrame()	Draw a standard selection frame in the specified state, with the specified inner and outer dimensions, and with the specified background color
DrawMenuGlyph()	Draws a menu glyph on a menu item control (for example, a check mark)
DrawMixedCheckBox	Draws a three-state check-box control

Table 7-6. *Basic ControlPaint Methods*

Method	Description
DrawRadioButton()	Draws a standard radio button control
DrawScrollButton	Draws a scroll button on a scroll bar control
DrawSizeGrip()	Draws the sizing grip that appears on the bottom right of some windows

Figure 7-27 shows the sample output for several ControlPaint methods, including check boxes of different sizes and states.

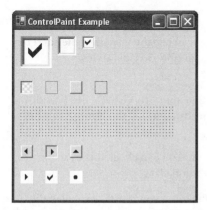

Figure 7-27. *Drawing pictures with ControlPaint*

Remember, this is a *picture* of a check box, not a check box! If you want it to change its state when the user clicks it, you need to manually repaint a new check box in a different state.

Visual Styles

A significant gap in the ControlPaint class is that it doesn't take visual style into account. If you're using Windows XP (or you have visual styles enabled for Windows 2003 Server), you have the ability to display modern interfaces with a slick new look. Painting an old-fashioned legacy control ruins the effect.

.NET 2.0 introduces a solution to this problem with a new System.Windows.Forms. VisualStyles namespace that wraps the visual styles API. Unfortunately, because the API uses a radically different model than ordinary control painting, it's not possible to merge the visual styles functionality into the ControlPaint class (which would be a cleaner result). However, the VisualStyleRenderer plays an analogous role—it renders user interface elements using the visual styles API.

The System.Windows.Forms.VisualStyles namespace includes all the ingredients you need to draw with a themed element. These details include the following:

- **VisualStyleInformation.** Provides static properties that return information about the current visual style environment, such as the chosen color scheme and the operating system support.

- **VisualStyleElement nested classes.** There's a separate nested class for each type of element you can paint. For example, VisualStyleElement.CheckBox.Button represents a check box in various states.

- **Enumerations.** There are many enumerations that you use in conjunction with the VisualStyleElement nested classes to set various properties.

- **VisualStyleRenderer.** This is the class that performs the actual work of painting the styled element onto a form. Plays a similar role to ControlPaint.

Visual Style Support

There's a significant catch to using visual styles. Before you can use the VisualStyleRenderer in an application, you need to be sure that your environment supports visual styles.

To have this support, four things need to be true:

- The application must be running on an operation that supports visual styles (Windows XP or Windows 2003 Server). You can determine this by checking the IsSupportedByOS property of the VisualStyleInformation class.

- Visual styles must be enabled in the operating system. You can check this by using the IsEnabledByUser property of the VisualStyleInformation class.

- Visual styles must be enabled for the application, meaning you must have called the Application.EnableVisualStyles() method. By default, when you create a new project in Visual Studio this line is added to the Program class.

- Visual styles must be applied to the client area of all application windows. You can determine this by checking the VisualStyleState property of the Application class, which must have the value VisualStyleState.ClientAreaEnabled or VisualStyleState. ClientAndNonClientAreasEnabled.

Rather than checking these details individually, you can rely on the Application.Render-WithVisualStyles property. If true, all of these conditions have been met. If any condition fails, visual styles cannot be used and this property returns false. Attempting to use visual styles when they aren't supported will lead to an exception, so you should always examine this property and degrade gracefully to a different set of drawing logic (such as the ControlPaint class) if visual styles aren't supported.

Drawing with the VisualStyleRenderer

Assuming visual styles are enabled, you begin by choosing the type of element you want to draw from the set of VisualStyleElement nested classes. Each nested VisualStyleElement class contains a group of static properties that allows you to retrieve the VisualStyleElement object.

For example, the VisualStyleElement.CheckBox.Button class provides static properties like CheckedDisabled, CheckedNormal, CheckedPressed, UncheckedDisabled, and so on. Each property returns a VisualStyle object that represents the element in the corresponding state.

```
VisualStyleElement element = VisualStyleElement.Button.CheckBox.CheckedNormal;
```

There are several dozen visual element classes. You can consult the MSDN Help to browse the full list.

Once you have the VisualStyle object you want, you can create a VisualStyleRenderer that wraps it. Before you do this, it's considered good practice to call the VisualStyleRenderer. IsElementDefined() method to make sure the renderer supports the element you've chosen (meaning it's supported by the current theme). For example, though there's a set of VisualStyleElement.Menu classes, none of the themes provided with current operating systems supports it.

```
if (VisualStyleRenderer.IsElementDefined(element))
{
    VisualStyleRenderer renderer = new VisualStyleRenderer(element);
    ...
```

■**Note** In theory, you could write your code generically to use visual styles for all elements when available. However, there is only one implementation of visual styles currently available (both Windows XP and Windows 2003 Server are the same), and future versions of Windows are likely to adopt a new drawing framework. That means in practice it's reasonable to code against the known visual style implementation and streamline your code.

The last step is to use the methods of the VisualStyleRenderer to create the output. The core VisualStyleRenderer methods are described in Table 7-7.

Table 7-7. *Essential VisualStyleRenderer Methods*

Method	Description
DrawBackground()	Draws the background for the current visual style element. In many cases, the background is the element—for example, the background of a push button creates the familiar white shaded button, and the background of a check box paints the check box. All you need to do after calling this method is (optionally) add text and a border.
DrawEdge()	Draws one or more edges of the specified bounding rectangle.
DrawText()	Draws text in the specified bounds using the appropriate font. The image is automatically adjusted based on the state of the item (for example, disabled).
DrawImage()	Draws the specified image within the specified bounding rectangle. The image is automatically adjusted based on the state of the item (for example, disabled).

Table 7-7. *Essential VisualStyleRenderer Methods (Continued)*

Method	Description
DrawParentBackground()	Draws the background of the control's parent in the specified area. Has no effect when painting directly to a form.
HitTestBackground()	Returns true if a specified point is contained in the background of the current visual style element. This is useful because, although you choose the bounding rectangle for the element, you don't necessarily know where the content is drawn.
IsElementDefined()	Returns true if the specified visual style element is defined by the current visual style. If it isn't, don't attempt to use any of the drawing methods—they won't produce any output.
SetParameters()	Sets the VisualStyleRenderer to use a different VisualStyleElement object.

Here's the remainder of the painting code. It displays a check box in a bordered and a text caption. The key methods are DrawBackground(), which creates the check box, DrawEdge(), and DrawTest().

```
...
Rectangle rectCheck = new Rectangle(10, 10, 50, 50);
Rectangle rectBox = new Rectangle(10, 10, 200, 50);
Rectangle rectText = new Rectangle(50, 25, 150, 25);
renderer.DrawBackground(e.Graphics, rectCheck);
renderer.DrawEdge(e.Graphics, rectBox,
   Edges.Bottom | Edges.Top | Edges.Left | Edges.Right,
   EdgeStyle.Etched, EdgeEffects.Flat);
renderer.DrawText(e.Graphics, rectText, "Styled checkbox", false,
   TextFormatFlags.Top);
}
```

Figure 7-28 shows the result.

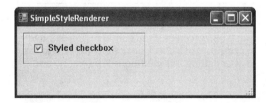

Figure 7-28. *Drawing pictures with VisualStyleRenderer*

▪**Note** Sadly, due to a bug in the .NET API for visual styles, the font is not always set correctly. Although this issue will be fixed in future releases, you can use the (somewhat awkward) workaround described at http://blogs.msdn.com/jfoscoding/articles/475517.aspx for now.

To get a better feeling for DrawTest() and the visual style elements that are available, be sure to browse the System.Windows.Form.VisualStyles namespace. You'll find classes that represent core controls (buttons, check boxes, text boxes, drop-downs, scroll bars, etc.) along with more modern controls (trees, panels, toolbars, and more). Regardless of the element, you use the same set of VisualStyleRenderer methods from Table 7-7 to render the output.

■**Tip** You can switch an existing VisualStyleRenderer object to use another element by calling the SetParameters() method and supplying the new VisualStyleElement object.

Using a Control Renderer

Adding the logic to painstakingly create a VisualStyleObject, check whether it's defined in the current theme, and then render it can become fairly time consuming. If you're planning to use the visual style support to build a unique custom control (like the examples in Chapter 12, which use visual styles in a charting control and a collapsible panel), you don't have any other option. However, if you simply want to create a basic ingredient like a button or check box, there is a shortcut. You can use one of the dedicated renderer classes defined in the System.Windows.Forms namespace.

The neat thing about many control renderers is that they work regardless of whether visual styles are available. Internally, they check the Application.RenderVisualStyles property and degrade to the classic Windows look if styles aren't supported. This simplifies the code you need to write dramatically.

.NET includes the following control renderers:

- ButtonRenderer

- CheckBoxRenderer

- GroupBoxRenderer

- RadioButtonRenderer

Here's an example of how you might use the CheckBoxRenderer inside a paint event handler:

```
CheckBoxRenderer.DrawCheckBox(e.Graphics, new Point(10,10),
  new Rectangle(10,10,110,15), "Style checkbox", this.Font, false,
  CheckBoxState.CheckedNormal);
```

There are also some control renderers that work only if visual styles are available (and they throw exceptions if styles aren't supported). That means it's up to you to check the Application. RenderVisualStyles property before you decide whether or not to use these renderers. They include the following:

- ComboBoxRenderer

- ProgressBarRenderer

- ScrollBarRenderer

- TabRenderer

- TextBoxRenderer

- TrackBarRenderer

The Last Word

In this chapter you learned how to use .NET's revitalized painting framework and the optimized techniques, including double buffering, that make drawing routines sharp and flicker-free. You also saw how to make shaped forms and considered topics you need to master if you want to develop owner-drawn controls, like hit testing and double buffering. The story doesn't end here—you'll see GDI+ at work throughout this book. Here are the most notable examples:

- Chapter 12 provides several practical examples of how you can use GDI+ to create owner-drawn controls.

- Chapter 23 uses owner-drawn controls to demonstrate modern skinned interfaces.

- Chapter 24 uses owner-drawn controls to implement a custom drawing program.

The GDI+ information in this chapter isn't comprehensive, and there are many more details about the platform that could easily occupy a complete book. If you want to explore more about GDI+, consider *Pro .NET Graphics Programming* (Apress). Another great resource for hard-core graphics programmers is the Paint.NET sample application (see http://www.eecs.wsu.edu/paint.net), which implements a feature-complete, modern drawing application using .NET.

Data Binding

Many Windows applications are really just attractive window dressing over a relational database. This is especially true of the internal software that powers most businesses. The chief responsibility of this type of software is to allow highly structured data entry and to generate reports that summarize vast quantities of information.

Of course, databases aren't only used for workflow and administrative software. Almost every application needs to connect to a data source and retrieve, format, and display information at some point. (Even an Internet e-commerce site is really just an interactive product catalog that draws information from one group of tables and logs transactions in another.) In this chapter, you'll consider the options you have for displaying data in a Windows application through *data binding*.

Data binding aims to reduce the amount of code you need to write to create forms that display and edit data. As you'll see in this chapter, you have a choice about how much functionality you code by hand and how much you allow Visual Studio to generate automatically. To create an application that's reasonably easy to change or enhance, you need to understand how to make this compromise.

■**Note** This chapter isn't meant as a primer on ADO.NET, the library .NET applications use to connect to relational databases. If you haven't used ADO.NET before, you may be interested in a dedicated book on the subject. Two good choices are *Microsoft ADO.NET Core Reference* (Microsoft Press) and *Pro ADO.NET* (Apress). However, if you are familiar with ADO.NET, you'll learn quite a bit in this chapter about the best ways to integrate relational data into a Windows Forms application.

In this chapter, you'll consider three fundamental topics:

- How to use .NET data binding to show the information from any data object in any control.

- How to use the .NET data source model to query data a database without writing any code—and whether you should rely on this approach in a serious application.

- How to design with data in mind, so you can keep your application ruthlessly organized and well encapsulated.

Introducing Data Binding

Traditionally, data binding has been viewed with a great deal of suspicion. Many developers feel that it's an inflexible, clumsy tool favored by beginning programmers and visual development tools. In most cases, they've been all too correct.

Data binding usually suffers from several well-known problems:

- **It's inflexible.** For example, you can only bind special controls to special objects—and when you do, you lose control of the process. In many cases, you need to either enable or disable entire features such as data editing because data controls don't allow you to participate in their work.

- **It's ugly.** When you bind to data, you often have to display all available rows and sacrifice any ability to format details like column widths or order. And if you hoped to convert a field made up of numeric constants into a friendlier representation, forget it.

- **It's fragile.** Data binding doesn't follow classic three-tier design. Instead, it binds database details directly to user interface logic. If the data source changes, or you need to create functionality that should be shared among different applications or environments, you are entirely on your own.

- **It's proprietary.** A fine-tuned data-binding solution is great—until your organization decides to upgrade to a newer programming tool or change programming languages. At this point, there is generally no migration path, because much of the logic is hard-coded in proprietary designer or project files. In some cases, you'll face the same problems if you simply switch from one relational database product to another (for example, you move from SQL Server to Oracle).

Does .NET suffer from the same problems? It all depends how you use data binding, and how you integrate it in the rest of your application. As you'll discover, it's possible to use data binding intelligently and flexibly, and avoid these problems. It's also possible to use data binding to build poorly designed applications that are all but impossible to change or optimize.

.NET Data Binding

It's important to realize that there are really two levels of .NET data binding:

- **Basic data binding (for data display).** This includes support for binding data objects to Windows Forms controls. Although this saves you from the hassle of writing display logic, you still need to manage the process that retrieves the data from the database (and commits changes).

- **No-code data binding (for data operations).** This adds support for automatically populating data objects based on a known data source, like a relational database. You also can apply changes in the same way. Using this level of support, you can theoretically avoid writing any database code at all.

The difference is important, because these two technologies have radically different consequences for the design of your application. It's almost always safe to use the first level. It gives you all the flexibility you need to display your data with an elegant, extensible model. On the other hand, if you use both levels of data binding you need to be very cautious. You run the risk of creating applications where database code is tightly bound to individual forms in your application, and routines for common tasks like handling errors are scattered throughout your application. You also make it more difficult to change or optimize your approach data access.

Figure 8-1 shows an example of the first approach—an application that retrieves data objects by hand, but uses data binding to get the information into various controls for display.

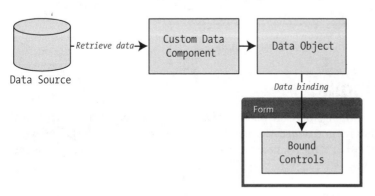

Figure 8-1. *Data binding in a .NET application*

In this example, a custom data access class (that you create) contains all the ADO.NET code. It contacts the database, performs a query, and transfers information into a data object (like the DataSet or a collection of objects). This data access class may be in the same assembly as the rest of your application, or for better componentization you can develop it in a separate class library project. Once the data object is returned, the information it contains is displayed in a form automatically, thanks to data binding. This automatic display works through various relationships between the data object and the controls on the form. These relationships are usually set up when the form is first created.

Figure 8-2 shows how no-code data binding works in a Windows application. The ingredients that are involved are similar to those in Figure 8-1—namely, there's a class to retrieve data and a class to represent that data. However, there are two significant differences. By default, all the objects are contained by the form that displays the data. Unfortunately, this makes it difficult to bind the data to other forms without duplicating code. More importantly, to create the application in Figure 8-1, you need to code the data access class by hand and choose a suitable data object. But when you use the approach shown in Figure 8-2, the choice is out of your hands. The data access logic and the data object are generated automatically in Visual Studio, and your options for customizing it are limited.

In this chapter, you'll start by exploring the first level (showing relational data in bound controls) and then consider whether or not it makes sense to use the second level (avoiding data access code altogether).

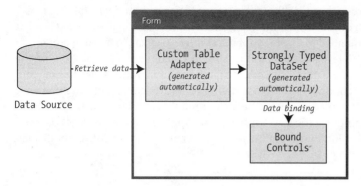

Figure 8-2. *No-code data binding in a .NET application*

Basic Data Binding

In the world of .NET data binding, there are *data providers* (the data objects that contain the information you want to show) and *data consumers* (the controls that display the bound data).

Figure 8-3 shows a snapshot of the relationship between data providers and data consumers.

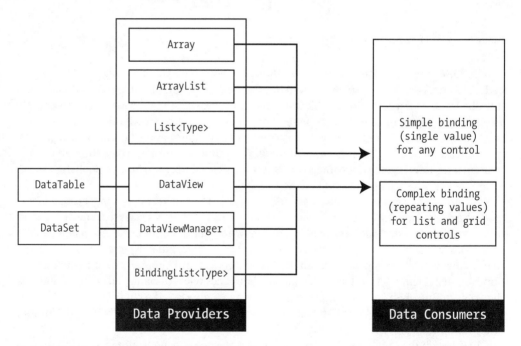

Figure 8-3. *Information flow in .NET data binding*

Data Consumers

Almost every control in .NET supports data binding in one form or another. However, different controls support data binding in different ways. For example, when binding to a text box, button, or image control, you will usually bind to the TextBox.Text, Button.Text, or PictureBox.Image property (although there are other possibilities, as you'll discover shortly). Each of these properties can bind to a single piece of information at a time through a process called *simple data binding*.

On the other hand, a control like ListBox or CheckedListBox can hold an entire list of data or the contents of a single field from a database. There are also rich controls like DataGridView that can display all the information from a DataSet on their own. All of these controls support *complex data binding*, which means they can show the values from more than one row in a data object.

Data Providers

You don't need to use any database code to take advantage of data binding. .NET allows controls to bind to any class that implements the IList interface.

Note IList is just a starting point. Other, more sophisticated interfaces extend IList with features for editing. As you'll see later in this chapter, interfaces like IBindingList and IEditableObject, allow two-way data binding, so you can modify a value in a control and have the control update the bound data object automatically. ADO.NET objects like the DataView support these interfaces, and you can implement them in your custom classes.

Data sources that are supported in Windows Forms data binding include:

- **DataColumn.** Represents a single value from a field.

- **DataView.** Represents a view onto a complete DataTable (which can include filtering and sorting settings). You can also bind to the DataTable directly, but when you use this approach .NET actually examines the DataTable.DefaultView property to get a DataView object, which it binds.

- **DataViewManager.** Represents a complete DataSet, which may contain several DataTable objects with information. You also can bind directly to a DataSet object, but when you use this approach .NET actually examines the DataSet.DefaultViewManager to get a DataViewManager object, which it binds.

- **Arrays and collections.** Represents a collection of virtually any type of object. You can use arrays, the ArrayList, and generic collections like List<T> and BindingList<T>. You can't use specialized collection types, like queues and hashtables. The best part is that you can fill the collection with your own custom data objects.

In the following examples, you'll begin by using the basic ADO.NET objects and then learn how create bindable custom objects.

A Data Access Component

Before continuing, it makes sense to introduce the database class that's used in the following examples. Here's the basic outline:

```
public class StoreDB
{
    public DataTable GetProducts()
    { ... }
}
```

When other forms need data, they call the StoreDB.GetProducts() method to retrieve a DataTable object. In this section, we're primarily interested with how ADO.NET objects like the DataTable and DataSet can be bound to Windows Forms controls. The actual process that deals with creating and filling these objects (as well as other implementation details, such as whether StoreDB caches the data over several method calls, whether it uses stored procedures instead of inline queries, whether it fetches the data from a local XML file when offline, and so on) isn't our focus.

However, just to get an understanding of what's taking place, here's the complete code:

```
public class StoreDB
{
    public DataTable GetProducts()
    {
        // Get the connection string from the .config file.
        string connectionString = Properties.Settings.Default.Store;

        // Create the ADO.NET objects.
        SqlConnection con = new SqlConnection(connectionString);
        SqlCommand cmd = new SqlCommand("GetProducts", con);
        cmd.CommandType = CommandType.StoredProcedure;
        SqlDataAdapter adapter = new SqlDataAdapter(cmd);

        // Fill a DataTable.
        DataSet ds = new DataSet();
        adapter.Fill(ds, "Products");
        return ds.Tables["Products"];
    }
}
```

■**Note** Currently, the GetProducts() method doesn't include any exception handling code, so all exceptions will bubble up the calling code. This is a reasonable design choice, but you may want to catch the exception in GetProducts(), perform cleanup or logging as required, and then rethrow the exception to notify the calling code of the problem. This design pattern is called *caller inform*.

This code retrieves a table of product information from the Store database, which is a sample database for the fictional IBuySpy store included with some Microsoft case studies. (You can get a script to install this database with the downloadable samples for this chapter.) The query is performed through a stored procedure in the database named GetProducts. The connection string isn't hard-coded—instead, it's retrieved through an application setting in the .config file for this application. (To view or set application settings, double-click the Properties ➤ Settings.settings node in the Solution Explorer.)

Figure 8-4 shows two tables in the Store database and their schema.

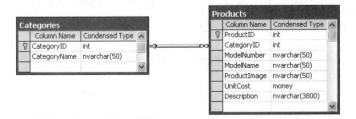

Figure 8-4. *A portion of the Store database*

You have several options for making the StoreDB class available to the forms in your application:

- The form could create an instance of StoreDB whenever it needs to access the database.

- You could change the methods in the StoreDB class to be static.

- You could create a single instance of StoreDB, and make it available through a static property in another class (following the "factory" pattern).

The first two options are reasonable, but both of them limit your flexibility. The first choice prevents you from caching data objects for use in multiple forms. Even if you don't want to use that approach immediately, it's worth designing your application in such a way that it's easy to implement later on. Similarly, the second approach assumes that you won't have any instance-specific state that you need to retain in the StoreDB class. Although this is a good design principle, there are some details (like the connection string) that you might want to retain in memory. If you convert the StoreDB class to use static methods, it becomes much more difficult to access different instances of the Store database in different back-end data stores.

Ultimately, the third option is the most flexible. It preserves the switchboard design, by forcing all the forms to work through a single property. Here's an example that makes an instance of StoreDB available through the Program class:

```
public static class Program
{
    private static StoreDB storeDB = new StoreDB();
    public static StoreDB StoreDB
    {
        get { return storeDB; }
    }
```

```
    [STAThread]
    static void Main()
    { ... }
}
```

Binding to a List (Complex Binding)

Binding to a list is one of the most common data-binding tasks. All the basic .NET list controls supply a DataSource property that accepts a reference to any IList data source.

Here's an example that binds a simple list to the ModelName column of the Products table:

```
private void SimpleListBinding_Load(object sender, EventArgs e)
{
    lstModelName.DataSource = Program.StoreDB.GetProducts();
    lstModelName.DisplayMember = "ModelName";
}
```

This is an example of complex binding because the model name of every product in the table is shown in the list control (see Figure 8-5).

Figure 8-5. *Complex binding to a DataView*

To make this work, you use two properties. The DataSource property is exposed by every control that uses complex binding. It accepts the data object, which must implement IList or one of its derived interfaces, as described earlier. The DisplayMember property names the field name that you want to display. The DisplayMember property is required in simple list controls, because they can show only one piece of information at a time.

In this example, the code appears to bind to a DataTable object, but it actually binds to the DataTable.DefaultView property. This property provides a DataView object that implements the required IList interface. For the most part, you can ignore this lower-level reality unless you want to use the DataView object to customize the displayed data. For example, the code that follows doesn't change the actual information in the DataTable, but it does ensure that only a subset of it will be shown in the list control:

```
DataTable dt = Program.StoreDB.GetProducts();

// Only include rows with a UnitCost value less than 5.
dt.DefaultView.RowFilter = "UnitCost < 5";

lstModelName.DataSource = dt;
lstModelName.DisplayMember = "ModelName";
```

Figure 8-6 shows the filtered list.

Figure 8-6. *Binding to a filtered DataView*

The DataView class provides other properties that allow you to implement sorting, and to specify whether the data-bound collection allows deletions, additions, and modifications (which don't apply to the list control because it never allows the modification of a bound data source). Taken together, these options (listed in Table 8-1) provide an extra layer of indirection that allows your code to be more flexible.

Table 8-1. *Useful DataView Properties*

Member	Description
RowFilter	A string that allows you to filter the results based on any field. This string works like a tiny snippet of SQL code, meaning that string values must be enclosed in single quotes, and you can use the operators like =, <, and >.
RowStateFilter	A combination of the values from DataViewRowState enumeration. This allows you to display rows that have been scheduled for deletion in the DataSet pending the next update (deleted rows are usually hidden).
Sort	Allows you to configure the sort order for the DataView. You can enter a combination of columns, separated by commas (as in "CategoryID, ModelName"). Append a space and the letters DESC after a column name to indicate descending (reverse) sort order.
Table	The DataTable object that contains the data used by this DataView.

> **Tip** As you might imagine, you can even create multiple DataView objects, allowing you to show data from the same underlying DataSet in multiple controls, but with different filtering or sorting options.

You also can bind through a DataSet instead of the DataTable. In this case, you need to supply the table name and the field name for the DisplayMember property, as shown here:

```
lstModelName.DataSource = ds;
lstModelName.DisplayMember = "Products.ModelName";
```

The end result is the same, but a DataSet.DefaultViewManager is used for the data binding. This property contains a DataViewManager object for the entire DataSet.

Binding to a Grid (Complex Binding)

.NET includes one bindable control that's head and shoulders above the rest. It's the DataGridView, and it has the ability to show every field of every record in a data source. That means with the following code, you'll end up with a grid like the one shown in Figure 8-7.

```
private void GridBinding_Load(object sender, EventArgs e)
{
    dataGridView1.DataSource = Program.StoreDB.GetProducts();
}
```

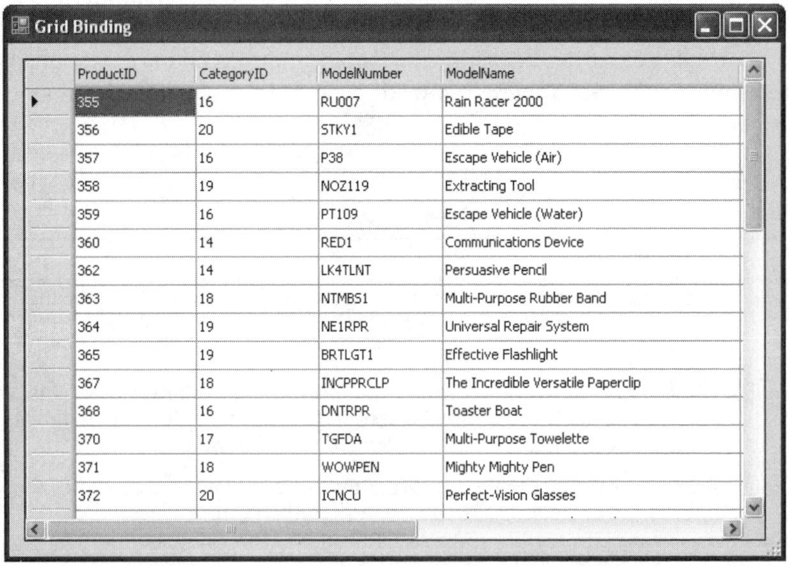

ProductID	CategoryID	ModelNumber	ModelName
355	16	RU007	Rain Racer 2000
356	20	STKY1	Edible Tape
357	16	P38	Escape Vehicle (Air)
358	19	NOZ119	Extracting Tool
359	16	PT109	Escape Vehicle (Water)
360	14	RED1	Communications Device
362	14	LK4TLNT	Persuasive Pencil
363	18	NTMBS1	Multi-Purpose Rubber Band
364	19	NE1RPR	Universal Repair System
365	19	BRTLGT1	Effective Flashlight
367	18	INCPPRCLP	The Incredible Versatile Paperclip
368	16	DNTRPR	Toaster Boat
370	17	TGFDA	Multi-Purpose Towelette
371	18	WOWPEN	Mighty Mighty Pen
372	20	ICNCU	Perfect-Vision Glasses

Figure 8-7. *Binding to a DataGridView*

The DataGridView has a significant amount of additional data-binding functionality built in. For example, you can edit any item in the list, add new items at the end, and remove an item by selecting it and pressing the Delete key. You also can apply sophisticated formatting and configure nearly every aspect of its behavior through properties. You'll learn about all these features in Chapter 15, which explores the DataGridView in detail. For now, it's just important to understand that the DataGridView is another example of complex binding.

Binding to Any Control (Simple Binding)

.NET list controls are designed for this type of data binding and provide a helpful DataSource property that's inherited from the base ListControl class. Other controls, like text boxes and buttons, don't add this feature. However, every control gains basic single-value data-binding ability from the Control.DataBindings collection.

Using this collection, you can link any control property to a field in a data source. For example, to connect a text box to a single field in a DataTable, you can use the following syntax (where dt is the DataTable object):

```
txtUnitCost.DataBindings.Add("Text", dt, "UnitCost");
```

The first parameter is the name of the control property as a string. (.NET uses reflection to find the matching property, and so it does not detect your mistakes at compile time.) The second parameter is the data source. The third parameter is the field in the DataSource that is used for the binding.

If you use this code statement on its own, you'll get a slightly perplexing result. The price of the first record in the DataTable will appear in the text box. However, there won't be any way to move to other items.

Programmers who are familiar with traditional data binding will probably expect that they need to add specialized navigation controls to the form. This isn't the case. Instead, you have two options—controlling navigation programmatically (which is described a little later in this chapter) or adding another control that uses complex binding to provide navigation.

For example, you can combine the list control example and the text box example to make this example more workable. Now, you can move from record to record simply by selecting items in the list box. When you do, all the other bound controls on the form are updated to show the values from the corresponding record. In other words, the form keeps track of your position, and all bound controls are synchronized to it.

To see this in action, consider the following form, which displays the information from a product record using a combination of three labels and a drop-down list control (see Figure 8-8). This list control allows navigation—when the user selects a different model name, the other data-bound controls are updated automatically.

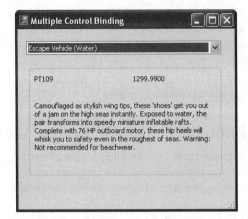

Figure 8-8. *Creating a record browser*

Here's the code that sets up the data bindings:

```
private void MultipleControlBinding_Load(object sender, EventArgs e)
{
    // Get the data object.
    DataTable dt = Program.StoreDB.GetProducts();

    // Use complex binding.
    cboModelName.DataSource = dt;
    cboModelName.DisplayMember = "ModelName";

    // Use simple binding.
    lblModelNumber.DataBindings.Add("Text", dt, "ModelNumber");
    lblUnitCost.DataBindings.Add("Text", dt, "UnitCost");
    lblDescription.DataBindings.Add("Text", dt, "Description");
}
```

Unusual Single-Value Binding

The nicest thing about single-value binding is that it can be used with almost any property. For example, you could set the background color of a text box, or specify the font. Unfortunately, there is no implicit type conversion when setting these specialized properties, which means you can't easily convert a string representing a font name into an actual font object.

The example that follows (Figure 8-9) demonstrates some of the extra effort you need to make if you want to bind one of these properties, and it makes for an interesting example of extreme data binding. Two list boxes are bound to the Font and ForeColor properties of a Label control. As you select different items in the list, the label changes automatically.

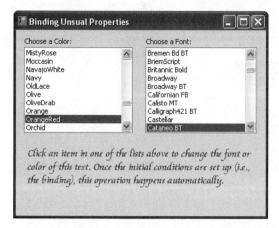

Figure 8-9. *Data binding with other text box properties*

The following code runs when this form first loads. To work, it requires that the System.Drawing and System.Drawing.Text namespaces be imported.

```
// These are our final data sources: two ArrayList objects.
List<Font> fontList = new List<Font>();
List<Color> colorList = new List<Color>();

// The InstalledFonts collection allows us to enumerate installed fonts.
// Each FontFamily needs to be converted to a genuine Font object
// before it is suitable for data binding to the Control.Font property.
InstalledFontCollection InstalledFonts = new InstalledFontCollection();
foreach (FontFamily family in InstalledFonts.Families)
{
    try
    {
        fontList.Add(new Font(family, 12));
    }
    catch
    {
        // We end up here if the font could not be created
        // with the default style.
    }
}

// To retrieve the list of colors, we need to first retrieve
// the strings for the KnownColor enumeration, and then convert each one
// into a suitable color object.
string[] colorNames;
colorNames = System.Enum.GetNames(typeof(KnownColor));
TypeConverter cnvrt = TypeDescriptor.GetConverter(typeof(KnownColor));
```

```
foreach (string colorName in colorNames)
{
    colorList.Add(
      Color.FromKnownColor(
        (KnownColor)cnvrt.ConvertFromString(colorName)));
}

// We can now bind both of our list controls.
lstColors.DataSource = colorList;
lstColors.DisplayMember = "Name";
lstFonts.DataSource = fontList;
lstFonts.DisplayMember = "Name";

// The label is bound to both data sources.
lblSampleText.DataBindings.Add("ForeColor", colorList, "");
lblSampleText.DataBindings.Add("Font", fontList, "");
```

You'll notice that the ForeColor and Font properties of the text box are simultaneously bound to two different data sources, which doesn't require any additional code. Some work is involved, however, to retrieve the list of currently installed fonts and named colors.

Common Data-Binding Scenarios

Simple (single-value) binding and complex (repeated-value) binding are the only two ingredients you need to enable a wide range of scenarios. In the following sections, you'll consider how to use data binding to edit records and how to handle formatting and validation.

Updating with Data Binding

As described earlier, you can perform basic binding with any IList data source. However, data sources that implement additional interfaces can gain some extra features. Four such interfaces are listed in Table 8-2.

Table 8-2. *Interfaces Used with Data Binding*

Interface	Description
IList	Allows simple data binding to a collection of identical types. (For example, you cannot bind to an ArrayList with different types of objects in it.)
IBindingList	Provides additional features for notification, for when the list itself has changed (for example, the number of items in the list increases) and for when the list items themselves change (for example, the third item in a list of customers has a change to its FirstName field).

Table 8-2. *Interfaces Used with Data Binding*

Interface	Description
IEditableObject	Allows permanent changes. For example, this allows a data-bound control to commit its changes back to the bound data object. This interface provides BeginEdit(), EndEdit(), and CancelEdit() methods.
IDataErrorInfo	Allows data sources to offer error information that a control can bind to. This information consists of two strings: the Error property, which returns general error message text (for example, "An error has occurred") and the Item property, which returns a string with a specific error message from the column (for example, "The value in the Cost column cannot be negative").

The DataView, DataViewManager, and DataRowView ADO.NET objects work together to implement all these interfaces. This means that when you bind to a DataSet, you acquire a much greater level of functionality. For example, if you modify the multiple control sample to use input controls, you will be able to make changes that permanently modify the DataSet. When you navigate to a changed record, you will see that its change persists. Furthermore, if multiple controls display the same data (for example, if you use a list control for navigation and allow the same field to be modified in a text box), they will all be updated with the new content when you browse back to the record. You can see this behavior with the product name field in the following example.

```
private void EditableBinding_Load(object sender, EventArgs e)
{
    DataTable dt = Program.StoreDB.GetProducts();

    cboModelName.DataSource = dt;
    cboModelName.DisplayMember = "ModelName";

    txtModelName.DataBindings.Add("Text", dt, "ModelName");
    txtModelNumber.DataBindings.Add("Text", dt, "ModelNumber");
    txtUnitCost.DataBindings.Add("Text", dt, "UnitCost");
    txtDescription.DataBindings.Add("Text", dt, "Description");
}
```

In this example, the code is largely unchanged. The key difference is that the Label controls are replaced with TextBox controls so the data object can be modified. Figure 8-10 shows the corresponding form.

Of course, a change made to the data set won't affect the original data source, it simply changes the linked DataRow object. Remember, the DataSet is always disconnected by nature. To commit changes, you need to add something like an update button, which would then presumably call a method like StoreDB.UpdateProducts(). This method would use the DataAdapter.Update() method to commit changes back to the database. But because this book only covers the user interface aspect of your code, we don't explore these details here.

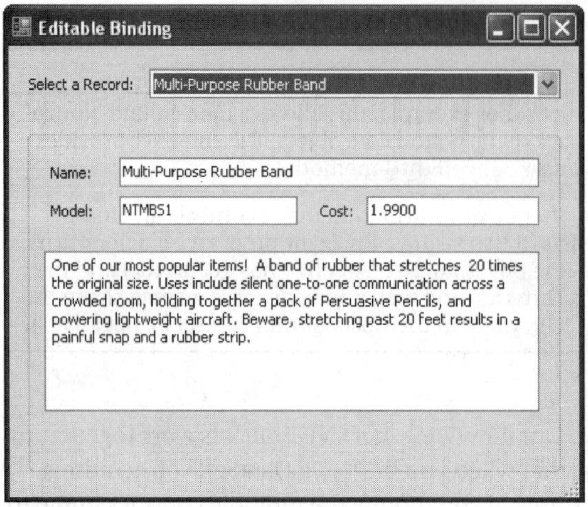

Figure 8-10. *An editable bound data source*

Formatting Data with a Format String

One limitation in your current example is that there is no way to handle data that need to be formatted before they can be displayed. For example, the UnitCost is displayed in the form 1.9900 instead of the more appropriate currency string $1.99.

Luckily, it's quite easy to change this detail. If the conversion you want to perform involves converting a number or date into an appropriate string representation, you can use an over-loaded version of the ControlBindingsCollection.Add() that accepts a format string.

For example, instead of using this code:

```
txtUnitCost.DataBindings.Add("Text", products, "UnitCost");
```

Use this:

```
txtUnitCost.DataBindings.Add("Text", products, "UnitCost", true,
  DataSourceUpdateMode.OnValidation, 0, "C");
```

There are several extra parameters at work here. The first new parameter (true) enables formatting. The next parameter specifies the default update mode, which applies changes to the bound object after validation is performed. This doesn't represent a change, but a value is required for this version of the Add() method. The following parameter (0) sets the value that's used if the bound field is null, and the final string sets the format (C for currency), which ensures the UnitCost field is displayed with a currency symbol and two decimal places (see Figure 8-11).

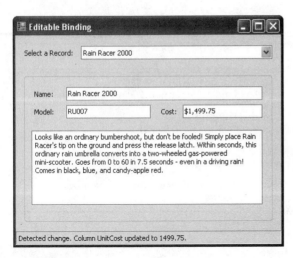

Figure 8-11. *Formatting numbers to strings*

You can learn about all the format strings that are available in the MSDN Help. However, Table 8-3 and Table 8-4 show some of the most common options you'll use for numeric and date values, respectively.

Table 8-3. *Numeric Format Strings*

Type	Format String	Example
Currency	C	$1,234.50 Brackets indicate negative values: ($1,234.50). The currency sign is locale-specific.
Scientific (Exponential)	E	1.234.50E+004
Percentage	P	45.6%
Fixed Decimal	F?	Depends on the number of decimal places you set. F3 formats values like 123.400. F0 formats values like 123.

Table 8-4. *Time and Date Format Strings*

Type	Format String	Example
Short Date	d	M/d/yyyy (for example: 10/30/2005)
Long Date	D	dddd, MMMM dd, yyyy (for example: Monday, January 30, 2005)
Long Date and Short Time	f	dddd, MMMM dd, yyyy HH:mm aa (for example: Monday, January 30, 2005 10:00 AM)

Table 8-4. *Time and Date Format Strings (Continued)*

Type	Format String	Example
Long Date and Long Time	F	dddd, MMMM dd, yyyy HH:mm:ss aa (for example: Monday, January 30, 2005 10:00:23 AM)
ISO Sortable Standard	s	yyyy-MM-dd HH:mm:ss (for example: 2005-01-30 10:00:23)
Month and Day	M	MMMM dd (for example: January 30)
General	G	M/d/yyyy HH:mm:ss aa (depends on locale settings) (for example: 10/30/2002 10:00:23 AM)

Note If you're using complex binding, you can't use the technique described here. However, many controls that support complex binding have similar features available to you. For example, the GridView allows you to define a format string for any column (as you'll see in Chapter 15). The ListBox allows you to supply a format string through the FormatString property (provided FormatStringEnabled is true).

Formatting Data with the Format and Parse Events

Format strings are great for tweaking numbers and dates. However, they don't help you with other values that might come out of a database in a less-than-professional state. For example, certain fields might use hard-coded numbers that are meaningless to the user, or they might use a confusing short form. If so, you need a way to convert these codes into a better display form. If you support editing, you also need to do the converse—take user-supplied data and convert it to a representation suitable for the appropriate field.

Fortunately, both tasks are fairly easy provided you handle the Format and Parse events for the Binding object. Format gives you a chance to modify values as they exit the database (before they appear in a data-bound control). Parse allows you to take a user-supplied value and modify it before it is committed to the data source. Figure 8-12 shows the process.

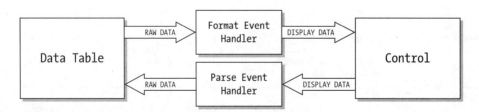

Figure 8-12. *Formatting bound data*

Here's an example that works with the UnitCost field and duplicates the previous example. It formats the numeric value as a currency string when it's requested for display in a text box.

The reverse process ensures that the final committed value doesn't use the currency symbol. To connect this logic, you need to begin by creating a Binding object, then register to receive its events, and finally add it to the DataBindings collection of the bound textbox. Notice that the following code adds a trick—it registers for the DataTable.ColumnChanged event. This way, you can verify what value is actually inserted into the DataTable.

```
// Create the binding.
Binding costBinding = new Binding("Text", dt, "UnitCost");

// Connect the methods for formatting and parsing data.
costBinding.Format += new ConvertEventHandler(DecimalToCurrencyString);
costBinding.Parse += new ConvertEventHandler(CurrencyStringToDecimal);

// Add the binding.
txtUnitCost.DataBindings.Add(costBinding);

// Register an event handler for changes to the DataTable (optional).
dt.ColumnChanged += new DataColumnChangeEventHandler(TableChanged);
```

The event-handling code for formatting simply returns the new converted value by setting the e.Value property.

```
private object previousUnitCost;

private void DecimalToCurrencyString(object sender, ConvertEventArgs e)
{
    if (e.DesiredType == typeof(string))
    {
        previousUnitCost = e.Value;

        // Use the ToString method to format the value as currency ("c").
        e.Value = ((decimal)e.Value).ToString("c");
    }
}

private void CurrencyStringToDecimal(object sender, ConvertEventArgs e)
{
    if (e.DesiredType == typeof(decimal))
    {
        // Convert the string back to decimal using the static Parse method.
        // Use exception handling code in case the text can't be interpreted
        // as a decimal.
        try
        {
            e.Value = Decimal.Parse(e.Value.ToString());
        }
```

```
    catch
    {
        e.Value = previousUnitCost;
    }
    }
}
```

The DataTable.ColumnChanged event handler is quite straightforward. It notes the changes by updating a label.

```
private void TableChanged(object sender, System.Data.DataColumnChangeEventArgs e)
{
    lblStatus.Text = "Detected change. Column " + e.Column.ColumnName;
    lblStatus.Text += " updated to " + e.ProposedValue.ToString() + ".";
}
```

Obviously, this approach requires a fair bit more code than the format string approach, and it doesn't add any new functionality. To see where the Format and Parse events really make sense, you need to consider an example that wouldn't be possible with format strings alone. The following section demonstrates some of these more interesting conversions.

Note Once again, this option isn't available with complex binding. Some controls provide support with their own events—for example, the DataGridView fires a CellFormatting event for each cell where you can perform similar adjustments. The ListBox has no such support.

Advanced Conversions

You can use a similar technique to handle more interesting conversions. For example, you could convert a column value to an appropriate string representation, straighten out issues of case, or ensure the correct locale-specific format for dates and times. Here's one example that compares hard-coded integers from the database against an enumeration:

```
private void ConstantToString(object sender, ConvertEventArgs e)
{
    if (e.DesiredType == typeof(string))
    {
        switch ((ProjectStatus)e.Value)
        {
            case ProjectStatus.NotStarted:
                e.Value = "Project not started.";
                break;
            case ProjectStatus.InProgress:
                e.Value = "Project in progress.";
                break;
```

```
            case ProjectStatus.Complete:
                e.Value = "Project is complete.";
                break;
        }
    }
}
```

■**Note** Be warned—this approach can lead you to mingle too many database details into your code. A better approach is to handle the problem at the database level, if you can. For example, if you use a list of numeric constants, create a table in the database that maps the numbers to text descriptions. Then, make this information available to your form either through a separate method in your data access class or by using a JOIN query when retrieving the data.

Now let's look at an additional trick that's useful when storing records that link to pictures. When storing a record that incorporates a graphic, you have two options. You can store the image as binary information in the database (which is generally less flexible but more reliable), or you can store the file name and ensure that the file exists in the appropriate shared directory. The next example (shown in Figure 8-13) uses the Format event to convert a picture name to the required Image object.

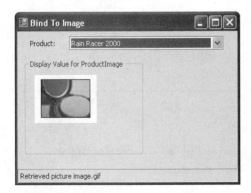

Figure 8-13. *Converting file names to image objects*

Unfortunately, data binding is always a two-way street, and if you implement a Format event handler, you need to create a corresponding Parse event handler to reverse your change. In our example, the Format event handler takes the file name and inserts the corresponding picture into a PictureBox. In the event handler, the code needs to take the picture, change back to the appropriate file name string, and insert this into the DataTable. This bidirectional conversion is required even though the application doesn't offer any way for the user to choose a new picture file and the content in the PictureBox can't be changed.

To make matters more complicated, there's no way to convert an image object back to the file name, so we have to fall back on another trick: storing the actual file name in the control for later retrieval.

Here's the data-binding code:

```
Binding pictureBinding = new Binding("Image", dt, "ProductImage");
pictureBinding.Format += new ConvertEventHandler(FileToImage);
pictureBinding.Parse += new ConvertEventHandler(ImageToFile);
picProduct.DataBindings.Add(pictureBinding);
```

And here is the formatting code (note that it requires the System.Drawing namespace to be imported):

```
private void FileToImage(object sender, ConvertEventArgs e)
{
    if (e.DesiredType == typeof(Image))
    {
        // Store the filename.
        picProduct.Tag = e.Value;

        // Look up the corresponding file, and create an Image object.
        try
        {
            lblStatus.Text = "Retrieved picture " + e.Value;
            e.Value = Image.FromFile(Application.StartupPath + "\\" + e.Value);
        }
        catch (System.IO.FileNotFoundException err)
        {
            lblStatus.Text = "Could not find picture " + e.Value;

            // You could return an error picture here.
            // This code uses a blank 1x1 pixel image.
            e.Value = new Bitmap(1,1);
        }
        catch (OutOfMemoryException err)
        {
            lblStatus.Text = "Picture " + e.Value + "has an unsupported format.";
            e.Value = new Bitmap(1,1);
        }

    }
}

private void ImageToFile(object sender, ConvertEventArgs e)
{
    if (e.DesiredType == typeof(string))
    {
        // Substitute the filename.
        e.Value = picProduct.Tag;
    }
}
```

This can only be considered a "conversion" in the loosest sense. What's really happening here is a file lookup. The process, however, is completely seamless. If you allow the user to dynamically choose a picture (maybe from a file or the clipboard), you could even create a corresponding Parse event handler that saves it to an appropriate directory with a unique name and then commits that name to the database.

■**Tip** The Format and Parse methods can run any .NET code. This provides an invaluable extra layer of indirection, and using it is one of the keys to making data binding work. With it, you can transform raw data into the appropriate presentation content.

Creating a Lookup Table

In the previous examples, the list control is a navigation control that allows the user to access any record. In some cases, this isn't the behavior you want. For example, you may want to use the list as an editing control. In that case, it should show the current value but contain a list of other possible values. Selecting a new value from the list doesn't perform record navigation—instead, it should update the data object.

Creating this effect isn't too difficult. For example, every product in the Products table is associated (by CategoryID) with a record in the Categories table (see Figure 8-4). Imagine you want to show the linked category for each product *and* allow the user to change it. Figure 8-14 shows one such example, where the user can browse to a record using one list and change the category using another.

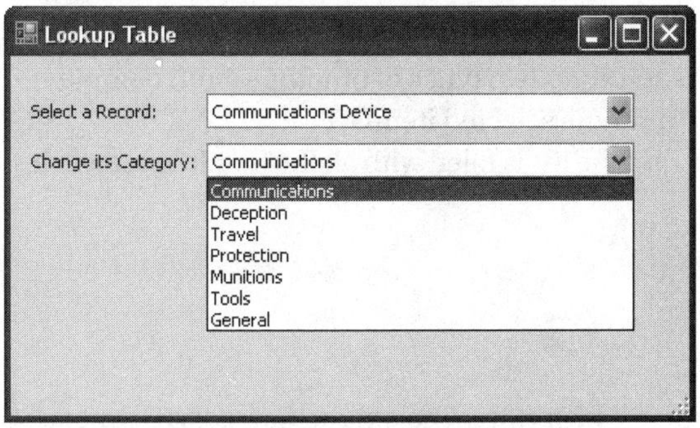

Figure 8-14. *A bound lookup list*

The easiest approach to create this example is to begin by using a JOIN query that ensures you retrieve the category information with each product, as with this stored procedure:

```
CREATE PROCEDURE GetProducts AS
SELECT * FROM Products INNER JOIN Categories ON Products.CategoryID =
Categories.CategoryID
GO
```

Next, you need to create a record in the StoreDB class that returns a DataSet with two tables—one with category information and one with product information. For example, you could create a method like this in the StoreDB class:

```
public DataSet GetCategoriesAndProducts()
{
    string connectionString = Properties.Settings.Default.Store;
    SqlConnection con = new SqlConnection(connectionString);
    SqlCommand cmd = new SqlCommand("GetProducts", con);
    cmd.CommandType = CommandType.StoredProcedure;
    SqlDataAdapter adapter = new SqlDataAdapter(cmd);

    DataSet ds = new DataSet();
    adapter.Fill(ds, "Products");
    cmd.CommandText = "GetCategories";
    adapter.Fill(ds, "Categories");

    return ds;
}
```

Here's how you can use this method:

```
DataSet ds = Program.StoreDB.GetCategoriesAndProducts();
```

To allow record navigation, you can bind a unique field like ModelName to a list box:

```
// Connect the product list used for navigation.
cboModelName.DataSource = ds.Tables["Products"];
cboModelName.DisplayMember = "ModelName";
```

To show category information, you have to set up two types of binding—both complex binding (to fill the list) and simple binding (to set the selected item).

First, you need to set the DataSource so that the list is filled with all the possible categories:

```
// Connect the category list used for editing.
cboCategory.DataSource = ds.Tables["Categories"];
cboCategory.DisplayMember = "CategoryName";
cboCategory.ValueMember = "CategoryID";
```

The trick here is the ValueMember property, with stores the unique CategoryID for each list item, but displays the CategoryName text through the familiar DisplayMember text.

Now, you need to use single binding to tie the SelectedValue property to the CategoryID field in the Products table:

```
cboCategory.DataBindings.Add("SelectedValue", ds.Tables["Products"],
  "CategoryID");
```

This is the technique that makes the example work. It ensures that every time you navigate to a new record, the list shows the category for that product. It also ensures that if you change the category selection, the product record is updated with a new CategoryID.

Row Validation and Changes

Now that you've seen how easy it is to commit changes to a bound DataTable, you're probably wondering what you can do to restrict the user's update ability—making sure some fields are read-only and others are bound by specific rules. This validation can be performed in exactly the same way it always is—by handling events like KeyPress in a text box or using the more-advanced validation techniques described in Chapter 18. After all, you're binding your fields to ordinary .NET controls—the only difference is that their changes are stored in the DataTable as soon as the user navigates to another record.

Another option is to handle the events raised by your bound data object. For example, if you're binding a DataTable, you can react to DataTable events like ColumnChanging. The advantage of this approach is that you create data-specific validation code that can be used no matter what control you end up binding to.

Here is an example that uses the ColumnChanging event and refuses to allow a change to the UnitCost column if the number is negative. Instead, it substitutes the existing value, effectively canceling the change.

```
private void TableChanging(object sender,
 System.Data.DataColumnChangeEventArgs e)
{
    if ((int)e.ProposedValue < 0)
    {
        e.ProposedValue = e.Row[e.Column.ColumnName];
    }
}
```

To use this code, you need to connect the event handler (typically at the same time you add the data binding):

```
dt.ColumnChanging += new DataColumnChangeEventHandler(TableChanging);
```

■**Note** Resist the urge to enter error-handling code into the Parse event handler. This method is purely designed to convert a value before attempting to store it. Instead, use the DataTable events or the editing events in the bound control.

This code is useful as a basic level of error protection, but it doesn't provide an easy way to notify the user about the error, because the user has more than likely already moved to another record. In some cases you may need to prevent the user from navigating to a new record after making invalid changes. To apply this logic, you need to take manual control of record navigation. This technique is explored in the next section, which considers what's really at work in data binding and shows how you can interact with it programmatically.

■**Tip** Some more-sophisticated controls, like DataGridView, have built-in support for handling data errors and validation through events. You'll learn about the DataGridView in detail in Chapter 15.

Data Binding Exposed

The secret behind data binding comprises two objects that you don't ordinarily see: Binding-Context and CurrencyManager (both of which are found in the System.Windows.Forms namespace).

Every form provides a single, default BindingContext object, which it creates automatically. In turn, every BindingContext provides a collection of zero or more BindingManagerBase objects. When you create a new form, its BindingContext will be empty. But once you start binding data objects (either through complex or simple binding), this changes. Ordinarily, you'll find one BindingManagerBase object for each bound data object. For example, if you bind a DataView to eight different controls, your form will have a BindingContext with *one* BindingManagerBase object (because there's a single DataView). This BindingManagerBase ensures that all the controls are synchronized—for example, it listens to a change of position in one control and updates the others accordingly. On the other hand, if you bind two different DataView objects to two different sets of controls, you'll wind up with two BindingManagerBase objects, one to synchronize each DataView.

■**Note** Technically, the BindingManagerBase doesn't communicate directly with the control. Instead, it interacts through the binding object that was created when you bound the control.

But there's another important detail. The BindingManagerBase is an abstract class, so it can't be created directly. Instead, the BindingContext actually contains instances of one of two classes that derived from BindingManagerBase—either PropertyManager or CurrencyManager. The difference depends on the type of data source. If you're using simple binding to display the properties of an ordinary object (one that doesn't support the interfaces in Table 8-2), the PropertyManager is used. This is a relatively rare occurrence. Usually, you're binding a DataView, DataViewManager, or collection of items, and the more capable CurrencyManager is used instead. In other words, the CurrencyManager is designed to work with a list of items.

The CurrencyManager object shoulders the responsibility for tracking the user's position in the bound data and synchronizing all the controls that are bound to it. To this end, the CurrencyManager provides a small set of properties, including Count, and the ever-important Position, which indicates an integer row index. It performs its work automatically. Figure 8-15 diagrams this relationship.

There are really only three reasons that you might want to access the data-binding objects:

- To programmatically control record navigation.

- To programmatically react to record navigation.

- To create a new BindingContext that allows you to store a different position to the same data.

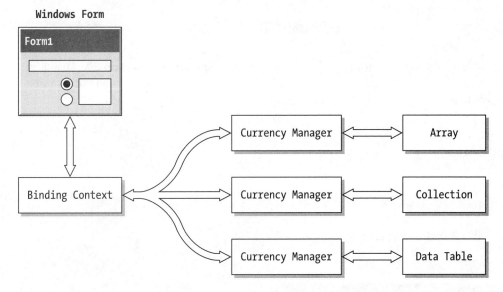

Figure 8-15. *Data binding under the hood*

Navigation with Data Binding

To navigate programmatically, you need to access the form's BindingContext object, find the correct CurrencyManager, and modify its Position property. Unfortunately, to find the correct CurrencyManager object, you need to submit the data object you used for your binding. That means you need to keep track of the data object in a form-level variable, or look up the CurrencyManager immediately after you perform the binding and track *it* in a form-level variable. The following example demonstrates the second technique.

First, create the variable for storing the CurrencyManager object:

```
// This is a CurrencyManager, but we don't need to perform a cast because
// the BindingManagerBase exposes all the properties we need to use.
private BindingManagerBase storeBinding;
```

Next, in the Form.Load event handler create the bindings and store a reference to the binding object. The only new line is highlighted in bold.

```
private void MultipleControlBinding_Load(object sender, System.EventArgs e)
{
    // Get table.
    DataTable dt = Program.StoreDB.GetProducts();

    // Set up bindings.
    cboModelName.DataSource = dt;
    cboModelName.DisplayMember = "ModelName";
    lblModelNumber.DataBindings.Add("Text", dt, "ModelNumber");
    lblUnitCost.DataBindings.Add("Text", dt, "UnitCost");
    lblDescription.DataBindings.Add("Text", dt, "Description");
```

```
    // Keep track of the currency manager.
    storeBinding = this.BindingContext[dt];
}
```

Now you can control the position through the storeBinding member variable. Here's an example with Previous and Next buttons that allow the user to browse through the data (see Figure 8-16):

```
private void cmdPrev_Click(object sender, System.EventArgs e)
{
    storeBinding.Position--;
}

private void cmdNext_Click(object sender, System.EventArgs e)
{
    storeBinding.Position++;
}
```

Figure 8-16. *Data binding with custom navigation controls*

Reacting to Record Navigation

As it stands, the navigation controls harmlessly fail to work if you try to browse past the bounds of the data source (for example, click the Previous button on the first record). However, a more intuitive approach would be to disable the controls at this position. You can accomplish this by reacting to the Binding.PositionChanged event.

First, you connect the event handler (after binding the data source):

```
storeBinding = this.BindingContext[dt];
storeBinding.PositionChanged += new EventHandler(Binding_PositionChanged);
```

The PositionChanged event doesn't provide you with any useful information (such as the originating page). But it does allow you to respond and update your controls accordingly. In the example below, the previous and next buttons are disabled when they don't apply.

```
private void Binding_PositionChanged(object sender, System.EventArgs e)
{
    if (storeBinding.Position == storeBinding.Count - 1)
    {
        cmdNext.Enabled = false;
    }
    else
    {
        cmdNext.Enabled = true;
    }

    if (storeBinding.Position == 0)
    {
        cmdPrev.Enabled = false;
    }
    else
    {
        cmdPrev.Enabled = true;
    }
}
```

If you want to be able to track the previous record, you need to add a form-level variable, and track it in the PositionChanged event handler. This technique has a few interesting uses, including validation (which you examine later in this chapter).

```
private int currentRecord;

private void Binding_PositionChanged(object sender, EventArgs e)
{
    // At this point, currentPage holds the previous page number.
    // Now we update currentPage:
    currentRecord = storeBinding.Position;
}
```

■Tip You could use the PositionChanged event handler to update the data source (the original database record or the XML file) if it has changed. By increasing the frequency of updates, you lower performance but reduce the chance of concurrency errors.

Creating Master-Detail Forms

Another interesting use of the PostionChanged event is to create master-detail forms. The concept is simple: you bind two controls to two different tables. When the selection in one table changes, you update the second by modifying the set of displayed rows with the RowFilter property.

This example uses two list controls, one that displays categories and one that displays the products in a given category (see Figure 8-17).

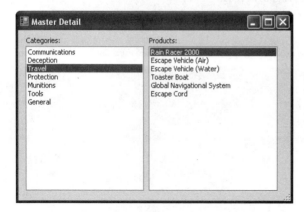

Figure 8-17. *Data binding with a master-detail list*

The lists are filled in the normal manner:

```
private BindingManagerBase categoryBinding;
private DataSet ds;

private void MasterDetail_Load(object sender, System.EventArgs e)
{
    ds = Program.StoreDB.GetCategoriesAndProducts();

    // Bind the lists to different tables.
    lstCategory.DataSource = ds.Tables["Categories"];
    lstCategory.DisplayMember = "CategoryName";

    lstProduct.DataSource = ds.Tables["Products"];
    lstProduct.DisplayMember = "ModelName";

    // Track the binding context and handle position changing.
    categoryBinding = this.BindingContext[ds.Tables["Categories"]];
    categoryBinding.PositionChanged += new EventHandler(Binding_PositionChanged);

    // Update child table at startup.
    UpdateProducts();
}
```

Now, when the PositionChanged event is detected for the category binding, the current view of products is automatically modified:

```
private void Binding_PositionChanged(object sender, System.EventArgs e)
{
    UpdateProducts();
}

private void UpdateProducts()
{
    string filter;
    DataRow selectedRow;

    // Find the current category row.
    selectedRow = ds.Tables["Categories"].Rows[categoryBinding.Position];

    // Create a filter expression using its CategoryID.
    filter = "CategoryID='" + selectedRow["CategoryID"].ToString() + "'";

    // Modify the view onto the product table.
    ds.Tables["Products"].DefaultView.RowFilter = filter;
}
```

The result is a perfectly synchronized master-detail list. You could adapt this example to work with two separate forms without much trouble. You simply need to design a way for the parent form to communicate with the child form, by setting a public property or calling a method.

Creating a New Binding Context

In the previous example, both controls were synchronized separately and had separate binding contexts because they were bound to two different tables (and hence two different DataView objects). In some cases, however, you might want the ability to bind to the same table (or any other data source) but at two different and independent positions. To accomplish this, you need to manually create an extra binding context.

Every control provides the BindingContext property. By default, each control checks its container, looking for a BindingContext to use. For example, a button in a group box checks the GroupBox.BindingContext property and uses the same context. The group box checks the BindingContext property of the containing form and uses that context. The end result is that every control acquires its BindingContext from the containing form.

You're free to change this behavior by creating your own BindingContext objects and assigning them to specific controls. The easiest way to do this is to place the controls that you want in a different binding context into a different container (like a group box). Next, you manually create a new BindingContext object for that container. Now, all the controls in that container will acquire the new context.

The code that follows carries out this operation for two list controls in different group boxes. The two list boxes are bound to the same data source but synchronized separately.

```
// Make sure all the controls in the second group box have a different binding.
grpB.BindingContext = new BindingContext();

DataTable dt = Program.StoreDB.GetProducts();

// Configure the first group.
lstModelNameA.DataSource = dt;
lstModelNameA.DisplayMember = "ModelName";

// Configure the second group.
lstModelNameB.DataSource = dt;
lstModelNameB.DisplayMember = "ModelName";
```

Figure 8-18 shows the separately synchronized panels.

Figure 8-18. *Separately synchronized view of the same data*

Validating Bound Data

Earlier in this chapter, you learned that one problem with ADO.NET data binding is validation. You can write specific error-handling code for each control, which is often a good approach, but one that creates extra code and ends up importing database details into your form code. Another approach is to handle the DataTable events like ColumnChanging, ColumnChanged, RowChanging, and RowChanged. The potential problem here is that the user may browse to another record, not realizing that invalid data have been rejected.

Taking control of data-binding navigation allows you to provide a more elegant solution. First, you create two form-level variables: one that tracks the current page and another that tracks the validity of the current record.

```
private int currentRecord;
private bool errFlag;
```

You also need to hook up the events for column changes and position changes:

```
storeBinding.PositionChanged += new EventHandler(Binding_PositionChanged);
dt.ColumnChanged += new DataColumnChangeEventHandler(TableChanged);
```

Next, you make the record navigation conditional on the current record being valid. If the errFlag member variable is set to true, the user is automatically sent back to the original page.

```
private void Binding_PositionChanged(object sender, System.EventArgs e)
{
    if (errFlag)
    {
        // Reset the page.
        storeBinding.Position = currentPage;
    }
    else
    {
        // Allow the page to change and update the currentPage variable.
        currentRecord = storeBinding.Position;
    }
}
```

Next, you add the validation code, which occurs in response to a table change. This event is fired when the user tabs to a new field after making a modification or tries to browse to a new record after making a modification. It always occurs before the PositionChanged event.

```
private void TableChanged(object sender, System.Data.DataColumnChangeEventArgs e)
{
    string errors = Program.StoreDB.ValidateProduct(e.Row);

    if (errors.Length == 0)
    {
        errFlag = false;
    }
    else
    {
        errFlag = true;
    }
    lblErrorSummary.Text = errors;
}
```

You'll notice that this form doesn't contain any database-specific code. Instead, the validation is performed by passing the current row to a special method provided by our database wrapper class. This method returns an error string or an empty string if the validation succeeded.

```
public string ValidateProduct(DataRow row)
{
    string errors = string.Empty;

    if (((decimal)row["UnitCost"]) <= 0)
    {
        errors += "* UnitCost value too low\n";
    }
```

```
    if (row["ModelNumber"].ToString().Length == 0)
    {
        errors += "* You must specify a ModelNumber\n";
    }
    if (row["ModelName"].ToString().Length == 0)
    {
        errors += "* You must specify a ModelName\n";
    }
    return errors;
}
```

The error message is displayed in the window. Everything works nicely together. Database validation code is in a database component, but record navigation is halted immediately if an error is found.

Figure 8-19 shows the final application detecting an error.

Figure 8-19. *Custom row validation with data binding*

Binding to Custom Objects

So far, you've concentrated exclusively on examples that bind controls to ADO.NET data objects. Surprisingly, you can use the same techniques to bind to collection of custom objects. There's no intrinsic advantage in taking this approach. However, it does give you a wide range of options when you decide how to model your application, where you want to place your validation logic, and so on.

To see how this works, it helps to consider a basic example. Here's a custom Product class that encapsulates the information for a single product in the Products table.

```csharp
public class Product
{
    private string modelNumber;
    public string ModelNumber
    {
        get { return modelNumber; }
        set { modelNumber = value; }
    }

    private string modelName;
    public string ModelName
    {
        get { return modelName; }
        set { modelName = value; }
    }

    private decimal unitCost;
    public decimal UnitCost
    {
        get { return unitCost; }
        set { unitCost = value; }
    }

    private string description;
    public string Description
    {
        get { return description; }
        set { description = value; }
    }

    public Product(string modelNumber, string modelName,
      decimal unitCost, string description)
    {
        ModelNumber = modelNumber;
        ModelName = modelName;
        UnitCost = unitCost;
        Description = description;
    }
    public Product() {}
}
```

This class doesn't include any special features (for example, the property procedures don't implement any validation and there aren't any helper methods). However, you could add these details without changing the example. The only requirement is that the information you want to display must be stored in *public properties*. The Windows Forms data binding infrastructure won't pick up private information or public member variables.

The next step is to modify the StoreDB.GetProducts() method so that it returns a collection of Product objects instead of a DataTable. Here's the revised code:

```
public class StoreDB
{
    public List<Product> GetProducts()
    {
        // Get the connection string from the .config file.
        string connectionString = Properties.Settings.Default.Store;

        // Create the ADO.NET objects.
        SqlConnection con = new SqlConnection(connectionString);
        SqlCommand cmd = new SqlCommand("GetProducts", con);
        cmd.CommandType = CommandType.StoredProcedure;

        List<Product> products = new List<Product>();
        try
        {
            con.Open();
            SqlDataReader reader = cmd.ExecuteReader();
            while (reader.Read())
            {
                // Create a Product object that wraps the
                // current record.
                Product product = new Product((string)reader["ModelNumber"],
                  (string)reader["ModelName"], (decimal)reader["UnitCost"],
                  (string)reader["Description"]);

                // Add to collection
                products.Add(product);
            }
        }
        finally
        {
            con.Close();
        }
        return products;
    }
}
```

You can now use this new version of the StoreDB class to create a quick data-bound list. In fact, you can exactly duplicate the result in Figure 8-5 (which binds to a DataTable) using the same code:

```
private void SimpleListBinding_Load(object sender, EventArgs e)
{
    lstModelName.DataSource = Program.StoreDB.GetProducts();
    lstModelName.DisplayMember = "ModelName";
}
```

Here, .NET uses reflection to examine the bound Product objects, searching for a property named ModelName. It then displays the value in the list.

However, there's a difference hidden behind the scenes. In the DataTable example, the list actually binds to DataRow objects and displays field values. In this example, the list binds to Product instances. When you retrieve the currently selected item, you'll find that it's a full Product object, complete with all the Product properties. This allows you to get other related information. To test this out, add the following code and attach it to the lstModelName.DoubleClick event that fires when an item in the list is double-clicked:

```
private void lstModelName_DoubleClick(object sender, System.EventArgs e)
{
    Product product = (Product)lstModelName.SelectedItem;
    MessageBox.Show(String.Format("Costs {0:C}", product.UnitCost));
}
```

Now when you double-click any item in the list, you'll see its price (Figure 8-20).

Figure 8-20. *Binding objects to a list*

The products collection works just as well if you want to create forms that have several data-bound controls. The only difference is that the object you bind is a List<Product> collection, not a DataTable:

```
// Get the data object.
List<Product> products = Program.StoreDB.GetProducts();

// Set up the bindings.
cboModelName.DataSource = products;
cboModelName.DisplayMember = "ModelName";

lblModelNumber.DataBindings.Add("Text", products, "ModelNumber");
lblUnitCost.DataBindings.Add("Text", products, "UnitCost");
lblDescription.DataBindings.Add("Text", products, "Description");
```

Even more impressively, you can bind these properties to edit controls (like text boxes) so the user can modify the properties. You can even handle the Format and Parse events to convert the data type representation that's shown in the form, as described earlier. However, there's no support for change events—if you want to react when the object is modified, you'll need to add your own event handling code.

■Note If one of your property procedures throws an exception when the user attempts to set an invalid value, no message is shown. Instead, the user is simply unable to move to another field or record until the problem is fixed. To improve this situation, you may want to raise an error event, which you can react to in your form to display information in another control (like a label). Additionally, some controls (like the DataGridView), support more sophisticated error reporting features and automatically raise an event when such problems occur.

Overriding ToString()

One interesting thing to note is what happens if you don't set the DisplayMember property. In this case, .NET simply calls the ToString() method of each object and uses that to provide the text. If the default implementation of ToString() hasn't been overriden, this text is the fully qualified class named, which means that every list appears exactly the same, as shown in Figure 8-21.

Figure 8-21. *Binding to a list of objects without DisplayMember*

However, you can put this behavior to good use by creating an object that overrides the ToString() method. This method could return some more useful information or a combination of different properties. Here's the code you would place inside the Product class:

```
public override string ToString()
{
    return string.Format("{0} ({1})", modelName, modelNumber);
}
```

This changes the text that's shown in the bound form, as shown in Figure 8-22.

Figure 8-22. *Overriding ToString() for a bound object*

■Tip The advantages that can be gained by these two techniques are remarkable. You can bind data without being forced to adopt a specific data access technology. If you don't like ADO.NET, it's easy to design your own business objects and use them for binding. Best of all, they remain available through the Items collection of the list, which means you don't need to spend additional programming effort tracking this information.

Supporting Grid Binding

The custom object approach is a little more limited if you bind it to the DataGridView control. The DataGridView control supports a range of enhanced data-binding functionality. For example, it allows the user to edit, add, and delete items. Unfortunately, none of this function-ality is available to your bound Product objects in the current example because they don't implement the necessary IBindingList interface. As a result, if you bind the current collection to the DataGridView, you're stuck with a read-only collection that doesn't allow editing, dele-tion, or insertion.

The IBindingList is actually responsible for supporting one or more of several optional features. These are described in Table 8-5. Notice that each feature is paired with a Boolean property that returns true if this feature is implemented, and false otherwise.

Table 8-5. *IBindingList Features*

Feature	Description	Property That Indicates Support
Change notification	Notifies controls when items or added, removed, or edited in the bound collection.	SupportsChangeNotification
New item insert	Allows a bound control like the DataGridView to insert a new item (when the user adds information at the bottom of the grid).	AllowNew
Item delete	Allows a bound control like the DataGridView to remove an item (when the user presses Delete).	AllowRemove
In-place editing of items	Allows a bound control like the DataGridView to perform in-place editing of an item. In other words, the various properties of the bound item can be changed.	AllowEdit
Searching	Your code can use the Find() method of the collection to locate a specific object.	SupportsSearching
Sorting	Your code can use the Sort() method of the collection to reorder the collection of objects. The DataGridView also can use this method to provide automatic sorting when column headers are clicked.	SupportsSorting

To create a collection of Product objects that supports some of these features, you could implement the IBindingList by hand. Fortunately, you don't need to because .NET provides a generic BindingList<T> collection in the System.ComponentModel namespace. This collection supports change notification, item insertion (provided the corresponding object has a default zero-parameter constructor), item deletion, and in-place editing of items. You can derive a new class from BindingList<T> if you want to support searching or sorting.

To see how this works, change your code to use the BindingList<T> collection instead of List<T>, as shown here:

```
public class StoreDB
{
    public BindingList<Product> GetProducts()
    {
        ...
        BindingList<Product> products = new BindingList<Product>();
        ...
    }
}
```

Now when you bind your control to the grid, you'll automatically get support for insertion, in-place editing, and deletion.

If you want to customize the way that the IBindingList features work, you can create a custom collection class by deriving from BindingList<T>. For example, imagine you create a Product class that doesn't have a default constructor. By default, the BindingList<T> collection won't allow new item creation. However, you can derive a class that will by manually setting AllowNew to true and overriding the AddNewCore() method, as shown here:

```
public class ProductList : BindingList<Product>
{
    public ProductList()
    {
        base.AllowNew = true;
    }

    protected override object AddNewCore()
    {
        // Create a new Product, and supply a unique model number
        // and some placeholder values.
        Product product = new Product(Guid.NewGuid().ToString(),
          "[ModelName]", 0, "[Description]");

        // Add the item to the collection.
        base.Items.Add(product);
        return product;
    }
}
```

Now you simply need to modify the StoreDB class to use the ProductList:

```
public class StoreDB
{
    public ProductList GetProducts()
    {
        ...
        ProductList products = new ProductList();
        ...
    }
}
```

There's no need to change any other part of your code. Because ProductList derives from BindingList<Product>, you can cast a ProductList object to a BindingList<Product> object if desired.

To see the difference in this example, fire up the DataGridView. Now when you scroll to the end and create a new record, you'll see your default values appear (Figure 8-23). The new record will be added to the collection, provided you edit at least one of the values.

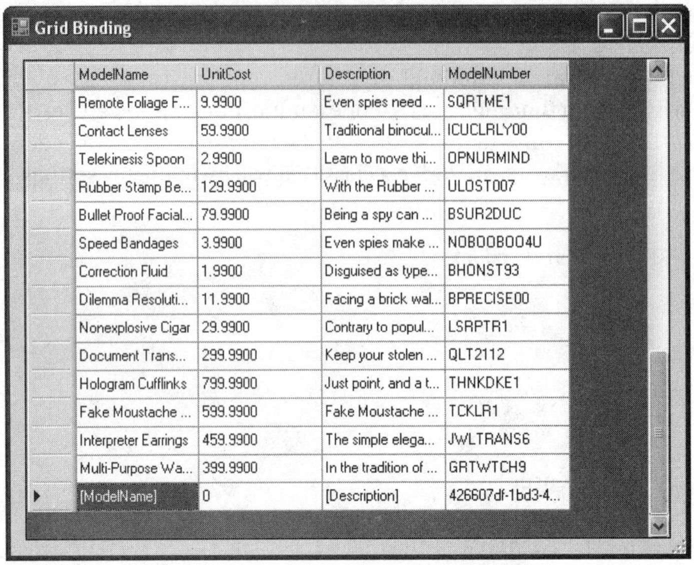

Figure 8-23. *Customizing the creation of bound objects*

Automatic Data Binding

The examples you've seen so far have used best design practices to retrieve their data from a dedicated class. This model is a bare minimum requirement for separating the user interface code from the data access code. By applying a proper separation, you make it easier to change the data access code without affecting the rest of your application, which is critical if the underlying data source changes or you just need to optimize performance (for example, by switching from ad-hoc queries to stored procedure calls).

That said, .NET 2.0 adds some time-saving features that allow you to effectively bypass this level and bring data straight into your application without writing a dedicated database wrapper component. These features are dangerous and in many cases should be avoided. In the following sections, you'll learn how they work and how you can use them intelligently without violating the basic tenets of good design.

Binding Directly to a Database (Table Adapters)

The automatic binding features all work through the Data Sources window in Visual Studio. The basic idea is that you define a data source (which can be an external database, a separate class, or a Web service) in this window. You can then bind these data sources more or less directly to a form.

The following steps take you through the simplest scenario, where you set up a data source for a database on the current computer or a local network.

1. Select Data menu ➤ Show Data Sources to show the Data Sources window (Figure 8-24).

2. Click the Add New Data Sources link.

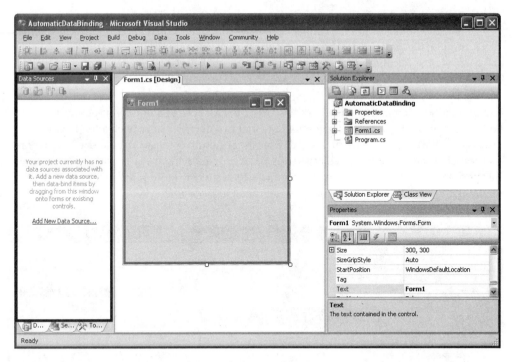

Figure 8-24. *The Data Sources window (without any data sources)*

3. You'll be given a choice of three data source types (see Figure 8-25). For this test, choose Database and click Next.

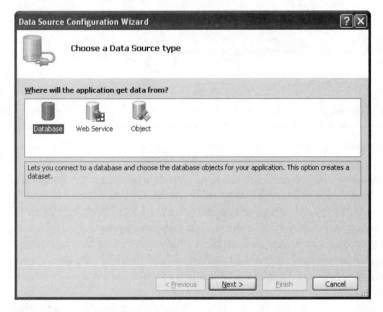

Figure 8-25. *Choosing a type of data source*

4. Follow the rest of the steps in the wizard to define the location of the database you want to use, whether or not the connection string should be stored in the application config- uration file (as it was for the StoreDB class), and what tables you'd like to make available to your application. At the end of the process, click Finish.

Figure 8-26 shows the result of creating a data source for the Products and Categories tables in the Store database. The two tables, with their associated columns, appear in the Data Sources window. The Solution Explorer shows that two new files have been added to the project—an XML schema (.xsd file) that defines the structure of these tables and a designer file that contains pages of automatically generated code for querying these two tables. The classes that perform this work (of querying the database for a specific table of records and optionally updating the table based on any changes) are called *table adapters*.

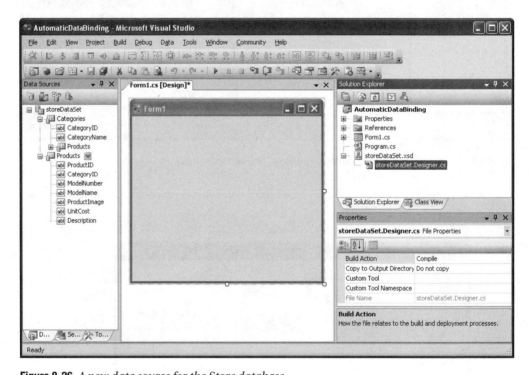

Figure 8-26. *A new data source for the Store database*

Here you'll encounter the first problem with automatic data binding in this simple scenario. The automatically generated code is created based on the tables you selected in the wizard. You don't have any ability to control how this code is generated. For example, you can't instruct the code to use a stored procedure (as the StoreDB class did) for optimum performance. You can't apply sorting or filtering clauses, and you can't control the concurrency strategy used for updating the data. If you edit the automatically generated code by hand, the changes you make will be wiped out if you need to regenerate the table adapters when the database schema changes (for example, a new table is added to the database) or a newer version of .NET is released. In the future, it's quite likely that the design-time support will improve and give you more options for configuring the generation of table adapters. However, this automatically generated code is still fundamentally limiting and unsuitable for large-scale applications where scalability and performance are key concerns.

From the Data Sources window, you can drag the full table or individual controls to any form. Before you take this step, you can click a drop-down arrow next to the table or form to configure how bound controls should be generated. For tables, you can choose to use the DataGridView for an all-in one view, which is the default choice (shown in Figure 8-27).

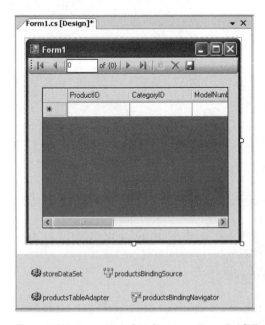

Figure 8-27. *Automatic binding to a DataGridView*

Alternatively, you can choose to bind individual controls (through simple binding), as shown in Figure 8-28. For each individual control, you can change among commonly used controls types like the TextBox, Label, LinkLabel, ListBox, and so on.

Either way, you'll end up with a few frills, like a navigation bar that allows you to add or remove records, move from one record to another, and so on. (You can create a ToolStrip with the same functionality by hand by using the code shown in this chapter.)

You'll also end up with something a lot less desirable—a slew of objects that appear directly on the form. These objects include an instance of the table adapter that queries the information and the DataSet that stores the retrieved information. You'll also get the BindingSource helper object (which allows you to quickly configure some aspects of the data-binding behavior, like whether new records are allowed) and the BindingNavigator that represents the navigation bar (and allows you to tweak its appearance).

This design is keenly undesirable because it embeds several data-specific objects directly in the form. That means that if you want to share data between forms, you need to perform wasteful trips back to the database. For each and every form that you want to connect in this way at design time, you'll end up with a duplicate copy of the table adapter, DataSet, and helper objects.

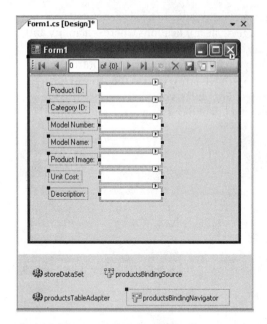

Figure 8-28. *Automatic simple binding to various controls*

If you look at the code for your form, you'll find that the data are queried when the form is loaded using the table adapters. Here's an example of what you'll see:

```
private void Form1_Load(object sender, EventArgs e)
{
    // TODO: This line of code loads data into the 'storeDataSet.Products' table.
    // You can move, or remove it, as needed.
    this.productsTableAdapter.Fill(this.storeDataSet.Products);
}
```

■**Note** It's worth noting that you don't need to connect your controls at design time. You can write code like this at any point to retrieve the data you need. For example, this allows you to put all your data into a single DataSet, which you can manually supply to each bound control. Unfortunately, if you take this approach you lose the ability to set up your data bindings at design time. In fact, if you sever the design-time connection between the bound control and its data source, all the data bindings are lost.

You can customize this section to perform your own error handling or logging. However, once again you are forced to place your database code in the form. This is one of only two areas of code that you can customize with automatic data binding. The other area is the code that saves the record and triggers and update when the user clicks a button in the navigation bar:

```
private void bindingNavigatorSaveItem_Click(object sender, EventArgs e)
{
    if (this.Validate())
    {
        this.productsBindingSource.EndEdit();
        this.productsTableAdapter.Update(this.storeDataSet.Products);
    }
    else
    {
        MessageBox.Show(this, "Validation errors occurred.", "Save",
            MessageBoxButtons.OK, MessageBoxIcon.Warning);
    }
}
```

This just isn't flexible enough for a professional application. In fact, trying to use this design is likely to leave you with an application that's poorly organized and difficult to maintain or optimize. In the following sections, you'll consider whether there's any way to redeem this design-time data-binding support.

Using a Strongly Typed DataSet

There is one feature that you get with automatically generated data sources that can be worthwhile—strongly typed DataSet classes.

When you add a data source, you end up with several new classes:

- One table adapter class for each table in the data source.

- One derived DataSet class for your database.

- One DataRow and one DataTable class for each table in the data source.

The table adapter encapsulates the data access logic. It plays the same conceptual role as StoreDB in the earlier examples, although it's much less flexible. You may use the table adapter for quick one-off mockups, but you're unlikely to use it in a large-scale application.

The DataSet, DataRow, and DataTable classes are data objects that model your data. They derive from the familiar DataSet, DataRow, and DataTable classes you already know, but they hard wire in the database schema. For example, in the previous example you'll end up with a ProductsDataTable and a ProductsDataRow class, which have the structure of the Products table hard wired into them.

These custom data classes have two advantages. First, when you query information from the database no schema information is needed because it's already in your objects. Thus, ADO.NET can fill the DataTable more efficiently (without making an initial query to determine the table schema). The other advantage is that it's easier to program with these classes because you can use strongly typed properties instead of string-based field and table lookup.

For example, you could take this code:

```
DataSet ds = Program.StoreDB.GetProducts();
foreach (DataRow row in ds.Tables["Products"])
{
    MessageBox.Show(row["ModelName"].ToString());
}
```

And change it to this:

```
StoreDataSet ds = Program.StoreDB.GetProducts();
foreach (ProductsDataRow row in ds.ProductsDataTable)
{
    MessageBox.Show(row.ModelName);
}
```

The second version is easier to write (thanks to IntelliSense) and any errors are caught at design time instead of runtime. But the real beauty is that you can use these features if you want or ignore them completely. Because ProductsDataTable derives from DataTable, ProductsDataRow derives from DataRow, and StoreDataSet derives from DataSet, the rest of your code can treat these objects as ordinary DataTable, DataRow, and DataSet instances, with the familiar string-based lookup.

In conclusion, you *might* choose to use the Data Sources window to create strongly typed data objects, which you can then use in your other data classes. However, this doesn't gain you the other benefits of automatic data binding. For example, you still don't have any way to set up bindings and data sources at design time. The cost to get these features is simply too great.

Binding Directly to a Custom Object

The automatic data-binding features in Visual Studio work much better when binding to custom objects. Now that you understand how data binding works in detail, you might still find that these features clutter your applications. However, they add some genuinely useful RAD capabilities without introducing the negative designs of automatic database binding.

■**Note** Unlike the automatic database binding, the object binding won't generate any data access for you. However, this gives you much more control (and allows you to write much better data access code).

The following example shows how you can set up object binding using the object example from before, which includes the StoreDB, Product, and ProductList classes:

1. If the object you want to bind to is in the current assembly, make sure you've compiled the assembly since you added it. If the object is in another assembly, make sure you've added a reference to that assembly.

2. Select Data ➤ Show Data Sources to show the Data Source window.

3. Click the Add New Data Sources link.

4. Choose Object and click Next.

5. Now you need to choose the *collection* object that holds the data you want to show (see Figure 8-29). This is the object that the controls bind to. In this example, you'll use the ProductList collection, not StoreDB.

6. Once you've made your choice, click Finish to end the wizard.

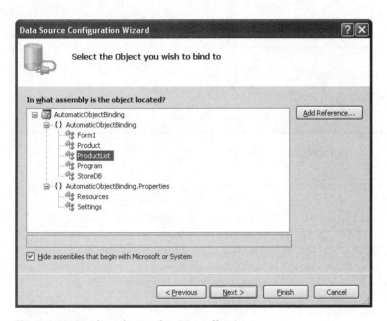

Figure 8-29. *Binding the ProductList collection*

When you take these steps, Visual Studio doesn't generate any new code (although it does record the information about the data source in the project file). To bind a form to your ProductList, choose the appropriate controls for each data member in the drop-down lists in the Data Sources window. Then, drag the controls to a form. Figure 8-30 shows one possible result.

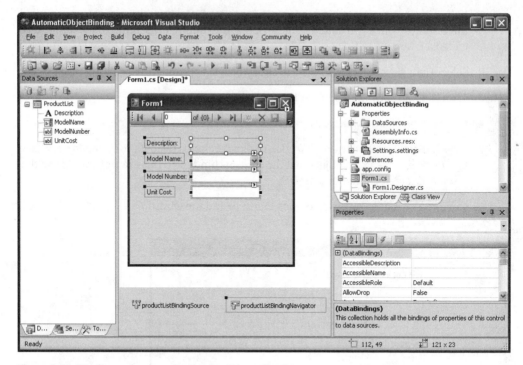

Figure 8-30. *Binding a form to the ProductList collection*

You'll still need to rearrange these controls to get the result you really want. Depending on your scenario, this might take longer than just designing the form from scratch. However, you do start off with a handy navigation bar that lets you move through the collection of product records.

When you run this application, you'll end up with a blank form. That's because Visual Studio has no idea how you plan to create a ProductList collection, and it doesn't generate any code. This is also the most flexible design, because it allows you to generate a ProductList collection in a variety of ways (from a database that gets every record, from a more targeted search, from a serialized file, and so on).

To complete this example, you need to add code like this, which uses the familiar StoreDB to return the ProductList:

```
private void Form1_Load(object sender, EventArgs e)
{
    productListBindingSource.DataSource = Program.StoreDB.GetProducts();
}
```

The great advantage here is that you don't need to write the code by hand that sets up your data bindings to the Product objects. Also, you only need to connect one object instead of wiring up the DataSource property of each individual control, which is a significant code savings.

You can use this approach to get better design-time support when using your own data access components. However, this a minor convenience compared to the promise of no-code data binding, which just won't be practical for most programmers.

Data-Aware Controls

Not all controls work well with data binding. For example, the popular TreeView and ListView controls need to be filled manually. In other circumstances, you may have controls that support data binding, but you want to take control of the entire process. Maybe you want to create a control that can't be filled all at once, but uses partial data reads or just-in-time queries to allow a user to browse through a large amount of data.

.NET provides many opportunities for data integration without data binding. One handy technique is using the Tag property. Every control provides the Tag property, but the .NET framework doesn't use it. Instead, you can use the Tag property to store any information or object you need. For example, you could use this property to store the relevant business object with each node in a TreeView, or a DataRow object with each row in a ListView.

■**Note** This example uses a GetProductsAndCategories() method that fills a DataSet with two DataTable objects and sets up a DataRelation between the two tables. The code is similar to what you've seen before— for the full details, see the online code or the next example, which presents the complete data access component.

The next example shows a TreeView that embeds the data it needs use the Tag property of each node. Here's the code needed to fill the TreeView (which could be placed in the Form.Load event handler):

```
DataSet ds = Program.StoreDB.GetProductsAndCategories();

// Add the records to the TreeView.
TreeNode nodeParent, nodeChild;
foreach (DataRow rowParent in ds.Tables["Categories"].Rows)
{
    // Add the category node.
    nodeParent = treeDB.Nodes.Add((string)rowParent["CategoryName"]);

    // Store the disconnected category information.
    nodeParent.Tag = rowParent;

    foreach (DataRow rowChild in rowParent.GetChildRows(relCategoryProduct))
    {
        // Add the product order node.
        nodeChild = nodeParent.Nodes.Add((string)rowChild["ModelName"]);

        // Store the disconnected product information.
        nodeChild.Tag = rowChild;
    }
}
```

When a node is selected, a generic code routine reads the accompanying DataRow and displays all the information it contains in a label. (This code reacts to the TreeView.AfterSelect event.)

```
private void treeDB_AfterSelect(object sender, TreeViewEventArgs e)
{
    lblInfo.Text = string.Empty;
    DataRow row = (DataRow)e.Node.Tag;

    StringBuilder sb = new StringBuilder();
    foreach (object field in row.ItemArray)
    {
        sb.Add(field.ToString());
        sb.Add("\n");
    }
    lblInfo.Text = sb.ToString();
}
```

The result, shown in Figure 8-31, is a TreeView that has easy access to the information for each node.

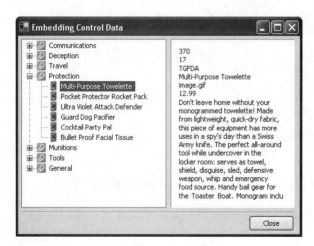

Figure 8-31. *A TreeView with embedded data*

A Decoupled TreeView with Just-in-Time Nodes

The preceding TreeView example requires very little information about the data source. Instead, it loops through the available fields to display a list of information. However, in doing so the control also gives up the ability to show the data in a more acceptable format. For example, fields that aren't important are always displayed, and the field order is fixed.

There is an elegant way to solve this problem. The next example shows a TreeView that still embeds data, but relies on the StoreDB class to transform the DataRow fields into display information (see Figure 8-32). Thanks to this approach, the TreeView doesn't need to handle the table hierarchy.

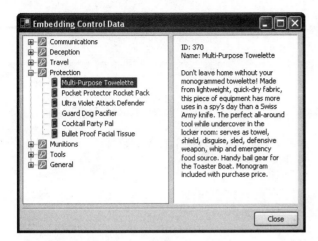

Figure 8-32. *A decoupled TreeView*

The form begins by filling the tree with a list of categories and adds dummy nodes under every level.

```
private void TreeViewForm_Load(object sender, System.EventArgs e)
{
    TreeNode nodeParent;
    foreach (DataRow row in Program.StoreDB.GetCategories().Rows)
    {
        // Add the category node.
        nodeParent =
          treeDB.Nodes.Add(row[StoreDB.CategoryField.Name].ToString());
        nodeParent.ImageIndex = 0;

        // Store the disconnected category information.
        nodeParent.Tag = row;

        // Add a "dummy" node.
        nodeParent.Nodes.Add("*");
    }
}
```

When a node is expanded and the TreeView.BeforeExpand event fires, the code calls the StoreDB with the selected category and requests more information. The StoreDB class then returns the information needed to add the appropriate child nodes. (It's up to you whether this step uses a previously cached product DataTable or fetches it at this exact moment, although the first approach is the fastest.)

```
private void treeDB_BeforeExpand(object sender, TreeViewCancelEventArgs e)
{
    TreeNode nodeSelected, nodeChild;
    nodeSelected = e.Node;
```

```
        if (nodeSelected.Nodes[0].Text == "*")
        {
            // This is a dummy node.
            nodeSelected.Nodes.Clear();

            foreach (DataRow row in
              Program.StoreDB.GetProductsInCategory((DataRow)nodeSelected.Tag))
            {
                string field = row[StoreDB.ProductField.Name].ToString();
                nodeChild = nodeSelected.Nodes.Add(field);

                // Store the disconnected product information.
                nodeChild.Tag = row;
                nodeChild.ImageIndex = 1;
                nodeChild.SelectedImageIndex = 1;
            }
        }
    }
}
```

When an item is selected, the code again relies on the ProductDatabase class to "translate" the embedded DataRow. In this case, the code responds to the TreeView.AfterSelect event:

```
private void treeDB_AfterSelect(object sender, TreeViewEventArgs e)
{
    lblInfo.Text = Program.StoreDB.GetDisplayText((DataRow)e.Node.Tag);
}
```

This pattern allows the StoreDB to handle its own data access strategy—it can fetch the information as needed with queries every time a node is expanded, or it can retain it in memory as a private member variable (as it does in this example). Even better, the StoreDB code is extremely simple because it doesn't need to convert ADO.NET objects into "business" objects. The TreeView can use and embed the ADO.NET objects natively, without needing to know anything about their internal field structures.

Here's the full StoreDB code for this example:

```
public class StoreDB
{
    public DataTable GetCategories()
    {
        string connectionString = Properties.Settings.Default.Store;
        SqlConnection con = new SqlConnection(connectionString);
        SqlCommand cmd = new SqlCommand("GetProducts", con);
        cmd.CommandType = CommandType.StoredProcedure;
        SqlDataAdapter adapter = new SqlDataAdapter(cmd);

        DataSet ds = new DataSet();
        adapter.Fill(ds, Tables.Product);
        cmd.CommandText = "GetCategories";
        adapter.Fill(ds, Tables.Category);
```

```
    // Set up a relation between these tables (optional).
    DataRelation relCategoryProduct = new DataRelation("CategoryProduct",
    ds.Tables[Tables.Category].Columns[CategoryField.ID],

    ds.Tables[Tables.Product].Columns[ProductField.CategoryID]);
    ds.Relations.Add(relCategoryProduct);
    return ds.Tables[Tables.Category];
}

public static class Tables
{
    public const string Product = "Products";
    public const string Category = "Categories";
}

public static class ProductField
{
    public const string Name = "ModelName";
    public const string Description = "Description";
    public const string CategoryID = "CategoryID";
}

public static class CategoryField
{
    public const string Name = "CategoryName";
    public const string ID = "CategoryID";
}

public DataRow[] GetProductsInCategory(DataRow rowParent)
{
    DataRelation relCategoryProduct = rowParent.Table.DataSet.Relations[0];
    return rowParent.GetChildRows(relCategoryProduct);
}

public string GetDisplayText(DataRow row)
{
    string text = "";

    switch (row.Table.TableName)
    {
        case Tables.Product:
            text = "ID: " + row[0] + "\n";
            text += "Name: " + row[ProductField.Name] + "\n\n";
            text += row[ProductField.Description];
            break;
    }
```

```
        return text;
    }
}
```

The ProductDatabase methods can be used easily with other controls. None of them are specific to the TreeView.

The Last Word

This chapter provided an in-depth examination of the inner workings of data binding. It also has considered the best practices you need to use for data binding without crippling your code and tying it too closely to the specific data-source details. In Chapter 15, you'll return to data binding and learn how you can create a rich data-bound form using only a single control: the new DataGridView.

PART 2

Custom Controls

CHAPTER 9

■ ■ ■

Custom Control Basics

Custom controls are a key theme in Windows Forms development. They can help you improve encapsulation, simplify your programming model, and make your user interface more "pluggable" (so that you can swap out a control and replace it with a completely different one without rewriting the rest of your application). Of course, custom controls have other benefits, including the way they can transform a generic window into a slick, modern interface with eye-catching graphics.

This chapter introduces the different types of custom controls and discusses the problems they solve. You'll learn the basic steps you need to create control projects and test them in Visual Studio. However, you won't actually create a realistic control. Instead, you'll get ready for the next four chapters, which build on these fundamentals to create some more practical controls.

Understanding Custom Controls

Generally, developers tackle custom control development for one of three reasons:

- To create controls that provide entirely new functionality or combine existing user inter-face elements in a unique way. For example, the .NET framework doesn't include any controls for charts, image thumbnails, or dockable windows—but that doesn't stop you from building your own.

- To create controls with a distinct original look, or ones that mimic the controls in a professional application that aren't available to the masses. Examples include shaped buttons and the infamous Outlook bar.

- To create controls that abstract away unimportant details and are tailored for a specific type of data. For example, if you're creating a file-browsing application, it's probably easier to program with a custom DirectoryTreeView control rather than the generic TreeView.

Creating custom controls in .NET is far easier than it is in COM-based frameworks like MFC or Visual Basic 6, where you typically need to use the ActiveX model. The ActiveX model has a cumbersome deployment model, poor versioning support (aka "DLL Hell"), and weak support for design-time features. In .NET, creating a custom control is often as easy as creating an ordinary class. You simply inherit from the best possible parent class and add the specific features you need. Best of all, thanks to .NET's deep language integration, you can share your control assemblies with other applications written in any .NET language.

THIRD-PARTY CONTROLS

The fact that custom controls are conceptually simple (and easy to deploy) doesn't mean you won't be forced to write a significant amount of code! If you want to create a rich, graphically intensive widget, you could easily write hundreds of lines of GDI+ code to perfect it. That's why you should consider some of the free and commercial controls that are available for Windows Forms.

There is a variety of options for popular control types like Outlook bars, dockable windows, and wizards. Some of the best are provided at Divelements (www.divil.co.uk) and Actipro (www.actiprosoftware.com). Another good option is Crownwood software (www.dotnetmagic.com), which includes complete source code for its products.

Finally, if you're interested in a free solution that can save you some money (or one you can extend to learn even more about .NET), check out the official Windows Forms community site (www.windowsforms.net), where an expansive control gallery provides free solutions and trial software.

Types of Custom Controls

Developers often make a distinction between three types of controls:

- **User controls.** These are the simplest type of control. They inherit from the System.Windows.Forms.UserControl class, and follow a model of composition. Usually, user controls combine more than one control in a logical unit (like a group of text boxes for entering address information). You'll learn about user controls in Chapter 10.

- **Derived controls.** With a derived control (also known as an inherited control), you choose the existing .NET control that is closest to what you want to provide. Then you create a custom class that inherits from the class you've chosen, and overrides or adds properties and methods. You'll see examples of this approach in Chapter 11.

- **Owner-drawn controls.** These controls use GDI+ drawing routines to generate their interfaces from scratch. Because of this, they tend to inherit from a more basic class that's farther down the control hierarchy, like System.Windows.Forms.Control. Owner-drawn controls require the most work, and provide the most flexibility. You'll see them at work in Chapter 12.

The distinction between the three control types is slightly exaggerated. For example, you can create a user control that paints itself with GDI+[1]. Similarly, instead of inheriting from Control, UserControl, or a full-fledged .NET control class, you can inherit from one of the intermediary classes to get a different level of support. For example, a control that needs the ability to contain other controls can inherit from ContainerControl.

---

1. This approach is slightly heavier than deriving from Control, but it does give you a few extra frills, like a built-in Load() method you can override to perform initialization.

Table 9-1 describes the classes you can inherit from when creating a custom control. The table is organized from general to specific. Figure 9-1 shows the relevant portion of the class hierarchy.

Table 9-1. *Base Classes for Custom Controls*

Class	Description	Examples
Component	A component is a designable class. You can drag and drop it onto the component tray at design time (see the next section for more information). However, a component is not a control, and as a result it doesn't get a piece of form real estate.	ToolTip, OpenFileDialog, Timer
Control	The first level of controls. Adds mouse support for standard events, along with keyboard handling. It's up to you to draw everything from scratch.	Owner-drawn controls (Chapter 12)
ScrollableControl	Adds support for scrolling. You shouldn't derive from this class directly. Instead, derive from ContainerControl or Panel.	
ContainerControl	Adds support for containing child controls and managing their focus.	GroupBox, Panel
UserControl	Adds the Load event for initialization, and provides design-time support you can use to lay out and configure child controls in Visual Studio.	User controls (Chapter 10)
Form and other control classes	You can derive from the Form class to create a reusable form template, or derive from an existing control to override and enhance its functionality.	Derived controls (Chapter 11)

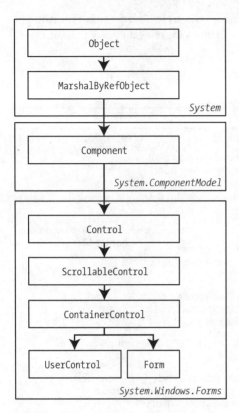

Figure 9-1. *The control base classes*

Custom Components

Along with custom controls, you can also create custom *components* that interact with your user interface. Technically, the .NET framework defines a component as a class that implements the System.ComponentModel.IComponent interface or that derives from another class that implements IComponent (such as System.ComponentModel.Component). If you dig into the .NET class library you'll discover the Control class derives from Component, which means that all controls are a type of component (as shown in Figure 9-1).

■Note Although controls are technically a type of component, when I refer to components in this book, I'm usually referring to components that *aren't* controls.

Component classes have two characteristics that distinguish them from noncomponent classes:

- **Components provide basic design-time support.** You can add component classes to the Toolbox in Visual Studio, and then drag and drop them onto a form. If you drop a control onto a form, it appears exactly where you've placed it. If you drop any other type of component on a form, it appears in the component tray under the form. Either way, you can configure it to your heart's content by selecting it and changing properties in the Properties window.

- **Components provide a deterministic way to release resources.** Because the IComponent interface extends the IDisposable interface, every component provides a Dispose() method. When this method is invoked, the component immediately frees the resources it uses.

Usually, you use custom components because you want to be able to drop an instance of your class onto a form at design time. For example, the OpenFileDialog, MenuStrip, and ImageList classes are components. Often, components have some hand in generating the user interface—as all these classes do. However, that doesn't need to be the case. In the Components tab of the Toolbox, you'll find classes like Timer, EventLog, and BackgroundWorker that don't have any visual representation at runtime.

Custom components often provide services used by other controls (like the validation classes in Chapter 18). One specialized example is extender providers like the ToolTip component, which extend other controls with additional properties. You'll learn how to create your own custom extender providers in Chapter 25.

Typically, if you want to create a custom component that's not a control, you'll derive your class from the Component class. The Component class provides a basic implementation of the IComponent interface. All you need to do is add your own properties and methods—there's no basic boilerplate code to write. Alternatively, you can implement IComponent by hand, but it's more work and doesn't add any benefit (other than giving you the flexibility to derive from another class).

There's one other advantage that you gain from creating a component instead of an ordinary class. Visual Studio gives all components a design surface. That means you can switch to design view, and drag and drop other controls onto the new component you're creating. You've seen this model in detail with forms, but with components it's more limited—in fact, all you'll see is a blank surface that looks like the component tray and fills the whole design window, as shown in Figure 9-2.

You can drop controls and components onto this component tray, and when you do, Visual Studio will generate the appropriate code and add it to the hidden InitializeComponent() method of your component class. If you're an unredeemable fan of dragging and dropping ADO.NET objects like SqlConnection and SqlCommand, this offers a great compromise. You can add these objects to a custom component and configure them at design time, rather than tightly coupling them to a single form in your application.

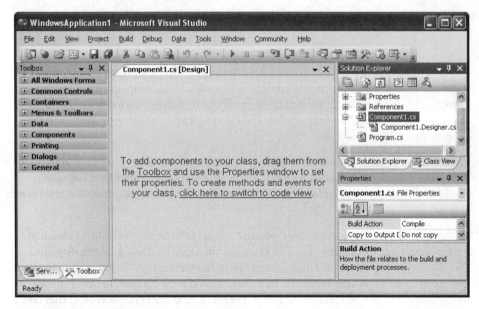

Figure 9-2. *The design surface of a component*

Control Projects

When designing a custom control or component, you could add the control or component class directly to your application project. However, this approach prevents you from reusing your class in multiple applications. A better, more component-based approach is to create a separate project for your custom control or component. You can then use it in any other project by adding a reference to the compiled DLL assembly. This separate control or component project is a library.

The Library Project

Typically, you'll create your control as either a Class Library Project (for components) or a Windows Control Library (for custom controls). The choice you make doesn't have much impact—essentially all the project type does is configure the default references and the namespaces that are initially imported into your project. The important fact is that either way you're creating a library project, which compiles into a DLL assembly instead of a stand-alone executable. This DLL can then be shared with any other project that needs to use the control. Figure 9-3 shows the option you need to select to create a Windows Control Library project.

When you begin your control project, you'll probably find that you need to add a few assembly references and import some namespaces. This is particularly the case if you're adding advanced design-time support for your controls, in which case you'll usually need a reference to the System.Design.dll and System.Drawing.Design.dll assemblies. (To add these references, just right-click the project in the Solution Explorer, select Add Reference, and find the assemblies in the list.)

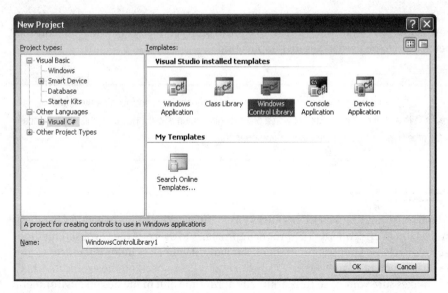

Figure 9-3. *Creating a control project*

Having accomplished this step, you'll probably want to import some namespaces in your code files so you don't have to type fully qualified names. Useful namespaces include System.Windows.Forms, System.ComponentModel, and System.Drawing. When building classes for design-time support, you'll need to rely on many more namespaces, as you'll see in Chapter 13. Remember that importing namespaces isn't required—it's just a convenience that helps trim long lines of code.

Once you've created the project, you can add your custom control or component classes. Generally, you'll place each control in a separate file. This isn't a requirement, but it makes it easier to work with your code when you start to add frills like design-time smarts.

To try this out, you can create the following exceedingly simple custom control that was first presented in Chapter 1. It extends the TextBox class so that it rejects non-numeric input:

```
public class NumericTextBox : TextBox
{
    protected override void OnKeyPress(KeyPressEventArgs e)
    {
        // Ignore all non-control and non-numeric key presses.
        if (!char.IsControl(e.KeyChar) && !char.IsDigit(e.KeyChar))
        {
            e.Handled = true;
        }

        // Call the implementation in the base TextBox class,
        // which raises the KeyPress event.
        base.OnKeyPress(e);
    }
}
```

To build your project at any time, right-click it in the Solution Explorer and choose Build. For obvious reasons, you can't launch a custom control project directly. Instead, your controls or components need to be used in another application.

Tip Visual Studio 2005 adds a feature that *does* allow you to launch user controls directly. It supplies a basic test harness (a form that shows the control with a property grid) automatically. However, this convenience doesn't work for other types of control projects or components.

The Disposable Pattern

If your class holds on to any unmanaged resources (like unmanaged memory or window handles), you need to clean them up properly. The proper approach is to override the Dispose() method, and make sure you release your resources there. Similarly, if your class holds references to any IDisposable classes, you need to override Dispose() and call Dispose() on those objects. This cleanup code makes sure your code runs optimally at runtime and in the design environment.

As long as you're deriving your class from Component or Control, it's very easy to add the Dispose() logic you need. Simply override the version of the method that takes a single Boolean parameter, as shown here:

```
protected override void Dispose(bool disposing)
{ ... }
```

The disposing parameter is an unusual ingredient—essentially, it indicates how your object was disposed. If the disposing parameter is true, your object has been properly released. In other words, some other piece of code explicitly called the Dispose() method. If disposing is false, you haven't had the same success—instead, your object was left floating in memory until the garbage collector eventually tracked it down and disposed it.

Note The dispose pattern isn't hard-wired into the common language runtime—instead, it's built into the Component class. If you inherit IComponent on your own, you'll need to re-create this pattern.

The reason you check the disposing parameter is to decide whether you should call the Dispose() method on other linked objects. If your object is being disposed properly (disposing is true), you should call the Dispose() method of the disposable objects that your class uses, so that they are cleaned up, as well. For example, if you're creating an owner-drawn control, you might have Pen and Brush objects that are held in member variables and need to be disposed. On the other hand, if the garbage collector is at work (disposing is false), these linked objects may or may not already be cleaned up, so you need to leave them alone to be safe.

Here's the structure you should use when you override Dispose():

```
protected override void Dispose(bool disposing)
{
    if (disposing)
    {
        // Call Dispose() on other linked objects.
        // For example: drawBrush.Dispose();
    }
    // Clean up any unmanaged resources.
}
```

Although it's not much work to write this basic conditional logic in the Dispose() method, Visual Studio will create it for you if you add a new component or user control by choosing Project ➤ Add Item. That's because components and user controls both have the ability to hold other components on their design surface (in the component tray). To make sure these objects are properly released, Visual Studio creates a component collection in your class:

```
private System.ComponentModel.IContainer components = null;
private void InitializeComponent()
{
    components = new System.ComponentModel.Container();
}
```

Visual Studio also adds cleanup code that calls Dispose() on every object in the component collection when your component or user control is disposed:

```
protected override void Dispose(bool disposing)
{
    if (disposing && (components != null))
    {
        components.Dispose();
    }
    base.Dispose(disposing);
}
```

There are two important details to keep in mind. First, the components collection contains only components that need to be disposed explicitly. If you add a component that doesn't hold onto any unmanaged resources, this component won't add itself to the component collection. Secondly, Visual Studio generates this boilerplate implementation of the Dispose() method only if you create a component or user control class using the Project ➤ Add Item menu command. If you type in the code by hand or create an ordinary class, you won't end up with the basic implementation of the Dispose() method. This isn't a problem, unless you start dropping components onto the design surface of your class, in which case you have no guarantee that these components will be cleaned up properly. But of course, now that you've read this, you won't make that mistake.

■**Note** To find the plumbing for the Dispose() method, you'll need to peek at the hidden designer file for your component. For example, if you create a component named Component1, Visual Studio creates a Component1.Designer.cs file with a partial definition of your class that fills in these details. (This is the same model Visual Studio uses with forms, which you saw in Chapter 1.) To see the designer file, just select Project ➤ Show All Files.

The Client Project

Once you've created the perfect control, you need an easy way to admire your work—and hunt for errors. Testing custom controls can be a little awkward. Visual Studio provides several options:

- You can add test forms directly to your control-class projects and remove them when they are no longer needed (or just set the Build Action to None instead of Compile, so that they are retained but not added to the compiled DLL).

- You can open two instances of Visual Studio, one with the control project, and one with the control test project. To use this approach, you need to add your control to the Toolbox manually.

- You can create a solution with two projects: one that tests the control, and one that uses the control. This is the easiest approach, because Visual Studio will temporarily add your control to the Toolbox automatically (as described in the next section). This approach also gives you a good separation between your control code and your test harness.

In order for you to use your control in another project, that project needs a reference to the compiled control assembly. When you add this reference, Visual Studio stores the location of the control assembly file. Every time you rebuild your client project, Visual Studio copies the latest version of the control assembly into the client's Bin directory, where the client executable resides. This ensures that you're always testing against the most recent build of a control.

Automatic Toolbox Support

Visual Studio 2005 introduces a time-saving feature that can let you start using custom controls without any extra configuration steps. To try this out, create a solution that contains two projects—the custom control-class library and the client application (see Figure 9-4).

This approach works because every time you compile a class library, Visual Studio scans through the classes it contains, and adds each component or control to a special temporary tab at the top of the Toolbox. You can then create instances of the control by dragging it to the design surface on a form. The first time you add a control to a project, Visual Studio adds a reference to the assembly where the control is defined, and copies this assembly to your project directory.

For example, if you open a project named CustomControl and it contains at least one component-derived class, Visual Studio will add a tab named CustomControl Components to the Toolbox, as shown in Figure 9-5. This tab remains as long as the project is open, and it's updated every time you compile the class library project.

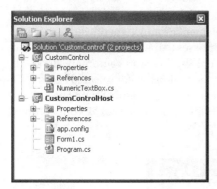

Figure 9-4. *A control-class library and client in the same solution*

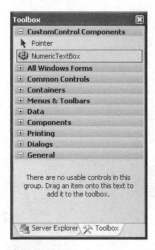

Figure 9-5. *Components and controls appear automatically in the Toolbox.*

When you actually deploy an application that uses a custom control, all you need to do is ensure that the required control DLL is in the same directory as the application executable. When you copy these files to another computer, you do not need to worry about registering them or performing additional steps. This is the infamous zero-touch deployment that has been heavily hyped with .NET.

Customizing the Toolbox

Visual Studio's automatic Toolbox support for custom controls offers the best solution if you're planning to reuse a control in just one or two projects. But in other cases, you'll want something a little more permanent. For example, you might decide a control is so useful you want to have the Toolbox item handy to insert it in any project, even if the library project with the custom control isn't open. In this case, you need to customize the Toolbox so it includes the custom control.

To add a component or control to the Toolbox, right-click the Toolbox, and select Choose Items. Then select the .NET Framework Components tab, and click the Browse button. Once

you double-click the appropriate assembly (for example, CustomControl.dll), Visual Studio
will examine its metadata to find all the classes that implement IComponent (including custom
component and custom controls). It adds each of these classes to the list and selects them. You
won't necessarily see the classes in the list, because Visual Studio doesn't automatically scroll
to the right place. Instead, you'll need to scroll through the list looking for selected items
(which are highlighted in blue). As a shortcut, you can click on the Assembly Name header to
sort the list by assembly. You can then scroll to your assembly, and you'll see all your controls
at once (see Figure 9-6).

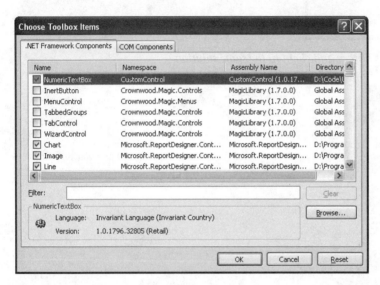

Figure 9-6. *Referencing an assembly with controls*

■Note In truth, not all components and controls will show up in the Choose Toolbox Items list. Component
or control classes that are decorated with the DesignTimeVisible(false) or ToolboxItem(false) attributes explicitly
prevent themselves from being placed in the Toolbox. As a result, they won't appear in the list.

Every selected item will be shown in the Toolbox. If you don't want one of the controls to
be added to the Toolbox, just remove the check mark next to its name. When you're finished,
click OK to continue and update the Toolbox with the currently selected controls.

Figure 9-7 shows the custom NumericTextBox control, which is added to the bottom of the
Toolbox alongside its .NET counterparts. If you haven't configured a custom icon, it appears
with the default gear icon. (Chapter 13 discusses how to choose a different Toolbox icon.) If you
want, you can reorganize the Toolbox by dragging your custom controls to another position or
another tab.

Figure 9-7. *A custom control in the Toolbox*

■**Note** The Toolbox is a user-specific Visual Studio setting, not a project-specific setting. This means that once you add a control to the Toolbox, it will remain there until you remove it, regardless of what project you are working with.

The GAC

If multiple applications need to use the same control, you can copy the appropriate assembly to each application directory. This gives you the freedom to update some applications with additional functionality without worrying about backward compatibility. It also simplifies deployment, and requires only a minuscule amount of extra disk space. For all these reasons, it's the favored approach.

Another option is to install your component to the Global Assembly Cache (the same repository that contains the core .NET assemblies). The Global Assembly Cache (or GAC) allows multiple versions of a component to be installed side by side. The GAC also ensures that every application uses the version of a control that it was compiled with, which almost completely eliminates versioning headaches. The disadvantage is that you now have an extra deployment step—you need to install the component into the GAC on each computer where it will be used. You also need to sign your versioned assembly using a private key to ensure that it has a unique identifier (and can't conflict with other components), and to ensure that no other organization can release a new control that claims to be yours. This process is the same for any shared component, whether it is a control or a business object.

Many factors that required a central repository for components in the old world of COM don't apply with .NET. If you just want to share a control between specific applications, you probably don't need the additional complexity of the GAC. On the other hand, if you are a tool vendor who creates, sells, and distributes custom controls, you may want to use the GAC to make your control available machine-wide. This process is well documented in the MSDN help, but the essential steps are explained in the following three sections.

■Tip You don't need to install your control to the GAC to use licensing (which is described in Chapter 13). In fact, I recommend that you don't place the controls developed in this chapter into the GAC unless you have a clear reason to do so. (For example, if you're creating a fairly complex component you want to sell as a third-party add-in.)

Creating a Key

Before you can install an assembly in the GAC, you need to sign it using the sn.exe command-line utility included with the .NET framework. To create a key, you use the -k parameter, and specify the name for your key, as shown here:

```
sn -k MyKey.snk
```

Each .snk file contains a private and a public key. Private and public keys provide a special time-honored form of encryption (called *asymmetric encryption*). Anything encrypted with a private key can be read only with the corresponding public key. Conversely, anything encrypted with a public key can be read only with the corresponding private key. The public key is typically made available to the world. The private key is carefully guarded. Public and private key encryption is sometimes used with e-mail. If you want to create a message that only a specific user can decipher, you would use that individual's public key to encrypt the message. If you want to create a message that anyone can read but no one can impersonate, you would use your own private key. Thus, asymmetric encryption can protect data *and* your identity.

In .NET, the private key is used to compile the assembly, and the public key is embedded inside the assembly. When an application uses your control, the common language runtime uses the public key to decode information from the manifest. Thus, no one else can create an update to your assembly because someone would need your original private key to encode it successfully.

■Tip You can create a strongly named component even if you don't intend to deploy it to the GAC. This has the advantage of guaranteeing your company's identity.

Applying a Key to a Control Assembly

To add the key to a control project, you need to add an attribute to the AssemblyInfo.cs file for your project. To find this file, look under the Properties node in the Solution Explorer.

The AssemblyInfo.cs file contains a variety of assembly attributes that configure assembly metadata, including details like versioning and product name. Here's the attribute you need to attach a key file:

```
[assembly: AssemblyKeyFile(@"c:\KeyFiles\MyKey.snk")]
```

If you specify a relative file name instead of the full path for the key file, the compiler looks in the \obj\Debug directory or the \obj\Release directory when you build the project, depending on whether you're compiling your code in debug or release mode. One easy way to get around this is to place the key file in the root project directory, and use the following attribute:

```
[assembly: AssemblyKeyFile(@"..\..\MyKey.snk")]
```

When you compile a project that has one of these attributes, the compiler searches for the key file. If it can't find the key file, it fails with an error message. If it does find the key file, the key information is added to the assembly metadata. .NET also supports delayed assembly signing, which allows you to add the strong name just before shipping the control. This is useful in a large organization, because it allows you to debug the control without requiring the private key. The assembly can then be signed just before it is released by the individual who guards the private key. Delayed assembly assignment requires a little more grunt work, and is described in the MSDN help.

Attaching Keys in Visual Studio

Visual Studio saves you from the trouble of using the sn command-line tool. Instead, it allows you to generate and attach a key file without leaving the development environment. To do so, double-click the Properties section in the Solution Explorer, and select the Signing tab. Select the check box "Sign the assembly" and then choose your key file in the drop-down list control. At this point, you can generate a new key (by selecting New) or browse to the location of an existing key file (by choosing Browse). Once you complete this step, the assembly key file will be added to the project and it will appear in the Solution Explorer.

Note that you don't need to add the AssemblyKeyFile attribute to your application when you use this approach. Instead, Visual Studio will take care of emitting the appropriate metadata when it compiles the assembly.

Installing a Control in the GAC

Now that your control assembly is signed, you can install it to the GAC using a dedicated setup program or the Global Assembly Cache tool (gacutil.exe) included with the .NET framework, as shown here:

```
gacutil /i CustomControl.dll
```

You can also drag and drop the assembly to the C:\[WindowsDir]\Assembly directory in Windows Explorer, which installs it automatically using a special plug-in. You'll see your assembly listed in the assembly list (see Figure 9-8), with its public key and version information. Life couldn't be easier.

If you install later versions of the same assembly in the GAC, the original version remains alongside the new version. Clients automatically use the assembly that they were compiled with (and raise an exception if they can't find the right version in the GAC). You can uninstall assemblies using the /u switch in the Global Assembly Cache tool, or by selecting the assembly in Windows Explorer and pressing the Del key.

■**Tip** There are many more options for configuring version policies using application configuration files. You can consult the MSDN reference or a book about .NET fundamentals for more information.

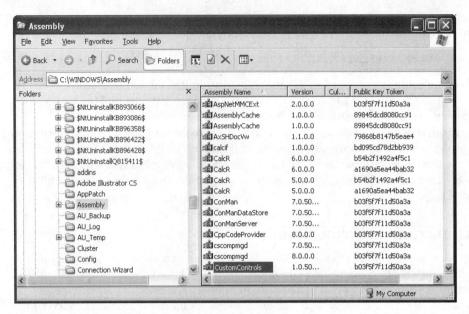

Figure 9-8. *A custom control assembly in the GAC*

The Last Word

This chapter introduced one of the most important ingredients in advanced user interfaces—custom controls. Now that you've digested the basics of creating, compiling, and consuming a custom control, it's time to look at some practical examples in the next three chapters. All of these custom controls are included with the downloadable code samples for this book

---

Note All the control projects in the samples have names that end with "Control" (as in DirectoryTreeControl), while the Windows Forms projects that test the controls have names that end with "Host" (as in DirectoryTreeHost). The easiest way to run these examples is to open the solution file that will open both projects at once.

CHAPTER 10

∎∎∎

User Controls

User controls allow you to build customized controls by combining the existing controls in the Windows Forms toolkit. Typically, a user control consists of a group of ordinary controls that are related in some way. For example, you might create a user control that models a simple record browser, combining navigation buttons with other display controls. Or, you could create a user control that wraps together related input fields and validators. The advantage is that you can build a user control in almost the same way as you build a full-fledged form.

Although user controls are the simplest type of custom control project, they suffer from some serious drawbacks:

- User controls make it a little too easy for developers to combine business logic with an inflexible block of user interface. For example, if the application programmer doesn't like the way individual text boxes are arranged in an address user control, there's no easy way to change it. Similarly, if the underlying business logic needs to change, the control needs to be rebuilt and redistributed. Although you can solve these problems with good design, user controls tend to be more fragile and less flexible than other types of custom controls.

- Unless you take additional steps, user controls hide all the properties and methods of their child controls. This is similar to the way ActiveX controls worked in Visual Basic 6.

That said, user controls are useful for quickly solving certain problems and creating composite controls. They also have one great benefit—you can use the design support in Visual Studio to add, configure, and lay out child controls inside a user control. This makes it possible to create a simple composite control very quickly.

Understanding User Controls

To add a user control to a .NET custom control project, right-click the Solution Explorer window and select Add ➤ User Control. Figure 10-1 shows a user control in the Solution Explorer.

To add a control to a user control, just drop it onto the design surface in the same way as you would a form. You can (and should) use anchoring and docking with the controls in your user control. That ensures that they always resize to fit the bounds of their container. Remember, the size of the user control is dictated by the application programmer.

You'll notice from the designer that a user control is halfway between an ordinary control and a form. It helps to imagine that a user control is just a reusable portion of a form. In fact, user controls inherit from all the same base classes as forms (described in Chapter 3).

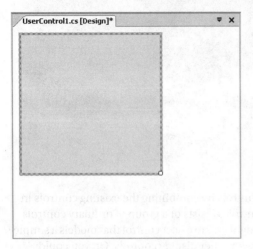

Figure 10-1. *A user control at design time*

To understand the strengths and limitations of user controls, it helps to consider a couple of examples. In this chapter, you'll see how to create and extend several user controls. First, you'll tackle a simple progress control that combines a progress bar and a label. Next, you'll tackle a more detailed thumbnail viewer. Finally, you'll consider a framework for building wizards that's based on user controls. Along the way you'll consider a few issues that are central to any custom control project, including proper encapsulation, events, and asynchronous support.

The Progress User Control

The first user control you'll consider is a simple coupling of a ProgressBar and Label control. This control solves a minor annoyance associated with the ProgressBar—there is no way to show a standard text description that indicates the percent of work complete. You can easily get around this limitation by adding a label to every form that uses the ProgressBar, and manually synchronizing the two. However, the Progress user control implements a standard, reusable solution.

Creating the Progress User Control

To begin, the user control is created with a label and a progress bar, as shown in Figure 10-2.

When you use the Progress control in a project, you'll discover that you can't access the ProgressBar or Label child controls directly. Instead, the only properties and methods that are available are those that belong to the user control itself, such as those that allow you to modify the default font and background color (as you can with a form), but not much more. To actually make the Progress user control functional, you need to wrap all the important methods and properties of the child controls with new methods and properties in the user control.

This delegation pattern can add up to a lot of extra code for an advanced control. Fortunately, when you create a user control you will usually restrict and simplify the interface so that it's more consistent and targeted for a specific use. For example, in the Progress user control you might decide not to allow the hosting form to set the font or background color for the label control.

Figure 10-2. *The progress control at design time*

■**Tip** If your user control contains several controls with the same properties (like Font), you need to decide whether to provide individual user control properties (NameFont, AddressFont, etc.) or set them all at once in a single property procedure. The UserControl class makes your job a little easier. It defines Font and ForeColor properties that are automatically applied to all the child controls unless they specify otherwise. (This is because these are *ambient properties*, which means they work in the same way in a form or any other type of container.) The UserControl class also provides BackColor and BackImage properties that configure the actual user control drawing surface.

The Progress user control provides access to three properties from the ProgressBar control (Value, Maximum, and Step) and the PerformStep() method. Here's the complete code for the Progress user control:

```
public partial class Progress : System.Windows.Forms.UserControl
{
    public int Value
    {
        get {return Bar.Value;}
        set
        {
            Bar.Value = value;
            UpdateLabel();
        }
    }
    public int Maximum
    {
        get {return Bar.Maximum;}
        set {Bar.Maximum = value;}
    }
```

```
public int Step
{
    get {return Bar.Step;}
    set {Bar.Step = value;}
}

public void PerformStep()
{
    Bar.PerformStep();
    UpdateLabel();
}

private void UpdateLabel()
{
    lblProgress.Text = (Math.Round((decimal)(Bar.Value * 100) /
        Bar.Maximum)).ToString();
    lblProgress.Text += "% Done";
}
}
```

Every time the progress bar changes (either by modifying the Value or invoking the PerformStep() method), the code calls a private method named UpdateLabel(), which changes the caption to reflect the current progress. This ensures that the label always remains completely synchronized with the progress bar.

Testing the Progress User Control

Testing this control is easy. All you need is a simple form that hosts the Progress user control and increments its value. In this case, a timer is used for this purpose. Each time the timer fires, the PerformStep() method increments the counter by its Step value:

```
private void tmrIncrementBar_Tick(object sender, System.EventArgs e)
{
    status.PerformStep();
    if (status.Maximum == status.Value)
        tmrIncrementBar.Stop();
}
```

■**Note** As discussed in the previous chapter, you can test a user control directly, just by running the user control project. Visual Studio provides a basic test form with a PropertyGrid. However, this isn't enough for a real test of the Progress control, because you need an automated way to increment the value multiple times.

The timer itself is enabled in response to a button click, which also configures the user control's initial settings:

```
private void cmdStart_Click(object sender, System.EventArgs e)
```

```
{
    tmrIncrementBar.Stop();

    // Reset the progress.
    status.Value = 0;
    status.Maximum = 20;
    status.Step = 1;

    // Start incrementing.
    tmrIncrementBar.Start();
}
```

Figure 10-3 shows the Progress control in the test application.

Figure 10-3. *The Progress user control in action*

The Back Door

Currently, the developer can access one back door in the Progress user control—the Controls collection. For example, a developer using the Progress control could dig through the Controls collection searching for the ProgressBar control. Once you find the ProgressBar control (either by looking for a specific name or by checking the class type), you can modify it directly, which means the label won't be refreshed. This technique is brittle because it leads to a tight coupling between the form and the inner workings of the user control, and therefore I strongly discourage it. However, it's important to realize this back door exists in case it could be used to introduce invalid data or cause an error you haven't anticipated.

■**Note** Of course, crafty developers are always trying out solutions to plug holes like these. One innovative solution is to override the CreateControlsInstance() method of the user control, which is called to create the control collection when the user control is instantiated. You can then replace the standard ControlCollection object with a read-only control collection that prevents direct access. This approach is detailed at `http:// www.martnet.com/~jfosler/articles/OverridingControlCollection.htm`. Although it's interesting, it isn't practical in most scenarios, because disabling the Controls collection breaks Visual Studio's design-time support, and makes it impossible to add controls to the user control design surface.

User Control Design

When creating any custom control, it helps to remember that you are designing a genuine class. As with any class, you should decide how it will communicate with other code and how it can encapsulate its private data *before* you begin writing the code. The best approach is to start by designing the control's interface. Figure 10-4 presents a UML (Unified Modeling Language) diagram that defines the interface for the Progress user control.

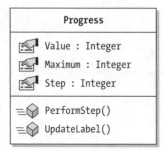

Figure 10-4. *The Progress control in UML*

There are no clear rules for designing custom controls. Generally, you should follow the same guidelines that apply to any type of class in a program. Some of the basics include the following:

- Always use properties in place of public class variables. Public variables don't give you the ability to implement any validation, event tracking, or type conversion, and they won't appear in the Properties window.

- If you provide a property, make it both readable and writable, unless there is a clear reason not to. Also, make sure that properties that can affect the control's appearance trigger a refresh when they are altered.

- Don't expose the inner workings of your control, such as the methods you use to refresh or manage the interface. Instead, expose higher-level methods that call these lower-level methods as required. Hide details that aren't important or could cause problems if used incorrectly. It's acceptable if private methods need to be used in a set order, but public methods should be able to work in any order.

- Wrap errors in custom exception classes that provide additional information to the application programmer about the mistake that was made.

- Always use enumerations when allowing the user to choose between two or more options (never fixed constant numbers or strings). Wherever possible, code so that invalid input can't be entered.

    When all other aspects of the design are perfect, streamline your control for performance. This means reducing the memory requirements, adding threading if it's appropriate, and applying updates in batches to minimize refresh times.

Finally, whenever possible, analyze the user interface for an application as a whole. You can then decide based on that analysis what custom controls can reduce the overall development effort.

An Automatic Progress Bar

Some applications use a different, less reliable type of progress. In these applications, once the progress bar reaches its maximum, it simply starts over at 0%. This approach is sometimes used in situations where you can't predict how long an operation will take (for example, if you're asynchronously retrieving information from a database or Web service). In these situations, the progress bar is simply intended to reassure the user that the application is still working, rather than to convey the actual amount of progress.

Converting the progress bar to use this type of behavior is easy—all you need to do is move the timer into the user control. Then, add a new PercentPerSecond property and remove the Maximum and Step properties. Whereas the Step property indicates the number of units that the progress bar should increment with each step, the PercentPerSecond property indicates the amount the progress bar should be incremented each second.

```
private int percentPerSecond = 5;
public int PercentPerSecond
{
    get {return percentPerSecond;}
    set
    {
        if (value < 0)
            throw new ArgumentException("Progress cannot go backward.");
        else if (value == 0)
            throw new ArgumentException("Progress must go on.");
        percentPerSecond = value;
    }
}
```

You'll notice that the PercentPerSecond property doesn't map directly to any of the properties in the child controls. Instead, it's a higher-level property that's stored by the user control. Using the PercentPerSecond property and a couple of internal details (like the maximum value and the timer interval), you can compute a suitable step value. This calculation takes place in the Start() method, which also enables the timer so the progress bar begins incrementing:

```
public void Start()
{
    // The maximum controls how fine-grained
    // the progress bar is. 200 is a good choice.
    Bar.Maximum = 200;

    // Calculation is based on a timer that
    // fires 10 times per second (an interval of 100).
    tmrIncrementBar.Interval = 100;
    decimal step = Math.Round((decimal)Bar.Maximum * PercentPerSecond / 1000);
    Bar.Step = (int)step;
```

```
    // Reset the progress and start counting.
    Bar.Value = 0;
    tmrIncrementBar.Start();
}

public void Stop()
{
    tmrIncrementBar.Stop();
    Bar.Value = 0;
}

public void Finish()
{
    tmrIncrementBar.Stop();
    Bar.Value = Bar.Maximum;
}
```

When the timer reaches the maximum value, the progress bar loops seamlessly back to start incrementing from zero again:

```
private void tmrIncrementBar_Tick(object sender, EventArgs e)
{
    Bar.PerformStep();
    if (Bar.Value == Bar.Maximum)
    {
        Bar.Value = 0;
    }
}
```

With a little imagination, you can come up with even more progress-bar behaviors. For example, you could design a "bouncing" progress bar that decrements progress when it reaches 100%, and then begins incrementing it again. And of course, you wouldn't need to create all of these options in separate controls. Instead, you can simply provide an enumerated value that lets the user choose an increment mode from one of the supported options.

Now that you've considered two versions of one of the simplest possible user controls, it's time to look at something a little more ambitious—and practical.

The Bitmap Thumbnail Viewer

The next user control creates a series of thumbnails that show miniature versions of all the bitmap files found in a specific directory. This type of control could be created in a more flexible way (and with much more code), by using the GDI+ drawing features. Instead, this example uses control composition, and dynamically inserts a PictureBox control for every image. This makes it easier to handle image clicks and support image selection. It also previews the techniques you'll see in Chapter 21, where a user interface is generated out of controls dynamically at runtime.

■**Note** If you're still interested in the GDI+ approach, don't worry—in Chapter 12 you'll learn the basics, and in Chapter 24 you'll see a full-scale drawing application that uses custom-drawn control objects.

Possibly the best aspect of the BitmapViewer user control is that it communicates with your program in both directions. You can tailor the appearance of the BitmapViewer by setting properties, and the BitmapViewer raises an event to notify your code when a picture is selected.

Creating the BitmapViewer User Control

The design-time appearance of the BitmapViewer is unremarkable (see Figure 10-5). It contains a single Panel control where all the picture boxes will be added. Alternatively, the picture boxes could be added directly to the Controls collection of the user control, but the Panel allows for an attractive border around the control. It also allows automatic scrolling support—as long as the Panel.AllowScroll is set to true, scroll bars are provided as soon as the image thumbnails extend beyond the bounds of the Panel. As with the previous example, the Panel is anchored to all sides for automatic resizing.

■**Note** The size of the user control in the user control designer sets the initial size that is used when the control is added to a form. This size can (and probably will) be changed by the developing using the control, but think of it as a reasonable default.

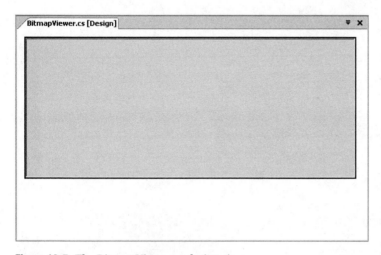

Figure 10-5. *The BitmapViewer at design time*

Unlike the Progress control, the BitmapViewer cannot just hand off its property procedures and methods to members in one of the composite controls. Instead, it needs to retain a fair bit of its own information. The following code shows the key private variables:

```
// The directory that will be scanned for image.
private string directory = "";

// Each picture box will be a square of dimension X dimension pixels.
private int dimension;

// The space between the images and the top, left, and right sides.
private int border = 5;

// The space between each image.
private int spacing;

// The images that were found in the selected directory.
private List<NamedImage> images = new List<NamedImage>();
```

Some of the values are user-configurable, while some are not. For example, the collection of images is drawn from the referenced directory. The property procedures for the modifiable values are shown here:

```
public string Directory
{
    get {return directory;}
    set
    {
        directory = value;
        GetImages();
        UpdateDisplay();
    }
}
public int Dimension
{
    get {return dimension;}
    set
    {
        dimension = value;
        UpdateDisplay();
    }
}
public int Spacing
{
    get {return spacing;}
    set
    {
        spacing = value;
        UpdateDisplay();
    }
}
```

■ **Note** For simplicity's sake, this code doesn't provide any error-handling logic. For example, all the integer properties in the BitmapViewer should be restricted to positive numbers. Ideally, the property procedure code should refuse negative numbers and raise an error to alert the developer if an attempt is made to set an invalid value.

Notice that every time a value is modified, the display is automatically regenerated by calling the UpdateDisplay() method. A more sophisticated approach might make this logic depend on a property like AutoRefresh. That way, the user could temporarily turn off the refresh, make several changes at once, and then re-enable it. Many collection-based Windows Forms controls use the SuspendLayout() and ResumeLayout() methods to implement this sort of performance optimization.

The set procedure for the Directory property also calls a special GetImages() method, which inspects the directory and populates the Images collection. You might expect that the Images collection contains Image objects, but this is not the case. To provide useful event information, the BitmapViewer needs to track the file name of every image it displays, along with the image data. To make this possible, you need to define another class that encapsulates this data, called NamedImage:

```
private class NamedImage
{
    private Image image;
    public Image Image
    {
        get {return image;}
        set {image = value;}
    }

    private string fileName;
    public string FileName
    {
        get {return fileName;}
        set {fileName = value;}
    }

    public NamedImage(Image image, string fileName)
    {
        Image = image;
        FileName = fileName;
    }
}
```

In this example, the NamedImage class is a private class nested inside the BitmapViewer control class. This means that NamedImage is used exclusively by the BitmapViewer, and not made available to the application using the BitmapViewer control.

The GetImages() method uses the standard .NET file and directory classes to retrieve a list of bitmaps. For each bitmap, a NamedImage object is created, and added to the Images collection:

```
private void GetImages()
{
    if (directory.Length != 0)
    {
        images.Clear();
        DirectoryInfo dir = new DirectoryInfo(Directory);
        foreach (FileInfo file in dir.GetFiles("*.bmp"))
        {
            images.Add(new
            NamedImage(Bitmap.FromFile(file.FullName),
            file.FullName));
        }
    }
}
```

The bulk of the work for the BitmapViewer takes place in the UpdateDisplay() method, which generates the picture boxes, adds them to the panel, and sets their tag property with the name of the corresponding file for later reference. The BitmapViewer is filled from left to right, and then row by row.

```
private void UpdateDisplay()
{
    // Suspend layout to prevent multiple window refreshes.
    pnlPictures.SuspendLayout();

    // Clear the current display.
    foreach (Control ctrl in pnlPictures.Controls)
    {
        ctrl.Dispose();
    }
    pnlPictures.Controls.Clear();

    // row and col will track the current position where pictures are
    // being inserted. They begin at the top-left corner.
    int row = border, col = border;

    // Iterate through the images collection, and create PictureBox controls.
    foreach (NamedImage image in images)
    {
        PictureBox pic = new PictureBox();
        pic.Image = image.Image;
        pic.Tag = image.FileName;
        pic.Size = new Size(dimension, dimension);
        pic.Location = new Point(col, row);
        pic.BorderStyle = BorderStyle.FixedSingle;
```

```
    // StretchImage mode gives us the "thumbnail" ability.
    pic.SizeMode = PictureBoxSizeMode.StretchImage;

    // Display the picture.
    pnlPictures.Controls.Add(pic);

    // Move to the next column.
    col += dimension + spacing;

    // Move to next line if no more pictures will fit.
    if ((col + dimension + spacing + border) > this.Width)
    {
        col = border;
        row += dimension + spacing;
    }
}
pnlPictures.ResumeLayout();
}
```

Notice that before the new controls are generated, the existing controls need to be disposed. If you simply call Panel.Controls.Clear() without explicitly disposing the controls, you won't reclaim all the unmanaged resources—in other words, your application will leak memory or control handles.

It's possible that the developer might want to trigger a refresh if the directory contents have changed, without needing to modify a property. To allow this, the UpdateDisplay() method is also made accessible through the public RefreshImages() method.

```
public void RefreshImages()
{
    GetImages();
    UpdateDisplay();
}
```

The OnSizeChanged() method is also overridden to ensure that the pictures are redrawn when the user control size changes. This ensures that the pictures are automatically adjusted (in rows and columns) to best fit the new size.

```
protected override void OnSizeChanged(System.EventArgs e)
{
    UpdateDisplay();
    base.OnSizeChanged(e);
}
```

Figure 10-6 shows a stripped-down UML diagram for the BitmapViewer control, in keeping with my philosophy of clearly defining the interfaces for custom controls. This diagram omits private members and members that have been inherited. It also shows two other class dependencies: the private NamedImage class and the PictureSelectedEventArgs class, which is introduced shortly as a means of passing event data to the application that hosts the BitmapViewer.

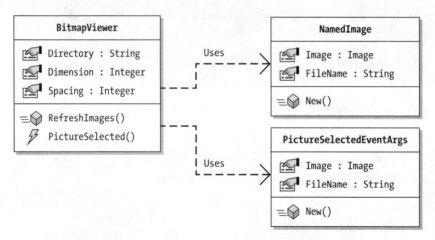

Figure 10-6. *The BitmapViewer in UML*

Testing the BitmapViewer Control

To see the final BitmapViewer control, follow these steps:

1. Compile the BitmapViewer control.

2. Create a new test project and add it to the solution.

3. Drop the BitmapViewer control onto the form using the Toolbox.

4. Set the appropriate properties, like Directory, Dimension, and Spacing. In Figure 10-7, a dimension of 80 and spacing of 10 is used. (You can modify the declarations of the corresponding private member variables to establish some reasonable default values.)

5. Set the Directory property. A good place to do this is in the Form.Load event handler.

Figure 10-7 shows the BitmapViewer test project. In this example, the BitmapViewer is docked to the form so you can change the size and see the image thumbnails being reorganized.

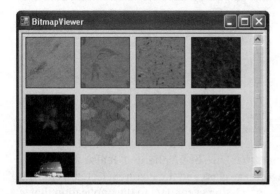

Figure 10-7 the *BitmapViewer in action*

BitmapViewer Events

To make the BitmapViewer more useful, you can add an event that fires every time a picture box is selected. Because the BitmapViewer is built entirely from PictureBox controls, which natively provide a Click event, no hit testing is required. All you need to do is register to handle the Click event when the picture box is first created in the UpdateDisplay() method.

```
pic.Click += new EventHandler(this.pic_Click);
```

To send an event to the application, the event must first be defined in the user control class. In this case, the event is named PictureSelected. In true .NET style, it passes a reference to the event sender and a custom EventArgs object that contains additional information.

```
public delegate void PictureSelectedDelegate(object sender,
  PictureSelectedEventArgs e);
public event PictureSelectedDelegate PictureSelected;
```

The custom PictureSelectedEventArgs object provides the file name of the picture that was clicked, which allows the application to retrieve it directly for editing or some other task. Here's the code:

```
public class PictureSelectedEventArgs : EventArgs
{
    private Image image;
    public Image Image
    {
        get {return image;}
        set {image = value;}
    }

    private string fileName;
    public string FileName
    {
        get {return fileName;}
        set {fileName = value;}
    }

    public PictureSelectedEventArgs(String fileName, Image image)
    {
        FileName = fileName;
        Image = image;
    }
}
```

The PictureBox.Click event handler changes the border style of the clicked picture box to make it appear "selected." If you were using GDI+, you could draw a more flexible focus cue, like a brightly colored outline rectangle.

The PictureBox.Click event handler then fires the event, with the required information.

```
private PictureBox picSelected;

private void pic_Click(object sender, System.EventArgs e)
{
    // Clear the border style from the last selected picture box.
    if (picSelected != null)
        picSelected.BorderStyle = BorderStyle.FixedSingle;

    // Get the new selection.
    picSelected = (PictureBox)sender;
    picSelected.BorderStyle = BorderStyle.Fixed3D;

    // Fire the selection event.
    PictureSelectedEventArgs args = new
      PictureSelectedEventArgs((string)picSelected.Tag, picSelected.Image);
    if (PictureSelected != null)
        PictureSelected(this, args);
}
```

The application can now handle this event. In the example shown here (and pictured in Figure 10-8), a message box is displayed with the file name information.

```
private void bitmapViewer1_PictureSelected(object sender,
  PictureSelectedEventArgs e)
{
    MessageBox.Show("You chose " + e.FileName);
}
```

Figure 10-8. *A BitmapViewer event*

Performance Enhancements and Threading

If you use the BitmapViewer with a directory that contains numerous large images, you'll start to notice a performance slowdown. One of the problems is that in its current form, the BitmapViewer stores the entire image in memory, even though it displays only a thumbnail.

A better approach would be to scale the image immediately when it is retrieved. This is accomplished using the Image.GetThumbnail() method.

In the code that follows, the GetImages() method has been rewritten to use this more memory-friendly alternative.

```
private void GetImages()
{
    if (directory.Length != 0)
    {
        images.Clear();
        DirectoryInfo dir = new DirectoryInfo(directory);
        foreach (FileInfo file in dir.GetFiles("*.bmp"))
        {
            Image thumbnail = Bitmap.FromFile(file.FullName).GetThumbnailImage(
                dimension, dimension, null, IntPtr.Zero);
            images.Add(new NamedImage(thumbnail, file.Name));
        }
    }
}
```

This technique also frees you up to use a simpler control than the PictureBox to show the picture, because the control no longer has to perform the scaling. However, it also means that you need to update the Dimension property procedure so that it calls the GetImages() method—otherwise, the image objects won't be the correct size. Here's the correction:

```
public int Dimension
{
    get {return dimension;}
    set
    {
        dimension = value;
        GetImages();
        UpdateDisplay();
    }
}
```

Using the cached image thumbnails, you could optimize the control even further by painting the image directly on the user control surface using the GDI+ drawing functions. In this case, you'd need to rely on hit testing to capture the user's mouse clicks. You'll learn more about mixing GDI+ with custom controls in Chapter 12, and in Chapter 24 you'll see an advanced example with a vector-based drawing program that compares both the control-based and the GDI+ approaches.

Assuming that the GetImages() method takes a significant amount of time, you might want to make another change to the BitmapViewer, and make the image retrieval asynchronous. With this design, the GetImages() code runs on a separate thread, and then automatically calls the UpdateDisplay() method when it's completed. That way, the user interface won't be tied up in the meantime. The remainder of this section walks you through the process.

First, ensure that none of the property procedures call GetImages() or UpdateDisplay(). This step simplifies life, because you won't need to catch actions that could trigger multiple updates at once (which won't cause an error if you code properly, but will bog down your code and introduce unnecessary flicker). Also, you should make sure that the Directory property is read-only. That's because you'll use another method—named StartLoadingImages()—to set the directory and explicitly start the refresh process.

```
public string Directory
{
    get {return directory;}
}

public void StartLoadingImages(string directory)
{
    this.directory = directory;
    GetImages();
}
```

Next, import the System.Threading namespace so you have the Thread class at your fingertips, and modify the GetImages() method so it starts the ReadImagesFromFile() method on a separate thread.

```
private void GetImages()
{
    Thread getThread = new Thread(new ThreadStart(this.ReadImagesFromFile));
    getThread.Start();
}
```

Finally, modify the file-reading code and place it in the ReadImagesFromFile() method. It's the ReadImagesFromFile() method that will do the real work of extracting the image data from the files and creating the thumbnails.

```
private void ReadImagesFromFile()
{
    lock (images)
    {
        images.Clear();
        if (directory != "")
        {
            Image thumbnail;
            DirectoryInfo dir = new DirectoryInfo(directory);
            foreach (FileInfo file in dir.GetFiles("*.bmp"))
            {
                thumbnail = Bitmap.FromFile(file.Name).GetThumbnailImage(
                  Dimension, Dimension, null, IntPtr.Zero);
                images.Add(new NamedImage(thumbnail, file.Name));
            }
        }
    }
}
```

```
    // Update the display on the UI thread.
    pnlPictures.Invoke(new MethodInvoker(this.UpdateDisplay));
}
```

Threading introduces potential pitfalls and isn't recommended unless you really need it. When implementing the preceding example, you have to be careful that the UpdateDisplay() method happens on the user-interface thread, not the ReadImagesFromFile() thread. Otherwise, a strange conflict could emerge in real-world use. Similarly, the lock statement is required to make sure that no other part of the control code attempts to modify the images collection while the ReadImagesFromFile() method is in progress. For a more detailed look at multithreading and the user-interface considerations it entails, refer to Chapter 20.

Simplifying Layout

When the BitmapViewer control renders itself, it determines where each picture box should be placed. There is a simpler approach—rather than calculating the coordinates of each child control by hand, you can use a more capable container control. One ideal choice is the FlowLayoutPanel.

To use the FlowLayoutPanel, you simply set the minimum space that needs to be kept around controls (by setting the Margin property of each control), the direction in which the controls should be ordered (by setting the FlowLayoutPanel.FlowDirection property), and whether controls should span multiple lines or columns (by setting the FlowLayoutPanel.WrapContents property). For example, if you use FlowDirection.LeftToRight and set WrapContents to true, the FlowLayoutPanel will order the picture boxes you add from left to right, and then on subsequent lines. This creates the same effect as the original version of the BitmapViewer, but you don't need to worry about explicitly setting the Position property of each PictureBox control, because the FlowLayoutPanel ignores this information.

To see this more realistic version of the BitmapViewer, which uses the FlowLayoutPanel and all the threading enhancements, refer to the code for this chapter in the Downloads section of the Apress Web site, www.apress.com. For more information about the FlowLayoutPanel, refer to Chapter 21, which deals with layout controls in much more detail and shows some other examples of dynamically generated user interfaces.

User Controls and Dynamic Interfaces

One interesting feature of user controls that you may not have considered is how they allow you to create a highly componentized and extremely flexible user interface. For example, user controls give you an easy way to build portal sites and other types of customizable applications where you can snap in different modules.

To create this sort of interface, you would create a separate user control for each module. For example, a financial application could have a range of available modules, like StockPickerModule, AccountViewerModule, HelpModule, NewsModule, and so on. The user could then choose what modules to show. Your application simply needs to load the selected modules and add them to the main form at runtime. To make the interface flow more smoothly, you'll probably also need the dynamic layout controls described in Chapter 21. They can help you manage the arrangement of different modules in a window without forcing you to write tedious and error-prone custom code for resizing and repositioning controls.

The reason user controls work so well with dynamic interfaces is because they allow you to build an entire portion of a window in one class. The design-time support for user control creation in Visual Studio makes it easy for another developer to create a module that could plug into any framework you create. Typically, you'll require that user controls implement an interface you recognize—that way you can perform basic interactions, like loading and saving data, or asking the control to initialize itself or perform cleanup.

In the following example, you'll see how you could build a system for creating multistep wizards based on user controls.

The Wizard Model

This example revolves around a single wizard form that contains the standard features (like Previous and Next buttons), and a panel that occupies most of the form. The logic for the Previous and Next buttons is hard-wired into the wizard form. However, for each step the wizard dynamically loads into the panel the user control that you supply. This approach allows unlimited customizability—quite simply, a developer using this model can put any type of content into the standardized wizard window. However, it also prevents the developer from tampering with any other aspect of the window.

▬**Note** There's another approach to solving this problem—visual inheritance. This technique (described in the next chapter) allows you to build a form template, which you can then reuse to create more-specialized forms. Form inheritance has some advantages over the user-control approach (it makes it easier to share and override bits of common functionality) and some disadvantages (it can't restrict changes to a single portion of the window).

Figure 10-9 shows the region of the wizard form that the dynamically loaded user control supplies.

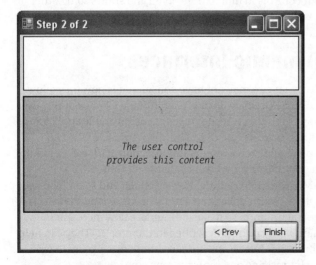

Figure 10-9. *The wizard model*

The Wizard Step

The wizard model is quite easy to create. A good starting point is to define an interface that all user controls must implement in order to be hosted in the wizard dialog. Here's a good beginning:

```
public interface IWizardItem
{
    string HeaderTitle {get;}

    Dictionary<string, string> GetValues();
    void ApplyValues(Dictionary<string, string> values);
}
```

This interface indicates that, at a minimum, every user control that's used with the wizard component must provide a HeaderTitle property (used to retrieve the header for the wizard step), and a method to save and restore values (the GetValues() and ApplyValues() methods). For the sake of simplicity and flexibility, settings are stored as a collection of name/value pairs. This allows the information from a wizard step to be retrieved, saved, and restored later. However, it also makes for more fragile code, because retrieving the wizard values involves searching for specific strings. You could address this problem by creating a more complex model that uses base classes or interfaces to standardize individual pieces of state information.

Figure 10-10 shows a simple example of a user control that implements the IWizardItem interface. It contains two text boxes, for supplying a first and last name. These two values need to be managed in the GetValues() and ApplyValues() methods.

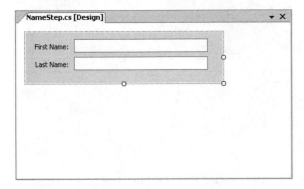

Figure 10-10. *The content for a wizard step*

Here's the complete code for this wizard step:

```
public partial class NameStep : UserControl, IWizardItem
{
    public string HeaderTitle
    {
        get { return "Please enter your first and last name."; }
    }
```

```
    // Store the state for this step.
    Dictionary<string, string> values = new Dictionary<string, string>();

    public Dictionary<string, string> GetValues()
    {
        values.Clear();
        values.Add("FirstName", txtFirstName.Text);
        values.Add("LastName", txtLastName.Text);
        return values;
    }

    public void ApplyValues(Dictionary<string, string> values)
    {
        this.values = values;
        txtFirstName.Text = values["FirstName"];
        txtFirstName.Text = values["LastName"];
    }
}
```

And just to make a more realistic test, you can quickly develop a second step, like the registration step shown in Figure 10-11.

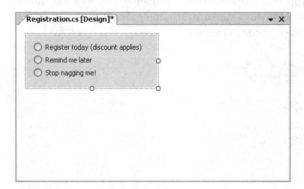

Figure 10-11. *A second wizard step*

This step tracks a single value—the currently selected radio button. Here's the code you need for this step:

```
public partial class RegistrationStep : UserControl, IWizardItem
{
    public string HeaderTitle
    {
        get { return "Select a registration method"; }
    }
```

```
Dictionary<string, string> values = new Dictionary<string, string>();
public Dictionary<string, string> GetValues()
{
    values.Clear();
    foreach (RadioButton opt in Controls)
    {
        if (opt.Checked)
        {
            values.Add(opt.Name, "True");
            break;
        }
    }
    return values;
}

public void ApplyValues(Dictionary<string, string> values)
{
    this.values = values;
    foreach (RadioButton opt in Controls)
    {
        if (values[opt.Name] != null)
        {
            opt.Checked = true;
            break;
        }
    }
}
}
```

The Wizard Controller

Now you can create the Wizard controller form that manages these use controls.

```
public partial class Wizard : Form
{ ... }
```

Three private variables track the current position, total number of steps, and the IWizardItem instances for each step:

```
private int currentStep;
private int totalSteps;
private List<IWizardItem> steps;
```

When the Wizard class is first instantiated, you need to supply the IWizardItem collection. At that point, the total number of steps is recorded, the current step is set to 1, and the work is handed off to the private ShowStep() method.

```
public Wizard(List<IWizardItem> steps)
{
    InitializeComponent();
    if (steps.Count > 0)
    {
        this.steps = steps;
        totalSteps = steps.Count;
        currentStep = 1;
        ShowStep();
    }
}
```

The ShowStep() method takes care of showing the current step, by getting the appropriate user control and inserting it into the automatic scrolling panel (after clearing the existing content). At the same time, the heading is applied and the button state is updated. For example, if you're on the first step, the Prev button is hidden. If you're on the last step, the Next button caption changes to Finish.

```
private void ShowStep()
{
    // Update buttons.
    cmdPrev.Visible = (currentStep != 1);
    if (currentStep == totalSteps)
      cmdNext.Text = "Finish";
    else
      cmdNext.Text = "Next >";

    // Get headings.
    lblHeader.Text = steps[currentStep - 1].HeaderTitle;
    Text = "Step " + currentStep.ToString() + " of " + totalSteps.ToString();

    // See if there's state to be restored.
    if (state != null && state[currentStep - 1] != null)
    {
        steps[currentStep - 1].ApplyValues(state[currentStep - 1]);
    }

    // Show step content.
    panelStep.Controls.Clear();
    UserControl ctrl = (UserControl)steps[currentStep - 1];
    panelStep.Controls.Add(ctrl);
}
```

Notice that in every step, the code checks the state collection to see if there are values to be applied to that step. The code for storing and maintaining this state collection is shown shortly.

The navigation buttons are quite straightforward. They simply adjust the current position and call the ShowStep() method. Here's the code for the Prev button:

```
private void cmdPrev_Click(object sender, EventArgs e)
{
    currentStep--;
    ShowStep();
}
```

The exception is the last step. When this is reached and the Finish button is clicked, all the state information is compiled into a collection and exposed through a property. The application that's calling the Wizard component could then store this for later use, or even serialize it to a file or some other storage location.

```
private void cmdNext_Click(object sender, EventArgs e)
{
    if (currentStep == totalSteps)
    {
        // The Finish button was clicked.
        // Save the state and close the form.
        state = new Dictionary<string, string>[totalSteps];
        for (int i = 0; i < totalSteps; i++)
        {
            state[i] = steps[i].GetValues();
        }
        Close();
    }
    else
    {
        currentStep++;
        ShowStep();
    }
}
```

```
private Dictionary<string, string>[] state;
public Dictionary<string, string>[] State
{
    get { return state; }
}
```

The final detail is a second constructor, which allows you to create a Wizard object with previous saved state information:

```
public Wizard(List<IWizardItem> steps, Dictionary<string, string>[] state) :
  this(steps)
{
    this.state = state;
}
```

▪**Note** Each time the user moves from one step to another, the controls are cleared out of the panel. However, they aren't disposed, and they remain in memory. This makes it easy to reload the controls if the user navigates back to the step. However, it's a good idea to explicitly dispose of all the controls when the Wizard component is disposed of. To do this, you can override the Dispose() method (as demonstrated in the online sample code available in the Downloads area of the Apress Web site, `www.apress.com`).

Testing the Wizard

You can now create a realistic test using the two wizard steps. All you need to do is create the array of steps, create a new instance of the Wizard, and then call the Wizard.ShowDialog() method, as shown here:

```
List<IWizardItem> items = new List<IWizardItem>();

items.Add(new NameStep());
items.Add(new RegistrationStep());
Wizard wizard = new Wizard(items);
wizard.ShowDialog();
```

Figure 10-12 shows the wizard at work. You'll notice that as you navigate from one page to the next, the values are restored automatically. In fact, if you close the wizard and then call ShowDialog() again to redisplay it, all the information remains intact.

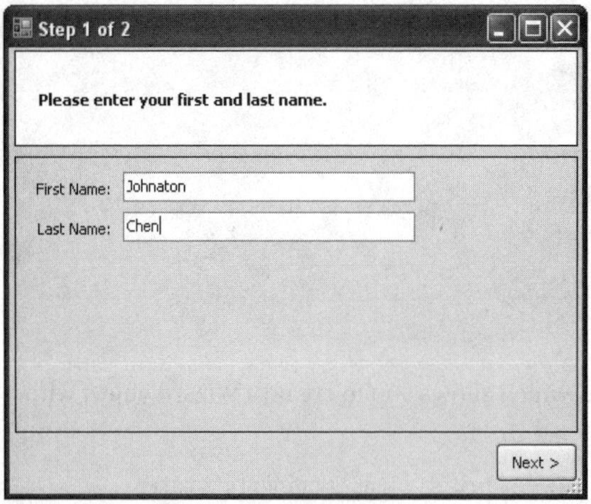

Figure 10-12. *The wizard at work*

By using the wizard model, you gain the ability to create a customized wizard without being forced to reinvent the wizard controller logic. Instead, you simply need to create the user interface for each step, and the logic that saves and restores their values. To complete the example shown in Figure 10-12, you'd need to retrieve the values at the end of the wizard process and perform the appropriate action.

Note For more examples of dynamic layout and highly modular forms, refer to Chapter 21. You can also read an interesting article at `http://msdn.microsoft.com/library/en-us/dnforms/html/winforms09212004.asp`. It shows a sample application in which user controls help to implement a Windows interface that's closer to a Web browser interface, complete with separate "pages" and navigation controls.

The Last Word

In this chapter, you learned how to master user interface controls and equip them with useful properties, methods, and events. In the next chapter, you'll consider a more powerful but more complex alternative—derived controls.

CHAPTER 11

■ ■ ■

Derived Controls

Derived controls provide an ideal way to take functionality from the existing .NET control classes and extend it. A derived control can be dramatically different from its predecessor, or it may just add a few refinements. Sometimes, derived controls are used to fasten a new feature onto an existing control (for example, you could create a TreeView that supports data binding). In other cases, derived controls customize more-general controls to work with specific types of data (like the Directory tree in this chapter). The only common thread is that all derived controls aim to avoid the heavy lifting by borrowing the features of another class.

The .NET class library is filled with examples of derived controls. For example, LinkLabel inherits from Label and CheckedListBox inherits from ListBox. In this chapter, you'll see how to create derived controls, and you'll use a similar technique to build customized form templates.

Understanding Derived Controls

To create a derived control, you simply create a class that inherits from a suitable parent control class. You can then override functionality you want to change and add the features you need.

Of course, derived controls often aren't this easy. Depending on the specific control, the functionality you want to change or extend might be buried deep within its inner workings, far beyond reach. A typical example of control functionality that can't be easily altered is control painting. For example, if you want to change the way a ListBox or TextBox is drawn on a form, you can't simply override the OnPaint() method, because the drawing takes place at a lower level (through Windows system calls). Instead, you need to look for a control class that supports an owner-draw mode (which is possible with the ListBox, but not possible with the Button), or you need to create a custom-drawn control from scratch. Chapter 12 explores the tricks and techniques of owner-drawn controls in detail.

Even if you don't want to change the appearance of a control, it's important to realize that every control wraps some sort of functionality that isn't extensible. This is often because the functionality is ingrained in the Windows API, but it's also possible that the developers of the control didn't anticipate the customization you want to add. Examples include the expansion and collapse behavior of nodes in a TreeView, the animation effects in a menu, and the selection behavior in the date controls. As a result, control authors who want to change this behavior must create custom controls that derive directly from the base Control class, and reimplement all the standard functionality, which can be quite a challenge.

■**Note** From .NET's point of view, there's no difference between deriving from the Control class and a higher-level control class like TreeView. However, for the purpose of this discussion there is an important conceptual difference. If you derive directly from Control, you are responsible for painting your control by hand in the OnPaint() method, or adding some child controls, at a bare minimum. If you derive from a class like Tree-View, you inherit a fully functioning control, and need to add or customize only the features that interest you.

Inherited controls (and the owner-drawn controls you'll see in the next chapter) are generally more powerful than user controls. They're also more likely to be used across applications (and even organizations, if you're a tool vendor), not just between different windows in the same program. Some of the reasons why programmers develop inherited controls include the following:

- **To add new functionality.** One example is the custom ComboBox in Chapter 18 that implements masking. Another example is a custom TreeView that supports node searching.

- **To implement a specific behavior.** One example is the simple TextBox shown in Chapter 9 that overrides OnKeyPress() to reject non-numeric characters.

- **To abstract away certain details.** For example, you might decide that you want to simplify the interface of a TreeView to deal with specific data structures. Rather than using the Nodes collection, you could add higher-level properties and methods that support the operations you need, and maintain the Nodes collection internally. You could use the same approach to react to actions in the base class and raise more meaningful custom events.

- **To set commonly used defaults.** For example, you might want to add a DataGridView that always has the same group of columns. To do this, you could configure the properties of your custom DataGridView in its constructor. These properties could still be changed by the consuming form, but the defaults would apply if they aren't.

Extending Controls

Chapter 9 showed the simplest possible example of a derived control—a NumericTextBox that extended the key-press behavior so that the control ignores all non-numeric characters. That simple example shows the basic approach to extending a derived control. You respond to events in the base class by overriding the corresponding On*Xxx*() method:

```
public class NumericTextBox : TextBox
{
    protected override void OnKeyPress(KeyPressEventArgs e)
    {
        // Ignore all non-control and non-numeric key presses.
        if (!char.IsControl(e.KeyChar) && !char.IsDigit(e.KeyChar))
        {
            e.Handled = true;
        }
    }
```

```
        // Call the implementation in the base TextBox class,
        // which raises the KeyPress event.
        base.OnKeyPress(e);
    }
}
```

When overriding a method in this way, you should always take care to call the base class implementation of the method. That's because the base class implementation might contain a key piece of functionality that must be executed for the control to function correctly. Often, the base class implementation does nothing more than raise the corresponding event. In this case, you need to call the base class method to make sure that the hosting form has the chance to respond to the event.

Usually, it doesn't matter whether you call the base class method before your custom code or after it. However, there are a few cases in which you might want to make sure your code has executed before the event is raised. For example, in an override OnLoad() event you might decide that you need to complete your initialization before allowing any other code to run.

■**Tip** In a very few rare cases, you might choose *not* to call the base class implementation, because the code you're adding is replacing some existing functionality. Although this isn't common, it is sometimes necessary.

Of course, instead of overriding the method you could handle the corresponding event directly—but you shouldn't. Not only is it extra hassle and a small bit of extra overhead to write the delegate code that wires up the event handler, but it can also cause problems if someone wants to create a customized control that derives from your derived control. The problem is that event handlers aren't guaranteed to be called in any specific order, so it's possible that the behavior of a control might change unexpectedly. (A well-designed control will be immune to this, but it's not always easy to anticipate how a custom control you create will be extended by others.) If you use method overriding, the overriding method always gets the first chance to handle the action, and explicitly calls the base class method when it should execute.

Of course, you aren't limited to override methods and properties. You can also add new properties, methods, and events to your derived control, just as you can with a user control.

Derived Controls or User Controls?

So, how do you know when to create a user control, and when you need a control that derives from another control class? It's not always an easy question to answer, because many problems can be solved with either approach. However, here are a few points that you should consider before embarking on a custom control project:

- User controls are well suited if you want to ensure that a block of interface is re-created *exactly* in more than one situation. Because a user control usually provides less-flexible configuration, it guarantees a more standardized appearance.

- If your control closely resembles an existing .NET control, consider whether you can derive it from an existing control class to simplify your life. With a user control, you'll need to spend more time creating new properties and methods to allow access to the members of the original control.

- User controls are generally easier and faster to program. If you don't anticipate reusing the control frequently in different scenarios and different programs, a user control may suffice. However, Visual Studio 2005 now includes better support for debugging other control types (such as the automatic Toolbox registration), so the gap is not as significant as it was in earlier versions of .NET.

- User controls don't provide a fine-grained level of reuse. User controls typically provide only a few members, and thus are not as configurable. The most flexible type of control is one that derives directly from the base Control class. Tool vendors and other advanced control programmers almost always take this approach.

- User controls are great for composite controls that wrap two or more existing .NET controls. However, for more flexibility you might want to consider creating separate derived controls. This approach gives you the ability to link the controls but make the relationship optional. The application programmer can then use them separately or together, and has complete freedom about how to integrate them into a user interface.

Now that you've had a quick overview of how derived controls work, consider a few examples that put it into practice.

The ProjectTree Control

The TreeView control provides a flexible model that allows it to be used in countless ways and with different types of data. But an individual TreeView in an application is generally used only in a set way, depending on the underlying data it represents. That means that it can make a good deal of sense to create a custom TreeView that exposes a fine-tuned, higher-level interface to your form. This approach can dramatically simplify and clarify your form code. The disadvantage is that the custom TreeView control you create is more tightly bound to a specific scenario or type of data.

For example, imagine you want to create a TreeView for a project-management system. It always uses two levels of nodes—a second level that contains the actual projects, and a first level that organizes the products into groups based on their status.

You could create a ProjectTree that "bakes in" this design. Your design goals would be as follows:

- Include all the resources (in this case the node pictures) in the control assembly.

- Create the first-level groupings automatically, and expose them as properties.

- Expose a method that lets the control consumer add projects without needing to go through the Nodes collection.

- Replace the AfterSelect event with a higher-level ProjectSelected event.

Figure 11-1 shows an example with a sample instance of the ProjectTree.

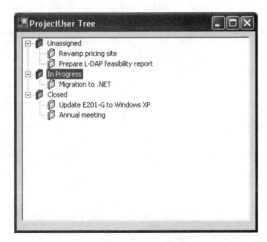

Figure 11-1. *A custom TreeView*

The ProjectTree could have been created as a user control, but the inheritance approach provides far more flexibility. For example, all the original TreeView events, properties, and methods are still available to the client code (unless you explicitly hide them). Best of all, you don't need to write any code to delegate the properties of your custom control class to an underlying control.

The first step to creating the ProjectTree is to define the custom control class, like this:

```
public class ProjectTree : TreeView
{ ... }
```

This creates a ProjectTree control that functions exactly like an ordinary TreeView. In the following sections, you'll build more functionality into the ProjectTree class.

The Data Class

Before you can write the code for the ProjectTree, you need to design the object model. In this example, the starting point is a Project class that represents the information for a single project. This class includes project name, description, and status information.

Here's the full code for the Project class:

```
public class Project
{
    // Use an enumeration to represent the three project status types.
    public enum StatusType
    { Unassigned, InProgress, Closed }

    private string name;
    public string Name
    {
        get { return name; }
        set { name = value; }
    }
```

```
    private string description;
    public string Description
    {
        get { return description; }
        set { description = value; }
    }

    private StatusType status;
    public StatusType Status
    {
        get { return status; }
        set { status = value; }
    }

    public Project(string name, string description, StatusType status)
    {
        Name = name;
        Description = description;
        Status = status;
    }
}
}
```

This Project class is tightly coupled to the ProjectTree. While a ProjectTree is physically a collection of TreeNode objects, logically it will be a grouping of Project instances.

Node Images

Before going any further, you need to embed the images you want to use for TreeView nodes into the custom control assembly. You could add these resources individually, but there's a shortcut. Because a custom control derives from Component, it provides a design-time surface (as described in Chapter 9), which is equivalent to the component tray on a form. That means you can switch to design view with your custom control, drop an ImageList onto it (see Figure 11-2), and add all the icons you need to the ImageList. The pictures that you add to the image list will be stored as an ImageStream resource, which is embedded in the control assembly automatically.

Figure 11-2. *Embedding an ImageList in a control*

You can link the ImageList to the ProjectTree by setting the ImageList property, either using the Properties window or a quick line of code in the ProjectTree constructor:

```
ImageList = imagesTree;
```

Sometimes, it's convenient to write this line of code using the base keyword, like this:

```
base.ImageList = imagesTree;
```

This emphasizes that the ImageList property is defined in the base class (in this case, the TreeView class), not your ProjectTree class. However, both approaches compile to exactly the same IL code.

Once you've set the ImageList, the ProjectTree control can choose to use these images when creating TreeNode objects by specifying an image index number. You can make this process easier by creating the following enumeration inside the ProjectTree class:

```
// Specific numbers correspond to the image index.
private enum NodeImages
{
    UnassignedGroup = 0, InProgressGroup = 1, ClosedGroup = 2,
    NormalProject = 3, SelectedProject = 4
}
```

Note As you can see, the ProjectTree is limiting projects to a small set of predefined categories. This improves the programming model, but it prevents you from reusing the control in different scenarios with different groupings. This tradeoff between convenience and flexibility is one of the recurring themes of custom control development. It's up to you to choose the best compromise.

Node Groups

The structure of the ProjectTree is also hard-wired. To help make this more flexible, you can create member variables that track the three key branches, and expose them as properties.

```
private TreeNode nodeUnassigned;
public TreeNode UnassignedProjectsNode
{
    get { return nodeUnassigned; }
}
private TreeNode nodeInProgress;
public TreeNode InProgressProjectsNode
{
    get { return nodeInProgress; }
}
```

```
private TreeNode nodeClosed;
public TreeNode ClosedProjectsNode
{
    get { return nodeClosed; }
}
```

When the ProjectTree is created, you can create these nodes, with the appropriate pictures, and then add them to the tree:

```
public ProjectTree() : base()
{
    // Set the images.
    ImageList = imagesTree;

    // Create the first level of nodes.
    nodeUnassigned = new TreeNode("Unassigned",
      (int)NodeImages.UnassignedGroup, (int)NodeImages.UnassignedGroup);
    nodeInProgress = new TreeNode("In Progress",
      (int)NodeImages.InProgressGroup, (int)NodeImages.InProgressGroup);
    nodeClosed = new TreeNode("Closed",
      (int)NodeImages.ClosedGroup, (int)NodeImages.ClosedGroup);

    // Add the project category nodes.
    Nodes.Add(nodeUnassigned);
    Nodes.Add(nodeInProgress);
    Nodes.Add(nodeClosed);
}
```

Adding Projects

When you use the ProjectTree control in a program, you don't add TreeNode objects. Instead, you add projects. Based on a Project object, the ProjectTree should be able to add the corresponding node to the correct branch, with the correct icon. Here's the method that makes it happen:

```
public void AddProject(Project project)
{
    TreeNode nodeNew = new TreeNode(project.Name,
      (int)NodeImages.NormalProject, (int)NodeImages.SelectedProject);

    // Store the project object for later use
    // (when the event is raised).
    nodeNew.Tag = project;
```

```
    switch (project.Status)
    {
        case Project.StatusType.Unassigned:
            nodeUnassigned.Nodes.Add(nodeNew);
            break;
        case Project.StatusType.InProgress:
            nodeInProgress.Nodes.Add(nodeNew);
            break;
        case Project.StatusType.Closed:
            nodeClosed.Nodes.Add(nodeNew);
            break;
    }
}
```

Now the client might use the custom ProjectTree like this:

```
Project projectA = new Project("Migration to .NET",
  "Change exsiting products to take advantage of new Windows Forms controls",
  Project.StatusType.InProgress);
Project projectB = new Project("Revamp pricing site",
  "Enhance the pricing website with ASP.NET", Project.StatusType.Unassigned);

tree.AddProject(projectA);
tree.AddProject(projectB);
```

The appeal of this approach is that the appropriate user interface class wraps many of the extraneous details and makes the rest of the code more readable.

To go along with this method, it makes sense to create a GetProject() method that searches for a node based on its name, and returns the corresponding Project object:

```
public Project GetProject(string name, Project.StatusType status)
{
    TreeNodeCollection nodes = null;

    switch (status)
    {
        case Project.StatusType.Unassigned:
            nodes = nodeUnassigned.Nodes;
            break;
        case Project.StatusType.InProgress:
            nodes = nodeInProgress.Nodes;
            break;
        case Project.StatusType.Closed:
            nodes = nodeClosed.Nodes;
        break;
    }
```

```
    foreach (TreeNode node in nodes)
    {
        // Test for a name match.
        if (node.Text == name)
        {
            // Get the Project object for this node.
            Project project = node.Tag as Project;
            if (project != null) return project;
        }
    }
    return null;
}
```

■**Note** At this point it may occur to you that the AddProject() and GetProject() methods are implementing a sort of virtual collection. A nicer way to expose this functionality is to do away with the Nodes collection altogether, and expose a ProjectTree.Projects collection that the application can interact with directly. The downside to this approach is that it requires more work—you need to create a custom collection, and your control needs to monitor the collection to determine when projects are added or removed. You'll see an example of a collection-based charting control in Chapter 12.

There's no limit to the possible features you can add to a TreeView class. For example, you can add special methods for sorting nodes, moving nodes, or presenting context menus. The danger is that you will make the control too specific, locking functionality into places where it can't be reused. Try to think of your custom TreeView as a generic TreeView designed for a specific type of data. Ideally, it should allow many different possible uses of that data. For example, the project-specific tree might be used in various windows to allow project managers to assign projects, programmers to prioritize their tasks, and managers to audit work and prepare company forecasts. If you've designed the ProjectTree well, it should support all of these uses. And no matter what the circumstance, you should never put business code into the control. For example, if a specific action should result in a database update, there's only one option—raise an event from your control and allow the code receiving that event to take care of the data source interaction.

Project Selection

The final ingredient is to replace the AfterSelect event, which fires whenever a node is clicked and provides the corresponding TreeNode object with a ProjectSelected event that provides the appropriate Project object. To implement this design, begin by creating a custom EventArgs object that the event will use to transmit the extra information:

```
public class ProjectSelectedEventArgs : EventArgs
{
    private Project project;
    public Project Project
    {
        get { return project; }
        set { project = value; }
    }

    public ProjectSelectedEventArgs(Project project)
    {
        Project = project;
    }
}
```

Now you can define the event signature:

```
// Define a higher-level event for node selection.
public delegate void ProjectSelectedEventHandler(
  object sender, ProjectSelectedEventArgs e);
```

and the event:

```
public event ProjectSelectedEventHandler ProjectSelected;
```

The next step is to override the OnAfterSelect() event, check that the selected node represents a project, and then raise the ProjectSelected event. There are several possible ways to determine if the node in question is a project node—for example, you can examine the node's parent to discover the category. In this case, the simplest approach is just to check the node's level. The first level (level 0) contains the project categories, and the second level (level 1) contains the projects.

```
// When a node is selected, retrieve the Project and raise the event.
protected override void OnAfterSelect(TreeViewEventArgs e)
{
    base.OnAfterSelect(e);

    // Check that at least one event listener is registered
    // before continuing.
    if (ProjectSelected != null)
    {
        if (e.Node.Level == 1)
        {
            Project project = (Project)e.Node.Tag;
            ProjectSelectedEventArgs arg = new ProjectSelectedEventArgs(project);
            ProjectSelected(this, arg);
        }
    }
}
```

This technique of intercepting events and providing more useful, higher-level events provides an easier model to program against. It also completes the ProjectTree class code.

A Custom TreeNode

The ProjectTree makes use of a handy but clumsy approach for linking Project objects to TreeNode objects—the TreeNode.Tag property. Although this works, it's not strongly typed, and it breaks down entirely if you need to associate two different objects with the same TreeNode. Another solution is to derive a custom TreeNode class that adds the properties you're interested in.

Here's an example:

```
public class ProjectTreeNode : TreeNode
{
    private Project project;
    public Project Project
    {
        get { return Project; }
    }

    public ProjectTreeNode(Project project, string text, int imageIndex,
        int selectedImageIndex) : base(text, imageIndex, selectedImageIndex)
    {
        this.project = project;
    }
}
```

Now you simply need to update the AddProject() method to use the ProjectTreeNode:

```
ProjectTreeNode nodeNew = new ProjectTreeNode(project, project.Name,
    (int)NodeImages.NormalProject, (int)NodeImages.SelectedProject);
```

and the OnAfterSelect() method:

```
Project project = ((ProjectTreeNode)e.Node).Project
```

You'll notice that the TreeNode still links to the Project object through a single member variable. Alternatively, you could abandon the Project class altogether, and add all the project properties (Name, Description, and Status) directly to the ProjectTreeNode class. However, this approach makes your solution more tightly coupled than it needs to be. It prevents you from reusing the Project data structure with other controls and other types of code, and it prevents you from adding properties or validation logic to the Project class without also modifying your custom control. For these reasons, it's best to keep the link between your control model and your data model as transparent as possible.

■**Tip** You might be tempted to track other information with ordinary TreeView controls by using derived TreeNode classes like ProjectTreeNode. This technique is perfectly acceptable—after all, a ProjectTreeNode is a genuine TreeNode. The only limitations are that you can't force a TreeView to reject other types of nodes, and you can't add custom TreeNode objects through the Properties window.

Design-Time Support

If you build the ProjectTree using just the information in this chapter, you'll discover that it works erratically in the design-time environment. To correct these glitches, hide the parts of the base TreeView class that you don't want accessible (like the Nodes collection), and make sure the ProjectTree works as seamlessly at design time as it does at runtime, you need to create an additional component called a control designer. You'll learn how to provide this missing ingredient in Chapter 13. For now, just keep in mind that the sample code for every control in this chapter includes a matching control designer.

The DirectoryTree Control

The next example is another custom control that derives from TreeView. However, this example— the DirectoryTree control—also changes the behavior of the control with just-in-time node creation.

The DirectoryTree control inherits from the standard TreeView and adds the features needed to display a hierarchical view of directories. Although .NET includes a similar component for selecting directories—the FolderBrowserDialog—it's a stand-alone dialog box, not a control, which means you can't show it in place on a form that you've designed. For that reason, the DirectoryTree is genuinely useful.

Perhaps most importantly, the DirectoryTree fills itself by reading subdirectories "just in time." That means that the control operates very quickly, even if the drive has tens of thousands of subdirectories. Only the expanded directory levels are actually shown. The collapsed branches all have a dummy node inserted. Every time a directory branch is expanded, the inherited control checks if a dummy node is present, and, if it is, the dummy node is removed and the directories are read from the disk.

Figure 11-3 shows the DirectoryTree on a form.

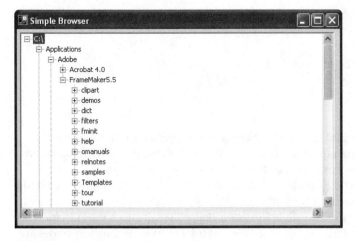

Figure 11-3. *The DirectoryTree in action*

Filling the Tree

The DirectoryTree control shows the directory tree for a single drive. The currently selected drive is stored as a single character (technically, a char). Another approach would be to use an instance of the System.IO.DirectoryInfo class to track or set the currently highlighted directory. That approach would provide better control for the application programmer, but it would complicate design-time support.

```
private char drive;
public char Drive
{
    get { return drive; }
    set
    {
        drive = value;
        RefreshDisplay();
    }
}
```

Whenever the Drive property is set, the RefreshDisplay() method is called to build the tree. The RefreshDisplay() method clears the current display, and then calls another method—named Fill()—to fill the root node. The reason that you need to split the logic into two methods is because Fill() needs to be called at different times to fill in different levels of the directory tree.

```
public void RefreshDisplay()
{
    // Erase the existing tree.
    Nodes.Clear();

    // Set the first node.
    TreeNode rootNode = new TreeNode(drive + ":\\");
    Nodes.Add(rootNode);

    // Fill the first level and expand it.
    Fill(rootNode);
    Nodes[0].Expand();
}
```

The RefreshDisplay() method is public so that you can trigger a refresh whenever it's needed. You could also use a component like the FileSystemWatcher to receive notification whenever directories are added or removed, and refresh the tree accordingly.

The Fill() method takes a single node, and fills in the first level of directories for that node. However, the Fill() method doesn't go any further to fill in deeper levels of nested subdirectories. If it did, the code would grind to a halt while the tree is being filled. Instead, the Fill() method adds an asterisk placeholder. The user won't see the asterisk because the directory nodes are initially in a collapsed state.

```
private void Fill(TreeNode dirNode)
{
    DirectoryInfo dir = new DirectoryInfo(dirNode.FullPath);

    foreach (DirectoryInfo dirItem in dir.GetDirectories())
    {
        // Add node for the directory.
        try
        {
            TreeNode newNode = new TreeNode(dirItem.Name);
            dirNode.Nodes.Add(newNode);
            newNode.Nodes.Add("*");
        }
        catch (Exception err)
        {
            // An exception could be thrown in this code if you don't
            // have sufficient security permissions for a file or directory.
            // You can catch and then ignore this exception.
        }
    }
}
```

The trick is that every time a subdirectory branch is expanded, that level is filled in first using the OnBeforeExpand() method. This just-in-time directory process unfolds speedily, so the user will never realize that it's taking place. (The only other possible step is to fill the tree asynchronously, which you could do using a technique similar to the BitmapViewer in the previous chapter.)

```
protected override void OnBeforeExpand(TreeViewCancelEventArgs e)
{
    base.OnBeforeExpand(e);

    // If a dummy node is found, remove it and read the real directory list.
    if (e.Node.Nodes[0].Text == "*")
    {
        e.Node.Nodes.Clear();
        Fill(e.Node);
    }
}
```

Directory Selection

The last step is to replace the AfterSelect event with a higher-level DirectorySelected event, just as in the ProjectTree. In this case, the DirectorySelectedEventArgs provides a single piece of information—the full path of the selected directory.

```
public class DirectorySelectedEventArgs : EventArgs
{
    private string directoryName;

    public string DirectoryName
    {
        get { return directoryName; }
        set { directoryName = value; }
    }

    public DirectorySelectedEventArgs(string directoryName)
    {
        DirectoryName = directoryName;
    }
}
```

Here's the DirectoryTree code that fires the DirectorySelected event:

```
public delegate void DirectorySelectedEventHandler(
  object sender, DirectorySelectedEventArgs e);
public event DirectorySelectedEventHandler DirectorySelected;

protected override void OnAfterSelect(TreeViewEventArgs e)
{
    base.OnAfterSelect(e);

    // Raise the DirectorySelected event.
    if (DirectorySelected != null)
    {
        DirectorySelected(this,
            new DirectorySelectedEventArgs(e.Node.FullPath));
    }
}
```

You can respond to the DirectorySelected event and perform additional work with the directory, like showing the files it contains in another control.

Deriving Forms

Just as you derive controls from existing control classes, you can also derive a new form from an existing form class. Of course, every form derives from the System.Windows.Forms.Form class, but you can add extra layers of inheritance to standardize form design. For example, you can create a custom form named MyFormTemplate (which derives from the Form class), and then derive additional forms from MyFormTemplate. This technique is called *visual inheritance*, although conceptually it isn't different from inheritance in any other scenario.

Visual inheritance has acquired a mixed reputation based on some of the idiosyncrasies it had in .NET 1.0. Problems included the following:

- Quirky design-time support, which sometimes necessitated closing and reopening a project to get past a cryptic error or see a change in the designer.

- Problems with anchored controls not being properly resized or relocated. This problem stemmed from the use of the SuspendLayout() and ResumeLayout() methods in the designer-generated code.

- Problems with control serialization, such as adding redundant lines in the designer-generated code for the derived form.

The good news is that these problems are ironed out in .NET 2.0, and Visual Studio now includes solid design-time support for visual inheritance.

Depending on how you use visual inheritance, you can accomplish two things:

- Use a common form template (appearance) for several different windows. This might be useful to create a wizard or standardized About window.

- Use form functionality in several different windows. This allows you to create a framework that you might use for different types of view windows in a Multiple Document Interface (MDI) application. Every window will have its own look, but it might reuse some of the same buttons to close the window or open a file.

As with any type of inheritance, visual inheritance gives you many different ways to customize how the descendent class can use, extend, or override the inherited class.

A Simple Derived Form

To create a simple example of form inheritance, you might create a wizard form like the one shown in Figure 11-4. It uses a blank header area for title text, a large surface area for additional content, and a Next button at the bottom. In this example (found in the downloadable code for this chapter at www.apress.com under the project name VisualInheritance), the base form is named Ancestor.

Figure 11-4. *An ancestor form for a wizard*

To create an inherited form that uses this form, you first need to compile the project. Then, right-click the project item in the Solution Explorer and choose Add ➤ New Item. Then, choose Inherited Form from the Add New Item dialog box. You'll be prompted to choose a new form name, and select the form you want to derive from (see Figure 11-5).

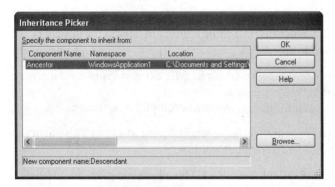

Figure 11-5. *Inheriting from a form*

■Tip As with inherited controls, it makes good sense to create two projects—a library that contains the form templates you want to reuse, and an application that contains the forms that derive from these templates.

Of course, you don't actually need to use the wizard to create an inherited form. All you really need to do is create a Form class, and change the standard class declaration (which inherits from the System.Windows.Forms class) to inherit from your custom class:

```
public partial class Descendent : VisualInheritance.Ancestor
```

Remember, Visual Studio 2005 uses partial classes to hide designer code, so you'll need to change the definition in both portions of the class. (For example, Descendant.cs and Descendant.Designer.cs.)

You'll notice that the inherited form contains all the controls that you defined in the original form, but it doesn't allow you to move them, change their properties, or add event handlers. You can, however, add new controls, write their event handlers, and change the size (or any other property) for your descendant form. In the basic example, this doesn't allow the flexibility you need. For example, the user needs to have some way to configure the text in the title area and override the behavior of the Next and Previous buttons. Fortunately, this is all easy if you understand a few basics about inheritance.

Making an Ancestor Control Available

By default, every control on the original ancestor form is declared with the private modifier. This keyword allows access to other forms in the same project, but it doesn't allow any access to your derived form. To change this state of affairs, simply modify the controls you want to configure to use the protected modifier instead. You can change the declaration by looking through the form code, or you can use the Properties window and look for the Modifiers property.

Technically, Modifiers isn't a real property of the control—instead, it's a design-time property added by Visual Studio. Whenever you change it, Visual Studio modifies the declaration of the control.

■**Tip** Whenever you change the ancestor form, you must recompile the project before you see the appropriate changes in the descendant form. Just right-click the project in the Solution Explorer and choose Build to create the assembly without launching it. You need to take this step regardless of whether the ancestor form is in an assembly separate from the descendant assembly, or in the same one.

Once you've changed the accessibility of the control and rebuilt the assembly that contains the ancestor form, you'll have much more freedom. In the descendant form, you can now configure any property of the inherited control, including its appearance and position (and you can even hide the control by settings its Visible property to false). The values that you've set in the ancestor form become the default values in the derived form. However, any changes you make in the derived form supersede these defaults, because they're applied in the derived form's InitializeComponent() method, which executes *after* the designer code in ancestor form.

Keeping a control private doesn't just affect whether you can change it. It also determines whether you can interact with the control *at all*. If the control is private to the ancestor form, you won't be able to access it at all in your derived form. As a result, you won't be able to respond to events, add items to a menu, or iterate through the Nodes property in a TreeView. However, you should think twice before changing the access modifier on your controls to solve these problems. If you make a change, you'll end up exposing the inner workings of your ancestor form and giving up all control over how it's used. As a result, the derived forms are likely to become tightly coupled to the low-level details of your ancestor form, limiting reuse and making it difficult to change or enhance your ancestor form. A far better solution is to expose just the details that are required by adding properties and methods to your form class, as described in the next section.

Adding a Property in the Ancestor Form

In the wizard example, creating protected-level controls isn't the best approach. Quite simply, it allows too much freedom to change the original layout. Take the header text, for example. The creator of the derived form should be able to enter custom text into the control, but other details (like its font, color, and position) shouldn't be modifiable, as they risk compromising the standardized layout you've established.

To code a better solution, you could create a property in the ancestor form. The client can then use this property to set the header text without being allowed any greater degree of control.

```
public string HeaderText
{
    get { return lblHeader.Text; }
    set { lblHeader.Text = value; }
}
```

Once you recompile, the HeaderText property will be available in your derived form. You can change it using code or, more conveniently, in the Properties window (see Figure 11-6). In fact, you can add other attributes to this property that configure the description it shows and the category it will appear in. See Chapter 13 for more on that topic.

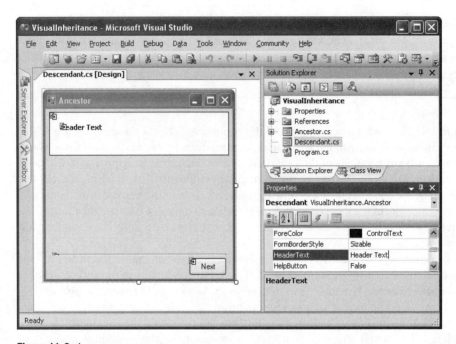

Figure 11-6. *A custom property*

Dealing with Events

Your base form might also contain event-handling logic. If this logic is generic (for example, it simply closes the form), it is suitable for all descendants. In the case of your Previous and Next buttons, clearly there is no generic code that can be written. Instead, the descendant needs to provide the event-handling code. Unfortunately, this raises the same problem as setting control properties. If you want the descendant form to handle an event in a control, you're forced to declare it as protected, which exposes it to unlimited modification.

There are two ways to code around this limitation:

- Define a new, higher-level event in the ancestor-form class. Handle the event of the child control in the ancestor class (like Button.Click), and raise the corresponding custom event (like AncestorForm.NextButtonClicked).

- Handle the event in your form class, but make the event handler explicitly overridable.

Both of these techniques give you the ability to perform some logic in the ancestor form (if required) and allow the derived form to respond, as well. The first approach offers the best design-time support, because you can hook up the event handler through the Properties window. However, the second approach offers an additional ability—you can force the derived form to override the method, ensuring it won't be ignored.

You've already seen the first approach at work with the two TreeView examples earlier in this chapter. For a change of pace, we'll consider the second technique.

The first step is to create the event handler in the ancestor form and declare that it can be overridden by marking it as protected and virtual. Here's an example:

```
protected virtual void OnNextButtonClick(object sender, EventArgs e)
{
    MessageBox.Show("Ancestor form event handler.");
}
```

■**Tip** It's a good idea to choose a more meaningful method name like OnNextButtonClick() rather than use the default event handler name like cmdNext_Click(). That's because in ordinary forms, the event handler name is an implementation that's internal to the form. But with visual inheritance, another class will see this method and override it.

You can now override this routine in your descendant form:

```
protected override void OnNextButtonClick(object sender, EventArgs e)
{
    MessageBox.Show("Descendant form event handler.");
}
```

Note that you do *not* connect this code by adding an event handler. That's because the original routine (the one you are overriding) is already connected to the event.

In some cases, you might want to execute both the extra code in the descendant form and the original code. You can accomplish this by using the base reference. The code that follows, for example, results in the display of two message boxes: one from the ancestor form, followed by one from the derived form.

```
protected override void OnNextButtonClick(object sender, System.EventArgs e)
{
    // Call the original version.
    base.OnNextButtonClick(sender, e);

    MessageBox.Show("Descendant form event handler.");
}
```

Finally, in some cases you might want to *force* an event handler to be overriden. For instance, in our example a wizard form can't be considered complete unless it has the necessary event-handling logic behind added to its Next button. However, it's impossible to code this logic at the ancestor level. To force the derived class to override this event handler (as a precautionary measure), you can declare the event handler with the abstract qualifier. In this case, you can't add a method body.

```
protected abstract void cmdNext_Click(object sender, System.EventArgs e);
```

For this to work, the ancestor-form class must also be declared abstract:

```
public abstract class Ancestor : System.Windows.Forms.Form
```

Be warned that this pattern confuses the Visual Studio IDE. You won't have any trouble designing an abstract form (the Ancestor form), but you won't be able to design any forms that inherit from it (the Descendant form). The reason lies deep in the Visual Studio design-time model. Essentially, while you are designing a form, Visual Studio instantiates the objects you're using in order to create the proper design-time representation. For example, if you're creating a form that contains two text box controls, Visual Studio creates two TextBox objects. However, the designer doesn't attempt to create the actual form you're designing. Instead, it creates an instance of the base form. Why? Remember, while you design a form, Visual Studio is continuously working, serializing your actions to code statements in the InitializeComponent() method. At the same time, Visual Studio applies your code to the live design-time version of your form. So there are two reasons Visual Studio doesn't create an instance of the form you're designing: It can't (because the code is constantly changing, and so it isn't yet compiled), and it doesn't need to (because it has the base class and all your customizations readily at hand).

The side effect of this model is that Visual Studio can't design a form that derives from an abstract form, because it can't create an instance of the base form. Microsoft is well aware of this problem, and has considered (but not yet implemented) compromises that would make it possible. Some of them are described at http://www.urbanpotato.net/Default.aspx/document/ 1772. And if you want to delve deep into the .NET designer infrastructure, you can actually code a complex workaround (http://www.urbanpotato.net/default.aspx/document/2001 shows how).

Of course, none of this affects the runtime performance of your form. If you derive a form from an abstract base class, you can still run it without a hitch. As a last resort, you can design your form without the abstract modifier, and then add it just before you compile and deploy your assembly.

■**Tip** One feature that isn't possible with form inheritance is to limit the derived form to inserting content in set areas of the form. For example, you might want to create a wizard template that inserts controls *only* in a predefined panel. Although this model isn't supported by visual inheritance, you can implement it yourself— in fact, you saw one possible approach with the wizard model in Chapter 10, which was based on user controls.

The Last Word

In this chapter, you walked through two custom TreeView controls that demonstrated how you could fine-tune existing .NET controls for specific scenarios. You also considered the advantages and limitations of visual inheritance, which offers an elegant way to create reusable form templates. In the next chapter, you'll step up to a more ambitious problem, and tackle controls that paint themselves from scratch.

■**Note** You're not finished with derived controls yet. Some of the best Windows Forms controls are designed with extensibility in mind. They allow you to customize the control by deriving another class that's used with the control, rather than an entirely new version of the complete control. You'll see this technique in Chapter 14 (to derive custom ToolStripItem controls that extend the ToolStrip and StatusStrip) and Chapter 15 (to derive a custom DataGridViewColumn that extends the DataGridView).

CHAPTER 12

■ ■ ■

Owner-Drawn Controls

In Chapter 7 you learned how to use GDI+ to draw text and complex shapes on a form by over-riding the OnPaint() method. Although this technique works perfectly well, most of the time you'll want to build an application out of smaller controls that paint themselves individually. Taken to its logical extreme, you can use this technique to build hand-tooled interfaces with the latest in eye-catching graphics (something you'll consider again in Chapter 23).

In this chapter, you'll start out on your journey to creating hand-drawn custom controls. First you'll consider controls that have built-in support for owner-drawing a portion of their interface. Then you'll graduate into custom controls that render their entire interface from scratch.

Understanding Owner-Drawn Controls

Many of the core Windows Forms controls are wrappers over the Win32 API. As a result, they don't render their interface directly, but rely on the work of the operating system. One side effect of this design is that there's no way to tailor the rendering of most simple controls, like the TextBox or Button. If you want to have a hand in the painting logic, you either need to build a custom control from scratch or find a control that explicitly gives you the ability to supply some of the drawing logic.

The following are some controls that support owner drawing:

- ListBox and ComboBox

- ListView and TreeView

- ToolTip

- MenuItem (which has been superseded by MenuStrip in .NET 2.0)

All controls that support owner drawing have either a Boolean OwnerDraw property (which you set to true), or a DrawMode property (which you set to one of several enumerated values to choose what drawing logic you want to supply). You then supply the drawing logic by responding to an event that supplies a Graphics object.

■**Note** Additionally, in Chapter 14 you'll learn how the ToolStrip and StatusStrip support a more loosely coupled model for owner drawing. These controls use a dedicated renderer class that controls the painting. This gives you the flexibility to tweak the visual appearance without needing to create an entirely new set of button controls.

A Simple Owner-Drawn ListBox

The standard ListBox control is fairly unimpressive. You can configure various properties that affect the whole control, like Font, ForeColor, and BackColor, but you can't change individual items independently. For example, you can't create a list box that contains pictures, formatted text, or colored item backgrounds. And while you could develop a custom list control from scratch, there's a fair bit of boilerplate code you would need to write for managing the scrolling and selection behavior.

Fortunately, an easier approach exists. You simply need to set the ListBox.DrawMode to DrawMode.OwnerDrawFixed or DrawMode.OwnerDrawVariable. The difference between the two owner-drawn options is that with fixed drawing each item in the list is the standard size (typically 13 pixels). With OwnerDrawVariable (the mode used in the following example), you can specify the height for each item independently.

Assuming you use OwnerDrawVariable, you need to handle two events: MeasureItem, in which you specify the size of an item row, and DrawItem, in which you use the GDI+ Graphics class to output images, shapes, or text.

The following example uses this approach to draw the simplest possible owner-drawn list box. All items are the same height (15 pixels). The text is displayed using the list box font, and obtained by calling ToString() on the list object. The background and foreground color depend on whether or not the item is selected.

```
private void listBox1_MeasureItem(object sender, MeasureItemEventArgs e)
{
    // Specify a fixed height.
    // (The default height depends on the system font settings,
    // but it usually 13 pixels.)
    e.ItemHeight = 15;
}

private void listBox1_DrawItem(object sender, DrawItemEventArgs e)
{
    // Draw the background.
    // The color (white or blue) depends on selection.
    e.DrawBackground();

    // Determine the forecolor based on whether or not
    // the item is selected.
    Brush brush;
    if ((e.State & DrawItemState.Selected) == DrawItemState.Selected)
    {
```

```
        brush = Brushes.White;
    }
    else
    {
        brush = Brushes.Black;
    }

    // Get the item text.
    string text = ((ListBox)sender).Items[e.Index].ToString();

    // Draw the item text.
    e.Graphics.DrawString(text, ((Control)sender).Font,
      brush, e.Bounds.X, e.Bounds.Y);
}
```

Tip If you use OwnerDrawFixed, you don't have the chance to specify the height of the items (because the MeasureItem event never fires). Thus, it makes sense to use OwnerDrawVariable to vary the height of items or just to apply a non-standard item height to all items.

A More Advanced Owner-Drawn ListBox

The previous example mimicked the basic list box. To create a more interesting owner-drawn list box, you can customize this code to apply different colors or formatting, or even draw bitmaps or shapes in the space provided. However, it's worth carefully considering how you want to model this control. In many cases, you'll want the ability to configure each item separately. Ideally, the object that represents each item in the list box should have its own formatting information. The list box could then read this information and use it to configure the painting process.

Note The custom-drawn content will not appear in the Visual Studio design-time environment. Instead, the list will be shown without any content.

To implement this design, you need to create a new class that encapsulates the list item data and the formatting information. Here's an example of a class that wraps any object and provides properties that allow you to set the foreground color, background color, and font:

```
public class FormattedListItemWrapper
{
    private object item;
    public object Item
    {
```

```
        get { return item; }
        set { item = value; }
    }

    private Color foreColor;
    public Color ForeColor
    {
        get { return foreColor; }
        set { foreColor = value; }
    }

    private Color backColor;
    public Color BackColor
    {
        get { return backColor; }
        set { backColor = value; }
    }

    private Font font;
    public Font Font
    {
        get { return font; }
        set { font = value; }
    }

    public override string ToString()
    {
        if (item == null)
        {
            return string.Empty;
        }
        else
        {
            return item.ToString();
        }
    }

    // (Constructors omitted.)
}
```

Remember, the standard ListBox accepts any object, and simply calls the ToString()
method to get the item text. To duplicate this functionality, the FormattedListItemWrapper
also wraps any object. When you call FormattedListItemWrapper.ToString(), it calls ToString()
on the wrapped object.

Although the FormattedListItemWrapper provides a Font, ForeColor, and BackColor
property, you don't need to use them all. If you don't set these properties, the ForeColor and
BackColor will contain the value Color.Empty, and the Font property will provide a null reference. The custom ListBox drawing logic should check for this possibility, and supply intelligent

defaults (such as the system colors and the ListBox font). You can easily extend the FormattedListItemWrapper to accommodate other details. For example, you can add an Image property to incorporate thumbnail images.

Once this class is in place, you need to rewrite the event-handling code for measuring the item. First, you need to check if the current item is a FormattedListItemWrapper instance. If it is, you can set the height based on the font. However, if it's a different type of item, or the FormattedListItemWrapper doesn't provide a font, you should revert to the standard size.

```csharp
private void listBox1_MeasureItem(object sender, MeasureItemEventArgs e)
{
    ListBox list = (ListBox)sender;
    FormattedListItemWrapper item =
      list.Items[e.Index] as FormattedListItemWrapper;

    if (item == null || item.Font == null)
    {
        // Use the default.
        e.ItemHeight = 15;
    }
    else
    {
        // Get the height from the current item's font.
        Font font = item.Font;
        e.ItemHeight = font.Height;
    }
}
```

The same process is used to draw the item. First, the code checks for a FormattedListItemWrapper. It then uses the corresponding settings or chooses sensible defaults, depending on what's available:

```csharp
private void listBox1_DrawItem(object sender, DrawItemEventArgs e)
{
    ListBox list = (ListBox)sender;
    FormattedListItemWrapper item =
      list.Items[e.Index] as FormattedListItemWrapper;

    Font font = null;
    Color foreColor = Color.Empty;
    Color backColor = Color.Emtpy;
    if (item != null)
    {
        font = item.Font;
        foreColor = item.ForeColor;
        backColor = item.BackColor;
    }
```

```
        // The font could be null if there is no ListItemWrapper or the
        // ListItemWrapper doesn't specify a font.
        if (font == null)
        {
            // Use the ListBox font if no custom font is provided.
            font = list.Font;
        }

        // The color could be empty if there is no ListItemWrapper or the
        // ListItemWrapper doesn't specify a color.
        Brush brush;
        if (foreColor == Color.Empty)
        {
            // Use the default color.
            brush = Brushes.Black;
        }
        else
        {
            // Use the custom color.
            brush = new SolidBrush(item.ForeColor);
        }

        // Override the color if the item is selected.
        // Alternatively, you could add SelectedForeColor and
        // SelectedBackColor properties to the wrapper.
        if ((e.State & DrawItemState.Selected) == DrawItemState.Selected)
        {
            brush = Brushes.White;
        }

        // Paint the background.
        if (backColor == Color.Empty)
        {
            e.DrawBackground();
        }
        else
        {
            Brush brushBackground = new SolidBrush(item.BackColor);
            e.Graphics.FillRectangle(brushBackground, e.Bounds);
        }

        // Draw the item text.
        string text = list.Items[e.Index].ToString();
        e.Graphics.DrawString(text, font,
          brush, e.Bounds.X, e.Bounds.Y);
    }
```

To create a simple test for this owner-drawn list box, try filling the list with a separate list item, one for each font installed on the system:

```
InstalledFontCollection families = new InstalledFontCollection();

foreach (FontFamily family in families.Families)
{
    try
    {
        Font font = new Font(family.Name, 12);
        FormattedListItemWrapper item = new FormattedListItemWrapper(
            family.Name, font);
        listBox1.Items.Add(item);
    }
    catch (ArgumentException err)
    {
        // An error occurs if the font doesn't support normal
        // typeface or 12-point size. Ignore this font.
    }
}
```

Figure 12-1 shows the resulting list box.

Figure 12-1. *Item-specific drawing in a list box*

Writing the correct code in the MeasureItem and DrawItem event handlers requires some tweaking of pixel offsets and sizes. Unfortunately, in the current implementation there is no easy way to reuse this logic for different windows (not to mention different applications). A better approach is to perfect your list box as a custom derived control, like the examples you saw in the previous chapter. Just set the OwnerDrawMode property in the constructor of your custom control, and override the OnMeasureItem() and OnDrawItem() methods to hard-wire the drawing logic into the control. You can then reuse the custom control in a variety of projects and scenarios.

An Owner-Drawn TreeView

The TreeView and the ListView are two controls that developers commonly want to change. In .NET 1.x, this feat ranged from difficult to nearly impossible because of the way the TreeView and ListView interact with the Win32 API. (In fact, overriding the OnPaint() method for these controls has no effect.) As a result, developers who needed to change an aspect of the control's appearance (for example, giving the TreeView the ability to support multiple selections) were forced to create look-alike custom controls from scratch. And although this approach works, it requires a hefty amount of code and some low-level message processing.

In .NET 2.0, the situation improves dramatically for both controls:

- The ListView provides a new OwnerDraw property. When true, you can handle the DrawColumnHeader, DrawItem, and DrawSubItem events to paint various parts of the control.

- The TreeView provides a new DrawMode property. You can set this property to OwnerDrawText if you just want to customize the appearance of the node content, or OwnerDrawAll if you want to draw everything, including node lines, the expand/collapse boxes, check boxes, and so on. Either way, you handle the DrawNode event to perform your drawing.

There's no reason to create an owner-drawn TreeView or ListView to add custom colors and fonts, as both the TreeNode and ListViewItem classes expose properties like ForeColor, BackColor, and Font. However, the TreeView still lacks multiselect functionality—a limitation that's corrected with the following owner-drawn TreeView.

This TreeView uses a DrawMode of OwnerDrawText so that the TreeView will paint the node lines, expand/collapse boxes, and check boxes, depending on the value of properties like ShowLines, ShowPlusMinus, ShowRootLines, and CheckBoxes.

The Custom TreeNode

The first step to create this TreeNode is to derive a new node class from the standard TreeNode. In this case, the goal is to give the TreeNode the ability to support multiple selection. Here's the declaration:

```
public class MultiSelectTreeNode : TreeNode
{ ... }
```

In the basic TreeNode class, the IsSelected property is read-only. The only way to set the selected node is through the TreeView.SelectedNode property. To get around this limitation, the MultiSelectTreeNode declares its own version of the new IsSelected property:

```
private bool selected = false;
public new bool IsSelected
{
    get { return selected; }
}
```

The TreeNode.IsSelected property isn't overridable, so the MultiSelectTreeNode falls back on a slightly awkward trick: declaring the IsSelected property with the new keyword. That indicates that the definition for MultiSelectTreeNode.IsSelected *hides* the underlying TreeNode.IsSelected property. For the most part, the MultiSelectTreeNode will behave exactly as expected. The only caveat is that if you cast a MultiSelectTreeNode object to the TreeNode type, you'll be able to access only the old single-select TreeNode.IsSelected property, which probably isn't what you want. To avoid this confusion, you'll need to make sure you always cast each node to the MultiSelectTreeNode type before inspecting its selected status.

To make a multiselect TreeView work, you need to track all the selected nodes in a collection. (The TreeView.SelectedNode property isn't of any use, because it allows for only one node to be selected at time.) Ideally, this collection would be built into a custom TreeView class. However, in this example you're using the standard TreeView, so you need to track the collection of selected nodes elsewhere. The most convenient approach is to store a reference to the collection in each MultiSelectTreeNode. That way, when the node is selected or unselected, it can insert itself in or remove itself from the collection.

```
private List<MultiSelectTreeNode> selectedNodes;
```

To create a MultiSelectTreeNode, you need to pass a reference to the collection through the constructor:

```
public MultiSelectTreeNode(string text,
  List<MultiSelectTreeNode> selectedNodes) : base(text)
{
    this.selectedNodes = selectedNodes;
}
```

This constructor accepts the selected node collection and the node text (which is passed along to the base TreeNode constructor). A well-rounded custom node class would probably duplicate many more of the constructors found in the base TreeNode class, so that you can create MultiSelectTreeNode objects with images and children in one step.

To select a node, you simply call the public Select() method. To remove the selection, you can call UnSelect(). Selecting a node doesn't automatically remove the selection from previously selected nodes.

```
public void Select()
{
    // Check if the selection is being changed.
    if (selected != true)
    {
        selected = true;
```

```
        // Update the collection.
        selectedNodes.Add(this);
        RepaintNode();
    }
}

public void UnSelect()
{
    // Check if the selection is being changed.
    if (selected != false)
    {
        selected = false;

        // Update the collection.
        selectedNodes.Remove(this);
        RepaintNode();
    }
}
```

Every time the selection status is changed, that region of the TreeView is invalidated so that the node is correctly painted:

```
private void RepaintNode()
{
    // TreeView will be null if the node hasn't been
    // added yet.
    if (base.TreeView != null && base.IsVisible)
    {
        // Repaint the node.
        base.TreeView.Invalidate(base.Bounds);
    }
}
```

By building this logic into the MultiSelectTreeNode class (rather than the TreeView or form), you ensure that the TreeView is always properly refreshed when you change the selection status of a node. Otherwise, the only nodes that will be repainted are the current node and the node that was clicked previously.

The Drawing Logic

The real work is the drawing logic in the TreeView.DrawNode event handler. We'll take a look at this code one piece at a time.

The first step is to confirm you are drawing a MultiSelectTreeNode. If you aren't, the standard drawing logic should be used. You can achieve this by setting the DrawTreeNodeEventArgs.DrawDefault property to true. This gives you the flexibility to customize the drawing for just some nodes:

```
private void treeView1_DrawNode(object sender, DrawTreeNodeEventArgs e)
{
    // Check for multiple selection support.
    MultiSelectTreeNode multiNode = e.Node as MultiSelectTreeNode;
    if (multiNode == null)
    {
        // No multiple selection support.
        e.DrawDefault = true;
    }
    ...
```

Otherwise, the first task is to determine the font and colors for the node. Here's where you consider the MultiSelectTreeNode.IsSelected property. When using default colors, you should check the Font, ForeColor, and BackColor properties of the node. If they aren't specified, you can fall back on the TreeView defaults.

```
    ...
    else
    {
        // Retrieve the node font. If the node font has not been set,
        // use the TreeView font.
        Font nodeFont = multiNode.NodeFont;
        if (nodeFont == null) nodeFont = treeView1.Font;

        // Create brushes for the background and foreground.
        Brush backBrush, foreBrush;
        if (multiNode.IsSelected)
        {
            foreBrush = SystemBrushes.HighlightText;
            backBrush = SystemBrushes.Highlight;
        }
        else
        {
            if (multiNode.ForeColor != Color.Empty)
                foreBrush = new SolidBrush(multiNode.ForeColor);
            else
                foreBrush = new SolidBrush(multiNode.TreeView.ForeColor);

            if (multiNode.BackColor != Color.Empty)
                backBrush = new SolidBrush(multiNode.BackColor);
            else
                backBrush = new SolidBrush(multiNode.TreeView.BackColor);
        }
        ...
```

The actual drawing logic is fairly straightforward. It draws the background, text, and focus rectangle (if appropriate), and then cleans up the brushes if necessary.

```
        ...
        // Draw the background of the selected node.
        e.Graphics.FillRectangle(backBrush, e.Bounds);

        // Draw the node text.
        e.Graphics.DrawString(e.Node.Text, nodeFont, foreBrush, e.Bounds);

        // If the node has focus, draw the focus rectangle.
        if ((e.State & TreeNodeStates.Focused) != 0)
        {
            using (Pen focusPen = new Pen(Color.Black))
            {
                focusPen.DashStyle = System.Drawing.Drawing2D.DashStyle.Dot;
                Rectangle focusBounds = e.Bounds;
                focusBounds.Size = new Size(focusBounds.Width - 1,
                  focusBounds.Height - 1);
                e.Graphics.DrawRectangle(focusPen, focusBounds);
            }
        }

        // Dispose brushes if they were created
        // just for this node.
        if (!multiNode.IsSelected)
        {
            backBrush.Dispose();
            foreBrush.Dispose();
        }
    }
}
```

Tracking Selected Nodes

To support this new drawing logic, the behavior of the TreeView also needs a little tweaking. Namely, you need to intercept node clicks and set or clear the MultiSelectTreeNode.IsSelected property. Selected nodes should also be tracked in a collection, which you can maintain as a form member variable, as shown here:

```
private List<MultiSelectTreeNode> selectedNodes =
  new List<MultiSelectTreeNode>();
```

You can't rely on the BeforeSelect and AfterSelect events, because these won't fire when the same node is clicked twice in a row. In a multiselect TreeView, multiple clicks like these can be used to toggle the selected state of an item. Instead, you need to rely on the NodeMouse-Click event, which fires every time a node is clicked. At this point, you can check the state of the Ctrl key. If it's held down, the click is being used to extend the current selection. If Ctrl isn't held down, the current selection is cleared. All of this is made easy thanks to the Select() and UnSelect() methods of the MultiSelectTreeNode.

Here's the complete code:

```
private void treeView1_MouseDown(object sender,
  MouseEventArgs e)
{
    // Test if the click was on a node.
TreeNode nodeHit = treeView1.HitTest(e.X, e.Y).Node;
if (nodeHit == null) return;

// Get the node that was clicked.
MultiSelectTreeNode multiNode = nodeHit as MultiSelectTreeNode;
    if (multiNode != null)
    {
        // Use advanced selection rules.
        if ((Control.ModifierKeys & Keys.Control) == 0)
        {
            // Ctrl is not held down.
            // Remove previous selection.
            foreach (MultiSelectTreeNode node in selectedNodes)
            {
                if (node != multiNode)
                {
                    node.UnSelect();
                }
            }
            // remove all nodes and keep only
            // the new clicked node
            selectedNodes.Clear();
            selectedNodes.Add(multiNode);
        }

        if (multiNode.IsSelected)
        {
            // Node is already selected.
            // Toggle it off.
            multiNode.UnSelect();
        }
        else
        {
            multiNode.Select();
        }
    }
}
```

There's one limitation in this approach—it doesn't change the node selection when the user moves from one node to another with the arrow keys. You would need to handle additional TreeView events to add such node-selection logic. You might also want to add more-intelligent selection logic, such as support for the Shift key, and give the user the ability to drag a selection square around several nodes at once (as in Windows Explorer).

Figure 12-2 shows the multiselect TreeView.

Figure 12-2. *An owner-drawn TreeView for multiple selection*

A Custom MultiSelectTreeView

Although the multiselect TreeView works well, it requires code in the form class. It's difficult to reuse this TreeView implementation without duplicating that code. To avoid this problem and perfect this example, it makes sense to derive a custom TreeView class that wraps the drawing and selection logic, and exposes a built-in SelectedNodes property. You can use the techniques described in the previous chapter to build this type of control.

Here's the basic outline:

```
public class MultiSelectTreeView : TreeView
{
    // Force the tree to use owner drawing.
    public MultiSelectTreeView()
    {
        base.DrawMode = TreeViewDrawMode.OwnerDrawText;
    }

    // Track the selected nodes.
    private List<MultiSelectTreeNode> selectedNodes =
      new List<MultiSelectTreeNode>();

    public ReadOnlyCollection<MultiSelectTreeNode> SelectedNodes
    {
        get
        {
            // Return a read-only wrapper for this collection.
            // The only way to change selection is through the
            // MultiSelectTreeNode methods.
            return selectedNodes.AsReadOnly();
        }
    }
}
```

```
    protected override void OnDrawNode(DrawTreeNodeEventArgs e)
    { ... }

    protected override void OnMouseDown(MouseEventArgs e)
    { ... }
}
```

You can also modify the MultiSelectTreeNode class. It no longer needs to track the selected node collection—instead, it can access this detail through the MultiSelectTreeView.

Hiding the SelectedNode property and making sure the TreeView accepts only MultiSelectTreeNode objects takes a bit more work. You'll learn about these design-time niceties in the next chapter. For the full details for this example, consult the online code.

Owner-Drawn Custom Controls

So far, you've seen examples that use owner drawing support to customize the appearance of existing controls. In the remainder of this chapter, you'll step up to a more challenging task— rendering entirely new controls from scratch.

Owner-drawn custom controls are one of the most ambitious projects a developer can undertake. This is not because they are conceptually tricky (although sometimes they may be), but because a moderately sophisticated control needs a great deal of basic code just to handle all aspects of its appearance. If you can create a control using composition (i.e., a user control) or by inheriting from a similar control class (as shown in Chapter 11), you'll save yourself some work. On the other hand, if you need complete control over drawing and behavior, or you want to introduce some of the unusual GDI+ features to your user interface, you need to create a control that performs its painting manually.

The prime advantage of GDI+ controls is freedom. The prime disadvantage of GDI+ controls is that they aren't nearly as autonomous as prebuilt controls. For example, with custom GDI+ controls you need to handle the following details manually:

- Scrolling support

- Focus cues (i.e., indicating when the control has focus)

- The "pushed" state appearance for a button control

- Special cues or "hot tracking" appearance changes when the mouse moves over the control

- Hit testing to determine if a click was made in an appropriate area

- Respecting and applying the Windows XP themes

The remainder of this chapter introduces several example controls that paint themselves without any outside help.

Double Buffering

In Chapter 7, you learned how to use double buffering with a form to dramatically reduce flicker. The same features are available in controls. However, they're exposed through protected members, which means you can turn on control double buffering only if you're *creating* a control (not if you're simply using it).

The easiest way to improve the drawing performance of a control that's made up of more than one element is to set the Control. DoubleBuffered property to true. Now, whenever you paint in the OnPaint() method, the Graphics object won't give you direct access to the surface of the control—instead, it wraps an in-memory bitmap. The image content won't be copied to the control until the method ends, at which point it is painted in a single step. A convenient place to turn on double buffering is in the control's constructor.

■**Note** Do *not* use the SetStyle() to apply the DoubleBuffer style. This has been superseded by the DoubleBuffered property, and is now considered obsolete.

In addition, you might want to set the ResizeRedraw property to true so that the control automatically invalidates itself if the size changes. This is useful if the drawing logic uses calculations that depend on the control's size. However, use it only if you need it. If you don't apply it, only newly exposed areas are painted, which often saves time.

The MarqueeLabel Control

The first type of GDI+ control that might occur to you to use is one that simply wraps one of the GDI+ drawing features you examined Chapter 7. For example, you might want to provide a simple shape control that renders a closed figure depending on the properties you set. Or, you might want to create a special type of label that paints itself with a textured brush, or a gradient that the developer can configure through the appropriate properties. That's the type of example considered next with the MarqueeLabel control.

The MarqueeLabel is a graphical control with a twist. It automatically refreshes its display in response to a timer, scrolling a line of text across the visible area. The control uses three significant properties: Text; ScrollTimeInterval, which determines how frequently the timer fires; and ScrollPixelAmount, which determines how much the text is scrolled with every timer tick. An additional private member variable, called position, is defined to track how far the text has scrolled. This property is not made available to the client (although it could be if you wanted to allow the text to be set at a specific scroll position).

Here's the property procedure code for the MarqueeLabel control:

```
private string text;
private int scrollAmount = 10;
private int position = 0;
private System.Windows.Forms.Timer tmrScroll;
```

```
public override string Text
{
    get { return text; }
    set
    {
        text = value;
        Invalidate();
    }
}

public int ScrollTimeInterval
{
    get { return tmrScroll.Interval; }
    set { tmrScroll.Interval = value; }
}

public int ScrollPixelAmount
{
    get { return scrollAmount; }
    set { scrollAmount = value; }
}
```

When the control is instantiated, it switches on double buffering:

```
public MarqueeLabel()
{
    InitializeComponent();

    DoubleBuffered = true;
    ResizeRedraw = true;
}
```

At runtime, you call the Scroll() method to turn the timer on:

```
public void Scroll(bool state)
{
    tmrScroll.Enabled = state;
}
```

Tip You can easily build a MarqueeLabel that starts scrolling automatically. However, to prevent it from also scrolling at design time (which is CPU-wasteful and distracting), you need to get a little more clever. Chapter 13 shows you how to add this support.

The timer simply increments the private position variable and invalidates the display with each tick:

```
private void tmrScroll_Tick(object sender, System.EventArgs e)
{
    position += scrollAmount;

    // Force a refresh.
    Invalidate();
}
```

The painting logic takes care of the rest. If the text has scrolled off the form, the position is reset. However, the new starting position is *not* (0, 0). Instead, the text is moved left by an amount equal to its length. That way, when the scrolling resumes, the last letter appears first from the left side of the control, followed by the rest of the text.

```
protected override void OnPaint(System.Windows.Forms.PaintEventArgs e)
{
    base.OnPaint(e);

    if (position > Width)
    {
        // Reset the text to scroll back onto the control.
        position = -(int)e.Graphics.MeasureString(text, Font).Width;
    }
    e.Graphics.DrawString(text, Font, new SolidBrush(ForeColor), position, 0);
}
```

The online samples for this chapter include a test program (shown in Figure 12-3) that allows you to try out the marquee control and dynamically modify its scroll speed settings.

Figure 12-3. *The MarqueeLabel test utility*

The GradientPanel Control

Many modern applications incorporate panels with rich gradient or blended backgrounds. The .NET framework doesn't include any such control, but using GDI+ you can easily develop your own.

The next example presents a control that's both an owner-drawn control *and* a derived control. The custom GradientPanel derives from Panel, which ensures you can add controls to it at design time without any extra steps, and gives automatic support for features like automatic scrolling. The custom GradientPanel class overrides OnPaintBackground() to fill the panel surface with a gradient based on two selected colors.

The Gradient Fill

In the GradientPanel, the first step is to create the required properties. In this case, you need to store information about the two colors for the gradient and the type of gradient to be used. Note that when set, the property procedures invalidate the display, ensuring that the gradient is repainted as needed.

```
private Color colorA = Color.LightBlue;
private Color colorB = Color.Purple;
private LinearGradientMode gradientStyle = LinearGradientMode.ForwardDiagonal;

public Color ColorA
{
    get { return colorA; }
    set
    {
        colorA = value;
        Invalidate();
    }
}

public Color ColorB
{
    get { return colorB; }
    set
    {
        colorB = value;
        Invalidate();
    }
}

public LinearGradientMode GradientFillStyle
{
    get { return gradientStyle; }
    set
    {
        gradientStyle = value;
        Invalidate();
    }
}
```

In the constructor, you can set the ResizeRedraw property to true:

```
public GradientPanel()
{
    ResizeRedraw = true;
}
```

You'll also need to invalidate the panel when the user scrolls down (assuming you've enabled scrolling by setting AutoScroll to true). There's no property to implement this behavior, so you'll need to override the OnScroll() method and invalidate the panel with the following code:

```
protected override void OnScroll(ScrollEventArgs se)
{
    Invalidate();
}
```

The Painting Process

The OnPaintBackground() code is fairly straightforward. It creates the LinearGradientBrush and fills the available control area.

```
protected override void OnPaintBackground(System.Windows.Forms.PaintEventArgs e)
{
    // To prevent flicker, don't call the base implementation
    // of OnPaintBackground(), which would paint a solid background using
    // the GradientPanel.BackColor.

    // Draw the gradient background.
    LinearGradientBrush brush = new LinearGradientBrush(
      ClientRectangle, gradient.ColorA, gradient.ColorB,
      gradient.GradientFillStyle);
    e.Graphics.FillRectangle(brush, ClientRectangle);
    brush.Dispose();
}
```

Figure 12-4 shows the GradientPanel on a form. Autoscroll is turned on, and a button and two labels have been added. The labels have a transparent background (Color.Transparent), so that the gradient shows through.

Note To make the GradientPanel work properly at design time with the Properties window, a few enhancements are needed. You'll explore those in Chapter 13.

Figure 12-4. *The GradientPanel*

Improving Performance

GDI+ controls suffer from one obvious limitation—they render themselves far slower than basic Windows controls. To compensate, you need to make sure your GDI+ code is as carefully optimized as can be.

In the GradientPanel class, two improvements are possible. The first step is to avoid continually re-creating resources (like brushes and pens) in the OnPaintBackground() method. A better approach is to create these ingredients only when required. In all likelihood, the control consumer will simply set the color properties once, so there's no need to generate a new brush each time the window is moved or the panel is scrolled. In the GradientPanel, the change won't make much difference, because the overhead required to create a single LinearGradientBrush object is trivial. However, if you created a more complex control with a collection of drawing resources, the difference would be more pronounced.

The first step is to create a private variable that stores the LinearGradientBrush object for the lifetime of the control and a property procedure that uses the lazy initialization pattern to create it only when it's requested.

```
private Brush gradientBrush;
private Brush GradientBrush
{
    get
    {
        if (gradientBrush == null)
        {
            gradientBrush = new LinearGradientBrush(
                ClientRectangle, gradient.ColorA, gradient.ColorB,
                gradient.GradientFillStyle);
        }
        return gradientBrush;
    }
}
```

Now, when setting the various properties you need to clear the gradient brush:

```
public Color ColorA
{
    get { return colorA; }
    set
    {
        colorA = value;
        if (gradientBrush != null)
        {
            gradientBrush.Dispose();
            gradientBrush = null;
        }
        Invalidate();
    }
}
```

The drawing code is simplified:

```
protected override void OnPaintBackground(System.Windows.Forms.PaintEventArgs e)
{
    // Draw the gradient background.
    e.Graphics.FillRectangle(GradientBrush, ClientRectangle);
}
```

The last step is to override the Dispose() method so that the gradient brush is properly disposed when the control is disposed. This is the best design because all brushes hold onto unmanaged resources, like many other GDI+ objects.

```
protected override void Dispose(bool disposing)
{
    if (disposing)
    {
        if (gradientBrush != null) gradientBrush.Dispose();
    }
    base.Dispose(disposing);
}
```

You'll notice that the Dispose() method disposes the brush only if the disposing argument is true. That's because this indicates that the GradientPanel was explicitly disposed by calling the Dispose() method. If disposing is false, it's been picked up by the garbage collector, and it's possible that the gradientBrush object has already been disposed.

■**Tip** If you have numerous resources that you want to generate on demand, it's easiest to create them all at once instead of maintaining them with separate property procedures. For example, you might want to create a method like RebuildResources() and call it when you start drawing. You could track if resources need to be re-created with a Boolean member variable like ResourcesDirty.

A more dramatic performance optimization is to bypass the rendering process altogether for subsequent paint using some form of caching. Caching becomes particularly important if you have a control that can render in several predetermined states (like a gel button) and the drawing logic is time-consuming. In this case, you can often optimize the painting code by holding onto the rendered picture and reusing it automatically when the panel is repainted if nothing has changed. This increases the complexity of the code, but it has the potential to give a much more significant performance boost. It works best when the ratio of control complexity to control size is high. That's because the more complex your control is, the more time you'll save by reusing the cached version rather than reconstructing it. The smaller your control, the smaller the cached memory footprint. The caching approach isn't appropriate for the GradientPanel (because it's large and not that complex), but you'll see this technique in action with custom buttons in Chapter 23.

The SimpleChart Control

The next control considered here is a simple charting tool. It's a good demonstration of how you can create a higher-level GDI+ control. Instead of representing a single label or button, it renders a complete display according to the supplied data.

The BarItem

The basis of the chart is a BarItem class that stores information for a single bar. This information consists of a numerical value and a short title that can be displayed along with the bar.

```
public class BarItem
{
    private string shortForm;
    public string ShortForm
    {
        get { return shortForm; }
        set { shortForm = value; }
    }

    private float barValue;
    public float Value
    {
        get { return barValue; }
        set { barValue = value; }
    }

    public BarItem(string shortForm, decimal value)
    {
        this.ShortForm = shortForm;
        this.Value = value;
    }
}
```

The data for a bar chart is made up of a collection of BarItem objects. The SimpleChart control provides a collection of BarItem objects through its Bars property. The client programmer must create and add the appropriate BarItem objects. A more sophisticated control might add dedicated UITypeEditors that allow BarItem objects to be created and added at design time. Chapter 13 demonstrates how to give this level of design-time sophistication to the SimpleChart control. The following, though, is our SimpleChart class:

```
public class SimpleChart : System.Windows.Forms.Control
{
    private List<BarItem> bars = new List<BarItem>();
    public List<BarItem> Bars
    {
        get { return bars; }
        set { bars = value; }
    }

    public SimpleChart()
    {
        DoubleBuffered = true;
    }

    // (Drawing logic omitted.)
}
```

Building the Chart

To use the SimpleChart, you must add one or more BarItem objects, and then call the public RebuildChart() method. This allows the client application to control exactly when the chart is generated.

Instead of using the RebuildChart() method, you could track changes to the BarItem collection, and fire an event to notify the SimpleChart. The SimpleChart could then rebuild the chart each time a bar is added, removed, or changed. However, this approach hampers performance, because it causes the chart to be recalculated multiple times—once each time a new bar is added. If you use this approach, you should also to provide a way to temporarily turn off automatic chart generation, as with the SuspendLayout() and ResumeLayout() methods exposed by many complex container controls. You'll see an example of this technique with a modified version of the GradientPanel control in the next chapter.

The RebuildChart() method steps through the data, determines the maximum BarItem value, and sizes all other bar items proportionally. Then, the RebuildChart() method creates a Rectangle object to represent the on-screen presence of each bar. Finally, the RebuildChart() method invalidates the control to trigger the painting logic.

```
private List<Rectangle> barRectangles = new List<Rectangle>();

public void RebuildChart()
{
    if (bars.Count == 0) return;
```

```
// Find out how much space a single bar can occupy.
int barWidth = (int)(Width / bars.Count);

// Set the maximum value on the chart.
decimal maxValue = 0;
foreach (BarItem bar in bars)
{
    if (bar.Value > maxValue)
    {
        maxValue = bar.Value;
    }
}

// Create the rectangle shapes and store them for later use.
// Clear any existing shapes.
barRectangles.Clear();

// Track the x-coordinate while laying out the bars.
int x = 0;
// Leave some space at the top.
int topMargin = 5;
// Leave some space between bars.
int barGap = 4;

foreach (BarItem bar in bars)
{
    int height = (int)(bar.Value / maxValue * (Height - topMargin));
    int top = Height - height;

    barRectangles.Add(new Rectangle(x + barGap / 2, top, barWidth - barGap,
        height));
    x += barWidth;
}

// Trigger a repaint.
Invalidate();
}
```

You might have expected to create the Rectangle objects as a part of the painting logic. However, doing so in the RebuildChart() method has several benefits. First of all, it improves performance, because the chart may be invalidated and refreshed multiple times (for example, when the form is minimized or resized) without needing to be rebuilt each time. Most importantly, it keeps the Rectangle objects around for hit testing later on. If you didn't create the Rectangle objects, you wouldn't be able to make the chart interactive.

Painting the Chart

The simplest part of the painting process is the OnPaintBackground() method, which fills the area behind the charts with a gentle blue gradient. To simplify this task, the region is filled using the VisualStyleRenderer class (described in Chapter 7), which uses Windows XP themes. Unfortunately, you can't assume that all computers support visual styles, so backup drawing logic uses a plainer solid fill if the operating system doesn't support themes or the user has switched them off.

```
protected override void OnPaintBackground(PaintEventArgs e)
{
    if (Application.RenderWithVisualStyles)
    {
        // Use part of the current theme.
        VisualStyleRenderer renderer = new VisualStyleRenderer(
          VisualStyleElement.ExplorerBar.NormalGroupBackground.Normal);
        renderer.DrawBackground(e.Graphics, e.ClipRectangle);
    }
    else
    {
        // Use a solid fill with the BackColor.
        Brush brush = new SolidBrush(base.BackColor);
        e.Graphics.FillRectangle(brush, e.ClipRectangle);
        brush.Dispose();
    }
}
```

The OnPaint() routine has the code for drawing the individual bars. It steps through the collection of bars and draws each one onto the form with the appropriate proportional size. To simplify the heavy lifting, the bars are drawn using the VisualStyleRenderer class. In this case, the Start bar style is used, which creates a bold blue bar if you're using the Default Windows XP theme. If visual styles aren't supported, more-straightforward shadowed rectangles are used instead. (You could create your own bar that mimics Windows XP visual styles, but it requires a significant amount of extra code.)

```
protected override void OnPaint(System.Windows.Forms.PaintEventArgs e)
{
    base.OnPaint(e);
    if (bars.Count == 0) return;

    foreach (Rectangle rect in barRectangles)
    {
        if (Application.RenderWithVisualStyles)
        {
            VisualStyleRenderer renderer = new VisualStyleRenderer(
              VisualStyleElement.StartPanel.UserPane.Normal);
            renderer.DrawBackground(e.Graphics, rect);
        }
```

```
        else
        {
            // Draw bar (two rectangles are used for a shadowed effect).
            int shadowMargin = 4;
            Rectangle rectShadow = rect;
            rectShadow.Offset(shadowMargin, shadowMargin);

            e.Graphics.FillRectangle(Brushes.White, rectShadow);
            e.Graphics.FillRectangle(Brushes.SteelBlue, rect);
        }
    }
}
...
```

The BarItem.ShortForm text is also drawn onto each bar in a second pass, which assures that long titles won't be obscured by adjacent bars. Finally, a bottom base line is added to frame the chart.

```
...
int index = 0;
foreach (Rectangle rect in barRectangles)
{
    // Get title.
    string text = bars[index].ShortForm;

    // Get the position.
    int textTopOffset = 10, textLeftOffset = 15;
    Point ptText = rect.Location;
    ptText.Offset(textTopOffset, textLeftOffset);

    // Draw the title.
    e.Graphics.DrawString(text, Font, Brushes.White, ptText);
    index++;
}

// Draw bottom line of the the grid.
Pen pen = new Pen(Color.Black, 3);
e.Graphics.DrawLine(pen, 0, base.Height - 1, base.Width,
    base.Height - 1);
pen.Dispose();
}
```

The code that follows creates a simple chart when the form first loads. The chart is shown in Figure 12-5 (in both its native themed look and the more basic style it uses when visual styles aren't available).

```
private void Form1_Load(object sender, System.EventArgs e)
{
    simpleChart1.Bars.Add(new BarItem("Sales 2002", 10000));
    simpleChart1.Bars.Add(new BarItem("Sales 2003", 20000));
    simpleChart1.Bars.Add(new BarItem("Sales 2004", 5000));
    simpleChart1.Bars.Add(new BarItem("Sales 2005", 27000));
    simpleChart1.RebuildChart();
}
```

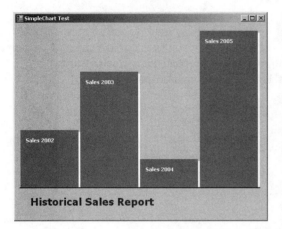 

Figure 12-5. *The SimpleChart, with and without visual styles*

If you want to start tweaking the SimpleChart control, there are several interesting avenues to explore. You might want to start by developing a better axis, allowing customizable bar captions, giving options for a legend and customizable title alignment, or creating a pie-chart mode. Adding these enhancements is relatively straightforward. However, even though it's conceptually easy to create a charting control, it can require a huge amount of drawing code. For that reason, it's worth considering third-party charting controls.

Making the Chart Interactive

Creating a charting control like SimpleChart is fairly easy because it doesn't need to interact with the user, receive focus, accept input, and so on. Instead, it draws itself in one pass and then sits on the form as a static piece of user interface.

However, thanks to the carefully segmented design of the SimpleChart, you can make it interactive without much extra work. The trick is to react to events like MouseMove and MouseClick, and test to see if the mouse is in the region of one of the bar rectangles. If it is, you can take additional steps, like firing a BarItemClick event to the application, showing a tooltip, or highlighting the selected bar.

The following example uses this approach to react to mouse movements. Each time the mouse moves over a bar item, the value of the corresponding BarItem object is shown in a tooltip, using a ToolTip component that's been added to the design surface of the SimpleChart control.

```
protected override void OnMouseMove(MouseEventArgs e)
{
    // Hit test all the bars.
    int index = 0;
    foreach (Rectangle rect in barRectangles)
    {
        if (rect.Contains(e.Location))
        {
            // Get matching value.
            string text = String.Format("{0:C}", bars[index].Value);

            // Get point relative to the top-left corner of the form
            // (currently the point is relative to the top-left corner
            // of the chart control).
            Point pt = e.Location;
            pt.Offset(base.Location);
            toolTip.Show(text, base.FindForm(), pt);
            return;
        }
        index++;
    }
    // No bar found.
    toolTip.Hide(base.FindForm());
}
```

Figure 12-6 shows the tooltip that appears.

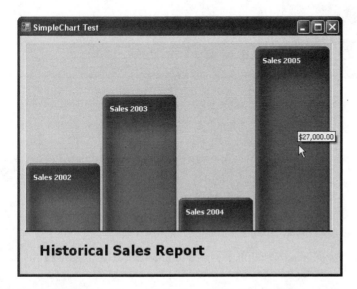

Figure 12-6. *Interacting with the bars in the SimpleChart*

You could easily extend this framework so the user can manipulate individual bar objects. A similar example in Chapter 23 demonstrates a dynamic drawing application in which shape objects can be manipulated freely.

The CollapsiblePanel Control

The last control you'll consider is a Windows XP standby that's finally available in the .NET world. It's a CollapsiblePanel developed by Microsoft and designed to mimic the Windows XP common task pane, which is shown on the side of many standard windows (see Figure 12-7).

Figure 12-7. *The common task pane in Windows XP*

This panel has several noteworthy features:

- It supports Windows XP themes, giving it a slick look with a detailed gradient background.

- It supports collapsing. When you click the arrow button in the top-right corner, the panel is reduced to just its header. You can click the arrow button again to expand the panel. In Figure 12-7, the Other Places panel is collapsed.

The .NET version of the collapsible panel duplicates this functionality (see Figure 12-8).

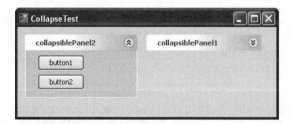

Figure 12-8. *The .NET CollapsiblePanel, expanded (left) and collapsed (right)*

The CollapsiblePanel is particularly useful when generating dynamic interfaces. For example, you can stack multiple CollapsiblePanel controls one on top of the other, and dock them all to the top of the form. This ensures that as one panel collapses, all the panels underneath shift up. To get even fancier, you can put CollapsiblePanel controls in the FlowLayoutPanel (discussed in Chapter 21). Then set the FlowLayoutPanel.Margin property to add a basic amount of space between each CollapsiblePanel, and set the FlowLayoutPanel.Padding property to add some space between the FlowLayoutPanel borders and the CollapsiblePanel controls inside. With this approach, you can duplicate the look of the Windows XP common tasks pane (see Figure 12-9).

Figure 12-9. *Dynamic interfaces with the CollapsiblePanel*

Although the code for the CollapsiblePanel is too long to repeat in its entirety (download the full code with the sample content for this book), it's fairly easy to pick out the important details using the concepts that you've explored in this chapter.

The CollapseButton

The CollapsiblePanel control is divided into two pieces (not including the classes for design-time support):

- The CollapsiblePanel derives from the base Panel class, and adds the custom drawing code and the collapsing logic.

- The CollapseButton represents the header of the panel, including the title and the arrow button shown in the top-left corner, which you can use to collapse and expand the panel.

Both of these controls draw their interfaces from scratch using the VisualStyleRenderer class, which means they are supported only in Windows XP. If you need to use this control with other types of clients, you'll need to extend the drawing logic to check for visual style support and gracefully downgrade.

The code for the button consists of a fair bit of painting logic. It adjusts the rendering depending on whether the mouse is hovering over the button, has just clicked it, and so on. Although this code is fairly lengthy (because of the range of possible states), the actual drawing process is straightforward because it's all built into the VisualStyleRenderer. For example, here's the code needed to paint a button if it's been pressed:

```
if (!collapsed)
{
    if ((State & StateButtonState.Pressed) != 0)
    {
        renderer = new VisualStyleRenderer(
          VisualStyleElement.ExplorerBar.NormalGroupCollapse.Pressed);
    }
    ...
}
else
{ ... }
```

Of course, the button does double duty as an expand button, as well. Note the slightly different VisualStyleElement you need to use to draw the "down" arrow button (rather than the "up" arrow button) if the panel is collapsed:

```
renderer = new VisualStyleRenderer(
  VisualStyleElement.ExplorerBar.NormalGroupExpand.Pressed);
```

There's also a fair bit of basic boilerplate code for handling mouse movements and mouse clicks, updating the state appropriately, and raising the related events. Most of this logic is standard for any button control. You can see the full code with the online content. For a walk-through of how to create a custom button, see Chapter 23.

Collapsing the Panel

The CollapsiblePanel class contains the most interesting logic. It provides a single CollapseButton that, when clicked, initiates the collapsing or expanding process. The button is configured in the control constructor.

```
private CollapseButton button;
private Timer timer;

public CollapsiblePanel()
{
    ResizeRedraw = true;
    DoubleBuffered = true;

    // Set up the button.
    button = new CollapseButton();
    button.Size = new Size(this.Width, 25);
    button.Location = new Point(0, 0);
    button.Font = new Font("Tahoma", 8.0f, FontStyle.Bold);
    button.Dock = DockStyle.Top;
    button.Click += new EventHandler(button_Click);
    base.Controls.Add(button);

    // Set up the timer.
    timer = new Timer();
    timer.Interval = 25;
    timer.Tick += new EventHandler(timer_Tick);
}
```

The automatic resizing is handled in much the same way as the scrolling in the MarqueeLabel. When the operation is started (either programmatically or by clicking the CollapseButton) a timer is switched on. Here's the (slightly shortened) code:

```
// Tracks collapsed/expanded state of control.
private bool collapsing;
// Track old height.
private int oldHeight;

private void button_Click(object sender, EventArgs e)
{
    if (!collapsing)
    {
        PerformCollapse();
    }
    else
    {
        PerformExpand();
    }
}
```

```
public void PerformCollapse()
{
    oldHeight = Height;
    collapsing = true;
    // Prevent child controls from being laid out until process is finished.
    SuspendLayout();
    timer.Enabled = true;
}

public void PerformExpand()
{
    collapsing = false;
    // Prevent child controls from being laid out until process is finished.
    SuspendLayout();
    timer.Enabled = true;
}
```

Each time the timer fires, the size of the panel is changed, until the process is complete and the timer can be disabled.

```
// Incremented to increase the speed of the resize as the process goes on.
private int accelerator;

private void timer_Tick(object sender, EventArgs e)
{
    if (collapsing)
    {
        // Collapse one increment.
        this.Size = new Size(this.Width, this.Height - 2 - accelerator);

        // Check if process is finished.
        if (this.Height <= 25)
        {
            this.Size = new Size(this.Width, 25);
            timer.Enabled = false;
            button.Collapsed = true;
            accelerator = 0;
            ResumeLayout();
        }
    }
    else
    {
        // Expand one increment.
        this.Size = new Size(this.Width, this.Height + 2 + accelerator);
```

```
    // Check if process is finished.
    if (this.Height >= oldHeight)
    {
        this.Size = new Size(this.Width, oldHeight);
        timer.Enabled = false;
        button.Collapsed = false;
        accelerator = 0;
        ResumeLayout();
    }
    }
    accelerator++;
}
```

Painting the Panel

The painting logic for the panel is surprisingly straightforward. Thanks to the visual renderer, there's not much work to do at all:

```
protected override void OnPaint(PaintEventArgs e)
{
    VisualStyleRenderer renderer = new VisualStyleRenderer(
      VisualStyleElement.ExplorerBar.NormalGroupBackground.Normal);
    renderer.DrawBackground(e.Graphics, e.ClipRectangle);

    if (!timer.Enabled) base.OnPaint(e);
}
```

If you wanted to make this control work without visual styles, you could simply fall back on the base implementation of the Panel.OnPaint() method, which fills a solid background with the background color. This wouldn't change the collapsing feature of the panel.

The Last Word

GDI+ controls represent the fusion of two remarkable features: a powerful drawing framework and .NET's simple and elegant class-based control development. The potential for owner-drawn .NET controls is limitless, and major tool vendors have developed countless complex .NET controls. Look for these on the Internet—some are even available to experiment with at no cost.

One topic that we haven't considered so far is Visual Studio's sometimes quirky design-time support of custom controls. The next chapter takes some of the controls you've been working with and develops the designers and type editors that allow them to behave properly in the IDE.

Design-Time Support for Custom Controls

The custom controls you have explored so far are full of promise. Being able to drop a tool-like directory browser or thumbnail viewer directly into your application without writing a line of extra code is a remarkable advantage.

However, even though your custom code might work perfectly at runtime, that doesn't mean it will behave itself at design time. Common problems include properties that you can't edit at design time, and properties that are mysteriously reset when you recompile the application. To correct these quirks, you need to apply attributes, create new classes, and write additional code to implement design-time support.

Overall, design-time issues fall into several categories:

- Allowing the developer to add your control to a form and configure it at design time.

- Ensuring the developer's configuration steps are properly serialized into the form code so the control can be successfully initialized when the program is executed.

- Ensuring the control behaves nicely at runtime. For example, you might want to select individual parts of the control, see a realistic representation of the runtime appearance, and so on.

- Giving design-time shortcuts for complex configuration tasks (right-click context menus, smart tags, advanced editors for specialized properties, and so on).

- Using licensing to differentiate between development and runtime use of a control, and restricting use according to your license policy.

In this chapter, you'll tackle the first three items on this list. In other words, you'll concentrate on using design-time support to make sure your control works as it should, and steers clear of common design-time problems. You won't consider adding frills like custom smart tags and designers—those topics are discussed in Chapter 26.

Design-Time Basics

Custom controls have two requirements. They need to interact with your code and the user at runtime, and they need to interact with Visual Studio and the developer at design time. These two tasks are related, but they can be refined and customized separately. Some of the most advanced Windows Forms controls include an impressive degree of design-time smarts.

You've already seen how Visual Studio gives a basic level of support to all custom controls by adding them to the Toolbox automatically when the project is compiled and by allowing you to drop them onto other forms. Once you insert a custom control, you can configure its properties in the Properties window. However, there's still a lot more that the design-time behavior of a control can offer.

Many of the techniques you'll see are niceties that make it easier to work with custom controls. For example, you might use design-time support to add descriptions in the Properties window or commands in a context menu for your control. However, there are other cases where design-time customization is required. For example, if you create a control that exposes complex objects as properties and you don't take any extra steps to add design-time support, the control will work erratically in the design-time environment. You might have trouble setting properties with the Properties window, or you might discover that when you do the information is abruptly wiped out. These quirks are a result of how Visual Studio serializes your control properties into source code, and you'll learn how to tackle these issues in this chapter.

Note This chapter talks about design-time control features as seen in Visual Studio. However, the .NET Framework actually provides a generic design-time model that can be used by third-party tools (like SharpDevelop). Other IDEs may not provide all the same services as Visual Studio, though. Generally, all IDEs will include at least a design surface and a Properties window.

The Key Players

In .NET, there's no single class that provides design-time support. Instead, there's a number of different ingredients involved. They include the following:

- **Attributes.** You apply attributes to parts of your control for several reasons. First, these attributes supply information that will be used in the Properties window. Second, attributes attach other design-time components to your control and configure how properties are serialized.

- **Type converters.** Type converters allow complex or unusual data types to be converted to and from representations in more common data types. For example, if you create a type editor that lets you convert a custom data type to and from a string representation, you can then view and edit a control property that uses that data type in the Properties window. Type converters can also play a role in code serialization by generating the initialization code required to instantiate a complex type.

- **Type editors.** Type editors provide a graphical interface for setting complex type values. For example, when you choose a color or font in the Properties window, you're making use of a type editor for that data type.

- **Control designers.** Control designers are the heavyweights of custom control development. Every control has a control designer that manages its design-time appearance and behavior. You can use a custom control designer to add frills like smart tags or manage more-complex details like the design-time selection behavior. You can also use a designer to hide properties in your control class at design time or add design-time-only properties.

In this chapter, you'll consider all of these ingredients. You'll begin by considering how you can outfit your control with a custom toolbox icon and proper support for the Properties window. Next, you'll learn how to shape basic control serialization into source code. Finally, you'll consider how to create type converters and type editors to deal with your custom data types. However, you won't look at custom control designers yet—you'll get that material in Chapter 26.

Basic Attributes

The first level of design-time support consists of control *attributes*—declarative flags that are compiled into the metadata of your custom control assembly. Attributes give you a way to add information that's related to a piece of code without forcing you to change the code or create a separate file in an entirely different format.

In .NET, attributes are used for a range of tasks. The key detail to understand about attributes is that they can be read and interpreted by different agents. For example, you can add attributes that give information to the common language runtime, the compiler, the debugger, or a custom tool. In this chapter, we're primarily interested in attributes that provide information to Visual Studio, and tell it how to work with a control at design time.

For an example, consider the Progress user control developed in Chapter 10. This control displays a synchronized label paired with a progress bar. To make it work, three properties were added: Value, Step, and Maximum. You may have noticed that these properties appear in the design window grouped under the generic Misc category without any additional information (see Figure 13-1).

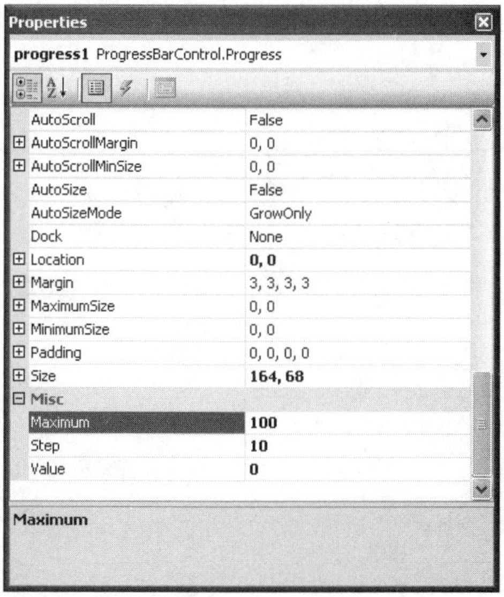

Figure 13-1. *Nondescript properties*

You can improve on this situation using attributes. For example, here's how you could place the Value property into the Behavior category:

```
[Category("Behavior")]
public int Value
{
    get { return Bar.Value; }
    set
    {
        Bar.Value = value;
        UpdateLabel();
    }
}
```

When you add more than one attribute, you can close them all in a single set of brackets (separated by commas), or you can place each one in its own set. Here's an example that adds a Description and Category attribute to the Value property:

```
[Description("The current value (between 0 and Maximum) which sets " +
 "the position of the progress bar")]
[Category("Behavior")]
public int Value
{ ... }
```

The result of applying these attributes is shown in Figure 13-2.

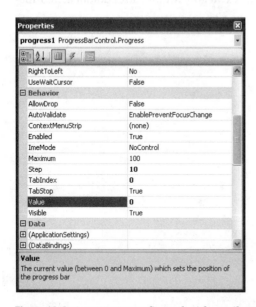

Figure 13-2. *A property configured with attributes*

All these attributes are found in the System.ComponentModel namespace, along with many more that allow you to configure aspects of your control's design-time behavior. Table 13-1 lists some of the attributes that affect the Properties window. You'll look at more attributes as this chapter progresses.

Table 13-1. *Attributes for Control Properties*

Attribute	Description
AmbientValue(true|false)	If true, indicates that the value for a property is derived from the control's container. For example, all controls have ambient Font, ForeColor, BackColor, and Cursor properties—if these values are not set, the values of the container are used automatically. The default is false.
Browsable(true|false)	If false, indicates that a property should not be shown in the Properties window. However, the property is still accessible through code and is still a candidate to be serialized into code if the value is different from the default value. The default is true.
Category("")	Sets the category under which the property appears in the Properties window. If a category with this name doesn't exist, it is created.
Description("")	Specifies the text description that will be displayed for this property in the Object Browser and the Properties window.
DesignOnly(true|false)	When set to true, the value of this property is not serialized even though it can be modified at design time. However, the attribute name is somewhat misleading—design-only properties can still be *read* at runtime. One example might be a property that determines how a control is localized. The default is false.
ImmutableObject(true|false)	When set to true on an object property, this attribute ensures that the subproperties of this object are displayed as read-only. For example, if you apply this to a property that uses a Point object, the X and Y subproperty will be read-only. The default is false.
MergableProperty(true|false)	Configures how the Properties window behaves when more than one instance of this control are selected at once. If false, the property is not shown. If true (the default), the property can be set for all selected controls at once.
NotifyParentProperty(true|false)	Set this to true to indicate that a parent property should receive notification about changes to the property's value (and update its display accordingly). For example, the Size property has two nested properties: Height and Width. These nested properties should be marked with this attribute. The default is false.
ParenthesizePropertyName(true|false)	When true, indicates that the property should be displayed with brackets around it in the Properties window (like the Name property). The default is false.
PasswordPropertyText(true|false)	When true, the value for this property will be displayed in the Properties window with bullets that mask the underlying value. This affects display only, and the real value is still visible in the serialized code. The default is false.

Table 13-1. *Attributes for Control Properties (Continued)*

Attribute	Description
ReadOnly(true|false)	When true, this property is read-only in the Properties window at design time and by default, its value is not serialized into code. The default is false.
RefreshProperties()	You use this attribute with a value from the RefreshProperties enumeration. It specifies whether the rest of the Properties window must be updated when this property is changed (for example, if one property procedure could change another property).

A few attributes can be applied to your custom control class declaration, rather than a specific property. These include two attributes that set the default event and property (as described in Table 13-2).

Table 13-2. *Basic Control-Class Attributes*

Attribute	Description
DefaultEvent	When the application programmer double-clicks your control, Visual Studio automatically adds an event handler for the default event.
DefaultProperty	The DefaultProperty is the property that is highlighted in the Properties window by default the first time the control is selected.

The Progress user control doesn't raise any new events, so the DefaultEvent attribute isn't of much use. However, here's how you could use these attributes with the DirectoryTree developed in Chapter 11:

```
[DefaultEvent("DirectorySelected")]
[DefaultProperty("Drive")]
public partial class DirectoryTree : TreeView
{ ... }
```

You can also use other advanced attributes to control serialization and type conversion, support licensing, and attach a control designer that manages one or more aspects of the control's design-time behavior.

Attributes and Inheritance

When you derive a control from a base class that has design-time attributes, the control inherits the design-time functionality of its parent, just like it inherits the methods and properties. If the parent class's implementation of the design-time attributes is sufficient for your control, you do not need to reapply them.

However, in some cases you might want to change the design-time behavior of an existing property. In this case, you must first override the property, and reapply the changed attributes or add the new ones.

Most of the properties in base classes like Control are marked as virtual, allowing you to change their behavior. However, this isn't always the case. For example, consider the Project-Tree example in Chapter 11. There, the tree is filled using higher-level methods, and you don't want the control consumer to see or be able to edit the Nodes property directly at design time. It might occur to you to solve this problem by overriding the Nodes property and using the Browsable attribute to hide it so it won't appear in the Properties window:

```
[Browsable(false)]
public override TreeNodeCollection Nodes
{ ... }
```

Unfortunately, the Nodes property isn't overridable, so this approach won't work. Instead, you need to disable design-time display of the directory tree altogether (as demonstrated in the sample code included for this chapter), or you need to use the more advanced technique of control designers. Chapter 26 shows a version of the DirectoryTree control that uses a control designer.

The Toolbox Bitmap

Adding a toolbox icon is refreshingly easy. All you need to do is add a bitmap to your project and ensure it has the same file name as your custom control class. This bitmap must meet a few basic criteria:

- It must be 16 pixels by 16 pixels. Otherwise, Visual Studio attempts to scale it, and the results will be ugly.

- It must use only 16 colors.

Once you add the file, use the Properties window to set the build action for it to Embedded Resource. Then recompile the control project. Figure 13-3 shows an example: the DirectoryTree control project with the required image file.

Figure 13-3. *Configuring a toolbox bitmap*

When you add the control to the toolbox (right-click it, select Choose Items, and browse to your control assembly), you'll see the new bitmap appear in the toolbox, as shown in Figure 13-4. However, the toolbox icons that are automatically added to the project-specific section of the toolbox always use the gear icon.

Figure 13-4. *A custom toolbox bitmap*

You can also attach a bitmap explicitly using the System.Drawing.ToolboxBitmap attribute. There are typically two reasons for taking this step—either you want to use a different name for your bitmap file, or you want to reuse an image from another control. For example, if you want to associate the image file DirTree.bmp with the DirectoryTree control, you'd add the DirTree.bmp image file as an embedded resource and then use the following attribute on the control to link the two:

```
[ToolboxBitmap(typeof(DirectoryTree), "DirTree.bmp")]
public class DirectoryTree : TreeView
{ ... }
```

Of, if you've placed your image in a project subfolder named images, you'd need to change your attribute as shown here:

```
[ToolboxBitmap(typeof(DirectoryTree), "images.DirTree.bmp")]
public class DirectoryTree : TreeView
{ ... }
```

For a more convenient shortcut, you can steal the toolbox bitmap from the standard TreeView control using this attribute:

```
[ToolboxBitmap(typeof(TreeView))]
public class DirectoryTree : TreeView
{ ... }
```

Debugging Design-Time Support

Developing good design-time support for your control requires a different set of considerations than creating its basic functionality. If you test your custom control in a project with the control source code, you are able to set breakpoints and use other debugging tricks. However, what if you want to use breakpoints to debug the design-time behavior? For example, you might want to test how your control reacts to selection or changes to values through the Properties window. You have a couple of options to perform this testing.

One good approach is to use .NET's specialized PropertyGrid control. This control is an exact replica of the Properties window contained in the Visual Studio environment. You can add this control to a form, and use it to run your custom control through its paces by modifying any of its properties. (This is a good habit to get into—if you try to set invalid property values, you'll probably discover that your control isn't as successful as you expect at rejecting them.) By default, the PropertyGrid control doesn't appear in the toolbox. To add it, you need to right-click the Toolbox, select Choose Items, and find it in the list. You can then drag the Property-Grid onto a test form.

The PropertyGrid provides properties that allow you to format its appearance and configure its display. The most important property is SelectedObject. When you set the SelectedObject to an instance of a control, the grid automatically fills with a list of all the available properties. (You can perform this step at design time using the Properties window or at runtime.) Now, when you change a property in the grid, it's applied to the control immediately. Figure 13-5 shows a test project that combines an instance of the DirectoryTree control with a PropertyGrid.

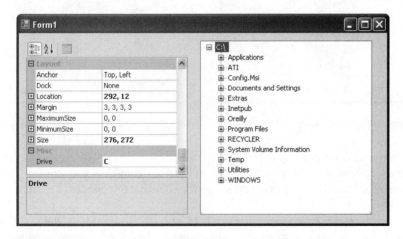

Figure 13-5. *Testing controls with the PropertyGrid*

■Tip Interestingly, you can use the PropertyGrid control with any object, regardless of whether it is a control, component, or simple class. The PropertyGrid allows you to modify any public property exposed by the class.

If you're working with a user control, you don't even need to create a test form, because Visual Studio has a convenient shortcut in store. Just launch your class library directly. Visual Studio automatically shows a sample form that hosts your user control and provides a PropertyGrid to tweak it. If your project has more than one user control, just choose the one you want to test from the drop-down list (as demonstrated in Figure 13-6) and click Load. Sadly, this won't work with any other type of control.

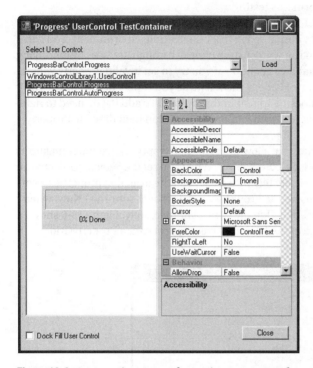

Figure 13-6. *Automatic support for testing user controls*

The PropertyGrid is useful for a variety of tasks, but it doesn't represent all of Visual Studio's design-time functionality. For example, you might want to debug how your control acts when it's resized on the form designer, or step through the code that implements a custom smart tag.

Microsoft offers an impressive component that can help you—the DesignModeDialog. The DesignModeDialog can create a design-mode representation of any form, complete with support for dragging, resizing, snap lines, and more. To use this component, simply instantiate a test form, as you would normally. You also need to add each of the properties you want to design to the DesignModeDialog.PropertiesToDesign collection. You can do this using the Properties window, but here's a code-only example:

```
DesignModeDialog dialog = new DesignModeDialog();

// Set the form you want to run in design mode.
dialog.HostForm = this;

// Specify the properties that should appear in the PropertyGrid.
dialog.PropertiesToDesign.Add("Items");
dialog.PropertiesToDesign.Add("AutoSize");
dialog.PropertiesToDesign.Add("Size");
dialog.PropertiesToDesign.Add("Text");
dialog.PropertiesToDesign.Add("Font");
dialog.PropertiesToDesign.Add("Location");
dialog.PropertiesToDesign.Add("ForeColor");
dialog.PropertiesToDesign.Add("BackColor");
dialog.PropertiesToDesign.Add("Anchor");
dialog.PropertiesToDesign.Add("Dock");
dialog.PropertiesToDesign.Add("ClientSize");

// Show the form with the design-time representation of the host form.
designModeDialog1.ShowDialog();
```

You don't need to specifically designate the controls you want to design. They're all designable.

The DesignModeDialog.ShowDialog() method opens a new window with a design-time view onto your form (see Figure 13-7). Essentially, the DesignModeDialog takes a snapshot of the parent form, clones all the controls, and then creates a new designer form that includes these exactly duplicated controls and a PropertyGrid to edit them. When the form is closed, all the changes are pushed back to the original control objects (although this obviously affects only the current in-memory instance of your application, not the serialized designer code you've created in Visual Studio).

The amazing thing about this designer form is that not only can you change properties using the PropertyGrid, but you can also drag, resize, and remove controls. (Smart tags and some other details don't work in the current implementation, however.) Keep in mind that as you make these changes, you're working with a copy of your form, not changing the actual code in your project.

The DesignModeDialog isn't a part of the .NET Framework, but is provided as a sample on the Microsoft community website www.windowsforms.net, and it's available with the sample code for this chapter (available in the Source Code area of the Apress Web site, www.apress.com).

Of course, there's no substitute for testing design-time support in the host that's used by almost every Windows developer—Visual Studio. So why not debug the Visual Studio IDE itself? To accomplish this, add your control to the toolbox, and then configure your custom control project to start Visual Studio (devenv.exe) when you run your project, as shown in Figure 13-8. Now when you run your project, it launches a second instance of Visual Studio. You can now set breakpoints in your control code or custom designer code that will be triggered as the control is manipulated in the IDE.

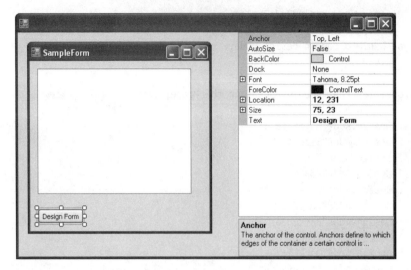

Figure 13-7. *Debugging an arbitrary form in design mode*

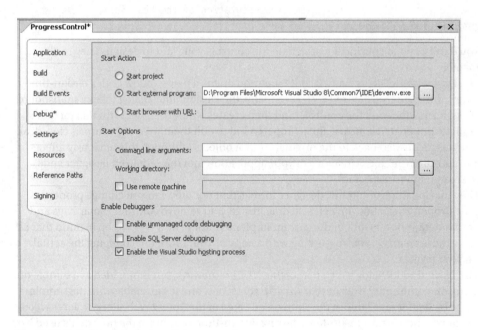

Figure 13-8. *Debugging design-time support*

Code Serialization

When you configure control properties in the Properties window, Visual Studio needs to be able to create the corresponding code statements in the InitializeComponent() method of the containing form. This process is called *code serialization*, and it often works automatically without a hitch. However, there's a fair bit you can do to optimize the process, and there's additional work you'll need to undertake if you use properties that are themselves complex types.

Basic Serialization

The basic serialization rules that Visual Studio follows are quite simple. Essentially, Visual Studio inspects the public read/write properties of a control and generates the corresponding statements that set them. Visual Studio doesn't respect the order in which you actually set the properties at design time. Instead, it simply sets properties in alphabetical order.

For example, if you drop a straightforward button onto a form, you'll generate serialized code that looks like this:

```
//
// button1
//
this.button1.Location = new System.Drawing.Point(84, 122);
this.button1.Name = "button1";
this.button1.Size = new System.Drawing.Size(85, 23);
this.button1.TabIndex = 0;
this.button1.Text = "Submit";
```

Fortunately, with a properly designed control (like the Button), Visual Studio won't attempt to serialize every property. If it did, the designer code for a simple form would be swamped with unnecessary code statements that simply apply default property values. However, the control projects that you've seen so far don't take this precaution, and you'll find that Visual Studio serializes *everything*, including the initial property values (the values that are set in your control's constructor and its member variable declarations). For example, when you add the Progress user control to a form, you'll see code like this:

```
//
// status
//
this.status.Location = new System.Drawing.Point(12, 8);
this.status.Maximum = 100;
this.status.Name = "status";
this.status.Size = new System.Drawing.Size(272, 88);
this.status.Step = 10;
this.status.TabIndex = 0;
this.status.Value = 0;
```

In this case, the Maximum, Step, and Value properties use the default values set in the control. However, Visual Studio doesn't know this, and so it adds the code to serialize this information, even though it isn't needed. To avoid this problem, you need to add a little more intelligence to your controls via the attributes shown in Table 13-3.

Table 13-3. *Serialization Attributes for Control Properties*

Attribute	Description
DefaultValue()	Sets the initial value that is used for this property when the control is created. As long as a control property matches the corresponding initial value, it's not serialized.
DesignerSerializationVisibility()	Configures whether or not a property should be serialized, and if it is, how it should be serialized. The DesignerSerializationVisibility() attribute is not taken into account if the property is decorated with the ReadOnly attribute.
Localizable(true|false)	When set to true, the design-time value for this property is stored in a resource file instead of in the generated code, when you're using a localized form. This makes it easy to swap the value later by introducing a new resource file. When the user configures properties that don't use this attribute, the appropriate code is inserted in the hidden designer region of the form, unless it requires a special data type (like an image) that must be stored in a resource file.

Default Values

You can avoid serializing long as a control property matches the unnecessary information by using the DefaultValue attribute. With this attribute, you specify a default value (using any basic .NET data type, like a string, integer, or Boolean value).

```
[DefaultValue(100)]
public int Maximum
{ ... }
```

Once this attribute is in place, Visual Studio will serialize the property only if the value is changed in the design-time environment. (A change can happen directly—the developer modifies the value in the Properties window—or indirectly—when the developer changes a different property or makes a selection in another designer window.) Keep in mind that the DefaultValue attribute doesn't apply the value; it simply determines serialization. In other words, if you specify a DefaultValue that isn't really the default, you'll run into trouble. For example, if you initialize the progress bar to have a Maximum of 100 and you specify the default value as 50, Visual Studio won't serialize the property if it's set to 50. However, when you run the form the real default of 100 will apply, wiping out your settings. Thus, you should always make sure that the DefaultValue attribute matches the actual default.

■**Tip** Using the DefaultValue attribute also allows the control consumer to reset a property value to its initial value at design time. To do so, just right-click on the property and choose Reset.

The DefaultValue attribute works wonders if you're using a simple data type, but what if you're dealing with a more sophisticated object like a Color or Font? Unfortunately, code like this won't work:

```
[DefaultValue(new Font("Tahoma", 8, FontStyle.Regular))]
```

The problem is you can't supply any nonconstant expression to an attribute constructor, which includes all objects. That's because the attribute information is evaluated when your code is compiled, not when the class is created.

But don't give up just yet. There is an overload to the DefaultValue constructor that's designed to tackle this problem. It accepts two parameters: the data type and a string representation of the value. Using this constructor, you could specify a default font like this:

```
[DefaultValue(typeof(Font), "Tahoma, 8pt")]
```

In this case, the string "Tahoma, 8 pt" can be converted into a Font object because the Font class has an associated type converter that performs the work. (You'll learn more about creating type converters later in this chapter.) If you don't have a type converter handy for your data type, you can't use the DefaultValue attribute at all. Instead, you'll have to use the technique described in the next section.

Incidentally, the Color type also has a type converter that allows you to supply a string with a color name, like this:

```
[DefaultValue(typeof(Color), "Purple")]
```

Making Serialization Decisions Programmatically

Usually, Visual Studio bases its decision about whether it should serialize a property on whether the current value matches the value specified by the DefaultValue attribute. However, this isn't always the best approach. Sometimes you might want make the decision to serialize or not to serialize based on a different condition.

For example, imagine you're creating a grid control that supports different configuration modes. In its default mode, this control needs to serialize every property value explicitly. However, it also supports an automatic mode that chooses property values based on the bound data source. When you use the automatic mode, you don't want to serialize the other property values. To implement this design, you need to add an optional method for each property named ShouldSerialize*PropertyName*(). This method returns true if the property should be serialized, or false if it shouldn't.

For example, if you have a property named Columns, you could add the following method:

```
private bool ShouldSerializeColumns()
{
    if (mode == CustomGrid.AutoGenerateProperties)
    {
        // Don't serialize the Columns property.
        return false;
    }
}
```

```
    else
    {
        // Serialize the Columns property.
        return true;
    }
}
```

Another reason to use this approach is if your default value is a complex object, not a simple data type. In that case, it's awkward to create the object and supply it in the constructor for the DefaultValue attribute. If you don't have a suitable type converter, you won't be able to do it at all. This limitation doesn't exist with the ShouldSerializeXxx() method, because it creates the default using pure code.

For example, consider a variant of the DirectoryTree control shown in Chapter 11 that uses a DriveInfo object instead of a char to track the currently selected drive. Here's how you might test if the drive object maps to the default drive (in this case, drive C:):

```
private bool ShouldSerializeDrive()
{
    if (Drive != null && Drive.Name != "C:")
        return true;
    else
        return false;
}
```

Once you understand the technique, you can simplify this syntax:

```
private bool ShouldSerializeDrive()
{
    return (Drive != null && Drive.Name != "C:")
}
```

■**Note** The ShouldSerializeXxx() method is called *after* the property is set, so you can retrieve it and examine it without a problem. It's called just before Visual Studio serializes the property value to the InitializeComponent() method.

In the previous example, the ShouldSerializeXxx() method checks if the current object wraps the default drive. Life gets a little more complicated if you want to check if several properties in an object match. For example, this code, which tests if the current Font matches a specified default value, is flawed:

```
private bool ShouldSerializeFont()
{
    // This compares the references, not the object content.
    return !(Font = new Font("Tahoma", 8, FontStyle.Bold));
}
```

The problem here is that the comparison checks to see if the two references are pointing to the same object in memory (which they aren't). But what you really want to do is compare the *content* of the two objects. Depending on the object you're dealing with, you may be able to make use of another helper method, or you may need to compare all the properties you're interested in yourself. Fortunately, the Font object provides an Equals() method that performs value comparison rather than reference comparison, and checks if two Font objects are equivalent. Here's the corrected code:

```
private bool ShouldSerializeFont()
{
    // This compares the content of the two Font objects.
    return !Font.Equals(new Font("Tahoma", 8, FontStyle.Bold));
}
```

The ShouldSerializeXxx() method simply instructs Visual Studio whether or not to serialize a value. If you use this method, you also need another method that works hand-in-hand with ShouldSerializeXxx(). It's the Reset*PropertyName*() method, and it's called when the property is reset (by right-clicking it in the Properties window and choosing Reset) and when the control is first created to get the initial property value.

Here's an example that sets the default value for the font:

```
public void ResetFont()
{
    Font = new Font("Tahoma", 8, FontStyle.Bold);
}
```

If you decide to use the ShouldSerializeXxx() and ResetXxx() methods, don't use the DefaultValue attribute. These methods supersede it.

Serialization Type

The DefaultValue attribute and the ShouldSerializeXxx() and ResetXxx() properties control when a property is serialized. However, you also use the DesignerSerializationVisibility attribute to prevent serialization or change how it takes place. You have three choices, listed in Table 13-4.

Table 13-4. *Values From the DesignerSerializationVisibility Enumeration*

Attribute	Description
Visible	This is the default value that applies if you don't add the DesignerSerializationVisibility attribute. In this case, the property should be serialized as usual.
Content	This value instructs Visual Studio to serialize the entire content of an object. You can use this value to serialize complex types with multiple properties.
Hidden	This value specifies that a property shouldn't be serialized at all.

For example, you could use this code to make sure a property isn't serialized:

```
[DesignerSerializationVisibility(DesignerSerializationVisibility.Hidden)]
public int Value
{ ... }
```

In this case, the property will still appear in the Properties window, and you will be able to modify its value. However, the change won't be persisted to code, so when you launch the application the property will revert to its default value.

■Tip Often, you'll use the Browsable attribute to hide properties that aren't serialized. If you use just the Browsable attribute to hide a property but you don't use the DesignerSerializationVisibility attribute to turn off serialization, the property value may still be serialized. For example, if you set another property that has the side effect of changing the nonbrowsable property, Visual Studio will still serialize its changed value, which is probably not what you want. Thus, it's a good idea to use the DesignerSerializationVisibility attribute to turn off serialization when using the Browsable attribute to hide a property.

Serialization isn't necessarily this easy. If one of your control properties is a nested object (rather than a simple data type like a string of an integer), you'll probably run into added difficulties. That's because creating the nested object might require the help of a specific constructor, or properties might need to be set in a certain order. For this to work, you not only need to set the DesignerSerializationVisibility to Content, but you also need to create a separate type converter that can generate the required code. You'll see this technique later in this chapter.

Batch Initialization

As you've seen, when control properties are serialized, they're ordered alphabetically. This can cause a problem if one property depends on another, and you've entered validation logic to reject values that don't make sense (as you should).

For example, you might create a control that exposes both a LowerBound and an UpperBound property. In this case, you'll want to ensure that the lower bound value is never greater than upper bound, and vice versa:

```
private int upperBound;
public int UpperBound
{
    get { return upperBound; }
    set
    {
        if (value < lowerBound)
            upperBound = value;
        else
            throw new ArgumentException(
              "UpperBound must be greater than LowerBound.");
    }
}
```

```
private int lowerBound;
public int LowerBound
{
    get { return lowerBound; }
    set
    {
        if (upperBound < value)
            lowerBound = value;
        else
            throw new ArgumentException(
                "UpperBound must be greater than LowerBound.");
    }
}
```

The problem occurs if you set both the UpperBound and LowerBound values at design time. Here's the designer code that will be generated:

```
control.LowerBound = 100;
control.UpperBound = 500;
```

This leads to an error because at the point when the lower bound is set, the upper bound is still 0.

There's no way to alter the order in which this serialized code is generated. However, you can give your control the ability to deal with out-of-order property setting by implementing ISupportInitialize. When you do, you'll be required to supply two methods—BeginInit(), which is called before any properties are set, and EndInit(), which is called after all properties are set. The serialized code becomes the following:

```
((ISupportInitialize)control).BeginInit();
control.LowerBound = 100;
control.UpperBound = 500;
((ISupportInitialize)control).EndInit();
```

On its own, this doesn't solve anything. However, you code around the problem by setting a member variable in the BeginInit() method that instructs the property procedures to skip their validation logic:

```
private bool intializing;
void ISupportInitialize.BeginInit()
{
    initializing = true;
}
```

Here's how you'd rewrite the property procedures so that it performs the check only if you're not currently in initialization mode:

```
public int UpperBound
{
    get { return upperBound; }
    set
    {
        if (initializing || (value < lowerBound))
            upperBound = value;
        else
            throw new ArgumentException(
                "UpperBound must be greater than LowerBound.");
    }
}
```

Now, in the EndInit() method you need to turn off initialization mode and check that the data is valid:

```
void ISupportInitialize.EndInit()
{
    initializing = false;
    if upperBound < lowerBound
        throw new ArgumentException(
            "UpperBound must be greater than LowerBound.");
}
```

■Tip Because the designer code explicitly casts your control reference to ISupportInitialize in order to access the BeginInit() and EndInit() methods, you're free to make them private (using explicit interface implementation, as shown in the previous example). This keeps them out of the public interface of your control, which is a little cleaner.

You can also use ISupportInitialize for the following reasons:

- To prevent invalidating an owner-drawn control multiple times when several properties are set in quick succession. Instead, just invalidate the display in EndInit().

- To vary initialization or behavior based on whether the control is in design mode. You can't query the DesignMode property in the constructor because the control isn't sited on the form yet. However, you can inspect the DesignMode property in the EndInit() method.

- To hook up event handlers or perform initialization that requires all the other properties to be already set.

For example, consider the MarqueeLabel control from Chapter 12. In order to make the MarqueeLabel start scrolling, you need to call the Scroll() method manually in your code. To simplify life, you could design the MarqueeLabel control so it starts scrolling immediately when it's created. However, this would cause it to scroll both at runtime and at design time, which is a waste of CPU time and an unnecessary distraction. Fortunately, there is a solution that lets you prevent design-time scrolling without forcing you to call the Scroll() method. You need to implement ISupportInitialize, and check the DesignMode property in the EndInit() method, as shown here:

```
void ISupportInitialize.EndInit()
{
    if (!DesignMode)
    {
        tmrScroll.Enabled = true;
    }
}
```

Localizable Properties

All of the Windows Forms controls included with .NET are highly localizable. That means you can use the technique described in Chapter 5 to localize a form, creating multiple versions for different cultures.

By default, when you create your own custom controls, none of the new properties you add is localizable. This significantly reduces their value in applications that need to be localized. Fortunately, there's no reason to stick with this limitation. You can easily create a localizable property just by adding the Localizable attribute.

For example, here are two string properties, only one of which is localizable:

```
private string nonLocalizableText;
public string NonLocalizableText
{
    get { return nonLocalizableText; }
    set { nonLocalizableText = value; }
}

private string localizableText;
[Localizable(true)]
public string LocalizableText
{
    get { return localizableText; }
    set { localizableText = value; }
}
```

To try this out, add this control to a form and set both properties. If you examine the serialized code, you won't notice any difference yet. Here's the sort of code you'll see:

```
this.localizableControl1.LocalizableText = "Test";
this.localizableControl1.Location = new System.Drawing.Point(21, 12);
this.localizableControl1.Name = "localizableControl1";
this.localizableControl1.NonLocalizableText = "Test";
this.localizableControl1.Size = new System.Drawing.Size(150, 150);
this.localizableControl1.TabIndex = 0;
```

However, if you start localizing your form (set the Localizable property of the form in the Properties window to true), the code changes immediately. Now this is all you'll see:

```
resources.ApplyResources(this.localizableControl1, "localizableControl1");
this.localizableControl1.Name = "localizableControl1";
this.localizableControl1.NonLocalizableText = "Test";
```

In other words, every property except Name and NonLocalizableText is localizable. These properties (including Location, Size, TabIndex, and LocalizableText) are all relocated into a .resx file for the form. You can browse them in Visual Studio to see the various values. The designer code uses the ComponentResourceManager.ApplyResources() method, which reflects on the control and fills in all its localizable properties.

As with serialization-to-code, Visual Studio serializes a localizable value only if it doesn't match the default value. Chapter 5 has more information about resources and localization.

Type Conversion

The Properties window deals seamlessly with common data types. String data doesn't present a problem, but the Properties window can also convert strings to other types. For example, if you look at the Font property, you'll see a value such as Tahoma, 8.25pt. You can enter any characters in this field, but if you try to commit the change (by pressing Enter or moving to another field) and you've included characters that can't be interpreted as a font, the change will be rejected.

This behavior is made possible by *type converters*, specialized classes that are designed for the sole purpose of converting a specialized data type to a string representation and back. Most of the core .NET data types have default type converters that work perfectly well. (You can find these type converters in the System.ComponentModel namespace.) However, if you create your own structures or classes and use them as properties, you may also want to create custom type converters to allow them to work in the Properties window. If you don't undertake this small effort, any property that uses a complex type will be uneditable.

Dealing with Nested Objects

In Chapter 12, you considered a GradientPanel control. Using this control, you can configure two colors, and the results appear immediately in the IDE.

However, there is an alternate design that you might want to use with the GradientPanel. Consider the ColorA, ColorB, and GradientFillStyle properties. These properties are really all parts of the same setting, and together they determine the background fill. If you wrapped these three settings into one class, they would be easier to find and set at design time, and easier to reuse in any other control that might need a gradient fill.

Here's how the custom class would look:

```
public class GradientFill
{
    private Color colorA = Color.LightBlue;
    private Color colorB = Color.Purple;
    private LinearGradientMode gradientStyle =
      LinearGradientMode.ForwardDiagonal;
```

```
[DefaultValue(typeof(Color), "LightBlue")]
public Color ColorA
{
    get { return colorA; }
    set { colorA = value; }
}

[DefaultValue(typeof(Color), "Purple")]
public Color ColorB
{
    get { return colorB; }
    set { colorB = value; }
}

[DefaultValue(typeof(LinearGradientMode), "ForwardDiagonal")]
public LinearGradientMode GradientFillStyle
{
    get { return gradientStyle; }
    set { gradientStyle = value; }
}
}
```

Now the new GradientPanel control doesn't need to define any of these properties. Instead, it defines a single GradientFill property. This property requires the DesignerSerializationVisibility attribute set to Content. This instructs Visual Studio to serialize all embedded child properties of the GradientFill class. Without it, you'll mysteriously lose the property values you set at design time.

```
private GradientFill gradient = new GradientFill();

[DesignerSerializationVisibility(DesignerSerializationVisibility.Content)]
public GradientFill GradientFill
{
    get
    {
        return gradient;
    }
    set
    {
        gradient = value;
        gradientBrush = null;
        Invalidate();
    }
}
```

Tip Notice that the GradientFill class uses the DefaultValue attribute, so its various subproperties aren't serialized if they match the default values.

Unfortunately, there's no way to set the GradientFill subproperties at design time. If you look in the Properties window, you'll see a piece of static text that shows the result of calling ToString() on the GradientFill object (see Figure 13-9). This provides the fully qualified class name, which isn't much help.

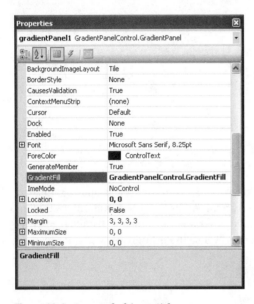

Figure 13-9. *A nested object without a type converter*

Creating a Type Converter

To solve this problem, you need to create a type converter, which is a specialized class that can convert a GradientFill object to a string, and then convert the string back to a live GradientFill object.

The first step is to create a custom class that derives from the base class System. ComponentModel.TypeConverter, as shown here:

```
public class GradientFillConverter : TypeConverter
{ ... }
```

By convention, the name of a type converter class is made up of the class type it converts, followed by the word "converter." Table 13-5 details the TypeConverter overridable methods.

Table 13-5. *TypeConverter Overridable Methods*

Method	Description
CanConvertFrom()	This method examines a data type, and returns true if the type converter can make the conversion from this data type to the custom data type.
ConvertFrom()	This method performs the conversion from the supplied data type to the custom data type.
CanConvertTo()	This method examines a data type, and returns true if the type converter can make the conversion from the custom object to this data type.
ConvertTo()	This method performs the conversion from the custom data type to the requested data type.

Remember, the key task of a type converter is to convert from your custom data type and a string representation. This example uses a string representation that includes all three values from the Gradient object, separated by commas and spaces:

```
ColorA, ColorB, LinearGradientMode
```

Here's an example:

```
LightBlue, Purple, ForwardDiagonal
```

Before attempting a conversion from a GradientFill object to a string, the Properties window will first query the CanConvertTo() method. If it receives a true value, it will call the actual ConvertTo() method. All the CanConvertTo() method needs to is check that the target type is a string.

```
public override bool CanConvertTo(ITypeDescriptorContext context,
  Type destinationType)
{
    if (destinationType == typeof(string))
        return true;
    else
        return base.CanConvertTo(context, destinationType);
}
```

Notice that if the target type isn't recognized, the type converter calls the base class implementation, which will either convert it, pass it to another class higher up the inheritance chain, or throw an error.

The ConvertTo() method is called if CanCovertTo() returns true. ConvertTo() simply checks that it can indeed convert to the desired type. If not, it calls the base class implementation of the ConvertTo() method (because presumably it was the base class that returned true from the CanCovertTo() method). If ConvertTo() is asked to convert a GradientFill into a string, it goes ahead by calling the implementation in the ConvertToString() method.

```
public override object ConvertTo(ITypeDescriptorContext context,
  CultureInfo culture, object value, Type destinationType)
{
    if (destinationType == typeof(string))
        return ConvertToString(value);
    else
        return base.ConvertTo(context, culture, value, destinationType);
}
```

The ToString() method builds the required string representation:

```
public string ConvertToString(object value)
{
    GradientFill fill = (GradientFill)value;
    ColorConverter converter = new ColorConverter();
    return String.Format("{0}, {1}, {2}", converter.ConvertToString(fill.ColorA),
        converter.ConvertToString(fill.ColorB), fill.GradientFillStyle);
}
```

Notice that this method makes use of the ColorConverter—an existing type converter that transforms colors into strings and back. This saves some work when converting the Gradient-Fill object. If you have a data type that has a type converter, but you don't know what the type converter class is, you can use the static TypeDescriptor.GetConverter() method. Here's an example:

```
TypeConverter converter = TypeDescriptor.GetConverter(typeof(Color));
```

Once you have the converter, you can call its ConvertToString() or ConvertFromString() method.

The exact same process occurs in reverse when converting a GradientFill object to a string. First the Properties window calls CanConvertFrom(). If it returns true, the next step is to call the ConvertFrom() method.

```
public override bool CanConvertFrom(ITypeDescriptorContext context,
  Type sourceType)
{
    if (sourceType == typeof(string))
        return true;
    else
        return base.CanConvertFrom(context, sourceType);
}

public override object ConvertFrom(ITypeDescriptorContext context,
  CultureInfo culture, object value)
{
    if (value is string)
        return ConvertFromString(value);
    else
        return base.ConvertFrom(context, culture, value);
}
```

The ConvertFromString() method does the actual work of decoding the string representation. If the string isn't in the format you need, the ConvertFromString() code raises an exception. Otherwise, it returns the new GradientFill object instance.

```
public GradientFill FromString(object value)
{
    string[] values = ((string)value).Split(',');
    if (values.Length != 3)
      throw new ArgumentException("Could not convert the value");

    try
    {
        GradientFill gradient = new GradientFill();

        // Retrieve the colors.
        ColorConverter converter = new ColorConverter();
        gradient.ColorA = (Color)converter.ConvertFromString(values[0]);
        gradient.ColorB = (Color)converter.ConvertFromString(values[1]);

        // Convert the name of the enumerated value into the corresponding
        // enumerated value (which is actually an integer constant).
        gradient.GradientFillStyle = (LinearGradientMode)Enum.Parse(
          typeof(LinearGradientMode), values[2], true);

        return gradient;
    }
    catch (Exception err)
    {
        throw new ArgumentException("Could not convert the value");
    }
}
```

Now that you have a fully functioning type converter, the next step is to attach it to the corresponding property.

Attaching a Type Converter

There are two ways to attach a type converter. The approach you should use in most cases is to link the custom type to the type converter by adding the TypeConverter attribute to the class declaration.

```
[TypeConverter(typeof(GradientFillConverter))]
public class GradientFill
{ ... }
```

Another option is to apply the TypeConverter attribute to the property in your custom control. This option is most suitable if your control needs to serialize a nested object in a different way than usual.

```
[TypeConverter(typeof(GradientFillConverter))]
[DesignerSerializationVisibility(DesignerSerializationVisibility.Content)]
public GradientFill GradientFill
{ ... }
```

If you use both approaches, the type converter that's attached to the property takes precedence when converting the data type to and from a string for display in the Properties window. However, this isn't the whole story.

As you'll learn a little later in this chapter, you can also use a type converter to convert an object into an InstanceDescriptor, which allows you to customize the way the object is serialized in the designer code. If you use this feature, the type converter that's attached to the class is the only type converter that has any bearing on the result. This behavior is necessary to avoid potential ambiguities (for example, if the same object is used for two properties, each of which uses a different type converter).

Now you can recompile the code and try using the GradientPanel control in a sample form. When you select a GradientPanel, you'll see the current value of the GradientPanel.GradientFill property in the Properties window (shown in Figure 13-10), and you can edit it by hand.

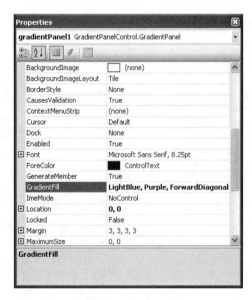

Figure 13-10. *A string representation of the GradientFill object*

Of course, unless you enter the correct string representation, you'll receive an error message, and your change will be rejected. In other words, this custom type converter gives you the ability to specify a GradientFill object as a string, but the process certainly isn't user-friendly. The next section shows you how to improve this level of support.

The ExpandableObjectConverter

A number of object properties are supported by Windows Forms controls. The best example is Font, which refers to a full-fledged Font object with properties like Bold, Italic, Name, and so on.

When you set the Font property in the Properties window, you don't need to type all this information in a single, correctly formatted string. Instead, you can expand the Font property by clicking the plus (+) box and editing all of the Font subproperties individually.

You can enable the same type of editing with your own custom object types. You actually have two choices—you can use the ExpandableObjectConverter directly, or you can create a custom type converter that derives from the ExpandableObjectConverter. If you use this approach, you'll have the benefit of the string representation and the ability to expand the property to see subproperties.

```
public class GradientFillConverter : ExpandableObjectConverter
{ ... }
```

Figure 13-11 shows the much more convenient interface of the Properties window.

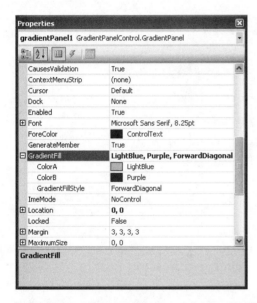

Figure 13-11. *Editing properties of the GradientFill object*

Solving the Refresh Problem with Events

This looks good at first pass, but there are still a few quirks. One problem is that when you change a subproperty, the string representation that's shown in the Format box isn't updated immediately. To solve this problem you need to apply the NotifyParentProperty and RefreshProperties attributes to the properties of the GradientFill class. Here's an example:

```
RefreshProperties(RefreshProperties.Repaint)]
[NotifyParentProperty(true)]
[DefaultValue(typeof(Color), "LightBlue")]
public Color ColorA
{ ... }
```

■**Tip** You can also add a Description attribute to the properties of the GradientFill class to configure the text that will appear in the lower Description pane of the Properties window.

This solves the refresh problem in the Properties window, but all the quirks still aren't worked out. Even though the property is correctly updated when you make a new selection (and the correct code is generated in the InitializeComponent() method), the Panel isn't refreshed on the design surface. That's because changing the properties of the GradientFill object doesn't invalidate the GradientPanel. Several workarounds are possible. One option is to define an event that can be fired from the GradientFill object and handled by the GradientPanel.

Here's the code you need in the GradientFill class:

```
public event EventHandler GradientChanged;

public Color ColorA
{
    get { return colorA; }
    set
    {
        colorA = value;
        OnGradientChanged(EventArgs.Empty);
    }
}
...
private void OnGradientChanged(EventArgs e)
{
    if (GradientChanged != null)
    {
      GradientChanged(this, e);
    }
}
```

In the GradientPanel, an event handler should be created and attached whenever the GradientPanel.GradientFill is set:

```
private EventHandler handlerGradientChanged;

public GradientFill GradientFill
{
    get { return gradient; }
    set
    {
        gradient = value;
        if (handlerGradientChanged != null) gradient.GradientChanged -=
handlerGradientChanged;
        handlerGradientChanged = new EventHandler(GradientChanged);
        gradient.GradientChanged += handlerGradientChanged;
        gradientBrush.Dispose();
```

```
        gradientBrush = null;
        Invalidate();
    }
}
```

When the event is received, the GradientChanged event handler simply needs to remove the current brush (so that it will be re-created with the new colors during the background painting), and invalidate the panel.

Solving the Refresh Problem with CreateInstance()

Another technique is to force the entire GradientFill object to be re-created every time a property changes. To implement this mechanism you need to override the GetCreateInstanceSupported() and CreateInstance() methods of the type converter. The GetCreateInstanceSupported() method returns a Boolean value that indicates whether the support for creating a GradientFill object is provided. The default is false.

```
public override bool GetCreateInstanceSupported(ITypeDescriptorContext context)
{
    // Always force a new instance.
    return true;
}
```

If GetCreateInstanceSupported() returns true, Visual Studio will call the CreateInstance() method to generate the GradientFill object whenever any of its properties are changed. This process is quite easy because the CreateInstance() method supplies a dictionary with name/value pairs for the current GradientFill object. These values are extracted through reflection. You can use them to generate the corresponding object instance, as shown here:

```
public override object CreateInstance(ITypeDescriptorContext context,
    IDictionary propertyValues)
{
    // Create the new instance.
    GradientFill fill = new GradientFill();
    fill.ColorA = (Color)propertyValues["ColorA"];
    fill.ColorB = (Color)propertyValues["ColorB"];
    fill.GradientFillStyle =
        (LinearGradientMode)propertyValues["GradientFillStyle"];
}
```

This solves the refresh problem with a little more overhead. Now the GradientFill object is re-created when any of its properties are changed.

Creating a Nested Object with a Constructor

With the GradientPanel, the three GradientFill properties are changed independently. As you modify them, Visual Studio generates code like this in the InitializeComponent() method:

```
this.gradientPanel1.GradientFill.ColorA = Color.Cyan;
this.gradientPanel1.GradientFill.ColorB = Color.Plum;
this.gradientPanel1.GradientFill.GradientFillStyle =
  LinearGradientMode.Horizontal;
```

This technique is great—when it works. In some cases, you can't alter the properties of a nested object in an arbitrary order. Instead, you need to create the object in one step using a specific constructor. Fortunately, by adding some additional intelligence to your type converter you can tell Visual Studio to take this step.

The trick is that you need to create a type converter that won't just convert between your object and a string. Instead, it will examine your object and return a System. ComponentModel.Design.Serialization.InstanceDescriptor. The InstanceDescriptor gives Visual Studio three key pieces of information:

- The method that must be called to create an object. Usually this is a constructor, but it could be a static method.

- The values that must be passed to the method as parameters.

- Whether additional persistence is required to capture the full state of the object.

With this information, Visual Studio can generate more-complex serialized code. To try this out, add the following constructors to the GradientFill class:

```
public GradientFill()
{}

public GradientFill(Color colorA, Color colorB,
  LinearGradientMode gradientFillStyle)
{
    ColorA = colorA;
    ColorB = colorB;
    GradientFillStyle = gradientFillStyle;
}
```

You now need to derive a new type converter. In the CanConvertTo() method, return true as long as the requested target is an InstanceDescriptor. If you want to also support conversion to the string data type, you can also add the same logic you used earlier, or you can derive your new custom type converter from the previous type converter so that any conversion it doesn't handle is forwarded to that class.

Here's the CanConvertTo() implementation you need:

```
public override bool CanConvertTo(ITypeDescriptorContext context,
  Type destinationType)
{
    if (destinationType == typeof(InstanceDescriptor))
        return true;
    else
        return base.CanConvertTo(context, destinationType);
}
```

Now the ConvertTo() method has the work of generating the InstanceDescriptor based on the supplied GradientFill object. There are two steps to generating the InstanceDescriptor. First, you need to create a System.Reflection.ConstructorInfo object that points to the constructor you want to use. To create the ConstructorInfo, you need to call the Type.GetConstructor() method on the GradientFill type.

Because a class can have more than one constructor, you need to specify the constructor you want to use by supplying an array of Type objects, one for each parameter the expected constructor should take. For example, to indicate that you want to call the GradientFill constructor with three parameters, you supply two Color types and the LinearGradientMode type, as shown here:

```
public override object ConvertTo(ITypeDescriptorContext context,
  CultureInfo culture, object value, Type destinationType)
{
    if (destinationType == typeof(InstanceDescriptor) &&
      value is GradientFill)
    {
        GradientFill gradient = (GradientFill)value;

        // Specify the three-parameter (Color-Color-LinearGradientMode)
        // constructor.
        ConstructorInfo ctor =
            typeof(GradientFill).GetConstructor(
                new Type[]
                {
                    typeof(Color),
                    typeof(Color),
                    typeof(LinearGradientMode)
                }
            );
        ...
```

The InstanceDescriptor wraps the ConstructorInfo object and the data that you want to pass to the constructor. To supply the data, you need to pass an object array, with one entry for each parameter. The parameters can be retrieved from the current gradient object:

```
        ...
        return new InstanceDescriptor(
            ctor,
            new object[]
            {
                gradient.ColorA,
                gradient.ColorB,
                gradient.GradientFillStyle
            }
        );
}
```

```
        else
        {
            return base.ConvertTo(context, culture, value, destinationType);
        }
    }
}
```

The last step is to change the DesignerSerializationVisibility for the property from Content to Visible. That way, the entire object will be serialized (triggering the type converter), not just the individual subproperties.

Once you've made these changes, the designer serialized code will use the GradientFill constructor, and generate code like this:

```
this.gradientPanel1.GradientFill.ColorA = new GradientFill(
    Color.Cyan, Color.Plum, LinearGradientMode.Horizontal);
```

Custom Serialization with CodeDOM

By using the serialization attributes, ShouldSerializeXxx() methods, and type converters, you have a good amount of control over how design-time changes are persisted into form code. For most cases, this level of control is enough. However, if you are developing extremely complex controls or commercial tools, you might need fine-grained control. You can get this through a .NET feature known as CodeDOM, although it's far from easy.

CodeDOM (code document object model) is a .NET API for generating code dynamically. What's unique about CodeDOM is that you create code constructs by instantiating and linking various objects, and these objects can create code in any supported language. That means a VB developer can use your control just as easily as a C# developer, because both languages have CodeDOM providers that allow CodeDOM objects to be serialized into their respective languages.

The problem is that serializing code with CodeDOM is far from trivial, and pitfalls abound. It's also incredibly tedious, and you'll quickly find that you need to construct quite a few objects just to model simple code statements. For a basic introduction to CodeDOM, refer to the MSDN article at http://msdn.microsoft.com/library/en-us/dndotnet/html/custcodegen.asp.

Providing Standard Values

The Properties window does a solid job of providing support for enumerations. For example, if you create a property that uses a custom enumeration, the Properties window automatically provides a drop-down list with the values from the enumeration.

For example, consider the DisplayStyle property shown here:

```
public enum DisplayStyle
{
    Standard,
    SpecialDirectoryPictures,
    AllDirectoryPictures
}
```

```
private DisplayStyle displayStyle;
public DisplayStyle DisplayStyle
{
    get { return displayStyle; }
    set { displayStyle = value; }
}
```

■**Tip** You can hide individual values in an enumeration from appearing in the Properties window. Just use the Browsable(false) attribute, as described in Table 13-1.

The enumerated values are shown in the Properties window (see Figure 13-12).

Figure 13-12. *Enumerations in the Properties window*

■**Note** Remember, even if you use an enumerated value, you still need to perform some error-checking in your property procedure. Though programmers won't be able to submit an invalid value through the Properties window, nothing prevents them from using code to directly set an integer value that doesn't correspond to a valid value in the enumeration.

What you probably don't realize is that you can supply a drop-down list of standard values for any control properties, even if it's not an enumeration. In fact, this trick is made possible with a custom type converter.

It all works through three overridable type converter methods that you haven't seen. The most important is GetStandardValues(), which returns a StandardValuesCollection (a type nested in TypeConverter from the System.ComponentModel namespace) that contains a list of all the items you want to show in the drop-down. However, for Visual Studio to use this functionality you also need to override GetStandardValuesSupported() and return true. Finally, if you want property settings to be limited to the list—in other words, you don't want the developer to supply a value that isn't in your standard value list at design time—you need to override GetStandardValuesExclusive() and return true.

To demonstrate how this works, the following example creates a type converter that shows a list of drive letters for the Directory.Drive property. Because the Drive property is really just a char, there's no need to waste time reimplementing the ConvertTo() and ConvertFrom() methods in the type converter. Instead, your custom type converter can derive directly from CharConverter. (The .NET Framework includes type converters for all common data types.)

Here's the full code:

```
public class DriveCharConverter : CharConverter
{
    // Cache the collection of values so you don't need to re-create it each time.
    private static StandardValuesCollection svc;

    // Advertise that the standard values are available.
    public override bool GetStandardValuesSupported(ITypeDescriptorContext context)
    {
        return true;
    }

    // Don't limit property values to the values in the list.
    public override bool GetStandardValuesExclusive(ITypeDescriptorContext context)
    {
        return false;
    }

    // Provide the list of standard values.
    public override StandardValuesCollection GetStandardValues(
        ITypeDescriptorContext context)
    {
        if (svc == null)
        {
            // First, build the list of values using any ICollection.
            // Make sure you use the right data type. In this case, Drive is a char,
            // so all values must be chars.
            ArrayList drives = new ArrayList();
            // Use exception-handling code here to prevent a file access error from
            // crashing the IDE.
            try
            {
                foreach (string drive in System.IO.Directory.GetLogicalDrives())
                {
                    drives.Add(drive[0]);
                }
                // Now wrap the real values in the StandarValuesCollection object.
                svc = new TypeConverter.StandardValuesCollection(drives);
            }
            catch {}
        }
```

```
        return svc;
    }
}
```

Figure 13-13 shows the result.

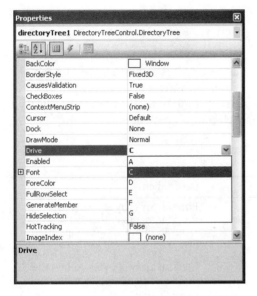

Figure 13-13. *A list of standard values for drives*

Type Editors

Type converters help you serialize your code, and allow unusual data types to be displayed in the Properties window as strings. However, that's not enough to guarantee the rich data type support that developers expect. Many data types can't be entered by strings, or if they can, it's too tedious to be required. The Windows Forms designer infrastructure solves this problem with type editors.

You've no doubt noticed that some richer object types have additional design-time support. For example, if you create a property that has a Font or Color data type, a color picker or font-selection dialog is used in the Properties window. Similar magic happens if you create a Collection property. This user interface is in addition to the string representation you see in the Properties window (as provided by the type converter).

These niceties are provided through UITypeEditor classes, which are dedicated components that generate the design-time user interface that allows the developer to set complex properties at design-time more easily.

Tip Type editors are particularly useful when you have classes that can't be reasonably represented as strings (like binary data), or have so many properties that setting individual properties is no longer practical. They also make sense for classes that have relationships between their properties that limit the properties from being set individually.

Using Prebuilt Type Editors

The base UITypeEditor class is found in the System.Drawing.Design namespace. You can inherit from this class to create your custom type editors, or you can use one of the derived classes that are provided with the .NET Framework. Table 13-6 shows a sampling of useful type editors (editors that are usable only with specific Web controls have been omitted).

Table 13-6. *UITypeEditors in the .NET Framework*

Class	Description
System.ComponentModel.Design.ArrayEditor	Edits an array by allowing the programmer to enter a list of strings. Used automatically for supported arrays.
System.ComponentModel.Design.BinaryEditor	Edits an array of bytes. Allows the developer to modify bytes in a hexadecimal view.
System.ComponentModel.Design.CollectionEditor	Edits a collection of items. Other controls usually derive custom collection editor classes from this class depending on the type of items they expose. You'll see an example of this technique in Chapter 26.
System.ComponentModel.Design.MultilineStringEditor	Displays a drop-down box that allows the developer to modify a long string with line breaks.
System.Drawing.Design.FontEditor	Allows the programmer to select and configure a font. Used automatically for font properties.
System.Drawing.Design.ImageEditor	Allows the programmer to create an Image object by selecting a bitmap or other supported file type from an open file dialog. You can also use similar editors like BitmapEditor, IconEditor, and MetafileEditor, which restrict the allowed file types.
System.Web.UI.Design.WebControls.RegexTypeEditor	Allows the programmer to choose a regular expression from a list of common choices. This UITypeEditor works with string properties.

Table 13-6. *UITypeEditors in the .NET Framework*

Class	Description
System.Windows.Forms.Design.MaskPropertyEditor	Allows you to set a string with a mask code (using the format specified by the MaskedTextBox control). Using this dialog box, you can choose from a list of presets, and test masks before applying them.
System.Windows.Forms.Design.FileNameEditor	Allows a fully qualified file name to be set by choosing a file from an open file dialog box. This type editor works with string properties.
System.Windows.Forms.Design.FolderNameEditor	Allows a directory path to be set by from a directory-browsing dialog box. This type editor works with string properties.
System.Windows.Forms.Design.ShortcutKeysEditor	Allows you to choose shortcut keys as a combination of values from the Keys enumeration.

You associate a property with a type editor using the Editor attribute. As with type converters, you can apply the Editor attribute to a class declaration or a property declaration. The correct approach depends on how specialized the underlying data type is.

For example, you'll always want to edit fonts in the same way, so the declaration for the Font class binds it to the FontEditor using the Editor attribute. On the other hand, some type editors work with more general types. An example is the RegexTypeEditor, which allows the programmer to choose a common regular expression for a control property, which is then stored as an ordinary string. Controls that provide strings with regular expression content must attach the type editor to the appropriate property using the Editor attribute. Here's an example:

```
private string regEx = String.Empty;

[Editor(typeof(System.Web.UI.Design.WebControls.RegexTypeEditor),
 typeof(UITypeEditor))]
public string ValidationExpression
{
    get { return regEx; }
    set { regEx = value; }
}
```

When the programmer clicks this property in the Properties window, an ellipsis (…) appears next to the property name. If the programmer clicks the ellipsis button, a full dialog appears with common regular expression choices (see Figure 13-14).

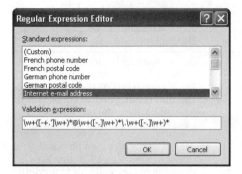

Figure 13-14. *The RegexTypeEditor*

■**Note** Interestingly, this type editor was originally designed for the validation controls provided with ASP.NET, and is provided alongside the Web controls in the .NET namespaces. However, it works equally well with a Windows control. You simply have to add the System.Design.dll assembly reference to your project.

Using Custom Type Editors

You can also develop your own custom type editor classes to allow special settings to be config-ured. For example, consider the TreeView control. Its Nodes property is a collection, but it doesn't use the standard System.ComponentModel.Design.CollectionEditor class. Instead, it uses the more specialized System.Windows.Forms.Design.TreeNodeCollectionEditor.

To create a custom type editor, you must first create a class that derives from System.Drawing.Design.UITypeEditor. You can then override the four methods shown in Table 13-7.

Table 13-7. *UITypeEditor Overridable Methods*

ClassMethod	Description
EditValue()	Invoked when the property is edited. Generally, this is where you would create a special dialog box for property editing.
GetEditStyle()	Specifies whether the type editor is a DropDown (provides a list of specially drawn choices), Modal (provides a dialog box for property selection), or None (no editing supported).
GetPaintValueSupported()	Use this to return true if you are providing a PaintValue() implementation.
PaintValue()	Invoked to paint a graphical thumbnail that represents the value in the Properties window.

You'll see three examples in the following sections.

A Modal Type Editor

A modal type editor shows an ellipsis (...) button next to the property value. When this button is clicked, a dialog box appears that allows the developer to change the property value (see Figure 13-15).

Figure 13-15. *The sign of a modal type editor*

To create a modal type editor, you need to create the dialog box form. To create a basic example, consider the DirectoryTree control first presented in Chapter 11. Although it isn't difficult to change the DirectoryTree.Drive property, it would be nice if you could run a little bit of extra code to find all the drives on the current computer, and allow the user to choose from them.

Here's a SelectDrive form that does exactly that. It gets an array of drives and shows them in a list. When the developer selects a new drive, the Select.DriveSelection property is updated. The OK button is set with a DialogResult of DialogResult.OK, so clicking it closes the window.

```
public partial class SelectDrive : System.Windows.Forms.Form
{
    // Store the selected drive.
    private char driveSelection;
    public char DriveSelection
    {
        get { return driveSelection; }
        set { driveSelection = value; }
    }
}
```

```
private void SelectDrive_Load(object sender, System.EventArgs e)
{
    string[] drives = System.IO.Directory.GetLogicalDrives();
    lstDrives.DataSource = drives;

    // Select the current drive.
    lstDrives.SelectedIndex = lstDrives.FindString(
      driveSelection.ToString());

    // Attach the event handler.
    // This step is performed after the selected index is set,
    // to prevent it from being overwritten as the list is built.
    lstDrives.SelectedIndexChanged += new
      EventHandler(lstDrives_SelectedIndexChanged);
}

private void lstDrives_SelectedIndexChanged(object sender,
 System.EventArgs e)
{
    driveSelection = lstDrives.Text[0];
}

// Allow quick select-and-close.
private void lstDrives_DoubleClick(object sender, EventArgs e)
{
    DialogResult = DialogResult.OK;
}
}
```

All the type editor needs to do is create an instance of the SelectDrive dialog box, show it, and then read the DriveSelection property once the dialog box is closed.

Here's the complete type editor code:

```
public class DriveEditor : UITypeEditor
{
    public override System.Drawing.Design.UITypeEditorEditStyle GetEditStyle(
     System.ComponentModel.ITypeDescriptorContext context)
    {
        // Use a dialog box for property editing.
        return UITypeEditorEditStyle.Modal;
    }

    public override object EditValue(
     System.ComponentModel.ITypeDescriptorContext context,
     System.IServiceProvider provider, object value)
    {
        SelectDrive frm = new SelectDrive();
```

```
            // Set current drive in window.
            frm.DriveSelection = (char)value;

            // Show the dialog box.
            if (frm.ShowDialog() == DialogResult.OK)
            {
                // Return the new value.
                return frm.DriveSelection;
            else
            {
                // Return the old value.
                return value;
            }
        }
    }

    public override bool GetPaintValueSupported(
      System.ComponentModel.ITypeDescriptorContext context)
    {
        // No special thumbnail will be shown in the Properties window.
        return false;
    }
}
```

The type editor is attached to the appropriate property using an Editor attribute:

```
[Editor(typeof(DriveEditor), typeof(UITypeEditor))]
public char Drive
```

Figure 13-16 shows the drive-selection window that appears when the user edits the Drive property.

Figure 13-16. *A custom drive-selection window*

One benefit to this design is that you can reuse this type editor with any drive property in any control. It's specific to the property data type, not the control.

An alternative approach is to use a DirectoryInfo object instead of an underlying char to represent the drive. Because the property editing is now handled by the type editor, there's no need to choose a basic type that can be edited with the default design-time support built into the property grid.

A Drop-Down Type Editor

Instead of showing a separate dialog box, a drop-down type editor shows a control in a drop-down box underneath the property. The drop-down box is sized to fit the initial size of the control you supply, but it will be resized if it can't fit due to screen size or window positioning.

The best way to prepare the content for the drop-down box is to create a user control. The type editor is then responsible for showing that user control in the drop-down box. For example, consider the Progress control first demonstrated in Chapter 10. It allows you to type any number into the Value property, although values that are higher than the maximum or lower than 0 will be rejected with an error message. To simplify editing, you might want to create a drop-down display that indicates the allowed range and lets the user set a value with a slider bar. Figure 13-17 shows a user control that provides this feature.

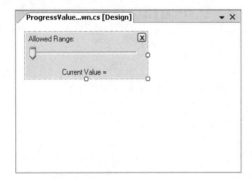

Figure 13-17. *The user control for a drop-down type editor*

Because this control is intended solely to be used at design-time, it makes sense to keep it out of the toolbox. You can accomplish this by adding the ToolboxItem attribute to the class declaration, and marking it false:

```
[ToolboxItem(false)]
public partial class ProgressValueDropDown : UserControl
{ ... }
```

The real trick in this example is that the user control you create for editing the property needs a way to receive information from the custom control object. To make this easier, you should add a constructor to your editing control that accepts all the information it needs. In this case, you need two details: the maximum and current values. (The Progress control in its current implementation forces developers to use a minimum of 0.)

Additionally, it's a common convention to accept an IWindowsFormEditorService object that represents the editing service in Visual Studio. (You'll learn more about design-time services in Chapter 26.) The reference to the editing service allows the control to close the drop-down after the editing is complete. In this example, it makes more sense to leave the drop-down open so the developer can try several settings, which means this detail isn't needed. However, it's useful to demonstrate it anyway, and it provides the functionality for the X button in the top-right corner.

Here's the constructor code and the details for storing the constructor-supplied information:

```
private int progressValue;
public int Value
{
    get { return progressValue; }
    set { progressValue = value; }
}

private IWindowsFormsEditorService editorService;

public ProgressValueDropDown(int value, int maximum,
 IWindowsFormsEditorService editorService)
{
    InitializeComponent();

    // Store this information for later use.
    Value = value;
    this.editorService = editorService;

    // Apply the current information.
    trackBar1.Maximum = maximum;
    lblRange.Text = "Allowed Range: (0, " + maximum.ToString() + ")";
    trackBar1.Value = value;

    trackBar1.SmallChange = 1;
    trackBar1.LargeChange = 5;
}

public ProgressValueDropDown()
{
    // Default constructor required for designing
    // this control in Visual Studio.
    InitializeComponent();
}
```

Every time the value in the track bar is changed, the Value property is updated:

```
private void trackBar1_ValueChanged(object sender, EventArgs e)
{
    Value = trackBar1.Value;
    lblValue.Text = "Current Value = " + trackBar1.Value.ToString();
}
```

Finally, when the X button is clicked the drop-down is closed. The developer can also close the drop-down by clicking the arrow next to the value (the same arrow that opens the drop-down region).

```
private void cmdClose_Click(object sender, EventArgs e)
{
    editorService.CloseDropDown();
}
```

The next step is to develop the type editor that uses this control. Here's the class declaration:

```
public class ProgressValueEditor : UITypeEditor
{ ... }
```

You can connect this type editor to the Progress.Value property using the Editor attribute, as in the previous example. All you need to do now is fill in the type editor code. This part is quite easy.

First, you choose the drop-down style:

```
public override System.Drawing.Design.UITypeEditorEditStyle GetEditStyle(
 System.ComponentModel.ITypeDescriptorContext context)
{
    return UITypeEditorEditStyle.DropDown;
}
```

Once again, you turn down thumbnails:

```
public override bool GetPaintValueSupported(
 System.ComponentModel.ITypeDescriptorContext context)
{
    return false;
}
```

Finally, in the EditValue() method you get the editor service, create an instance of the ProgressValueDropDown control, and add it to the Properties window using the IWindowsFormsEditorService.DropDownControl() method, as shown here:

```
public override object EditValue(
 System.ComponentModel.ITypeDescriptorContext context,
 System.IServiceProvider provider, object value)
{
    if (provider != null)
    {
        IWindowsFormsEditorService editorService =
          provider.GetService(typeof(IWindowsFormsEditorService))
          as IWindowsFormsEditorService;

        if (editorService != null)
        {
```

```
            // Create the editing control.
            Progress ctrl = (Progress)context.Instance;
            ProgressValueDropDown selectionControl =
              new ProgressValueDropDown(
                (int)value, ctrl.Maximum, editorService);

            // Show the editing control.
            editorService.DropDownControl(selectionControl);
            value = selectionControl.Value;
        }
    }
    return value;
}
```

Figure 13-18 shows the drop-down editor in the Properties window.

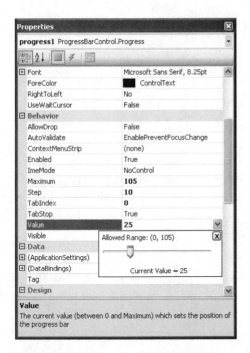

Figure 13-18. *A drop-down type editor*

Painting a Thumbnail

Type editors also give you the chance to get a little fancy by creating a custom thumbnail of the gradient in the Properties window. You might use this trick with the GradientPanel control. To add this extra bit of finesse, all you need to do is create a type editor for the GradientFill class, and override the PaintValue() method. Here's the complete code:

```
public class GradientFillEditor : UITypeEditor
{
    public override bool GetPaintValueSupported(
     System.ComponentModel.ITypeDescriptorContext context)
    {
        return true;
    }

    public override void PaintValue(
     System.Drawing.Design.PaintValueEventArgs e)
    {
        GradientFill fill = (GradientFill)e.Value;
        LinearGradientBrush brush = new LinearGradientBrush(e.Bounds,
            fill.ColorA, fill.ColorB, fill.GradientFillStyle);

        // Paint the thumbnail.
        e.Graphics.FillRectangle(brush, e.Bounds);
    }
}
```

Finally, attach the type editor to the GradientFill class with an Editor attribute:

```
[TypeConverter(typeof(GradientFillConverter))]
[Editor(typeof(GradientFillEditor), typeof(UITypeEditor))]
public class GradientFill
```

The GradientPanel now retains its effortless design-time support, with the added frill of a thumbnail gradient in the Properties window next to the GradientFill property (see Figure 13-19). You can also reuse the GradientFill and GradientFillEditor to add similar features to countless other custom control projects.

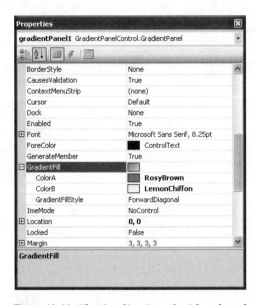

Figure 13-19. *The GradientPanel with a thumbnail gradient*

The Last Word

This chapter covered a lot of ground about custom controls, with the goal of getting you up to speed on all the essentials. First, you learned about the basic set of attributes that go into every custom control. Next, you took an in-depth look at code serialization, and how to take control with attributes, the ShouldSerializeXxx() methods, and custom type converters. Finally, you examined type editors, which allow you to provide a slick editing interface for complex properties.

The story doesn't end here, however. In Chapter 26 you'll revisit design-time support and consider some new topics. Namely, you'll focus on control designers, which allow you to influence your control's design-time behavior, show smart tags, and hide (or add) properties. You'll also see a more advanced serialization example that demonstrates how you can add design-time support for a collection control.

PART 3

Modern Controls

■■■

CHAPTER 14

Tool, Menu, and Status Strips

■NET 2.0 does something that's more than a little surprising with its toolbar, status bar, and menu controls—it tosses out the .NET 1.x standbys and replaces them with an entirely new model. The old controls like the ToolBar, StatusBar, and MainMenu are still available (right-click the toolbox and select Choose Items to hunt for them), but they're intended only for backward compatibility. Now, a new set of classes that includes System.Windows.Forms.ToolStrip and two other derived classes (MenuStrip and StatusStrip) provides a completely new model for toolbars and menus.

The natural question is, Why reinvent the wheel? The legacy ToolBar, StatusBar, and MainMenu classes were based on some of the older corners of the Win32 API, and developers were quick to complain that they were out of place among the slick themed and skinned interfaces popular in modern applications like Microsoft Office. Theming support was entirely absent, which meant that there was no way to harmonize these controls with the Windows XP user interface, and there was no little or no support for reordering buttons, rearranging side-by-side toolbars, or customizing the button-drawing process. In fact, even painting a thumbnail image next to a menu item required custom painting code with the .NET 1.x MainMenu.

For the .NET 2.0 release, the Windows Forms development team was faced with the significant task of bringing these out-of-date controls up to a respectable level. Rather than rework each control separately, they set out to build a new model that could be leveraged for each of these scenarios. That new model revolves around the ToolStrip control. Its many features include a slick modern look, support for themes and customizable rendering, and the ability for the user to drag, rearrange, and customize toolbars effortlessly. In this chapter, you'll examine the ToolStrip in detail, and use it to create toolbars, status bars, and menus.

ToolStrip Basics

The ToolStrip is the basis of the StatusStrip, MenuStrip, and ContextMenuStrip controls you'll consider in this chapter, and a slick stand-alone control of its own. To get off to a quick start with ToolStrip, drag it onto a form, select it, and choose Insert Standard Items from the smart tag. This adds a basic set of buttons including File, Open, Save, and Print, the editing commands Cut, Copy, and Paste, and a Help button.

When you run this example, you'll immediately notice that the ToolStrip sports a slick new interface that's far better than the miserably out-of-date ToolBar. Some of its niceties include:

- It's flat, so there aren't any visible button edges (although you can add etched separator lines).

- It supports hot tracking, so as you hover over a button, it's highlighted.

- It supports Windows XP themes, so the gradient background that's painted as the bar background automatically uses the active color scheme.

- It provides automatic overflow menus. That means when the windows resized so that not all the buttons can fit, an arrow icon is added at the end of the menu. If you click that arrow, you'll see a drop-down menu with the missing items (see Figure 14-1). You can disable the overflow behavior by setting CanOverflow to false.

Overall, the ToolStrip closely matches the polished toolbars introduced in Microsoft Office XP (and present in later versions).

Figure 14-1. *Automatic overflow menus in the ToolStrip*

Figure 14-1 shows a standard horizontal ToolStrip, which is what you get when you first drop a ToolStrip onto a form. However, you can change the direction using the ToolStrip. LayoutStyle property, using any of the options described in Table 14-1.

Table 14-1. *LayoutStyle Values (from the ToolStripLayoutStyle Enumeration)*

Value	Description
HorizontalStackWithOverflow	Arranges items in a horizontal line from left to right, adding any leftovers to the overflow menu (on the right).
VerticalStackWithOverflow	Arranges items in a single column of buttons, and adds an overflow menu to the bottom if needed.
StackWithOverflow	Uses either HorizontalStackWithOverflow or VerticalStackWithOverflow, depending on whether the ToolStrip is docked to the top or side of its container. This is the default.

Table 14-1. *LayoutStyle Values (from the ToolStripLayoutStyle Enumeration)*

Value	Description
Flow	Tiles items from left to right and then downward to fill the available space. No overflow menu is created—instead, the ToolStrip is enlarged to fit all the items.
Table	Arranges items in a grid, from left to right and then down. To make this work, you need to cast the ToolStrip.LayoutSettings to TableLayoutSettings, and then set the desired number of columns. The ToolStrip is then expanded (with new rows) to fit all the items.

Usually, when you use horizontal layout you'll want to dock the ToolStrip to the top or bottom of your form. When you use a vertical layout you'll dock to the left or right sides. In fact, when you set the ToolStrip.Dock property, the ToolStrip automatically sets the LayoutStyle property to match (although you can modify it afterward).

■Tip Although docked horizontal and vertical toolbars are most common, you don't need to dock your ToolStrip anywhere. If you don't, it remains fixed in place on the form wherever you've positioned it, just like any other control. Later in this chapter, you'll learn to use the ToolStripContainer to allow users to rearrange ToolStrip controls.

The ToolStrip is outfitted with a wide range of features, and it's impossible to introduce them all at once. Instead, the following sections will take you through a series of common ToolStrip tasks, from the relatively simple (for example, handling button clicks) to the much more complex (customizing the painting logic).

The ToolStripItem

At its heart, the ToolStrip is a collection of ToolStripItem objects, which are exposed through the ToolStrip.Items property. Each ToolStripItem represents a separate element on the ToolStrip bar, like a button, combo box, text box, label, or separator. You can select each ToolStripItem individually in to configure it or attach event handlers.

The ToolStripItem class inherits from Component, and defines a basic set of properties for controlling the font (Font), colors (BackColor and ForeColor), the displayed content (Image and Text), the ToolTipText, the state of the item (Visible and Enabled), and so on. You'll consider many of these properties in the following sections.

In the simple example shown in Figure 14-1, all the ToolStripItem objects are either buttons (instances of ToolStripButton) or separators (instances of ToolStripSeparator). Both of these classes derive from ToolStripItem, along with several other supported ToolStripItem types. Table 14-2 lists all the ToolStripItem classes that are recommended for use with the ToolStrip.

Later in this chapter, you'll learn about ToolStripItem classes that are tailored for status bars and menus, and you'll see how to create your own custom ToolStripItem classes.

Table 14-2. *ToolStripItem Derived Classes*

Class	Description
ToolStripButton	Represents an item on the ToolStrip that the user can click. You can place text or image content (or both) on the button.
ToolStripLabel	Represents a non-selectable item on the ToolStrip. It can include text or an image (or both). However, if you set the IsLink property to true, the ToolStripLabel is rendered like a hyperlink, and is selectable. (You'll still need to handle the Click event to perform the appropriate action.)
ToolStripSeparator	Separates adjacent ToolStrip items into groups with a thin engraved line. Even though this ingredient doesn't seem terribly important, it can still raise events like any other ToolStripItem.
ToolStripControlHost	An item that hosts another Windows Form control. You can use the ToolStripControlHost to display just about any control in the ToolStrip, or you can use one of the classes that are derived from it (ToolStripComboBox, ToolStripTextBox, or ToolStripProgressBar) to get a specific control with strongly typed properties.
ToolStripDropDownItem	An item that displays a drop-down menu. When using the ToolStripDropDownItem, you actually have two very similar options, depending on what ToolStripDropDownItem-derived class you choose. ToolStripDropDownButton gives you a button with a tiny arrow icon (and your own text or image). When this button is clicked, the drop-down menu appears. ToolStripSplitButton looks similar, but it separates the drop-down button from your content with a thin solid line. Typically, you use ToolStripSplitButton when you want to give the ability to provide several functions through one button. The user can push on the button to get a drop-down menu and select an option from it to apply.

The easiest way to add ToolStrip items is to use the Visual Studio designer. Just select Edit Items from the ToolStrip smart tag. You'll see a designer that lets you add new ToolStripItem objects, configure them, and rearrange their order (see Figure 14-2).

Although the ToolStrip class manages the heavy lifting, including painting, keyboard handling, and mouse input, the ToolStripItem determines the content and some aspects of the layout, and fires its own events.

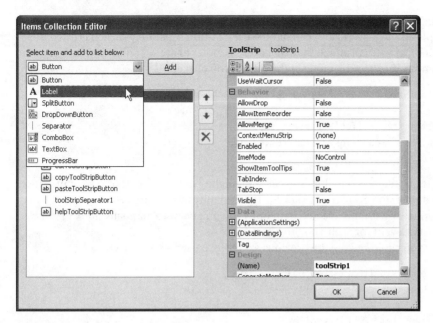

Figure 14-2. *Designing a ToolStrip*

ToolStripItem Events

Every ToolStripItem supports a small set of events. In fact, even noninteractive ToolStripItem instances (like separators and labels) fire the ToolStripItem events. These events closely match the events provided by the base Control class and don't hide any surprises. Table 14-3 lists the most useful ones.

Table 14-3. *ToolStripItem Events*

Event	Description
Click	Occurs when the ToolStripItem is clicked.
DoubleClick	Occurs when the ToolStripItem is double-clicked with the mouse. Because double-clicks can mask single-clicks, and because there's rarely any reason to double-click a part of the ToolStrip, double-clicks are disabled by default. They won't be raised unless you set ToolStripItem.DoubleClickEnabled to true.
DragDrop, DragEnter, DragLeave, DragOver, GiveFeedBack	Allow you to manage drag-and-drop operations, much as you would with any other control. For more information, see the section about these events in Chapter 4.
MouseMove, MouseEnter, MouseHover, MouseLeave, MouseDown, MouseUp	Allow you to track the state of the mouse and handle mouse clicks.

To implement most of the functionality behind a typical ToolStrip, you'll simply react to the ToolStripItem.Click event. You can handle each button separately (which is often the clearest approach), or you can attach the same event handler to every ToolStripItem. Here's an example that simply displays the name of the button you clicked:

```
private void ToolStripButton_Click(object sender, EventArgs e)
{
    ToolStripItem item = (ToolStripItem)sender;
    MessageBox.Show("You clicked " + item.Name);
}
```

An alternate approach is possible. You can handle the ToolStrip.ItemClicked event, which fires when any item in the ToolStrip is clicked. This is handy in scenarios where you need to perform a generic task with the selected item but you don't want to manually hook up the ToolStripItem.Click event for each ToolStripItem.

Here's how you could rewrite the previous example to use this approach:

```
private void ToolStrip_ItemClicked(object sender,
 ToolStripItemClickedEventArgs e)
{
    ToolStripItem item = e.ClickedItem;
    MessageBox.Show("You clicked " + item.Name);
}
```

ToolStripItem Display Styles

There are several different ways to display a ToolStripItem, based on the DisplayStyle property, which takes a value from the ToolStripItemDisplayStyle enumeration. You can display just an image (Image), just text (Text), nothing at all (None, the oddest option), or image and text (ImageAndText).

■Tip The ToolStrip is optimized so it doesn't attempt to lay out content if the corresponding property is null—for example, if you have an image set but no text, TextAndImage and ImageOnly render the same.

The default DisplayStyle depends on the type of item. For example, a ToolStripButton starts off in image mode, while a ToolStripLabel uses ImageAndText. The DisplayStyle has no meaning for the ToolStripSeparator and ToolStripControlHost (and this Property doesn't appear in their Properties Window for these items).

When you use ImageAndText, you have the flexibility to choose how the two components are arranged. By default, the image appears on the left and the text on the right. However, you can change this relationship with the TextImageRelation property. Supported values include:

- ImageBeforeText (the default)

- TextBeforeImage

- ImageAboveText

- TextAboveImage

- Overlay (which superimposes the text over your image).

Figure 14-3 shows a test program included with the code for this chapter that lets you try out different text-alignment options.

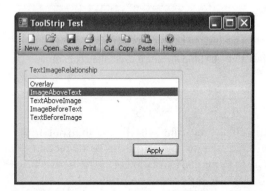

Figure 14-3. *Image above text and other alignment options*

■**Tip** It's a common technique in applications like Internet Explorer and Office to mix image-only buttons with other buttons that include image and text. Usually, the images that include text represent less common commands that need some identification.

ToolStripItem Images

Each ToolStripItem supports an image through its Image property. However, the ToolStrip assumes that all images are the same size. This size is dictated by the ToolStrip.ImageScalingSize dimensions. This size is initially 16x16 pixels, although you can change the scaling size to any dimensions you want.

Problems occur if there's a mismatch between the scaling size and the actual size of an image. If the image doesn't match the scaling size of the ToolStrip, the ToolStrip needs to scale the image to fit, with unimpressive results. To turn off this automatic scaling behavior, change each ToolStripItem.ImageScaling property from SizeToFit to None. Now the image for each ToolStripItem image will be kept at its native size, no matter what the ImageScalingSize of the ToolStrip imposes.

You can actually set two images in each ToolStripItem—one in the foreground (through the Image property) and one in the background (through the BackgroundImage property). You can use this in conjunction with BackgroundImageLayout (which allows you to tile, stretch, or zoom the image) to place an image behind your text and any foreground image. You can even set the ImageTransparent property to one of the colors in your foreground image to allow the background to bleed through (although this effect is never as polished as when you prepare the images ahead of time with the right background color, using a professional drawing program that applies anti-aliasing).

ToolStripItem Text

Each ToolStripItem supports an arbitrary amount of text through its Text property. However, text is never wrapped in a ToolStrip item, so it's a good idea to keep it as short as possible. A single word is ideal—any more should go into the tooltip.

■**Note** The ToolStrip gives you a range of tooltip possibilities. If you don't set anything in the ToolTipText property, the ToolStripItem will use its Text property for tooltip text. To disable this behavior, set the AutoToolTip property to false. To turn off tooltips for the entire ToolStrip in one step, set the ToolStrip. ShowItemToolTips property to false.

The text in a ToolStripItem is rendered horizontally, regardless of whether the ToolStrip itself is horizontal or vertical. However, you can rotate the text by setting the TextDirection property (of the ToolStrip or a single ToolStripItem) to Vertical90 (a rotation of 90°) or Vertical270 (a rotation of 270°) rather than the default, Horizontal. Images are never rotated.

Figure 14-4 shows an example with two vertical ToolStrip objects. The one displays images and text with the normal text direction. The one of the right shows images only, but adds two labels with a TextDirection of Vertical90.

Figure 14-4. *Rotated text labels*

■**Note** Rotated text is uncommon in professional Windows application, but it does crop up from time to time (usually with the objective of saving space). In Office, toolbars rotate text by default when they're in the vertical orientation. One example is the List toolbar in Microsoft Excel 2003, which has 90°-rotated text on two items.

The ToolStripItem supports quick-access keys, which let the user trigger a command using an Alt key combination. To define a quick-access key, add the ampersand (&) before the key you want to use in the text. For example, &New makes Alt+N the quick-access key. The quick-access key is active only if the ToolStripItem.DisplayStyle is set to an option that shows the text.

■**Note** As with menus, the appearance of underlining in the ToolStrip depends on the "Hide underlined letters for keyboard navigation until I press the Alt key" operating system setting. You can configure this setting in the Display section of the Control Panel. If this option is set, underlining won't appear until you press Alt.

ToolStripItem Size and Alignment

Ordinarily, each ToolStripItem is sized to fit its content (text and image). The only changes you make are through the Margin property of each ToolStripItem, which allows you to increase spacing between the edges of the ToolStrip and adjacent items.

You can turn off the automatic sizing by setting the ToolStripItem.AutoSize property to false. You then have the freedom to change the Size property to set the exact size of the ToolStripItem. If the ToolStripItem is too small to accommodate all its content, part of the content will be truncated at the end. Text in a ToolStripItem is never wrapped.

If you make the ToolStripItem much larger than its content, the text and images will be centered inside its bounds. However, you can fine-tune this alignment using the ImageAlign and TextAlign properties, and change it so that the content is aligned along one of the edges.

Figure 14-5 shows some of your alignment options. Keep in mind that all of the buttons in this example use the default TextImageRelation.ImageBeforeText, so the image is always to the left of the text. You can change the TextImageRelation property to get even more positioning flexibility.

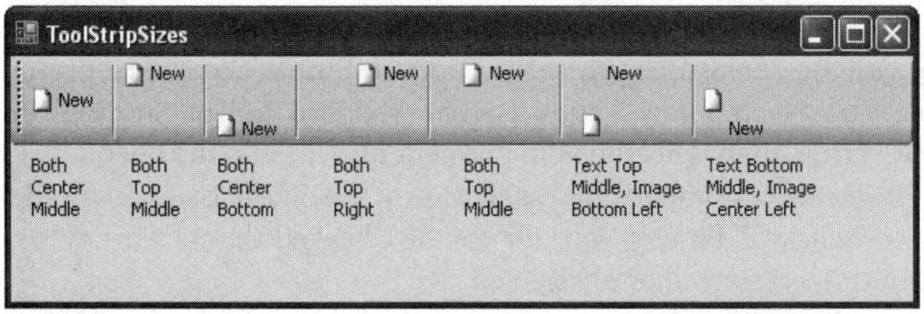

Figure 14-5. *Explicitly sizing and aligning the ToolStripItem*

The ImageAlign and TextAlign properties determine the alignment of content inside a ToolStrip. You also can change how different items are aligned with respect to each other. Ordinarily, all items are ordered starting at the left edge of the ToolStrip (or the top edge in a vertical ToolStrip). Items are arranged according to the order they have in the ToolStrip.Items collection. However, you can set some items to stick to the end of the ToolStrip (the right edge in a horizontal ToolStrip or bottom of a vertical ToolStrip) by setting the ToolStripItem. Alignment property from Left to Right. (Of course, if your ToolStrip is docked to the side of a form, an Alignment value of Right places it at the bottom of the ToolStrip rather than the right side.) This technique is occasionally useful to separate a few buttons, like a Help icon.

Figure 14-6 shows an example that has three buttons aligned to the end of the ToolStrip. When more than one button is aligned to the end, the buttons are attached in the order they appear in the collection, so the first is the farthest right, the next button is just to the left, and so on.

Figure 14-6. *Aligning items on both ends*

It's important to understand not only how the ToolStripItem is sized, but also how the containing ToolStrip is sized. Once again, there's an automatic option and a manual option, depending on the value of the ToolStripItem.AutoSize property. By default, this property is true, and a horizontal ToolStrip is heightened (while a vertical ToolStrip is widened) to fit the dimensions of the largest item. However, if you turn off the AutoSize property you can set the size precisely through the Size property. As long as you have a LayoutStyle of HorizontalStackWithOverflow, VerticalStackWithOverflow, or StackWithOverflow, an overflow menu is added for any items that don't fit in the ToolStrip. But if you're using Flow layout, items that don't fit are simply left out.

Creating a ToolStrip Toggle Button

A toggle button is a button that has two states—and ordinary unselected state and a selected state. When a toggle button is in its selected state, it remains highlighted even when the mouse is not hovering over it. The user can turn a toggle button on or off by clicking it once.

Toggle buttons are easy with the ToolStrip because the ToolStripButton class adds several properties for managing them. The selected state is known as checked, and the ToolStripButton adds a Checked property that, if true, highlights the item permanently. To add the on/off behavior, you simply set the CheckOnClick property to true. That way, the button is automatically switched on or off when the user clicks it. Finally, you can use the CheckedChanged event to react in your code when the button is selected or unselected.

Some toggle buttons are used in groups. For example, in Microsoft Word there are a set of justification buttons, and only one can be selected at a time. To implement this design, the CheckOnClick property isn't enough—instead, when a button in the group is clicked you need to handle the CheckedChanged event, and manually set the Checked property of the other buttons to false.

Creating a ToolStrip Link

Most ToolStrip examples are filled with ToolStripButton objects. However, you also can use the ToolStripLabel to fire commands by setting the IsLink property to true, thereby turning it into a link (see Figure 14-7). You can set the LinkBehavior property to control how the link is under-lined (AlwaysUnderline, NeverUnderline, HoverUnderline, or SystemDefault). You also can determine the colors of the link in both its initial and visited state by setting LinkColor and VisitedLinkColor. Finally, you can read or set the Boolean LinkVisited property to determine whether or not the link is in its visited state.

Figure 14-7. *A ToolStripLabel as a link*

Links are sometimes used to start a new process (for example, launching a browser to display a help or update page). For example, if you place a target URL into the Tag property of a ToolStripLabel, you can use this code to launch it with the default browser:

```
private void ToolStripLinkLabel_Click(object sender, EventArgs e)
{
    ToolStripLabel lbl = (ToolStripLabel)sender;
    try
    {
        Process.Start(new ProcessStartInfo(lbl.Tag.ToString()));
    }
    catch (Exception err)
    {
        MessageBox.Show("Error launching browser.");
    }
}
```

If you want to attach more information, and aren't happy with passing it through the weakly typed Tag property, you can always develop a custom ToolStripItem that derives from ToolStripLinkLabel. You'll learn how to develop custom ToolStripItem classes later in this chapter.

The ToolStripContainer

So far, the ToolStrip examples you've seen have used docked ToolStrip objects. This is a quick way to build simple forms, and it's ideal if you intend to have only a single ToolStrip visible. However, there's another option—you can embed your ToolStrip inside a ToolStripContainer.

The ToolStripContainer allows more than one docked ToolStrip control to share space. For example, imagine you create a control with three ToolStrip objects. If you dock them all to the top, they appear in three separate rows, one above the other, depending on the order in which you created them. The first created object is at the top, because it has the lowest z-index. (See Chapter 2 for a more detailed discussion about z-order.) To change this, you can right-click the control you want on top and select Bring To Front.

But what do you do if you want more than one ToolStrip control appear on the same row, side by side but similarly docked to the top edge? You could avoid docking altogether and position them absolutely, but this causes tremendous headaches with ToolStrip resizing. Namely, you'll need to tweak the ToolStrip size to accommodate newly added buttons, and write code to manage overflow menus and implement the proper sizing behavior when the window is resized. Fortunately, the ToolStripContainer saves you the trouble with an elegant solution.

Essentially, the ToolStripContainer is a group of five panels. There are four ToolStripPanel controls, one for the top, bottom, left, and right edges, and a ContentPanel for the center region, where you can place the rest of the window content. Figure 14-8 shows this design. Usually, you'll dock the ToolStripContainer to fill the form, so that its edges are the same as the form's edges.

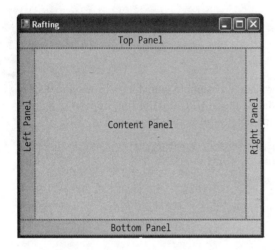

Figure 14-8. *The ToolStripContainer at design time*

When the ToolStripContainer is first created, these four panels are hidden. However, as soon as you place a ToolStrip on one of the edges, the closest panel is resized to fit the ToolStrip. The neat part of this design is the fact that the ToolStrip objects don't use any docking—instead, they're placed in terms of the panel, and the panel is docked in the right place. By default, the ToolStripContainer panels use a shaded background like the ToolStrip.

Figure 14-9 shows a ToolStripContainer with several identical ToolStrip objects. To make it easier to see the different panels, the background color of the content panel has been set to white. Now, you can place more than one ToolStrip on the same row or column, and you also can click on the ToolStrip sizing grip at runtime and drag it from one place to another. A user can apply this technique to rearrange a group of adjacent ToolStrip objects, or to drag a ToolStrip from one panel to another (for example, from the top of the window to the right side). The ToolStripContainer provides the necessary dragging cues. For example, as you drag the ToolStrip, a rectangle outline shows you the new position. When you approach one of the sides, the ToolStrip snaps neatly into place with the correct orientation.

■**Tip** You can set the ToolStrip.Stretch property to true to force a ToolStrip to fill the whole row (for a horizontal ToolStrip) or column (for a vertical ToolStrip). This property is intended primarily for displaying menus. It has no effect unless the ToolStrip is inside a ToolStripPanel.

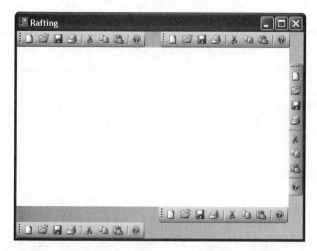

Figure 14-9. *Rearranging ToolStrip objects at runtime*

If you want to add a ToolStrip into a ToolStripContainer at design time, you first must expand the panel where you want to place it. To do this, use the arrow buttons that appear along each edge of the ToolStripContainer. These buttons are a design-time convenience, and they don't appear at runtime. For example, if you want to add a ToolStrip to the right edge, start by clicking the right arrow button to expand the panel. You can then drop the ToolStrip into the exposed panel area. When you first add the ToolStripContainer, the top panel begins with its surface exposed.

Tip You can add a ToolStripContainer directly from the Visual Studio toolbox. However, if you have an existing ToolStrip that you want to place into a ToolStripContainer, just select it and choose Embed in ToolStripContainer from the smart tag. Visual Studio will create a new ToolStripContainer and place your existing ToolStrip inside.

Restricting the ToolStripContainer

By default, the user is allowed to drag any ToolStrip in a ToolStripContainer, and dock it to any side. ToolStrip objects outside a ToolStripContainer are immovable.

You can restrict this freedom in several ways. If you want to restrict docking to certain areas, you can disable some of the ToolStripContainer panels by setting their visibility to false. The ToolStripContainer gives you four properties to serve this purpose: TopToolStripPanelVisible, BottomToolStripPanelVisible, LeftToolStripPanelVisible, and RightToolStripPanelVisible. For example, if you set BottomToolStripPanelVisible to false, no ToolStrip will appear in the bottom panel and the user won't be able to drag another ToolStrip into that area.

■**Tip** You can create a form that allows the user to rearrange ToolStrip objects but restricts them to the top of the window by setting every visibility property to false, except for TopToolStripPanelVisibility.

You also can fix an individual ToolStrip in place by setting the ToolStrip.GripStyle property to Hidden. Without the grip, there's no way for the user to drag the ToolStrip out of its startup position.

Configuring the ToolStripContainer Panels

The ToolStripContainer doesn't expose much of a programming model. However, it does let you customize the five panels it wraps through several properties.

The four side panels are instances of the ToolStripPanel control, which has the built-in collapse/expand behavior you saw in the previous example. The ToolStripPanel doesn't derive from the Panel control, although it has a similar lineage. To get access to these panels, you use the TopToolStripPanel, BottomToolStripPanel, LeftToolStripPanel, and RightToolStripPanel properties.

The center panel is an instance of the ToolStripContentPanel, which does derive from the Panel control. You add the rest of your window content here. You can access it through the ContentPanel property.

So what can you do once you have access to these controls? Primarily, you'll want to change the background color, set a background image, or use the RenderMode property to change how the panel is painted (a technique discussed later in this chapter). You can access all of these panels at design time with the Properties window through the properties of the ToolStripPanel, or you can choose them from the drop-down list box in the Properties window.

■**Note** The ToolStripContainer doesn't make much sense on an MDI parent because of the content region. However, if you want a similar experience (namely, the ability to let the user rearrange multiple ToolStrip controls), you can add one or more ToolStripPanel controls directly to your MDI form. Unfortunately, the ToolStripPanel doesn't appear in the Toolbox, so you'll need to do it in code.

Floating ToolStrips

Now that you understand how the ToolStripContainer functionality is built using separate panels, you might not be as surprised to learn about the one key limitation of the ToolStripContainer— it doesn't support floating ToolStrip objects. If you start dragging a ToolStrip and try to release it anywhere except one of the four edges—for example, in the content panel or outside the window—nothing happens.

However, you can code your own solution. For example, you could use the fake drag-and-drop technique from Chapter 4 to change the position of the ToolStrip as the user drags it with the mouse. However, this isn't quite as easy as it should be. The problem is that the ToolStrip mouse events (like MouseDown) only fire when they aren't handled by any other part of the

ToolStrip. Unfortunately, when the user clicks the ToolStrip grip, the sizing grip handles the click and the event isn't passed on to your code.

The only way to code around this problem is to create a custom ToolStrip control that overrides the corresponding mouse methods. For example, the following code listing shows a custom ToolStrip that overrides OnMouseDown and checks if the click was made inside the sizing grip region. If it was, the control creates a new form and moves the ToolStrip from the current form to the new (floating) form.

```
public class FloatToolStrip : ToolStrip
{
    public event EventHandler Undocked;

    protected override void OnMouseDown(MouseEventArgs mea)
    {
        if (this.GripRectangle.Contains(mea.Location))
        {
            Point location = PointToScreen(Point.Empty);

            // For more control, this would be a custom form.
            // You could then event handlers that would react when
            // it is dragged to an edge, and redock it automatically.
            floatForm = new Form();
            floatForm.StartPosition = FormStartPosition.Manual;
            floatForm.Owner = this.FindForm();
            Point pt = location;
            pt.Offset(5, 5);
            floatForm.Location = pt;
            floatForm.Text = this.Text;
            floatForm.FormBorderStyle = FormBorderStyle.FixedToolWindow;
            floatForm.ClientSize = this.Size;

            // A control can be contained in only one form. This moves
            // the ToolStrip out of the original form and into the floating form.
            floatForm.Controls.Add(this);
            floatForm.Show();

            // Raise the event to notify the form.
            if (Undocked != null) Undocked(this, EventArgs.Empty);
        }
        else
        {
            // Perform the normal mouse-click handling.
            base.OnMouseDown(mea);
        }
    }
}
```

```
        private Form floatForm;
        public Form FloatForm
        {
            get { return floatForm; }
        }
    }
```

Now you can recompile your application and add this custom ToolStrip from the Toolbox. You'll have all the same design support for configuring the FloatToolStrip and adding ToolStrip-Item objects inside.

Figure 14-10 shows how this code can create a rudimentary floating ToolStrip.

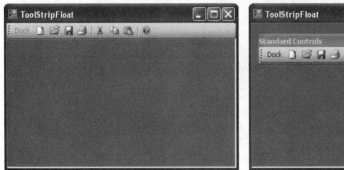

Figure 14-10. *Floating the ToolStrip in a tool window*

You can try out the complete example with the downloadable code for this chapter, available in the Source Code area at www.apress.com.

The StatusStrip and MenuStrip

So far, you've learned the ToolStrip essentials, including how to control the layout, handle ToolStripItem events, and use the ToolStripContainer to add drag-and-rearrange support. Now, it's time to consider how the ToolStrip model enables status bars and menus.

The basic idea behind the ToolStrip model is that you can add the same ToolStripItem objects to different top-level containers. If you need a toolbar, the top-level container is the ToolStrip. If you need a status bar, the StatusStrip item makes more sense. And if you need a menu, the MenuStrip or ContextMenuStrip containers make sense. All the top-level containers provide a very similar model, with essentially the same set of features. However, the default rendering is slightly different, and some ToolStripItem objects are intended only for certain top-level containers. In truth, there's no absolute limitation—you can add menu items to the ToolStrip and status panels to a MenuStrip. However, you're encouraged not to (and this option isn't available in the designers you use at design time).

Table 14-4 shows the full list of ToolStripItem classes, and indicates what container supports them. Remember, this table is based on intended usage and design-time support—you can break the rules if you want and treat every container in the same way.

Table 14-4. *ToolStripItem Container Support*

Class	Recommended in ToolStrip	Recommended in MenuStrip	Recommended in StatusStrip
ToolStripButton	Yes	No	No
ToolStripComboBox	Yes	Yes	No
ToolStripSplitButton	Yes	No	No
ToolStripLabel	Yes	No	No
ToolStripSeparator	Yes	Yes	No
ToolStripDropDownButton	Yes	No	No
ToolStripTextBox	Yes	Yes	Yes
ToolStripMenuItem	No	Yes	No
ToolStripStatusLabel	No	No	Yes
ToolStripProgressBar	Yes	No	Yes

■**Note** There's one other class that derives from ToolStrip: the ToolStripDropDownMenu. This class represents a submenu for a menu item or a drop-down button, as you'll see later in this chapter.

Creating a Status Bar

The StatusStrip is essentially a subset of the ToolStrip control. Although it can be used in a ToolStripContainer, it's almost always docked to the bottom of the window, where it can provide long-term status information. By default, the StatusStrip doesn't use the themed background of the ToolStrip (although you can change this by shifting the RenderMode to Professional). The StatusStrip rendering is also tweaked a bit—it adds a shaded line above the status bar, and a sizing grip for the window at the right side (which you can hide by setting SizingGrip to false).

Because a status bar is most commonly used to show information, not to provide commands, you'll probably add more label items than you would with an ordinary ToolStrip. In fact, there's a customized ToolStripStatusLabel control that's tailored for the StatusStrip. It inherits from the ToolStripLabel, changes some defaults, and adds four new properties: Alignment, BorderStyle, BorderSides, and Spring.

■**Tip** In some applications, like the Microsoft Office applications, double-clicking on a label in the status bar is a shortcut for a commonly used feature.

The BorderStyle and BorderSides properties allow you to create a border around your label. With status bars, it's a common convention to separate several pieces of information graphically. You can set the BorderStyle property to one of the options in Table 14-5.

Table 14-5. *BorderStyle Values (from the Border3DStyle Enumeration)*

Value	Description
Adjust	The border is drawn just *outside* the control bounds. This way, you have free rein to perform custom drawing inside (by responding to the ToolStripItem.Paint event).
Bump	The inner and outer edges of the border have a raised appearance.
Etched	The inner and outer edges of the border have an etched (engraved) appearance.
Flat	The border has no three-dimensional effects. (This is the BorderStyle default for the ToolStripStatusLabel.)
Raised	The border has raised inner and outer edges.
RaisedInner	The border has a raised inner edge and no outer edge.
RaisedOuter	The border has a raised outer edge and no inner edge.
Sunken	The border has sunken inner and outer edges.
SunkenInner	The border has a sunken inner edge and no outer edge.
SunkenOuter	The border has a sunken outer edge and no inner edge.

You can then set the BorderSides property to indicate on which edges the border should be drawn. For example, you can choose to enclose the label completely, or just draw a vertical separator line. Figure 14-11 shows a test program included with downloadable code for this chapter that lets you try out different border options.

The other new property in ToolStripStatusLabel is Spring. If Spring is true, the ToolStripStatusLabel automatically expands to fill any leftover space in the StatusStrip. Unless you change the TextAlign and ImageAlign properties, the content is centered in the middle of the item. If you have more than one ToolStripStatusLabel with Spring set to true, any extra space is divided between them proportionately. Figure 14-12 shows this spring behavior in action.

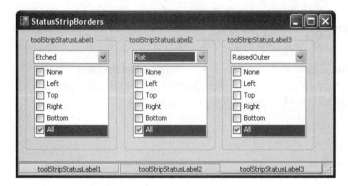

Figure 14-11. *Borders with the ToolStripStatusLabel*

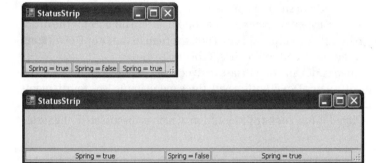

Figure 14-12. *A StatusStrip with two springing labels*

THE PROPER PLACE FOR A STATUS BAR

A status bar is ideal for displaying small amounts of information throughout the life of the application. This information should never be critical or take the place of informative messages or progress indicators, as many users won't notice it. This information should also be kept to a minimum to prevent a cluttered interface. Some possible status bar information includes:

- **Information about the application mode or operating context.** For example, if your application can be run by many different types of users, you might use a status bar panel to provide information about the current user level (e.g., Administrator Mode). Similarly, a financial application might provide a label indicating U.S. Currency Prices if it's possible to switch regularly between several different pricing modes.

- **Information about the application status.** For example, a database application might start by displaying Ready or Connected To... when you first log in, and then display Record Added when you update the database. This technique avoids stalling advanced users with a confirmation window where they need to click an OK button, but it can also easily be missed, leaving it unsuitable for some situations.

- **Information about a background process.** For example, Microsoft Word provides some information about print operations while they are being spooled in its status bar.

- **Information about the current document.** For example, most word processors use a status bar to display the current page count and the user's position in the document. Windows Explorer uses the status bar to display ancillary information like the total number of files in a folder.

ToolStrip Menus

Just as in Microsoft Office applications, the ToolStrip can accommodate drop-down menu items. You simply need to add one of the items that derives from ToolStripDropDownItem (either ToolStripDropDownButton or ToolStripSplitButton) to your ToolStrip.

The ToolStripDropDownItem adds a small set of members. The most important is the DropDownItems collection, which accepts a collection of ToolStripItem objects for the drop-down menu. The interesting part is that you can add any ToolStripItem to the DropDownItems collection. This means that you can add menu commands, ToolStripTextBox, ToolStripComboBox, and (through code) any other class derived from ToolStripItem.

Figure 14-13 shows a ToolStripDropDownButton with three menu items. The fourth menu item is being chosen from a drop-down list that provides four options. The only ingredient in this list that you haven't yet considered is the ToolStripMenuItem, which is discussed in the next section.

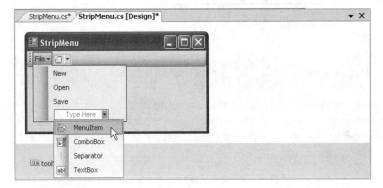

Figure 14-13. *Designing a drop-down ToolStrip menu*

Along with the DropDownItems collection, the ToolStripDropDownItem class also adds a DropDownDirection property you can set (in code) to influence where the menu is displayed, and a set of events (DropDownOpening, DropDownOpened, DropDownClosing, and DropDownClosed) that you can handle to add, hide, insert, or remove menu items on the fly. Finally, it includes a ShowDropDown() method you can call to pop open the menu programmatically, and a DropDownItemClicked event that fires when any of the items in the DropDownItems collection is clicked.

■**Tip** Often, you won't handle the DropDownItemClicked event, which fires when any item in the submenu is clicked. Instead, you'll create separate event handlers that respond to the ToolStripItem.Click event of each menu item. This helps keep your user interface code more encapsulated. For example, it allows you to easily add new menu items and move them between menus without needing to change your code.

The ToolStripMenuItem

The ToolStripMenuItem represents a command in a menu. It renders differently depending on whether it's part of a submenu, or a top-level menu item in a MenuStrip control. When it's in a submenu, the ToolStripMenuItem renders a margin on the left where thumbnail images are displayed for each command (if supplied).

The ToolStripMenuItem derives from the ToolStripDropDownItem, which means you can create a submenu by adding items to the ToolStripMenuItem.Items collection. The ToolStripMenuItem also adds properties for managing shortcut keys and for supporting checked menu items and MDI (Multiple Document Interface) applications. You'll learn more about MDI menu merging and window lists in Chapter 19. Table 14-6 has the full details.

Table 14-6. *ToolStripMenuItem Members*

Member	Description
Checked	If true, a check mark is shown in the margin to the left of the menu item. Keep in mind that you can't simultaneously use check marks and images because they are both displayed in the same margin space. If you do, the image will overwrite the check mark.
CheckOnClick	If true, the check mark is automatically switched on or off when the user selects the menu item.
CheckedChanged event	Handle this event to respond when the item is checked or unchecked.
IsMdiWindowListEntry	Returns true if this is an autocreated menu item that's part of a MDI window list. You'll learn about this feature in Chapter 19.
ShortcutKeys	Specifies the shortcut key, using a combination of values from the Keys enumeration. For example, set this to Keys.Control | Keys.N if you want the key sequence Ctrl+N to activate this command automatically.
ShowShortcutKeys	If true, the shortcut key is automatically displayed at the right of the menu item, and right-justified.
ShortcutKeyDisplayString	If ShowShortcutKeys is true and a value is supplied for ShortcutKeyDisplayString, this value is used instead of the shortcut key. For example, if you want the shortcut key text to appear as Ctrl+Shift+N instead of the default Shift+Ctrl+N, you can use this property.

■**Tip** You also can use quick-access keys (called *mnemonics*) with a menu item. Simply add the ampersand character before the access key (as in E&xit, which makes "x" the access key).

If the menu grows too large to fit the current screen resolution, scroll buttons are automatically added to the top and bottom. Here's an example that tests this feature by adding a series of menu items, one for each font installed on the computer:

```
private void stripMenu_Load(object sender, EventArgs e)
{
    // Create the font collection.
    InstalledFontCollection fontFamilies = new InstalledFontCollection();

    // Iterate through all font families.
    foreach (FontFamily family in fontFamilies.Families)
    {
        try
        {
            // Create a ToolStripMenuItem that will display text in this font.
            ToolStripMenuItem item = new ToolStripMenuItem(family.Name);
            item.Font = new Font(family, 8);

            mnuFont.DropDownItems.Add(item);
        }
        catch
        {
            // An error will occur if the selected font does
            // not support normal style (the default used when
            // creating a Font object). This problem can be
            // harmlessly ignored.
        }
    }
}
```

Figure 14-14 shows the result.

Figure 14-14. *Scroll buttons in a long menu*

Multicolumn Menus

Interestingly, the drop-down menu exposed by the ToolStripDropDownItem is a complete, independent ToolStrip. You can get a reference to this sub-ToolStrip through the ToolStripDropDownItem.DropDown property. Technically, this is an instance of a ToolStrip-derived class, with the confusingly similar name ToolStripDropDown. The ToolStripDropDownItem makes this child ToolStrip available through the ToolStripDropDownItem.DropDown property.

This opens up some interesting possibilities. For example, you can change the ToolStrip.Opacity property to create a semi-transparent drop-down menu. Here's how:

```
toolStripDropDownButton1.DropDown.Opacity = 0.5;
```

Or, you could create a multicolumn table layout as shown here:

```
// Create a new drop-down menu.
ToolStripDropDown menu = new ToolStripDropDown();

// Copy the existing items.
ToolStripItem[] items =
  new ToolStripItem[fileToolStripMenuItem.DropDown.Items.Count];
fileToolStripMenuItem.DropDown.Items.CopyTo(items, 0);

// Transfer the items into the drop-down menu.
foreach (ToolStripItem item in items)
{
    if (!(item is ToolStripSeparator)) menu.Items.Add(item);
}

// Adjust the layout of the new menu.
menu.LayoutStyle = ToolStripLayoutStyle.Table;
 ((TableLayoutSettings)menu.LayoutSettings).ColumnCount = 2;

// Attach it to the File menu.
fileToolStripMenuItem.DropDown = menu;
```

Figure 14-15 shows the result.

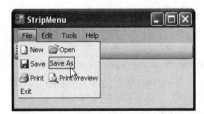

Figure 14-15. *A menu with two columns*

A Main Menu

Now that you've learned how to create a drop-down menu in a ToolStrip, you know almost everything you need to know to create main menus and context menus. Both controls use a similar set of ToolStripMenuItem objects. The only difference is the top-level container.

To create a main menu, you begin by adding a MenuStrip to your form. It's usually enough to dock the MenuStrip to the top of your window, above any other docked ToolStrip objects. However, the MenuStrip can be placed in a ToolStripContainer so that you can place a ToolStrip and MenuStrip side by side, and you can drag a MenuStrip from one place to another (as you can in Microsoft Office). However, by default the MainMenu.GripStyle property is set to Hidden and the MenuStrip is fixed in place. The Stretch property is also set to true so the menu expands to the full width of the window.

By default, when you add a MenuStrip to your form, Visual Studio sets the Form.MainMenuStrip property to point to your menu. By taking this step, your MenuStrip is assigned to be the form's main menu, which means it responds to the Alt key. However, it is valid (although unusual) for a form to have more than one MenuStrip. In this case, although all menus are displayed, only the Form.MainMenuStrip can handle the Alt key (and only one menu will use the MDI menu merging feature described in Chapter 19).

Once you've added the MenuStrip, you must create the menu structure by adding ToolStripMenuItem objects. One difference between the MenuStrip and the ToolStrip is the fact that the top-level menu headings in the MenuStrip are all ToolStripMenuItem objects. In fact, *every* menu item in a MenuStrip is a ToolStripMenuItem. You don't use the ToolStripDropDownButton or ToolStripSplitButton.

Figure 14-16 shows a basic main menu.

Figure 14-16. *The default rendering for a MenuStrip*

■**Tip** You can quickly create a standard menu with commonly used menu commands using the Insert Standard Items link from the MenuStrip smart tag.

The MenuStrip derives from ToolStrip. Although it tweaks the rendering, it adds only two new members: the MenuActivate and MenuDeactive events. MenuActivate fires when the menu is opened using the mouse or keyboard, and MenuDeactivate fires when it closes. This event isn't terribly useful because it fires for any menu in the ToolStrip. ToolStripMenuItem events like DropDownOpening and DropDownClosing (for submenus) and Click (for individual menu items) are more useful.

There's one possible point of confusion with the MenuStrip. Because the MenuStrip derives from ToolStrip, it provides an Items collection that contains the top-level menu entries (like File, Edit, Tools, Help, and so on). Each of these entries is represented by a ToolStripMenuItem instance. The items inside each menu (like the New, Open, and Close commands in the File menu) are also ToolStripMenuItem objects. However, because ToolStripMenuItem derives from ToolStripDropDownMenuItem, the name of this collection changes, and these items are stored in the ToolStripMenuItem.DropDownItems collection. Figure 14-17 shows this organization.

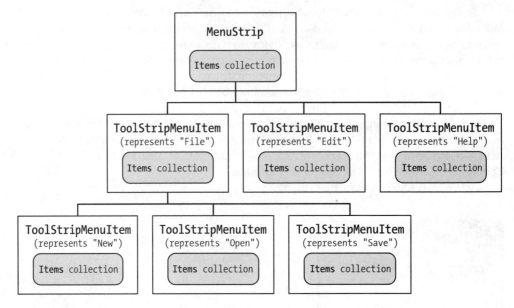

Figure 14-17. *The object model for a simple menu*

When you add a MenuStrip to a form, the Form.MenuStrip property is automatically set to point to that MenuStrip object. You probably won't need to use this property in your code (because the menu is already defined as a member variable of your form class), but it's required to support menu keyboard commands and MDI menu merging (which you'll see in Chapter 19).

■**Note** Unlike the legacy MainMenu control, when you add a MenuStrip to a form it's inserted into the Forms.Controls collection like any other ToolStrip or control. The MenuStrip also uses the client area of the form (whereas the MainMenu used the nonclient area). This gives you more options—for example, you can place other controls on top of the MenuStrip, you can add several MenuStrip controls to the same form, or you can add a MenuStrip to another container, like a Panel.

A Context Menu

Applications use two kinds of menus—main menus and context menus. Context menus are "pop up" menus that provide additional options, usually when the user right-clicks a part of the window.

In .NET 2.0, you model context menus using the ContextMenuStrip class, which derives from ToolStripDropDownMenu. When you add a ContextMenuStrip object to your form, it appears in the component tray. When you select the menu, it appears at the top of the form and you can design it in the same way as a MenuStrip for the main menu.

At runtime, your ContextMenuStrip won't appear. You have two choices to display it. The easiest approach is to associate it with another control by setting the Control.ContextMenuStrip property to your ContextMenuStrip object. When the user right-clicks the control, your context menu appears automatically.

Using a control's ContextMenu property is really just a convenience. You can display a context menu at any time, in response to any event using the ContextMenuStrip.Show() method. Here's an example that opens a context menu when the user right-clicks a control, just as if you set the Control.ContextMenuStrip property:

```
private void listBox_MouseUp(object sender, MouseEventArgs e)
{
    if (e.Button == MouseButtons.Right)
    {
        contextMenuStrip1.Show((Control)sender, e.X, e.Y);
    }
}
```

Sometimes, you might want to show a subset of a main menu in a context menu. Unfortu-nately, there's no way to set this up at design time. Even at runtime, your options are limited. You can't copy ToolStripMenuItem objects from one menu, because a ToolStripMenuItem can be a member of only one menu (and when you add it to another, it's removed from the first). There's also no Clone() method to allow you to duplicate entries with their event handlers intact. However, you can respond to the Opening event to copy a set of items into a context menu, and then react to Closed to copy them back the main menu.

■**Tip** For an example that shows how you could create a custom ToolStripMenuItem control that *does* support cloning, check out `http://blogs.msdn.com/jfoscoding/articles/475177.aspx`.

In many scenarios, you'll have a single context menu that you bind to several controls. In this situation, you'll probably want to tailor the menu depending on which control currently has focus. For example, you might choose to hide or disable certain options. This process is easy thanks to the ContextMenuStrip.SourceControl property, which always returns a reference to the control that was just clicked to display the context menu. You can examine the SourceControl property just before the menu is shown by reacting to the ContextMenuStrip. Opening event. You can test for specific controls by comparing the SourceControl reference to the corresponding member variable, or you can test the type of control based on class, as shown here:

```
private void contextMenuStrip_Opening(object sender, CancelEventArgs e)
{
    // Enable everything.
    foreach (ToolStripItem item in contextMenuStrip.Items)
    {
        item.Visible = true;
    }
```

```
    // Disable what isn't appropriate.
    if (contextMenuStrip.SourceControl is Label)
    {
        mnuCut.Visible = false;
        mnuPaste.Visible = false;
    }
}
```

ToolStrip Customization

Now that you've mastered the essentials of the ToolStrip, you're ready to consider a few more advanced scenarios. In this section, you'll have a tour of a variety of different ways to extend the ToolStrip, from fine-tuning the behavior of the overflow menu to creating your own ToolStripItem classes.

Hosting Other Controls in the ToolStrip

Sometimes, you'll want to put controls other than buttons and labels in a ToolStrip. The ToolStripControlHost makes this feat easy. You simply create a new instance of a ToolStripControlHost and pass any Control-derived class in the constructor. You can then add the ToolStripControlHost to the ToolStrip.

Here's an example that uses this technique to add a DateTimePicker to a ToolStrip:

```
DateTimePicker dt = new DateTimePicker();
dt.Value = DateTime.Now;
dt.Format = DateTimePickerFormat.Short;
ToolStripControlHost item = new ToolStripControlHost(dt);
toolStrip.Items.Add(item);
```

■**Tip** If you want to slot the new ToolStripControlHost into a specific place in an existing ToolStrip, use the Insert() method instead of Add(). This allows you to supply an index number for the position.

Because the ToolStripControlHost.AutoSize property is set to true by default, the ToolStripItem automatically fits the exact size of the hosted control. Depending on the control you're hosting, you may need to set its BackgroundColor to Color.Transparent to make it look respectable. You may also need to set the AutoSize property to true to make sure its bounds are only as large as its content.

Figure 14-18 shows an example of a hosted control sandwiched between two ordinary buttons.

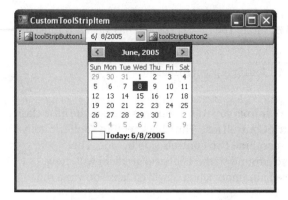

Figure 14-18. *A DateTimePicker in a ToolStrip*

There are a few minor disadvantages to using the ToolStripControlHost:

- You can add only a single control. However, there's a workaround. If you want to place an arrangement with more than one control, you need to create a container control (like a Panel or UserControl) that has these controls. Then, use that container in the ToolStripControlHost.

- You need to create it and add the control to your ToolStrip programmatically because there's no design-time support. However, you can easily derive a custom ToolStripItem from ToolStripControlHost (as explained in the next section).

- You don't have strongly typed access to the hosted control. You need to cast the ToolStripControlHost.Control property to the right type to get access to control-specific members.

The ToolStripControlHost does one very smart thing—it provides numerous members that wrap basic properties and events from the Control class members. That means you can access properties like Text, Font, and ForeColor, and events like GotFocus, LostFocus, and KeyPress for the hosted control. If you need something more specific, you need to cast the Control property.

Here's an example of both approaches:

```
MessageBox.Show("The current date is " + item.Text);
MessageBox.Show("The current date format is " +
  ((DateTimePicker)item.Control).Format.ToString());
```

.NET includes a rich set of controls that complement the ToolStrip. With the ToolStripControlHost you have the ability to use any control or combination of controls to create custom menu items, toolbar buttons, and tool windows.

Creating a Custom ToolStripItem

If you want to improve the design-time support and add strongly typed properties to your item, there's an easy answer—just create a custom ToolStripItem class that derives from ToolStripControlHost.

To use this approach, you begin by deriving your custom ToolStripItem. In this example, the ToolStripItem renders itself as a CheckBox followed by a TextBox. The CheckBox must be checked to type into the TextBox.

```
public class CheckTextBoxToolStripItem : ToolStripControlHost
{ ... }
```

Next, you use constructor to create the controls you want, and pass them to the base class constructor, thereby initializing the ToolStripControlHost. The CheckTextBoxToolStripItem uses a FlowLayoutPanel as an easy way to combine two controls side by side. The FlowLayoutPanel is given a transparent background so the ToolStrip gradient will show through, and the CheckBox is set to size itself automatically so it will collapse down to the smallest possible width.

```
// Controls in this item.
private FlowLayoutPanel controlPanel;
private CheckBox chk = new CheckBox();
private TextBox txt = new TextBox();

public CheckTextBoxToolStripItem() : base(new FlowLayoutPanel())
{
    // Set up the FlowLayouPanel.
    controlPanel = (FlowLayoutPanel)base.Control;
    controlPanel.BackColor = Color.Transparent;

    // Add two child controls.
    chk.AutoSize = true;
    controlPanel.Controls.Add(chk);
    controlPanel.Controls.Add(txt);
}
```

Now you need to add properties, methods, and events to wrap the members of the hosted control. You can do this in almost exactly the same way as in the user control examples demonstrated in Chapter 10.

In this example, a single TextEnabled property wraps the CheckBox.Checked property:

```
public bool TextEnabled
{
    get { return chk.Checked; }
    set { chk.Checked = value; }
}
```

Finally, it's important to attach event handlers to any events in the hosted control that you need to intercept. Although you could perform this step in the constructor, the ToolStripControlHost has two dedicated methods that make it easy—OnSubscribeControlEvents and OnUnsubscribeControlEvents.

The CheckTextBox handles the CheckBox.CheckedChange event to update the state of the TextBox:

```
protected override void OnSubscribeControlEvents(Control control)
{
    base.OnSubscribeControlEvents(control);
    chk.CheckedChanged += new EventHandler(CheckedChanged);
}

protected override void OnUnsubscribeControlEvents(Control control)
{
    base. OnUnsubscribeControlEvents(control);
    chk.CheckedChanged -= new EventHandler(CheckedChanged);
}

private void CheckedChanged(object sender, EventArgs e)
{
    // Enable or disable the TextBox according to the
    // current CheckBox selection.
    txt.Enabled = TextEnabled;
}
```

■**Tip** If you need to put a ProgressBar, TextBox, or ComboBox into a ToolStrip, .NET already includes ToolStripControlHost-derived items that wrap these controls. These are the ToolStripComboBox, ToolStripTextBox, and ToolStripProgressBar.

Design-Time Support for a Custom ToolStripItem

The real miracle is how easily your custom ToolStripControlHost can plug into the design-time ToolStrip architecture. All you need to do is carry out a few simple steps.

First, add a reference to the System.dll assembly. Next, import the System.Windows. Forms.Design namespace. Now you can use the ToolStripItemDesignerAvailability attribute to specify what types of ToolStrip-derived classes your custom item supports. Because you've derived from ToolStripControlHost, which doesn't appear at design time at all, the default visibility of your class is none. Here's a quick change that allows your custom ToolStripItem to be added to a ToolStrip or StatusStrip at design time:

```
[ToolStripItemDesignerAvailability(ToolStripItemDesignerAvailability.ToolStrip |
 ToolStripItemDesignerAvailability.StatusStrip)]
public class CheckTextBoxToolStripItem : ToolStripControlHost
{ ... }
```

Finally, just rebuild your application and click the Edit Items link in the ToolStrip smart tag. At the bottom of the list of options, you'll see your newly created class (see Figure 14-19).

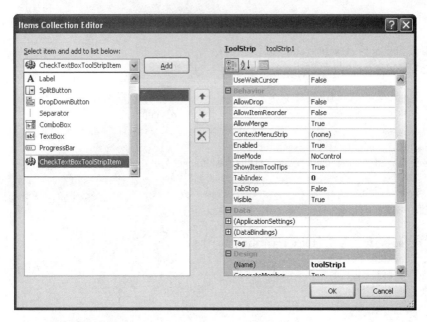

Figure 14-19. *Adding a custom ToolStripItem at design time*

Once you add your custom ToolStripItem, you can configure it in the Properties window. All the design-time skills you learned in Chapter 13 still apply. That means you can use attributes to customize the default gear icon, add descriptions for your properties, control how property values are serialized, and so on.

This integration makes it effortless to create custom ToolStripItem objects with design-time integration for menus, toolbars, and status bars. In fact, this model is so easy and elegant, it's hard not to wish for something comparable to give you design-time support for custom items in other collection-base controls, like the TreeView and ListView.

Tip If you want to set a custom item for your ToolStripItem, just use the ToolboxBitmap attribute, which is described in Chapter 13.

Creating an Owner-Drawn ToolStripItem

The design-time integration of custom ToolStripItem classes isn't limited to those that wrap other Windows Forms controls. In fact, you can create an owner-drawn ToolStripItem by deriving directly from ToolStripItem or ToolStripButton and overriding the OnPaint() method.

```
public class CustomToolStripButton : ToolStripButton
{
    protected override void OnPaint(PaintEventArgs pe)
    {
        pe.Graphics.Clear(Color.Red);
    }
}
```

Once again, you can add the ToolStripItemDesignerAvailability attribute to configure design-time support. Without it, the design time support of your class is based on the class you derive from, so if you derive from ToolStripButton, your custom item will appear in all the same designers as ToolStripButton.

In some cases, you might want to render with some of the normal rendering support, but add additional content. For example, you might use this technique to add custom-drawn content to a ToolStripItem while keeping the standard gradient background used by the rest of the ToolStrip. To accomplish this, you need to access the renderer for the current ToolStrip and then call one of its public methods, depending on what item you want to draw. For example, here's a custom-drawn item that uses the background that's being rendered for the rest of the ToolStrip where it's located.

```
public class CustomToolStripButton : ToolStripButton
{
    protected override void OnPaint(PaintEventArgs pe)
    {
        Parent.Renderer.DrawButtonBackground(
          new ToolStripItemRenderEventArgs(pe.Graphics,this));

        pe.Graphics.DrawEllipse(Pens.Blue, 0, 0, this.Width, this.Height);
        pe.Graphics.FillEllipse(Brushes.Yellow, 0, 0, this.Width, this.Height);
    }
}
```

You'll learn more about renderers and the methods they provide later in this chapter.

Taking Control of Overflow Menus

As you saw at the beginning of this chapter (in Figure 14-1), the ToolStrip uses an overflow menu when there isn't enough room to show all the buttons at once. By default, items are dropped off the end of the ToolStrip and added into the overflow menu. But more sophisticated programs that use overflow menus (like Microsoft Office) take a different approach—they selectively eliminate commands that are deemed to be less important. You can implement the same sort of logic with the .NET ToolStrip. In fact, there are several options, depending on how much control you want.

At the highest level, you can prevent items from being placed in an overflow menu by setting the ToolStripItem.Overflow to Never (the default value is AsNeeded). A ToolStripItem configured in this way will remain on the ToolStrip as other AsNeeded items are dropped into the overflow menu. If there are several items set to not overflow and the ToolStrip can't accommodate all of them, the items just won't appear at all. You have one other choice—if you set ToolStripItem.Overflow to Always the item will remain permanently in the overflow menu, regardless of how much space there is.

In some situations, you might want even more fine-grained control. For example, maybe you want to show image and text buttons when space allows, but remove the text captions when the ToolStrip shrinks to prevent the need for an overflow menu. The basic technique is to react to the ToolStrip.LayoutCompleted event, which fires after all the items have been arranged and the overflow menu has been created. You then have two possibilities for determining what items overflowed.

Your first option is to check the ToolStrip.OverflowButton property to get access to the overflow menu. You can test its HasDropDownItems property to check whether there is anything in the overflow menu. Alternatively, you can loop through the ToolStrip.Items collection (which still contains all the items) and check the ToolStripItem.Placement property of each item. If it returns ToolStripItemPlacement.Overflow, this item has been relocated to the overflow menu.

This task is conceptually quite straightforward, although in practice the code can become quite convoluted. The following example implements a basic approach to custom overflow menus. If possible, it tries to fit all buttons with text and images. If that doesn't work, it takes the first button on the right and switches the display style to text-only. As the ToolStrip continues to shrink, it removes all the images one-by-one. If you shrink the ToolStrip beyond this point, it starts switching the text-only buttons to the even more compact image-only display (see Figure 14-20). The same logic unfolds in reverse when you expand the ToolStrip.

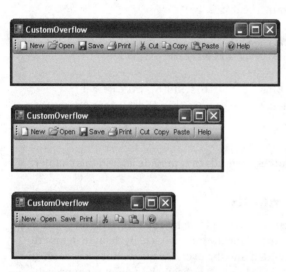

Figure 14-20. *Advanced ToolStrip configuration at runtime*

To implement this design, you need to handle two ToolStrip events: Layout and LayoutCompleted. The LayoutCompleted event fires when the layout has been finished and the overflow menu has been created. At this point, you can check to see if an overflow menu exists. If it does, you can try selectively reducing the buttons to a smaller display format.

```
private void toolStripOverflow_LayoutCompleted(object sender, EventArgs e)
{
    // Check if the overflow menu is in use.
    if (toolStrip1.OverflowButton.HasDropDownItems)
    {
```

```
        // Step backwards.
        for (int i = toolStrip1.Items.Count - 1; i >= 0; i--)
        {
            ToolStripItem item = toolStrip1.Items[i];
            if (!(item is ToolStripSeparator))
            {
                if (item.DisplayStyle == ToolStripItemDisplayStyle.ImageAndText)
                {
                    item.DisplayStyle = ToolStripItemDisplayStyle.Text;
                    return;
                }
            }
        }
        // If we reached here, all buttons are shrunk to text.
        // Try reducing them further.
        for (int i = toolStrip1.Items.Count-1; i >= 0; i--)
        {
            ToolStripItem item = toolStrip1.Items[i];
            if (!(item is ToolStripSeparator))
            {
                if (item.DisplayStyle == ToolStripItemDisplayStyle.Text)
                {
                    item.DisplayStyle = ToolStripItemDisplayStyle.Image;
                    return;
                }
            }
        }
        // If we reach here, the bar is fully collapsed.
    }
}
```

The Layout event fires at the beginning of the resize process. At this point, you can attempt to expand the ToolStrip if space allows. Here's the code:

```
private void toolStripOverflow_Layout(object sender, LayoutEventArgs e)
{
    if (toolStrip1.DisplayRectangle.Width > MeasureToolStrip())
    {
        // Right now everything fits.
        // Check if a larger size is appropriate.
        foreach (ToolStripItem item in toolStrip1.Items)
        {
            if (!(item is ToolStripSeparator))
            {
```

```
                    // Look to expand any image-only buttons.
                    if (item.DisplayStyle == ToolStripItemDisplayStyle.Image)
                    {
                        item.DisplayStyle = ToolStripItemDisplayStyle.Text;
                        return;
                    }
                }
            }
        }
        // If we reach here, there are no image-only buttons.
        // Look to expand any text-only buttons.
        foreach (ToolStripItem item in toolStrip1.Items)
        {
            if (!(item is ToolStripSeparator))
            {
                if (item.DisplayStyle == ToolStripItemDisplayStyle.Text)
                {
                    item.DisplayStyle = ToolStripItemDisplayStyle.ImageAndText;
                    return;
                }
            }
        }
        // If we reach here, the bar is fully expanded.
    }
}
```

Although this design works, it does have a few idiosyncrasies. It the user jerks the border quickly enough, the ToolStrip size can be collapsed dramatically without the Layout and LayoutCompleted events firing enough times to update all the buttons. The result is that all the buttons won't be resized and an overflow menu will be present. A more sophisticated implementation would need to calculate the available space and determine which buttons to expand, and it would take dramatically more code.

Allowing Runtime Customization

In applications like Microsoft Office, the toolbars are highly customizable. You can switch toolbars into a design mode, and then rearrange and remove items. You've already seen how you can use a ToolStripContainer to let users rearrange ToolStrip objects. It's also no stretch of the imagination to design a menu that allows users to selectively show and hide specific ToolStrips. But what about customizing the buttons on a single ToolStrip?

It turns out that the ToolStrip has a minimal level of built-in support for runtime customization. If you set ToolStrip.AllowItemReorder to true, the user can rearrange items on a ToolStrip by holding down the Alt key, and clicking and dragging the items to a new position. Although this process works quite well, it's completely uncustomizable. You can't change the hotkey, programmatically switch into reorder, or allow reorder of just certain buttons. The reorder feature also won't allow a user to drag an item off a ToolStrip, or move it from one ToolStrip to another. You might think you could add these features, but unfortunately the model is locked up tight. When the user holds down Alt to begin reordering items, the ToolStrip blows right past events like MouseDown and ItemClicked, so there's no way for your code to get involved.

■**Note** You can still handle events like DragDrop and DragEnter to allow the user to drag other types of items onto a ToolStrip.

If you're happy with the reordering functionality, you'll be pleased to find that there's built-in support for persisting and restoring the order of items in a ToolStrip. This functionality comes from the ToolStripManager, which is a helper class that you'll use later in this chapter to implement custom rendering. The ToolStripManager also includes static methods for a few other tasks, like searching for a specific ToolStrip, or merging the buttons on separate ToolStrip instances.

The ToolStripManager works on a form-by-form basis, using the static SaveSettings() and LoadSettings() methods. To save the settings for all the reordered ToolStrip objects on a form, you supply a reference to the form and a key name:

```
ToolStripManager.SaveSettings(this, this.Name);
```

To restore the settings, you can use this code:

```
ToolStripManager.LoadSettings(this, this.Name);
```

Settings are stored in an automatically generated user-specific directory in a subfolder of c:\Documents and Settings\[userName]\Local Settings\Application Data.

If the built-in ToolStrip customization features don't fit your needs, you may want to implement a dedicated dialog box for adding, removing, and rearranging the items in a ToolStrip. The Windows Forms team has made an interesting customization sample available that creates a dialog box that's quite similar to the one used in Office applications (see Figure 14-21).

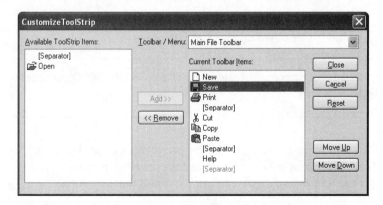

Figure 14-21. *Advanced ToolStrip configuration at runtime*

The code for this dialog box is quite lengthy, but it provides an impressive level of features, with support for multiple toolbar editing, canceling, and requesting the full set of allowed menu items from the client program. The complete code for this component is available with the downloadable code samples for this chapter.

Customizing the ToolStrip Rendering

The ToolStrip uses a completely different rendering model than other controls that support owner drawing. Although the ToolStripItem does provide an OnPaint() method that can perform custom painting, by default a separate renderer class does all the work. The renderer paints the text and image content, and other details like the gradient background to the sizing grips, high-lighting, and drop-down buttons.

Here's how it works. The ToolStripRenderer defines an abstract base class for all renderers. To create a renderer, you simply need to derive from ToolStripRenderer and override its various methods. In fact, .NET includes two renderer classes that derive from ToolStripRenderer:

- **ToolStripSystemRenderer.** This renderer paints the ToolStrip according to operating system settings and colors.

- **ToolStripProfessionalRenderer.** This renderer paints the ToolStrip with a slick Office XP-style look and support for Windows XP themes.

You have several options for choosing the renderer that's active for a given ToolStrip. For absolute control, you can programmatically set the ToolStrip.Renderer property to the renderer object you want to use. This gives you the flexibility to individually configure each ToolStrip, StatusStrip, and MenuStrip to use a different renderer. Here's an example:

```
toolStrip1.Renderer = new ToolStripSystemRenderer();
```

You can set the renderer for a drop-down submenu, but the syntax is a little different. There is no Renderer property in the ToolStripDropDownItem itself, because the ToolStripDropDownItem is rendered according to the renderer that the parent ToolStrip uses, like all ToolStripItems. However, you can use the ToolStripDropDownItem. DropDown.Renderer property to set the renderer for just the drop-down items:

```
toolStripDropDownItem1.DropDown.Renderer = new ToolStripSystemRenderer();
```

■**Tip** If you don't explicitly set the drop-down renderer, the renderer from the top-level container automatically cascades down to any submenus.

The ToolStrip isn't the only class with a RenderMode property. You also need to set the RenderMode of the panels in a ToolStripContainer if you want the renderer to paint the appropriate type of background. Here's an example that changes just one of the five panels:

```
toolStripContainer.LeftToolStripPanel.Renderer = new ToolStripSystemRenderer();
```

Of course, in an application with dozens of different ToolStrip and ToolStripContainer objects, it doesn't make much sense to create new renderer instances for each one. To simplify life, the ToolStrip adds the RenderMode property, which springs into effect if the Renderer property isn't set.

```
toolStrip.RenderMode = ToolStripRenderMode.System;
```

The RenderMode property accepts one of three values, as detailed in Table 14-7.

Table 14-7. *RenderMode Values (from the ToolStripRenderMode Enumeration)*

Member	Description
Professional	The ToolStrip uses a common instance of the ToolStripProfessionalRenderer.
System	The ToolStrip uses a common instance of the ToolStripSystemRenderer.
Custom	The rendering work is performed by the renderer set in the Renderer property. You can't set a RenderMode of Custom directly; instead, the ToolStrip sets it when you supply a custom renderer.
ManagerRenderMode	The work is offloaded to a helper class called the ToolStripManager, which supplies the right renderer.

By default, every ToolStrip and MenuStrip you create has a RenderMode of Manager and uses the ToolStripManager. The StatusStrip and ToolStripContentPanel have a default RenderMode of System.

■**Tip** The ToolStripPanel (used for the sides of the ToolStripContainer) and the ToolStripContentPanel (used for the center region of the ToolStripContainer) also provide the Renderer and RenderMode properties, allowing you to customize how their background is painted in the same ways you customize the ToolStrip itself.

The ToolStripManager

The ToolStripManager allows you to set a renderer that will be used by multiple ToolStrip objects in your application. This gives you the ability to transform the look of your entire interface by modifying a single line code. Figure 14-22 shows this model.

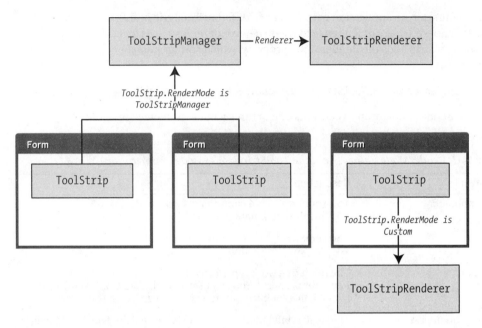

Figure 14-22. *How the ToolStripManager interacts with the ToolStrip*

The model is actually quite simple. The ToolStripManager provides three static properties that deal with rendering: the familiar Renderer and RenderMode properties, and a Boolean VisualStylesEnabled property. (If you turn off visual styles, the renderer will use the default system colors instead of the XP theme colors.) At any time, you can modify either the RenderMode or the Renderer property. When you do, all objects that use a RenderMode of ToolStripManager are updated immediately.

Figure 14-23 shows an example where you can dynamically switch renderers and the entire form is updated.

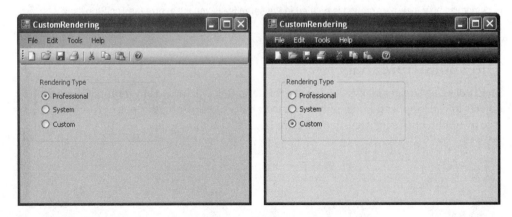

Figure 14-23. *Changing the renderer dynamically*

Here's the straightforward code that makes it work:

```
private void optPro_CheckedChanged(object sender, EventArgs e)
{
    ToolStripManager.RenderMode = ToolStripManagerRenderMode.Professional;
}

private void optSys_CheckedChanged(object sender, EventArgs e)
{
    ToolStripManager.RenderMode = ToolStripManagerRenderMode.System;
}

private void optCust_CheckedChanged(object sender, EventArgs e)
{
    ToolStripManager.Renderer = new CustomRenderer();
}
```

The only detail this example doesn't show is how the CustomRenderer class was built. You'll explore that topic in the next section.

■**Note** The ToolStripManager.RenderMode property is not identical to the ToolStrip.RenderMode property. Technically, it uses the ToolStripManagerRenderMode enumeration rather than the ToolStripRenderMode enumeration. The only difference is the ManagerRenderMode option is left out (because it doesn't apply).

Customizing a Renderer

There are two approaches to creating a custom renderer. You can derive from one of the existing renderers, or you can derive from the abstract ToolStripRenderer class. Either way, you need to override only the methods that have the functionality you want to change.

Table 14-8 lists the methods you can override.

Table 14-8. *Overridable Methods in the ToolStripRenderer*

Method	Description
OnRenderToolStripBackground	Draws the basic background for the entire ToolStrip.
OnRenderToolStripBorder	Draws the border around the ToolStrip.
OnRenderItemBackground	Draws the background of a ToolStripItem (over which its content is superimposed). This is used only if the more-specific background-rendering methods don't apply to this item.
OnRenderButtonBackground	Draws the background for a ToolStripButton.
OnRenderDropDownButtonBackground	Draws the background for a ToolStripDropDownButton.

Table 14-8. *Overridable Methods in the ToolStripRenderer (Continued)*

Method	Description
OnRenderSplitButtonBackground	Draws the background for a ToolStripSplitButton.
OnRenderLabelBackground	Draws the background for a ToolStripLabel.
OnRenderToolStripStatusLabelBackground	Draws the background for a ToolStripStatusLabel.
OnRenderMenuItemBackground	Draws the background for a ToolStripMenuItem.
OnRenderOverflowButtonBackground	Draws the background for an overflow button.
OnRenderItemImage	Draws an image on a ToolStripItem.
OnRenderItemText	Draws text a ToolStripItem.
OnRenderSeparator	Draws a ToolStripSeparator.
OnRenderGrip	Draws the grip handle for moving a ToolStrip.
OnRenderStatusStripSizingGrip	Draws the window-sizing grip shown at the corner of a StatusStrip.
OnRenderArrow	Draws the drop-down arrow used on some items.
OnRenderItemCheck	Draws an image on a ToolStripItem that indicates the item is in a selected state.
OnRenderImageMargin	Draws the shaded margin where an image is placed (usually next to a menu item).
OnRenderToolStripContentPanelBackground	Draws the background for the content panels in a ToolStripContainer.
OnRenderToolStripPanelBackground	Draws the background for one of the side panels in a ToolStripContainer.

For example, the following custom renderer changes the background of the whole ToolStrip and the background of all ToolStripButton items. Notice that this code needs to account for whether the button is currently highlighted.

```
public class CustomRenderer : ToolStripRenderer
{
    protected override void OnRenderToolStripBackground(
      ToolStripRenderEventArgs e)
    {
        LinearGradientBrush brush = new LinearGradientBrush(e.AffectedBounds,
          Color.DarkGray, Color.Black, 90);
        e.Graphics.FillRectangle(brush, e.AffectedBounds);
        brush.Dispose();
    }
```

```
protected override void OnRenderButtonBackground(
  ToolStripItemRenderEventArgs e)
{
    // Check if the item is selected or hovered over.
    if (e.Item.Selected || e.Item.Pressed)
    {
        LinearGradientBrush brush = new LinearGradientBrush(e.Item.Bounds,
          Color.DarkBlue,
          Color.DarkGreen, 90);
          e.Graphics.FillRectangle(brush, 0, 0, e.Item.Width, e.Item.Height);
    }
}
...
```

The drawing code uses various gradients, and darkens the overall color scheme considerably. To compensate, the renderer also changes the way text is drawn, switching the text color to white.

```
...
protected override void OnRenderItemText(ToolStripItemTextRenderEventArgs e)
{
    e.TextColor = Color.White;
    base.OnRenderItemText(e);
}
}
```

Note that the OnRenderItemText() is the only method that calls the base class implementation from ToolStripRenderer. As a rule of thumb, you never need to call the base class implementation unless you want to trigger the normal drawing logic. In the case of OnRenderItemText(), you can make use of a shortcut by changing the text color and then launching the normal text painting operation.

Changing the Colors of the ProfessionalToolStripRenderer

In the previous example, you saw how you can get complete rendering control by creating a custom renderer for the ToolStrip. However, in some cases a custom renderer is more than you need. For example, you might want to perform the standard drawing logic but simply tweak the colors that are used. In this case, there's a shortcut.

By default, the ToolStripProfessionalRenderer chooses colors that match the visual style settings on a Windows XP computer. If you're using the default blue scheme, that means the colors are blue and (for highlighting) orange. If the current operating system isn't Windows XP, or you've set ToolStripManager.VisualStylesEnabled property to false, you'll get back to the more familiar grey and blue system colors.

However, the ToolStripProfessionalRenderer gives you another choice. You can explicitly specify the colors when you create the ToolStripProfessionalRenderer, by supplying a color table to the constructor. Here's an example:

```
toolStrip1.Renderer = new ToolStripProfessionalRenderer(new CustomColorTable());
```

The only trick is to create the class for the color table. To do this, you simply need to derive from ProfessionalColorTable and override the properties that correspond to the colors you want to change. For example, the following CustomColorTable class changes the colors used for the basic ToolStrip gradient shown on the ToolStrip background and behind all image and text content. It doesn't change the highlight gradient colors which are used when you move the mouse over a button.

```
public class CustomColorTable : ProfessionalColorTable
{
    public override Color ToolStripGradientBegin
    { get { return Color.FromArgb(50, 50, 50); } }

    public override Color ToolStripGradientMiddle
    { get { return Color.FromArgb(60, 50, 50); } }

    public override Color ToolStripGradientEnd
    { get { return Color.LimeGreen; } }
}
```

Customizing every color in a ToolStrip can take some time. The ProfesionalColorTable class defines more than fifty color properties, all of which you can override.

The Last Word

In this chapter, you took a close look at the different strip controls provided in .NET, including the ToolStrip, StatusStrip, MenuStrip, and ContextMenuStrip. You learned how to use their many features to control formatting and layout, and how to extend the way the strip controls are drawn, how they are customized by the user, and how they use the overflow menu. The ToolStrip is one of the most impressive additions to the .NET Windows Forms toolkit. It's rivaled only by another new control—the DataGridView, which you'll explore in the next chapter.

■ ■ ■

CHAPTER 15

The DataGridView

The first two releases of the .NET Framework (.NET 1.0 and .NET 1.1) left a glaring gap in the data-binding picture. Although developers had a flexible, configurable model for linking almost any control to almost any data source, they didn't have a practical way to display full tables of information. The only tool included for this purpose was the DataGrid control, which worked well for simple demonstrations but was woefully inadequate for real-world code. Most developers found that the DataGrid was awkward to use, inflexible, and almost impossible to customize. Oddly enough, the DataGrid lagged far behind its ASP.NET counterpart, making it more difficult to display rich data-bound tables in a Windows application than in a web page.

Filling this gap is a key goal for .NET 2.0, and Microsoft's taken up the challenge with an entirely new grid control—the DataGridView. The DataGridView has two overall goals. First of all, it aims to support common tasks like master-details lists, validation, and data formatting without requiring you to write more than a few of lines of code. More importantly, it's designed from the ground up with extensibility in mind, so that you can integrate the specialized features you need without resorting to low-level hacks and "black magic" programming.

This chapter dissects the DataGridView. You'll begin by considering how it works with basic data-binding tasks, and then delve deeper into more advanced customization.

The DataGrid Legacy

Developers have been using grid controls for years. In the pre-.NET world, developers often relied on ActiveX controls like the MSFlexGrid, which provides a solid formatting model and access to individual cells. Though controls like the MSFlexGrid still can be used in .NET, they obviously can't support .NET data binding. If you want to use them, you'll need to write painstaking code to iterate through the rows of your data source and copy values into the grid.

The DataGrid was the first native .NET solution for a data-bound list control, and it's included with every version of the .NET Framework. The DataGrid has an almost deceptive appearance of simplicity—although you can bind data with a single line of code, you might need to write dozens more to accomplish a seemingly easy task like applying a custom background color to a cell. In fact, the first edition of this book included a mere seven pages of information about the DataGrid, because most developers outgrew its feature set long before they had the chance to use it in a realistic application.

Some of the limitations of the DataGrid include:

- **Limited ability to customize its appearance.** Some details, like column formatting, are fairly easy to change. Other details, like individual cell formatting, are much more challenging and require writing custom DataGridColumnStyle classes. Still other details, like formatting an entire row or modifying the appearance of table links, are nearly impossible.

- **No easy way to display pictures in cells.** Again, if you want to use this feature you'll need to implement it yourself with a custom DataGridColumnStyle class that contains dozens of lines of code.

- **Limited support for formatting text and numbers.** You can use the standard number formats, but if you need to apply a custom format—for example, "translating" a numeric status code into a text string—you're on your own.

- **Limited ability to access individual cells.** The DataGrid doesn't make it easy to change or read arbitrary cell values. Instead, you need to work through the bound data source. If you want to display information in a DataGrid *without* using data binding, you're out of luck.

- **Limited support for modifying the DataGrid programmatically.** Tasks like changing column order or adding custom button columns are impossible.

- **No ability to customize the DataGrid error messages.** If the user attempts to make an invalid edit to a cell, you're stuck with cryptic error messages provided by the .NET Framework.

For most developers, the best they could hope for was to discover these issues before committing their applications to use the DataGrid. Needless to say, the third-party control market had great success selling custom grid controls for .NET 1.0 and 1.1.

Introducing the DataGridView

The DataGridView is the .NET 2.0 answer to the DataGrid fiasco. It demonstrates what some call the traditional Microsoft approach—when the first product disappoints, keep working until the next one is perfect. And, although the DataGridView might not be perfect, it's dramatically better than the DataGrid, and it's one of the most sophisticated controls in the Windows Forms package.

Some of the enhancements you'll find in the DataGridView include:

- **Extensive visual customization.** The DataGridView won't force you to accept default formatting for your cell data, fonts, colors, or justification.

- **Performance.** The DataGridView is optimized to work faster than the DataGrid, especially when painting cells.

- **Events, events, and more events.** You can "plug in" to all of the major DataGridView operations, including sorting, filtering, validation, record insertions, and error handling. In other words, if the default behavior isn't what you want, you can code your own.

- **Programmability.** The DataGridView exposes a richer, more logical object model than the DataGrid. It gives you the ability to interact with individual cells, columns, and rows.

- **Flexible sizing.** The DataGridView includes built-in functionality to size columns according to cell contents, saving you the heavy lifting of calculating text widths for different fonts.

It's worth noting that the DataGridView isn't designed to solve every problem you might encounter displaying data. It doesn't provide the following features:

- **Spreadsheet-like behavior.** Tables and spreadsheets look similar, but they serve fundamentally different purposes and need a different set of features. For spreadsheet functionality, consider using Excel automation.

- **Reporting.** The DataGridView has no ability to format data in a rich document-like format or print its data. If you need this capability, you're better off working with Crystal Reports.

- **Hierarchical data views.** Hierarchical controls show more than one set of data and help illustrate the relationship. Some hierarchical controls use a collapsible display, while others (like the DataGrid) use link-based navigation. Unfortunately, allowing hierarchical data can complicate controls horribly, and there's no standard, one-size-fits-all representation.

Tip Though the DataGridView doesn't natively support hierarchical data, you can create forms that do. The most common approach is to use multiple DataGridView controls that work together. You'll see this technique later in this chapter with the master-details list example.

The DataGridView and Very Large Data Sources

The DataGridView is designed from the ground up to display large amounts of data efficiently, without draining away vast amounts of memory. Depending on your needs, you may need to follow certain best practices to make sure your use of the DataGridView is scalable.

The DataGridView scalability features revolve around three key concepts:

- **Shared row state.** The DataGridView automatically shares as much memory as possible between rows that have similar state. For example, if there is a large group of rows that have the same long string value in a column, the DataGridView will store only one copy of that data. Sharing is implemented automatically, but the actions you take can affect it. For example, there are numerous actions that can cause a shared row to become unshared (like accessing the object for that row directly). The MSDN Help has a full list of such actions, and you'll learn about the most common pitfalls as you consider various topics in this chapter.

- **Shared styles.** The DataGridView uses a style-based model, which allows you to define one set of formatting presets and apply them to groups of cells, entire rows, columns, or the complete DataGridView. This is much more efficient than tracking separate style information for each cell.

- **Virtual mode.** The DataGridView supports a virtual mode where data are fetched as they are needed (for example, as the user scrolls down through the grid). You can implement virtual mode in the DataGridView in much the same way that you implement it with the ListView. See Chapter 6 for a full description, or refer to the online samples for a basic demonstration.

This architecture ensures that the DataGridView won't break down when dealing with huge lists of information. Although this chapter doesn't specifically deal with large data strategies (for example, you'll probably need to develop your own custom caching mechanism), you will learn about the considerations you need to watch to make sure the DataGridView's memory use remains as compact as possible.

DATA BINDING AND THE DATA MODEL

The examples in this chapter follow the data-binding approach of Chapter 8. That means that we'll work with the Store database. However, we'll fill this database using a separate service provider component (the StoreDB class), so that the data access code can be tested and fine-tuned separately. We won't use the automatic data binding described in Chapter 8. Though it provides some design-time niceties, it's not worth sacrificing the flexibility of the service provider model. In professional applications, it's generally more important to have optimized performance, a clean component-based separation on layers, and a range of techniques to deal with errors. As a result, hand-written data access code is preferred over designer-generated data access code.

There's another hidden stumbling block that you'll face with DataGridView if you plan to use strongly typed data access code. The problem occurs when you want to manipulate individual columns in the DataGridView. To do this, you need to use the field name, which the DataGridView retrieves from your data source automatically. Here's an example:

```
DataGridView.Columns["OrderID"].ReadOnly = true;
```

This is weakly typed code, because the field name ("OrderID") is an ordinary string. A minor error in the field name won't be caught at design time—instead, it will appear as an unexpected runtime error. With additional effort, you can sidestep this problem using constants or a strongly typed DataSet (both of which are described in Chapter 8) to look up the proper field name. Here's an example:

```
DataGridView.Columns[storeDs.Orders.OrderIDColumn.ColumnName].ReadOnly = true;
```

This code is safer, but it's a little less compact. This approach isn't used in this chapter, because it can lead to confusion when you're first learning the DataGridView object model. However, you can adopt this approach in production applications to prevent errors.

Bare-Bones Data-Binding

The best way to get acquainted with the DataGridView is to try out it without configuring a single property. Just like the DataGrid, you can bind a DataTable object (or an object derived from DataTable) using the DataSource property. Here's an example that uses the StoreDB class (which is included with the online samples and discussed in Chapter 8):

```
dataGridView1.DataSource = Program.StoreDB.GetProducts();
```

Unlike the DataGrid, the DataGridView can show only a single table at a time. If you bind an entire DataSet, no data will be displayed, unless you set the DataMember property with the name of the table you want to show.

```
dataGridView1.DataSource = Program.StoreDB.GetProductsAndCategories();
dataGridView1.DataMember = "Products";
```

■**Tip** As explained in Chapter 8, binding a DataTable actually binds the linked DataView object returned by the DataTable.DefaultView property. You can use this fact to customize the sort order and filter out rows, or you can programmatically create and bind a new DataView. Additionally, the DataGridView supports binding to collections of custom objects. For example, you can use the alternate version of the StoreDB class (discussed in Chapter 8) that returns a custom ProductList object instead of an ordinary DataSet or DataTable.

The basic DataGridView is shown in Figure 15-1 with a table of order records. Its appearance follows a few straightforward rules:

- The DataGridView creates one column for each field in the data source.

- The DataGridView creates column headers using the field names. The column headers are fixed, which means they won't scroll out of view as the user moves down the list.

- The DataGridView supports Windows XP visual styles. You'll notice that the column headers have a modern flat look and become highlighted when the user moves the mouse over them.

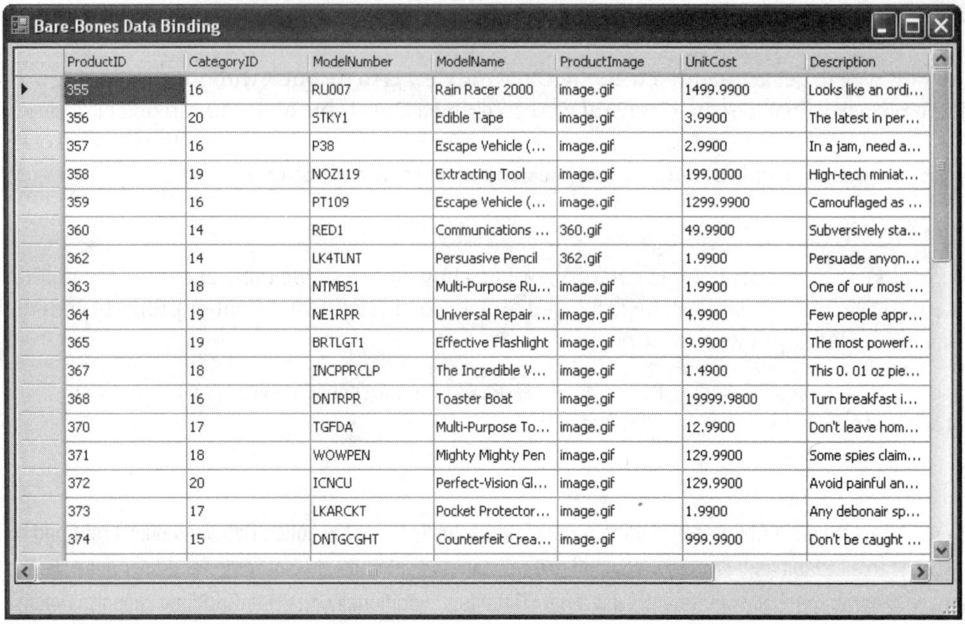

Figure 15-1. *A DataGridView with no customization*

The DataGridView also includes quite a bit of default behavior that you might not notice immediately. Here's what you'll see if you follow the simple approach shown previously to bind a DataGridView without performing any additional customization.

- The DataGridView allows different types of selection. Users can highlight one or more cells, or multiple rows or columns, by clicking and dragging. Clicking the square at the top left of the DataGridView selects the entire table.

- Using the Tab key moves you from one cell to another inside the DataGridView. To tab out of the DataGridView press Ctrl+Tab or set the StandardTab property to true, which reverses this behavior (so Ctrl+Tab moves from cell to cell, and Tab moves out of the DataGridView control).

- The DataGridView has automatic tooltips that show the full text content when the user hovers over a cell with the mouse pointer. Although this feature is quite convenient for truncated values, it can slow down performance if you have extremely large fields, in which case you'll want to set ShowCellToolTips to false.

- The DataGridView supports automatic sorting. The user can click on a column header once or twice to sort values in ascending or descending order based on the values in that field. By default, the sort takes the data type into account and is alphabetic or numeric. Alphabetic sorts are case sensitive.

- The DataGridView supports an autosizing feature. Users can double-click on the column divider between headers, and the column on the left will be automatically expanded or contracted to fit the cell content. (Users also can freely resize rows and columns by dragging on the edges of the row or column header.)

- The DataGridView allows in-place editing. To initiate editing, the user can double-click in a cell, press F2, or start typing in a new value (by typing in a letter, number, or symbol). The only exceptions are read-only properties and fields that have DataColumn. ReadOnly set to true (like the ProductID field in the current example). Similarly, the user can remove rows (by selecting the record and pressing Delete) and insert new ones (by scrolling to the blank bottom record and typing in it).

■**Note** To support sorting and in-place editing with a collection of custom objects, you need to use (or create) a collection that implements IBindingList. See Chapter 8 for details.

These basic characteristics are highly configurable. In the following sections, you'll learn how to tailor this built-in behavior. But first, it's worth taking a quick look at the DataGridView object model.

The DataGridView Objects

The DataGridView is a complex control that exposes dozens of properties, methods, and events. However, there are a few key collections that you should learn about to make the most of other features. These collections (Columns and Rows) allow you to work with the entire set of data that's displayed in the DataGridView.

The Columns property provides a collection of DataGridViewColumn objects, one for each field or property in the bound data object. The Rows property provides a collection of DataGridViewRow objects, each of which references a collection of DataGridViewCell objects with the actual data. Figure 15-2 diagrams the relationship along with three additional details—the collections that let you retrieve selection information (as described in the next section).

Generally, you'll turn to the DataGridViewColumn object to configure column display properties, formatting, and header text. You also may use it to fine-tune sizing or sorting for a specific column, or to hide a column you don't want to see in the grid (set Visible to false). You'll use the DataGridViewRow and DataGridViewCell objects to retrieve the actual data from the bound record. When you modify the data in a DataGridViewCell, it's treated in the same way as a user edit: The appropriate DataGridView change events are fired, and the underlying data source is modified.

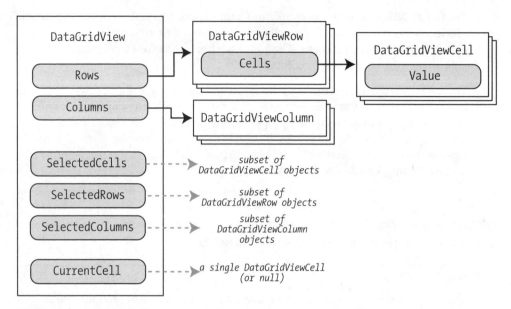

Figure 15-2. *The DataGridView objects*

The DataGridViewRow

Now that you understand the DataGridView object model, you can easily create code that iterates over the table. The following example displays the ProductID (in the debug window) of each item that has a value in the UnitCost field greater than 50.

```
foreach (DataGridViewRow row in dataGridView1.Rows)
{
    if (!row.IsNewRow && Convert.ToInt32(row.Cells["UnitCost"].Value) > 50)
    {
        // You can retrieve a field value by index position or name.
        Debug.WriteLine(row.Cells["ProductID"].Value);
    }
}
```

Note that the code needs to test the DataGridView.IsNewRow property to make sure that the blank new row placeholder (which is at the bottom of the grid) is not included in the search. If the DataGridView.AllowUserToAddRows property is false, this row won't appear and so this test isn't necessary.

There's one limitation with this code—it isn't scalable if you're working with extremely large grids. That's because iterating over the Rows collection causes each row to become *unshared*, which means it's created as a separate object with its own independent state. If you aren't binding extremely large tables of data, this isn't a consideration. However, it's rare that you need to iterate over all the rows in a DataGridView. As you'll see in this chapter, you can usually manipulate specific rows by responding to DataGridView events or calling DataGridView methods. Both of these techniques allow you to manipulate a relatively small subset of rows, thereby leaving the untouched rows in a memory-friendly shared state.

■**Note** Formatting information isn't directly stored in the DataGridViewCell, DataGridViewColumn, and DatGridViewRow objects. Instead, there's a separate style model that you'll learn about later in this chapter, which revolves around the DataGridViewCellStyle class.

The DataGridView Column

Here's a similar approach that hides all columns and then shows just the ProductID and Description column. This code performs its task by enumerating over the available DataGridViewColumn objects, and then directly accessing the desired columns by name.

```
foreach (DataGridViewColumn col in dataGridView1.Columns)
{
    col.Visible = false;
}

// You can retrieve a column by index position or name.
dataGridView1.Columns["ProductID"].Visible = true;
dataGridView1.Columns["Description"].Visible = true;
```

■**Tip** Another approach for removing columns is to use the Remove() method of the columns collection. However, setting the visible property gives you the flexibility to hide and then re-show a column.

It's worth noting that there are several different classes that derive from DataGridView-Column. These classes can control the way values are painted and edited in a cell. The .NET includes six prebuilt DataGridView column classes, which are listed in Table 15-1.

Table 15-1. *Classes Derived from DataGridViewColumn*

Class	Description	Corresponding Cell Class
DataGridViewButtonColumn	Displays text as a clickable button. You'll see this type of column used later in this chapter to create a master-details view with two forms.	DataGridViewButtonCell
DataGridViewLinkColumn	Displays text as a clickable link. The functionality of this column is similar to the DataGridViewButtonColumn.	DataGridViewLinkCell
DataGridViewCheckBoxColumn	Displays a check box. This column is automatically used for Boolean data fields.	DataGridViewCheckBoxCell

Table 15-1. *Classes Derived from DataGridViewColumn (Continued)*

Class	Description	Corresponding Cell Class
DataGridViewComboBoxColumn	Displays a drop-down list box. We'll use this type of column in a later example to restrict user selections.	DataGridViewComboBoxCell
DataGridViewImageColumn	Displays an image. We'll use this type of column later in this chapter to load custom pictures.	DataGridViewImageCell
DataGridViewTextBoxColumn	Displays plain text, and uses a text box when the user edits the cell value. This is the default column type for most fields.	DataGridViewTextBoxCell

Column Headers

Another reasonable change is to clean up the header text shown in each column. For example, the title "Order Date" looks more professional than the field name OrderDate. This change is easy enough to make. You simply need to retrieve the appropriate DataGridViewColumn from the DataGridView.Columns collection, and modify the header cell accordingly:

```
dataGridView1.Columns["OrderID"].HeaderCell.Value = "Order ID";
```

Writing this sort of code risks embedding a lot of database-specific code into your form class, which is never a good idea. One possible solution is to add read-only variables to another class with the correct field names. In some cases, an even easier alternative is possible. For example, consider the SplitStringByCase() method shown next. It splits a string into separate words by inserting a space before each new capital letter.

```
private string SplitStringByCase(string inputString)
{
    System.Text.StringBuilder sb = new System.Text.StringBuilder();

    // Add first character.
    sb.Append(inputString[0]);

    // Add middle characters. Insert space before capitals.
    for (int i = 1; i < inputString.Length - 1;  i++)
    {
        char c = inputString[i];
        // Skip existing spaces (if any).
        if (c == ' ')
        {
            sb.Append(c);
            i++;
            sb.Append(Char.ToUpper(inputString[i]));
            continue;
        }
```

```
        if (Char.IsUpper(c))
            sb.Append(" ");
        sb.Append(c);
    }

    // Add last character.
    sb.Append(inputString[inputString.Length - 1]);
    return sb.ToString();
}
```

Using this method, you can iterate over the columns of any table in the Store database and create readable header text. Here's the generic code you'll need:

```
// Clean up all the columns.
foreach (DataGridViewColumn col in dataGridView1.Columns)
{
    col.HeaderCell.Value = SplitStringByCase(col.HeaderText);
}
```

If you're looking for an even more elegant solution, you can use regular expressions through the Regex class in the System.Text.RegularExpressions. Although the regular expression you need is a little tricky to decipher, using it is extremely easy:

```
// Adjust the header text through a regular expression.
string regularExpression = @"(\p{Ll})(\p{Lu})|_+", "$1 $2";
foreach (DataGridViewColumn col in dataGridView1.Columns)
{
    col.HeaderText = Regex.Replace(col.HeaderText, regularExpression);
}
```

Creating an Unbound Grid

Now that you understand the object model of the DataGridView, you can modify the structure of any grid and even create a new grid programmatically. This latter technique is known as creating an *unbound* grid, and it's occasionally useful if you want to use the DataGridView simply as a way to display some static information that isn't represented by an existing collection or DataTable.

To create an unbound grid, you start with a blank DataGridView and begin adding the columns you need. Here's an example that adds several columns:

```
DataGridViewTextBoxColumn col1 = new DataGridViewTextBoxColumn();
col1.Name = "ProductID";
col1.HeaderText = "Product ID";
dataGridView1.Columns.Add(col1);

// The easiest way to add a column, with name and header text.
dataGridView1.Columns.Add("ModelName", "Model Name");
dataGridView1.Columns.Add("Description", "Description");
dataGridView1.Columns.Add("UnitCost", "Unit Cost");
dataGridView1.Columns["UnitCost"].ValueType = typeof(decimal);
```

Once the columns are in place, you can generate new rows. The Add() method of the rows collection makes this easy—all you need to do is supply a list of values in the correct order.

```
// Fill in a row of data (as a list of values).
dataGridView1.Rows.Add(100, "Emergency Travel Gear",
  "Be prepared for vacation disasters.", 34.44m);

// Add another row (the hard way).
DataGridViewRow row = (DataGridViewRow)dataGridView1.Rows[0].Clone();
row.SetValues(
  101, "Supreme Flight", "Sail over the trees with this glider.", 138.25m);
dataGridView1.Rows.Add(row);
```

Figure 15-3 shows the grid this code creates.

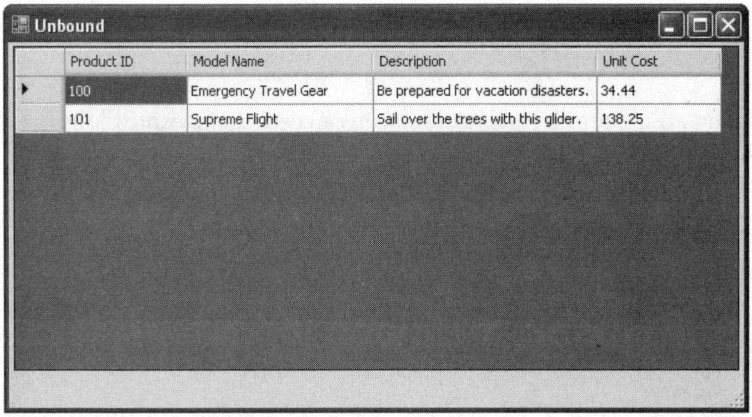

Figure 15-3. *An unbound DataGridView*

Finally, it also makes sense to disable other DataGridView features you don't need, like editing support.

```
// Disable editing features.
dataGridView1.AllowUserToAddRows = false;
dataGridView1.AllowUserToDeleteRows = false;
dataGridView1.EditMode = DataGridViewEditMode.EditProgrammatically;
```

This isn't a requirement. You could allow editing and even respond to editing actions using various DataGridView events. You'll learn more about editing later in this chapter.

Tip When creating an unbound grid, you can define all the columns at design time. Just click the ellipsis next to the Columns property in the Properties window to launch the designer you need.

Cell Selection

By default, the DataGridView allows free selection. Users can highlight individual cells, groups of cells, all the cells at once (by clicking the square in the top-right of the grid), or one or more rows (by clicking in the row header column). Depending on the selection mode, users may even be able to select one or more columns by selecting the column headers. You can control this behavior by setting the DataGridView.SelectionMode property with one of the values from the DataGridViewSelectionMode enumeration, as described in Table 15-2.

Table 15-2. *SelectionMode Values*

Value (from the DataGridViewSelectionMode enumeration)	Description
CellSelect	The user can select cells, but not full rows or columns. The user will be able to select multiple cells if DataGridView.MultiSelect is true.
FullColumnSelect	The user can select full columns only, by clicking on the column header. The user will be able to select multiple columns if DataGridView.MultiSelect is true. When this mode is used, clicking on a column header will not sort the grid. To clear the current selection, click on a cell.
FullRowSelect	The user can select full rows only, by clicking on the row header. The user will be able to select multiple rows if DataGridView.MultiSelect is true. To clear the current selection, click on a cell.
ColumnHeaderSelect	The user can use CellSelect or FullColumnSelect selection modes. When this mode is used, clicking on a column header will not sort the grid.
RowHeaderSelect	The user can use CellSelect or FullRowSelect selection modes. This is the default selection mode.

Note No matter what selection mode you use, the user will always be able to select the entire table by clicking the top-right square, unless you have set MultiSelect to false (or you have chosen not to display the column or row headers).

The DataGridView makes it easy to retrieve the selected cells using three properties: SelectedCells, SelectedRows, and SelectedColumns. SelectedCells always returns a collection of DataGridViewCell objects, regardless of the selection mode being used. SelectedRows, on the other hand, only returns information if a full row has been selected using the row header. SelectedColumns only returns information if a full column has been selected using the column header.

To drive this point home, you can create a simple DataGridView test that checks the current selection using all the selection properties. Here's the code you need:

```
StringBuilder info = new StringBuilder();
info.Append(String.Format("Selected Cells: {0}",
  dataGridView1.SelectedCells.Count));
info.Append(Environment.NewLine);
info.Append(String.Format("Selected Rows: {0}",
  dataGridView1.SelectedRows.Count));
info.Append(Environment.NewLine);
info.Append(String.Format("Selected Columns: {0}",
  dataGridView1.SelectedColumns.Count));
info.Append(Environment.NewLine);

// Display the selection information.
txtSelectionInfo.Text = info.ToString();
```

To report some additional information, you can retrieve the actual values from the selected cells. You can start with any of the three selection properties, but using the SelectedCells property will always work, regardless of the selection mode:

```
info.Append("Values: ");
info.Append(Environment.NewLine);
foreach (DataGridViewCell cell in dataGridView1.SelectedCells)
{
    info.Append(String.Format("  {0} at ({1}, {2})",
      cell.Value, cell.RowIndex, cell.ColumnIndex));
    info.Append(Environment.NewLine);
}
```

■**Tip** DataGridViewCell.Value grabs the underlying value from the bound data object. If you use DataGridViewCell.FormattedValue instead, you'll receive the representation of the value that's currently displayed in the grid. For example, the value 10 might be displayed as the formatted value $10.00, depending on the formatting you've applied.

Figure 15-4 shows this code at work.

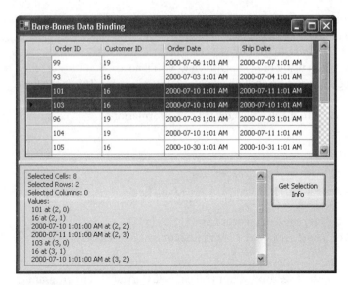

Figure 15-4. *Retrieving selection information*

■**Tip** Instead of responding to a button click, you can respond immediately when the selection changes by handling the SelectionChanged event.

In this example, each cell is treated individually, and identified with a column and row index number. You can retrieve information about the cell field or row by retrieving the corresponding DataGridViewColumn or DataGridViewRow object from the DataGridView. For example, here's how you restrict the display to selected cell values that are in the column corresponding to the ProductID field:

```
foreach (DataGridViewCell cell in DataGridView.SelectedCells)
{
    if (DataGridView.Columns[cell.ColumnIndex].Name == "ProductID")
    {
        info.Append(cell.Value) ;
        info.Append(Environment.NewLine);
    }
}
```

In row selection mode, life is even easier. The DataGridViewRow object provides a Cells property that lets you retrieve individual cell values using the field name:

```
foreach (DataGridViewRow row in DataGridView.SelectedRows)
{
    info.Append(row.Cells["ProductID"].Value);
    info.Append(Environment.NewLine);
}
```

Remember, the SelectedRows collection is only filled when you select entire rows. Other selected cell and columns won't appear.

It's just as easy to retrieve a reference to the current cell using the CurrentCell or CurrentCellAddress properties. When using the DataGridView, you'll notice that the current cell is surrounded by a focus rectangle, which looks like a black dotted square. This is the location where the user is currently positioned.

Here's the code you need to add to display the current cell information:

```
if (dataGridView1.CurrentCell != null)
{
    info.Append(String.Format("Current Cell Value: {0}",
        dataGridView1.CurrentCell.Value));
    info.Append(Environment.NewLine);
    info.Append(String.Format("Current Cell Location: ({0}, {1})",
        dataGridView1.CurrentCellAddress.X, dataGridView1.CurrentCellAddress.Y));
}
```

The CurrentCellAddress property is read-only, but you can use CurrentCell to programmatically change the current location. Once you do, the DataGridView is scrolled so that the current location is visible.

```
// Move to the fourth cell in the eleventh row.
DataGridView.CurrentCell = DataGridView.Rows[10].Cells[3];
```

You also can scroll the DataGridView by setting the DataGridView.FirstDisplayedCell property with the index number of the row that should be positioned at the top of the display.

■**Tip** To programmatically change the selection in a grid, you can modify the Selected property of a DataGridViewCell, DataGridViewRow, or DataGridViewColumn. The DataGridView itself also exposes SelectAll() and ClearSelection() methods for quickly selecting and deselecting the entire table without needing to iterate over each cell.

It's worth considering some of the limitations of cell selection with the DataGridView. Most significantly, if you enumerate over the SelectedCells property, you'll wind up unsharing all the rows you touch. In fact, it's best to avoid cell selection altogether if you can, and use row selection or column selection instead. Finally, you can check if the user has selected the entire grid (typically by clicking the box in the top-right corner) by calling the DataGridView.AreAllCellsSelectedMethod(). Use this method before you enumerate over a collection of rows, columns, or cells, to prevent needlessly unsharing rows.

Navigation Events

The DataGridView is packed full of events, including several navigation events that allow you to respond when the user moves from one cell to another, from one row to another, or abandons the control entirely. The event arguments indicate the relevant cell. Table 15-3 has more information.

Table 15-3. *Navigation Events*

Event	Description
Enter and Leave	Enter fires when the user moves to the DataGridView from another control on the form, and Leave fires when the user heads to another control.
RowEnter and RowLeave	These events fire when the user moves from one row to another. RowLeave also fires when the user clicks on another control on the form.
CellEnter and CellLeave	These events fire when the user moves from one cell to another (regardless of whether or not the cell is in the same row). CellLeave also fires when the user clicks on another control on the form.
CellClick	The user selects a cell by clicking on it with the mouse.
SelectionChanged	The currently selected cells have changed (usually the result of the user clicking with the mouse, moving with the arrow keys while holding Shift down, although the selection also can also be set programmatically).

For example, when the user clicks a new cell in the same row, the events unfold like this:

1. CellLeave (for the current cell)

2. CellEnter (for the new cell)

When the user moves to a cell in another row, the navigation events fire in this order:

1. CellLeave

2. RowLeave

3. RowEnter

4. CellEnter

And if the user moves from the DataGridView to another control (like a text box on the form), the events fire in this order:

1. CellLeave

2. RowLeave

3. Leave

Column-Based Sorting

As you learned earlier, the DataGridView has built-in sorting support. When you click a column, values are ordered according to the data type (numerically or alphabetically in ascending order) and a sorting glyph appears in the column header (an arrow pointing up). Click again, and the sort order is reversed and the sorting glyph becomes an arrow pointing down. Figure 15-5 shows a grid sorted by CustomerID.

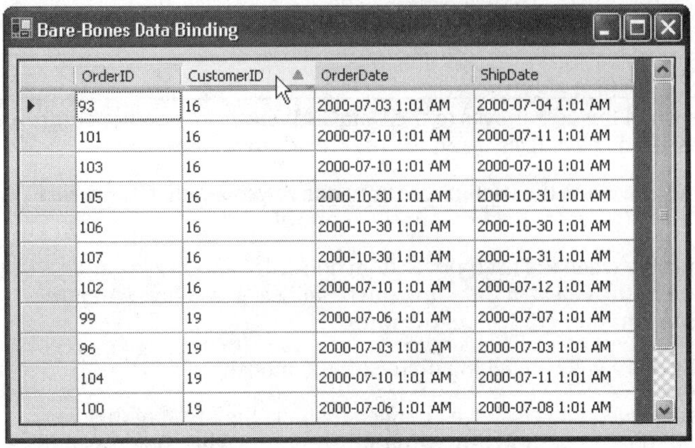

Figure 15-5. *Sorting the DataGridView*

Sorting is controlled on a column-specific basis, according to the DataGridViewColumn. SortMode property, which takes one of three values: Automatic (the default), NotSortable (no sorting is performed), and Programmatic (no sorting is performed, but space is reserved for the sorting glyph, which you can use if you perform your own custom sorting).

There are several cases in which you might choose to perform custom sorting. Here are some examples:

- You want to sort non-text-box columns. For example, Boolean fields are (by default) not sorted.

- You want to format the display value (using the CellFormatting event described later), but you want to sort according to the original value. For example, you might want to replace status numbers with descriptive text or icons, but sort based on the underlying number.

- You want to implement more sophisticated sorting logic that takes several values into consideration or arranges values in a way other than strictly alphabetic or numeric.

The first scenario is the easiest to implement. All you need to do is change the SortMode property of the appropriate column:

```
dataGridView1.Columns["InStock"].SortMode = DataGridViewColumnSortMode.Automatic;
```

Custom sorting requires a little more work to implement. First, turn off automatic sorting for the columns in question. This code turns off automatic sorting for all columns:

```
foreach (DataGridViewColumn col in dataGridView1.Columns)
{
    col.SortMode = DataGridViewColumnSortMode.Programmatic;
}
```

Now when the user clicks on the column header for these columns, it will have no effect. Next, handle the DataGridView.ColumnHeaderMouseClick event. Check if the mouse click was on one of the columns that you want to sort programmatically. If it is, perform your sorting now by calling DataGridView.Sort(). Here's an example that always sorts columns in ascending order:

```
private void dataGridView1_ColumnHeaderMouseClick(object sender,
  DataGridViewCellMouseEventArgs e)
{
    dataGridView1.Sort(dataGridView1.Columns[e.ColumnIndex],
      ListSortDirection.Ascending);
}
```

This overload of the Sort() method accepts a DataGridViewColumn and a sort order. Clearly, it doesn't allow much customization. For more control, you need to use the Sort() method overload that accepts a custom IComparer object. This IComparer must compare two DataGridViewRow objects and determine which should occur first in the sort. This exact technique is demonstrated with the ListView control in Chapter 6.

Note The DataGridView also provides a SortCompare event. However, this event only fires if you've created an unbound grid. In this (relatively uncommon) situation, you can perform the comparison between two rows in the SortCompare event handler by modifying the event arguments, rather than by creating a custom IComparer.

Formatting the DataGridView

One of the most important aspects of rich data controls is formatting—how you can tailor their appearance to suit your needs. On this score, the DataGridView is remarkably flexible. It introduces a new style-based system that allows you to apply formatting changes coarsely (for best performance) or make them as fine-grained as you need. You also have built-in support for adjusting column widths, rearranging, hiding, and freezing columns in place, and using specialized column types to show buttons and images. In this section, you'll learn how to use all of these features.

Column and Row Resizing

The default appearance vof the DataGridView is a modest improvement over the DataGrid. But with a few quick refinements, you can greatly improve it.

One problem is that the DataGridView gives a default standard width to all columns regardless of their content. As a result, the initial appearance of the bound grid in Figure 15-1 is less than perfect, with the ModelName and Description columns too small for the data they contain.

Fortunately, you can use some powerful automatic resizing functionality that's built into the DataGridView. Your first decision is whether you want to control sizing for the entire control or fine tune individual columns. The following sections explore your options.

Setting an Automatic Resize Mode for the Entire Grid

The simplest approach is to set a resizing behavior that applies to all columns using the AutoSizeColumnsMode property. Your options are shown in Table 15-4.

Table 15-4. *AutoSizeColumnsMode Values*

Value	Description
None	The column widths are not adjusted automatically. Extra content is clipped (with an ellipsis added to indicate the missing content). This is the default.
AllCells	Each column is sized just large enough to fit the largest value, including header cells.
AllCellsExceptHeader	Each column is sized just large enough to fit the largest value, excluding header cells.
ColumnHeader	Each column is sized just large enough to fit the text in the header.
DisplayedCells	Similar to AllCells, except the DataGridView only considers the rows that are currently visible at the time the property is set. This option is used to improve performance for large grids. The assumption is that the first subset of values has a fairly representative set of widths.
DisplayedCellsExceptHeader	The same as DisplayedCells, except it doesn't take the header cell into consideration.
Fill	Column widths are adjusted so that all columns exactly fill the available DataGridView. If the grid is resized, all the columns change proportionately. You can adjust the MinimumWidth and FillWeight properties of each column to make some columns wider than others.

■**Tip** Using the AllCells criteria to sort a small table works perfectly well. However, if you have an extremely large table (one with thousands of rows), it introduces a noticeable delay because the width of every value in the table needs to be examined. In these cases, it much more practical to compromise and use the DisplayedCells value instead. This only examines the width of the values in the rows that are currently visible in the DataGridView.

Setting the AutoSizeColumnsMode at any time triggers the DataGridView to resize its columns immediately. Figure 15-6 shows a simple test application in action, changing the grid from AutoSizeColumnsMode.None to AutoSizeColumnsMode.Fill and then to AutoSizeColumnsMode.DisplayCells (in which case the last column is too wide to fit in the grid, and scroll bars are added).

If you use Fill mode, users are still allowed to resize columns (assuming you haven't changed the Resizable property of any DataGridViewColumn objects). When a column is resized, all the following columns are expanded or shrunk proportionately to fit the remaining space. If you resize the last column, all the other columns are resized proportionately.

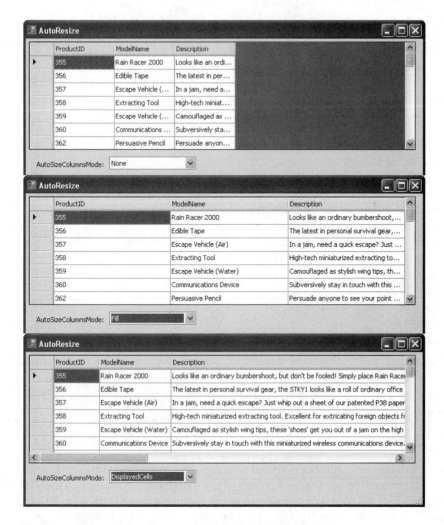

Figure 15-6. *Automatic column resizing in the DataGridView*

Setting an Automatic Resize Mode for Individual Columns

If you don't want all columns to be resized in the same way, you can adjust the AutoSizeMode property of the DataGridViewColumn object for each column. For example, you could size one column to None and another column to DisplayedCells. (The default value is NotSet, in which case the value is inherited from the DataGridView.AutoSizeColumnsMode property.)

A more interesting scenario occurs if you're using proportional fill. In many cases, you'll want to make some columns larger than others or limit them so they can't shrink beyond a certain minimum. This is easy to accomplish through the FillWeight and MinimumWidth properties.

Initially, the FillWeight of every column is 100. If you set the FillWeight of another column to 200, you create a column that's twice as wide. A FillWeight of 50 is half as large as the default. The FillWeight is only important in a relative sense, unlike the MinimumWidth property, which sets an absolute minimum width in pixels.

Here's an example that configures these details:

```
// Retrieve the columns you need to work with.
DataGridViewColumn colID = dataGridView1.Columns["ProductID"];
DataGridViewColumn colModel = dataGridView1.Columns["ModelName"];
DataGridViewColumn colDesc = dataGridView1.Columns["Description"];

// Give much more weigth to the description.
colID.FillWeight = 25;
colModel.FillWeight = 25;
colDesc.FillWeight = 100;

// However, keep a minimum width that ensures
// the first two columns are readable.
// Another option in this scenario is to only
// assign fill mode to the description column.
colID.MinimumWidth = 75;
colModel.MinimumWidth = 125;
colDesc.MinimumWidth = 100;
```

Note Unfortunately, you must configure column properties using code. Although the DataGridView does provide design-time support for modifying the Columns property, unless you're using the automatic data-binding features discussed in Chapter 8 (which aren't suitable for most large-scale projects), you won't be able to add or modify bound columns.

When the user resizes a column, the FillWeight changes. As a result, additional resize operations (on other columns or the whole grid) will work a little differently. For example, if the user expands the first column, it's automatically given a correspondingly larger FillWeight. If the user then resizes the whole form (and by extension, the DataGridView), the first column gets the same larger proportion of space.

There's no need to use Fill mode with every column. You can use Fill mode with just one column. The fill behavior still works the same—the remaining space in the DataGridView is divided among all Fill mode columns.

Tip If you don't want to use Fill mode for the whole grid, but you want to make sure the DataGridView background isn't visible, you can configure the last column to spring to fill the remaining space. All you need to do is set the AutoSizeColumnsMode of that column to Fill.

Manual Sizing

Automatic resizing is preferred because it's the most flexible approach. However, you can use fixed pixel widths instead. Just set the AutoSizeColumnsMode to None (either for individual columns or for the entire grid) and then set the DataGridViewColumn.Width property with the width in pixels.

User Sizing

By default, the DataGridView allows the user to resize columns that have an AutoSizeColumnsMode of None or Fill. If you are using another option (like DisplayedCells), resizing is disabled. (However, you'll learn how to work around this limitation in the next section.)

If you want to prevent the user from resizing columns or rows altogether, set the AllowUserToResizeRows and AllowUserToResizeColumns properties for your DataGridView to false. You also can restrict the user from resizing individual columns or rows by setting the Resizable property of the corresponding DataGridViewColumn or DataGridViewRow.

Programmatic Resizing

The DataGridView also allows you to trigger autosizing for specific columns or the entire grid by calling one of the following methods:

- AutoResizeColumn()

- AutoResizeColumns()

- AutoResizeRow()

- AutoResizeRows()

- AutoResizeColumnHeadersHeight()

- AutoResizeRowHeadersWidth()

There are a couple of common reasons that you might choose to use these methods. First of all, there is a possible performance consideration. The DataGridView performs automatic column resizing at several points, including after a column sort and a cell edit. If you've used a resize mode like AllCells, this could be impractically slow. In this case, you might choose to perform your sorting exactly when you want it by calling the appropriate method.

Another reason you might use programmatic resizing is to get around the problem that automatically resized columns don't allow user resizing. If you use a resize mode other than None or Fill, the user won't be able to adjust the column widths. This might be a problem in some situations—for example, if you want the user to be able to collapse a column to see more information without scrolling. To get around this problem, you can leave the default resizing mode to None, but call one of the resizing methods when the form first loads.

Here's an example that resizes the third column:

```
dataGridView1.AutoResizeColumn(2, DataGridViewAutoSizeColumnMode.AllCells);
```

And here's an example that resizes the whole grid:

```
dataGridView1.AutoResizeColumns(DataGridViewAutoSizeColumnMode.AllCells);
```

Keep in mind that this method needs to be invoked after you bind the data, or it won't have any effect. You also might want to use it after user editing (perhaps in response to an event like DataGridView.CellValueChanged).

Resizing Rows

The DataGridView provides a similar model for resizing rows. Your options are identical to those shown in Table 15-4, and you can resize the height all the rows in the grid or specific rows automatically or manually. The only difference is the name of the properties and methods that you use. For example, the AutoSizeRowsMode property configures automatic resizing for the DataGridView, and the DataGridViewRow.Height property allows you to set a specific pixel height.

There are only three reasons that you'll want to resize a row:

- You've enlarged the font size, so the text is being clipped at the bottom. (Similarly, if you reduce the font size, you might resize the row to get rid of the extra space.)

- You're using a different column type, like an image, and the content extends beyond the bounds of the standard row height.

- You're using wrapped text, and you want to show several lines at once.

The first two options are fairly straightforward. Wrapped text is a little more interesting. It works through the style model described in the next section. The basic approach is that you set the columns that you want to wrap. Then, you set the column width. Finally (and optionally), you use automatic row resizing to heighten the row to fit all the text.

Here's an example that ensures you can always see the full description text. The Description column is set to use DataGridViewAutoSizeColumnMode.Fill, and the automatic row size adjusts the row height as necessary.

```
DataGridViewColumn colDesc = dataGridView1.Columns["Description"];

// Give it as much width as possible.
colDesc.AutoSizeMode = DataGridViewAutoSizeColumnMode.Fill;

// Wrap to fit the bounds of the column.
colDesc.DefaultCellStyle.WrapMode = DataGridViewTriState.True;

// Use row autosizing to show all the text.
dataGridView1.AutoSizeRowsMode = DataGridViewAutoSizeRowsMode.DisplayedCells;
```

Figure 15-7 shows how this grid adapts as it is resized.

In this example, the automatic row resizing only takes displayed cells into consideration. Try the same example (included online) with AllCells resizing, and you'll notice more lethargic performance.

■**Note** You'll see the DataGridViewTriState enumeration used in some places where you might expect to find ordinary Boolean values. The three values are True, False, and NotSet (which inherits values from the containing object). For example, a value of NotSet allows a cell to inherit settings from a row, the row to inherit them from the grid, and so on.

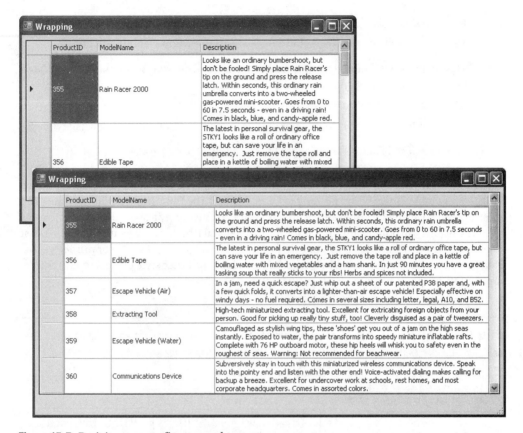

Figure 15-7. *Resizing rows to fit wrapped text*

DataGridView Styles

One of the challenges of designing the DataGridView was to create a formatting system that was flexible enough to apply different levels of formatting, but remained efficient for very large tables. For flexibility, the best approach is to allow the developer to configure each cell individually. But for efficiency, this approach can be disastrous. A table with thousands of rows will have tens of thousands of cells, and maintaining distinct formatting for each cell is sure to waste vast expanses of memory.

To solve this problem, the DataGridView adopts a multilayered model using DataGridViewCellStyle objects. A DataGridViewCellStyle object represents the style of a cell, and it includes details like color, font, alignment, wrapping, and data formatting. You can create a single DataGridViewCellStyle to specify the default formatting for an entire table. Additionally, you can specify the default formatting for a column, row, and individual cell. The more fine-grained your formatting is and the more DataGridViewCellStyle objects you create, the less scalable solution will be. But if you use primarily column-based and row-based formatting, and only occasionally format individual cells, your DataGridView won't require much more memory than the DataGrid.

When the DataGridView displays a cell, it examines the DataGridViewCellStyle objects in this order:

1. The style for the specific cell: DataGridViewCell.Style.

2. The default style for all cells in that row: DataGridViewRow.DefaultCellStyle.

3. The default styles defined by the grid for normal and alternating rows: DataGridView. RowsDefaultColumnStyle or DataGridView.AlternatingRowsDefaultColumnStyle, depending on whether the row is even or odd numbered.

4. The default style for cells in that column: DataGridViewColumn.DefaultCellStyle.

5. The default style defined by the grid for all cells: DataGridView.DefaultCellStyle.

The items higher in the list have the greatest priority in the case of any overlap. However, styles aren't applied in an all-or-nothing fashion. Instead, the DataGridView looks at the properties of each style object. For example, imagine you want to apply a special forecolor to a specific cell, but you don't want to change any other details. In this case, you can attach a style object through the DataGridViewCell.Style property and set just the ForeColor property. The DataGridView will use that color, but continue checking the other style objects to find the appropriate background color, font, and so on.

■**Tip** None of these styles apply to row or column headers. To change the appearance of these cells, use the ColumnHeadersDefaultCellStyle and RowHeadersDefaultCellStyle properties of the DataGridView.

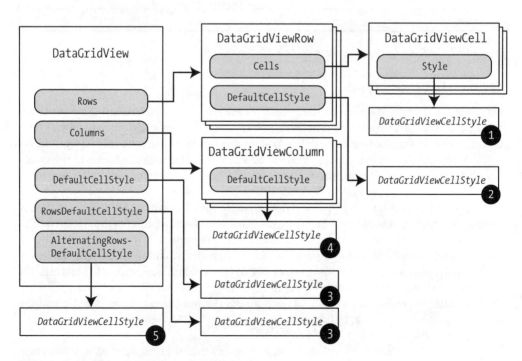

Figure 15-8. *The DataGridView and CellStyle objects*

Figure 15-8 shows how you can set cell styles using the DataGridView objects. The numbers represent the order that the DataGridView checks for styles.

The DataGridViewCellStyle defines two types of formatting: data and appearance. Data formatting describes how the data-bound value will be modified before it is displayed. This typically includes using formatting strings to turn numeric or date values into text. To use data formatting, you simply set the format specifier or custom format string using the DataGridViewCellStyle.Format property. You can use all the format specifiers listed in Chapter 8 (see Tables 8-3 and 8-4).

For example, the following code snippet formats all the numbers in the UnitCost column so that they are displayed as currency values, with two decimal places and the appropriate currency symbol defined in the regional settings:

```
dataGridView1.Columns["UnitCost"].DefaultCellStyle.Format = "C";
```

Appearance formatting includes the cosmetic niceties like color and font. For example, the following code right-aligns the UnitCost cells, applies a bold font, and changes the cell background to yellow:

```
dataGridView1.Columns["UnitCost"].DefaultCellStyle.Font =
  new Font(DataGridView.Font, FontStyle.Bold);
dataGridView1.Columns["UnitCost"].DefaultCellStyle.Alignment =
  DataGridViewContentAlignment.MiddleRight;
dataGridView1.Columns["UnitCost"].DefaultCellStyle.BackColor = Color.LightYellow;
```

Figure 15-9 shows the formatted UnitCost column.

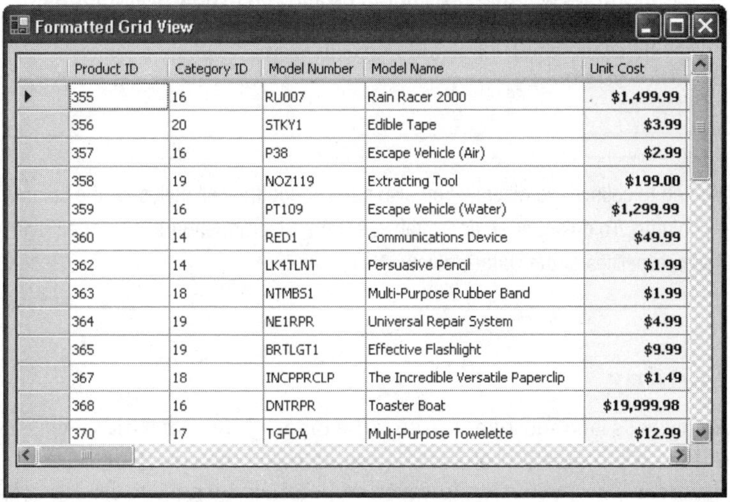

Product ID	Category ID	Model Number	Model Name	Unit Cost
355	16	RU007	Rain Racer 2000	$1,499.99
356	20	STKY1	Edible Tape	$3.99
357	16	P38	Escape Vehicle (Air)	$2.99
358	19	NOZ119	Extracting Tool	$199.00
359	16	PT109	Escape Vehicle (Water)	$1,299.99
360	14	RED1	Communications Device	$49.99
362	14	LK4TLNT	Persuasive Pencil	$1.99
363	18	NTMBS1	Multi-Purpose Rubber Band	$1.99
364	19	NE1RPR	Universal Repair System	$4.99
365	19	BRTLGT1	Effective Flashlight	$9.99
367	18	INCPPRCLP	The Incredible Versatile Paperclip	$1.49
368	16	DNTRPR	Toaster Boat	$19,999.98
370	17	TGFDA	Multi-Purpose Towelette	$12.99

Figure 15-9. *A formatted currency column*

Table 15-5 lists all the DataGridViewCellStyle properties.

Table 15-5. *DataGridViewCellStyle Properties*

Property	Description
Alignment	Configures how text will be justified inside the cell.
BackColor and ForeColor	Sets the color of the cell background and the cell text.
Font	Sets the font used for the cell text.
Format	A format string that configures how data source values are formatted for display. Usually, you'll use this to convert numeric or date values to the appropriate string representation.
FormatProvider	A custom IFormatProvider object that configures how data source values are formatted for display.
NullValue	The data that will be displayed in the grid for any null values in the data source.
DataSourceNullValue	The value that will be committed back to the data source if a control is empty or null.
Padding	Sets the spacing between the cell content and the borders of the cell, on one or more sides.
SelectionBackColor and SelectionForeColor	Sets the cell background and text colors for selected cells.
WrapMode	Determines whether text should be allowed to flow over multiple lines, if the row is high enough to accommodate it. Otherwise, text will be truncated. By default, no cells wrap.

Tip Your formatting isn't limited to cells in the display. You also can change the cell styles for the column headers and the row selection column. To do so for an entire table, set the ColumnHeadersDefaultCellStyle and RowHeadersDefaultCellStyle properties of the DataGridView.

Custom Cell Formatting

The first choice for formatting cells is to set styles through the higher-level DataGridView, DataGridViewColumn, and DataGridViewRow objects. These styles are then used for the entire grid, entire columns, or entire rows, respectively. However, sometimes you need to set the style for specific, individual cells. For example, you might want to flag data in a column that is greater or less than a certain value, such as due dates that have passed on a project schedule list or negative rates of return on a sales analysis. In both of these cases, you'll need to format the individual cell.

Using your knowledge of the DataGridView object model, you might be tempted to iterate through the collection of cells in a specific column looking for the values you want to highlight. This approach will work, but it's not the best choice. The key problem is that if the user edits the data or if your code changes the bound data source, the cell highlighting won't be updated to match.

Fortunately, the DataGridView provides a CellFormatting event just for this purpose. CellFormatting fires just before the cell value is painted. It gives you the chance to update the cell style based on its content.

Here's an example that flags prices above or equal to $1,000.

```
private void DataGridView_CellFormatting(object sender,
  System.Windows.Forms.DataGridViewCellFormattingEventArgs e)
{
    // Check if this is in the column we want.
    if (dataGridView1.Columns[e.ColumnIndex].Name == "UnitCost")
    {
        // Check if the value is large enough to flag.
        if (Convert.ToInt32(e.Value) >= 1000)
        {
            e.CellStyle.ForeColor = Color.Red;
            e.CellStyle.BackColor = Color.Yellow;
            e.CellStyle.Font =
                new Font(dataGridView1.DefaultCellStyle.Font, FontStyle.Bold);
        }
    }
}
```

The formatted DataGridView is shown in Figure 15-10.

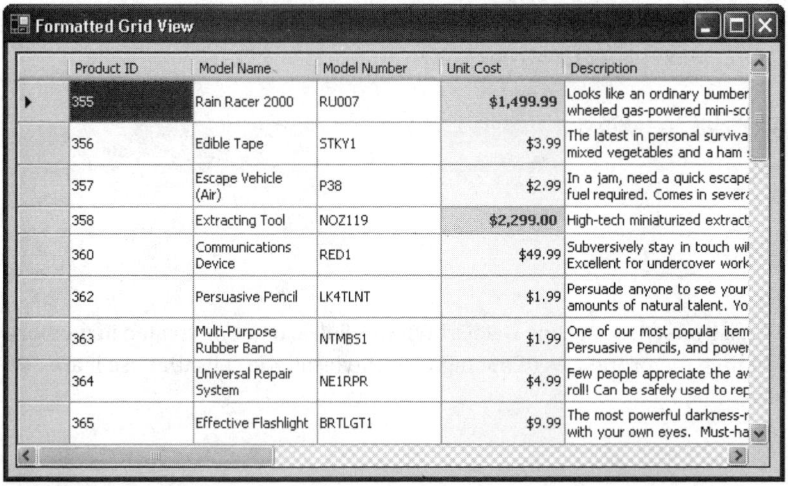

Figure 15-10. *Highlighting large prices with cell-based formatting*

■**Note** Due to the architecture of the DataGridView, the CellFormatting event fires every time a cell becomes visible—when you resize the window, minimize and maximize it, scroll through the list, move your mouse over cells, and so on. To ensure optimum performance, you shouldn't perform any time-consuming operations in the CellFormatting event. For example, if you need to perform a complex calculation, perform it ahead of time and store the value for later use in the CellFormatting event.

Notice in this code that the cell data is retrieved through the TableCellFormattingEventArgs object that's passed to the event handler. This object is also used to specify the new style information. This approach is important because cell objects are often created on demand. If you don't directly manipulate the individual DataGridViewCell object for a cell, .NET may not need to create it, which reduces the overall memory use of your application.

You can further improve performance by reusing the same DataGridViewCellStyle object with multiple cells. First, define the DataGridViewCellStyle as a member variable of the form class:

```
DataGridViewCellStyle highPriceStyle = new DataGridViewCellStyle();
```

In your Form.Load event handler, configure this style accordingly:

```
highPriceStyle.ForeColor = Color.Red;
highPriceStyle.BackColor = Color.Yellow;
highPriceStyle.Font = new Font(dataGridView1.DefaultCellStyle.Font,
  FontStyle.Bold);
```

Now you can apply this style to multiple cells in the CellFormatting event handler:

```
private void DataGridView_CellFormatting(object sender,
  System.Windows.Forms.DataGridViewCellFormattingEventArgs e)
{
    if (dataGridView1.Columns[e.ColumnIndex].Name == "UnitCost")
    {
        if (Convert.ToInt32(e.Value) >= 1000)
        {
            e.CellStyle = highPriceStyle;
        }
    }
}
```

This is known as a *shared* style. Only one DataGridViewCellStyle object is created in memory. Additionally, if you change the properties of the highPriceStyle, all the cells that use it are affected automatically.

■**Note** The DatGridViewCellStyle object won't be garbage collected as long as it is used by at least one cell or referred to by a member variable in your form class.

You also can use this technique to apply the same formatting to multiple columns. Create the DataGridViewCellStyle object in the same way, configure it, and then set it to multiple columns using the DataGridViewColumn.DefaultCellStyle property.

Hiding, Moving, and Freezing Columns

Styles aren't the only detail that influences the appearance of your grid. You also can hide columns, move them from place to place, and "freeze" them so that they remain visible even as the user scrolls to the right. These features are all provided through the properties of the DataGridViewColumn class, as detailed in Table 15-6.

Table 15-6. *Appearance-Related DataGridViewColumn Properties*

Property	Description
DisplayIndex	Sets the position where the column will appear in the DataGridView. For example, a column with a DisplayIndex of 0 is automatically shown in the leftmost column. Initially, the DisplayIndex matches the index of the DataGridViewColumn object in the DataGridView.Columns collection.
Frozen	If true, the column will remain visible and fixed the left side of the table, even if the user scrolls to the right to view additional columns. All columns to the left are automatically also frozen.
HeaderText	Sets the text that will appear in the column header.
Resizable and MinimumWidth	Set Resizable to false to prevent the user from resizing a column, or set MinimumWidth to the minimum number of pixels that will be allowed.
Visible	Set this to false to hide a column.

For example, the following code rearranges the columns of a DataGridView bound to the Products table:

```
dataGridView1.Columns["ProductImage"].Visible = false;
dataGridView1.Columns["CategoryID"].Visible = false;
dataGridView1.Columns["ModelNumber"].DisplayIndex = 4;

dataGridView1.Columns["ProductID"].Frozen = true;
dataGridView1.Columns["ProductID"].Resizable = false;
```

When you change the display index, the existing columns are moved out of the way. For example, in the preceding code the columns that currently have a DisplayIndex of 4 or later are automatically changed to have a DisplayIndex of 5 and later.

■Tip If you are simultaneously hiding and rearranging rows, you'll need to set the DisplayIndex property as though all the rows are visible. The DisplayIndex of a column won't change when you hide a column.

Some of these techniques can be applied to rows using the properties of the DataGridViewRow object. For example, you can freeze rows (they'll remain at the top of the grid as you scroll down), and you can set DataGridViewRow.Visible to false to hide a row. This gives you the ability to implement more advanced filtering than what's available with properties like DataView.RowFilter (described in Chapter 8). Simply loop through the collection of rows looking for those you'd like to hide.

For example, here's a function that filters out strings containing the words "warning" or "danger":

```
private bool TestForWords(string stringToTest)
{
    stringToTest = stringToTest.ToLower();
    return (stringToTest.Contains("warning") || stringToTest.Contains("danger"));
}
```

And here's the code that hides any row that has these words in the description:

```
// Remove cells with the objectionable description.
foreach (DataGridViewRow row in DataGridView.Rows)
{
    if (TestForWords(Convert.ToString(row.Cells["Description"].Value)))
        row.Visible = false;
}
```

You'll also need to respond to the CellValueChanged event to check whether you need to filter new or modified rows.

Note This approach isn't as efficient as setting a filter string for the DataView, but it allows you far more possibilities. If you're binding to a DataTable, you may want to consider using the DataView.RowFilter property instead, as described in Chapter 8.

Using Image Columns

One of the column types provided for the DataGridView is the DataGridViewImageColumn, which displays a picture in the bounds of the cell. You can set the DataGridViewImageColumn. Layout property to configure how the picture is shown in the cell—whether it is stretched to fit, or simply cropped if it's too large.

One extremely straightforward way to use images in a DataGridView is to add an unbound DataGridViewImageColumn. In this case, the column data won't be drawn from the underlying data source. Instead, you can set images programmatically. You might use this approach is to distinguish between new and changed rows, or to flag important rows. You might even use the DataGridViewImageColumn to display a generic image next to every row just to improve the appearance of the control. The next example demonstrates this technique with a column that shows a starburst icon next to new or modified rows.

First of all, define the images that you want to use as form member variables, so that they are available to all event-handling code:

```
private Image genericImage;
private Image newImage;
```

When the application first loads, you can configure these images by loading them from a file or, more practically, by retrieving the image from an embedded resource or an ImageList:

```
genericImage = imageList.Images[1];
newImage = imageList.Images[0];
```

Next, create the image column. In this example, the image column is in the leftmost position of the DataGridView, and always shows the default genericImage:

```
// Bind the grid.
dataGridView1.DataSource = Program.StoreDB.GetProducts();

// Create the image column.
DataGridViewImageColumn imageCol = new DataGridViewImageColumn();
imageCol.DefaultCellStyle.Alignment = DataGridViewContentAlignment.MiddleCenter;
imageCol.ImageLayout = DataGridViewImageCellLayout.Normal;
imageCol.Frozen = true;
imageCol.Name = "Image";
imageCol.HeaderText = "";

// Move the column to the left, and move the ProductID
// column out of the way.
imageCol.DisplayIndex = 0;
dataGridView1.Columns["ProductID"].DisplayIndex = 1;

// By default, show the generic image.
imageCol.Image = genericImage;

// Add the image column to the grid.
dataGridView1.Columns.Add(imageCol);
```

Finally, you can respond to the CellValueChanged event, and update the image to show that the row has been modified. In a more sophisticated scenario, you might want to check other criteria for the modified row before deciding how to change the image.

```
private void DataGridView_CellValueChanged(object sender,
  System.Windows.Forms.DataGridViewCellEventArgs e)
{
    if (e.RowIndex != -1)
    {
        // Retrieve the image column for this row.
        DataGridViewImageCell col =
          (DataGridViewImageCell)dataGridView1.Rows[e.RowIndex].Cells["Image"];

        // Set the image.
        col.Value = newImage;
    }
}
```

Figure 15-11 shows the DataGridView with two modified rows. Note that the DataGridView correctly handles background selection, changing the color of the image background appropriately. This works because the ImageList control defines the background color as transparent using the TransparentColor property.

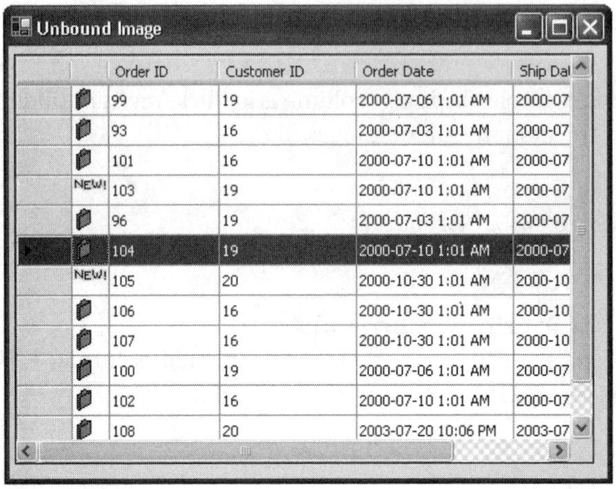

Figure 15-11. *Using an image to represent row state*

■Tip Unfortunately, the DataGridView doesn't have any built-in way to show both image content and text in a single cell. However, you can easily add this ability using custom painting, as described later in this chapter.

A more sophisticated way to use image columns is to display picture data that relates to an actual record. There are two ways to do this. The simple approach requires no extra code, and takes place automatically if you are showing a column that has the Image data type. For example, consider the pub_info table in the pubs sample database that's included with all installations of SQL Server. It includes a logo field that holds a 16-byte picture. If you retrieve this information and bind it to a DataGridView, the DataGridView automatically uses a DataGridViewImageColumn to show it.

However, displaying an image isn't always this easy. Sometimes, you might need your code to explicitly translate the binary data in a portion of a binary column to create the picture. Or, your database record might simply store the file name of the image file you want to show. In these cases, you need an extra manual step, where your code must retrieve and supply the required data.

To implement this design, you need to respond to the CellFormatting event. In this event, you set the Image object for the cell. You can create this Image object based on binary data in the database, or using a filename specified in another field, which is the approach we'll use in the next example with the Products table.

The Products table includes a ProductImage field that specifies the file name for a picture of the product. The following code binds the DataGridView to the Products table, hides the ProductImage field, and creates a new image column where the linked picture will be displayed.

```
// Bind the grid.
dataGridView1.DataSource = Program.StoreDB.GetProducts();

// Hide the column with the image file name.
dataGridView1.Columns["ProductImage"].Visible = false;

// Create a new image column.
DataGridViewImageColumn imageCol = new DataGridViewImageColumn();
imageCol.DefaultCellStyle.Alignment = DataGridViewContentAlignment.MiddleCenter;
imageCol.ImageLayout = DataGridViewImageCellLayout.Normal;
imageCol.Name = "Image";
dataGridView1.Columns.Add(imageCol);

// Make sure pictures are visible.
dataGridView1.AutoSizeRowsMode = DataGridViewAutoSizeRowsMode.AllCells;
```

Next, the CellFormatting event handler looks for the file specified for each record and, if it can be found, loads it into the cell:

```
private void DataGridView_CellFormatting(object sender,
  System.Windows.Forms.DataGridViewCellFormattingEventArgs e)
{
    // Check if it's the Image column.
    if ((dataGridView1.Columns[e.ColumnIndex].Name == "Image"))
    {
        // Set the value based on the hidden ProductImage column.
        string fileName = Application.StartupPath + "\\" +
          dataGridView1.Rows[e.RowIndex].Cells["ProductImage"].Value;
        if (File.Exists(fileName))
        {
            e.Value = Image.FromFile(fileName);
        }
        else
        {
            // (You could supply a default picture here.)
        }
    }
}
```

Figure 15-12 shows the DataGridView with product images.

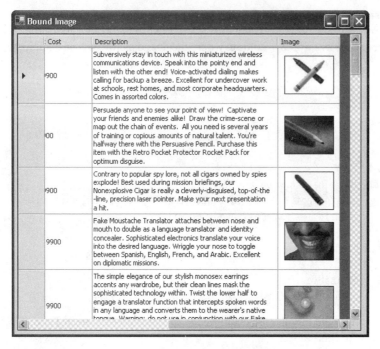

Figure 15-12. *Displaying images from a hidden column*

DISPLAYING UNBOUND DATA

When designing the DataGridView, Microsoft developers considered common data-binding scenarios—especially those that the DataGrid couldn't tackle. One of these is displaying nonbound data. You can apply the same technique used to create an image column to add multiple columns to a DataGridView that doesn't have any bound data source. The DataGridView will even support editing and row insertions (depending on the AllowUserToAddRows and ReadOnly properties). It's up to you whether you want to use this approach to show unbound data, or programmatically create a new DataTable to use with the DataGridView.

For optimum performance, don't use this approach to implement calculated columns with bound data. Instead, you should add calculated columns directly to the underlying DataTable, and set the DataColumn. Expression property so that the column value is calculated automatically. This technique is demonstrated in Chapter 8.

Using Button Columns

Another type of column you might want to add manually is the DataGridViewButtonColumn, which displays a button next to every item. You can respond to a click of this button and use it to start another action or show a new form. For example, a button column might be used to allow a user to purchase an item or see related rows in another table. The following example demonstrates this latter approach with a master-details form.

In a master-details form, you show two tables of data. When the user makes a selection from the first, you show the related rows in a second. In the Chapter 8, you saw an example with a single form that allowed users to browse products by category. Using the DataGridViewButtonColumn, you can implement a slightly different approach.

First, bind the grid and add the new column. When configuring the DataGridViewButtonColumn, you need to specify a name and the button text:

```
DataSet ds = Program.StoreDB.GetCategoriesAndProducts();
dataGridView1.DataSource = ds.Tables["Categories"];

DataGridViewButtonColumn detailsCol = new DataGridViewButtonColumn();
detailsCol.Name = "Details";
detailsCol.Text = "Details...";
detailsCol.UseColumnTextForButtonValue = true;
detailsCol.HeaderText = "";
DataGridView.Columns.Insert(DataGridView.Columns.Count, detailsCol);
```

Figure 15-13 shows the grid with the new column.

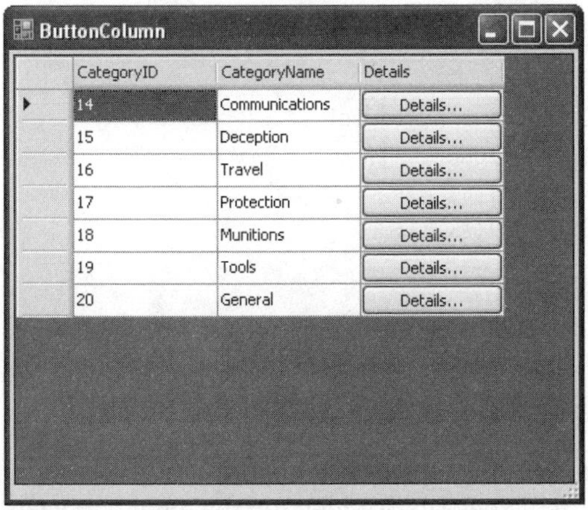

Figure 15-13. *Adding a button column*

Here's the code that reacts to this event handler, creates a new form, copies the CategoryID of the selected item to a property of the new form, and then displays it modally:

```
private void DataGridView_CellClick(object sender,
  System.Windows.Forms.DataGridViewCellEventArgs e)
{
    if (dataGridView1.Columns[e.ColumnIndex].Name == "Details")
    {
        // Create the new form.
        ChildForm frm = new ChildForm();

        // Provide the OrderID to the new form.
        frm.CategoryID = Convert.ToInt32(
          dataGridView1.Rows[e.RowIndex].Cells["CategoryID"].Value);
```

```
        // Show the form.
        frm.ShowDialog();
        frm.Dispose();
    }
}
```

The ChildForm.CategoryID property sets up the DataGridView on the new form using the DataView.RowFilter property:

```
private int categoryID;

public int CategoryID
{
    get
    {
        return categoryID;
    }
    set
    {
        categoryID = value;
        DataSet ds = Program.StoreDB.GetCategoriesAndProducts();
        dataGridView1.DataSource = ds.Tables["Products"];
        ds.Tables["Products"].DefaultView.RowFilter =
            "CategoryID =" + categoryID.ToString();
    }
}
```

Editing and Validation with the DataGridView

The DataGrid was notoriously inflexible with user input, offering little opportunity to customize how cells were validated and errors were reported. The DataGridView, on the other hand, lets you control its behavior in a variety of ways. First of all, you can use the editing properties in Table 15-7 to configure editing support for the DataGridView.

Table 15-7. *Editing Properties of the DataGridView*

Property	Description
AllowUserToAddRows	If this property is set to true, the bottom of the grid will show an extra blank row with an asterisk in the row header. The user can type values here to create a new row.
AllowUserToDeleteRows	If this property is set to true, the user can delete entire rows just by selecting the row (typically by clicking on the row header), and pressing the Delete key on the keyboard.

Table 15-7. *Editing Properties of the DataGridView*

Property	Description
ReadOnly	If this property is set to true, the user will not be able to type in any row. This also effectively disables row insertion—even though the user can scroll to the new record marker at the bottom grid, there's no way to type anything in. You also can set the ReadOnly property of individual DataGridViewColumn, DataGridViewRow, or DataGridViewCell objects to make specific columns read-only.
EditMode	Sets the conditions under which a cell will switch to edit mode. The default (EditOnKeystrokeOrF2) switches the row into edit mode when the user types a character or presses F2. Depending on the value you use, the DataGridView can be configured to put a cell into edit mode immediately when the user navigates to it (EditOnEnter), or it can prevent all user-initiated edits (EditProgrammatically), in which case you can choose to start an edit by calling DataGridView.BeginEdit(). You also can EditOnKeystroke or EditOnF2 to restrict the default editing behavior to use either the F2 key or character keystrokes, but not both.

■**Note** If you use any EditMode value other than EditProgrammatically, the user *also* can initiate an edit by double-clicking the cell with the mouse.

When the user is editing a cell, the row header will display an editing icon that looks like a pencil, although this too is configurable (just set ShowEditingIcon to false).

The user can cancel an edit by pressing the Esc key. If the EditCellOnEnter property is set to true, the cell will remain in edit mode, but all changes will be discarded. To commit a change, the user simply needs to move to a new cell (just pressing Enter will take care of that) or change focus to another control. If your code moves the position of the current cell, this also will commit the change.

To prevent a cell from being edited, you can set the ReadOnly property of the DataGridViewCell, DataGridViewColumn, DataGridViewRow, or DataGridView (depending on whether you want to prevent changes to that cell only, all cells in that column, all cells in that row, or all cells in the table, respectively). Values are automatically read-only if the underlying property or field in the data object is read-only.

You also can start and stop cell edits programmatically, using the BeginEdit(), CancelEdit(), CommitEdit(), and EndEdit() methods of the DataGridView.

Editing Events

The DataGridView also exposes several events during the edit process, as detailed in Table 15-8.

Table 15-8. *DataGridView Editing Events*

Event	Description
CellBeginEdit	Raised when the cell enters edit mode. You can examine the cell, and use the DataGridViewCellCancelEventArgs object to cancel the edit if needed.
CellEndEdit	Raised when a cell exits edit mode, either because the change has been cancelled or committed. However, you don't receive any information about why the edit was cancelled, and you won't have the opportunity to prevent the cancellation.
UserAddedRow	Raised when a user navigates away from a newly entered row, after the validation events and CellEndEdit.
UserDeletingRow	Raised when a user initiates an edit by selecting a row and pressing the Del key. At this point, you still have the chance to cancel the delete.
UserDeletedRow	Raised after the delete operation is complete and the row has been removed from the grid.

For example, if you want to show a confirmation dialog box when a user attempts to remove a row, you could use the following event handler:

```
private void DataGridView_UserDeletingRow(object sender,
 DataGridViewRowCancelEventArgs e)
{
    string id = e.Row.Cells["ProductID"].FormattedValue.ToString();
    string name = e.Row.Cells["ModelName"].FormattedValue.ToString();

    DialogResult result = MessageBox.Show(
      "Are you sure you want to delete product " + id + " - " + name + "?",
      "Delete?", MessageBoxButtons.OKCancel);

    if (result == DialogResult.Cancel)
    {
        // Cancel the delete operation.
        e.Cancel = true;
    }
}
```

Default Values for New Rows

Ordinarily, when the user begins adding a new row, the values of that new row are filled in with any defaults defined in the data source. (For example, if you're binding to a custom data object that sets certain defaults in its constructor, the constructor determines what text appears in the fields.)

However, in many cases you need a more flexible, decoupled approach that allows you to set defaults that apply only to the DataGridView. This is actually quite easy to accomplish—all you need to do is handle the DefaultValuesNeeded event. The DefaultValuesNeeded event supplies you with the appropriate DataGridView row object. You simply need to fill in each of the fields.

Here's an example:

```
private void dataGridView1_DefaultValuesNeeded(object sender,
    System.Windows.Forms.DataGridViewRowEventArgs e)
{
    e.Row.Cells["ProductID"].Value = Guid.NewGuid.ToString();
    e.Row.Cells["ModelName"].Value = "[Enter Name]";
    e.Row.Cells["Image"].Value = "noimage.gif";

    ...
}
```

Incidentally, you also can supply default formatting for new cells. Just set the properties of the DataGridView.RowTemplate object. Any property values you don't set are inherited from the styles associated with the corresponding DataGridViewColumn and the DataGridView.

Handling Errors

By default, the DataGridViewTextBoxColumn allows users to enter any characters, including those that might not be allowed in the current cell. For example, a user might type non-numeric characters in a numeric field, or specify a value that violates a ForeignKeyConstraint or UniqueConstraint defined in the DataSet. The DataGridView handles these problems in different ways:

- If the edited value can be converted into the required data type (for example, the user has typed text into a numeric column), the user won't be able to commit the change or navigate to another row. Instead, the change must be cancelled, or the value must be edited.

- If the editing attempt causes an exception, the change will be cancelled immediately after the user attempts to commit it by navigating to another row or pressing Enter. Exceptions can be thrown from the property procedure code of a bound object, or generated if you violate a constraint in a bound DataTable.

These common sense defaults work well for most scenarios. However, if necessary, you also can participate in the handling of errors by responding to the DataGridView.DataError event, which fires when the DataGridView intercepts an error from the data source (for example, entering a string instead of a number or violating a constraint in the underlying DataTable).

For example, the following DataError event handler catches both of the errors described above when the user edits the CategoryID field of the Products table:

```
private void DataGridView_DataError(object sender,
    System.Windows.Forms.DataGridViewDataErrorEventArgs e)
{
    // Check if it's an error during the commit stage.
    if ((e.Context & DataGridViewDataErrorContexts.Commit) ==
      DataGridViewDataErrorContexts.Commit)
```

```
    {
        // Check the column.
        if (dataGridView1.Columns[e.ColumnIndex].Name == "CategoryID")
        {
            // Check if it's a constraint exception.
            if (e.Exception is System.Data.InvalidConstraintException)
            {
                MessageBox.Show("This category does not exist.");
                // The following two lines suppress the exception for this error
                // and cancel the attempted action (like row navigation) so focus
                // remains on the cell. However, these are the defaults, so these
                // lines aren't required.
                e.ThrowException = false;
                e.Cancel = true;
            }
            // Check if it's a formatting exception.
            else if ((e.Exception.InnerException != null) &&
              (e.Exception.InnerException is FormatException))
            {
                MessageBox.Show("This field can only contain numbers.");
                e.ThrowException = false;
                e.Cancel = true;
            }
        }
    }
}
```

The DataError event isn't limited to dealing with exceptions that occur in the underlying data source. In fact, it's a catch-all event that fires when exceptions occur in a variety of situations. You can determine what the exception is by investigating the DataGridViewDataErrorContexts property of the DataGridViewDataErrorEventArgs object passed to the event handler. This provides a combination of enumeration values that represent exactly what's taking place. Table 15-9 lists the possible values.

Table 15-9. *DataGridViewDataErrorContexts Values*

Value	Description
Display	An error occurred when attempting to paint the cell or calculate the cell's tooltip. Several different factors can cause a display error. For example, if there's a problem formatting a value for display in a cell, you'll see both the Formatting and Display error values.
Commit	An error occurred when committing changes to the underlying data object. As with a Display error, a Commit error can occur for a variety of reasons, so this value is usually combined with additional error values from this enumeration.

Table 15-9. *DataGridViewDataErrorContexts Values*

Value	Description
Parsing	An error occurred when converting the cell's FormattedValue into its Value. Parsing errors usually indicate problems with user-supplied data. Common situations that can cause the Parsing value include errors when committing, ending, or canceling an edit. The Parsing flag is usually combined with other error values.
Formatting	An error occurred when converting the cell's Value into a FormattedValue. This is the reverse of the Parsing error.
CurrentCellChange	An error occurred when the cursor moved to another cell (at which point the DataGridView may commit an edit and perform validation). The CurrentCellChange value is usually combined with another error value.
LeaveControl	An error occurred when the DataGridView lost focus (at which point the DataGridView may commit an edit and perform validation). The LeaveControl value is usually combined with another error value.
RowDeletion	An error occurred when deleting a row. The underlying data object may have thrown an exception (for example, perhaps the deletion would violate a foreign key constraint).
ClipboardContent	An error occurred when copying content to the clipboard, because the cell value could not be converted to a string.
InitialValueRestoration	An error occurred when restoring a cell to its previous value. This value indicates that a cell tried to cancel an edit and the rollback to the initial value failed. This can occur if the cell formatting changed so that it is incompatible with the initial value.
PreferredSize	An error occurred when calculating the preferred size (height and width) of a cell when resizing a column or row.
Scroll	An error occurred when scrolling a new portion of the grid into view.

For example, you could take advantage of this context information to change the behavior of the DataGridView if the user is attempting to change focus to a different control on the form. In this case, it might be appropriate to simply display the error message in a status bar, but revert to the original value (rather than force the user to cancel the change or edit the value). To do this, you need to set the DataGridViewDataErrorEventArgs.Cancel property to false, as shown here:

```
if ((e.Context & GridViewDataErrorContexts.LeaveControl) ==
  GridViewDataErrorContexts.LeaveControl)
{
    e.Cancel = false;
}
```

Validating Input

Validation is a slightly different task than error handling. With error handling, you deal with the problems reported by the data source. With validation, you catch your own custom error conditions—for example, data that may be allowed in the data source, but doesn't make sense in your application.

When the user commits a change by navigating to a new cell, the DataGridView control raises the CellValidating and CellValidated events. These are followed by the RowValidating and RowValidated events, which only occur when the user navigates to another row. You can respond to these events, check if the user-entered values are correct, and perform any required post-processing. If a value is invalid, you have a choice of how you want to respond.

The most intrusive approach is to stop the user with a message box. Here's an example:

```
private void DataGridView_CellValidating(object sender,
    System.Windows.Forms.DataGridViewCellValidatingEventArgs e)
{
    // Check if it's a column you want to validate.
    if (dataGridView1.Columns[e.ColumnIndex].Name == "ProductImage")
    {
        // Apply the appropriate rule.
        if (System.IO.Path.GetExtension(e.FormattedValue.ToString()) != ".gif")
        {
            // There's a problem. Alert the user and cancel navigation.
            MessageBox.Show("Invalid product image.");
            e.Cancel = true;
        }
    }
}
```

By setting the Cancel property of the DataGridViewCellValidatingEventArgs object to true, you force the cell to stay in edit mode so the invalid data is not committed to the underlying data source.

Tip If you decide to use the aggressive message box approach, it may make sense to wait until the user has finished editing the entire row. Although this introduces the possibility of multiple errors, it also reduces the number of annoying message boxes that the user will see. To implement this approach, just respond to the RowValidating event instead of the CellValidating event, check every column of the current row, and present a message box with a bulleted list of all the problems you've found.

Almost everyone hates to be interrupted by a message box with error information. A more elegant approach is to set some error text to alert the user. The error text can be placed in another control, or it can be shown in the DataGrid using the ErrorText property of the corresponding DataGridViewRow and DataGridViewCell.

Usually, you'll use both of these properties in conjunction, and set an error message in both the row and cell. Here's an example that prevents file names that don't have the correct extension from being used in the ProductImage field:

```
private void DataGridView_CellValidating(object sender,
  System.Windows.Forms.DataGridViewCellValidatingEventArgs e)
{
    if (dataGridView1.Columns[e.ColumnIndex].Name == "ProductImage")
    {
        if (System.IO.Path.GetExtension(e.FormattedValue.ToString()) != ".gif")
        {
            dataGridView1.Rows[e.RowIndex].ErrorText = "Invalid Product Image";
            dataGridView1.Rows[e.RowIndex].Cells[e.ColumnIndex].ErrorText =
                "The file name must end with '.gif'.";
        }
    }
}
```

The ErrorText settings follow two rules:

- When DataGridViewCell.ErrorText is set, an exclamation icon appears in the cell. Hovering over this icon with the mouse reveals the error message. To hide these error icons, set ShowCellErrors to false.

- When DataGridViewRow.ErrorText is set, an exclamation icon appears in the row header at the left of the row. Hovering over this icon with the mouse reveals the error message. To hide these error icons, set ShowRowErrors to false.

Figure 15-14 shows the row and cell error icons.

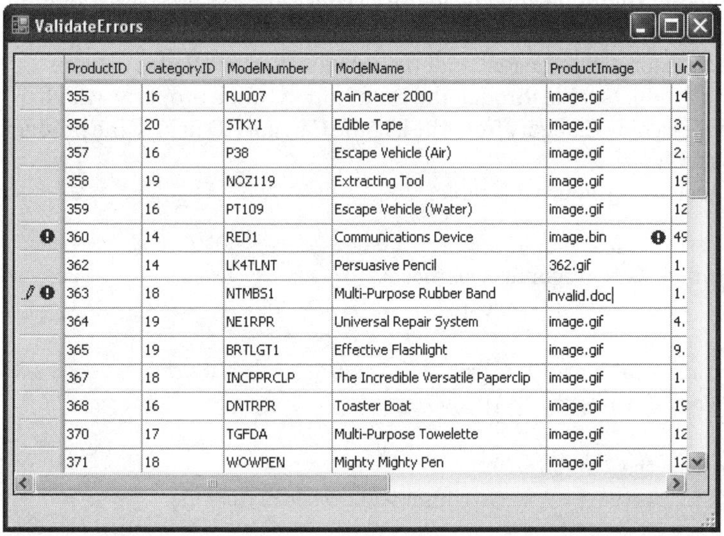

Figure 15-14. *Setting row and cell errors*

■Note Error messages that are set in the cell are only visible while the cell is not being edited. That means if you set cell error text *and* cancel the change, the user will remain in error mode and won't see the message. You can resolve this problem by setting error text for the row or in another control.

Constraining Choices with a List Column

Using validation, you can catch any error conditions. However, this approach isn't necessarily the best, because it allows the user to enter invalid input and then tries to correct it after the fact. A better solution is to restrict the user from entering any invalid input in the first place.

One common example is when you need to constrain a column to a list of predefined values. In this scenario, it's easiest for the user to choose the correct value from a list, rather than type it in by hand. Best of all, you can implement this design quite easily using the DataGridViewComboBoxColumn.

The list of items for the DataGridViewComboBoxColumn can be added by hand using the Items collection, much as you would with a ListBox. Alternatively, you can bind the DataGrid-ViewComboBoxColumn to another data source. In this case, you specify the data source using the DataSource property, and indicate what value should be displayed in the column using the DisplayMember property and what value should be used for the underlying column value using the ValueMember property.

For a demonstration, consider the next example, which works with the Products table. Every record in this table is linked to a record in the Categories table through its CategoryID field. To change the category of a product, the user must remember the correct ID and enter it in the CategoryID field. A better solution would be to use a DataGridViewComboBoxColumn that is bound to the Categories table. This column would use CategoryName as the display member, but would have CategoryID as the real underlying value. Best of all, this column would still be bound to the Products table through the DataProperyName property, which means when the user chooses a new Category from the list, the CategoryID field of the product record is changed automatically.

Here's the code you need to configure this table:

```
// Bind the grid.
DataSet ds = Program.StoreDB.GetCategoriesAndProducts();
dataGridView1.DataSource = ds.Tables["Products"];

// Remove the auto-generated CategoryID column.
dataGridView1.Columns.Remove("CategoryID");

// Create a list column for the CategoryID.
DataGridViewComboBoxColumn listCol = new DataGridViewComboBoxColumn();
listCol.DisplayIndex = 0;
listCol.HeaderText = "Category";

// This column is bound to the Products.CategoryID field.
listCol.DataPropertyName = "CategoryID";
```

```
// The list is filled from the Categories table.
listCol.DataSource = ds.Tables["Categories"];
listCol.DisplayMember = "CategoryName";
listCol.ValueMember = "CategoryID";

// Add the column.
dataGridView1.Columns.Add(listCol);
```

Figure 15-15 shows the new category column.

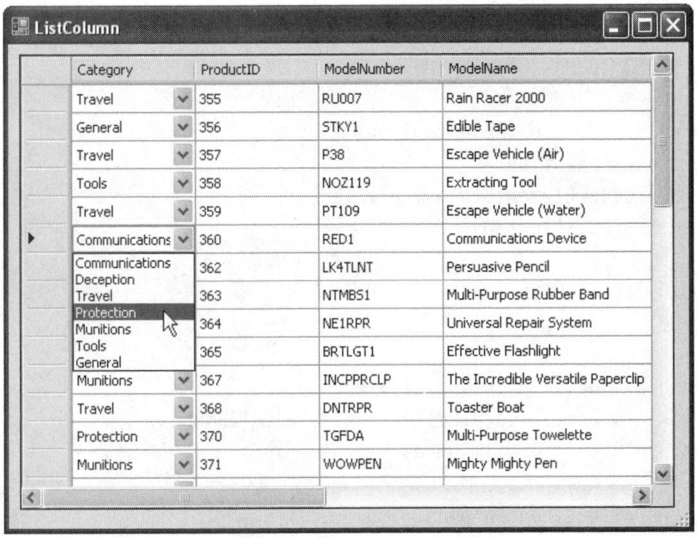

Figure 15-15. *Setting values through a list column*

DataGridView Customization

The most impressive feature of the DataGridView is its support for customization. You can extend the DataGridView to suit your needs, and you can implement these extensions in a flexible and reusable way. Although many of the possible avenues for customization are outside the scope of this book (for example, you can fine tune details as minute as the asterisk symbol shown in the new record placeholder by deriving a custom class), the following sections will give you an overview of some common scenarios where customization makes sense.

Custom Cell Painting

Although the DataGridView supports images, there are still cases where you'll want to display different types of content or apply custom formatting that isn't directly supported. For example, you might want to mingle text and graphics, draw shapes, or add a background behind the cell content. All of these details can be handled using the GDI+ drawing tools you learned about in Chapter 7. All you need to do is handle the CellPainting event (or the RowPrePaint and RowPostPaint events to apply drawing effects for the entire row). All of these events provide a drawing surface through the Graphics property of the appropriate EventArgs object.

The following example shows how you can handle the CellPainting event to fill a background gradient behind the cell content of the first column. The only caveats are that you need to explicitly set the DataGridViewCellPaintingEventArgs.Handled property to true to prevent the DataGridView from performing its own painting logic over the top of yours, and you need to paint both the background and the cell content.

Here's the drawing logic:

```
private void DataGridView_CellPainting(object sender,
 DataGridViewCellPaintingEventArgs e)
{
    // Only paint the desired column and
    // don't paint headers.
    if ((e.ColumnIndex == 0) && (e.RowIndex >= 0))
    {
        // If the cell is selected, use the normal painting
        // instead of the custom painting.
        if ((e.State & DataGridViewElementStates.Selected) !=
         DataGridViewElementStates.Selected)
        {
            // Suppress normal cell painting.
            e.Handled = true;

            // Get the rectangle where painting will take place.
            Rectangle rect = new Rectangle(e.CellBounds.X, e.CellBounds.Y,
              e.CellBounds.Width - 1, e.CellBounds.Height - 1);

            // Render the custom cell background.
            using (LinearGradientBrush brush = new LinearGradientBrush(rect,
              Color.White, Color.YellowGreen, 35f))
            {
                e.Graphics.FillRectangle(brush, rect);
            }

            // Render the standard cell border.
            using (Pen pen = new Pen(dataGridView1.GridColor))
            {
                e.Graphics.DrawRectangle(pen, e.CellBounds.X - 1,
                    e.CellBounds.Y - 1, e.CellBounds.Width, e.CellBounds.Height);
            }

            // Render the cell text.
            string cellValue = e.FormattedValue.ToString();

            // Set the alignment settings. Unfortunately, there's no
            // straightforward way to get the cell style settings and
            // convert them to the text alignment values you need here.
```

```
        StringFormat format = new StringFormat();
        format.LineAlignment = StringAlignment.Center;
        format.Alignment = StringAlignment.Near;

        using (Brush valueBrush = new SolidBrush(e.CellStyle.ForeColor))
        {
            e.Graphics.DrawString(cellValue, e.CellStyle.Font, valueBrush,
              rect, format);
        }
      }
    }
  }
}
```

Figure 15-16 shows the result.

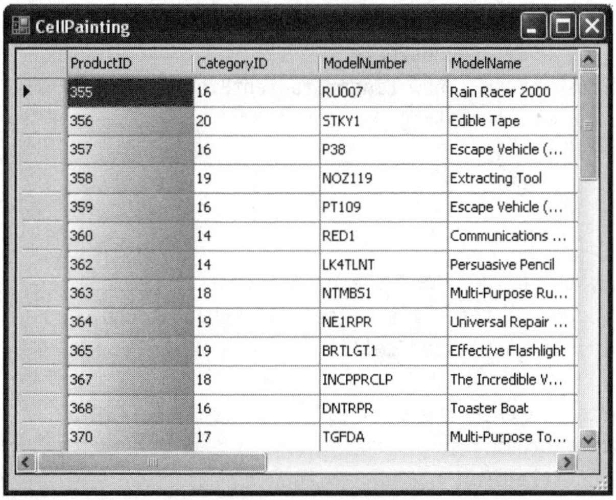

Figure 15-16. *Custom painting in a cell*

The CellPainting event provides several shortcuts so you don't need to re-create basic functionality. For example, the DataGridViewCellPaintingEventArgs class provides a PaintContent() and a PaintBackground() method. You can call these to paint part of the cell—for example, if you're interested in adding a fancy background but you don't want to bother drawing the cell text by hand. For even more control, you can use the Paint() method, which accepts a combination of values from the DataGridViewPaintParts enumeration. This combination of values tells the DataGridView exactly what to paint, and it can include the Background, Border, ContentBackground, ContentForeground, ErrorIcon, Focus, and SelectionBackground.

Using the DataGridViewCellPaintingEventArgs.Paint() method, it's possible to simplify the previous example as shown here:

```
private void DataGridView_CellPainting(object sender,
 DataGridViewCellPaintingEventArgs e)
{
    // Paint only the desired column and
    // don't paint headers.
    if ((e.ColumnIndex == 0) && (e.RowIndex >= 0))
    {
        // If the cell is selected, use the normal painting
        // instead of the custom painting.
        if ((e.State & DataGridViewElementStates.Selected) !=
         DataGridViewElementStates.Selected)
        {
            e.Handled = true;

            // Render the custom cell background.
            Rectangle rect = new Rectangle(e.CellBounds.X, e.CellBounds.Y,
              e.CellBounds.Width - 1, e.CellBounds.Height - 1);
            using (LinearGradientBrush brush = new LinearGradientBrush(rect,
              Color.White, Color.YellowGreen, 35f))
            {
                e.Graphics.FillRectangle(brush, rect);
            }

            // Paint the cell text, the border, and the error icon (if needed).
            // Don't worry about the focus rectangle or selection background,
            // because we aren't painting selected cells.
            e.Paint(e.ClipBounds,
              DataGridViewPaintParts.ContentForeground |
              DataGridViewPaintParts.Border |
              DataGridViewPaintParts.ErrorIcon |
              DataGridViewPaintParts.Focus);
        }
    }
}
```

Custom Cells

Throughout this chapter, you've seen a range of ways to extend the DataGridView by handling various cell-based events. In all of these examples, you place your event handling code in the form. This works perfectly well, but it's not terribly convenient if you want to reuse the same DataGridView in more than one form or, more likely, you want to reuse the same formatting, painting, or validation technique in different columns, forms, and even applications.

If you've perfected a piece of custom DataGridView functionality that you want to reuse, you can create a custom DataGridViewCell that encapsulates that logic. You can derive directly from the DataGridViewCell class, which is an abstract base class. Depending on your needs, you might be able to save some work by deriving from one of the higher-level cell classes like DataGridViewImageCell or DataGridViewTextBoxCell (as in the next example).

For example, here's a custom DataGridViewCell that applies the shaded background you saw in the previous example—with a twist. Now the shaded background is only applied for the cell over which the user hovers the mouse.

```
public class GradientRolloverCell : DataGridViewTextBoxCell
{
    private static int inCell = -1;

    protected override void OnMouseEnter(int rowIndex)
    {
        inCell = rowIndex;

        // Invalidate the cell.
        this.DataGridView.InvalidateCell(this.ColumnIndex, rowIndex);
    }

    protected override void OnMouseLeave(int rowIndex)
    {
        // Invalidate the cell.
        this.DataGridView.InvalidateCell(this.ColumnIndex, rowIndex);
    }

    protected override void Paint(System.Drawing.Graphics graphics,
      System.Drawing.Rectangle clipBounds, System.Drawing.Rectangle cellBounds,
      int rowIndex, DataGridViewElementStates cellState, object value,
      object formattedValue, string errorText, DataGridViewCellStyle cellStyle,
      DataGridViewAdvancedBorderStyle advancedBorderStyle,
      DataGridViewPaintParts paintParts)
    {
        // Is the mouse hovering over this cell?
        if (inCell == rowIndex)
        {
            // (Perform the gradient painting shown earlier.)
        }
        else
        {
            // Perform the standard painting.
            base.Paint(graphics, clipBounds, cellBounds, rowIndex, cellState,
              value, formattedValue, errorText, cellStyle, advancedBorderStyle,
              paintParts);
        }
    }
}
```

You also can override methods like PaintErrorIcon() and PaintBorder() to customize these details in the visual representation of your cell. (Although a bug that's present in the first release on .NET 2.0 ensures that PaintErrorIcon() isn't actually called.)

You can't place a custom DataGridViewCell directly into a DataGridView. Instead, you need to place your cell into a column, then add that column to the grid. To create a custom column, you simply need to derive a class from DataGridViewColumn.

In your custom column class, you can override functionality, add useful properties, or just set reasonable defaults in the constructor. However, in this case all you need to do is associate the custom cell with the custom column. You can achieve that with the single line of code in the constructor shown here:

```
public class GradientRolloverColumn : System.Windows.Forms.DataGridViewColumn
{
    public GradientRolloverColumn()
    {
        base.CellTemplate = new GradientRolloverCell();
    }
}
```

This code sets the DataGridViewColumn.CellTemplate property to an instance of your custom DataGridViewCell. In other words, the DataGridViewColumn will use this class every time the DataGridView asks it to create a new cell.

The final step is to add the custom column into the grid. Here's the code that accomplishes this task:

```
// Hide the ordinary version of this column.
dataGridView1.Columns[0].Visible = false;

// Create custom column.
GradientBackgroundColumn colGradient = new GradientBackgroundColumn();
colGradient.DataPropertyName = dataGridView1.Columns[0].DataPropertyName;
colGradient.HeaderText = dataGridView1.Columns[0].HeaderText;
colGradient.Width = dataGridView1.Columns[0].Width;
colGradient.ReadOnly = dataGridView1.Columns[0].ReadOnly;
colGradient.ValueType = dataGridView1.Columns[0].ValueType;
colGradient.DisplayIndex = 0;

// Add the custom column.
dataGridView1.Columns.Add(colGradient);
```

The custom column class is also a great place to define properties that should apply to all your custom cells. For example, instead of hard-coding the gradient color, you can add a property in the column class:

```
public class GradientRolloverColumn : System.Windows.Forms.DataGridViewColumn
{
    public GradientRolloverColumn(Color gradientColor)
    {
        GradientColor = gradientColor;
        base.CellTemplate = new GradientRolloverCell();
    }
```

```
    private Color color;
    public Color GradientColor
    {
        get { return color; }
        set { color = value; }
    }
}
```

You can retrieve a reference to the parent column using the DataGridViewCell.
OwningColumn property. In this example, you need to cast the column to the correct type
and retrieve the color in your drawing logic:

```
Color gradientColor;
GradientRolloverColumn gradientColumn = this.OwningColumn as GradientRolloverColumn;
if (gradientColumn != null)
{
    gradientColor = ((GradientRolloverColumn)base.OwningColumn).GradientColor;
}
else
{
    gradientColor = defaultGradientColor;
}
backgroundBrush = new LinearGradientBrush(rect, Color.White, gradientColor, 35f);
```

When you create the column, you can choose the desired color for the background fill:

```
GradientRolloverColumn colGradient =
  new GradientBackgroundColumn(Color.SlateBlue);
```

It's important to realize that custom cell and column classes aren't reserved for scenarios
where you want to perform custom drawing. They're equally useful if you want to encapsulate
validation, formatting, or error handling logic in a reusable package.

Custom Cell Edit Controls

One interesting use of custom cells is to create custom editing controls for that cell. Ordinarily,
the DataGridView limits you to ordinary text boxes, check boxes, and drop-down lists. However,
you might want to use another editing control, like the DateTimePicker, as shown in Figure 15-17.

The basic model is the same as what you learned in the previous section. In other words,
you need to create a custom DataGridViewCell class, plus a custom DataGridViewColumn that
uses the cell. The difference is in the custom DataGridViewCell class, which can override several
methods to control editing behavior.

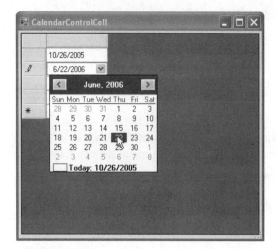

Figure 15-17. *Editing dates with a custom cell*

The key ingredient is the EditType property. This property returns the type of editing control that the cell uses. For example, if you derive a custom cell from DataGridViewTextBoxCell, the default editing control is DataGridViewTextBoxEditingControl. Here's how you would override that property to use something different:

```
public class CalendarCell : DataGridViewTextBoxCell
{
    public override Type EditType
    {
        get
        {
            return typeof(CalendarEditingControl);
        }
    }
    ...
}
```

Of course, it's up to you to create the CalendarEditingControl (as you'll see shortly). But first, you need to specify the underlying type of data that the cell stores. It's no longer strings—now it's instances of DateTime.

```
    ...
    public override Type ValueType
    {
        get
        {
            return typeof(DateTime);
        }
    }
    ...
```

Next, you need to override the InitializeEditingControl() method to configure the editing control when the cell switches into editing mode. This is the point at which you need to copy the value from the cell into the editing control.

```
...
public override void InitializeEditingControl(int rowIndex, object
  initialFormattedValue, DataGridViewCellStyle dataGridViewCellStyle)
{
    base.InitializeEditingControl(rowIndex, initialFormattedValue,
      dataGridViewCellStyle);
    CalendarEditingControl ctl =
      (CalendarEditingControl)DataGridView.EditingControl;
    ctl.Value = (DateTime)this.Value;
}
...
```

And last of all, you can override the DefaultNewRowValue property to set the default content that should appear in this column when a new row is inserted.

```
...
public override object DefaultNewRowValue
{
    get
    {
        // Use the current date and time as the default value.
        return DateTime.Now;
    }
}
}
```

Now the only remaining task to create the example shown in Figure 15-16 is to build the custom CalendarEditingControl. This step is quite easy, although there's a fair bit of boilerplate code to write. The basic technique is to derive a new class from the .NET control that you want to use. For example, in this case you need the editing features of the DateTimePicker, so it makes sense to derive from the DateTimePicker control class. However, there's another ingredient every control needs to work as an editing control for the DataGridView—it must implement IDataGridViewEditingControl.

Here's the class declaration you need:

```
public class CalendarEditingControl : DateTimePicker, IDataGridViewEditingControl
{ ... }
```

The rest of the work is to implement the IDataGridViewEditingControl members. Most of these are quite straightforward. For example, you need properties that expose the linked DataGridView, the current row index:

```
private DataGridView dataGridView;
public DataGridView EditingControlDataGridView
{
    get { return dataGridView; }
    set { dataGridView = value; }
}

private int rowIndex;
public int EditingControlRowIndex
{
    get { return rowIndex; }
    set { rowIndex = value; }
}
```

Notice you don't need to supply any real code, other than a private variable to track each of these details. The DataGridView takes care of setting these properties when it creates an editing control.

Along with these basics are some more important details. For example, whenever the value changes in your editing control, you need to call the DataGridView.NotifyCurrentCellDirty() method to notify the DataGridView (which will then display the pencil icon next to that cell). In the case of the DateTimePicker, the easiest way to implement this step is to override the OnValueChanged() method:

```
// This is the only member in CalendarEditingControl that's not implemented
// to satisfy the IDataGridViewEditingControl interface.
protected override void OnValueChanged(EventArgs eventargs)
{
    // Notify the DataGridView that the contents of the cell
    // have changed.
    valueChanged = true;
    this.EditingControlDataGridView.NotifyCurrentCellDirty(true);
    base.OnValueChanged(eventargs);
}

private bool valueChanged = false;
public bool EditingControlValueChanged
{
    get { return valueChanged; }
    set { valueChanged = value; }
}
```

Notice that you also need to implement the EditingControlValueChanged property to track whether the control value has changed.

Another property you need to implement is EditingControlFormattedValue. This property allows your control to receive a formatted string from the cell, which it must convert into the appropriate DateTime value and display.

```
public object EditingControlFormattedValue
{
    get { return this.Value.ToShortDateString(); }
    set
    {
        string newValue = value as string;
        if (newValue != null)
            this.Value = DateTime.Parse(newValue);
    }
}

public object GetEditingControlFormattedValue(
  DataGridViewDataErrorContexts context)
{
    return EditingControlFormattedValue;
}
```

Two more interesting methods are ApplyCellStyleToEditingControl() and EditingControlWantsInputKey(). In ApplyCellStyleToEditingControl(), you configure the control to match the style properties of the DataGridViewCell. In EditingControlWantsInputKey(), you define what keystrokes your control should handle.

```
public void ApplyCellStyleToEditingControl(
  DataGridViewCellStyle dataGridViewCellStyle)
{
    this.Font = dataGridViewCellStyle.Font;
    this.CalendarForeColor = dataGridViewCellStyle.ForeColor;
    this.CalendarMonthBackground = dataGridViewCellStyle.BackColor;
}

public bool EditingControlWantsInputKey(
  Keys key, bool dataGridViewWantsInputKey)
{
    // Let the DateTimePicker handle the keys listed.
    switch (key & Keys.KeyCode)
    {
        case Keys.Left:
        case Keys.Up:
        case Keys.Down:
        case Keys.Right:
        case Keys.Home:
        case Keys.End:
        case Keys.PageDown:
        case Keys.PageUp:
          return true;
        default:
          return false;
    }
}
```

The remaining members of IDataGridViewEditingControl don't need any real code in this example. They simply give you the opportunity to configure the DateTimePicker when it enters edit mode, force the DataGridView to reposition the control when the value changes, and set the edit cursor.

```
public void PrepareEditingControlForEdit(bool selectAll)
{}

public bool RepositionEditingControlOnValueChange
{
    get { return false; }
}

public Cursor EditingPanelCursor
{
    get { return base.Cursor; }
}
```

The Last Word

This chapter provided a close look at the DataGridView, one of .NET's most anticipated new controls. As you've seen in this chapter, the DataGridView works well in a variety of scenarios and offers rich support for common scenarios, formatting, customization, different column types, and editing. Unlike the original DataGrid, the DataGridView really does offer an all-in-one data display solution for Windows Forms applications.

CHAPTER 16

■ ■ ■

Sound and Video

Great user interfaces don't stop at buttons and text boxes. They include multimedia features like soundtracks and even live video. One of the most glaring omissions in the first versions of .NET was the lack of any controls for dealing with audio. This gap forced developers to dig into the Windows API just to play simple sounds and beeps. Fortunately, .NET 2.0 addresses this problem with a new SoundPlayer control that lets you play WAV files synchronously or in the background.

Sadly, the SoundPlayer control is still a limited solution. If you need something a little more sophisticated, like the ability to play MP3 audio or host a movie window, you still need to step outside the .NET Framework and use the unmanaged DirectShow library that's included with Windows. In this chapter, you'll learn how to use both the SoundPlayer control and DirectShow.

The SoundPlayer

Playing a sound in Windows has never been difficult. Programmers in just about any language can rely on the unmanaged PlaySound() function in the Windows API. Life gets even easier in .NET 2.0, which includes a simple SoundPlayer class that wraps the PlaySound() function. The SoundPlayer is found in the new System.Media namespace, which is largely slated for future use. Currently, it contains only three types: SoundPlayer, SystemSounds, and SystemSound. You'll see all of these classes in this chapter.

Note In order to use the SoundPlayer, you must create it manually in code. Although the SoundPlayer is derived from the Component class and therefore has rudimentary design-time features, Microsoft chose to explicitly hide it from the Toolbox using the ToolboxItem attribute. This decision was made because there isn't any design-time support for wiring up media files to the Sound Player in Visual Studio. In other words, even if you could add the SoundPlayer to the component tray, you would still need to write code to configure it.

Aside from convenience, the chief benefit of the SoundPlayer class is that it supports .NET stream objects. That means you don't have to store your audio in separate files. Instead, you can extract it from a variety of different sources, like a binary field in a database, or a resource file that's embedded inside your application assembly. The key drawback of the SoundPlayer is the fact that it can play only the WAV audio format. If you want to play other types of multimedia, like MP3 or WMA files, you need to use a different solution.

To play a sound with the SoundPlayer, you follow several steps:

1. First, specify the sound content by setting either the Stream or the SoundLocation property. If you have a Stream-based object that contains WAV audio content, use the Stream property. If you have a file path or URL that points to a WAV file, use the SoundLocation property.

2. Once you've set the Stream or SoundLocation property, you can tell SoundPlayer to actually load the audio data by calling the Load() or LoadAsync() method. The Load() method is the simplest—it stalls your code until all the audio is loaded into memory. LoadAsync() quietly carries out its work on another thread and fires the LoadCompleted event when it's finished.

■**Note** Technically, you don't need to use Load() or LoadAsync(). The SoundPlayer will load the audio data if needed when you call Play() or PlaySync(). However, it's a good idea to explicitly load the audio—not only does that save you the overhead if you need to play it multiple times, but it also makes it easy to handle exceptions related to file problems separately from exceptions related to audio-playback problems.

---

3. Now you can call PlaySync() to pause your code while the audio plays, or you can use Play() to play the audio on another thread, ensuring that your application's interface remains responsive. Your only other option is PlayLooping(), which plays the audio asynchronously in an unending loop (perfect for those annoying soundtracks). To halt the current playback at any time, just call Stop().

The SoundPlayer also exposes two less-useful events. These are the SoundLocationChanged and StreamChanged events, which fire when your code changes the SoundLocation or Stream property of the SoundPlayer.

■**Tip** If you're hunting for WAV files to test out with the SoundPlayer, look for the Media directory in the Windows directory, which holds WAV files for all the Windows system sounds.

Synchronous and Asynchronous Playback

The following code snippet shows the simplest approach to load and play a sound synchronously:

```
SoundPlayer player = new SoundPlayer();
player.SoundLocation = Application.StartupPath + "\\test.wav";
try
{
    player.Load();
}
catch (System.IO.FileNotFoundException err)
{
    // An error will occur here if the file can't be found.
}

try
{
    player.PlaySync();
}
catch (FormatException err)
{
    // A FormatException will occur here if the file doesn't
    // contain valid WAV audio.
}
```

The asynchronous pattern for playing audio is similar, except that you can't assume the audio is available and ready to play until the LoadCompleted event fires. You can handle the LoadCompleted event to take the next step, such as enabling playback controls on your form or playing the sound.

Here's an example that uses the asynchronous pattern. The process begins when the form first loads:

```
private SoundPlayer player = new SoundPlayer();

private void SoundTestForm_Load(object sender, EventArgs e)
{
    // Attach the event handler.
    player.LoadCompleted += new AsyncCompletedEventHandler(player_LoadCompleted);

    player.SoundLocation = Application.StartupPath + "\\test.wav";
    try
    {
        player.LoadAsync();
    }
    catch (FileNotFoundException err)
    {
        // An error will occur here if the file can't be found.
    }
}
```

```
private void player_LoadCompleted(object sender, AsyncCompletedEventArgs e)
{
    try
    {
        player.PlaySync();
    }
    catch (Exception err)
    {
        // A FormatException will occur here if the file doesn't
        // contain valid WAV audio.
    }
}
```

You can see both techniques in the sample audio player included with this chapter's samples, which are available in the Source Code area of the Apress Web site, www.apress.com (see Figure 16-1).

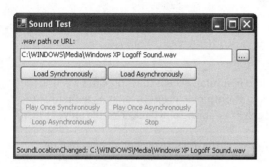

Figure 16-1. *A SoundPlayer test utilty*

Of course, you don't need to load the SoundPlayer audio from a file. If you've created small sounds that are played at several points in your application, it may make more sense to embed the sound files into your compiled assembly as resources. This technique, which was discussed in Chapter 5, works just as well with sound files as it does with images. For example, if you add the ding.wav audio file with the resource name Ding (just browse to the Properties ➤ Resources node in the Solution Explorer and use the designer support), you would use this code to play it:

```
SoundPlayer player = new SoundPlayer();
player.Stream = Properties.Resources.Ding;
player.PlaySync();
```

■Note The SoundPlayer class doesn't deal well with large audio files, because it needs to load the entire file into memory at once. You might think that you can resolve this problem by submitting a large audio file in smaller chunks, but the SoundPlayer wasn't designed with this technique in mind. There's no easy way to synchronize the SoundPlayer so that it plays multiple audio snippets one after the other, because it doesn't provide any sort of queuing feature. Each time you call PlaySync() or PlayAsync(), the current audio playback is stopped. Workarounds are possible, but you'll be far better off using the DirectX libraries discussed later.

System Sounds

One of the shameless frills of the Windows operating system is its ability to map audio files to specific system events. .NET includes a new System.Media.SystemSounds class that allows you to access the most common of these sounds, and use them in your own applications. This technique works best if all you want is a simple chime to indicate the end of a long-running operation, or an alert sound to indicate a warning condition.

Unfortunately, the SystemSounds class is based on the MessageBeep Win32 API, and as a result it provides access to only the following generic system sounds:

- Asterisk

- Beep

- Exclamation

- Hand

- Question

The SystemSounds class provides a property for each of these sounds, which returns a SystemSound object you can use to play the sound through its Play() method. For example, to sound a beep in your code, you simply need to execute this line of code:

```
SystemSounds.Beep.Play();
```

To configure what WAV files are used for each sound, select the Sounds and Audio Devices icon in the Control Panel.

Advanced Media with DirectShow

The SoundPlayer and SystemSounds classes are easy to use, but they're relatively underpowered. In today's world, it's much more common to use compressed MP3 audio for everything except the simplest of sounds, instead of the original WAV format. But if you want to play MP3 audio or MPEG video, you need to turn to the world of unmanaged code.

The solution is the Quartz COM component. This component is a key part of DirectX, and it's included with Windows Media Player and the Windows operating system. (The same component is also known by the more marketing-friendly term DirectShow, and previous versions were called ActiveMovie.) You can find the Quartz component by looking for a like-named quartz.dll in the Windows System32 directory.

Using Quart.dll Through Interop

Before you can use the Quartz component, you need to generate an interop assembly that can handle the interaction between your .NET application and the unmanaged Quartz library. One easy approach is to generate an interop assembly using the Type Library Importer utility (tlbimp.exe). Just open a command-prompt window (preferably by choosing Programs ➤ Microsoft Visual Studio 2005 ➤ Visual Studio Tools ➤ Visual Studio Command Prompt, which sets the path variable so that the tlbimp.exe utility is always available). Then enter the following command, where [WindowsDir] is the path for your installation of Windows:

```
[WindowsDir]/tlbimp quartz.dll /out:QuartzTypeLib.dll
```

You can then add a reference to this interop class to your .NET project. Just right-click your project in the Solution Explorer, and choose Add Reference from the context menu. Select the .NET tab, click Browse, and select the QuartzTypeLib.dll assembly that you created. Alternatively, you can let Visual Studio .NET generate the interop class on its own. To do this, simply right-click your project in the Solution Explorer and choose Add Reference. Then click the Browse tab and select the quartz.dll file in the System32 directory inside your Windows directory.

Note You can also find the quartz.dll library in the list of known COM components, under the name ActiveMovie.

Playing MP3, MIDI, WMA, and More

Once you've added a reference to the Quartz component, you can use it to play a wide range of audio files. Essentially, you can play any audio supported by Windows Media Player. This includes the following:

- **MP3**, the high-quality compressed audio format that made song pirating famous.

- **WMA** (Windows Media Audio), Microsoft's MP3 clone that can be used in conjunction with strict licenses.

- **MIDI**, the lightweight format that stores a sequence of notes rather than digital audio. When you play a MIDI file, the sequence of notes is synthesized using whatever capability your sound card has. MIDI files were once the easiest way to play high-quality music (with the right equipment). But now that hard drives have grown, and compressed digital audio formats like MP3 are practical, MIDI is used more commonly by music professionals than by computer hobbyists or gamers.

Of course, you can also use Quartz to play a basic WAV audio file.

To play an audio file with Quartz, you use the IMediaControl interface. IMediaControl is fairly easy to use, but its cryptically named methods can be somewhat confusing at first. To load an audio file, you use the RenderFile() method. You can then control its playback using methods like Run(), Stop(), and Pause(). The actual playback always takes place on a separate thread, so it won't block your code.

The following example shows the form code you can use to play an audio file. The audio is started when a Play button is clicked, and stopped when a Pause button is clicked.

```
// The FilgraphManager is the central source for all other interfaces.
private QuartzTypeLib.FilgraphManager graphManager;

// The IMediaControl interface allows you control playback.
private QuartzTypeLib.IMediaControl mc;
```

```csharp
private void cmdPlay_Click(object sender, System.EventArgs e)
{
    if (mc == null)
    {
        // This audio is being played for the first time.

        // Get access to the IMediaControl interface.
        graphManager = new QuartzTypeLib.FilgraphManager();
        mc = (QuartzTypeLib.IMediaControl)graphManager;

        // Load the file.
        try
        {
            mc.RenderFile(Application.StartupPath + "\\test.mp3");
        }
        catch (System.IO.FileNotFoundException err)
        {
            MessageBox.Show("File not found.");
            return;
        }
    }

    // Start playing the audio asynchronously.
    try
    {
        mc.Run();
    }
    catch (System.Runtime.InteropServices.COMException err)
    {
        // Indicates a problem interpreting the file.
        MessageBox.Show("COM error.");
    }
}

private void cmdPause_Click(object sender, System.EventArgs e)
{
    if (mc != null) mc.Pause();
}

private void Form_Closed(object sender, System.EventArgs e)
{
    if (mc != null) mc.Stop();
}
```

The Quartz component provides quite a bit more functionality that's hidden in this example. For instance, you might want to control volume and position, and respond to events. To perform any of these tasks, you need to first define a few more interfaces. Add these at the form level so they're accessible in all your event handlers:

```
// IBasicAudio exposes Volume and Balance properties.
private QuartzTypeLib.IBasicAudio audio;

// IMediaPosition exposes the CurrentPosition property.
private QuartzTypeLib.IMediaPosition position;

// IMediaEventEx allows you to receive events, including when playback stops.
private QuartzTypeLib.IMediaEventEx mEventEx;
```

As with the IMediaControl interface, you can access all of these interfaces through the central FilgraphManager. You simply need to cast the object to the required interface before you load the file. You can place this code immediately after you create the FilgraphManager.

```
audio = (QuartzTypeLib.IBasicAudio)graphManager;
position = (QuartzTypeLib.IMediaPosition)graphManager;
mEventEx = (QuartzTypeLib.IMediaEventEx)graphManager;
```

For example, using the IMediaPosition interface you can add a Stop button that resets the position to the beginning of the file:

```
private void cmdStop_Click(object sender, EventArgs e)
{
    if (mc != null) mc.Stop();
    position.CurrentPosition = 0;
}
```

Tracking Position

Another reason you might go to all the trouble of defining the additional interfaces is to measure the duration of a file and track the current position of playback.

The IMediaPosition.Duration property retrieves the total length of the file (in seconds). Here's the code you could use to display the total duration of the file in hours, minutes, and seconds just before you start playing it:

```
statusLabel1.Text = "Total: " + ConvertTimeToString((int)position.Duration);
```

This code employs the private ConvertTimeToString() method shown here:

```
private string ConvertTimeToString(int seconds)
{
    int hours = seconds / 3600;
    int minutes = (seconds  - (hours * 3600)) / 60;
    seconds = seconds - (hours * 3600 + minutes * 60);
    return String.Format("{0:D2}:{1:D2}:{2:D2}", hours, minutes, seconds);
}
```

Even better, to ensure the progress stays up-to-date as you play a file, you can add a simple timer that checks the IMediaPosition.Position property every 500 milliseconds and updates the status bar accordingly:

```
private void timerPosition_Tick(object sender, System.EventArgs e)
{
    if (position != null)
    {
        statusLabel2.Text = "Current: " +
            ConvertTimeToString((int)position.CurrentPosition);
    }
}
```

Now, just start the timer immediately after you start the playback:

```
timerPosition.Start();
```

And stop the timer before the playback is stopped or paused:

```
timerPosition.Stop();
```

Figure 16-2 shows the media player application so far.

Figure 16-2. *A Quartz-based media player*

Looping Audio

Another reason you might want to use some of the extender interfaces is to receive a notification when the file is complete. Because the Quartz component doesn't provide any way to loop your audio, you could use this point to restart the playback process.

This technique is a little more awkward because the only way you can receive the notification you need is to override the WndProc() method of the form. WndProc() fires every time a Windows notification message is received by your window. When you override WndProc(), you need to check if the message is one that specifically interests you and, if not, pass it along to the .NET Framework.

Here's the code you need to check for the audio completion message and restart playback so it loops forever:

```
private const int WM_APP = 0x8000;
private const int WM_GRAPHNOTIFY = WM_APP + 1;
private const int EC_COMPLETE = 0x01;
```

```
protected override void WndProc(ref Message m)
{
    // Check if it's a notification message from the Quartz component.
    if (m.Msg == WM_GRAPHNOTIFY)
    {
        int lEventCode;
        int lParam1, lParam2;

        try
        {
            // Retrieve the message.
            mEventEx.GetEvent(out lEventCode, out lParam1,
              out lParam2, 0);
            mEventEx.FreeEventParams(lEventCode, lParam1, lParam2);

            // Check if it's the end-of-file message.
            if (lEventCode == EC_COMPLETE)
            {
                // Restart the playback.
                mc.Stop();
                position.CurrentPosition = 0;
                mc.Run();
                MeasureProgress();
            }
        }
        catch (Exception)
        {
            // Never throw an exception from WndProc().
            // You may want to log it, however.
        }
    }
    // Pass the message along to .NET.
    base.WndProc(ref m);
}
```

There's only one catch. In order to receive the completion message, you need to tell the Quartz component to notify you when playback is finished. To do this, call the SetNotifyWindow() method of the IMediaEventEx interface, and pass the low-level handle of the window that needs to receive the message. You should perform this step before you start playback (in other words, before you call the IMediaControl.Run() method), using a line of code like this:

```
mEventEx.SetNotifyWindow((int) this.Handle, WM_GRAPHNOTIFY, 0);
```

Now your audio will loop continuously. You can try out the complete sample application with the downloadable code for this chapter (in the Source Code area at www.apress.com).

Showing MPEG and Other Video Types

The Quartz component also works with video files. You can use it to play common types of video like MPEG, AVI, or WMV). In fact, you use the exact same methods of the IMediaControl interface to load and play a movie. If you try out the application shown in the previous example with an MPEG file, a stand-alone window will automatically appear showing the video. You can use all of the same techniques to adjust the sound, change the position, and loop the video.

The only difference occurs if you want to show the video window inside your application interface (rather than in a separate stand-alone window). In this case, you need use the IVideoWindow interface.

As with the other interfaces, you can cast the FilgraphManager to the IVideoWindow interface. Using the IVideoWindow interface, you can bind the video output to a control on your form, such as a Panel or a PictureBox. To do so, set the IVideoWindow.Owner property to the handle for the control, which you can retrieve using the Control.Handle property. Then, call IVideoWindow.SetWindowPosition() to set the window size and location.

The following example plays a video file and shows it in a PictureBox on your form.

```
private const int WS_CHILD = 0x40000000;
private const int WS_CLIPCHILDREN = 0x2000000;

private QuartzTypeLib.IMediaControl mc;
private QuartzTypeLib.IVideoWindow videoWindow = null;

private void Form1_Load(object sender, System.EventArgs e)
{
    // Load the movie file.
    FilgraphManager graphManager = new FilgraphManager();
    videoWindow = (IVideoWindow)graphManager;
    mc = (IMediaControl)graphManager;
    graphManager.RenderFile(Application.StartupPath + "\\test.mpg");

    // Attach the view to a PictureBox on the form.
    try
    {
        videoWindow.Owner = (int) pictureBox1.Handle;
        videoWindow.WindowStyle = WS_CHILD | WS_CLIPCHILDREN;
        videoWindow.SetWindowPosition(
          pictureBox1.ClientRectangle.Left, pictureBox1.ClientRectangle.Top,
          pictureBox1.ClientRectangle.Width, pictureBox1.ClientRectangle.Height);
    }
    catch
    {
        // An error can occur if the file does not have a video
        // source (for example, an MP3 file.)
        // You can ignore this error and still allow playback to
        // continue (without any visualization).
    }
```

```
    // Start the playback (asynchronously).
    mc.Run();
}

private void Form1_Closing(object sender,
 System.ComponentModel.CancelEventArgs e)
{
    mc.Stop();
}
```

You can use the SetWindowPosition() method to change the size of your video window even while playback is in progress. In the preceding example, the PictureBox is anchored to all sides of the form, so it changes size as the form is resized. You need to respond to the PictureBox.SizeChanged event to change the size of the corresponding video window so it matches the new size of the PictureBox.

```
private void pictureBox1_SizeChanged(object sender, System.EventArgs e)
{
    if (videoWindow != null)
    {
        try
        {
            videoWindow.SetWindowPosition(
                pictureBox1.ClientRectangle.Left, pictureBox1.ClientRectangle.Top,
                pictureBox1.ClientRectangle.Width,
                pictureBox1.ClientRectangle.Height);
        }
        catch
        {
            // Ignore the exception thrown when resizing the form
            // when the file does not have a video source.
        }
    }
}
```

■Note If you want to go one step further and use advanced DirectX features for rendering three-dimensional graphics and mixing multiple audio sounds at once, you may be interested in the managed DirectX SDK (software development kit). This toolkit is large and complex, and it requires a client that has DirectX 9 (older computers need not apply), but it's also stocked full of powerful functionality for building cutting-edge games and other graphically rich applications. You can find out more at Microsoft's DirectX Developer Center (http://msdn.microsoft.com/directx), or you can read a dedicated book on the topic.

Figure 16-3 shows a sample video being played in this application.

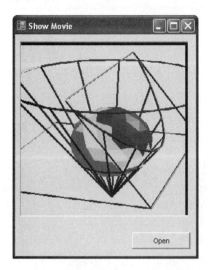

Figure 16-3. *Playing video with DirectShow*

The Last Word

In this chapter, you learned how to play sound with the simple SoundPlayer, and step up to more ambitious audio and video with the unmanaged Quartz component. Unfortunately, sound and video are two areas where the Windows Forms toolkit still has some significant gaps.

In the next chapter, you'll learn about a much more impressive addition to the .NET Framework—the WebBrowser control.

CHAPTER 17

The WebBrowser

The WebBrowser control is another new frill in .NET 2.0. Essentially, the WebBrowser allows you to embed a full-featured Internet Explorer inside any window. This feat was technically possible in previous versions of .NET using interop and the Internet Explorer ActiveX control. However, the interop approach suffered from a few annoying quirks that the WebBrowser control deftly avoids. The WebBrowser control also adds a remarkable piece of new functionality: the ability to interact with the contents of a Web page programmatically using a specially crafted *document object model* (DOM). In other words, you can access individual HTML elements on a Web page, tweaking their text, changing their position, or inserting new markup. You can even handle JavaScript events that originate from a Web page in your form code. If you're willing to invest a fair bit of work, you could use these features to build something really unique, like a next-generation help engine, a screen-scraping Web browser, or a blended interface that incorporates both Windows and Web controls.

WebBrowser Basics

Some of the most innovative applications weave together Windows controls and Web-style interfaces. With the new WebBrowser control, .NET gives you a tool that you can use to build your own Web-enabled interfaces. You can use the WebBrowser to display a Web site or an ordinary HTML file on the current computer, which makes it a great tool for serving up user information and sophisticated help.

The WebBrowser displays a standard Internet Explorer window. That means that WebBrowser has all the features and frills of IE, including JavaScript, Dynamic HTML, ActiveX controls, and plug-ins. However, the WebBrowser window doesn't include additional details like a toolbar, address bar, or status bar (although you can add all of these ingredients to your form using other controls like the ToolStrip). Best of all, the WebBrowser has a respectable .NET interface, with a solid complement of methods, a rich event model, and some extended functionality that allows you to manipulate HTML pages as a collection of objects.

Note The WebBrowser isn't written from scratch in managed code. It's actually a wrapper for the shdocvw.dll COM component, which provides the actual Web-browsing functionality. However, the WebBrowser is far superior to using interop on your own. That's because the WebBrowser control supports features that don't quite work right with an automatically generated shdocvw.dll wrapper.

Navigating to a Page

Once you've placed the WebBrowser control on a window, you need to point it to a document. Usually, you'll supply a URL that points to a local or remote location. However, you can also submit a complete HTML document, content and all, as a long string or a Stream-based object.

The WebBrowser control gives you the choice of three properties:

- **Url.** Set this to a remote URL (http://mysite.com/mypage.html) or a fully qualified file path (file:///c:\mydocument.text). You must use a Uri object (which you can create from a string).

- **DocumentText.** Set this with a string containing the HTML document you want to show. This provides some interesting options, like the dynamic HTML editor shown in Figure 17-1, which creates a Web page by copying the HTML entered in a text box in the DocumentText property of a WebBrowser window.

- **DocumentStream.** Set this with an object that derives from Stream and contains the HTML document. This allows you to open a file and feed it straight into the WebBrowser for rendering, without needing to hold the whole HTML content in memory at once.

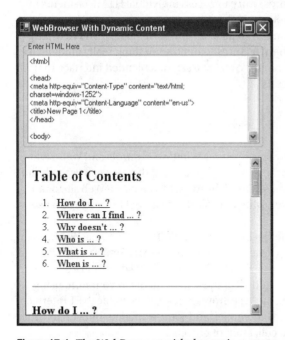

Figure 17-1. *The WebBrowser with dynamic content*

■**Note** All three navigation properties are writable and readable. That means you can set a URL, wait for the page to load, and then retrieve the raw HTML from the DocumentText property (and the title from DocumentTitle). If a document couldn't be loaded and an error page is shown, this property returns an empty string.

In addition to these properties, you can navigate to a URL using several different methods, the most useful of which is Navigate(). Navigate() is particularly interesting because it provides several overloaded versions. One of these allows you to specify a Boolean new Window parameter. Set this to true, and the WebBrowser will launch a stand-alone Internet Explorer window (complete with toolbars, address bars, and more).

```
webBrowser1.Navigate("http://www.prosetech.com", true);
```

This stand-alone browser will be out of your control, and you won't be able to send it to specific pages or receive events for it.

Another overloaded version of the Navigate() method lets you update a single frame in the current document. In this case, you specify a targetFrameName parameter. The WebBrowser loads the new URL into this frame, provided it exists, in the current document.

```
webBrowser1.Navigate("http://www.prosetech.com", "bodyFrame");
```

This command is particularly handy if you want to control different parts of a complex Web page independently.

Table 17-1 lists all the navigation methods of the WebBrowser control.

Table 17-1. *Navigation Methods for the WebBrowser*

Method	Description
Navigate()	Moves to the new URL you specify. If you use one of the overloaded methods, you can choose to load this document into a specific frame or a stand-alone IE window. You can also use one of the overloads that allows you to supply data that will be posted to the server.
GoBack() and GoForward()	Moves to the previous or next document in the navigation history. If you try to move back while on the first document, or try to move forward while on the most recent document, the method returns false and has no effect.
GoHome() and GoSearch()	Moves to the designated home page or search page, as configured in the computer's Internet settings.
Refresh()	Reloads the current document.
Stop()	Stops downloading the document if it is not yet complete. The partial version will still be shown (or an error page if the server couldn't be contacted at all). It also ends playing any background sounds or animations on the page.

■**Note** You can also direct the WebBrowser to a directory. For example, set the Url property to file:///c:\. In this case, the WebBrowser window becomes the familiar Explorer-style file browser, allowing the user to open, copy, paste, and delete files. However, the WebBrowser doesn't provide events or properties that allow you to restrict this ability (or even monitor it), so tread carefully!

All WebBrowser navigation is asynchronous. That means your code continues executing while the page is downloading. If you want to determine if the page is finished, you can check the IsBusy property (which should be false). For more information, check the ReadyState property, which provides one of the values from Table 17-2.

Table 17-2. *Values for the WebBrowserReadyState Enumeration*

Value	Description
UnInitialized	No document is currently loaded.
Loading	A download has been initiated.
Loaded	Contrary to what you might expect, the document's not finished yet. However, the WebBrowser control has initialized the new document and started retrieving the data it needs.
Interactive	The document's still not finished, but there is enough data to display some of it and allow limited user interaction. For example, the user can click on any hyperlinks that have been displayed so far.
Complete	The document is fully loaded. On a typical connection, the WebBrowser will pass through the Loaded, Interactive, and Complete stages quite quickly.

WebBrowser Events

If you want your application to perform respectably, you won't waste time querying the IsBusy and ReadyState properties. Instead, you'll wait for a WebBrowser event to fire that indicates the document is complete. With this approach, your user interface remains responsive, and the user has the ability to click other buttons or interact with the partially downloaded Web page.

To master the WebBrowser, you need to understand its event model. The WebBrowser events unfold in this order:

- **Navigating** fires when you set a new Url, or the user clicks a link. You can inspect the Url, and cancel navigation by setting e.Cancel to true.

- **Navigated** fires after Navigating, just before the Web browser begins downloading the page.

- **ProgressChanged** fires periodically during a page download, and gives you information about how many bytes have been downloaded and how many are expected in total. You can use this event to update a status bar or some sort of progress control. Just keep in mind that the numbers you receive are not always accurate, and you need to continually check both the current value and the maximum value. For example, a ProgressChanged event fires at the beginning of every page request with a max value of 10,000, and may be adjusted to a more accurate page size shortly thereafter.

- **DocumentCompleted** fires when the page is completely loaded. This is your chance to process the page.

These are the core WebBrowser events. In addition, you may be interested in handling the events shown in Table 17-3.

Table 17-3. *Additional WebBrowser Events*

Event	Description
FileDownload	This event occurs just before a file download starts. You can cancel the download by setting e.Cancel to true.
NewWindow	This event occurs just before a new stand-alone Internet Explorer window opens in response to the overloaded Navigate() method, or if the user right-clinks a link and chooses Open in New Window. You can cancel this operation by setting e.Cancel to true.
CanGoBackChanged and CanGoForwardChanged	Occurs when the CanGoBack and CanGoForward properties change. These properties are simple Boolean values that indicate if there is a previous or subsequent entry in the navigation history. You can use these events to keep the state of any custom forward or backward buttons synchronized.
DocumentTitleChanged	Occurs when the document title changes as a result of downloading the page. At this point, you can display the document title somewhere else (Internet Explorer shows it in the title bar).
StatusTextChanged	Occurs whenever the WebBrowser has new status text. The status text is displayed at the bottom of a typical Internet Explorer window in the status bar, and it indicates the current state, as well as the destination of a hyperlink when the user hovers over it with the mouse. By default, this text doesn't appear in the WebBrowser control, but you can receive it from the StatusText property every time this event fires and display it somewhere else on your form.
EncryptionLevelChanged	Occurs when the user navigates to or from a site that uses SSL (Secure Sockets Layer) to encrypt communication between the client and server.

A WebBrowser Example

The following code shows a form that hosts a WebBrowser, and is armed with a simple status bar and progress bar. The key point in this example is the event handler for the Navigating event. It demonstrates how you can stop the user from surfing to pages you don't want them to access. In this example, any page that's not on the msdn.microsoft.com domain is prohibited. This example also shows how to show the Internet Explorer status text, and use a progress bar to show the amount of a page that's been downloaded so far.

```
public partial class WebBrowserRestricted : System.Windows.Forms.Form
{
    private void WebBrowserRestricted_Load(object sender, System.EventArgs e)
    {
        webBrowser.Navigate("http://msdn.microsoft.com");
    }
}
```

```csharp
private void webBrowser_Navigating(object sender,
  System.Windows.Forms.WebBrowserNavigatingEventArgs e)
{
    // Here you decide whether to allow navigation to the selected page.

    // Check the domain.
    // In this case, allow only the home site.
    if (e.Url.Host != "msdn.microsoft.com")
    {
        MessageBox.Show("Site restricted for demonstration purposes.");
        e.Cancel = true;
    }
}

private void webBrowser_Navigated(object sender,
  System.Windows.Forms.WebBrowserNavigatedEventArgs e)
{
    // Show the progress bar.
    progressBar.Visible = true;
}

private void webBrowser_ProgressChanged(object sender,
  System.Windows.Forms.WebBrowserProgressChangedEventArgs e)
{
    // Update the progress bar.
    progressBar.Maximum = (int)e.MaximumProgress;
    if (e.CurrentProgress >= 0 && e.CurrentProgress <= e.MaximumProgress)
    {
        progressBar.Value = (int)e.CurrentProgress;
    }
}

private void webBrowser_DocumentCompleted(object sender,
  System.Windows.Forms.WebBrowserDocumentCompletedEventArgs e)
{
    // Hide the progress bar.
    progressBar.Visible = false;
}

private void webBrowser_StatusTextChanged(object sender, System.EventArgs e)
{
    // Display the text that IE would ordinarily show
    // in the status bar.
    statusBar.Text = webBrowser.StatusText;
}
```

```
    private void webBrowser_NewWindow(object sender,
      System.ComponentModel.CancelEventArgs e)
    {
        // Never allow external windows.
        e.Cancel = true;
    }
}
```

Figure 17-2 shows the Web browser in action.

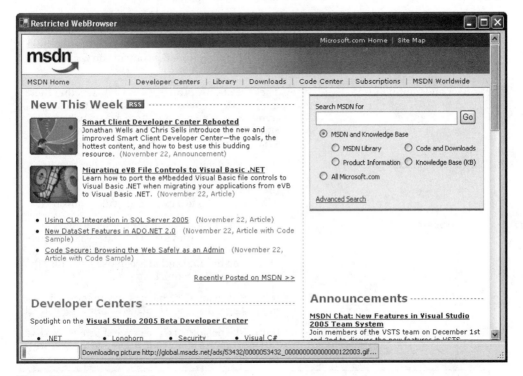

Figure 17-2. *A custom Web browser*

Printing, Saving, and Fine-Tuning

You can set a slew of miscellaneous WebBrowser properties to customize its behavior. It's important to consider these carefully, not because you might need to access additional features, but because they let you clamp down on the open-ended nature of the Internet Explorer window. For example, if you're worrying about users dragging and dropping links or right-clicking to get extended options, you can set the AllowWebBrowserDrop and IsWebBrowserContextMenuEnabled properties to false to disable this functionality completely, ensuring that your WebBrowser window shows only the content you want it to. Table 17-4 lists these properties, all of which require a true or false value.

Table 17-4. *Miscellaneous WebBrowser Properties*

Property	Description
AllowNavigation	If false, no navigation is allowed. If the user clicks a link no action will be taken. However, you can still set the Url or DocumentText properties to perform programmatic navigation.
AllowWebBrowserDrop	If true (the default), the WebBrowser control will automatically load and render any document dropped on it. Set this to false to stop the user from navigating away from the content you want to show. The default is true.
CanGoBack and CanGoForward	These read-only properties indicate whether there are previous or subsequent entries in the navigation history. You can use these events to keep the state of any custom forward or backward buttons synchronized.
IsWebBrowserContextMenuEnabled	If true (the default), users can right-click on a link to see other options (including those that allow them to save the target or open in a new, stand-alone window). Set this to false to restrict these possibilities.
ScriptErrorsSuppressed	If false (the default), the WebBrowser displays an alert window if it tries to run invalid JavaScript code. Usually, you'll want this to be true while testing, and false when the application is deployed, because this error information won't help the user.
ScrollBarsEnabled	If true (the default), scroll bars will be shown if the page is larger than the size of the WebBrowser control.
WebBrowserShortcutsEnabled	If true (the default), users can use shortcut keys like Ctrl+N to open a new window. Disable this feature to restrict these possibilities.

In addition, the WebBrowser lets you programmatically access some of the options you've seen in the Internet Explorer menu. Two particularly useful features are the ability to print and save documents. For example, if you use the WebBrowser to show a collection of Web pages with online help, you can add a Print button to your form that calls the WebBrowser's PrintDialog() or Print() method to send the content directly to the printer without any headaches. Table 17-5 lists these useful methods, which you might want to use from your own custom toolbar buttons.

Table 17-5. *Miscellaneous WebBrowser Methods*

Method	Description
Print()	Sends the currently loaded document to the default printer. For a less drastic approach, use ShowPrintDialog() instead.
ShowPageSetupDialog()	Shows the Internet Explorer Page Setup dialog box, allowing the user to change options like page orientation and margins.
ShowPrintDialog()	Shows the Internet Explorer Print dialog box, allowing the user to choose a printer and optionally print the current document.
ShowPrintPreviewDialog()	Shows a Print Preview window that allows the reader to see the printed output, change printer settings, and even print the document. Unlike the other windows, the Print Preview window is always shown modelessly, meaning it doesn't stop your code or prevent the user from accessing the current window in your application.
ShowPropertiesDialog()	Shows the Properties dialog box, which has basic information about the URL, the page size, when the page was last updated, and server certificates.
ShowSaveAsDialog()	Shows the Internet Explorer Save As dialog box, allowing the user to choose a file name and save the current document.

Blending Web and Windows Interfaces

So far, you've seen how you can use the WebBrowser to embed Web content inside a window. This technique works wonders if you need to show an application help file, or direct the user to a Web site with product updates, discussion groups, or late-breaking news. However, the WebBrowser control actually goes quite a bit further with features that let you break down the boundaries between Web content and your C# code. This interaction works two ways:

- You can create C# code that browses through the tree of HTML elements on a page. You can even modify, remove, or insert elements as you go.

- You can create a Web page that triggers the C# code in your application in response to a specific action, like clicking on a button.

   In both cases, you use a programming model that's similar to the HTML DOM used in Web browser scripting languages like JavaScript. In the following sections, you'll see both techniques.

Build a DOM Tree

The starting point for exploring the content in a Web page is the WebBrowser.Document property. This property provides an HtmlDocument object that models the current page as a hierarchical collection of HtmlElement objects. You'll find a distinct HtmlElement object for each tag in your Web page, including paragraphs (<p>), hyperlinks (<a>), images (<img>), and all the other familiar ingredients of HTML markup.

The WebBrowser.Document property is read-only. That means that although you can modify the linked HtmlDocument, you can't create a new HtmlDocument object on the fly. Instead, you need to set the Url, DocumentText, or DocumentStream property (or use the Navigate() method) to load a new page. Once a document is loaded, you can access the Document property.

■**Tip** Building the HtmlDocument takes a short but distinctly noticeable amount of time for a typical Web page. The WebBrowser won't actually build the HtmlDocument for the page until you try to access the Document property for the first time.

Each HtmlElement object has a few key properties:

- TagName is the actual tag, without the angle brackets. For example, an anchor tag takes this form <a href="...">...</a>, and has the tag name A.

- Id contains the value of the id attribute, if specified. Often, elements are identified with unique id attributes if you need to manipulate them in an automated tool or server-side code.

- Children provides a collection of HtmlElement objects, one for each contained tag.

- InnerHtml shows the full content of the tag, including any nested tags and their content.

- InnerText shows the full content of the tag and the content of any nested tags. However, it strips out all the HTML tags.

- OuterHtml and OuterText play the same role as InnerHtml and InnerText, except they include the current tag (rather than just its contents).

To get a better understanding of InnerText, InnertHtml, and OuterHtml, consider the following tag:

```
<p>Here is some <i>interesting</i> text.</p>
```

The InnerText for this tag is:

```
Here is some interesting text.
```

The InnerHtml is:

```
Here is some <i>interesting</i> text.
```

Finally, the OuterHtml is the full tag:

```
<p>Here is some <i>interesting</i> text.</p>
```

In addition, you can retrieve the attribute value for an element by name using the HtmlElement.GetAttribute() method.

To navigate the document model for an HTML page, you simply move through the Children collections of each HtmlElement. The following code performs this task in response to a button click, and builds a tree that shows the structure of elements and the content on the page (see Figure 17-3).

```
private void cmdBuildTree_Click(object sender, System.EventArgs e)
{
    // Show the title.
    this.Text = webBrowser.Document.Title;

    // Analyzing a page takes a nontrivial amount of time.
    // Use the hourglass cursor to warn the user.
    this.Cursor = Cursors.WaitCursor;

    // Process all the HTML elements on the page.
    ProcessElement(webBrowser.Document.Body.Children, treeDOM.Nodes);

    this.Cursor = Cursors.Default;
}

private void ProcessElement(HtmlElementCollection elements,
  TreeNodeCollection nodes)
{
    // Scan through the collection of elements.
    foreach (HtmlElement element in elements)
    {
        // Create a new node that shows the tag name.
        TreeNode node = new TreeNode("<" + element.TagName + ">");
        nodes.Add(node);

        if ((element.Children.Count == 0) && (element.InnerText != null))
        {
            // If this element doesn't contain any other elements, add
            // any leftover text content as a new node.
            node.Nodes.Add(element.InnerText);
        }
        else
        {
            // If this element contains other elements, process them recursively.
            ProcessElement(element.Children, node.Nodes);
        }
    }
}
```

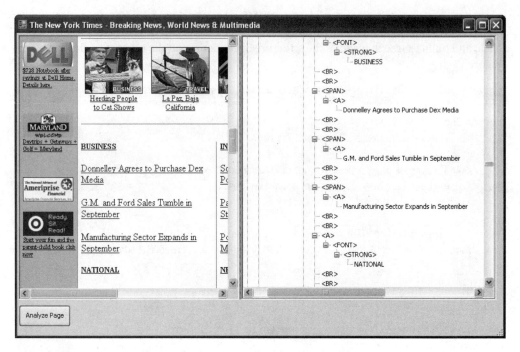

Figure 17-3. *A tree model of a Web page*

If you want to find a specific element without digging through all the layers of the Web page, you have a couple of simpler options. First of all, you can use the HtmlDocument.All collection, which allows you to retrieve any element on the page using its id attribute. If you need to retrieve an element that doesn't have an id attribute, you can also use the HtmlDocument method GetElementsByTagName(), as demonstrated in the next example.

Extract All Links

The next example shows how you can use screen scraping to extract just those elements that interest you. In this case, the task is to retrieve all the hyperlinks on a page by searching for anchor tags. Remember, a typical anchor tag looks like this:

```
<a href="http://www.mysite.com/mypage.html">Click here!</a>
```

The hyperlink destination (which is found in the href attribute of the anchor tag) is then added to a list box, but the inner text is ignored. Here's the complete code:

```
private void cmdGetAllLinks_Click(object sender, System.EventArgs e)
{
    if (webBrowser.ReadyState == WebBrowserReadyState.Complete)
    {
        // Use an hourglass mouse pointer, because it takes a short delay
        // to build the document tree.
        this.Cursor = Cursors.WaitCursor;
        lstLinks.Items.Clear();

        HtmlElementCollection elements =
          webBrowser.Document.GetElementsByTagName("A");
        foreach (HtmlElement element in elements)
        {
            lstLinks.Items.Add(element.GetAttribute("href"));
        }

        this.Cursor = Cursors.Default;
    }
}
```

To make the example more interesting, every time the user clicks a link in the list box, the corresponding item is modified in the Web page. In this case, a string of three angle brackets (>>>) is inserted to mark the selected hyperlink. When a new selection is made, the previous hyperlink is returned to normal.

```
HtmlElement previous = null;

private void lstLinks_SelectedIndexChanged(object sender, System.EventArgs e)
{
    HtmlElementCollection elements =
     webBrowser.Document.GetElementsByTagName("A");

    if (previous != null) previous.InnerText = previous.InnerText.Substring(3);

    previous = elements[lstLinks.SelectedIndex];
    previous.InnerText = ">>>" + previous.InnerText;
}
```

Figure 17-4 shows the form at work.

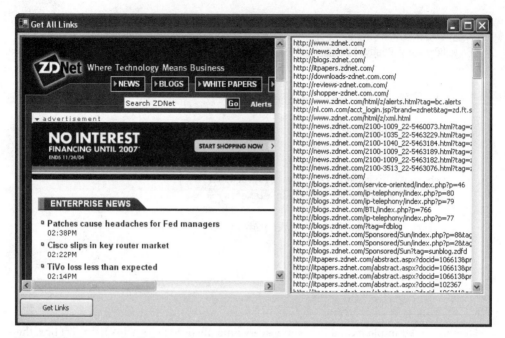

Figure 17-4. *Hunting for links in a page*

■Tip This example matches selected indexes by index number position. However, if you're specifically creating pages to use with the WebBrowser control, you'll save yourself some work by adding the id attribute to all the elements you want to work with. You can then use GetElementById() to retrieve elements with a specific ID. Or, if you want to find the element at a specific coordinate in the control (perhaps so you can update some other control while the user hovers over a portion of a Web page), use the GetElementFromPoint() method.

This example shows how the HtmlDocument works in both directions. Not only can you use it to retrieve information, but you can also use it as in interface for modifying parts of a page, perhaps to keep it synchronized with your application. There's no limit to how you can alter a page or insert content using the HtmlElement.CreateElement() method. However, unfortunately you can't create an HtmlDocument by hand. Instead, you always need to load data into a WebBrowser window, and then retrieve the current HtmlDocument from the Document property.

Scripting a Web Page with .NET Code

The last trick you'll see with the WebBrowser is something even more intriguing: the ability to react to Web-page events in your Windows code.

The WebBrowser makes this technique remarkably simple. All you need to do is specify the object that will receive scripted events. You do this by setting the WebBrowser.ObjectForScripting property. Here's an example that sets this reference to the current form:

```
private void ScriptedMenu_Load(object sender, System.EventArgs e)
{
    webBrowser.ObjectForScripting = this;
    webBrowser.Navigate("file:///" + Application.StartupPath + @"\\sample.htm");
}
```

Additionally, you need to add the ComVisible attribute to your form to allow the Web page to see it:

```
[ComVisible(true)]
public class ScriptedMenu : System.Windows.Forms.Form
{ ... }
```

In the Web page, you use JavaScript code to trigger the event. All you need to do is use the window.external object, which represents the linked .NET object. Using this object, you specify a method that you want to trigger; for example, use window.external.HelloWorld() if there's a public method named HelloWorld in the .NET object.

■**Caution** If you use this option, make sure that your class doesn't include any other public methods that aren't related to Web access. A nefarious user could theoretically find the HTML source, and modify it to call a different method than the one you intend. Ideally, the scriptable class should contain only Web-related methods to ensure security.

To build the JavaScript command into your Web page, you first need to decide what Web-page event you want to react to. Most HTML elements support a small number of events, and some of the most useful include the following:

- **onFocus** occurs when a control receives focus.

- **onBlur** occurs when focus leaves a control.

- **onClick** occurs when the user clicks a control.

- **onChange** occurs when the user changes the value of certain controls.

- **onMouseOver** occurs when the user moves the mouse pointer over a control.

To write a JavaScript command that responds to one of these events, you simply add an attribute with that name to the element tag. For example, if you have an image tag that looks like this

```
<img border="0" id="img1" src="buttonC.jpg" height="20" width="100">
```

you can add an onClick attribute that triggers the HelloWorld() method in your linked .NET class whenever the user clicks the image:

```
<img onClick="window.external.HelloWorld()" border="0" id="img1"
 src="buttonC.jpg" height="20" width="100">
```

Figure 17-5 shows an application that puts it all together. In this example, a WebBrowser control shows a local HTML file that contains four buttons, each of which is a graphical image. This page uses Dynamic HTML effects so that the buttons slide onto the page from different sides of the screen. The buttons also light up as the user hovers over them, changing their position.

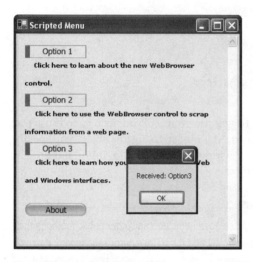

Figure 17-5. *An HTML menu that triggers .NET code*

But when the user clicks a button, the image uses the onClick attribute to trigger a form-level method called WebClick():

```
<img onClick="window.external.WebClick('Option1')' ... >
```

The WebClick() method then takes over. It could show another Web page, open a new form, or modify part of the Web page. In this example, it simply displays a message box to confirm that the event has been received:

```
public void WebClick(string source)
{
    MessageBox.Show("Received: " + source);
}
```

You'll notice this example introduces one new feature—parameters. The images pass hard-coded strings to the WebClick() method. By examining this string, it's possible to determine which button triggered the method, without needing to create a separate method for each button. Another way that you can use this feature is to pass user-supplied information to your application, as you'll see in the next section.

■**Tip** Scripting a window also comes in handy if you're using a WebBrowser control to show product documentation. Using this feature, you can place a link that says "Do it for me" at the bottom of a how-to topic. When the user clicks that link, it can trigger a method in your code that performs the action the user was reading about. The secret to making this strategy work is to make sure that you don't script individual forms. Instead, create an application-wide class that's dedicated to handling Web events. That way it doesn't matter what window is active when the user clicks the link.

Interestingly, this ability to jump between the bounds of the HTML document and managed .NET code works both ways. You can call any script that's embedded in the HTML document courtesy of the WebBrowser.Document.InvokeScript() method, which takes two parameters. The first parameter is the name of the script function that you want to execute in the HTML page, and the second is an array of strings, one for each argument in the function.

For example, imagine you want to trigger the following Web-page script function (which displays a message box using the JavaScript alert() function:

```
<script>
  function ShowMessage(message) {
    alert(message);
  }
</script>
```

You can call this script through the WebBrowser using this code statement:

```
webBrowser1.Document.InvokeScript("ShowMessage",
  new string[] { "This script was called by C#" });
```

This gives you the flexibility to control what happens in your .NET application, but code the Web-page-manipulation functions in the HTML document, where they may be easier to write. It also helps remove some of the messy HTML details from your form code, and create pages that are more logically encapsulated.

■**Caution** Keep in mind that unless your HTML document is compiled into your assembly as an embedded resource or retrieved from some secure location (like a database), it may be subject to client tampering. For example, if you store HTML documents as separate files, users can easily edit them. If this is a concern, use the embedding techniques described in Chapter 5. You can create file resources, retrieve them as strings, and assign them using the WebBrowser.DocumentText property.

Scripting an HTML Form

HTML pages can use HTML form controls. These are special tags that represent user-interface widgets like buttons, check boxes, text boxes, and options. These elements are always placed inside a <form> tag. In your .NET code, you'll want to examine the user-supplied information in these controls.

There are two basic approaches to retrieving a value. The following example—a customer feedback form shown in Figure 17-6—demonstrates both of them.

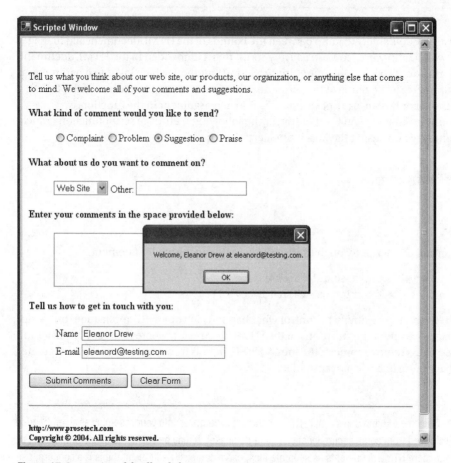

Figure 17-6. *A scripted feedback form*

The most straightforward approach is to create a method that accepts all the required information as separate parameters. For example, imagine you want to retrieve the customer name and e-mail address. First, create a form method that accepts the two string parameters you need. (Every object passed from an HTML page is usually in the form of a string.)

```
public void Feedback(string userName, string email)
{
    MessageBox.Show("You are " + userName + " at " email + ".");
}
```

Next, you need to look at the HTML for that portion of the page. In this case, it's wrapped inside a table. The two text boxes are represented by <input> tags of type text, one with the name UserName and the other with the name UserEmail.

```
<table>
    <tr>
        <td>Name</td>
        <td><input type="text" size="35" maxlength="256" name="UserName"></td>
    </tr>
    <tr>
        <td>E-mail</td>
        <td><input type="text" size="35" maxlength="256" name="UserEmail"></td>
    </tr>
</table>
```

To retrieve the current value for either of these elements in your JavaScript command, you simply need to access the value property. For example, UserName.value will contain the text that's currently entered in the user name text box.

Armed with this information, you can add an onClick attribute to the Submit Comments button that triggers the Feedback() method and passes the two important pieces of information. Here's what it looks like:

```
<input onClick="window.external.Feedback(UserName.value, UserEmail.value)"
 type="submit" value="Submit Comments">
```

Generally, this is the best approach. However, you can also retrieve information from the page using the HtmlDocument model. In this case, you need to check the value attribute, which will have the information you need once the page has been submitted. Here's an example that grabs the text from the comment box:

```
string comments = webBrowser.Document.All["Comments"].GetAttribute("value");
```

Or to test if the Complaint radio button is selected, use the following:

```
if (webBrowser.Document.GetElementById("Complaint").GetAttribute("checked")
    == "True")
```

The Last Word

In this chapter you learned about the new WebBrowser control, which allows you to display Web pages and control navigation. On its own, the WebBrowser provides some useful features, but some of the most interesting possibilities arise when you use scripting and the HtmlDocument object model to fuse together the world of the Web with the managed world of .NET code. Using these features you can create small-scale solutions (like a startup window that shows an animated company logo by displaying a Web page that uses Macromedia Flash) or more ambitious projects (like a next-generation help engine that allows users to read documentation and trigger application tasks).

PART 4

Windows Forms Techniques

■■■

CHAPTER 18

Validation and Masked Editing

In any realistic application, you need to have some sort of error-checking hard-wired into the user-interface code. If you don't code this logic properly or if you put it in the wrong place, you may frustrate users, complicate the business process, and even lose data.

In this chapter, you'll learn about all the options for preventing and responding to input errors in a Windows application. First, you'll take a look at how you can use *validation events* to react to mistakes before they become serious problems. Next, you'll learn how to extend your validation techniques to flag errors politely with the ErrorProvider, and check complex text patterns with *regular expressions*.

In the second half of this chapter, you'll learn about an elegant way to solve validation problems by creating custom validation components. Best of all, you'll learn how to reuse these components to make all your forms bulletproof. Finally, you'll take a close look at the new MaskedTextBox control, which can help you prevent errors before they happen. You'll even learn how to harness the MaskedTextProvider to create your own custom masked controls.

Validating at the Right Time

Before you write any validation code, you need to decide where it fits into your application. In a stand-alone application, this decision is usually fairly easy. But in a distributed application that might invoke remote objects, contact a database server, or use a Web service, there are several options—and they're far from equal.

For example, consider an application designed for entering sales invoices. Once a sales invoice is complete, the application sends the data to a Web service (or some other type of server-side component), and the Web service stores the invoice information in a central database. A naive programmer might try to code all the validation logic in the Web service. This approach makes the validation code easier to monitor and change. However, it also introduces a few dangerous headaches:

- **Error notifications will occur too late.** By the time the Web service identifies the problem and returns an error message to the client, the user will have already moved on (mentally at least), and will be frustrated to take a few steps back or—even worse—restart the process. This problem is particularly severe if you need a multistep process to create an invoice. In this case, it's more than likely that the user will have long forgotten about the choices made in the first few steps. Even worse, the user may no longer have the information needed to correct the error. (For example, the customer who made the purchase might have already left the store.)

- **Error notifications can't be fine-grained.** If the invoice has multiple mistakes, it's difficult to explain each one effectively. A generic "invalid invoice" message is no help to anyone, and it only increases the likelihood that the invoice information won't be submitted successfully.

- **The error-checking overhead isn't trivial.** If an invoice has an error, the application needs to waste a trip to the Web service to perform error-checking. If an invoice has more than one error, you may need to make several round-trips before you can submit a single invoice, multiplying the overhead of the application. Calling a remote computer takes a nontrivial amount of time, particularly if you're working over a slow network connection or the wide Internet.

Overall, checking for errors on the Web server makes the system slightly less scalable. But the most significant change is the fact that the system becomes less robust—in other words, it has less ability to let users correct problems and get their work done successfully.

In scenarios like these, the best solution is to validate *twice* (as shown in Figure 18-1). The first validation happens in the client application and should be as comprehensive as possible, enforcing maximum field lengths, checking for non-numeric input, and so on. Very few invalid invoices should clear the client validation process. Next, the Web service side can perform its own set of validation checks. These validation checks serve two purposes—they are a failsafe guarantee that grossly incorrect or malicious data can't be submitted, and they perform any checks that the client can't. For example, you might want to examine the order history in the database to verify that a customer doesn't have any outstanding payments before you allow an invoice to continue. To increase performance (by avoiding an extra round-trip) or tighten security, you might choose to perform this check on the server instead of the client. Server-side checking also allows you to update business rules without rolling out new client updates.

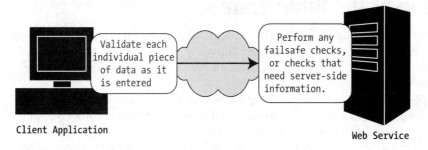

Figure 18-1. *A sensible approach to validation*

■**Tip** If your validation requirements are complex, you might need a way for the client to periodically down-load a list of rules from the server. This approach makes sure the latest validation rules are always in effect, without forcing you to update clients manually. One of the simplest ways to do this is to use a DataSet that is configured with all the database schema information, including data types and maximum field lengths. However, this won't help you validate more-complex rules (like making sure a phone number field has the right format).

Validation Events

The perfect Windows application would make it impossible for the user to enter any syntactically invalid information; this is achieved by using the right set of controls, checking key presses, and limiting choices. Of course, sometimes this task is too daunting and you need to settle on the next best thing, which is checking for errors after the fact. If you take this approach, it's important that you report any error as soon as possible, preferably before the user continues to enter more information. The easiest way is to react to *validation events*.

Validation events are designed to let you check information as soon as it is entered, rather than waiting for the whole form to be submitted. This kind of instantaneous error-checking is very useful, for the following reasons:

- Without it, users might be afraid to submit a form because they know there is a possible error.

- Users might enter several pieces of invalid data at the same time. If you don't check the data until the form is submitted, your program will have to find some way to report all the mistakes at once.

- By the time users submit a form, they might have already forgotten about the particular field they entered incorrectly.

The validation events avoid these problems by checking the field as soon as the user is finished entering information in it and changes focus to another control (either to enter new information, like choosing a text box, or to perform an action, like clicking a button).

The Validation Event Sequence

When you navigate from one control to another, a series of events unfolds. For example, if you move from TextBox1 to TextBox2 by pressing the Tab key, here are the events that fire:

1. Leave (TextBox1)

2. Enter (TextBox2)

3. LostFocus (TextBox1)

4. GotFocus (TextBox2)

The same pattern plays out when you change focus using other keys (like Shift+Tab), or when your code calls the Control.Select() or Control.SelectNextControl() methods, or sets the ContainerControl.ActiveControl property.

Oddly enough, if you change focus using the mouse or by calling the Control.Focus() method, the order of events shifts slightly so that the LostFocus event occurs earlier:

1. LostFocus (TextBox1)

2. Leave (TextBox1)

3. Enter (TextBox2)

4. GotFocus (TextBox2)

It may seem tempting to write "do-it-yourself" validation by responding to a control's LostFocus event. Unfortunately, this approach is dangerous, because it's not safe to change the focus inside a LostFocus event handler. If you try to direct the user back to the original control, or if you change the focus in another way (for example, by showing a message box), you'll end up triggering an additional LostFocus event from the target control. If both controls have invalid data, they may fight endlessly among themselves, trying to move the focus somewhere else and trapping your program in an endless loop.

Tip If you don't want to perform validation, but you simply want to update some part of your user interface when focus changes from one control to another, you still shouldn't use the GotFocus and LostFocus events. Instead, use the safer Enter and Leave events. You'll notice that both GotFocus and LostFocus are hidden from the Properties window to prevent accidental usage.

.NET handles this problem with the Validating and Validated events. These events occur between the Leave and Enter events. For example, if you tab from one text box to another, here's the sequence of events that occurs:

1. Leave (TextBox1)

2. Enter (TextBox2)

3. Validating (TextBox1)

4. Validating (TextBox2)

5. LostFocus (TextBox1)

6. GotFocus (TextBox2)

The Validated event allows you to respond to correctly entered data. The Validating event is more useful. It allows you to verify the data and, if it fails the test, stop the focus from moving to the new control.

Validation takes place only if the source control (the control to be validated) has the CausesValidation property set to true. In addition, the validation won't take place until the focus changes to a control that *also* has its CausesValidation property set to true. If either one has a CausesValidation of false, the validation events are suppressed, but the other events (like Enter and Leave) still fire. Table 18-1 shows some examples of what can happen when tabbing from one control to another.

Table 18-1. *.NET Validation*

Source Control Status	Destination Control Status	Result
CausesValidation is false	Doesn't matter	Validation code is ignored.
CausesValidation is true	CausesValidation is true	Validation is performed for the source control.
CausesValidation is true	CausesValidation is false	Validation is postponed until the focus changes to a CausesValidation control. At this point, all the controls that need to be validated are validated in order until one is found with invalid input and the process is canceled.

Finally, it's important to note that you can switch off this behavior entirely by setting the Form.AutoValidate property to AutoValidate.Disable. In this case, the validation events will never be fired, no matter what you set for the CausesValidation property of your controls. You can set the AutoValidate property for any container control (panels, group boxes, and so on). Use AutoValidate.Inherit to acquire the settings from the parent control or form.

Handling Validation Events

The program shown in Figure 18-2 uses validation to verify that neither text box is left blank. If the user tries to change focus without entering any information, a message box appears, and the focus is reset to the empty text box.

Figure 18-2. *A validation example*

All that's necessary to implement this behavior is to set the CausesValidation property for both text boxes to true, and handle the TextBox.Validating event. The validation code for this application is shown here:

```
private void txtName_Validating(object sender,
 System.ComponentModel.CancelEventArgs e)
{
    if (((TextBox)sender).Text.Length == 0)
    {
        MessageBox.Show("You must enter a first and last name.", "Invalid Input",
                    MessageBoxButtons.OK, MessageBoxIcon.Warning);
        e.Cancel = true;
    }
}
```

You can handle the Validating event for both text boxes with the same event handler, provided you write your code generically. That means you shouldn't hard-code the control you want to check—instead, retrieve a reference from the sender parameter, as in the preceding example.

Tip You can alter this behavior using the Form.AutoValidate property. As discussed earlier, you can prevent your validation code from running altogether (with AutoValidate.Disable). You can also allow your validation code to run, but ignore any cancel requests so that the user is allowed to tab from one control to the next (use AutoValidate.EnableAllowFocusChange). The default is AutoValidate.EnablePreventFocusChange.

Note that if you cancel a focus change in the Validating event, no other events will fire for the target control. For example, if you move to a control with invalid input and then click a button, the Button.Click event won't fire.

Tip There's a potential catch in the validation example shown here. For validation to work, the focus needs to begin on one of the text boxes. If the focus begins on another control (like the button), the user can close the form or click the button without triggering the validation events. That's because validation takes place only when you navigate *away* from the control that performs the validation. To avoid any problem, make sure you set the focus to start on the correct input control or use the Control.Select() method when the form loads.

Closing a Form with Validating

There's one interesting quirk in the previous example. If the user attempts to close the form with the top-right close button (or by pressing Alt+F4), this action also triggers validation. If validation fails, the form won't close.

This behavior is reasonable, but it complicates your life if you need to let users escape from a form without filling in all the controls. One solution is to create a Cancel button that closes the form, and set its CausesValidation property set to false. However, this is only part of the solution.

By setting CausesValidation to false, you allow the focus to change to the Cancel button, and you allow its Button.Click event to fire. However, when your code uses the Form.Close() method to close the form, the validation code still springs into action, preventing the form from closing.

```
private void cmdClose_Click(object sender, EventArgs e)
{
    // This triggers validation.
    this.Close();
}
```

There are two solutions. The first choice is to change the Form.AutoValidate setting before you attempt to close the form. For example, this event handler will breeze past any validation routines:

```
private void cmdClose_Click(object sender, EventArgs e)
{
    this.AutoValidate = AutoValidate.Disable;
    this.Close();
}
```

There's another option. When the validation code sets the cancel flag, it indicates that the form should not be allowed to close. However, you still have the chance to override this decision by handling FormClosing. At this point, you can clear the cancel flag if you want, allowing the form to close. Here's an example that lets the user decide:

```
private void Form1_FormClosing(object sender, FormClosingEventArgs e)
{
    // If e.Cancel is true, the cancel flag has been set by a validation routine.
    if (e.Cancel)
    {
        DialogResult result = MessageBox.Show(
            "There are still errors on the form. Do you wish to close the form?",
            "Errors found", MessageBoxButtons.YesNo);
        if (result == DialogResult.Yes) e.Cancel = false;
    }
}
```

This approach is quite a bit different than the first solution, because it ensures that your validation code runs.

The ErrorProvider

Interrupting users with a message box is a crude way of pointing out an error. It's not likely to get users on your side, and you won't find it in any modern Windows application. A much better approach is to provide some kind of on-screen indication about the problem, like an explanatory error message next to the incorrect input.

The .NET Framework provides an elegant way to accomplish this: ErrorProvider control. The ErrorProvider has a simple role in life—it can display an error icon (which looks like a red exclamation point) next to any control. Typically, you'll show the error icon next to a control that has invalid input. You'll also specify a detailed text message. The error message appears in a tooltip if the user hovers over the error icon with the mouse pointer (see Figure 18-3).

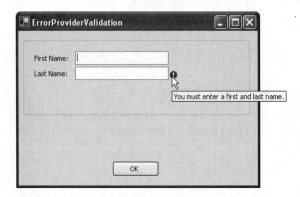

Figure 18-3. *The ErrorProvider*

The ErrorProvider is a provider control—a special type of user-interface ingredient introduced in Chapter 4. Like all other providers, you add a single instance of the ErrorProvider to the form you want to validate. You can then use that instance to display an error icon next to any control. To add the ErrorProvider, you can drag it from the Toolbox into the component tray, or you can create it manually in code. In the latter case, make sure you create a member variable to track it so you can access it later.

Showing Error Icons

To show an error icon next to a control, you use the ErrorProvider.SetError() method. The following code segment shows the same text box validation code as in the previous example, which reacts to the TextBox.Validating event. However, the code has been rewritten so that it doesn't stop the user from moving to the new control. Instead, if validation fails, it simply indicates the error using the error icon.

```
private void txtName_Validating(object sender,
 System.ComponentModel.CancelEventArgs e)
{
    Control ctrl = (Control)sender;
    if (ctrl.Text.Length == 0)
    {
        errProvider.SetError(ctrl, "You must enter a first and last name.");
    }
    else
    {
        errProvider.SetError(ctrl, "");
    }
}
```

To hide the error icon you must explicitly clear the error message when validation succeeds.

■**Note** This example uses the time-honored TextBox. However, there's no reason you can't validate other input controls, like lists, check boxes, radio buttons, and more, using the exact same Validating event and ErrorProvider control.

In this example, the validation event doesn't cancel the user's action. This is a more user-friendly alternative, but it also means that when the user clicks OK to submit the form, you need to explicitly check if there are any errors before continuing. Here's an example that verifies there are no errors attached to either text box:

```
private void cdmOK_Click(object sender, System.EventArgs e)
{
    if (errProvider.GetError(txtFirstName).Length == 0 &&
        errProvider.GetError(txtLastName).Length == 0)
    {
        this.Close();
    }
    else
    {
        MessageBox.Show("You still have invalid input.", "Invalid Input",
                    MessageBoxButtons.OK, MessageBoxIcon.Warning);
    }
}
```

If you have a lot of controls, it makes more sense to iterate through the whole collection, rather than code-checking each control individually. In the following example, the validation controls are all contained inside a single group box named grpValidation, so the code iterates its collection of child controls.

```
private void cmdOK_Click(object sender, System.EventArgs e)
{
    bool invalidInput = false;
    foreach (Control ctrl in grpValidation.Controls)
    {
        if (errProvider.GetError(ctrl).Length != 0)
        {
            invalidInput = true;
            break;
        }
    }
```

```
    if (invalidInput)
    {
        MessageBox.Show("You still have invalid input.", "Invalid Input",
                    MessageBoxButtons.OK, MessageBoxIcon.Warning);
    }
    else
    {
        this.Close();
    }
}
```

This approach still has one limitation. Because validation is performed only when the focus changes, the error icon doesn't disappear when the user corrects a problem. Instead, it remains until the user moves to another control and validation is triggered. If you want a different behavior, you can skip using the validation events altogether. For example, you can perform your validation by reacting to the TextBox.TextChanged event every time the user presses a key.

Customizing Error Icons

The ErrorProvider control can serve any number of input controls on the same form, and display as many simultaneous error icons and warning messages as needed. By default, every warning icon appears to the immediate right of the input control. However, enterprising developers will be happy to find out that they can tweak the error icon's appearance to better fit in with their applications.

The ErrorProvider control provides two methods that let you specify how an error icon should be aligned with a control, and how much spacing there should be between the icon and the control (see Table 18-2).

Table 18-2. *ErrorProvider Appearance-Related Methods*

Method	Extended Property	Description
SetIconAlignment()	IconAlignment	Determines where the error icon will appear for a specific control, using one of the values from the ErrorIconAlignment enumeration. The default is MiddleRight, which means the icon appears on the right side of the control, centered between the top and bottom edge. You can easily flip the icon to any other side.
SetIconPadding()	IconPadding	Determines the amount of space, in pixels, that will be left between the icon and the aligned edge of a specific control. By default this is 0, which still leaves a few pixels between the control and the icon.

As you probably remember from Chapter 4, there are always two ways to interact with an extender provider: you can call its methods explicitly in your code, or you can configure the corresponding extended property at design time for the extended control. For example, instead of calling the SetError() method to show an error message in a TextBox, you can select the TextBox at design time and modify the Error property in the Properties window. The Error property doesn't really exist—instead, it's just provided as a design-time convenience. When you set it, Visual Studio adds the required statement that invokes the SetError() method to your form initialization code. It doesn't make sense to set the Error property at design time, because as soon as the Error string is set, the error icon appears. However, it makes good sense to set the IconAlignment and IconPadding properties at design time if you need to use them. That way you can set up everything properly ahead of time without resorting to code.

In addition to the extended properties, the ErrorProvider has a few useful properties of its own. These properties allow you to control how the error icon blinks, and even to replace the familiar red exclamation mark with something more customized (see Table 18-3).

Table 18-3. *ErrorProvider Appearance-Related Properties*

Property	Description
BlinkRate	Determines the rate, in milliseconds, at which the error icon should flash (assuming the BlinkStyle is set to allow flashing). The default is 250 milliseconds, which means the error icon blinks to get attention once every 250 milliseconds (or four times a second).
BlinkStyle	Determines when the error icon blinks, using one of the values from the ErrorBlinkStyle enumeration. You can choose to never blink (NeverBlink), always blink (AlwaysBlink), or blink only the first time an error is set and when a new error message is set (BlinkIfDifferentError). The nice thing about BlinkIfDifferentError (the default) is that the blinking continues for only a few seconds before stopping automatically— enough to catch the user's attention without becoming an eyesore.
Icon	A System.Drawing.Icon object that's shown for the error icon. If you don't like the red exclamation mark, this is the property you need to change. In .NET 2.0, the ErrorIcon got a minor facelift so that it has a more shaded, three-dimensional look than it did in previous versions.
SetIconPadding() IconPadding	Determines the amount of space, in pixels, that will be left between the icon and the aligned edge of the control. By default this is 0, which still leaves a few pixels between the control and the icon.

■**Note** The ErrorProvider properties are applied automatically for every control that you use with the ErrorProvider. That means that if you want to have the ability to show error icons with more than one icon, you need to add more than one ErrorProvider. And if you want to change something more substantial about the ErrorProvider, like showing error messages in the status bar, a balloon tip, or a different control, you'll need to create your own custom provider, as described in Chapter 28.

Regular Expressions

The ErrorProvider control is an ideal way to weave error feedback into your application. However, writing the actual validation code can still be painful and time-consuming. One way to streamline your work is to use the .NET regular expression classes, which allow you to search text strings for specific patterns.

A *regular expression* is a formula for matching complex text patterns. Using the ordinary methods of the String class, you can search for a series of specific characters (for example, the word "hello") in a string. Using a regular expression, however, you can search a string for any word that is five letters long and begins with an *h*.

Regular Expression Basics

All regular expressions are made up of two kinds of characters: literals and metacharacters. *Literals* represent a specific defined character. *Metacharacters* are wildcards that can represent a range of values. Regular expressions gain their power from the rich set of metacharacters that they support.

Two examples of regular-expression metacharacters include \s (which represents any white-space character) and \d (which represents any digit). Using these characters, you can construct the following expression, which will successfully match any string that starts with the numbers 333, followed by a single white-space character and any three numbers. Valid matches include 333 333, 333 945, but not 334 333 or 3334 945.

```
333\s\d\d\d
```

You can also use the plus (+) sign to represent a repeated character. For example, 5+7 means "any number of *5* characters, followed by a single *7*." The number 57 matches, as does 555557. You can also use the brackets to group together a subexpression. For example, (52)+7 would find match any string that starts with a sequence of 52. Matches include 527, 52527, 52552527, and so on.

You can also delimit a range of characters using square brackets. [a-f] would match any single character from *a* to *f* (lowercase only). The following expression would match any word that starts with a letter from *a* to *f*, contains one or more letters, and ends with "ing"—possible matches include *acting* and *developing*.

```
[a-f][a-z]+ing
```

This discussion just scratches the surface of regular expressions, which constitute an entire language of their own. However, you don't need to learn everything there is to know about regular expressions before you start using them. In fact, many programmers simply look for useful prebuilt regular expressions on the Web. Without much trouble, you can find examples for e-mails, phone numbers, postal codes, and more, all of which you can drop straight into your applications.

■**Tip** To learn about regular expression, you might be interested in a dedicated book like the excellent *Mastering Regular Expressions* (O'Reilly).

Table 18-4 shows a brief list of some common regular-expression metacharacters. You can use these characters to create your own regular expressions. However, it's often easier to look up a prebuilt regular expression that suits your data using the Internet or a dedicated book on the subject.

Table 18-4. *Regular-Expression Metacharacters*

Character	Rule
*	Represents zero or more occurrences of the previous character or subexpression. For example, a*b matches aab or just b.
+	Represents one or more occurrences of the previous character or subexpression. For example, a+b matches aab but not a.
( )	Groups a subexpression that is treated as a single element. For example, (ab)+ matches ab and ababab.
{m}	Requires *m* repetitions of the preceding character or group. For example, a{3} matches aaa.
{m, n}	Requires *n* to *m* repetitions of the preceding character or group. For example, a{2,3} matches aa and aaa but not aaaa.
|	Represents either of two matches. For example, a|b matches a or b.
[ ]	Matches one character in a range of valid characters. For example, [A-C] matches A, B, or C.
[^]	Matches a character that is not in the given range. For example, [^A-C] matches any character except A, B, and C.
.	Represents any character except newline.
\s	Represents any white-space character (like a tab or space).
\S	Represents any non–white-space character.
\d	Represents any digit character.
\D	Represents any character that is not a digit.
\w	Represents any alphanumeric character (letter, number, or underscore).
^	Represents the start of the string. For example, ^ab can find a match only if the string begins with ab.
$	Represents the end of the string. For example, ab$ can find a match only if the string ends with ab.
\	Indicates that the following character is a literal (even though it might ordinarily be interpreted as a metacharacter). For example, use \\ for the literal \ and use \+ for the literal +.

Table 18-5 shows a few regular expression examples to get you started.

Table 18-5. *Sample Regular Expressions*

Content	Regular Expression	Description
Email address*	\S+@\S+\.\S+	Check for an "at" symbol (@), a dot (.), and only allow non–white-space characters.
Password	\w+	Any sequence of word characters (letter, space, or underscore).
Specific-length password	\w{4,10}	A password that must be at least four characters long, but no longer than ten characters.
Advanced password	[a-zA-Z]\w{3,9}	As with the specific-length password, this regular expression will allow four to ten total characters. The twist is that the first character must fall in the range of a–z or A–Z (that is, it must start with a letter).
Another advanced password	[a-zA-Z]\w*\d+\w*	This password starts with a letter character, followed by zero or more word characters, a digit, and then zero or more word characters. In short, it forces a password to contain a number somewhere inside it. You could use a similar pattern to require two numbers or any other special charactesr.
Limited-length field	\S{4,10}	Like the password example, this allows four to ten characters, but it allows special characters (asterisks, ampersands, and so on).
Social Security number	\d{3}-\d{2}-\d{4}	A sequence of three, two, then four digits, with each group separated by a dash. A similar pattern could be used when requiring a phone number.

* There are many different ways to validate e-mail addresses, with regular expressions of varying complexity. See www.4guysfromrolla.com/webtech/validateemail.shtml for a discussion of the subject and numerous examples.

Validating with Regular Expressions

To validate regular expressions in .NET, you can use the Regex class from the System.Text. RegularExpressions namespace. When you create this class, you specify the regular expression you want to use as a constructor argument. You can then call the IsMatch() method to check if a given string (like the text in a text box) matches the regular expression.

■**Tip** When you use validation with the Regex class, make sure your expression starts with the ^ metacharacter (representing the start of the string) and ends with the $ metacharacter (representing the end of the string). Otherwise, the IsMatch() method will search for matching text *anywhere* inside the string you specify, ignoring any invalid characters at the start or end of the string, which isn't the behavior you want.

The following example puts regular expressions to work with the ErrorProvider. In this case, the regular expression validates an e-mail address by verifying that it contains an "at" symbol (@) and a period (.) and doesn't include spaces or special characters. The validation is performed in the TextChanged event handler, which ensures that the error provider icon is updated immediately after any change.

```
private void txtEmail_TextChanged(object sender, System.EventArgs e)
{
    System.Text.RegularExpressions.Regex regex;
    regex = new System.Text.RegularExpressions.Regex(@"^\S+@\S+\.\S+$");

    Control ctrl = (Control)sender;
    if (regex.IsMatch(ctrl.Text))
    {
        errProvider.SetError(ctrl, "");
    }
    else
    {
        errProvider.SetError(ctrl, "Not a valid email.");
    }
}
```

■**Tip** In C#, you can precede a string with the "at" symbol (@)to indicate that it is a string literal. In this case, all character sequences that start with a backward slash (\) will be interpreted as backslashes, not special escape sequences. This is very useful when dealing with regular expressions and file paths, which use the backslash character frequently.

Many programmers create their own resource classes to group together the regular expressions they need to use. One example is shown below.

```
public class RegularExpressions
{
    public const string Email = @"^\S+@\S+\.\S+$";

    // 4-10 character password that starts with a letter.
    public const string Password = @"^[a-zA-Z]\w{3,9}$";

    // A sequence of 3-2-4 digits, with each group separated by a dash.
    public const string SSN = @"^\d{3}-\d{2}-\d{4}$";
}
```

Once you have created this type of resource class, you can use it easily to create a Regex object:

```
Regex expression = new Regex(RegularExpressions.Email);
```

Custom Validation Components

The validation solutions you've seen so far work well, but they tend to be code-heavy. To validate different controls, you almost always need to create separate Validating event handlers, because each control requires its own validation logic and its own error message. Clearly, in an application with dozens of forms and hundreds of input controls, this approach isn't very convenient because it forces you to write a huge amount of custom validation code.

You might try to solve this by writing generic validation routines that handle the Validating event for multiple controls. Unfortunately, there's no easy way to keep track of the error message and validation rules that you want to apply for each control. If you needed only one control-specific piece of information, you could store it in the handy Control.Tag property. For example, you could use the Tag property to store an error message for each control, or a custom regular expression to use for validation. Unfortunately, you can't store both pieces of information—at least not without making it impossible for developers to enter the validation expression and error-message information using the Properties window at design time, which is the real goal.

Fortunately, there is a solution, and it already exists in the .NET Framework. Unfortunately, the solution is designed for a completely different platform—ASP.NET Web pages. Although you can't use the ASP.NET validation controls in a Windows Forms application, you can learn a lot about the best way to encapsulate validation logic. With a little additional effort, you can even build your own set of validation controls that provides the same functionality.

■**Note** There is another potential solution that's not pursued in this chapter—you could create a custom extender provider to implement the customized validation. This extender provider could work like the ErrorProvider, but perform the validation *as well* as the error display. You'll learn more about extender providers in Chapter 25, and you can find a detailed example of this technique (in VB code) at `http://msdn.microsoft.com/library/en-us/dnadvnet/html/vbnet04082003.asp`.

Understanding the ASP.NET Validation Controls

The goal of the ASP.NET validation controls is to create a straightforward, reusable validation framework that allows you to set validation rules *declaratively*. In other words, you drag a validator onto a form, connect it to an existing control, and set a few properties to determine how the validation will be performed. All of these steps unfold at design time. Best of all, you don't need to write any validation code at all.

Clearly, validation controls allow you to be more productive. Validation controls also simplify your application because they encapsulate common validation tasks like checking for blank values, comparing numbers, and using regular expressions. Because the validation controls handle this basic infrastructure, you don't need to write (and repeat) this code yourself. Considering that validation code is usually scattered throughout countless different forms, you can see how validation controls can help you dramatically cut down the total amount of code in your application.

ASP.NET provides five core validators, which are shown in Table 18-6.

Table 18-6. *ASP.NET Validator Controls*

Control Class	Description
RequiredFieldValidator	Validation succeeds as long as the input control doesn't contain an empty string.
RangeValidator	Validation succeeds if the input control contains a value within a specific numeric, alphabetic, or date range.
RegularExpressionValidator	Validation succeeds if the value in an input control matches a specified regular expression.
CompareValidator	Validation succeeds if the input control contains a value that matches the value in another, specified input control.
CustomValidator	Validation is performed by an event handler you write.

Each validation control can be bound to a single input control. In addition, you can apply more than one validation control to the same input control to provide multiple types of validation. Each validator provides its own set of properties that are specific for that type of validation. For example, if you use a RangeValidator, you need to set the upper and lower limits. Once you've configured these bounds and connected the RangeValidator to another control, the validation happens automatically.

You can follow this model to build powerful validators for Windows applications. In this case your validators won't be controls, but components that derive from the System.ComponentModel.Component class, and can be dropped into a form's component tray at design time. The first step to building these components is to create a class library project where you'll place all your validation code. Once that's in place, you can continue with the following sections to create the validator classes you need.

Building the BaseValidator

In the ASP.NET world, each validator inherits form a base class named BaseValidator. The BaseValidator class defines the basic features needed to connect to an input control and store an error message. This functionality is generic, and can be reused in every validator. If you follow the same pattern, you'll have an easy time creating a wide range of custom validators.

The BaseValidator needs a few basic ingredients:

- It needs to inherit from Component so that it can be placed in the component tray.

- It needs to create an ErrorProvider behind the scenes for flagging invalid controls, and expose any ErrorProvider properties you should be able to change, like Icon.

- It needs to let you specify an error message.

- It needs to allow you to bind it to a specific control. When you do, it should automatically register itself to receive the Validating event for that control.

- It needs to respond to the Validating event, perform validation, and display the error icon if needed.

- Additionally, it needs to provide a Validate() method so you can trigger validation programmatically if needed, and it needs to expose an IsValid property so you can check what the validation outcome was.

Keep in mind that the BaseValidator doesn't actually perform the validation, because it doesn't know what type of validation you want. Instead, it calls an abstract method named EvaluateIsValid() method. The validator classes that inherit from BaseValidator override this method to implement the appropriate validation logic. In other words, the BaseValidator defines the infrastructure for binding to a control and performing validation, but the derived classes add the actual validation code. Figure 18-4 diagrams this interaction.

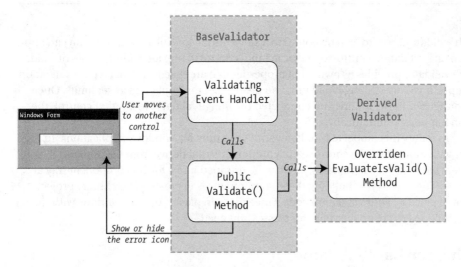

Figure 18-4. *How the BaseValidator plugs in to a form*

The following code listings dissect the BaseValidator class piece by piece. First of all, the BaseValidator is defined as an abstract class so that it can't be instantiated directly:

```
public abstract partial class BaseValidator : System.ComponentModel.Component
{ ... }
```

Internally, the BaseValidator stores a private instance of an ErrorProvider, along with an error message and an IsValid property that reflects whether validation has failed. Here are the basic properties:

```
// Use an internal error provider to show error icons.
private ErrorProvider errorProvider = new ErrorProvider();

// Expose whatever ErrorProvider settings you want the
// user to be able to modify (like Icon, BlinkStyle, and BlinkRate).
// This class exposes only Icon.
```

```
public Icon Icon
{
    get { return errorProvider.Icon; }
    set { errorProvider.Icon = value; }
}

// This is the error message that will be shown if validation fails.
private string errorMessage;
public string ErrorMessage
{
    get { return errorMessage; }
    set { errorMessage = value; }
}

// This property allows you to check if validation succeeded.
// The safest option is to default to false, and assume that
// any unvalidated data is not valid.
private bool isValid = false;
public bool IsValid
{
    get { return isValid; }
}
```

The ErrorProvider also gives you the option to stop focus changes when an error is detected:

```
private bool cancelFocus = false;
public bool CancelFocusChangeWhenInvalid
{
    get { return cancelFocus; }
    set { cancelFocus = value; }
}
```

Whenever a control is assigned to the BaseValidator, the BaseValidator connects to that control's Validating event (unless the application is in design mode).

```
// This is the control that will be validated.
// The ReferenceConverter allows the user to choose a control from
// a drop-down list with all the controls on the form.
private Control controlToValidate;
[TypeConverter(typeof(ReferenceConverter))]
public Control ControlToValidate
{
    get { return controlToValidate; }
    set
    {
```

```
        // Detach event handler from previous control.
        if ((controlToValidate != null) && (!DesignMode))
        {
            controlToValidate.Validating -= new
                CancelEventHandler(ControlToValidate_Validating);
        }

        controlToValidate = value;
        // Hook up the control's Validating event.
        if ((controlToValidate != null) && (!DesignMode))
        {
            controlToValidate.Validating +=
                new CancelEventHandler(ControlToValidate_Validating);
        }
    }
}
```

When the Validating event fires, the BaseValidator simply calls the public Validate()
method, and optionally stops the focus from changing.

```
// Validate the control when the Validating event fires.
private void ControlToValidate_Validating(object sender, CancelEventArgs e)
{
    Validate();

    // Cancel the focus change if the data is invalid,
    // and this is the configured behavior.
    if (!isValid && cancelFocus) e.Cancel = true;
}
```

In turn, the Validate() method calls the abstract EvaluateIsValid() method, which each
validator overrides with its custom validation code. Then, depending on the success or failure
of validation, the error icon is updated.

```
// This is a public method so that validation can be triggered
// manually if you want, not just in response to the Validating event.
public bool Validate()
{
    // Validate the control (using whatever functionality
    // is provided in the derived class).
    isValid = EvaluateIsValid();

    if (isValid)
    {
        // Clear the error message.
        errorProvider.SetError(controlToValidate, "");
    }
```

```
    else
    {
        // Display the error message.
        errorProvider.SetError(controlToValidate, errorMessage);
    }
    return isValid;
}

// This is the method where the derived classes will
// execute their validation logic.
protected abstract bool EvaluateIsValid();
```

All in all, this gives you a solid framework for building custom validation controls, as demonstrated in the next section.

■**Note** It's worth pointing out that this design has one limitation—if a control is already valid when you attach it to a validator, the IsValid property will still return false. That's because validation won't be performed until the user tabs over to the control and moves away, so that the Validating event fires. There are two possible work-arounds. You can trigger the validation as soon as the control is connected (which has the disadvantage of showing the error icon immediately), or you can make sure you call the Validate() method of each validator before you check the IsValid property (for example, when the user clicks the OK button to move on to another form).

Building Three Custom Validators

With the BaseValidator in place, it's surprisingly easy to create new validators. The first validator that you'll consider is the RequiredFieldValidator, which simply checks that the control text is not blank. Here's the code in full:

```
public class RequiredFieldValidator : BaseValidator
{
    protected override bool EvaluateIsValid()
    {
        // This is valid, as long as the value is not blank.
        return (ControlToValidate.Text.Trim().Length != 0);
    }
}
```

■**Note** Because the BaseValidator is an abstract class, the Visual Studio designer won't allow you to use the design surface of derived classes like the RequiredFieldValidator. This is a known limitation of Visual Studio (and the same problem is discussed for forms at the end of Chapter 11). However, it's not a significant problem, because you don't need to use the design surface of this component. Instead, edit the code directly. If you do want to use the design surface, you can modify the BaseValidator class so it isn't abstract.

The RegularExpressionValidator is almost as straightforward. It adds a property where the user can supply a regular expression, and overrides the EvaluateIsValid() method with the code needed to verify the expression against the control text. Here's what it looks like:

```
public class RegularExpressionValidator : BaseValidator
{
    // Store the regular expression.
    private string validationExpression;
    public string ValidationExpression
    {
        get { return validationExpression; }
        set { validationExpression = value; }
    }

    // Validate with the regular expression.
    protected override bool EvaluateIsValid()
    {
        // Don't validate if empty (that's a job for the RequiredFieldValidator).
        if (ControlToValidate.Text.Trim().Length == 0) return true;

        // Evaluate the regular expression.
        Regex regex = new Regex(validationExpression);
        return regex.IsMatch(ControlToValidate.Text);
    }
}
```

You'll notice that the RegularExpressionValidator returns true if it encounters a blank value. That's the same way that ASP.NET validators work, and it gives you the flexibility to deal with optional information. Essentially, the RegularExpressionValidator checks a control if it contains a value. If it doesn't contain a value but it should, you need to use both the RegularExpressionValidator and the RequiredFieldValidator on the same control.

The final validator you'll consider is the RangeValidator, which checks that a value is between a specified minimum and maximum. The RangeValidator is slightly more complicated, because it needs to support different types of data. In this example, it works for string comparisons, floating point numbers, and integers, although you could easily extend it to work with dates and other values. Here's the enumeration that defines supported data types:

```
public enum ValidationDataType
{
    Integer,
    Double,
    Text
}
```

The minimum and maximum values in the RangeValidator are stored as strings until the actual comparison is performed. Here's the basic set of properties for the RangeValidator:

```
public class RangeValidator : BaseValidator
{
    // Determines how the ranges are compared
    // (numerically or alphabetically).
    private ValidationDataType validationDataType;
    public ValidationDataType Type
    {
        get { return validationDataType; }
        set { validationDataType = value; }
    }

    // Set a minimum and maximum allowed value.
    // You could add checks to make sure the minimum value
    // isn't greater than the maximum value.
    private string minimumValue = "";
    public string MinimumValue
    {
        get { return minimumValue; }
        set { minimumValue = value; }
    }

    private string maximumValue = "";
    public string MaximumValue
    {
        get { return maximumValue; }
        set { maximumValue = value; }
    }

    // Check if the value falls in the range.
    protected override bool EvaluateIsValid()
    { ... }
}
```

When the EvaluateIsValid() method is triggered, the RangeValidator checks what type of comparison is needed. If necessary, it performs a data type conversion. It also checks for decimals if the value is supposed to be an in integer.

```
protected override bool EvaluateIsValid()
{
    // Don't validate if empty (that's a job for the RequiredFieldValidator).
    if (ControlToValidate.Text.Trim().Length == 0) return true;
```

```
    switch (validationDataType)
    {
        case ValidationDataType.Double:
        case ValidationDataType.Integer:
            if (validationDataType == ValidationDataType.Integer)
            {
                // Check there's no decimal point.
                if (ControlToValidate.Text.IndexOf(".") != -1) return false;
            }

            try
            {
                double valD = Double.Parse(ControlToValidate.Text);
                return ((valD >= Double.Parse(minimumValue)) &&
                        (valD <= Double.Parse(maximumValue)));
            }
            catch
            {
                // The text can't be converted to a number
                return false;
            }
        case ValidationDataType.Text:
            string valS = ControlToValidate.Text;
            return ((String.Compare(valS, minimumValue) >= 0) &&
                    (String.Compare(valS, maximumValue) <= 0));
        default:
            return false;
    }
}
```

You could use this model to build many more custom validators. But first, continue to the next section to see these three in action.

Using the Custom Validators

It's easy to use all of the custom validation components that were built in the last section. All you need to do is compile the class library project; the components it contains are automatically added to the Toolbox in Visual Studio (as described in Chapter 9). Then, you can drag validator components into the component tray, one for each control you want to validate. To configure how the validation works, adjust the appropriate properties (like the regular expression or maximum and minimum allowed values) using the Properties window.

Figure 18-5 shows several custom validators on a form.

Figure 18-6 shows the validators at work at runtime, with no validation code required.

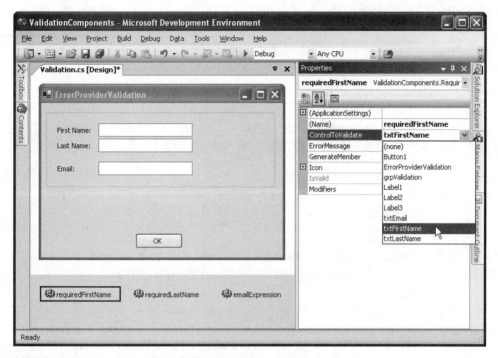

Figure 18-5. *Connecting custom validators*

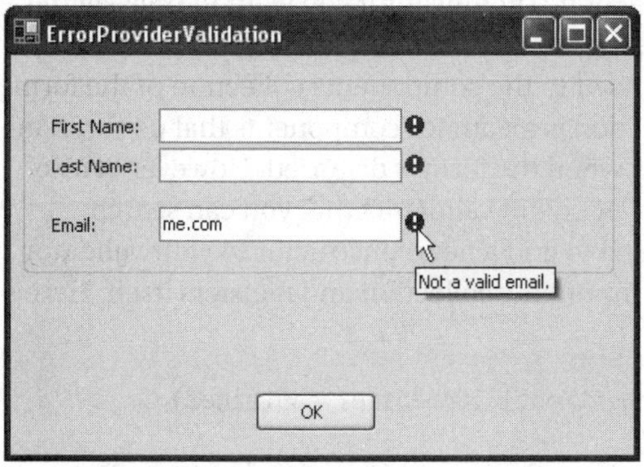

Figure 18-6. *Automatic validation*

Remember, the validation controls have a single goal in life—to check input values and display the error icons when they're needed. The validator controls won't stop the user from changing focus or clicking another button (although you could certainly modify the BaseValidator to add this optional functionality).

As a result, when the user finishes the form and clicks OK to continue, you need to check that there isn't any invalid input. You also need to make sure that every validator has been triggered at least once. Here's the basic pattern you'll use:

```
private void cmdOK_Click(object sender, System.EventArgs e)
{
    // Make sure all the validation is performed.
    requiredFirstName.Validate();
    requiredLastName.Validate();
    emailExpression.Validate();

    // Check that all the controls are valid.
    if (requiredFirstName.IsValid && requiredLastName.IsValid
        && emailExpression.IsValid)
    {
        this.Close();
    }
    else
    {
        MessageBox.Show("You still have invalid input.", "Invalid Input",
                        MessageBoxButtons.OK, MessageBoxIcon.Warning);
    }
}
```

Unfortunately, the more validators you add, the longer this code becomes. Even worse, it's all too easy to forget to check one of the validators and accept invalid information.

To solve this problem, you need a generic way to scan all the validators on a form and check that each one is valid. But because the validators aren't controls (instead, they're components), they won't be stored in the Form.Controls collection. That means if you want to track all the validators that are associated with a form, you need to add this logic yourself.

One solution is to tell the validator to add itself to the components collection of the form that hosts it. Technically, the components collection is meant for components that use unmanaged resources and need to receive notification when the form is disposed. However, it also gives you an easy way to create a form-wide collection of validators that you can search.

To implement this solution, you simply need to add a new constructor to your validator classes. This constructor accepts the form's components collection and registers itself. Here's an example for the RequiredFieldValidator:

```
public RequiredFieldValidator(System.ComponentModel.IContainer container)
{
    container.Add(this);
}
```

Provided this constructor is available, Visual Studio will automatically use it. You can then scan the components collection to perform form-wide validation, as shown here:

```
bool invalidInput = false;

// Make sure all the validation is performed.
foreach (IComponent component in formComponents.Components)
{
```

```
    BaseValidator validator = component as BaseValidator;
    if (validator != null)
    {
        validator.Validate();
        if (!validator.IsValid) invalidInput = true;
    }
}
```

Of course, there's no good reason to put all this validation code in the client. Instead, you can add a helper method to the BaseValidator class that performs this check. Here's an example:

```
public static bool IsFormValid(IContainer formComponents)
{
    bool invalidInput = false;

    // Maybe nothing to validate...
    if (formComponents == null)
    {
        return(true);
    }

    // Make sure all the validation is performed.
    foreach (IComponent component in formComponents.Components)
    {
        BaseValidator validator = component as BaseValidator;
        if (validator != null)
        {
            validator.Validate();
            if (!validator.IsValid) invalidInput = true;
        }
    }
    return !invalidInput;
}
```

Now you can call this method in your client to check the form, with less hassle:

```
private void cmdOK_Click(object sender, EventArgs e)
{
    if (BaseValidator.IsFormValid(this.components))
    {
        this.Close();
    }
    else
    {
        MessageBox.Show("You still have invalid input.", "Invalid Input",
            MessageBoxButtons.OK, MessageBoxIcon.Warning);
    }
}
```

Masked Edit Controls

The best possible way to prevent invalid input is to make it impossible for users to enter it in the first place. You accomplish this by forcing users to choose from lists, ignoring invalid key presses, and using specialized controls. Specialized controls can include the date controls described in Chapter 4, your own custom controls, or the MaskedTextBox, one of .NET's newest additions.

A *masked* text box is a text box that automatically formats input as it's entered. For example, if you type 1234567890 into a masked edit control that uses a U.S. telephone number mask, the number will be displayed as the string (123) 456-7890. Masked edit controls have numerous advantages:

- **They provide more guidance.** When empty, a masked edit control shows all the literal values, along with placeholders where the user supplied values need to go. For example, the phone number control shows the text string (___) ___-____ when it's empty, clearly indicating what type of information it needs.

- **They make data easier to understand.** Many values are easier to read and interpret when formatted a certain way. Examples include social security numbers, phone numbers, zip codes, and IP addresses.

- **They prevent errors.** Masks not only enforce details like data length and format, they also reject invalid characters (like letters in a phone number or a second decimal place in a number).

One of the most interesting aspects of a masked edit control is the way it avoids *canonicalization errors*, which occur when there is more than one way of representing the same information. One example of a canonicalization error is when a date is entered in day-month format when your code expects month-day. Phone numbers can also suffer from canonicalization errors. For example, your code might assume that the user will enter a series of ordinary numbers, and fail if the user adds dashes or forgets to include the area code. Masked edit controls neatly sidestep many of these problems.

Masked edit controls are nothing new—in fact, they've been a part of Access and Visual Basic (thanks to an ActiveX control) for years. However, .NET 1.0 and 1.1 didn't include any native support for masks. In .NET 2.0, the new MaskedTextBox provides a text box that offers support for masks.

■**Note** The MaskedTextBox functionality is completely new. It is not a wrapper on the somewhat quirky ActiveX control used in previous versions of Visual Basic, although the masking language is very similar.

Creating a Mask

You can set the mask for a MaskedTextBox using one of several prebuilt choices at design time. Just click the ellipsis (...) next to the Mask property in the Properties window (or click Set the Mask Associated with This Control in the smart tag for the MaskedTextBox). A dialog box named Input Mask will appear (see Figure 18-7), with a list of commonly used masks (for phone numbers, zip codes, dates, and so on). When you select a mask from the list, the mask appears in the Mask text box. You can try out the mask in a sample MaskedTextBox using the Try It text box.

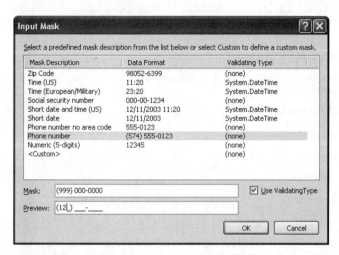

Figure 18-7. *Choosing a mask at design time*

You can also set your own custom mask, either by customizing a mask in the Input Mask dialog box, or writing one from scratch. Every mask is built out of two types of characters: *placeholders*, which designate where the user must supply a character, and *literals*, which are used to format the value.

For example, the mask 990.990.990.990 represents an IP address. The periods (.) are literals that are always displayed. The user can't delete, modify, or move them. In fact, as the user types, the cursor automatically jumps over the literal characters. The 0 and 9 characters are placeholders. 0 represents a required number, and 9 represents an optional number. Thus, the IP address mask requires four numbers separated by periods, each with one to three digits.

On a form, the MaskedTextBox displays all the literal characters, and puts a *prompt character* where each placeholder is defined. For example, if you have the mask 990.990.990.990 and you are using the underscore for your prompt character (which is the default), the text box initially shows ___.___.___.___ on the form. You can change the prompt character by modifying the PromptChar property.

Table 18-7 shows the characters you can use to build a custom mask.

Table 18-7. *Basic Properties of the MaskedTextBox*

Character	Description
0	Required digit (0–9).
9	Optional digit or space. If left blank, a space is inserted automatically.
#	Optional digit, space, or plus/minus symbol. If left blank, a space is inserted automatically.
L	Required ASCII letter (a-z or A-Z)
?	Optional ASCII letter.

Table 18-7. *Basic Properties of the MaskedTextBox (Continued)*

Character	Description
&	Required Unicode character. Allows anything that isn't a control key, including punctuation and symbols.
C	Optional Unicode character.
A	Required alphanumeric character (allows letter or number, but not punctuation or symbols).
a	Optional alphanumeric character.
.	Decimal placeholder.
,	Thousands placeholder.
:	Time separator.
/	Date separator.
$	Currency symbol.
<	All the characters that follow will be converted automatically to lower-case as the user types them in. (There is no way to switch back to mixed-case entry mode once you use this character.)
>	All the characters that follow will be converted automatically to upper-case as the user types them in.
\	Escapes a masked character, turning it into a literal. Thus, if you use \&, it is interpreted as a literal character &, which will be inserted in the text box.
All other characters	All other characters are treated as literals, and are shown in the text box.

> **Note** The mask characters that the MaskedTextBox uses bear no relation to the regular expression language! Using regular expressions to write masks would be horrendously complex, and Microsoft developers chose to go with a simpler, more familiar masking syntax.

Editing with the MaskedTextBox is quite intuitive. The user can move to any position in the text box, and delete or insert characters (in which case existing characters are moved to the right or left, provided they are allowed in their new position). The MaskedTextBox even supports cutting and pasting text. Optional characters can be ignored (the user can just skip over them using the arrow keys) or space characters can be inserted in their place.

The MaskedTextBox makes interesting use of the Text property. If you set the Text property, the MaskedTextBox treats it as though you were typing each character in the string one by one into the text box. If it finds any invalid character, it simply ignores it (without raising an exception).

For example, if you have the phone number mask (000)-000-0000, the best way to set a phone number through the Text property is like this:

```
maskedTextBox.Text = "2121234567";
```

Which is displayed as (212)-123-4567. However, you can also use this syntax:

```
maskedTextBox.Text = "(212)-123-4567";
```

Typically, the only reason you'd use this approach is if you're binding the text box to a data value that's already formatted.

Finally, you can even break the rules altogether and supply invalid characters, like this:

```
maskedTextBox.Text = "((212))123!!";
```

The invalid characters are silently discarded, so the text box now displays (212)-123-___ (the last four numbers haven't been supplied). You can change this behavior to some extent using the RejectInputOnFirstFailure property described in Table 18-8.

Reading from the Text property is another issue. The format you get depends on the TextMaskFormat property, which takes one of four values from the MaskFormat enumeration: IncludePromptAndLiterals (the default), IncludeLiterals, IncludePrompt, and ExcludePromptAndLiterals. For example, if you have the phone number shown previously (which contains literals and user supplied values), IncludePromptAndLiterals and IncludeLiterals return (212)-123-4567, while IncludePrompt and ExcludePromptAndLiterals return 2121234567. On the other hand, if you have a partially filled out phone number, the IncludePromptAndLiterals and IncludePrompt values will include that prompt character. That means IncludePromptAndLiterals will be (212)-123-___ while IncludePrompt is 212123____. The formats that don't include the prompt character just substitute spaces instead.

The MaskedTextBox Class

The MaskedTextBox derives from TextBoxBase, an ancestor of the TextBox control. As a result, the MaskedTextBox includes most of the same properties as the TextBox. (One notable exception is the MultiLine property, which isn't used.) The MaskedTextBox also offers several new ingredients, as shown in Table 18-8.

Table 18-8. *Basic Properties of the MaskedTextBox*

Property	Description
Mask	Specifies the pattern that the input must match, complete with literal values. For example, the mask (000)-000-0000 defines a phone number. The zeroes represent digits the user must enter, and the other characters are placeholders that are always shown. (999)-000-0000 defines a phone number where the area code is optional.
PromptChar	Every required value in the MaskedTextBox is displayed with a prompt character until the user enters a value. The default prompt character is the underscore (_), so a mask for a telephone number displays (___)-___-____ while empty. Whatever you do, make sure you don't use a PromptChar that you are already using as a literal, as that will cause complete confusion!
Text	By default, the Text property returns everything you see in the masked text box, including prompt characters and literals. However, you can configure this using the TextMaskFormat property. You can also use the Text property to set the text, in which case invalid characters are ignored.

Table 18-8. *Basic Properties of the MaskedTextBox (Continued)*

Property	Description
TextMaskFormat	Determines the format of the Text property. You can use one of four values from the MaskFormat enumeration— IncludePromptAndLiterals (the default), IncludeLiterals, IncludePrompt, and ExcludePromptAndLiterals.
CutCopyMaskFormat	Similar to TextMaskFormat, but determines the text that's copied to the clipboard when you use a cut or copy operation.
AllowPromptAsInput	In some cases, you might allow the user to enter the same character you use as the prompt character. For example, the C placeholder accepts any character, including the underscore, which is the default prompt character. In this situation, you can set AllowPromptAsInput to false to prevent the user from being allowed to use the prompt character as a value.
InsertMode	Accepts a value from the MaskedTextBoxInsertMode enumeration. This can set the text box to always be in insert mode (On), always stay in overwrite mode (Off), or vary depending on the state of the Insert key (InsertKeyMode).
HidePromptOnLeave	Hides the prompt characters when the control doesn't have focus (spaces are shown in their place).
PasswordChar and	If you want all user-supplied values to be hidden from view, you can either supply a password character, or set UseSystemPasswardChar to true to use the standard Unicode dot.
BeepOnError	If the user inputs an invalid character and BeepOnError is true, the MaskedTextBox will play the standard error sound.
RejectInputOnFirstFailure	Some operations transfer multiple characters into the MaskedTextBox at once. Two common examples are pasting from the clipboard, and setting the Text property. In either case, if RejectInputOnFirstFailure is true, the MaskedTextBox will stop processing the remaining values when it encounters the first error. The MaskInputRejected event is raised only once. If RejectInputOnFirstFailure is false (the default), the MaskedTextBox tries to process each character individually.
ResetOnPrompt	If true (the default), if the user types the prompt character over an existing value, the existing value is deleted. If false, the prompt character is treated as a normal key press (which usually means it isn't allowed).
ResetOnSpace	If true (the default), if the user types the space character over an existing value, the existing value is deleted. If false, the prompt character is treated as a normal key press (which usually means it isn't allowed).
SkipLiterals	If true (the default) and the cursor is positioned just before a literal character, the user can type in that literal, and the cursor will move forward one space. For example, if a user is entering a phone number and the cursor is positioned just before the dash (-) and the user types in a dash character, the cursor will move past the dash. If SkipLiterals is false, typing in the dash at this point has no effect, and the cursor remains in the same position until the next number is entered. The "skip ahead" behavior is just a cue for the user—either way, typing the literal has no effect on the value, and users never *need* to type in a literal.

Table 18-8. *Basic Properties of the MaskedTextBox (Continued)*

Property	Description
ValidatingType and FormatProvider	These allow you to get strongly typed values from the MaskedTextBox. ValidatingType is a Type object that represents the data type the value should be converted into. When the mask is complete, you can retrieve this value in the TypeValidationCompleted event. If you need to convert a text string into a value and the standard Parse() method can't do it, you can specify a custom FormatProvider to use for the operation.
MaskCompleted and MaskFull	MaskCompleted returns true if there are no empty required characters in the mask (meaning the user has entered the required value). MaskFull returns true if there are no empty characters in the mask at all (including optional values). If your mask doesn't include optional values, MaskCompleted and MaskFull will always be the same.
MaskInputRejected event	Fires whenever an invalid character is entered. MaskInputRejectedEventArgs provides the position where the error occurred, and a MaskedTextResultHint that may provide more information about why the error occurred.
TypeValidationCompleted event	Fires when the mask is complete. At this point, you can check whether the entered value was successfully converted to the ValidatingType, and retrieve it.

MaskedTextBox Events

One of the more useful features of the MaskedTextBox is the ability to convert the user's information to strongly typed values by setting the ValidatingType property. For example, imagine you've chosen a mask that expects a date in a standard form recognized by the DateTime.Parse() method. In this case, just set the ValidatingType property like this:

```
maskedTextBox.ValidatingType = typeof(DateTime);
```

Once the mask is complete, you can retrieve the converted value by responding to the TypeValidationCompleted event. At that point, you can check the IsValidInput property of the TypeValidationEventArgs object, and if it's true you can retrieve the properly converted object from the ReturnValue property. Here's an example:

```
private DateTime dateVal;

private void maskedTextBox1_TypeValidationCompleted(object sender,
  System.Windows.Forms.TypeValidationEventArgs e)
{
    if (e.IsValidInput)
    {
        // The value can be successfully converted to a date.
        dateVal = (DateTime)e.ReturnValue;
        MessageBox.Show("You have correctly entered a date value.");
    }
```

```
    else
    {
        dateVal = DateTime.MinValue;
        MessageBox.Show("Your value fits the mask, but it isn't a valid date.");
    }
}
```

If you use a custom type, you need to equip your type with a static Parse() method that converts a string (supplied as the only parameter) to the appropriate object instance. Here's the signature you need to follow:

```
public static MyType Parse(string s)
{ ... }
```

The MaskedTextBox will find this method (using reflection), and call it when the mask is complete, just before the TypeValidationCompleted event fires.

■**Note** The online examples for this chapter include an IP address sample that creates an IP object after a mask is completed.

You can also respond to a MaskInputRejected event, which fires whenever the user enters an invalid character that's discarded. Unfortunately, the MaskInputRejected event doesn't provide any information about what the problem is, but it might still be useful if you want to show a generic error message. The following code shows a tooltip when an error occurs, and clears it the next time a change is successfully committed.

```
private void maskedTextBox1_MaskInputRejected(object sender,
    MaskInputRejectedEventArgs e)
{
    // Show an error notification.
    Control control = (Control)sender;
    toolTip1.Show("That character is not allowed in this text box.",
        control, new Point(control.Height, control.Height+1));
}

private void maskedTextBox1_TextChanged(object sender, EventArgs e)
{
    // Hide any error messages.
    toolTip1.Hide((IWin32Window)sender);
}
```

Figure 18-8 shows the result.

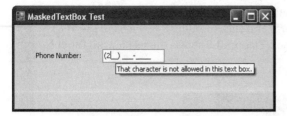

Figure 18-8. *Catching invalid characters in a mask*

Registering a Custom Mask

If you've created a custom mask that you'd like to reuse or share with others, you can use a
handy extensibility system through the MaskDescriptor. The basic idea is that you create a
MaskDescriptor class that provides your mask, the associated data type, and some other
descriptive information like the mask name and a sample of a valid value. Once you create the
MaskDescriptor, other controls can read and use the information. Currently, there's only one
.NET piece that uses MaskDescriptor classes—the MaskPropertyEditor that displays the Input
Mask dialog box where you can choose a mask at design time.

When you display the Input Mask dialog box, the MaskProperty editor searches the current
assembly (and all referenced assemblies) for classes that derive from MaskDescriptor. Whenever
it finds one, it adds it to the list of allowed masks.

For example, you could create the following IPv5MaskDescriptor class to describe a mask
that represents IPv5 network addresses:

```
public class IPv5MaskDescriptor : MaskDescriptor
{
    public override string Mask
    {
        get { return "099.099.099.099"; }
    }

    public override string Name
    {
        get { return "IPv5 IP address"; }
    }

    public override string Sample
    {
        get { return "128.128.1.0"; }
    }

    public override Type ValidatingType
    {
        get { return typeof(IPv5); }
    }
}
```

To try this out, add it to a project, rebuild the assembly (choose Build ➤ Rebuild Solution). Then select a MaskedEditTextBox on a form and click the ellipsis (…) next to the Mask property to show the Input Mask dialog box. Figure 18-9 shows the result, with the custom IPv5MaskDescriptor first in the list.

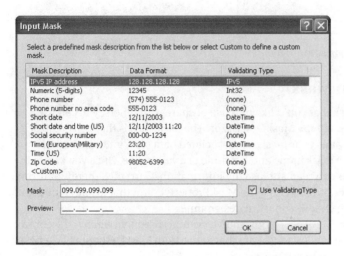

Figure 18-9. *Plugging a custom mask into the Input Mask dialog box*

Creating Custom Masked Controls

The MaskedTextBox control doesn't actually include the functionality needed to validate masks. Instead, the MaskedTextBox control relies on a more generic service provided by another class—the MaskedTextProvider class in the System.ComponentModel namespace. You can use the MaskedTextProvider to implement your own masked control, although the process probably won't be easy because it needs you to have fine-grained control over the display and keyboard handling of the control.

To create a custom masked control, you need to follow these guidelines:

- Create a control that maintains an instance of MaskedTextProvider internally. The MaskedTextProvider is stateful—it maintains the text that the user has entered into the mask so far.

- Whenever the custom control receives a key press, determine the attempted action and pass it on to the MaskedTextProvider using methods like Add(), Insert(), Remove(), and Replace(). The MaskedTextProvider will automatically ignore invalid characters.

- After you've sent a change to the MaskedTextProvider, call MaskedTextProvider.ToDisplayString() to get the latest text. You can then refresh your custom control. Ideally, you'll update just those characters that have changed, although that often isn't when you're deriving from other controls, in which case you may need to replace all the text in one operation, which might cause flicker.

The difficulty in using the MaskedTextProvider is keeping track of all the low-level details, like the user's current position in the input string.

The following example creates a custom ComboBox control that uses this principle to support masking in a combo box. First of all, you need to create a class that derives from ComboBox, create the private MaskedTextProvider member, and expose the Mask and MaskCompleted properties.

```
public class MaskedComboBox : ComboBox
{
    private MaskedTextProvider maskProvider = null;

    public string Mask
    {
        get
        {
            if (maskProvider == null)
            {
                return "";
            }
            else
            {
                return maskProvider.Mask;
            }
        }
        set
        {
            if (value.Length == 0)
            {
                maskProvider = null;
                this.Text = "";
            }
            else
            {
                // This is necessary because the Mask property is read-only.
                maskProvider = new MaskedTextProvider(value);
                this.Text = maskProvider.ToDisplayString();
            }
        }
    }

    public bool MaskCompleted
    {
        get { return maskProvider.MaskCompleted; }
    }

    // (Other code omitted.)
}
```

The next step is to create two useful private functions that you'll need to rely on. First, the SkipToEditableCharacter() method returns the edit position where the cursor should be positioned. You need to call this at various times as the user moves through the mask to make sure you skip over mask characters. MaskedTextProvider.FindEditPostionFrom() performs the hard work, finding the next valid insertion point to the right of the current cursor position.

```
private int SkipToEditableCharacter(int startPos)
{
    int newPos = maskProvider.FindEditPositionFrom(startPos, true);
    if (newPos == -1)
    {
        // Already at the end of the string.
        return startPos;
    }
    else
    {
        return newPos;
    }
}
```

Another important private method is RefreshText(), which gets the most recent text from the MaskedTextProvider, displays it in the current control, and resets the cursor to the correct position.

```
private void RefreshText(int pos)
{
    this.Text = maskProvider.ToDisplayString();

    // Position cursor.
    this.SelectionStart = pos;
}
```

The final detail is to override OnKeyDown() and OnKeyPress(). You can use OnKeyPress() to react to ordinary characters and the Backspace key. However, when inserting a character you need to take special care to find out whether the Insert key is currently on. Notice that the code sets the e.Handled property to true so the key won't be processed any further by the base ComboBox class.

```
[DllImport("user32.dll")] extern static int GetKeyState(int key);

protected override void OnKeyPress(KeyPressEventArgs e)
{
    if (maskProvider != null)
    {
        int pos = this.SelectionStart;
```

```
        // Deleting a character (backspace).
        // Currently this steps over a format character
        // (unlinked MaskedTextBox, which steps over and
        // deletes the next input character).
        // You could use the private SkipToEditableCharacter()
        // method to change this behavior.
        if ((int)e.KeyChar == (int)Keys.Back)
        {
            if (pos > 0)
            {
                pos--;
                maskProvider.RemoveAt(pos);
            }
        }
        // Adding a character.
        else if (pos < this.Text.Length)
        {
            pos = SkipToEditableCharacter(pos);

            // Overwrite mode is on.
            if (GetKeyState((int)Keys.Insert) == 1)
            {
                if (maskProvider.Replace(e.KeyChar, pos))
                {
                    pos++;
                }
            }
            // Insert mode is on.
            else
            {
                if (maskProvider.InsertAt(e.KeyChar, pos))
                {
                    pos++;
                }
            }

            // Find the new cursor position.
            pos = SkipToEditableCharacter(pos);
        }
        RefreshText(pos);
        e.Handled = true;
    }

    base.OnKeyPress(e);
}
```

The OnKeyDown() method allows you to handle special extended keys, like Delete.

```
protected override void OnKeyDown(KeyEventArgs e)
{
    int pos = this.SelectionStart;

    // Deleting a character (Delete key).
    // Currently this does nothing if you try to delete
    // a format character (unliked MaskedTextBox, which
    // deletes the next input character).
    // You could use the private SkipToEditableCharacter
    // method to change this behavior.
    if ((int)e.KeyCode == (int)Keys.Delete && pos < (this.Text.Length))
    {
        if (maskProvider.RemoveAt(pos))
        {
            RefreshText(pos);
        }
        e.Handled = true;
    }
    base.OnKeyDown(e);
}
```

Figure 18-10 shows the MaskedComboBox at work.

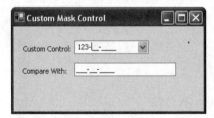

Figure 18-10. *Entering data in a custom masked combo box*

This lengthy code still doesn't provide all the functionality you probably want. For example, you may want to handle the WM_PASTE message by overriding the WndProc() method so that you can accept pasted text. You might also want to add logic to the OnKeyDown() method to handle keystrokes when text is selected (like Delete).

The Last Word

This chapter gave an in-depth look at different validation techniques, from the simple (validation events and the ErrorProvider) to the most sophisticated (regular expressions, custom validation components, and masked controls). For more tips about preventing invalid input and managing complexity, refer to Appendix A, which gives a basic user-interface design primer.

CHAPTER 19

■ ■ ■

Multiple and Single Document Interfaces

As long as developers have had graphical windows to play with, there have been heated debates about the best ways to organize these windows into applications. Although there are hundreds of possibilities, most user interfaces tend to fall into one of three categories:

- **MDI (multiple document interface).** MDIs start with a single container window that represents the entire application. Inside the container window are multiple child windows. Depending on the type of application, these child windows might represent different documents the user is editing at the same time or different views of the same data. Visual Studio is an MDI application.

- **SDI (single document interface).** SDIs can open only a single document at a time. Notepad is an example of an SDI application—if you want to open two text files at once, you need to fire up two instances of Notepad.

- **MFI (multiple frame interface).** MFIs place each document into a completely separate window, which gets a separate button on the taskbar. When you open multiple documents in an MFI application, it looks as though there are multiple instances of the application running at once (similar to an SDI application). However, the underlying architecture is different. Word is an MFI application—even though each document has its own separate window, you can use the Window menu to jump from one to another, because they're really all part of one application.

In this chapter, you'll learn how to use these different models, and you'll learn about the specific MDI features that are included in .NET. You'll also learn how to use basic window management and synchronization with the document-view architecture.

The Evolution of Document Interface Models

Early Windows applications were only designed to deal with one task a time. For example, if you wanted to edit two text files, you opened two instances of Notepad. This is still the way that many small-scale Windows applications work today, including the Calculator, Paint, and Notepad accessories that are included with Windows. (All the examples you've seen in this book so far are SDI applications.)

Soon after, the first MDI applications appeared. MDI applications were perfect for document-centric applications, because they allowed you to work with several documents in a single work environment (see Figure 19-1). The hallmarks of a typical document-centric MDI application include a main window, a common set of toolbars, and a top-level Window menu. The Window menu provides a list of all the open documents, and allows you to switch from one to another quickly. Often, MDI applications let you tile or cascade child windows to view several documents side by side. They may also include floating or dockable tool windows that provide access to additional features.

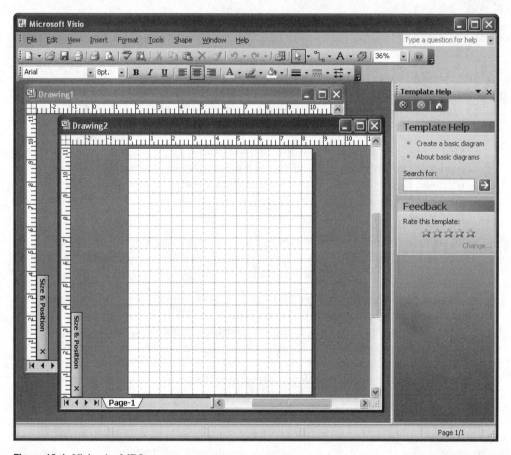

Figure 19-1. *Visio: An MDI*

There are essentially two types of MDI applications:

- **Document applications.** These applications use a single application window to contain multiple identical document windows. In a word processing program, this might provide a simple way for a user to work with several files at once.

- **Workspace applications.** These applications provide several different windows (which correspond to different features) that can all be displayed simultaneously. For example, you might create a project management program that allows you to simultaneously browse through a list of users, enter new projects, and report software bugs. This could be modeled in an Explorer-style SDI application, but the user would be able to perform only one task at a time.

MDI applications remained the de facto standard until the last few years. In a drive to streamline and simplify Windows applications, Microsoft has quietly created a hybrid approach—MFI applications.

In an MFI application, multiple documents are displayed in separate windows, as though they were separate instances of the same application, although only one instance is actually running (see Figure 19-2). Each window has its own copy of the application menu and toolbars. For example, Internet Explorer is an MFI application—if you want to open several pages at once, the pages appear in several windows, each of which is shown on the taskbar. Microsoft Word also has become an MFI application, although it was one of the earliest MDI examples in the Windows world. Most other word processors and document applications use MDIs. Excel straddles the fence—it allows you to manipulate several spreadsheet windows in the same main window (like an MDI application) but it also adopts the MFI convention of adding a separate button to the taskbar for each open document.

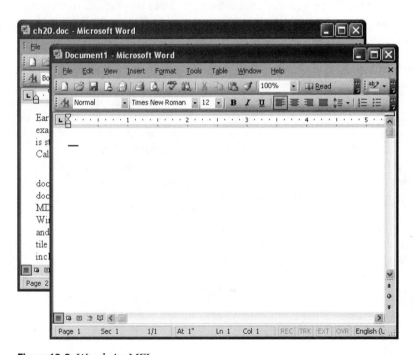

Figure 19-2. *Word: An MFI*

■Tip When planning your own applications, it's always good to survey the landscape and study the models used in today's most popular applications. That tells you what interfaces are the most successful and, more important, what the average user is most familiar with.

The debate among MDI, SDI, and MFI is sometimes heated.[1] There is no clear standard, although Microsoft officially states that MFI and SDI are easier to use and preferred. The best design depends on the purpose of your application and the user it is designed to serve. If you are dealing with advanced users who need to manage several views simultaneously, an MDI is often better than scattering multiple windows across the taskbar. On the other hand, if you are creating a small application for a novice user, it may be clearer to follow a simpler MFI or SDI design.

There are also architectural considerations. MDI design is usually one of the easiest models to implement, because programming frameworks like .NET include extensive support for it. SDI design is even easier, but if you need to support certain features (like drag-and-drop between windows, or some other form of document interaction), life gets more complicated because you need to deal with cross-application communication. In .NET, this involves using the set of features known as *remoting*.

Finally, if you use an MFI design, you may have substantial issues keeping different windows and views synchronized. There's no prebuilt MFI framework in .NET, so you'll need to build your own, and make sure it adheres to convention (so it doesn't confuse the user).

Recently, some applications have revamped the look of MDI. The best example is Visual Studio, which provides a unique user interface with tabbed and grouped windows. The basic principle of MDI—hosting several different windows in one large container—remains unchanged, but the style is streamlined. FrontPage is another example of an MDI application that displays child windows using a set of tabs. Unfortunately, tabbed windows are higher level features that are not trivial to create and completely absent from .NET. If you want this functionality, you'll probably need to use a third-party component (as discussed at the end of this chapter).

At the other end of the spectrum, many newer applications are adopting conventions from the world of the Web to create modular, flow-based applications. Creating these types of applications is more complicated because you need to build your own window management system. However, it allows highly configurable displays that can adapt to different content, different types of users, and different screen resolutions. There are a whole set of acronyms used to describe these Web-like applications—Microsoft sometimes uses the term IUI (inductive user interface). For more about these techniques, refer to Chapter 21.

---

1. One of the key features driving savvy Web surfers away from Internet Explorer to the upstart Firefox, for example, is the latter's use of tabbed windows (MDI design) to show multiple pages at once. To some users, this relatively minor feature is more important than any consideration about security, spyware, or compatibility!

MDI Essentials

In .NET, there is no sharp distinction between ordinary forms and MDI forms. In fact, you can transform any form into an MDI parent at design time or runtime by setting the IsMdiContainer container. You can even change a window back and forth at will, which is a mind-expanding trick never before allowed.

```
this.IsMdiContainer = true;
```

When displayed as an MDI container, the form's surface becomes a dark gray open area where other windows can be hosted. To add a window as an MDI child, you simply set the form's MdiParent property on startup:

```
Child frmChild = new Child();
frmChild.MdiParent = this;
frmChild.Show();
```

Ideally, you perform this task before you display the window, but with .NET you don't need to. In fact, you can even have more than one MDI parent in the same project, and move a child from one parent to the other by changing the MdiParent property.

Figure 19-3 shows two different views of an MDI parent with a contained MDI child.

Figure 19-3. *An MDI child*

One of the most unusual features of an MDI parent in .NET is that they can display any type of control. Traditionally, MDI parents only support docked controls like toolbars, status bars, and menus. With an MDI parent created in .NET, however, you can add any other type of control, and it remains fixed in place (or anchored and docked), suspended "above" any other MDI child windows.

This trick can be used to create a bizarre window like that shown in Figure 19-4 or a unique type of floating tool window (although you'll need to add the "fake" drag-and-drop support, as described in Chapter 4).

Figure 19-4. *Suspended controls*

■**Tip** MDI child forms can be minimized or maximized. When maximized, they take up the entire viewable area, and the title name appears in square brackets in the MDI container's title bar. When minimized, just the title bar portion appears at the bottom of the window. You can prevent this behavior by disabling the ShowMaximize or ShowMinimize properties for the child form.

Finding Your Relatives

If you display multiple windows in an SDI application, you need to carefully keep track of each one, usually by storing a form reference in some sort of static application class. With MDIs, you don't need to go to this extra work. That's because it's easy to find the currently active MDI window, the MDI parent, and the full collection of MDI children.

Consider the next example, which provides a ToolStrip with two buttons: New and Close. The New button creates an MDI child window, while the Close button always closes the currently active window (see Figure 19-5). You don't need to write any extra code to track the currently active child. Instead, it is provided through the ActiveMdiChild property of the parent form.

Here's the code:

```
private int mdiIndex = 0;

private void cmdNew(object sender, EventArgs e)
{
    // Show a new child form.
    Child frmChild = new Child();
    frmChild.MdiParent = this;

    mdiIndex++;
    frmChild.Text = "MDI Child #" + mdiCount.ToString();

    frmChild.Show();
}
```

```
private void cmdClose(object sender, EventArgs e)
{
    // Close the active child.
    if (ActiveMdiChild != null)
        ActiveMdiChild.Close();
}
```

The event handlers are treated as user interface "commands" (hence the names cmdClose and cmdNew). That's because they aren't linked to just one control. Instead, clicks on the menu and the ToolStrip are handled by the same event handlers.

Figure 19-5. *Working with the active child*

■**Tip** You also can set the active MDI form using the Form.Activate() method. This is similar to setting the focus for a control. It automatically moves the appropriate child form to the top of all other child forms and sets the focus to the most recently selected control on that form. Additionally, you can find the control that has focus on an MDI form by reading the ActiveControl property.

Synchronizing MDI Children

The MdiParent property allows you to find the MDI container from any child. The ActiveMdiChild property allows you to find the active child from the parent form. The only remaining gap to fill is retrieving the full list of all MDI children. You can accomplish this using the MdiChildren property, which provides an array of form references. (That's right, an array—not a collection, which means you can't use methods like Add() and Remove() to manage MDI children.)

The next example shows how you can use the MdiChildren array to synchronize MDI children. In this example, every child shows a text box with the same content. If the text box content is modified in one window, the custom RefreshChildren() method is called in the parent form.

```
private bool isUpdating;

// Triggered in response to the TextBox1.TextChanged event.
private void textBox1_TextChanged(object sender, System.EventArgs e)
{
    // The reference to the MDI parent must be converted to the appropriate
    // form class to access the custom RefreshChildren() method.
    Parent parent = base.MdiParent as Parent;

    if (parent != null && !isUpdating)
    {
        parent.RefreshChildren(this, textBox1.Text);
    }
}
```

The RefreshChildren() method in the MDI parent form steps through all the child windows and updates each one, except the original sender. It also stores the current text in a private member variable, so it can assign it automatically to newly created windows.

```
private string synchronizedText;

public void RefreshChildren(Child sender, string text)
{
    // Store text for use when creating a child form, or if needed later.
    synchronizedText = text;

    // Update children.
    foreach (Child frm in this.MdiChildren)
    {
        if (frm != sender)
        {
            frm.RefreshText(text);
        }
    }
}
```

The refreshing is performed through the RefreshText() method provided by each child window. It takes special care to avoid triggering another refresh by disabling the event handler for the duration of the task.

```
public void RefreshText(string text)
{
    // Disable the event to prevent an endless string of updates.
    isUpdating = true;

    // Update the control.
    textBox1.Text = text;
```

```
    // Reenable the event handler.
    isUpdating = false;
}
```

Finally, when the parent creates a new child window, it sets the last synchronized text into the text box using this line of code:

```
frmChild.RefreshText(synchronizedText);
```

This example shows how synchronization can be implemented using the MdiChildren property. However, the potential drawback of this technique is that it forces every window to be updated even if the change only affects one or two. This is suitable if all windows are linked together, but is not useful if the user is working in multiple independent windows. A more scalable approach is introduced later when you explore document-view architecture.

MDI Window List

By convention, MDI applications often provide a menu that lists all the open document windows, and provides options for automatically tiling or cascading them. Adding these features in .NET is easy.

To create an MDI child window list, simply add a MenuStrip, and then insert one Tool-StripMenuItem for the list. Typically, this ToolStripMenuItem will display the text "&Window". Once you've created this menu item, set the MenuStrip.MdiWindowListItem to the top-level ToolStripMenuItem you created. You can perform this step using the Properties window, which will give you a drop-down list of all the ToolStripMenuItem objects that are a part of the menu.

Once you've established this link, the Windows Forms engine automatically adds one item to the bottom of the submenu for each child window (using the title bar for the menu text) and places a check mark next to the window that is currently active (see Figure 19-6). The user also can use the menu to move from window to window, without any required code.

Figure 19-6. *The MDI child list*

■Note The MDI window list is always added at the bottom of the menu. There is no way to add other menu items after the list.

There's a trick here. If you want to put additional options in the same menu that has the window list (for example, options to rearrange the windows, as you'll see in the next section), you'll probably want to add a separator between your items and the window list. However, you don't want this separator to appear if there are no children, because it looks odd at the bottom of the menu.

The easiest solution is to handle the DropDownOpening and DropDownClosed events of the ToolStripMenuItem for the Window menu, and hide or show the separator as required. The following code implements a reasonably generic approach that works even if you change the number of items in the menu or the variable name of the separator.

```
private void windowToolStripMenuItem_DropDownOpening(object sender, EventArgs e)
{
    if (this.MdiChildren.Length == 0)
    {
        // There are no children.
        // The last item in the menu must be a separator. Hide it.
        int lastItem = windowToolStripMenuItem.DropDown.Items.Count - 1;
        windowToolStripMenuItem.DropDown.Items[lastItem].Visible = false;
    }
}

private void windowToolStripMenuItem_DropDownClosed(object sender, EventArgs e)
{
    if (this.MdiChildren.Length == 0)
    {
        int lastItem = windowToolStripMenuItem.DropDown.Items.Count - 1;
        windowToolStripMenuItem.DropDown.Items[lastItem].Visible = true;
    }
}
```

MDI Layout

If you want to add the support for tiling and cascading windows, you'll probably also add these options to this menu. Every MDI container supports a LayoutMdi() method that accepts a value from the MdiLayout enumeration, and arranges the windows automatically.

For example, here's the code to tile windows horizontally in response to a menu click in the Parent form:

```
private void mnuTileH_Click(object sender, System.EventArgs e)
{
    this.LayoutMdi(MdiLayout.TileHorizontal);
}
```

Of course, it's just as easy to create your own custom layout logic. Here's the code for a menu option that minimizes all the open windows:

```csharp
private void mnuMinimizeAll_Click(object sender, System.EventArgs e)
{
    foreach (Form frm in this.MdiChildren)
    {
        frm.WindowState = FormWindowState.Minimized;
    }
}
```

Figure 19-7 summarizes some of the layout options.

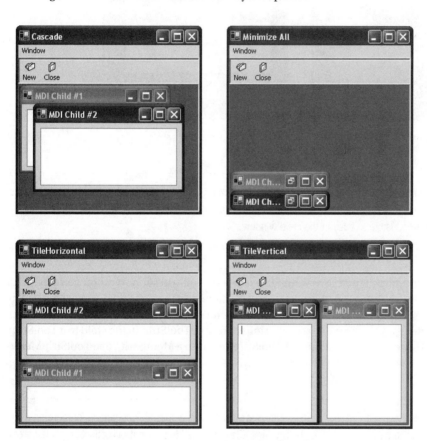

Figure 19-7. *Different layout options*

Merging Menus

Another unique characteristic of MDI applications is their treatment of menus. If you create a child form with a menu, that menu is added to the main menu when the child form is displayed. This behavior allows you to provide different options depending on the current view, but presents a centralized menu to the user.

Using the default menu behavior, menu items from the child form are added to the right of the predefined menu items in the parent (and removed from the child menu). This merging process happens whenever the child form gets focus (is activated). As you move from one child to another, the menus are adjusted automatically.

Figure 19-8 shows an example with a child menu named Document.

Figure 19-8. *Merged menus*

■**Tip** Even if you merge every top-level menu in a child window, the MenuStrip container remains, with its shaded background. Fortunately, there's an easy workaround. If you plan to merge the entire menu, you should set MenuStrip.Visible to false in the child window.

Interestingly enough, both the MenuStrip *and* the ToolStrip support menu merging. However, you can only merge between top-level containers of the same type. For example, you perform menu merging to move a menu from the MenuStrip on the child to the MenuStrip on the parent. Similarly, you can move a ToolStripItem from a ToolStrip in the child to a ToolStrip in the parent. However, you can't move a ToolStripItem into a MenuStrip, or a ToolStripMenu-Item into an ordinary ToolStrip through merging.

■**Tip** If you use merging with the ToolStrip and there is more than one possible destination for merging, your ToolStripItem objects are merged into the *last* ToolStrip (the one added to the Controls collection of the parent form last).

Menu merging revolves around three properties: AllowMerge, MergeAction, and MergeIndex. For any merging to happen, the AllowMerge property of both top-level containers needs to be set true (which is the default value). For example, if you're performing merging between two main menus, the MenuStrip.AllowMerge property of both the source and destination menus must be true.

Next, you need to consider the MergeAction and MergeIndex properties of the menu items in the *child*. (The MergeAction and MergeIndex properties of the menu items in the *parent* have no effect.) The most important of the two properties is MergeAction, which determines how each individual menu item is merged. It takes one of the values shown in Table 19-1. MergeIndex is only used if you use a MergeAction of Insert.

Table 19-1. *Values from the MergeAction Enumeration*

Value	Description
Append	Adds the child menu to the end of the parent menu. If you append several items, their order in the parent menu is the same as their order was in the child menu. The menu disappears from the child window.
Replace	Searches for a matching item in the parent menu. If it finds a matching item, the parent menu (and its subitems) is replaced with the child menu (and its subitems). If no match is found, the menus aren't merged. The menu disappears from the child window.
Insert	Inserts the child item into the parent menu at the position indicated by the MergeIndex property. For example, if the property is 0, the merged item will be placed first in the menu. If the property is second, the merged item will be placed between the original first and second items, and so on. The menu disappears from the child window.
Remove	Searches for a matching item in the parent menu. If a match is found, that item is removed from the parent. However, the menu remains in the child.
MatchOnly	Searches for a matching item in the parent menu, but doesn't perform any merging. This option is primarily useful for combining top-level menus or nested structures. For example, if you create a top-level File menu with a MatchOnly merge, and you place other items into this menu with other merge types (like Append or Insert), these subitems will be relocated into the parent's File menu, if it exists. However, the top-level File menu will remain in the child window.

Merging Nested Menus

Using the Append and Insert merge options, it's easy to insert new menus from the child into the parent (as described in Table 19-1). Merging submenus together takes a little more work.

For example, imagine you have a File menu in the parent, with a few basic commands (New, Open, Save, a separator, and Quit). When a child is activated, you want to add the Print command just after the Save command. To make this work with menu merging, take these steps:

1. Make sure both MenuStrip controls have AllowMerge set to true (the default).

2. Add a File menu to the child.

3. Set the MergeAction of the File menu to MatchOnly.

4. Add a Print menu item to the child's File menu.

5. Set the MergeAction of the File menu to Insert, and set the MergeIndex to 3, so it appears fourth on the list.

6. If you don't want the empty File menu to appear on the child form, set the top-level File menu on the child by setting ToolStripMenuItem.Visible to false or hide the entire child MenuStrip by setting its Visible property to false. Either way, the merged items will still appear in the parent menu.

Programmatic Merging

In some cases, you might want to perform merging only when certain conditions are true. In this case, the MergeAction and MergeIndex properties will be too simple to provide the functionality you want. However, you can still perform programmatic merging using the ToolStripManager.

The ToolStripManager is a utility class made of static methods. In Chapter 14, you learned how to use it to save ToolStrip settings and change the ToolStrip renderer for your application. The ToolStripManager also includes two functions for programmatic menu merging: Merge() and RevertMerge().

Merge() combines two ToolStrip controls using the MergeAction and MergeIndex properties described earlier. Here's the syntax:

```
ToolStripManager.Merge(toolStripSource, toolStripTarget)
```

This method returns true if merging is successful, and the target menu has been changed. If the merge process failed or no action was performed (perhaps because one of the menus has AllowMerge set to false), it will return false. You may want to handle the Form.Activated or Form.Enter event to perform merging.

RevertMerge() reverses this step. You can call it in response to the Form.Leave event.

```
ToolStripManager.RevertMerge(toolStripTarget, toolStripSource)
```

■**Tip** There's no need to use menu merging, particularly if your child windows have essentially the same set of menu options. In that case, it's easiest to create your menu in the parent, and hide or show certain options (or entire ToolStrips) when different child windows are activated (by responding to the Form.Activated event). However, if your child windows have a mix of different menu commands, menu merging may be worthwhile.

Managing Interface State

When creating MDI applications, you'll often find that you have more than one control with equivalent functionality. For example, you may find that the buttons in the ToolStrip duplicate options in the main menu.

To resolve this problem, Windows Forms would need a *commanding model*. This model would allow you to define a single command (like opening a document) and then map this command to different controls. Although .NET doesn't yet include this feature, you can create a reasonable solution by adding an extra layer of code. One easy technique is to hand off the work to another method. Thus, both the toolbar button-click and the menu-click event handler forward requests for a new document to a form-level or application class method like NewDocument(). Here's how it works:

```
public partial class MDIParent : System.Windows.Forms.Form
{
    private void cmdNew_Click(object sender, EventArgs e)
    {
        ApplicationTasks.NewDocument(this);
    }

    private void mnuNew_Click(object sender, EventArgs e)
    {
        ApplicationTasks.NewDocument(this);
    }
}

public static class ApplicationTasks
{
    public static void NewDocument(Form parentForm)
    {
        // (Code implementation here.)
    }
}
```

■Tip This switchboard pattern is an all-purpose approach that works with any control. Of course, with the ToolStrip and MenuStrip it gets even easier. Because these are two variants of the same control, the event handler signatures for the Click event are identical, which means in this special case you can handle both clicks in one event handler. However, you should still separate the implementation code into a separate class like ApplicationTasks, so you have the flexibility of triggering this action through another path.

Life becomes a little trickier when you need to handle the enabled/disabled state for these controls. For example, rather than performing error-checking to verify there is an active document when the user clicks Save, you should disable the Save button and menu option unless a document is available. The problem is that you not only have to disable the menu option, you also need to ensure that the corresponding toolbar button (or any other control that provides the same functionality) becomes disabled or enabled at the same time. Otherwise, mysterious bugs can creep into your application, where controls allow a function to be attempted when the document is in an invalid state. If you are performing all your testing with the menu bar, you might not even notice this vulnerability, because it's exposed solely through the toolbar.

Generally, you'll need a dedicated controller class to manage the state for your application. One option is to provide higher-level methods or properties in the controller class that automatically disable or enable related controls. Then your code will call one of these methods instead of manually interacting with the appropriate controls.

Here's how a controller class like this might look:

```
public class MDIMainStateController
{
    private MDIParent MDIMain;
    public MDIMainStateController(MDIParent mainForm)
    {
        MDIMain = mainForm;
    }

    public bool NewEnabled
    {
        get
        {
            return MDIMain.mnuNew.Enabled;
        }
        set
        {
            MDIMain.mnuNew.Enabled = value;
            MDIMain.cmdNew.Enabled = value;
        }
    }
}
```

This is typical of many programming solutions: it works by adding another layer of indirection. The MDIMainStateController acts as a layer between the form and the user interface code. When you want to remove the ability for the user to create new documents, you simply use a single line of code:

```
controller.NewEnabled = false;
```

As with many programming tasks, the trick is in managing the details. The controller class technique works well and helps tame the inevitable complexity of your user interface. However, you need to design with this technique in mind from the beginning, even if your application only exposes a few simple options.

■**Tip** For an example of a commanding architecture that's implemented through a custom component, check out www.codeproject.com/cs/miscctrl/actionlist.asp.

Document-View Architecture

Many developers will recognize document-view architecture as a staple of MFC design. In .NET, the emphasis is less critical because custom form classes can be equipped with most of the intelligence they need (as you saw in the multiple-window refresh example), and don't require an additional separation between the document and the view. Tasks that typically required views, like scrolling, are dealt with effortlessly with the built-in smarts of most .NET controls.

On the other hand, there are several scenarios that are particularly well suited to a dedicated document-view architecture:

- When you are working with complex documents that require helper methods to perform tasks like preparing the information for display.

- When you are providing more than one view of the same document.

- When you want the flexibility to provide different views in separate windows or in a single window.

When discussing MDIs, a *document* is the actual underlying data. For example, with Microsoft Word the document is the memo, report, or resume the user is composing. The document often encapsulates document persistence—for example, it might provide methods that save and re-create the document (possibly with the help of another class). The *view* is a window onto the document. For example, the view in Microsoft Word might just include the page that is currently being edited (which can be scrolled to different pages).

A typical document-view application uses the following ingredients:

- A document class.

- A document view class that references an instance of a document.

- An MDI child class that hosts the view.

- An MDI container that holds all the MDI children.

Why would a document require more than one view? It's easy to think of a view as a window onto a different part of a document, but a view also can correspond to a *representation* of the document. For example, you could have an editing view where changes are made and a print preview that shows the final layout. Both views represent the same data in different ways and must be synchronized. However, they can't be cleanly dealt with in a single class. Similarly, you might have a document object that corresponds to a large amount of information from a database. You could simultaneously view this as a grid of records and as a diagram with two different views. Yet another example is an HTML file, which can be viewed as straight text or marked-up content. And of course there are Windows forms, which can be viewed in Visual Studio as design surfaces or pure code files.

A Document-View Ordering Program

Our next example presents a fairly sophisticated model that supports real-time previews using the document-view architecture. It includes the following ingredients:

- An Order document object that contains a list of OrderItem objects.

- Two view objects: OrderPrintPreview and OrderGridView. Both derive from the User-Control class, but they could be implemented just as easily using a Panel or some other control.

- A Child form class, which can display either of the two view objects.

- A main Parent class, which provides a toolbar and the event handling logic that creates the document objects and displays the child windows.

- Resource classes, like Product, which represents an individual product, and PriceList, which provides a static GetItem() method that accepts a product ID and returns a Product object with product information.

Figure 19-9 shows the relationship of some of the classes in this example.

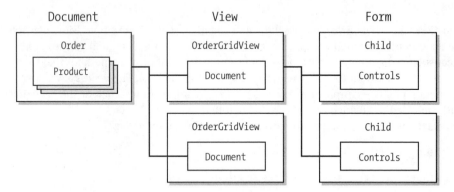

Figure 19-9. *The document-view architecture in the ordering program*

The Document Class

The heart of this application is the document class called Order, which represents a collection of items in a sales order. Because this is a fairly long piece of code, it helps to attack it piecemeal.

Note In a large-scale solution, it may make sense to create a Document class and derive the Order class from that class, or to design an IDocument interface that standardizes basic methods like Save() and Open(). However, this example keeps the classes to a bare minimum needed to illustrate the document-view pattern.

The Order class requires the help of several other data classes to model all the information that represents an order. The first such ingredient is the Product class, which represents an item in the catalog.

```
public class Product
{
    private int id;
    private string name;
    private string description;
    private decimal price;
    // (Public properties ID, Name, Description, and Price omitted.)
```

```
    public Product(int id, string name, string description, decimal price)
    {
        ID = id;
        Name = name;
        Description = description;
        Price = price;
    }
}
```

In an order, each product is identified solely by its product ID. The OrderItem class wraps this information and represents a single line item in an order:

```
public class OrderItem
{
    private int id;
    // (Public property ID omitted.)

    public OrderItem(int id)
    {
        ID = id;
    }
}
```

The OrderItem doesn't record the price because the application always uses the current price for an order. (If the application were intended to show historical information about past orders, you would need this information.) To keep things simple, the OrderItem also can only represent a single unit of any particular item.

Finally, the Order class contains a collection of OrderItem objects. The Order class is created as a custom collection by deriving from the CollectionBase class. This trick provides an added benefit to all clients, ensuring that they can easily iterate through the order items using foreach syntax. It also prevents deficient code from trying to add any objects other than OrderItem instances.

Here's the basic framework for the Order class:

```
public class Order : CollectionBase
{
    private string lastFilename = "[New Order]";
    public string LastFileName
    {
        get { return lastFilename; }
        set { lastFilename = value; }
    }

    public void Add(OrderItem item)
    {
        this.List.Add(item);
        OnDocumentChanged(new EventArgs());
    }
```

```
public void Remove(int index)
{
    // Check to see if there is an item at the supplied index.
    if (index > (this.Count - 1) || index < 0)
        throw new System.IndexOutOfRangeException();
    else
        base.List.RemoveAt(index);
    OnDocumentChanged(new EventArgs());
}

public OrderItem this[int index]
{
    get { return (OrderItem)base.List[index]; }
    set { base.List[index] = value; }
}

public event EventHandler DocumentChanged;
protected void OnDocumentChanged(System.EventArgs e)
{
    // Note that this currently occurs as items are added or removed,
    // but not when they are edited. To overcome this would require adding
    // an additional OrderItem change event.
    if (DocumentChanged != null)
        DocumentChanged(this, e);
}
}
```

The OnDocumentChanged() method is a critically important ingredient. This is the key that allows other views to update themselves when the list of items in the order is changed (either by adding a new item or removing an existing one).

The Order class also includes two additional document-specific methods—Save() and Open()—which transfer the data to and from a file.

```
public void Open(string filename)
{
    using (FileStream fs = new FileStream(filename, FileMode.Open))
    {
        StreamReader r = new StreamReader(fs);
        do
        {
            this.Add(new OrderItem(int.Parse(r.ReadLine())));
        } while (r.Peek() != -1);
```

```
        r.Close();
    }


    // By placing this last we ensure that the file will not be updated
    // if a load error occurs.
    // (The exception itself is handled by the calling code).
    this.LastFileName = filename;
}

public void Save(string filename)
{
    using (FileStream fs = new FileStream(filename, FileMode.Create))
    {
        StreamWriter w = new StreamWriter(fs);
        foreach (OrderItem item in this.List)
        {
            w.WriteLine(item.ID);
        }
        w.Close();
    }

    // Note: a real pricing program would probably store the price in the file
    // (required for orders) but update it to correspond with the current
    // price for the item when the file is opened.

    // By placing this last we ensure that the file will not be updated
    // if a save error occurs.
    this.LastFileName = filename;
}
```

All in all, the Order class is really built out of three parts: It contains data (the collection of OrderItem objects), it provides the functionality for saving and opening files, and it provides the DocumentChanged event that will prompt the appropriate views to update themselves when any changes are detected.

The OrderGridView Class

The OrderGridView presents a ListView that displays all the order items and provides support for adding and removing items. The view is created as a user control, which allows it to hold various combined controls and be tailored at design time. The ListView is anchored so that it grows as the dimensions of the user control expand (see Figure 19-10).

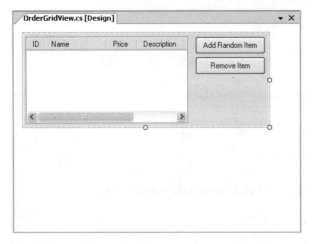

Figure 19-10. *The OrderGridView*

```
public partial class OrderGridView : System.Windows.Forms.UserControl
{
    private Order document;
    public Order Document
    {
        set
        {
            // Store a reference to the document, attach the event handler,
            // and refresh the display.
            document = value;
            document.DocumentChanged += new EventHandler(RefreshList);
            RefreshList();
        }
        get { return document; }
    }

    public OrderGridView()
    {
        InitializeComponent();
    }

    // This constructor calls the default constructor to make sure the controls
    // were added at design-time are created.
    public OrderGridView(Order document) : this()
    {
        Document = document;
    }
```

```csharp
private void RefreshList(object sender, System.EventArgs e)
{
    RefreshList();
}

private void RefreshList()
{
    // Update the ListView control with the new document contents.
    if (list != null)
    {
        // For best performance, disable refreshes while updating the list.
        list.SuspendLayout();
        list.Items.Clear();

        // Step through the list of items in the document.
        Product itemProduct;
        ListViewItem itemDisplay;
        foreach (OrderItem item in this.Document)
        {
            itemDisplay = list.Items.Add(item.ID.ToString());
            itemProduct = PriceList.GetItem(item.ID);
            itemDisplay.SubItems.Add(itemProduct.Name);
            itemDisplay.SubItems.Add(itemProduct.Price.ToString());
            itemDisplay.SubItems.Add(itemProduct.Description);
        }
        list.ResumeLayout();
    }
}

// Triggered when the Add button is clicked.
private void cmdAdd_Click(object sender, System.EventArgs e)
{
    // Add a random item.
    Random randomItem = new Random();
    Document.Add(new OrderItem(randomItem.Next(1, 4)));
}

// Triggered when the Remove button is clicked.
private void cmdRemove_Click(object sender, System.EventArgs e)
{
    // Remove the current item.
    // The ListView Is configured for single-selection only.
    if (list.SelectedIndices.Count == 1)
    {
        Document.Remove(list.SelectedIndices[0]);
    }
}
}
```

Most of the forms and user controls in this example provide non-default constructors—that is, custom constructors that accept one or more arguments. This makes it easy for your code to correctly create and configure the form or user control in one step, supplying the necessary document. However, the zero-argument constructor is still required because it's used by Visual Studio to create the user control or form at design time. You also need to call this constructor to make sure the controls you added at design time are instantiated at runtime. You achieve this by adding the colon after the constructor declaration, followed by the keyword "this" and any parameters to indicate the constructor you want to use. (Alternatively, you could call the InitializeComponent() method directly from your constructor.)

Note If you want to add the OrderGridView at design time, make sure you subsequently set the Document property somewhere in your code to supply the document and attach the event handlers.

Our simple example doesn't provide an additional product catalog—instead, a random order item is added every time the Add button is clicked. It also doesn't include any code for editing items. None of these details would change the overall model being used.

You also should notice that the RefreshList() method handles the DocumentChanged event, ensuring that the list is rebuilt if any change is made by any view (or even through code).

The OrderPrintPreview Class

The OrderPrintPreview class is also a user control, but it contains only a single instance of the PrintPreview control. Once again, this example is intentionally crude. You can easily add other controls for zooming, moving from page to page, and otherwise configuring the print preview. Similarly, the printed output is very basic and doesn't include details like an attractive title or letterhead. Figure 19-11 shows the OrderPrintPreview view in action.

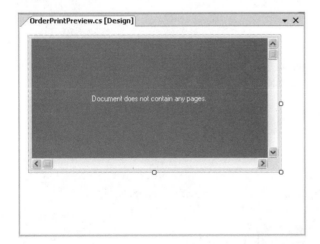

Figure 19-11. *The OrderPrintPreview*

The OrderPrintPreview class follows a similar design to the OrderGridView. A reference to the document is set in the constructor, and the RefreshList() method handles the DocumentChanged event. The only difference is that the RefreshList() needs to initiate printing using a PrintDocument instance. The PrintDocument.PrintPage event handler writes the output to the preview window.

```csharp
public partial class OrderPrintPreview : System.Windows.Forms.UserControl
{
    private Order document;
    public Order Document
    {
        set
        {
            // Store a reference to the document, attach the event handler,
            // and refresh the display.
            document = value;
            document.DocumentChanged += new EventHandler(RefreshList);
            printDoc.PrintPage += new PrintPageEventHandler(PrintDoc);
            RefreshList(this, null);
        }
        get { return document; }
    }

    private PrintDocument printDoc = new PrintDocument();

    public OrderPrintPreview(Order document) : this()
    {
        // Store a reference to the document, attach the document event handlers,
        // and refresh the display.
        Document = document;
    }

    private void RefreshList(object sender, System.EventArgs e)
    {
        RefreshList();
    }

    private void RefreshList()
    {
        Preview.Document = printDoc;
        Preview.InvalidatePreview();
    }

    // Tracks placement while printing.
    private int itemNumber;

    // The print font.
    private Font printFont = new Font("Tahoma", 14, FontStyle.Bold);
```

```
private void PrintDoc(object sender,
  System.Drawing.Printing.PrintPageEventArgs e)
{
    // Tracks the line position on the page.
    int y = 70;

    // Step through the items and write them to the page.
    OrderItem item;
    Product itemProduct;

    for (itemNumber = 0; itemNumber < Document.Count; itemNumber++)
    {
        item = Document[itemNumber];
        e.Graphics.DrawString(item.ID.ToString(), printFont,
                            Brushes.Black, 70, y);
        itemProduct = PriceList.GetItem(item.ID);
        e.Graphics.DrawString(itemProduct.Name, printFont,
                            Brushes.Black, 120, y);
        e.Graphics.DrawString(itemProduct.Price.ToString(), printFont,
                            Brushes.Black, 350, y);

        // Check if more pages are required.
        if ((y + 30) > e.MarginBounds.Height &&
         itemNumber < (Document.Count - 1))
        {
            e.HasMorePages = true;
            return;
        }

        // Move to the next line.
        y += 20;
    }

    // Printing is finished.
    e.HasMorePages = false;
    itemNumber = 0;
}
}
```

■**Tip** Printing operations are threaded asynchronously, which allows you to code lengthy RefreshList() code without worrying. However, if you create other views that need to perform time-consuming work in their automatic refresh routines (like analyzing statistical data), you should perform the work on a separate thread, and callback at the end to display the final results.

The Child Form Class

So far, everything is designed according to the document-view ideal. Most of the data manipulation logic is concentrated in the Order class, while most of the presentation logic is encapsulated in the view classes. All that's left for the child form is to create the appropriate view and display it. You do this by adding an additional constructor to the form class that accepts an Order document object.

```
public partial class Child : System.Windows.Forms.Form
{
    public enum ViewType
    {
        ItemGrid,
        PrintPreview
    }

    public Order Document;

    public Child(Order doc, ViewType viewType) : this()
    {
        // Configure the title.
        this.Text = doc.LastFileName;
        this.Document = doc;

        // Create a reference for the view.
        // This reference can accommodate any type of control.
        Control view = null;

        // Instantiate the appropriate view.
        switch (viewType)
        {
            case ViewType.ItemGrid:
                view = new OrderGridView(doc);
                break;
            case ViewType.PrintPreview:
                view = new OrderPrintPreview(doc);
                break;
        }

        // Add the view to the form.
        view.Dock = DockStyle.Fill;
        this.Controls.Add(view);
    }
}
```

One advantage to this design is that you can easily create a child window that hosts a combination of views (for example, grid views for two different orders, or a grid view and print preview for the same document). You even have the flexibility to change the interface to an SDI style.

The Parent Form Class

The MDI parent provides a toolbar with basic options and the typical event handling logic that allows users to open, close, and save documents. This code follows true "switchboard" style and relies heavily on the other classes to actually perform the work.

```csharp
public partial class Parent : System.Windows.Forms.Form
{
    private string lastDir = "C:\\Temp";

    private void cmdOpen(object sender, EventArgs e)
    {
        OpenFileDialog dlgOpen = new OpenFileDialog();
        dlgOpen.InitialDirectory = lastDir;
        dlgOpen.Filter = "Order Files (*.ord)|*.ord";

        // Show the open dialog.
        if (dlgOpen.ShowDialog() == DialogResult.OK)
        {
            Order doc = new Order();

            try
            {
                doc.Open(dlgOpen.FileName);
            }
            catch (Exception err)
            {
                // All exceptions bubble up to this level.
                MessageBox.Show(err.ToString());
                return;
            }

            // Create the child form for the selected file.
            Child frmChild = new Child(doc, Child.ViewType.ItemGrid);
            frmChild.MdiParent = this;
            frmChild.Show();
        }
    }

    private void cmdNew(object sender, EventArgs e)
    {
        // Create a new order.
        Order doc = new Order();
        Child frmChild = new Child(doc, Child.ViewType.ItemGrid);
        frmChild.MdiParent = this;
        frmChild.Show();
    }
```

```csharp
private void cmdSave(object sender, EventArgs e)
{
    // Save the current order.
    if (ActiveMdiChild != null)
    {
        SaveFileDialog dlgSave = new SaveFileDialog();
        Order doc = ((Child)this.ActiveMdiChild).Document;
        dlgSave.FileName = doc.LastFileName;
        dlgSave.Filter = "Order Files (*.ord)|*.ord";

        if (dlgSave.ShowDialog() == DialogResult.OK)
        {
            try
            {
                doc.Save(dlgSave.FileName);
                ActiveMdiChild.Text = dlgSave.FileName;
            }
            catch (Exception err)
            {
                // All exceptions bubble up to this level.
                MessageBox.Show(err.ToString());
                return;
            }
        }
    }
}

private void cmdClose (object sender, EventArgs e)
{
    if (ActiveMdiChild != null)
        ActiveMdiChild.Close();
}

private void cmdPreview(object sender, EventArgs e)
{
    // Launch a print preview child for the active order.
    if (base.ActiveMdiChild != null)
    {
        Order doc = ((Child)base.ActiveMdiChild).Document;

        Child frmChild = new Child(doc, Child.ViewType.PrintPreview);
        frmChild.MdiParent = this;
        frmChild.Show();
    }
}
}
```

One interesting detail is the event handling code for the preview button. It determines whether there is a current document and, if there is, it opens a preview window with the same underlying document object.

Figure 19-12 shows the finished application with its synchronized views. You can peruse the full code in the DocumentView project included with the samples for this chapter.

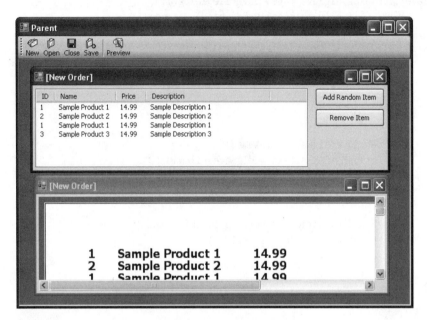

Figure 19-12. *Synchronized views on the same document*

■**Note** Because this application makes a clean separation of documents and windows, you can use this approach in other types of applications. For example, tabbed interfaces and MDI interfaces don't have the same mapping between documents and windows. Multiple documents can be placed on the same window, in different tabs. However, you can still use this model to create a tabbed MDI application because you can place multiple user controls in different tabs of the same window.

Multiple-Document SDI Applications

SDIs are easy to create—up until this chapter, every application you've seen has been a straightforward SDI application. However, modern MFI applications implement a few new twists. For example, some MFI applications include a Window menu that lists all of the open documents. When you select a document from the list, the appropriate window appears in the foreground. This behavior is implemented in Microsoft Word and several other Office applications.

Unlike the MDI window list, a window list in an MFI application needs to be implemented by hand. Essentially, it's up to you to build a replacement for the ActiveMdiChild and MdiChildren properties and the Window menu.

The following example shows a replacement class called DocumentManager. It has the following responsibilities:

- Track all the document forms that are currently open.

- Keep track of which form currently is activated.

- Create and update a window menu with a list of open document forms.

- Allow an automatic shutdown when the last document form is closed.

The DocumentManager class tracks the collection of open forms and the active form using private member variables, as shown here:

```
public class DocumentManager
{
    // Track the open documents.
    private Dictionary<Form, string> documents =
      new Dictionary<Form, string>();
    public Dictionary<Form, string> Documents
    {
        get { return documents; }
    }

    // Track the form that has focus.
    private Form activeDocumentForm;
    public Form ActiveDocumentForm
    {
        get { return activeDocumentForm; }
    }
    ...
```

Notice that the documents collection doesn't just store a list of form objects. Instead, it keeps a dictionary of document names, indexed by form reference. This is important because the document name is used to fill in the Window menu that lets the user switch from one document to another. In this example, the document name is by default the same as the form caption text—it's the full file path for the document.

To register a form, you need to call a dedicated DocumentManager.AddForm() method. This adds the form to the collection, and hooks up the events it needs to listen for.

```
    ...
    public void AddForm(Form form)
    {
        if (!documents.Contains(form))
        {
            documents.Add(form);
```

```
        // Watch for events that require a document list update.
        form.Activated += new EventHandler(Form_Activated);
        form.Closed += new EventHandler(Form_Closed);
        form.TextChanged += new EventHandler(Form_TextChanged);

        // Raise an event to indicate a new document has been added to the list.
        OnWindowListChanged();
    }
}
...
```

The rest of the DocumentManager class consists of reacting to these events. For example, when a form is activated, the DocumentManager class has to change the ActiveDocumentForm property to reflect the change.

```
...
private void Form_Activated(object sender, EventArgs e)
{
    activeDocumentForm = (Form)sender;
}
...
```

When a form is closed, the DocumentManager class has to remove the document from the document list. It also gives an option to end the application when the last document form is closed, provided the QuitWhenLastDocumentClosed property is true.

```
...
private void Form_Closed(object sender, EventArgs e)
{
    documents.Remove((Form)sender);

    if (documents.Count == 0 && quitWhenLastDocumentClosed)
    {
        Application.Exit();
    }

    // Raise an event to indicate a document has been removed from the list.
    OnWindowListChanged();
}

// Provide an automatic shut-down feature when
// last document is closed, if desired.
private bool quitWhenLastDocumentClosed = true;
public bool QuitWhenLastDocumentClosed
{
    get { return quitWhenLastDocumentClosed; }
    set { quitWhenLastDocumentClosed = value; }
}
...
```

Next, when a form caption changes, the Form.TextChanged event makes sure the window list is updated accordingly.

```
...
private void Form_TextChanged(object sender, EventArgs e)
{
    Form form = (Form)sender;
    documents[form] = form.Text;

    // Raise an event to indicate a window name has changed.
    OnWindowListChanged();
}
...
```

Finally, the OnWindowListChanged() method raises an event whenever the window list changes. The child window can react to this event to update its Window menu.

```
...
public event EventHandler<WindowListChangedEventArgs> WindowListChanged;

public void OnWindowListChanged()
{
    if (WindowListChanged != null)
    {
        WindowListChanged(this,
            new WindowListChangedEventArgs(documents));
    }
}
}
```

The WindowListChangedEventArgs class isn't shown here. It simply defines a custom EventArgs that includes a property for the dictionary of window information.

It's easy to plug this simple framework into any application. For example, consider the document-view sample demonstrated in the previous section. To convert it to a multiple document MFI application, you need to start by creating a DocumentManager instance. You can store this as a static member variable in the Program class, so it's readily available to the rest of your code:

```
private static DocumentManager documentManager = new DocumentManager();
public static DocumentManager DocumentManager
{
    get { return documentManager; }
}
```

Here's the interesting part: You need to move the toolbars and menus that are a part of the Parent form into the Child form. In this revamped version of the application, there won't be a parent any longer—instead, there'll simply be a collection of child windows representing separate documents, which are tracked and coordinated by the DocumentManager behind the scenes.

However, this design change doesn't mean you should move all of the code from the Parent form into the Child form. Instead, it makes sense to use a more factored design and move the code for creating and saving documents into a new ApplicationTasks class. Here's the basic outline:

```
public class ApplicationTasks
{
    public void Open()
    {...}

    public void New()
    {...}

    public void Save()
    {...}

    public void Preview()
    {...}
}
```

The code for all of these methods is almost identical to the code you used in the MDI version of this application. The only change is that you can't use properties like ActiveMdiChild and MdiChildren. Instead, you need to use the corresponding DocumentManager versions. That means you need to replace code like this:

```
Child frmChild = new Child(doc, Child.ViewType.ItemGrid);
frmChild.MdiParent = this;
frmChild.Show();
```

with this:

```
Child frmChild = new Child(doc, Child.ViewType.ItemGrid);
Program.DocumentManager.AddForm(frmChild);
frmChild.Show();
```

You also need to convert every reference to ActiveMdiChild to Program.DocumentManager.ActiveDocumentForm.

You expose the ApplicationTasks class to the rest of your application in the same way that you exposed the DocumentManager—through a static property in the Program class:

```
private static ApplicationTasks appTasks = new ApplicationTasks();
public static ApplicationTasks AppTasks
{
    get { return appTasks; }
}
```

Now when the user clicks a toolbar button in the child, your event handler simply calls the corresponding method in ApplicationTasks, as shown here:

```
private void cmdOpen_Click(object sender, EventArgs e)
{
    Program.AppTasks.Open();
}
```

You'll also need to add just a little more logic—namely, the event handler that reacts to the DocumentManager.WindowListChanged event to update the Window menu, and the event handler that reacts to clicks in the Window menu and activates the corresponding form:

```
public void WindowListChanged(object sender, WindowListChangedEventArgs e)
{
    windowToolStripMenuItem.DropDownItems.Clear();
    foreach (KeyValuePair<Form,string> name in e.WindowNames)
    {
        ToolStripItem menuItem =
            windowToolStripMenuItem.DropDownItems.Add(name.Value);
        menuItem.Tag = name.Key;
    }
}

private void windowToolStripMenuItem_DropDownItemClicked(object sender,
  ToolStripItemClickedEventArgs e)
{
    // Show the linked form.
    ((Form)e.ClickedItem.Tag).Activate();
}
```

And with this modest rearrangement, you now have a fully functioning MFI application, as shown in Figure 19-13. For the full code, refer to the downloadable examples for this chapter, in the DocumentViewMFI folder.

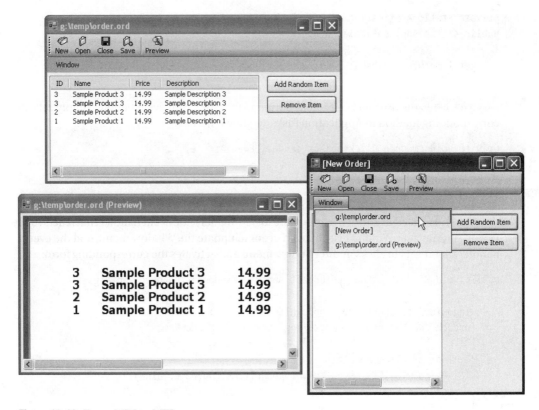

Figure 19-13. *From MDI to MFI*

Gaps in the Framework

So far, you've seen what you can do with .NET. Unfortunately, there are a few challenges that aren't nearly as easy to deal with.

Almost everyone expects an MDI to support dockable windows and toolbars—floating controls that can be latched into place or left hovering above your application. Unfortunately, designing this type of interface is surprisingly awkward. Windows (and previous application frameworks) do not provide native support for most of these features. Instead, the developer has to resort to some creative coding to implement a solution. As a side effect, docked and floating windows often look different in every Windows application that uses them—even if these applications are written by Microsoft programmers. Every solution has drawbacks and advantages.

A good case in point is Visual Studio 2003, which has a completely different docking archi-tecture than Visual Studio 2005. Even though both interfaces look similar, there are significant behind-the-scenes differences. For example, Visual Studio 2003 only shows the window border while dragging, while Visual Studio 2005 shows the contents (with a bit of transparency). Another difference is in Visual Studio 2003, windows aren't pulled out of a docked position based on the amount they are dragged, but also the speed at which the user drags them. Thus, a quick jerk will dislodge a docked form, while a slow pull will leave it in place. This behavior changes in Visual Studio 2005. Unfortunately, docked windows are a nonstandardized area of Windows programming, and one where the .NET Framework still comes up short.

The previous edition of this book presented a hand-crafted docking strategy. However, there's one universal truth about handmade docking—it's easy to do a simple mock-up, but very difficult to polish it up into a practical, robust solution. The code for the custom docking is still available with the downloadable code for this chapter if you want to start exploring your options. However, we won't consider it any detail in this book. As a professional developer, you'll be better served by leveraging more full-featured, third-party components than struggling to cobble together your own solution.

So where should you look to fill this gap? It all depends on the features you need and the amount you're willing to pay.

The Windows Forms control gallery is a good first stop, particularly if you're on a budget. Look under the Custom Forms ➤ Docking Windows category at www.windowsforms.net/ControlGallery. You'll find some freely usable examples and a few free trials. However, there's no quality guarantee.

Professional solutions for docking windows are provided by www.dotnetmagic.com, www.divil.co.uk, and www.actiprosoftware.com.

You also may decide to turn to these component vendors to find controls for implementing tabbed interfaces, which are another common user interface convention that has no built-in .NET support. Tabbed interfaces are a way to update class MDIs, and applications like Visual Studio uses them to show several open documents without confusing the ideas of documents and windows.

■**Tip** If you follow good design practices and make sure your applications are well encapsulated (with business logic divided from user interface logic), you should be able to move from one implementation of docking windows to another without changing crucial pieces of your code.

The Last Word

This chapter explored MDI programming and design. The chapter began with an introduction to .NET's effortless MDI features, and showed how to use menu merging, simple synchronization, and MDI layout styles. It continued in more detail with a sophisticated example of document-view architecture, which provides the freedom to create multiple synchronized views hosted in separate windows or the same window. Finally, the chapter ended by considering some of the missing ingredients in the Windows Forms toolkit.

CHAPTER 20

Multithreading

One of the great advantages of rich client applications is their support for *asynchronous operations*—in other words, their ability to perform multiple tasks at the same time and still remain responsive. The same feat isn't possible in a typical server-side Web application. Although Web browsers are themselves multithreaded pieces of software, most Web applications strictly separate the work that's done in the browser from the work that's done on the server, for both security and compatibility reasons. As a result, there's little (if any) support for background processing. Even if the server-side application uses multiple threads, the user is still stuck waiting until all the work is completed before the final HTML for the page is rendered, sent back, and displayed in the browser.[1]

In a Windows client application, running multithreaded code is as easy as instantiating an object and calling a method. However, multithreading *safely* isn't as clear-cut. Several issues can trip you up, including passing data from one thread to another, updating controls from the proper thread, and properly cleaning up when the work is finished.

In this chapter, you'll learn about these techniques and consider several ways to implement multithreading. You'll look at a simple application that calculates prime numbers by brute force and see how to implement it with asynchronous delegate calls, the new BackgroundWorker component, and the Thread class.

Multithreading Basics

A *thread* is an independent unit of execution. A complex application can have dozens of threads executing simultaneously.

You can take a quick count of the threads that are currently running in an application by using the Task Manager. Just call it up (with Shift+Ctrl+Esc), switch to the Processes tab, and choose View ➤ Select Columns from the menu. Add a check mark in the Thread Count check box, and click OK. Now you'll see a list of processes, with the total threads for each process (see Figure 20-1).

---

1. Enterprising Web developers often try to work around these problems with JavaScript code that runs on the client and manages a background task by making multiple requests. However, trying to make these kludges reliable and scalable is a small nightmare.

Figure 20-1. *The current processes and thread use*

■**Tip** If you want to take a deeper look under the hood, with more thread details for currently running applications, you can use a utility such as the free Process Explorer (available from www.sysinternals.com). For example, Process Explorer lets you see when a thread was created, the name of the thread's starting method, and even the current call stack.

When you program with threads, you write your code as though each thread were running independently. Behind the scenes, the Windows operating system gives each thread a brief unit of time (called a *time slice*) to perform some work, and then it freezes the thread in a state of suspended animation. A little bit later (perhaps only a few milliseconds), the operating system unfreezes the thread and allows it to perform a little more work.

This model of constant interruption is known as *preemptive multitasking*. It takes place completely outside the control of your program. Your application acts (for the most part), as if all its threads were running simultaneously, and each thread carries on as though it's an independent program performing some task.

The Goals of Multithreading

Multithreading increases complexity. If you decide to use multithreading, you'll need to code carefully to avoid minor mistakes that can lead to mysterious errors later on. Before you split your application into separate threads, carefully consider whether the additional work is warranted.

There are essentially three reasons for using multiple threads in a program:

- **Making the client more responsive.** If you run a time-consuming task on a separate thread, the user can still interact with your application's user interface to perform other tasks. You can even give the user the ability to cancel the background work before it's complete.

- **Completing several tasks at once.** On its own, multithreading doesn't improve performance for the typical single-CPU computer. (In fact, the additional overhead needed to track the new threads decreases it slightly.) However, certain tasks can involve a high degree of latency, such as fetching data from an external source (Web page, database, or a file on a network) or communicating with a remote component. While these tasks are underway, the CPU is essentially idle. Although you can't reduce the wait time, you can use the time to perform other work. For example, you might send requests to three Web services at the same time to reduce the total time taken, or you might perform CPU-intensive work while waiting for a call to complete.

- **Making a server application scalable.** A server-side application needs to be able to handle an arbitrary number of clients. Depending on the technology you're using, this might be handled for you (as it is if you're creating an ASP.NET Web application). In other cases, you might need to create this infrastructure on your own—for example, if you're building a peer-to-peer file sharer with the .NET networking classes.

In this chapter, you'll consider only the first two options. The issue of programming a threaded server requires a closer look at distributed programming. For more information, refer to *Microsoft .NET Distributed Applications* (Microsoft Press).

■**Tip** Remember, multithreading *doesn't* improve performance if both of your threads are competing for the same resource. For example, if you have a CPU-intensive task, splitting this task into two threads won't help it finish any sooner, because both threads will get approximately half of the CPU resources (in time slices).

Options for Asynchronous Programming

As all programmers know, there are several ways to solve most problems. In keeping with this principle, .NET provides several tools for multithreaded programming. Each approach has its own strengths and weaknesses.

Your options include the following:

- **Asynchronous delegate calls.** The delegate type has built-in support for asynchronous use. That means you can launch any method on a separate thread. The code runs on one of the free threads that the common language runtime (CLR) reserves in a handy thread pool. This approach is straightforward and convenient.

- **The BackgroundWorker component.** It's easy enough to get code to run on a separate thread, but it's not as easy to manage threading issues such as synchronization. To help you avoid these challenges, .NET 2.0 introduces a new higher-level model with the BackgroundWorker component, which allows you to write multithreaded code just by responding to a couple of events that fire when the task starts and when it finishes. This approach is the simplest, but also the least flexible.

- **The System.Threading.Thread class.** For more control, you can spawn a new thread at will by creating a Thread object. The Thread object is tied to a single method, which it launches when you call Thread.Start(). When the method ends, the thread is destroyed. This approach is the most powerful, but it also requires the most work to implement.

These three approaches differ in how they are implemented by the CLR, how you write your code, and what features are available. A serious .NET programmer needs to be familiar with all three. In the rest of this chapter, you'll work through examples that put all three of these techniques to the test. Along the way, you'll develop a simple asynchronous application, making it increasingly more sophisticated (and more complex).

TIMERS

You can avoid threading concerns altogether using the System.Windows.Forms.Timer component. However, the Timer doesn't offer true multithreaded execution. Instead, it waits for an idle moment in your application, at which point it triggers the Timer.Tick event handler.

The advantage of the Timer is that your time code always executes on the main user interface thread, thereby sidestepping synchronization problems and other headaches. However, this also introduces a number of limitations. For example, if your Timer event handling code performs a time-consuming task, the user interface will lock up until it's finished. Thus, the timer doesn't help you make a user interface more responsive, and it doesn't allow you to collapse the waiting time for high-latency operations. To get this functionality, you need real multithreading.

.NET actually provides several different timers, some of which *do* execute on other threads (which also means they introduce the threading complexities you'll learn about in this chapter). You can learn more about .NET timers from an *MSDN Magazine* article at `http://msdn.microsoft.com/msdnmag/issues/04/02/TimersinNET`. But before you do, read through this chapter to get a handle on the essentials of multi-threading and synchronization.

Asynchronous Delegates

As you already know, delegates are type-safe function pointers that form the basis for .NET events. You create a delegate that references a specific method, and then you can call that method through the delegate.

The first step is to define the delegate at the namespace level (if it's not already present in the .NET class library). Here's a delegate that can point to any method that accepts a single integer parameter and returns an integer:

```
public delegate int DoSomethingDelegate(int input);
```

Now consider a class that has a method that matches this delegate:

```
public class MyObject
{
    public int DoubleNumber(int input)
    {
        return input * 2;
    }
}
```

You can create a delegate variable that points to a method with the same signature. Here's the code:

```
MyObject myObj = new MyObject();

// Create a delegate that points to the myObj.DoubleNumber() method.
DoSomethingDelegate doSomething = new DoSomethingDelegate(myObj.DoubleNumber);

// Call the myObj.DoubleNumber() method through the delegate.
int doubleValue = doSomething(12);
```

What you may not realize is that delegates also have built-in threading smarts. Every time you define a delegate (such as DoSomethingDelegate in the above example), a custom delegate class is generated and added to your assembly. (A custom delegate class is needed because the code for each delegate is different, depending on the signature of the method you've defined.) When you call a method through the delegate, you are actually relying on the Invoke() method of the delegate class.

The Invoke() method executes the linked method synchronously. However, the delegate class also includes methods for asynchronous invocation—BeginInvoke() and EndInvoke(). When you use BeginInvoke(), the call returns immediately, but it doesn't provide the return value. Instead, the method is simply queued to start on another thread. When calling BeginInvoke(), you supply all the parameters of the original method, plus two additional parameters for an optional callback and state object. If you don't need these details (described later), simply pass a null reference.

```
IAsyncResult async = doSomething.BeginInvoke(12, null, null);
```

BeginInvoke() doesn't return the return value of the underlying method. Instead, it returns an IAsyncResult object that you can examine to determine when the asynchronous operation is complete. To pick up the results later on, you submit the IAsyncResult object to the matching EndInvoke() method of the delegate. EndInvoke() waits for the operation to complete if it hasn't already finished and then provides the real return value. If any unhandled errors occurred in the method that you executed asynchronously, they'll bubble up to the rest of your code when you call EndInvoke().

Here's the previous example rewritten to call the delegate asynchronously:

```
MyObject myObj = new MyObject();

// Create a delegate that points to the myObj.DoubleNumber() method.
DoSomethingDelegate doSomething = new DoSomethingDelegate(myObj.DoubleNumber);

// Start the myObj.DoubleNumber() method on another thread.
IAsyncResult async = doSomething.BeginInvoke(originalValue, null, null);

// (Do something else here while myObj.DoubleNumber() is executing.)

// Retrieve the results, and wait (synchronously) if they're still not ready.
int doubleValue = doSomething.EndInvoke(async);
```

■**Note** Most of the time, the EndInvoke() method takes a single parameter—the IAsyncState object. However, if your method uses out or ref parameters, the EndInvoke() method will also be responsible for supplying these values. As a result, you'll need to supply all these parameters to EndInvoke(), followed by the IAsyncState parameter.

To gain some of the benefits of multithreading with this technique, you could call several methods asynchronously with BeginInvoke(). You could then call EndInvoke() on all of them before continuing. The assumption in this case is that you need to perform every task before continuing. It doesn't matter what order you use, because you'll always need to wait for the slowest method. But in a more sophisticated application, you'll want to have different tasks running over different periods of time, and you'll need a way to check their status or react when they are complete, as described in the next section.

ASYNCHRONOUS DELEGATES UNDER THE HOOD

When you invoke a delegate asynchronously, no new thread is created. Instead, the CLR automatically assigns a free thread from a small thread pool that it maintains. Typically, this thread pool starts with one thread and increases to a maximum of about 25 free threads on a single-CPU computer. As a result, if you start 50 asynchronous operations, one after the other, the first 25 will complete first. As soon as one ends, the freed thread is used to execute the next asynchronous operation .

Usually, this is exactly the behavior you want, because it allows you to avoid worrying about creating too many threads, in which case none get enough access to the CPU and the overhead is multiplied. However, if you really want the ability to create new threads at will, or you want to be able to pause, prioritize, or abort an in-progress thread, you'll need to tackle the more advanced Thread class that's described later in this chapter.

Polling and Callbacks

When you call EndInvoke(), the call becomes synchronous. That means that if the underlying method hasn't returned by the time you call EndInvoke(), your code simply waits for it to finish, as it would if you called Invoke().

If you want to check whether the method is actually complete before you call EndInvoke(), you can check the IsCompleted property of the IAsyncResult object that's returned from the BeginInvoke() method. You can check this information repeatedly (for example, in a loop while you do some other work in bite-sized pieces). This approach is known as polling, and it's usually not terribly efficient. Here's an example that uses it:

```
IAsyncResult async = doSomething.BeginInvoke(12, null, null);

// Loop until the method is complete.
while (!async.IsCompleted)
{
    // Do a small piece of work here.
}
int doubleValue = doSomething.EndInvoke(async);
```

A better approach is to use a callback to react immediately when an asynchronous task is complete. Callbacks allow you to separate the code for different tasks, and they can simplify your application significantly. To use a callback, you must first create a method that accepts a single parameter of type IAsyncResult, as shown here:

```
private void MyCallback(IAsyncResult async)
{ ... }
```

The IAsyncResult object is the same object you receive when you call BeginInvoke(). It's provided to your callback so that you can easily complete the call—just call EndInvoke() and submit the IAsyncResult object.

To use a callback, you need to pass a delegate that points to your callback method as the second-to-last parameter when you call BeginInvoke():

```
doSomething.BeginInvoke(12, new AsyncCallback(this.MyCallback), null);
```

In this case, the BeginInvoke() will still return the same IAsyncResult object, but the code doesn't need to use it to monitor progress because the CLR will automatically call the callback method as soon as the asynchronous operation is complete.

Callbacks don't provide any information about why they were triggered. They don't even provide the delegate object that you used to start the asynchronous processing. That means that if you're handling several asynchronous tasks with the same callback, you can't easily tell which operation has completed when the callback fires. To get around this limitation, you can send an additional object using the last parameter of the BeginInvoke() method. This object is then provided through the IAsyncResult.AsyncState parameter in the callback method. You can use any object, including an instance of a custom class that records the details of the original operation. One useful trick is to provide the original delegate object (in this case, the doSomething delegate) as part of that custom class. This way, you can easily complete the call in the callback by calling EndInvoke() on the provided delegate. Otherwise, it's up to you to keep the delegate reference around for later.

Here's an example that starts an asynchronous task with a callback and sends an additional state parameter. In this example, the state object is simply the delegate that made the call:

```
doSomething.BeginInvoke(originalValue,
  new AsyncCallback(this.MyCallback), doSomething);
```

And here's how you can retrieve the result in the callback:

```
private void MyCallback(IAsyncResult async)
{
    // Retrieve the delegate.
    DoSomethingDelegate doSomething = (DoSomethingDelegate)async.AsyncState;

    // Use it to retrieve the result.
    int doubleValue = doSomething.EndInvoke(async);
    // (Do something with the retrieved information.)
}
```

It's important to realize that callbacks are actually executed on the same thread as the asynchronous delegate, *not* the main thread of your application.

This fact can cause a host of problems if you don't take it into account. For example, if you try to update an existing object, you could run into synchronization problems (where two threads try to update the same data at once). Similarly, you can't modify the properties of an existing UI control from a separate thread, or you may introduce other obscure errors and trigger unexpected exceptions. The only solution to these problems is to marshal your call to the right user interface thread, or use some type of synchronization. You'll see examples of both these techniques in the following section, as you apply the delegate approach to a more realistic example.

Note You might think that you could solve the thread communication problem by firing an event from your worker thread. Unfortunately, this has the exact same limitation as the callback—the event handler will still execute on the same thread, which isn't the main thread of your application.

Multithreading in a Windows Application

The asynchronous delegate example demonstrates how to execute code on a separate thread. However, this example is wide open to some of the nastier problems of multithreading. The worst part about all these problems is they usually don't appear immediately. Instead, they occur only sporadically under certain conditions, making them difficult to diagnose and solve.

To tackle these problems, it helps to consider a sample application. The basic ingredient for any test is a time-consuming process. The following example uses a common algorithm for finding prime numbers in a given range called the *sieve of Eratosthenes*, which was invented by Eratosthenes himself in about 240 BC. With this algorithm, you begin by making a list of all the integers in a range of numbers. You then strike out the multiples of all primes less than or equal to the square root of the maximum number. The numbers that are left are the primes.

The Worker Component

In this chapter, you won't go into the theory that proves the sieve of Eratosthenes, or see the fairly trivial code that performs it. (Similarly, you won't worry about optimizing it or comparing it against other techniques.) However, you will see how to perform the sieve of Eratosthenes algorithm on a background thread.

The full code is available with the online examples for this chapter. It takes this form:

```
public class Worker
{
    public static int[] FindPrimes(int fromNumber, int toNumber)
    {
        // Find the primes between fromNumber and toNumber,
        // and return them as an array of integers.
    }
}
```

The FindPrimes() method takes two parameters that delimit a range of numbers. The code then returns an integer array with all the prime numbers that occur in that range. The Worker class is compiled into a separate DLL assembly. You can then reference it in your client application.

To try out the Worker component, you can call the FindPrimes() method synchronously. Figure 20-2 shows a simple test form after a successful search has finished.

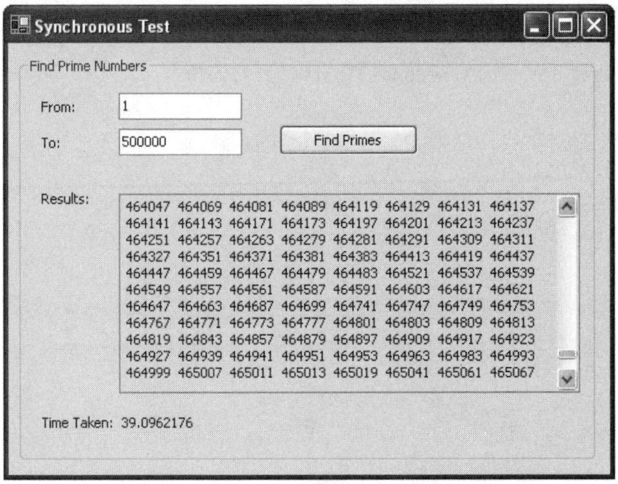

Figure 20-2. *A synchronous test of a long-running operation*

When you specify a search range and click Find Primes, the following code runs:

```
private void cmdFind_Click(object sender, EventArgs e)
{
    this.UseWaitCursor = true;
    txtResults.Text = "";
    lblTimeTaken.Text = "";

    // Get the search range.
    int from, to;
    if (!Int32.TryParse(txtFrom.Text, out from))
    {
        MessageBox.Show("Invalid From value.");
        return;
    }
    if (!Int32.TryParse(txtTo.Text, out to))
    {
        MessageBox.Show("Invalid To value.");
        return;
    }

    // Start the search for primes and wait.
    DateTime startTime = DateTime.Now;
    int[] primes = Worker.FindPrimes(from, to);

    // Display the time for the call to complete.
    lblTimeTaken.Text =
      DateTime.Now.Subtract(startTime).TotalSeconds.ToString();

    // Paste the list of primes together into one long string.
    StringBuilder sb = new StringBuilder();
    foreach (int prime in primes)
    {
        sb.Append(prime.ToString());
        sb.Append("  ");
    }
    txtResults.Text = sb.ToString();

    this.UseWaitCursor = false;
}
```

This code runs without a hitch, but it also locks the user out while the work is in progress. If you start dragging the form around the screen while the Worker is searching for primes, you may see some erratic behavior. For example, the window may become a blank surface, indicating that the form hasn't yet responded to the Windows message asking it to repaint itself, or it may display the "Not Responding" message in the caption (see Figure 20-3). To improve on this situation, you need multithreading.

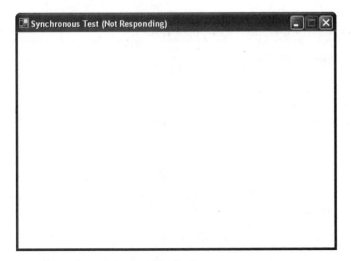

Figure 20-3. *An unresponsive user interface*

The Asynchronous Call

There are several ways to translate this example into a multithreaded application. Using asynchronous delegates, you can launch the Worker.FindPrimes() method on another thread. However, a much better approach is to wrap the call to Worker.FindPrimes() with another method in the form. This allows you to separate the code for updating the user interface from the code that actually performs the prime-number search, which is a key design goal. It also provides you with an extra layer of flexibility. This extra layer comes in handy if the signature of the FindPrimes() method changes. Figure 20-4 shows this design.

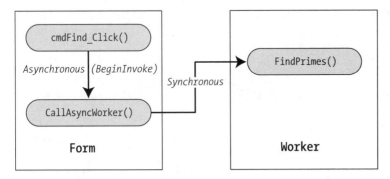

Figure 20-4. *Calling a component asynchronously*

Here's the form method that you need. It simply calls the Worker.FindPrimes() method (synchronously), and then updates the user interface with the results.

```
private void CallAsyncWorker(int from, int to)
{
    // Start the search for primes and wait.
    DateTime startTime = DateTime.Now;
    int[] primes = Worker.FindPrimes(from, to);

    // (Update the user interface.)
}
```

Because you're calling the CallAsyncWorker() method asynchronously, you need to create a delegate for it that has the same signature:

```
private delegate void CallAsyncWorkerDelegate(int from, int to);
```

Now you can invoke the CallAsyncWorker() method on another thread when the user clicks the Find Primes button. Here's the code you need:

```
private void cmdFind_Click(object sender, EventArgs e)
{
    // Disable the button.
    cmdFind.Enabled = false;

    txtResults.Text = "";
    lblTimeTaken.Text = "";

    // Get the search range.
    int from, to;
    if (!Int32.TryParse(txtFrom.Text, out from))
    {
        MessageBox.Show("Invalid From value.");
        return;
    }
    if (!Int32.TryParse(txtTo.Text, out to))
    {
        MessageBox.Show("Invalid To value.");
        return;
    }

    // Start the search for primes on another thread.
    CallAsyncWorkerDelegate doWork = new
      CallAsyncWorkerDelegate(CallAsyncWorker);
    doWork.BeginInvoke(from, to, null, null);
}
```

Notice that this example disables the button so that only one asynchronous operation can be performed at a time. The button will be re-enabled when the asynchronous task is completed.

Marshalling Calls to the Right Thread

This example leaves out one detail—the code for updating the user interface. The problem is that .NET controls exhibit *thread affinity*, which means that their properties and methods can be called only by code running on the same thread that created the control. As a result, you can't modify the lblTimeTaken or txtResults controls from the CallAsyncWorker() method.

A new debugging feature in .NET 2.0 helps you spot threading errors. By default, every Windows control included with .NET throws an InvalidOperationException when it's accessed from the wrong thread. (You can disable this behavior by setting the static Control.CheckForIllegalCrossThreadCalls to false.) However, it's important to realize that this is a debugging convenience, and these checks aren't made in a release-mode build. Furthermore, third-party controls are unlikely to provide the same nicety. As a result, you need to be conscious of when you cross a thread boundary. If you do access a control from another thread, you will run into unpredictable errors that can crash your application or freeze your user interface. Worst of all, these types of errors happen sporadically, which makes them very difficult to diagnose.

Fortunately, all .NET controls provide two members that you *can* access from other threads. These include:

- **InvokeRequired.** This property returns true if the current code is running on a thread other than the one that created the control, in which case you can't directly manipulate the control.

- **Invoke().** This method allows you to fire a method on the correct user interface thread, so you can manipulate the control without causing an error.

You can use the Invoke() method to solve the problem in the current example. You just need to break your code down so that the user interface update happens in a separate method.

Here's an UpdateForm() method you could use for updating the interface (with the corresponding delegate):

```
private delegate void UpdateFormDelegate(TimeSpan timeTaken, string primeList);

private void UpdateForm(TimeSpan timeTaken, string primeList)
{
    lblTimeTaken.Text = timeTaken.TotalSeconds.ToString();
    txtResults.Text = primeList;

    cmdFind.Enabled = true;
}
```

Now you can call the UpdateForm() method from the CallAsyncWorker() method using Control.Invoke(). Here's how you need to revise the code:

```
private void CallAsyncWorker(int from, int to)
{
    // Start the search for primes and wait.
    DateTime startTime = DateTime.Now;
    int[] primes = Worker.FindPrimes(from, to);
```

```
        // Calculate the time for the call to complete.
        TimeSpan timeTaken = DateTime.Now.Subtract(startTime);

        // Paste the list of primes together into one long string.
        StringBuilder sb = new StringBuilder();
        foreach (int prime in primes)
        {
            sb.Append(prime.ToString());
            sb.Append(" ");
        }

        // Use the Control.Invoke() method of the current form,
        // which is owned by the same thread as the rest of the controls.
        this.Invoke(new UpdateFormDelegate(UpdateForm),
            new object[] {timeTaken, sb.ToString()} );
    }
```

The nice part about the Invoke() method is that it supports methods with any signature. All you need to do is pass a delegate and supply an object array with all the parameter values.

Notice that the CallAsyncWorker() method also performs the work of building the string of primes. That's because the UpdateForm() method fires on the user interface thread (when it's idle), temporarily interrupting your application. To ensure that the application remains responsive, you need to reduce the amount of work you perform here as much as possible.

This completes the example. Figure 20-5 shows the three steps. First the button is clicked, launching the event handler (step 1). Next, the CallAsyncWorker() is invoked asynchronously (step 2), and it calls the FindPrimes() method (step 3). Finally, CallAsyncWorker() retrieves the result and calls the UpdateForm() method on the user interface thread (step 4). Steps 1 and 4 are on the user interface thread, while the shaded portion (steps 2 and 3) execute on a single thread borrowed from the CLR's thread pool.

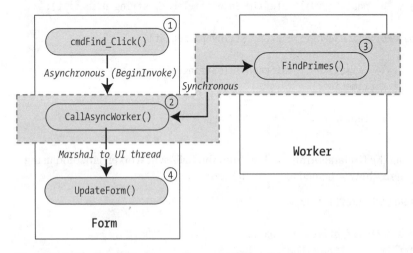

Figure 20-5. *Dealing with an asynchronous task safely*

To test this example, run the application and start a prime search. While it's underway, you still can click on other controls, and drag the form around the screen. Of course, to prevent synchronization problems or unintended side effects, you need to make sure your user interface is in a state where only the supported commands are available. For example, the Find Primes button is disabled in this example because we've chosen to allow only one search at a time.

If you like, you can rewrite UpdateForm() method to make it self-sufficient, so that it automatically marshals itself to the user interface thread as needed. This is a common pattern in Windows Forms applications that's easy to implement.

```
private void UpdateForm(TimeSpan timeTaken, string primeList)
{
    if (this.InvokeRequired)
    {
        this.Invoke(new UpdateFormDelegate(UpdateForm),
          new object[] {timeTaken, primeList} );
    }
    else
    {
        lblTimeTaken.Text = timeTaken.TotalSeconds.ToString();
        txtResults.Text = primeList;
        cmdFind.Enabled = true;
    }
}
```

Now you can call UpdateFormDelegate() directly. If you call UpdateFormDelegate() from the user interface thread, the code will run ordinarily. If you call it from another thread, the method will call itself on the correct thread, taking care of the marshalling automatically.

CONTROL.INVOKE() UNDER THE HOOD

In .NET, there is no general-purpose way to trigger code on specific threads. The Control.Invoke() method is a special exception to this rule that makes writing multithreaded Windows applications much easier.

When you call Control.Invoke(), the code checks that the control is created and its Windows handle exists. If its handle exists, the rest of the process is straightforward. The Invoke() method uses the GetWindowThreadProcessId() Win32 API function to find the thread ID for the control, and then compares that value against the currently executing one using GetCurrentThreadId(). This stage determines whether or not marshalling is needed.

Life becomes much more ugly if the control's handle isn't created yet. In this case, the Invoke() method walks the control hierarchy trying to find out if the control's parent (or its parent's parent, and so on), have been created yet. If they have, the Invoke() method grabs that thread ID. If you're facing erratic behavior or you think your Control.Invoke() method is taking longer than it should because you're using Invoke() on a control that is created dynamically, you have two possible solutions. You can access the Control.Handle property in your code before you call the Invoke() method, which ensures that the control handle is created. (Of course, you'll need to access Control.Handle from the main application thread.) Or, you can skip directly to the parent by calling the Invoke() method of a container control or the hosting form.

Continued

Finally, to marshal your call, Control.Invoke() posts a message to the message queue for the user interface thread (using the Win32 API function PostMessage). As with any other event in a Windows application,
this message isn't handled until your application has an idle moment. In other words, if your main thread is
tied up with some intensive processing and you use Control.Invoke(), the call may be deferred for some time.
Similarly, when your call does execute, it will temporarily take control away from your main thread. For the
same reason, make sure that you perform any processor-intensive work on the separate thread before you use
Control.Invoke().

For a more detailed look at the implementation behind Control.Invoke(), refer to Justin Rogers's post at
`http://weblogs.asp.net/justin_rogers/articles/126345.aspx`.

Locking and Synchronization

The technique shown in the previous example works great when you want to perform a single
asynchronous task and update the user interface once it completes. However, in many situations
you'll simply want to take the data that the asynchronous worker provides, and store it somewhere for later use. One reason to take this step is to avoid interrupting other work the user is
performing. For example, consider an application that shows a product catalog in a grid control.
You might fetch an updated DataSet from a Web service, but you probably don't want to refresh
the grid immediately. That's because the user might be looking at a specific row, or even
performing an edit. Instead, a better approach is to provide a message in a status bar informing
the user that new data is available, and allow the user to click a button to refresh the grid at the
right time.

The problem with this type of scenario is that you need a place to store the data until you
decide to display it. A form member variable makes perfect sense for this storage. However, it
also introduces a new problem—thread synchronization.

The problem is that it's not safe for you to access any data from more than one thread.
That's because there's a possibility that both the main thread and your asynchronous thread
would try to manipulate the same object at the same time, which leads to unpredictable
behavior and, occasionally, incorrect or corrupted data.

There are two ways to resolve this problem:

- **Use the Control.Invoke() method.** The Control.Invoke() method can marshal your code
  to the main thread, where it's safe to update the form-level variable. However, this
  approach requires a free time slice on the user interface thread, potentially slowing
  performance. It's also awkward to manage if you have several asynchronous tasks taking
  place at once.

- **Use locking.** This way, you ensure that you gain exclusive access to the variable for a
  short time. If another thread tries to access the same object, it will be forced to wait.

Locking is easily implemented in C# through the lock statement. The lock statement gains
exclusive access to any reference type. When you use the lock statement, the object is automatically released when you exit the block, even if it's the result of an unhandled error.

```
lock (myObj)
{
    // (Do something with myObj.)
}
```

When creating a lock, make sure you lock the smallest object with the least visibility for the shortest amount of time to ensure that other parts of the application that might also use the object aren't blocked. It's also a good idea to avoid locking multiple objects at once using nested lock statements, as this can lead to *deadlock* situations, in which two threads are trapped waiting for each other to release a lock they need.

To see locking in action, consider the next version of the prime-number search form. Instead of showing the new results immediately when the search is finished, it shows a notification in the status bar. When the user double-clicks that panel, the data is displayed.

To make this possible, you need to create a form-level variable for storing the data returned by the asynchronous worker.

```
private string primeList = string.Empty;
```

Now the CallAsyncWorker() method needs to store the prime-number list as soon as the operation is complete. To safeguard, this step, the primeList object is locked before it's accessed:

```
// (Call FindPrimes() to get the prime list.)

// Store the prime list in the form.
lock (primeList)
{
    primeList = sb.ToString();
}

// (Invoke NotifyComplete() on the right thread to update the form.)
```

■**Tip** Although this example locks a string, it's more common to lock a custom object that wraps several pieces of information. The only limit to the lock statement is that it won't work with value types (such as integers and Boolean values). You always need to wrap these inside another object.

The CallAsyncWorker() method no longer calls the UpdateForm() method to apply the changes. Instead, it calls another custom method—NotifyComplete()—which displays the status text. Figure 20-6 diagrams the revised model.

Because the NotifyComplete doesn't require any arguments, you don't need to define a specific delegate type for it. Instead, you can use the generic MethodInvoker delegate, which works with any parameter-less method.

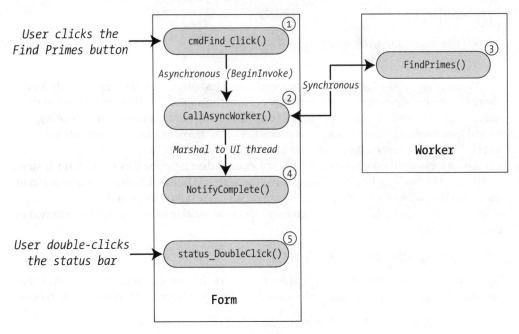

Figure 20-6. *Using a notification instead of an automatic refresh*

Here's how you call NotifyComplete() on the user interface thread:

```
this.Invoke(new MethodInvoker(NotifyComplete));
```

The NotifyComplete() method displays the status message, sets a flag to indicate that the data's available, and re-enables the Find Primes button:

```
private bool dataAvailable = false;

private void NotifyComplete()
{
    dataAvailable = true;
    statusPanel.Text = "Double-click panel to see new prime list.";
    cmdFind.Enabled = true;
}
```

Figure 20-7 shows the notification message.

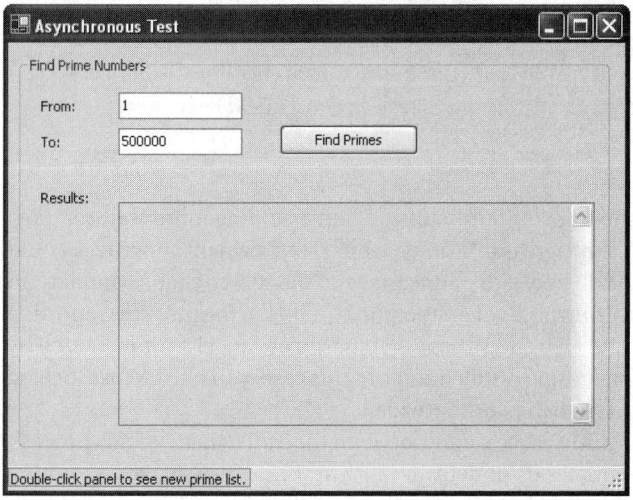

Figure 20-7. *Notfiyng the user when a result is ready*

When the status bar is double-clicked, the cached information is inserted into the txtResults text box. This part is easy, because it doesn't require any synchronization:

```
private void status_DoubleClick(object sender, EventArgs e)
{
    if (dataAvailable)
    {
        dataAvailable = false;
        lock (primeList)
        {
            txtResults.Text = primeList;
            primeList = string.Empty;
        }
        statusPanel.Text = string.Empty;
    }
}
```

Remember, locking only works if you use it in *every* place you try to access the shared object. For example, if your main application thread needs to modify the primeList string, it must also use the lock statement. You don't need to worry about synchronized access to the status bar text and the dataAvailable variable because the code that interacts with these details always runs on the main thread.

■**Tip** The System.Threading namespace includes other classes you can use for fine-grained control over locking behavior, such as Monitor and ReaderWriterLock. These classes aren't discussed in this book. For more information, consult a dedicated book about .NET multithreading or the MSDN Help.

At this point, you've learned enough about threading to begin adding more features. For example, you could add a method for progress reporting, which your asynchronous task could call periodically to provide information about the percentage of the search that's complete so far. In this case, you need to use the Control.Invoke() method to marshal the progress reporting to the user interface thread. You could also allow the user to pause or cancel a prime search by designating a form-level variable for passing notifications. In this case, you need to use locking to make sure the data is handled correctly by both threads.

Both of these improvements require adding additional methods. To manage this process effectively, you shouldn't add these methods directly to the form class. Instead, you should create a dedicated asynchronous controller class. The form can call the asynchronous controller class, and the controller class can then manage the asynchronous operation with the worker class.

There are two ways you can go about building this design. The simplest is to use the BackgroundWorker component (described in the next section), which provides high-level management and neatly hides the threading details. A more powerful option is to create a custom-threaded class, a task you'll consider at the end of this chapter.

The BackgroundWorker Component

Realizing that the challenges of multithreaded programming weren't for everyone, Microsoft programmers added the System.ComponentModel.BackgroundWorker component to .NET 2.0. The BackgroundWorker component gives you a nearly foolproof way to run a time-consuming task on a separate thread. Under the hood, it works the same way as the delegate approach you've been considering, but the marshalling issues are abstracted away with an event-based model.

To use the BackgroundWorker, you begin by creating an instance (either programmatically in your code, or by dragging it onto a form at design time). You then connect it to the appropriate event handlers, and start it on its way by calling the RunWorkerAsync() method.

When the BackgroundWorker begins executing, it grabs a free thread from the CLR thread pool, and then fires the DoWork event from this thread. You handle the DoWork event and begin your time-consuming task. However, you need to be careful not to access shared data (such as form-level variables) or controls on the form. If you do, all the same locking and synchronization considerations apply. Once the work is complete, the BackgroundWorker fires the RunWorkerCompleted event to notify your application. This event fires on the original thread, which allows you to access shared data and update controls freely, without incurring any problems.

As you'll see, the BackgroundWorker also supports two more frills—progress events and cancel messages. In both cases the threading details are hidden, making for easy coding.

A Simple BackgroundWorker Test

To try out the BackgroundWorker, it makes sense to use it with the prime-number search example. The first step is to create a custom class that allows you to transmit the input parameters to the BackgroundWorker. When you call BackgroundWorker.RunWorkerAsync(), you can supply any object, which will be delivered to the DoWork event. However, you can supply only a single object, so you need to wrap the to and from numbers into one class, as shown here:

```
public class FindPrimesInput
{
    private int from;
    public int From
    {
        get { return from; }
        set { from = value; }
    }

    private int to;
    public int To
    {
        get { return to; }
        set { to = value; }
    }

    public FindPrimesInput(int from, int to)
    {
        From = from;
        To = to;
    }
}
```

Now, drop a BackgroundWorker component onto your form. When the user clicks the Find Primes button, create a new FindPrimesInput object, and submit it to the worker using the BackgroundWorker.RunWorkerAsync() method, as shown here:

```
// Start the search for primes on another thread.
FindPrimesInput input = new FindPrimesInput(from, to);
backgroundWorker.RunWorkerAsync(input);
```

Once the BackgroundWorker acquires the thread, it fires the DoWork event. You can handle this event to call the Worker.FindPrimes() method. The DoWork event provides a DoWorkEventArgs object, which is the key ingredient for retrieving and returning information. You retrieve the input object through the DoWorkEventArgs.Argument property, and return the result by setting the DoWorkEventArgs.Result property.

```
private void backgroundWorker_DoWork(object sender, DoWorkEventArgs e)
{
    // Get the input values.
    FindPrimesInput input = (FindPrimesInput)e.Argument;

    // Start the search for primes and wait.
    int[] primes = Worker.FindPrimes(input.From, input.To);

    // Paste the list of primes together into one long string.
    StringBuilder sb = new StringBuilder();
    foreach (int prime in primes)
    {
        sb.Append(prime.ToString());
        sb.Append("  ");
    }

    // Return the result.
    e.Result = sb.ToString();
}
```

Once the method completes, the BackgroundWorker fires the RunWorkerCompletedEventArgs from the user interface thread. At this point, you can retrieve the result from the RunWorkerCompletedEventArgs.Result property. You can then update the interface and access form-level variables without worry.

```
private void backgroundWorker_RunWorkerCompleted(object sender,
  RunWorkerCompletedEventArgs e)
{
        if (e.Error != null)
    {
        // An error was thrown by the DoWork event handler.
        MessageBox.Show(e.Error.Message, "An Error Occurred");
        primeList = "";
        statusPanel.Text = "";
    }
    else
    {
        primeList = (string)e.Result;
        statusPanel.Text = "Double-click panel to see new prime list.";
    }
    cmdFind.Enabled = true;
}
```

Notice that you don't need any locking code, and you don't need to use Control.Invoke().

Tracking Progress

The BackgroundWorker also provides built-in support for tracking progress, which is useful for keeping the client informed about how much work has been completed in a long-running task.

To add support for progress, you need to first set the BackgroundWorker. WorkerReportsProgress property to true. Actually, providing and displaying the progress information is a two-step affair. First, the DoWork event handling code needs to call the BackgroundWorker.ReportProgress() method and provide an estimated percent complete (from 0 to 100). You can do this as often as you like. Every time you call ReportProgress(), the BackgroundWorker fires the ProgressChanged event. You can react to this event to read the new progress percentage and update the user interface. Because the ProgressChanged event fires from the user interface thread, there's no need to use Control.Invoke().

Supporting this pattern in the current example is a little more work. Currently, the majority of the work is performed in response to a single method call—Worker.FindPrimes(). But to provide progress information, you need to call ReportProgress() during the prime search. To make this possible, you must split the search into several pieces, or give the Worker class the ability to report progress. In this example, you'll see the second approach.

To add support to the Worker class, start by adding a third parameter to the FindPrimes() method, as shown here:

```
public static int[] FindPrimes(int fromNumber, int toNumber,
  System.ComponentModel.BackgroundWorker backgroundWorker)
{ ... }
```

The FindPrimes() method is also changed to report progress periodically. Reporting progress usually involves a calculation, an event, and a refresh of the form's user interface. As a result, you want to cut down the rate of progress reporting to one or two updates per second. In the FindPrimes() method, progress is reported only in one-percent increments:

```
int iteration = list.Length / 100;
for (int i = 0; i < list.Length; i++)
{
    ...
    // Report progress only if there is a change of 1%.
    // Also, don't bother performing the calculation if there
    // isn't a BackgroundWorker or it doesn't support progress notifications.
    if ((i % iteration == 0) &&
      (backgroundWorker != null) && backgroundWorker.WorkerReportsProgress)
    {
        backgroundWorker.ReportProgress(i / iteration);
    }
}
```

Now the only remaining step is to respond to the ProgressChanged event and update a progress control in the status bar:

```
private void backgroundWorker_ProgressChanged(object sender,
  ProgressChangedEventArgs e)
{
    progressPanel.Value = e.ProgressPercentage;
}
```

Figure 20-8 shows the progress meter while the task is in progress.

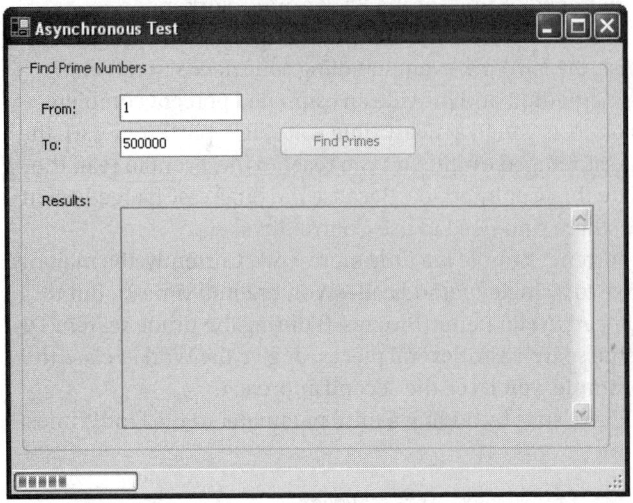

Figure 20-8. *Tracking progress for an asynchronous task*

This approach breaks the clean separation between data processing and the user interface layer, and it tightly couples your Worker component to a particular asynchronous implementation (in this case, the one provided by the BackgroundWorker component). Ideally, you could avoid this complexity by using an interface (say, IReportProgress) that could be implemented by the BackgroundWorker and other classes. Sadly, the BackgroundWorker doesn't use any such interface. The only way to properly correct the problem is to create your own asynchronous implementation that does use an interface (see the section on custom-threaded classes later in this chapter).

However, you can improve the situation a bit by making sure the BackgroundWorker supports alternate approaches, including invocation without a BackgroundWorker. To keep compatibility with the earlier examples, you can add an overload to the FindPrimes() method that takes the original two parameters. It can then call the other version of FindPrimes() to perform the actual work:

```
public static int[] FindPrimes(int fromNumber, int toNumber)
{
    return FindPrimes(fromNumber, toNumber, null);
}
```

The Worker component is still tightly coupled to the BackgroundWorker, but by factoring your code a bit more and providing overloaded versions of the FindPrimes()method, you buy yourself some valuable flexibility.

Supporting a Cancel Feature

It's just as easy to add support for canceling a long-running task with the BackgroundWorker. The first step is to set the BackgroundWorker.WorkerSupportsCancellation property to true.

To request a cancellation, your form needs to call the BackgroundWorker.CancelAsync() method. In this example, the cancellation is requested when a Cancel button is clicked:

```
private void cmdCancel_Click(object sender, EventArgs e)
{
    backgroundWorker.CancelAsync();
}
```

Nothing happens automatically when you call CancelAsync(). Instead, the code that's performing the task needs to explicitly check for the cancel request, perform any required cleanup, and return. Here's how you can add this code to the FindPrimes() method so that it checks just before it reports progress:

```
for (int i = 0; i < list.Length; i++)
{
    ...
    if ((i % iteration) && (backgroundWorker != null))
    {
        if (backgroundWorker.CancellationPending)
        {
            // Return without doing any more work.
            return;
        }
        if (backgroundWorker.WorkerReportsProgress)
        {
            backgroundWorker.ReportProgress(i / iteration);
        }
    }
}
```

The code in the DoWork event handler also needs to explicitly set the DoWorkEventArgs.Cancel property to true to complete the cancellation. You can then return from that method without attempting to build up the string of primes.

```
private void backgroundWorker_DoWork(object sender, DoWorkEventArgs e)
{
    FindPrimesInput input = (FindPrimesInput)e.Argument;
    int[] primes = Worker.FindPrimes(input.From, input.To,
      backgroundWorker);

    if (backgroundWorker.CancellationPending)
    {
        e.Cancel = true;
        return;
    }

    // (Code for building the prime list.)
}
```

Even when you cancel an operation, the RunWorkerCompleted event still fires. At this point, you can check if the task was canceled, and handle it accordingly.

```
private void backgroundWorker_RunWorkerCompleted(object sender,
  RunWorkerCompletedEventArgs e)
{
    primeList = "";
    statusPanel.Text = "";
    if (e.Cancelled)
    {
        MessageBox.Show("Search cancelled.");
    }
    else if (e.Error != null)
    {
        MessageBox.Show(e.Error.Message, "An Error Occurred");
    }
    else
    {
        primeList = (string)e.Result;
        statusPanel.Text = "Double-click panel to see new prime list.";
    }
    cmdFind.Enabled = true;
}
```

Now the BackgroundWorker component allows you to start a search and end it prematurely.

The Thread Class

At first, the BackgroundWorker component seems like the perfect solution to building multi-threaded applications, and in many cases it is. The BackgroundWorker component makes particularly good sense when you have a single long-running task that executes in the background. But the BackgroundWorker doesn't provide some features, such as the following:

- The ability to manage multiple asynchronous tasks at once. For example, you can't run multiple prime-number queries at once (at least not without some ugly workarounds).

- The ability to communicate in ways other than sending a progress report or cancellation request. For example, you can't pause an in-progress task or supply new information. You're limited to the features baked into the BackgroundWorker.

- The ability to directly access and manipulate details about the background thread (such as its priority).

If you're creating an application that needs these features, you need to step up to the System.Threading.Thread class. The Thread class represents a new thread of execution. To use the Thread class, you begin by creating a new Thread object, at which point you supply a delegate to the method you want to invoke asynchronously. As with the delegate examples and the

BackgroundWorker, a Thread object can point to only a single method. However, there's one basic limitation—this method must accept no parameters and have no return value. In other words, it must match the signature of the System.Threading.ThreadStart delegate.

```
ThreadStart asyncMethod = new ThreadStart(myMethod);
Thread thread = new Thread(asyncMethod);
```

Once you've created the Thread object, you can start it on its way by calling the Thread.Start() method. This method returns immediately, and your code begins executing asynchronously on a new thread (not one of the threads in the CLR thread pool).

```
thread.Start();
```

When the method ends, the thread is destroyed and cannot be reused.

Table 20-1 lists the key properties of the Thread class.

Table 20-1. *Thread Properties*

Property	Description
IsAlive	Returns true unless the thread is stopped, aborted, or not yet started.
IsBackground	A thread is either a background thread or a foreground thread. Background threads are identical to foreground threads except they can't prevent a process from ending. After all the foreground threads in your application have terminated, the CLR automatically aborts all background threads that are still alive.
Name	Enables you to set a string name that identifies the thread. This is primarily useful during debugging.
Priority	You can set a ThreadPriority to change the priority of your thread at any time. Valid values are Highest, AboveNormal, Normal (the default), BelowNormal, Lowest. Thread priorities are important in a relative sense. For example, if your application has an AboveNormal thread, it gets many more time slices in which to execute than a BelowNormal thread in your application (or other applications). However, be careful about relying on high priority levels, as they may compromise the performance of other currently running applications or system services. It is usually a good idea to set a lower priority to your worker thread in order to have a more responsive user interface.
ThreadState	A combination of ThreadState values, which indicate whether the thread is started, running, waiting, a background thread, and so on. You can poll this property to find out when a thread has completed its work.
CurrentThread (static)	Returns a Thread object for the current thread (where your code is executing).

The Thread class also provides some useful methods for controlling threads. These are listed in Table 20-2.

Table 20-2. *Thread Methods*

Method	Description
Abort()	Kills a thread using the ThreadAbortException. As a rule of thumb, it's better to use message passing to make sure a thread ends politely in response to a cancellation request.
Interrupt()	If the thread is currently waiting (using synchronization code), blocked, or sleeping, this method puts it back on track.
Join()	Waits until the thread terminates (or a specified timeout elapses).
ResetAbort()	If the thread calls this method when handling the ThreadAbortException, the exception will not be thrown again and the thread will be allowed to continue living.
Resume()	Returns a thread to life after it has been paused with the Suspend() method.
Start()	Starts a thread executing for the first time. You cannot use Start() to restart a thread after it ends.
Suspend()	Pauses a thread for an indefinite amount of time (until Resume() is called). This method is risky, because the code may be anywhere when you pause it, and it may even be holding onto a lock. It's often better to create your own thread communication mechanisms, so that your threaded code can pause itself (using the Thread.Sleep() method) on request .
Sleep()	Pauses the current thread for a specified number of milliseconds. This method is static.

In the next example, you'll see how to build a threading system for performing an arbitrary number of simultaneous prime-number searches.

Creating a ThreadWrapper

Because the Thread class supports only methods with no parameters and no return value, it's common to put the code you want to execute in a separate class. You can then add properties to that class for the input and output information.

A common design in .NET applications is to create a Worker class that encapsulates the code for performing your specific task *and* the thread object. That way, you don't need to track both the worker and the thread objects separately.

Before you create your thread wrapper, it makes good sense to factor out all the threading essentials into a base class. That way you can use the same pattern to create multiple asynchronous tasks without recoding it each time. This approach also gives you the benefit of defining a standard interface.

We'll examine the ThreadWrapper base class piece by piece. First of all, the ThreadWrapper is declared abstract so that it can't be instantiated on its own. Instead, you need to create a derived class.

```
public abstract class ThreadWrapper
{ ... }
```

The ThreadWrapper defines two public properties. Status returns one of three values from an enumeration (Unstarted, InProgress, or Completed). ID returns an automatically generated unique ID, which is useful for tracking the task when several are underway at once.

```
// Track the status of the task.
private StatusState status = StatusState.Unstarted;
public StatusState Status
{
    get { return status; }
}

// Use a unique ID to track the task later, if needed.
private Guid id = Guid.NewGuid();
public Guid ID
{
    get { return id; }
}
```

The ThreadWrapper wraps a Thread object. It exposes a public Start() method which, when called, creates the thread and starts it off:

```
// This is the thread where the task is carried out.
private Thread thread;

// Start the new operation.
public void Start()
{
    if (status == StatusState.InProgress)
    {
        throw new InvalidOperationException("Already in progress.");
    }
    else
    {
        // Initialize the new task.
        status = StatusState.InProgress;

        // Create the thread and run it in the background,
        // so it will terminate automatically if the application ends.
        thread = new Thread(StartTaskAsync);
        thread.IsBackground = true;

        // Start the thread.
        thread.Start();
    }
}
```

The thread executes a private method named StartTaskAsync(). This method farms the work out to two other methods—DoTask() and OnCompleted(). DoTask() performs the actual work (calculating the prime-numbers). OnCompleted() fires a completion event or triggers a callback to notify the client. Both of these details are specific to the particular task at hand, so they're implemented as abstract methods that the derived class will override:

```
private void StartTaskAsync()
{
    DoTask();
    status = StatusState.Completed;
    OnCompleted();
}

// Override this class to supply the task logic.
protected abstract void DoTask();

// Override this class to supply the callback logic.
protected abstract void OnCompleted();
```

This completes the ThreadWrapper.

Creating the Derived Task Class

Now that you have the thread wrapper in place, you can derive a new class that overrides DoTask() and OnCompleted() to perform the prime-number calculation:

```
public class EratosthenesTask : ThreadWrapper
{ ... }
```

The first order of business is getting the input information into the EratosthenesTask class. The easiest approach is to require that the from and to numbers be supplied as constructor arguments:

```
private int fromNumber, toNumber;

public EratosthenesTask(int from, int to)
{
    this.fromNumber = from;
    this.toNumber = to;
}
```

This solves the problem of getting the input information into the class. But how do you get the result out? The thread wrapper needs to fire some sort of completion event. You could require the client to supply a callback as a constructor argument. However, this example uses an event instead:

```
public event FindPrimesCompletedEventHandler Completed;
```

The event signature defines two parameters—the sender and a FindPrimesCompletedEventArgs object that wraps the information about the search range and final prime-number result list.

```
public delegate void FindPrimesCompletedEventHandler(object sender,
   FindPrimesCompletedEventArgs e);
```

Now, you simply need to override the DoTask() and OnCompleted() methods to fill in the blanks. The DoTask() method performs the search and stores the prime list in a variable:

```
private string primeList;

protected override void DoTask()
{
    // Start the search for primes and wait.
    int[] primes = Worker.FindPrimes(from, to);

    // Paste the list of primes together into one long string.
    StringBuilder sb = new StringBuilder();
    foreach (int prime in primes)
    {
        sb.Append(prime.ToString());
        sb.Append("  ");
    }

    // Store the result.
    string primeList = sb.ToString();
}
```

Notice that in this example, the work is farmed out to the Worker component. This makes for a more streamlined design and simpler coding. However, you might want to change this design to put the prime search code into the DoTask() method. This way, you can add support for progress reporting and cancellation. (The downloadable samples for this chapter [in the Source Code area of the Apress Web site] use this approach.)

The OnCompleted() method fires the event:

```
protected override void OnCompleted()
{
    if (Completed != null)
        Completed(this,
            new FindPrimesCompletedEventArgs(fromNumber, toNumber, primeList));
}
```

The next ingredient is to create the form that lets the user launch the prime-number searches.

Creating and Tracking Threads

In this example, the user can launch multiple searches using an MDI interface (see Figure 20-9). Each search is run by a separate instance of the EratosthenesTask class. The MDI form tracks all these wrappers and responds to the completion callback to show the results. The number of ongoing tasks is indicated in the status bar.

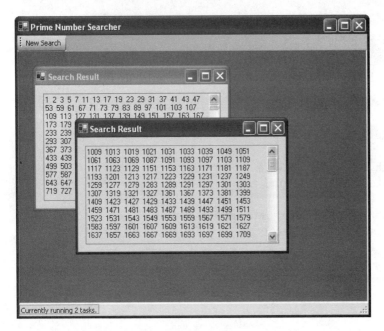

Figure 20-9. *Performing multiple searches*

To make this work, you need to use a collection that keeps track of all the wrappers that are currently performing searches. You can add this collection as a member variable to the MDI form:

```
List<EratosthenesTask> workers = new List<EratosthenesTask>();
```

The window you've seen in previous example, which included both the search parameters and the search results, now needs to be split into two separate windows. AsyncTestQuery is the window where the user will define the range for a new search. AsyncTextResult is the window that shows the result of a search.

When the user launches a new search, you need to show a search window. Once the user clicks OK, you can continue by creating the wrapper, adding it to the collection, and getting it started with the EratosthenesTask.Start() method.

```
private void cmdNewSearch_Click(object sender, EventArgs e)
{
    // Create the window with the controls for choosing the search range.
    AsyncTestQuery search = new AsyncTestQuery();

    // Show the window and wait for OK or Cancel.
    if (search.ShowDialog() == DialogResult.OK)
    {
        // Create the wrapper.
        EratosthenesTask worker = new EratosthenesTask(search.From, search.To);
        worker.Completed += new FindPrimesCompletedEventHandler(WorkerCompleted);
```

```
        // Register the wrapper.
        lock (workers)
        {
            workers.Add(worker);
            statusPanel.Text =
                String.Format("Currently running {0} tasks.", workers.Count);
        }

        // Start the asynchronous task.
        worker.Start(search.From, search.To);
    }
    search.Dispose();
}
```

Notice that when you access the collection, you need to use locking to make sure it's not accessed by another thread at the same time.

When the task is completed, it triggers the WorkerCompleted() event handler. This callback removes the wrapper from the collection, and then calls the private ShowResults() method on the user interface thread.

```
private void WorkerCompleted(object sender, FindPrimesCompletedEventArgs e)
{
    // Stop tracking the worker.
    lock (workers)
    {
        workers.Remove((EratosthenesTask)sender);
    }

    // Show the results (on the user interface thread).
    this.Invoke(new FindPrimesCompletedEventHandler(ShowResults),
      new object[] {sender, e} );
}
```

The ShowResults() method handles the job of showing the results. It creates a new window as an MDI child, and displays the prime list in it. It also updates the status bar to reflect the fact that the number of ongoing tasks has been reduced by one.

```
private void ShowResults(object sender, FindPrimesCompletedEventArgs e)
{
    // Create the window with the controls for showing the search result.
    AsyncTestResult result = new AsyncTestResult();
    result.Text = String.Format("Primes From {0} To {1}",  e.From, e.To );

    // Pass the data to the result window, and show it as an MDI child.
    result.ShowList(e.primeList);
    result.MdiParent = this;
    result.Show();
```

```
    // Update the status information.
    lock (workers)
    {
        statusPanel.Text = String.Format("Currently running {0} tasks.",
          workers.Count);
    }
}
```

Improving the Thread Wrapper

This example sketched out the bare skeleton you need to create a respectable solution. You can add a lot more functionality to the thread wrapper implementation. For example, the base ThreadWrapper class could be enhanced to support task stopping, either politely (through a cancel request message that you must heed in the DoTask() method), or impolitely (by aborting the thread).

Here's the rough outline for a stop feature. Simply add this code to the ThreadWrapper base class and customize the protected variables in the EratosthenesTask class as required.

```
// Flag that indicates a stop is requested.
private bool requestCancel = false;
protected bool RequestCancel
{
    get { return requestCancel; }
}


// How long the thread will wait (in total) before aborting a thread
// that hasn't responded to the cancellation message.
// TimeSpan.Zero means polite stops are not enabled.
private TimeSpan cancelWaitTime = TimeSpan.Zero;
protected TimeSpan CancelWaitTime
{
    get { return cancelWaitTime; }
    set { cancelWaitTime = value; }
}


// How often the thread checks to see if a cancellation
// message has been heeded.
private int cancelCheckInterval = 5;
protected int CancelCheckInterval
{
    get { return cancelCheckInterval; }
    set { cancelCheckInterval = value; }
}
```

```
public void StopTask()
{
    // Perform no operation if task isn't running.
    if (status != StatusState.InProgress) return;

    // Try the polite approach.
    if (cancelWaitTime != TimeSpan.Zero)
    {
        DateTime startTime = DateTime.Now;
        while (DateTime.Now.Subtract(startTime).TotalSeconds > cancelWaitTime)
        {
            // Still waiting for the time limit to pass.
            // Allow other threads to do some work.
            Thread.Sleep(TimeSpan.FromSeconds(cancelCheckInterval));
        }
    }

    // Use the forced approach.
    thread.Abort();
}
```

You could use a similar approach to implement the Pause() and Resume() methods.

The next refinement is progress tracking. If your derived class supports progress reporting, it should set the SupportsProgress property to true. It can then supply the percentage complete through the protected progress variable.

```
private bool supportsProgress = false;
protected bool SupportsProgress
{
    get { return supportsProgress; }
    set { supportsProgress = value; }
}

protected int progress;
public int Progress
{
    get
    {
        if (!supportsProgress)
          throw new InvalidOperationException(
            "This worker does not report progess.");
        else
          return progress;
    }
}
```

You'll see progress reporting in the next example.

Task Queuing

There's still a lot more you can do with this example. One improvement would be to implement some form of task queuing. This approach prevents the possibility that the user might start a huge number of threads running simultaneously, ensuring that none can get enough system resources to finish their work (a problem known as *thread starvation*). Instead, you allow only a set number of threads to work at once. Once you reach the limit, you add any additional requests to a queue and execute them only when a thread becomes available.

To manage this work, you need to replace the simple collection of worker threads (from the previous example) with a dedicated class that wraps the queuing and thread management work. This model requires too much code to show it all here, but you can see the complete code in the downloadable examples for this chapter.

■**Note** You can also use the ThreadPool class from the System.Threading namespace for a simple implementation of thread queuing that uses threads from the CLR's pool. However, the ThreadPool doesn't give you much flexibility—for example, you can't stop tasks, report progress, control how many tasks execute at once, and change priorities. However, the ThreadPool implementation is still better than the example you'll consider in this section in one respect. Because it reuses threads for more than one task, you avoid the overhead of creating new threads.

The basic idea is that your form uses a new TaskManager class. The TaskManager class derives from Component, so it can be added to a form at design time. This makes it easy to hook up event handlers.

```
public class TaskManager : System.ComponentModel.Component
{ ... }
```

The TaskManager allows you to choose how many tasks can be performed at a time through a MaxThreads property:

```
private int maxThreads = 2;
public int MaxThreads
{
    get { return maxThreads; }
    set { maxThreads = value; }
}
```

The TaskManager class wraps three ThreadWrapper collections. These collections reflect tasks that are queued, currently underway, and completed:

```
// Track ongoing workers.
List<ThreadWrapper> workers = new List<ThreadWrapper>();

// Track queued requests.
List<ThreadWrapper> workersQueued = new List<ThreadWrapper>();

// Task completed requests.
List<ThreadWrapper> workersCompleted = new List<ThreadWrapper>();
```

To add a new task to the queue, the client simply calls EnqueueTask(). This method doesn't start the work—instead, it adds it to the collection of queued requests.

```
public void EnqueueTask(ThreadWrapper task)
{
    lock (workersQueued)
    {
        workersQueued.Add(task);
    }
}
```

The magic happens in the AllocateWork() method, which runs continuously on a low-priority thread. The TaskManager doesn't actually create this thread and start allocating work until the client calls StartAllocatingWork().

```
private Thread allocateWork;
private bool working = false;
private Control invokeContext;

public void StartAllocatingWork(Control invokeContext)
{
    if (!working)
    {
        this.invokeContext = invokeContext;
        allocateWork = new Thread(new ThreadStart(AllocateWork));
        allocateWork.Priority = ThreadPriority.BelowNormal;
        allocateWork.IsBackground = true;
        working = true;
        allocateWork.Start();
    }
}
```

There's another important detail here. When the client calls AllocateWork(), it passes in a reference to the current form. The TaskManager uses this to call Control.Invoke() before raising any events. That way, the events are always raised on the user interface thread, and the client application is completely insulated from the threading complexities.

The AllocateWork() method has the bulk of the work. It walks through the three collections of ThreadWrapper objects. It performs its work in a continuous loop, sleeping for a few seconds after each pass to allow other threads to do some work.

```
private void AllocateWork()
{
    while (true)
    {
        // (Allocate work, check for completed items, and report progress here.)
        Thread.Sleep(TimeSpan.FromSeconds(5));
    }
}
```

The AllocateWork() method performs three tasks in its loop. First it removes completed tasks and fires the appropriate completion events.

```
for (int i = workers.Count-1; i >= 0; i--)
{
    if (workers[i].Status == StatusState.Completed)
    {
        ThreadWrapper worker = workers[i];
        lock (workersCompleted)
        {
            workersCompleted.Add(worker);
        }
        workers.Remove(worker);

        // Fire notification event on the user interface thread.
        invokeContext.Invoke(new WorkerCompletedEventHandler(OnWorkerCompleted),
         new object[] {this,
            new WorkerCompletedEventArgs((EratosthenesTask)worker)});
    }
}
```

This code loops through the collection in reverse order, so that a single pass can remove entries without rearranging the items that haven't been scanned yet. You'll notice that the collection isn't locked while it's being scanned. That's because the AllocateWork() method is the only piece of code that touches this object. On the other hand, the workersCompleted collection does need locking, because you may want to provide another method that extracts this information later on.

If you haven't reached the maximum number of in-progress tasks, the next step is to move tasks from the queue to the current collection, and start them:

```
// Allocate new work while threads are available.
while (workersQueued.Count > 0 && workers.Count < maxThreads)
{
    ThreadWrapper task = null;
    lock (workersQueued)
    {
        task = workersQueued[0];
        workersQueued.RemoveAt(0);
    }
    workers.Add(task);
    task.Start();
}
```

Once again, you don't need to lock the workers collection, but you do need to lock the workersQueued collection, because the application could be in the process of queuing up a new task.

Finally, progress notifications are fired for all the tasks that are in progress.

```
// Report progress.
for (int i = workers.Count - 1; i >= 0; i--)
{
    ThreadWrapper worker = workers[i];
    // Fire notification event.
    invokeContext.Invoke(
     new ReportWorkerProgressEventHandler(OnReportWorkerProgress),
     new object[]{this,
        new ReportWorkerProgressEventArgs(worker.ID, worker.Progress)});
}
```

There are different ways to accomplish this step, each with its own compromises. In the design used here, a separate event is fired for each in-progress task. This allows you to keep the threading code and the user interface code well separated, but it may not perform well for applications that queue up a long list of tasks, because the client will be forced to search for the matching task request each time the event fires. In this case, you might consider a compromise such as passing all the status information at once, or even giving your task objects a reference to a control the TaskManager can update directly. This approach is messier, but it may allow you to keep the application more responsive.

The end result is that once you have the TaskManager code in place, you can create an application that allows you to start and monitor multiple tasks, as shown in Figure 20-10. When a task is completed, simply double-click the item to see the prime list.

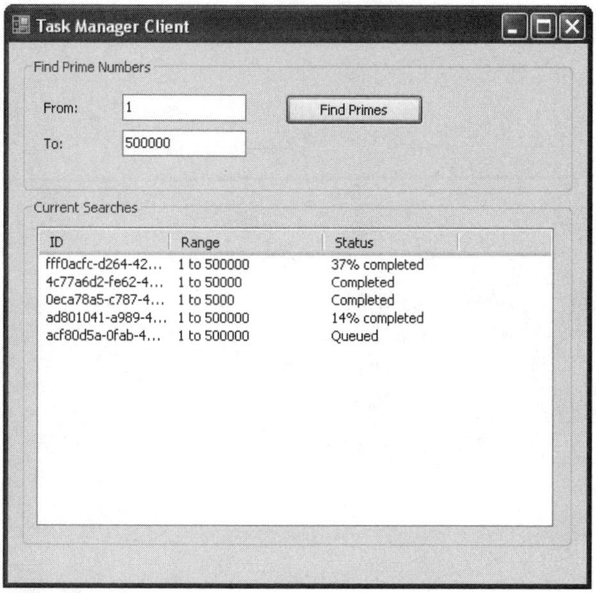

Figure 20-10. *Testing the Task Manager*

The Last Word

In this chapter, you've seen a variety of techniques for multithreading, ranging from the relative simplicity of asynchronous delegates and the BackgroundWorker to much more advanced designs with thread wrappers and task managers.

Think twice before letting loose with multithreading, as it increases the complexity associated with every aspect of your application, from design to debugging. If you need multithreading to ensure a responsive application (and Windows applications often do), use it judiciously—in other words, run only the most time-consuming, long-running operations in the background, and make the rest of your application synchronous. Multithreading definitely isn't for the faint of heart, and creating a real-world task manager (such as the one demonstrated in this example) requires a thorough understanding of the subtleties involved.

■ ■ ■

CHAPTER 21

Dynamic Interfaces and Layout Engines

One of the most common questions in any Windows programming language is how to add a control to a window dynamically—in other words, while the program is executing. For example, you might want to create a program that generates tailored forms based on the information in an XML file. This sort of task is surprisingly easy in .NET, because there isn't a sharp distinction between control creation at runtime and control creation at design time. In fact, in .NET programming, *every* control is created through code. As you learned in Chapter 1, when you add a control to a form and configure its properties, Visual Studio generates the appropriate code statements and adds them to a designer file. By studying this automatically generated code, you can quickly learn how to create and add any control you need at runtime.

Of course, creating a dynamic user interface is about much more than instantiating a control object at runtime. It's also a philosophy that breaks free of the shackles of visual design tools and allows you to generate user interfaces based on database records, user preferences, or localization needs.

In this chapter, you'll start with dynamic menus and a button generator, and then dive into more advanced examples. For example, you'll see an application that builds made-to-measure windows based on survey definitions in a file, and another that creates a flexible portal-style interface out of multiple modules. Along the way, you'll learn about the new .NET 2.0 layout panels, which provide a flexible framework that can help you manage how dynamically inserted content is organized in a window.

The Case for Dynamic User Interface

Before you start writing any code, you need to decide how dynamic your user interface should be. This chapter offers examples that do little more than add a few simple elements to a form, and others that build the Window dynamically from scratch. So which approach is best?

As usual, it all depends on your project and design goals. To determine where dynamic user interface fits in, you need to consider the role of the user interface designer. Some of the reasons that programmers rely on Visual Studio to create their interface include:

- **It hides the messy code details.** User-interface code is difficult to manage due to the sheer amount you need to implement even basic designs. Because Windows Forms controls don't provide constructors that allow important properties to be set, it takes several lines that set multiple properties to fully configure an average control.

- **It saves time.** The design-time environment makes it faster to create and maintain an interface. You can apply changes directly, with little chance of error.

- **It supports localization.** As described in Chapter 5, it's easy to localize the properties of the controls on your form at design time. Just set Form.Localizable to true, set the Language property, and enter your values.

Overall, it's far easier to create a user interface with precision and cosmetic appeal using the IDE. On the other hand, there are some things that user interfaces designed in the IDE don't handle well:

- **Adaptable user interfaces.** In some cases, you want the user interface to change according to distinct rules. For example, you might need to adjust the UI to suit different user skill levels, different permissions, or different languages. In these situations, you can stick with a static user interface and write a great deal of "control tweaking" code, or consider a more radical solution that builds the whole interface dynamically. The latter approach takes longer to code initially, but it may end up being more manageable in the long run.

- **Customizable user interfaces.** Many applications give the user the ability to customize some aspects of the UI. In some cases, your product might be so customizable that you need to include a separate administrative module that allows nonprogrammers to define or modify certain aspects of the interface. Once again, if the changes are relatively minor you can tweak the existing UI, but if they're more substantial (for example, if the user chooses different modules to show on a main window) a dynamic interface will be much easier.

- **Wizards.** If this type of UI, you need to show different content in a region of the form (usually a panel) as the user moves from one step (or "page") to the next. Chapter 10 presented a solution to this problem that makes use of user controls.

- **Drawing and diagramming tools.** Most drawing tools don't just paint static content. Instead, they let users create independent objects (ranging from lines of texts to geometric shapes). If you're creating an application like this, you'll want to consider custom drawing or owner-drawn controls (as demonstrated in Chapter 24).

Code that dynamically creates a user interface is almost always more work to create and more difficult to maintain. But as you'll see in this chapter, a dynamic interface also can result in an application that's much more flexible and much more adaptable to different needs and changing content.

Dynamic Content

When discussing dynamic interfaces, it's often useful to draw a distinction between those that simply tailor the content of existing controls and those that actually create and add new controls. The first case—dynamic content—is obviously simpler and can appear in just about any situation. Some examples include applications that need to be localized or configured for different sets of users, or applications that are heavily data-driven (like a program for browsing an online product catalog).

One of the simplest examples of dynamic content is the average About box (shown in Figure 21-1). It rarely makes sense to hard-code information like a program's version directly into the user interface of a window, because it cannot be guaranteed to remain correct (and it can be extremely tedious to synchronize if you use auto-incrementing version numbers). Instead, this information should be retrieved dynamically:

```
lblProductName.Text = Application.ProductName;
lblProductVersion.Text = "Version: " + Application.ProductVersion.ToString();
lblPath.Text = "Executing in: " + Application.ExecutablePath;
```

Figure 21-1. *Dynamic content in the About box*

Usually, you'll decide between dynamic content and dynamic control creation based on the type of information you need to display and how much it varies.

An Adaptable Menu Example

A more interesting example of dynamic content is an adaptable menu. Some Windows programming frameworks (like MFC) include the concept of changing a menu as different controls get focus. Although .NET doesn't include this functionality, you can build it yourself.

Before you begin, you need to consider how your menu will vary. Key considerations include whether you need to change one submenu or several; whether you need to change toolbars as well as menus; and whether you want to replace the menu with a completely different one, or simply add or hide individual items.

Once you've identified your design, you need to decide how to implement it. You'll need to react to the focus events Enter and Leave to change the menu as the user moves from one control to another. To actually change the menu, you can use one of three common techniques:

- **Programmatic menu merging.** In this case, you use the ToolStripManager.Merge() method to trigger automatic menu merging. Menu merging is described in Chapter 19.

- **Replacing submenus with context menus.** In this case, you create multiple context menus, and simply assign them to parts of the main menu.

- **Hiding and showing individual items.** In this case, you simply tweak the Enabled or Visible property of the appropriate ToolStripMenuItem object.

The following example uses the second (context menu) approach. The next section shows a more ambitious example that uses the third approach.

When designing an adaptable menu, you don't necessarily need to tailor the menu for individual controls. It many cases, you'll only want to have a small set of menus, and use each one for a group of controls. The easiest way to implement this design is to arrange your controls into some sort of container, like a panel.

Consider the form shown in Figure 21-2. The second top-level menu varies depending on whether the focus is somewhere in the first panel or somewhere in the second.

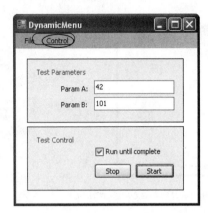

Figure 21-2. *A menu that changes according to control focus*

Implementing this example is easy. The trick is that you can replace a top-level menu item with a context menu using code like this:

```
mnuTopLevel.DropDown = mnuContext.DropDown;
```

Assuming mnuTopLevel is a top-level menu (like File) in a MenuStrip, and mnuContext is a ContextMenuStrip, this single line populates the top-level menu with all the items in the context menu.

The problem with this approach is that it doesn't change the top-level menu text. This example works around this limitation by binding to the first item in the context menu, rather than the entire context menu. In other words, it uses code like this:

```
// Get the first item in the menu.
ToolStripMenuItem item = (ToolStripMenuItem)mnuContext.Items[0];

// Copy the subitems from this item into the top-level menu.
mnuTopLevel.DropDown = item.DropDown;

// Copy the text from this item into the top-level menu.
mnuReplaceable.Text = item.Text;
```

This design assumes the menu you're moving into the top level is a submenu of the first item in the context menu. This allows you to define the menu items and the menu text.

Using this approach makes it easy to create the context menus and attach event handlers at design time. It's also easy to associate each menu with its corresponding panel through the Control.ContextMenuStrip property. In fact, you can use as many menus and panels as you want without complicating the design. Every panel can use the same code in the same event handler to perform the swap:

```
private void panel_Enter(object sender, EventArgs e)
{
    Panel panel = (Panel)sender;
    mnuTopLevel.DropDown = panel.ContextMenuStrip;
    ToolStripMenuItem item = (ToolStripMenuItem)panel.ContextMenuStrip.Items[0];
    mnuTopLevel.DropDown = item.DropDown;
    mnuTopLevel.Text = item.Text;
}
```

If you decide to use an alternate approach (for example, menu merging with the ToolStripManager), you'll need to devise a way to associate a ToolStrip with a control, or you'll be forced to hard-code these relations in your form, which makes your code longer and much more difficult to maintain. This challenge is a prime candidate for a custom property extender (as described in Chapter 25). With a custom property extender, you could add properties like AssociatedToolStrip and MergeToolStripOnFocus to *every* panel control. Once you set these properties, the property extender takes care of listening for the focus change events, getting the related ToolStrip, and performing the merge operation. To learn more about how to implement a property extender, see Chapter 25.

A Database-Driven Adaptable Menu

It's all well and good to assemble a menu out of bits and pieces in response to specific events, but it's even more interesting if the information is drawn from an external source. The following example uses a database table that maps user levels to control access permissions. Depending on the user type, some options may be disabled or hidden entirely.

The database uses three tables (see Figure 21-3). Controls lists the names of available controls in the user interface, Levels lists the supported user levels, and Controls_Levels specifies what controls are allowed for a given user level (using a special State field that indicates 0 for normal, 1 for hidden, and 2 for disabled). All controls are enabled by default, so the only records that need to be added to Controls_Levels are those that specifically hide or disable controls. In a full-blown application, there would probably also be a Users table that indicates what level each user has.

Figure 21-3. *Tables mapping control access permissions*

In this example, the database is configured with the information for two user levels: User and Admin. The different menu structures these users will see are shown in Figure 21-4.

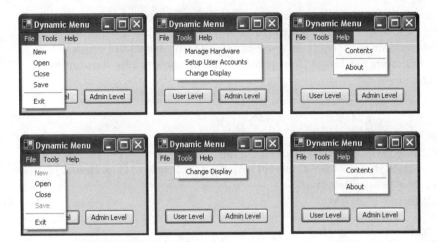

Figure 21-4. *Different menu structures*

By pulling all the user permission logic out of the user interface and placing it in the database, it becomes very easy to write a small amount of generic code that automatically configures the user interface for the user who is currently logged on:

```
// Get permissions for an Admin-level user.
DataTable dtPermissions =
  DBPermissions.GetPermissions(DBPermissions.Level.Admin);

// Update the menu with these permissions.
MenuLockDown.SearchMenu(MainMenuStrip.Items, dtPermissions);
```

The DBPermissions class uses a static GetPermissions() function that returns a table with all the security information for the specified user level. To remove the chance of error, it also uses an enumeration that defines the different levels of user access in the database.

```
public class DBPermissions
{
    public enum State
    {
        Normal = 0,
        Disabled = 1,
        Hidden = 2
    }

    public enum Level
    {
        Admin,
        User
    }
```

```
    private static SqlConnection con = new SqlConnection(
        Properties.Settings.Default.DBConnectionString);

    public static DataTable GetPermissions(Level userLevel)
    {
        // Permissions isn't actually a table in the data source.
        // Instead, it's a view that combines the important information
        // from all three tables using a Join query.
        string selectPermissions =
            "SELECT * FROM Permissions WHERE LevelName=@LevelName";
        SqlCommand cmd = new SqlCommand(selectPermissions, con);
        SqlParameter param = new SqlParameter("@LevelName",
            Enum.GetName(typeof(Level), userLevel));
        cmd.Parameters.Add(param);

        SqlDataAdapter adapter = new SqlDataAdapter(cmd);
        DataSet ds = new DataSet();
        adapter.Fill(ds, "Permissions");

        return ds.Tables["Permissions"];
    }
}
```

Finally, the SearchMenu() function recursively tunnels through the menu, hiding or disabling controls as indicated in the permissions table.

```
public class MenuLockDown
{
    public static void SearchMenu(ToolStripItemCollection items,
     DataTable dtPermissions)
    {
        DataRow[] rowMatch;

        foreach (ToolStripItem item in items)
        {
            // Skip separators and other controls
            ToolStripMenuItem mnuItem = item as ToolStripMenuItem;
            if (mnuItem != null)
            {
                // See if this menu item has a corresponding row.
                rowMatch = dtPermissions.Select("ControlName = '" +
                    mnuItem.Name + "'");

                // If it does, configure the menu item state accordingly.
                if (rowMatch.GetLength(0) > 0)
                {
                    DBPermissions.State state;
                    state = (DBPermissions.State)int.Parse(
                        rowMatch[0]["State"].ToString());
```

```
                switch (state)
                {
                    case DBPermissions.State.Hidden:
                        mnuItem.Visible = false;
                        break;
                    case DBPermissions.State.Disabled:
                        mnuItem.Enabled = false;
                        break;
                }
            }
            else
            {
                mnuItem.Visible = true;
                mnuItem.Enabled = true;
            }

            // Search recursively through any submenus.
            if (mnuItem.DropDownItems.Count > 0)
            {
                SearchMenu(mnuItem.DropDownItems, dtPermissions);
            }
        }
    }
}
```

Best of all, if the permissions need to change or another access level needs to be added, only the database needs to be modified. An application created in this way is easy to maintain without painful recompiles and redeployment.

Our example dynamically configures menus, but there are other approaches. For example, you could disable controls in a form (at which point you would probably want to add a FormName field to the Controls table). Chapter 22 demonstrates a similar technique with dynamic help content. You also could use a similar model to create localizable content for your menus. Instead of mapping controls to user levels with a State field, you would use a Text field that would be applied to the control's Text property.

Note You can even extend this system to make a radically configurable interface supporting user-selected themes, but beware of going too far. The more variation your application supports, the more difficult it is to create support material and solve problems in the field. This is the classic flexibility-versus-ease-of-use dilemma.

Creating Controls at Runtime

Creating a control at runtime involves a few simple steps:

1. Create the control object as you would any other class.

2. Set the properties for the control (including basics like size and position).

3. Add the control object to the Controls collection of a container control, like a Form, GroupBox, Panel, or TabPage.

4. If you want to handle any of the control's events, use the appropriate delegate code to hook up your event handler.

To demonstrate this process, consider the sample button generator program shown in Figure 21-5. This program creates a button at the specified position every time the user clicks the Create button. An event handler is attached to the Click event for each new button, ensuring that .NET can capture user clicks (and display a brief user message at the bottom of the window).

```
public partial class ButtonMaker : Form
{
    private int buttonCount = 0;

    private void cmdCreate_Click(object sender, System.EventArgs e)
    {
        buttonCount++;

        // Create the button.
        Button newButton = new Button();
        newButton.Text = "Button " + buttonCount.ToString();

        // You could set the Left and Top properties separately,
        // but setting both at once (through the Location property)
        // is more efficient.
        newButton.Location = new Point(
          Int32.Parse(txtLeft.Text). Int32.Parse(txtTop.Text));

        // Attach the event handler.
        newButton.Click += new EventHandler(ButtonHandler);

        Controls.Add(newButton);
    }

    private void ButtonHandler(object sender, System.EventArgs e)
    {
        lblStatus.Text = " You clicked ... ";
        lblStatus.Text += ((Button)sender).Text;
    }
}
```

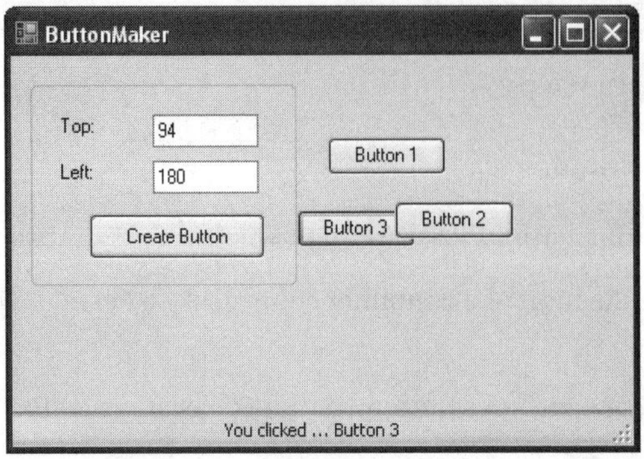

Figure 21-5. *A dynamic button generator*

One of the key challenges with this approach is that you need to place each control exactly. If you have a modestly detailed user interface, you'll need some extremely messy calculations to determine the correct coordinates and size for each element. One way to deal with these problems is to use a control layout engine, as described in the next section.

■**Tip** The button generator is a proof-of-concept example. On its own, it doesn't do anything useful. In the following sections, you'll see how you can adapt the same technique to create a much more practical application.

Managing Control Layout

If you're creating highly dynamic forms, you need a way to create the controls and a technique to ensure they all end in the right place. You could calculate control sizes and positions by hand, but it can quickly lead to complex and convoluted code. Another solution is to use one of .NET's layout panels. These container controls, which are new in .NET 2.0, automatically organize all the contained child controls based on specific rules.

The control layout panels extend the possibilities for form layout, but they also complicate your application. As a general rule of thumb, you shouldn't use a control layout engine if you can get all the functionality you need using docking, anchoring, the Control.AutoSize property, and container controls like the Panel and SplitContainer (which are described in Chapter 3). These controls allow you to create a wide range of control layouts, and are easy to work with at design time. However, if you need to programmatically create a highly configurable interface or you need one of the specific resizing behaviors discussed in the following sections, you can consider using a specialized layout control instead.

■**Note** If you've programmed with Java before, the idea of layout managers is nothing new. Some of the layout managers provided for Java containers include FlowLayout (similar to a word processor), BorderLayout (which divides the screen into five zones), CardLayout (like a stack of cards layered on top of each other), GridLayout (which allows one component per equal-sized cell), and GridBagLayout (which adds support for variable control sizes and location with a grid). Although the layout ability in .NET resembles the Java approach in several ways, it also provides much more impressive design-time support.

The Layout Event

As you've seen, the .NET forms architecture provides support for laying out controls using coordinates in a grid. This approach, combined with the built-in support for docking and anchoring, gives developers a rich layout environment.

However, there are times when the use of the Dock and Anchor properties alone is not necessarily the best approach. For example, you may need a container control that automatically lays out child controls according to different rules, perhaps adjusting them to accommodate the width of the largest control or shrinking them to fit the size of the container, to name just two possibilities.

The basic starting point in extending control layout is the Control.Layout event (or, equivalently, the Control.OnLayout() method). This event occurs in container controls and forms when they need to update the position or size of their child controls. Several factors can trigger the Layout event, including when child controls are added or removed, when a child control is resized or moved, and when the bounds of the container are changed.

■**Note** You can temporarily suspend the Layout event using the SuspendLayout() and ResumeLayout() methods, which are handy to optimize performance if you need to perform several operations. Each will trigger a layout operation, such as moving and resizing a control. However, the SuspendLayout() and ResumeLayout() methods are only one level deep. In other words, if you have a TopPanel that contains an InnerPanel control and you call TopPanel.SuspendLayout(), layout events will still take place for the InnerPanel.

To extend Windows Forms layout, you can create a *layout manager*—a specialized class that connects itself to the action by listening for layout events from the container control. When a layout event fires, the layout manager can iterate through all the items in the Controls collection of the container and arrange them accordingly. Depending on the layout manager, this may mean ignoring the Location property and even the Size property of each control. It also could involve inspecting other extended properties.

A Simple Hand-Made Layout Manager

The following SingleLineFlowLayoutManager is an example of a simple layout manager
that tracks one associated control. When the Layout event of that control fires, the
SingleLineFlowLayoutManager lays out the controls it contains, placing one control per
line from top to bottom. It also gives each control the width of the container. The
SingleLineFlowLayoutManager also includes a single property—Margin—that lets you
set the spacing between lines.

```
public class SingleLineFlowLayoutManager
{
    private Control container;

    // Instead of using a simple integer, you could use a full Padding structure.
    private int margin;
    public int Margin
    {
        get { return margin; }
        set
        {
            margin = value;
            container.PerformLayout();
        }
    }

    public SingleLineFlowLayoutManager(Control container, int margin)
    {
        this.container = container;
        this.margin = margin;

        // Attach the event handler.
        container.Layout += new LayoutEventHandler(UpdateLayout);

        // Refresh the layout.
        container.PerformLayout();
    }

    private void UpdateLayout(object sender,
     System.Windows.Forms.LayoutEventArgs e)
    {
        int y = 0;
        foreach (Control ctrl in container.Controls)
        {
            y += Margin;
```

```
            // For maximum efficiency, set the
            // size and location in one step through
            // the Bounds property.
            ctrl.Bounds = new Rectangle(Margin, y,
                container.Width - Margin*2, Margin);
        }
    }
}
```

The bulk of the work is performed in the UpdateLayout() method, which adjusts the position of the controls in the container. The client doesn't need to call this method manually. Instead, once the layout manager is connected to the correct container, it fires automatically as controls are added or removed. The UpdateLayout() method arranges controls with a fixed height and uses the width of the container. Many more alternatives are possible—for example, you could record the width of the largest child control and resize all the other controls and the container itself to match.

To trigger the layout when the layout manager is first created, the code uses the PerformLayout() method. PerformLayout() plays the same role with layout as Invalidate() does with custom drawing. When you call it, you notify the control that its layout is no longer valid, and it must fire its Layout. It's more efficient to call PerformLayout() than to launch directly into your layout code (mainly because it helps multiple layouts in a row when they aren't needed).

The following form code shows how easy it is to use the layout manager. It adds several check box controls to a TabPage container when a form is loaded. Because a layout provider is being used, the client doesn't need to worry about details like the position or size of the child controls—they are organized automatically.

```
private void Form_Load(object sender, System.EventArgs e)
{
    // Create and attach the layout manager.
    SingleLineFlowLayoutManager layoutManager =
        new SingleLineFlowLayoutManager(tabPage1, 20);

    // Add 10 sample check boxes.
    CheckBox chkbox;

    for (int i = 1; i < 11; i++)
    {
        chkbox = new CheckBox();
        chkbox.Name = "checkBox" + i.ToString();
        chkbox.Text = "Setting " + i.ToString();
        tabPage1.Controls.Add(chkbox);
    }
}
```

Without the layout manager, all the check boxes would just be layered on top of each other with the default size and the coordinates (0, 0). Figure 21-6 shows the result with the SingleLineFlow layout manager.

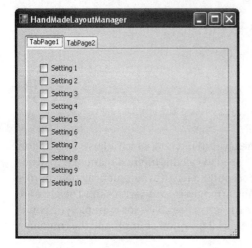

Figure 21-6. *The SingleLineFlowLayoutManager in action*

To take a look at what's really going on behind the scenes, you can add some quick-and-dirty debugging code to the SingleLineFlowLayoutManager.UpdateLayout() method:

```
private void UpdateLayout(object sender,
  System.Windows.Forms.LayoutEventArgs e)
{
    string debugMessage = "Called: " +
      "\n Affected Control: " + e.AffectedControl.Name +
      "\n Affected Property: " + e.AffectedProperty;
    Debug.WriteLine(debugMessage);
    ...
}
```

You'll find that when the form first loads, the UpdateLayout() method runs (in response to the Layout event) 12 times. The first time occurs when the SingleLineFlowLayoutManager is created and calls PerformLayout(). It displays this debug message:

```
Called:
 Affected Control: tabPage1
 Affected Property: Bounds
```

The next 10 times occur after each check box is added. The AffectedControl property indicates the control that's been added, and the AffectedProperty property explains the reason for the layout (the control has a new parent—the tab page).

```
Called:
 Affected Control: checkBox1
 Affected Property: Parent
Called:
 Affected Control: checkBox2
 Affected Property: Parent
...
```

Finally, the layout code fires again when the form becomes visible:

```
Called:
Affected Control: tabPage1
Affected Property: Visible
```

If you switch to the second tab and back again, the layout code runs once more with the same message, which indicates that the tab page has become visible again.

To optimize your layout code, you may choose to ignore some layout operations or perform less work depending on the type of action that triggered the layout. However, it's usually difficult and unreliable to code this logic, particularly because LayoutEventArgs.AffectedProperty returns a simple string and isn't guaranteed. In fact, the AffectedControl and AffectedProperty are set by the caller when calling PerformLayout():

```
control.PerformLayout(control, "Parent")
```

If you don't supply these parameters, the control defaults to the control on which you're calling PerformLayout(), and the AffectedProperty string defaults to Bounds.

A safer optimization is to use the SuspendLayout() and ResumeLayout() methods. By placing these calls before and after you add the check boxes, you can reduce the number of layout events from 12 to 3.

```
// Create and attach the layout manager.
SingleLineFlowLayoutManager layoutManager =
  new SingleLineFlowLayoutManager(tabPage1, 20);

tabPage1.SuspendLayout();
// (Add 10 sample checkboxes.)
tabPage1.ResumeLayout();
```

■ **Note** Remember, it won't help to call SuspendLayout() on the entire tab control because that will only suppress layout events for controls that are directly contained by the TabControl (namely, TabPage controls). It won't affect the controls inside each TabPage.

Problems with the Simple Layout Manager

The SimpleFlowLayoutManager is a good example of custom layout logic, but it has a few glaring issues:

- The layout manager doesn't give a good design-time representation of what the form will look like. That's because the layout logic isn't performed until the layout manager class is created at runtime. As a result, the child controls won't be organized in the IDE view at design time. Instead, they will be reorganized when the program is launched and your code attaches the layout manager.

- The code is still quite simple. You could extend this example layout manager so that it lays out controls in multiple columns or a fixed-size table. However, it will take more time and code.

- The layout manager treats all controls equally. In some cases, you'll want a more customizable layout that takes individual control settings into account. For example, the default layout provided by Windows Forms gives every control a Size and a Location property that is used to determine where the control is placed in the container. You might want to add other layout properties (for example, a Justification, Column, or LayoutListPriority property) to standard controls, which your layout manager could then take into account. To achieve this, you would need to design your layout manager as a custom extender provider (see Chapter 27).

In .NET 1.x, there was no alternative to creating custom layout classes by hand. However, .NET 2.0 adds a new layout engine system that solves these problems.

Layout Engines

.NET 2.0 extends the layout system with *layout engines*. Layout engines play the same role as the custom layout manager shown in the previous example, with a few minor differences:

- All layout engines inherit from the abstract base class LayoutEngine in the System. Windows.Forms.Layout namespace. (You won't actually see the basic set of layout engine classes in this namespace, because they are hidden, internal classes.) When inheriting from LayoutEngine, the class must override two methods: InitLayout() and Layout().

- Layout engines don't link themselves to controls. Instead, wherever possible controls bind themselves to layout engines. This allows a single layout manager to be reused for multiple controls, saving memory. To accommodate this design, each control has a LayoutEngine property, which provides a reference to the layout engine that should be used for organizing child controls.

■**Note** In some cases, controls and layout engines do have a one-to-one relationship. One key example is the ToolStrip, which has its own layout manager that implements details like the overflow menu.

By default, the Control.LayoutEngine is set to an instance of the internal DefaultLayout class (from the System.Windows.Forms.Layout namespace). This class implements the dock-and-anchor functionality you learned about in Chapter 3.

The Control.LayoutEngine property is protected and read-only, so you don't set it directly. Instead, to bind a control to a layout engine, you must derive a new control class. Because the chief goal of a layout engine is to organize child controls, you would only use this technique to create new types of containers. For example, you might design a new type of custom toolbar, and override its Control.LayoutEngine property so it returns a custom layout engine object that can organize the individual toolbar buttons the way you want.

Later in this chapter, you'll consider how to create and use a custom layout manager. But in most cases, you won't need to go to this work because .NET includes two all-purpose container controls that implement specialized layout: FlowLayoutPanel and TableLayoutPanel.

The FlowLayoutPanel and TableLayoutPanel controls are hard wired to use a corresponding layout engine to organize their child controls. (These are the FlowLayout and TableLayout classes, respectively. Both are in the System.Windows.Forms.Layout namespace, but they're internal, so you won't be able see them.) Additionally, both FlowLayoutPanel and TableLayoutPanel implement IExtenderProvider, which allows them to add layout-related properties to other controls. For example, if you drag a button into a TableLayoutPanel and check the Properties window, you'll find that it has several new properties, like RowSpan and ColumnSpan. Using these properties, you can give the layout engine additional information that it can use when performing the layout.

Figure 21-7 shows the interaction of the layout engines, controls, and layout panels.

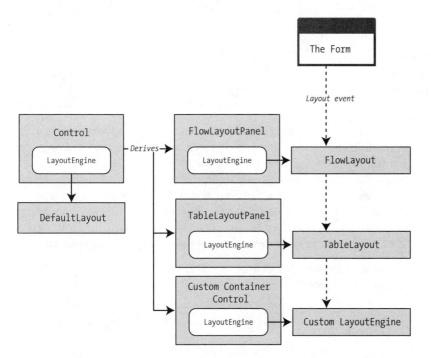

Figure 21-7. *Layout engines in .NET 2.0*

Creating a Custom Layout Engine

Before we consider the FlowLayoutPanel and TableLayoutPanel controls, it's worth taking a deeper look at how layout engines plug into controls.

It's surprisingly easy to transform the SingleLineFlowLayoutManager demonstrated in the previous example into a legitimate layout engine. The first step is to create a class that derives from the abstract LayoutEngine class (in the System.Windows.Forms.Layout namespace):

```
public class SingleLineFlowLayoutEngine : LayoutEngine
{ ... }
```

You can add a Margin property and a basic constructor to this class, just as you did with the SingleLineFlowLayoutManager. But the real work is done by overriding the Layout() method. This method is triggered automatically in response to a Layout event in the linked control (unless SuspendLayout() has been called, in which case the call is deferred until ResumeLayout() is called).

```
public override bool Layout(object container, LayoutEventArgs layoutEventArgs)
{
    Control parent = container as Control;

    int y = 0;
    foreach (Control ctrl in parent.Controls)
    {
        y += Margin;
        ctrl.Bounds = new Rectangle(Margin, y, parent.Width - Margin*2, Margin);
    }

    // Return true if the layout should be performed again
    // by the parent.
    return parent.AutoSize;
}
```

This code implements the same logic you saw earlier—each control is spaced out in a separate line. You can easily choose to take other properties (such as the parent's padding, and the margins or anchor settings of each child control) into account.

The final step is to connect this layout engine to a control. You can do this only by deriving a new control class and assigning to the LayoutEngine property. For example, you could create a derived panel control or user control that uses this technique. But the easiest test is to change the layout manager of a form. Because every form you create in Visual Studio is a custom class that derives from Form, you're able to override the LayoutEngine property, as shown here:

```
private SingleLineFlowLayoutEngine layoutEngine = null;
public override LayoutEngine LayoutEngine
{
    get
    {
        if (layoutEngine == null)
        {
            // Create a layout manager that uses a 20-pixel margin.
            layoutEngine = new SingleLineFlowLayoutEngine(20);
        }
        return layoutEngine;
    }
}
```

Now the controls in this form are automatically laid out by the SingleLineFlowLayoutEngine.

The FlowLayoutPanel

There are two panel controls for custom layout. The FlowLayoutPanel is the simpler of the two. The FlowLayoutPanel arranges controls one after the other in the available space. It's similar to the approach usually used with web pages, where each element is positioned immediately after the preceding element.

To try out a FlowLayoutPanel, drag it onto a form and start adding some controls. The FlowLayoutPanel adds two new properties to the Panel class:

- **FlowDirection.** This property determines how the controls are laid out in sequence (for example, from top to bottom). Table 21-1 lists the supported values.

- **WrapContents.** If true, this allows the layout control to wrap controls once they extend beyond the boundary specified by FlowDirection. For example, if you're laying out items from left to right and you set WrapContents to true, items will be added in a new left-to-right row underneath when the first row is full. If WrapContents is false, everything will be added into the first row, but items that extend beyond the boundaries of the panel will be clipped or hidden.

Table 21-1. *Values for the FlowDirection Enumeration*

Value	Description
BottomUp	Elements flow from the bottom of the panel to the top.
LeftToRight	Elements flow from the left edge of the panel to the right. This is the default.
RightToLeft	Elements flow from the right edge of the panel to the left.
TopDown	Elements flow from the top of the panel to the bottom.

Once you're familiar with these two properties, there's not much more you need to know about the FlowLayoutPanel. Figure 21-8 shows two examples where multiple buttons are placed in FlowLayoutPanel. In the first case, wrapping is enabled. In the second, it isn't. In both examples, a border is displayed around the FlowLayoutPanel, although this isn't required.

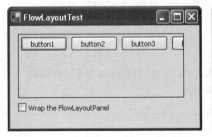 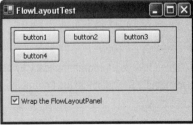

Figure 21-8. *Wrapping the contents of a FlowLayoutPanel*

When you add FlowDirection to the mix, you have a few more interesting possibilities. Figure 21-9 shows two different wrapping orders.

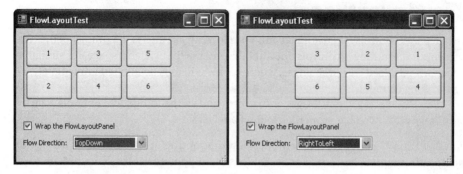

Figure 21-9. *Changing the flow direction*

The FlowLayoutPanel follows a single, simple rule—controls can never overlap. That means if you are wrapping multiple lines of controls, the second line is space according to the highest control in the first line (as shown in Figure 21-10). No attempt is made to make all the lines the same height—if you need that sort of functionality, you need the TableLayoutPanel instead.

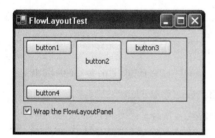

Figure 21-10. *Spacing different-sized controls*

The order of controls in the FlowLayoutPanel is determined by the z-order (first described in Chapter 2). The controls are laid out in order from lowest to highest z-index. Ordinarily, the z-index is incremented for each new control you create at design time, which means the controls you add first appear first in the FlowLayoutPanel (assuming FlowDirection is LeftToRight or TopDown). To change the order, you can drag and drop child controls inside the FlowLayoutPanel. Their z-indexes will be adjusted automatically.

■**Tip** You also can change the order programmatically by calling the ControlCollection.SetChildIndex() method, as in flowLayoutPanel1.SetChildIndex(myControl, newIndex).

The FlowBreak Extended Property

The FlowLayoutPanel implements IExtenderProvider, which allows it to extend other controls on the form. It adds a single property to all its child controls: a Boolean property named FlowBreak.

If FlowBreak is set to true and the FlowLayoutPanel.WrapContents property is also true, the next control is wrapped to the following line, even if there is sufficient space remaining. In that way, FlowBreak is a handy tool for separating groups of controls without relying on the FlowLayoutPanel borders alone. FlowBreak is false by default, and it has no effect if WrapContents is false.

Figure 21-11 shows an example.

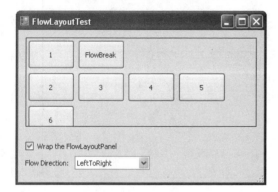

Figure 21-11. *A flow break*

Margins and Padding

As you've seen in the previous examples, the FlowLayoutPanel leaves some spacing between its child controls, and between the child controls and its borders. It does this by respecting the Margin and Padding properties.

You first learned about Margin and Padding in Chapter 3, but these properties have an increased significance with the FlowLayoutPanel and TableLayoutPanel. In the examples you've seen so far (a FlowLayoutPanel that contains numerous buttons), here's how these properties come into effect:

- The FlowLayoutPanel.Padding adds space between the panel edges and the buttons inside. You can adjust the Top, Bottom, Left, and Right properties of the padding separately.

- The Button.Margin property adds space between one button and adjacent buttons (or the edges of the panel). As with padding, the Margin property has Top, Bottom, Left, and Right properties.

The Padding and Margin settings are cumulative. For example, if button1 is on the left and button2 is adjacent on the right, the space between them is the sum of button1.Margin.Right and button2.Margin.Left. Similarly, if button1 is the first control in flowPanel, the space between the left edge is the sum of button1.Margin.Left and flowPanel.Padding.Left. Figure 21-12 illustrates how this works.

By default, controls like the button have a margin of 3, and the FlowLayoutPanel has no padding.

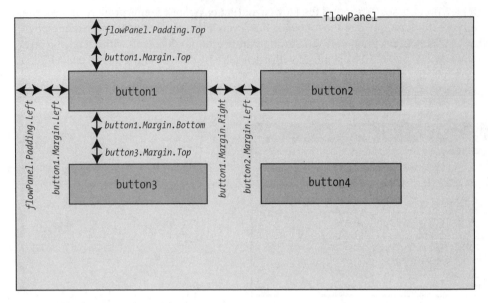

Figure 21-12. *How margins affect the FlowLayoutPanel*

Automatic Scrolling and Sizing

You've seen how the FlowLayoutPanel can use automatic wrapping to place controls on multiple lines. However, whether you've enabled WrapContents or not, once the controls reach the bounds of the panel they'll be cut off.

There are two ways around this problem, and both were introduced in Chapter 3. One option is to use automatic scrolling by setting the FlowLayoutPanel.AutoScroll property to true. This has one of two effects:

- If WrapContents is false and AutoScroll is true, a horizontal scroll bar is added that allows you to scroll from side to side.

- If WrapContents is true and AutoScroll is true, a vertical scroll bar is added that allows you to scroll down to see the remaining controls.

Either way, the AutoScroll property gives you a convenient solution to handling dynamic content that can expand greatly.

Your other option is to use the FlowLayoutPanel.AutoSize property to use automatic sizing. In this case, the FlowLayoutPanel determines the minimum size that's required to show all its child controls and expands itself accordingly, either horizontally (if WrapContents is false) or vertically (if WrapContents is true). If you use this approach, you also can use the MaximumSize property to constrain the FlowLayoutPanel's growth at some predetermined maximum size.

Automatic sizing is most often useful if you want to arrange more than one FlowLayoutPanel inside another layout container. For example, imagine you have a form that contains a Flow-LayoutPanel. This FlowLayoutPanel contains other FlowLayoutPanel controls (each of which might represent a different module in a portal-style application). These child panels are hidden, shown, and resized depending on various user options. In this situation, you might decide to use automatic scrolling with the parent FlowLayoutPanel and use automatic sizing with the child panels.

■**Tip** Sometimes it gets a little tricky to lay out detailed interfaces with the layout controls. The problem is that you'll often end up with many nested layers. For example, you might have a FlowLayoutPanel that contains other panels, which in turn contain still more panels, which then contain ordinary .NET controls. To get an overview of these levels of hierarchy, you can use the Document Outline window. Just choose View ➤ Other Windows ➤ Document Outline. The Document Outline window also allows you to rearrange the order of controls in their container. This is important because order determines layout in controls like the FlowLayoutPanel and TableLayoutPanel, unlike other .NET containers

---

The TableLayoutPanel

The TableLayoutPanel is a more advanced layout control. It arranges controls in a grid with a fixed number of rows and columns. Each control occupies a single cell. You have the ability to set how the rows and columns are sized for a variety of effects.

Table 21-2 gives you an at-a-glance look at the properties of the TableLayoutPanel.

Table 21-2. *TableLayoutPanel Properties*

Property	Description
ColumnCount	Sets the number of columns that are in the table.
RowCount	Sets the number of rows that are in the table.
ColumnStyles	Provides a collection of ColumnStyle objects, one for each row in the table. Each ColumnStyle object has two properties: Width and SizeType. Width sets the preferred width, while SizeType indicates the sizing mode. Depending on the sizing mode, the width of the column may be expanded, as you will soon see.
RowStyles	Provides a collection of RowStyle objects, one for each row in the table. Each RowStyle object has two properties: Height and SizeType. Height sets the preferred height, while SizeType indicates the sizing mode. Depending on the sizing mode, the height of the row may be expanded.
GrowStyle	The GrowStyle property sets how the table will expand itself when more controls are added programmatically. You can use one of three enumeration values, including AddRows (insert new rows for the added controls), AddColumns (insert new columns), or FixedSize (throw an exception if you try to add a control to a full table).
CellBorderStyle	Sets the border that will be shown around the TableLayoutPanel and between each cell. You can use etched (Inset), embossed (Outset), solid lines (Single), or no lines (None, the default).

To try out the TableLayoutPanel, begin by dragging it onto a form. The TableLayoutPanel starts out with two columns and two rows, for a total of four cells. You can adjust the number of cells by modifying the RowCount and ColumnCount properties.

Tip Visual Studio shows the column and row borders at design-time with dotted lines, but you also can set the CellBorderStyle property to any value other than none if you want to show lines at runtime. This makes it easier to debug your layout.

Once you have the right size of table, you can drag controls into the TableLayoutPanel (see Figure 21-13). Each control occupies one cell in the table. If you want to put more than one control into a single cell, just wrap your controls into a container control. For example, you could create a TableLayoutPanel with four cells, and put an ordinary Panel in each cell with an unlimited number of additional controls.

Figure 21-13. *Tiling controls in a table*

This example shows the basic model of the TableLayoutPanel, but it doesn't explain how you can control the sizing behavior of the rows, columns, and individual controls. To master these details, you need to understand how the TableLayoutPanel works with styles, as described in the next section.

Row and Column Styles

To get the result you want with the TableLayoutPanel, you need to independently define the behavior of each row and column. You do this through a style-based model. Essentially, every column is paired with a matching ColumnStyle object. Every row is matched with a RowStyle object. You configure these style objects through the ColumnStyles and RowStyles properties of the TableLayoutPanel. In an attempt to simplify this model, Visual Studio doesn't expose these two collections directly in the Properties window. Instead, it lets you configure them through two linked virtual properties, named Columns and Rows or through the direct "Edit Rows and Columns…" link in the Action pane.

For example, imagine you create a 2 x 3 table by setting the ColumnCount and RowCount properties. Visual Studio will add the code required to create two RowStyle and three

ColumnStyle objects. RowStyle and ColumnStyle objects are exceedingly simple—in fact, they only have two properties each. The RowStyle class provides a Height property that sets the preferred height, while the ColumnStyle class provides a Width property. Both include a SizeType property, which determines how the Height or Width should be interpreted, and how the row should be resized when the TableLayoutPanel changes size.

There are three possible values for SizeType, as shown in Table 21-3.

Table 21-3. *Values from the SizeType Enumeration*

Property	Description
Absolute	The Height or Width property is interpreted as the exact number of pixels to size the row or column.
Percent	The Height or Width property is interpreted as a percentage of the height or width of the containing TableLayoutPanel when sizing the row or column.
AutoSize	The row or column is sized to match the largest cell. For example, a column is widened to fit its widest control and a column is heightened to fit its tallest control.

Visual Studio includes a handy designer that lets you tweak these values at design time. Just click the ellipsis (...) next to the Rows or Columns property, and you'll see the Column and Row Styles dialog box shown in Figure 21-14.

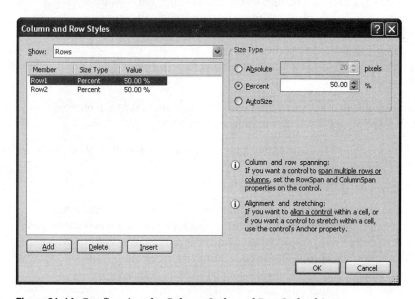

Figure 21-14. *Configuring the ColumnStyle and RowStyle objects*

You'll quickly see how to use the RowStyle and ColumnStyle objects to create simple fixed or proportional layouts. For example, you can assign absolute sizes to every column (with a SizeMode of Absolute) or proportional sizes (with a SizeMode of Percent). However, it's less clear what happens if you set more than size mode for your rows or columns. To understand what happens, you need to understand how the TableLayoutPanel creates its grid. It follows these steps:

1. It allocates space for all absolute-sized columns (or rows).

2. It allocates space for all autosized columns (or rows).

3. It distributes the remaining space the percentage-sized columns or rows. It attempts to meet the percentage sizes they request, but may not.

4. If extra space is left over, the last column (or row) is enlarged to fill it.

■**Note** For the remainder of the discussion, we'll consider column sizing for simplicity's sake. However, all these details apply equally to row sizing.

This sequence leads to a few important consequences. First of all, if you have absolute-sized columns or autosized columns that don't fit (the TableLayoutPanel is too small), they are cut off at the end. (This is a case where you might want to switch on autoscrolling by setting the TableLayoutPanel.AutoScroll property).

The TableLayoutPanel is more flexible with percentage-sized columns. For example, if a column requests 50 percent of the width of the panel, but only 10 percent is available, the column is resized to fit. Similarly, if you have several columns and their combined percentages are more than 100 percent, the TableLayoutPanel normalizes them to 100 percent (and divides whatever space is available proportionately).

Finally, step 4 may lead to the last column being wider than you want. To fix this problem, you have two options:

- You can size your table to exactly fit the total widths of all the columns. (One easy way to accomplish this is to set the TableLayoutPanel.AutoSize property to true.)

- You can add another dummy column that's empty, but is just intended to fill space.

Generating New Columns and Rows

In the design environment, Visual Studio ensures that you have exactly the right number of RowStyle and ColumnStyle objects based on the values you set for RowCount and ColumnCount. However, this isn't a necessity. For example, you can add cells programmatically just by setting the RowCount and ColumnCount properties in code. Similarly, new cells will be added if you add new controls the TableLayoutPanel.Controls collection.

This raises a couple of interesting questions—if you add controls to the TableLayoutPanel, are they placed in new rows or new columns? And what styles are applied?

The TableLayoutPanel.GrowStyle property answers the first question. It determines whether new controls are placed in rows (AddRows) or columns (AddColumns) or disallowed completely (FixedSize), which means an exception will be thrown if you attempt to add a control to the Controls collection.

The GrowStyle property only comes into play when you're adding to the Controls collection. It doesn't have any effect if you resize the table using the RowCount and ColumnCount properties.

■Note Keep in mind that when you use a GrowStyle of AddRows or AddColumns, the overall size of the TableLayoutPanel will increase. To deal with this, you might need to use the AutoScroll or AutoSize properties of the TableLayoutPanel.

The next issue is the row and column styles that are used for dynamically added rows, and this is governed by a simple default. When you add a column or row (either by adding a control or by changing the RowCount or ColumnCount properties), it's automatically assumed to have a SizeMode of AutoSize. If this isn't what you want, you can add a corresponding RowStyle or ColumnStyle object to the RowStyles or ColumnStyles collection.

Positioning Controls

So far, you've seen how you can configure the sizing of rows and columns. But what about the individual controls inside each cell?

By default, controls appear in the top-left corner of the cell that contains them. As with the FlowLayoutPanel, you can use the Margin properties of each control to add spacing between the cell edges and the control edges. You also can use the TableLayoutPanel.Padding property, but it's less useful. It sets the space between the borders of the TableLayoutPanel and the grid of cells inside.

To change the alignment of a control in its cell, you use the familiar Anchor and Dock properties. By default, all controls are docked to the top left of the cell, but you can easily make a control that is:

- Centered inside a cell (set Anchor to None).

- Fills the available space in a cell (set Dock to Fill, or set Anchor to Left, Right, Top, and Bottom).

- Absolutely positioned (set Anchor to Top and Left, and then set the Left and Top components of the Margin property to nudge the control into place).

As you learned in Chapter 3, Dock and Anchor apply to the container. In this case, the container is the cell, so the control shrinks or expands as the cells shrinks or expands. The cell shrinks or expands to fit the row height and column width. And as you learned earlier, the row height and column width are either fixed or may vary with the size of the TableLayoutPanel, depending on the SizeMode property.

Figure 21-15 shows some examples with differently aligned controls. Remember, you also can place an entire panel inside a cell if you want to align a combination of controls. Mastering this combination of layout panels, nested panels, and anchoring and docking isn't always easy, but it will give you virtually limitless possibilities for creating dynamic interfaces.

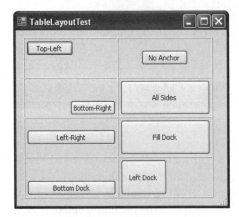

Figure 21-15. *Aligning controls inside a cell*

■**Note** You can look at almost any user interface and envision how it can be laid out with a TableLayoutPanel. However, be careful that you don't needlessly complicate your life. Microsoft architects recommend that you only use the TableLayoutPanel if you need the TableLayoutPanel resizing functionality or if you're generating your controls programmatically.

Extended Properties with the TableLayoutPanel

The TableLayoutPanel also doubles as a property extender (by implementing IExtenderProvider). As a result, it adds virtual properties to all the child controls you place inside it. These properties are listed in Table 21-4.

Table 21-4. *Extended Properties for TableLayoutPanel Children*

Property	Description
Column	Indicates the zero-based column index where the control is positioned. You also can set this value programmatically to move a control to a new location in the table. If you move a control farther down a table, all the cells in between are left blank.
Row	Indicates the zero-based row index where the control is positioned. You also can set this value programmatically to move a control to a new location in the table. If you move a control farther down a table, all the cells in between are left blank.
ColumnSpan	Indicates the number of columns that this control spans (the default is 1). For example, if you set ColumnSpan to 2, the control will occupy two cells (its own cell and the one on the right). If you specify a ColumnSpan greater than the number of columns on the right, the control is bumped to the next row. If you specify a ColumnSpan greater than the total number of columns in the table, the control occupies the entire row.

Table 21-4. *Extended Properties for TableLayoutPanel Children*

Property	Description
RowSpan	Indicates the number of rows that this control spans (the default is 1). For example, if you set RowSpan to 2, the control will occupy two cells (its own cell and the one below it). If you specify a RowSpan greater than the number of rows below, the control is bumped to a new column.
CellPosition	Provides a TableLayoutPanelCellPosition you can use to set both the Row and Column at once for optimum performance. In the Properties window, this extended property appears with the name Cell.

Figure 21-16 shows an example of cell spanning. Notice that if you set the TableLayoutPanel.CellBorderStyle to a value other than None, the control in the spanned cell is superimposed over the border. You can use column and row spanning simultaneously. In this case, the control fills a block of cells RowSpan x ColumnSpan in size.

The layout panels are extremely flexible, and you can use them to create a wide range of effects. Unfortunately, it's not immediately obvious what approach you should take with the layout panels, and a property-by-property description does little to fill in the blanks. Instead, the following sections give you an example-based approach, leading you through common solutions that the layout panels can provide.

Figure 21-16. *Row and column spanning*

Layout Panel Examples

TableLayoutPanel: A Localizable Dialog Box

Imagine you have a simple dialog box that you need to localize. This dialog box has three buttons, arranged one on top of the other. Using the AutoSize property described in Chapter 3, it's fairly easy to make these buttons expand to fit their content. However, it's not as easy to make sure all three buttons have the *same* size. Ideally, you'd like to make all the buttons take the size of the largest automatically sized button so they line up neatly. Figure 21-17 shows the desired result.

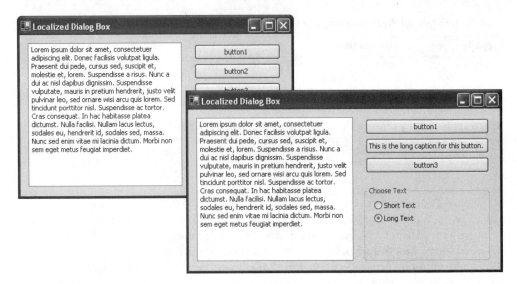

Figure 21-17. *A resizable column of buttons*

To implement this design, follow these steps:

1. Add a TableLayoutPanel for the three buttons. Define the basic structure by setting RowCount to 3 and ColumnCount to 1, and add the three buttons.

2. Edit the RowStyles collection of the TableLayoutPanel (which is exposed in the Properties window as the Rows collection) so that each row has an Absolute size of 30 pixels. This is because the buttons should all have the same height (if you want to allow different fonts and character sets for other languages, this isn't necessarily true). To make sure the last row isn't stretched, make sure the TableLayoutPanel height is equal to three rows' heights (in this case, 90 pixels).

3. Edit the ColumnStyles collection of the TableLayoutPanel so that the single column uses AutoSize, which allows the table to grow with the buttons. Also set the initial width of the TableLayoutPanel (such as 100 pixels).

4. Add a button in each cell.

5. Change each button by setting the AutoSize property to true (so the button can grow with its caption text), and set the Dock property to Fill (so that the button expands to fill the full cell). This step implements the basic design. If the content of any button is extended, the button will resize to fit. This action will widen the column, and the other buttons will follow suit because of to their docking properties.

6. Finally, to get everything to display correctly, you need to make sure the TableLayoutPanel and the containing form also expand as the column expands. To achieve this, set the AutoSize property of both to true.

To fine-tune this example, you might want to adjust the Margin property of the TableLayoutPanel so that the controls it contains line up with other anchored controls on the form. (The example in Figure 21-17 uses 10 pixels rather than the default 3.)

TableLayoutPanel: BiPane Proportional Resizing

Although anchoring and docking give you a great deal of control, there is some behavior they can't accomplish on their own. One example is resizing adjacent controls *proportionately*. For example, consider a window that's split into two panels. With anchoring, you can configure one panel to enlarge as the form is widened. However, you can't get both panels to resize to split the new space equitably. As a result, the proportions of the window change. (Windows Explorer is one example of this behavior. As you resize the window, the width of file list changes, but the width of the directory tree does not.) In conventional Windows applications, this problem is usually dealt with by a splitter bar, which lets the user explicitly change the portion of the window allocated to each panel as needed.

Another option is to use the TabelLayoutPanel to implement proportional resizing. Figure 21-18 shows an example.

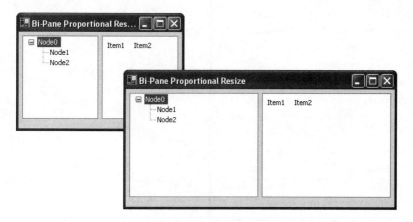

Figure 21-18. *Proportional resizing*

To implement this design, follow these steps:

1. Add a TableLayoutPanel. Define the basic structure by setting RowCount to 1 and ColumnCount to 2.

2. Size the TableLayoutPanel to fill most of the form, and then set its Anchor property so it's anchored to all four sides of the form and will grow as the form is resized.

3. Add a control on each side (such as a TreeView on the left and ListView on the right). Set the Dock property of each control to Fill. If you wanted to add multiple controls, you would use Panel controls instead and add anchored controls inside each panel.

4. Edit the ColumnStyles collection of the TableLayoutPanel (which is exposed in the Properties window as the Columns collection) so that each column uses SizeType.Percent. You can then choose appropriate percentages (in this example the space is split with the 50 percent columns).

TableLayoutPanel: A List of Settings

The TableLayoutPanel makes great sense for columns of settings that need to be laid out in a grid. To model this sort of window, you could use a two-column TableLayoutPanel with labels on the left and an input control (text box, drop-down list box, etc.) on the right. The label column should size to fit the largest label. The text box column should fill all the remaining space. Figure 21-19 shows an example.

Figure 21-19. *A list of settings*

To implement this design, follow these steps:

1. Add a TableLayoutPanel. Define the basic structure by setting RowCount to 1 and ColumnCount to 2.

2. Size the TableLayoutPanel to fill most of the form, and then set its Anchor property so it's anchored to all four sides of the form and will grow as the form is resized. Don't add any controls—instead, the labels and buttons will be inserted programmatically.

3. Edit the ColumnStyles collection of the TableLayoutPanel. The first column should use AutoSize resizing mode so that it grows to fit the largest label. The sizing mode for the second column isn't important, as it will automatically be sized to fit whatever space remains.

4. Edit the RowStyles collection of the TableLayoutPanel. Set the first (and only) row to AutoSize resizing mode.

Now you can insert the controls when the form loads. In this example, the controls are hard-coded, but you could easily generate them based on the information in a database or file (as demonstrated later in this chapter):

```
private void Form_Load(object sender, EventArgs e)
{
    // Reduce the number of times the layout logic is executed.
    tableLayoutPanel1.SuspendLayout();

    // Add the controls.
    for (int i=1; i<15; i++)
    {
        // Create an autosizing label for the left column.
        Label lbl = new Label();
        lbl.Text = "This is Setting " + i.ToString();
        lbl.AutoSize = true;
        lbl.Margin = new Padding(3, 7, 3, 3);

        // Create a text box that's docked to fill up the entire second column.
        TextBox txt = new TextBox();
        txt.Dock = DockStyle.Fill;

        // Add the controls
        tableLayoutPanel1.Controls.Add(lbl);
        tableLayoutPanel1.Controls.Add(txt);
    }

    tableLayoutPanel1.ResumeLayout();
}
```

Note In this example, the layout logic is performed when the Form.Load event fires. For best performance, you should perform this task even earlier. That's because when the Form.Load event fires, the handles have already been created for the form and the TableLayoutPanel. A better place to perform initialization like this is in the Form constructor, immediately after InitializeComponent() is called to create the control objects.

You can easily extend this example to use even more columns. For example, you could create a four-column table with two pairs of settings, or you could add a third column with a button, as shown in Figure 21-20. In this example, the label column sizes to the largest label, the button column sizes to the fixed button size, and the text box column in between takes the remaining space.

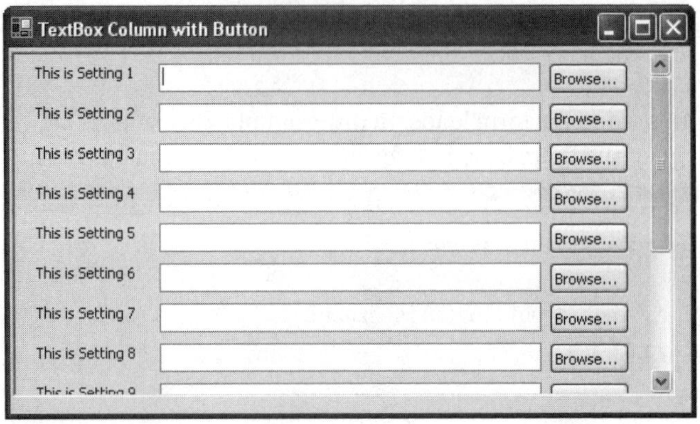

Figure 21-20. *A more-detailed list of settings*

To create this window, you simply need to add a third AutoSize column. You can then dock a newly created button in the column, as shown here:

```
Button cmd = new Button();
cmd.Text = "Browse...";
cmd.Width = 60;
tableLayoutPanel1.Controls.Add(cmd);
```

One other frill is added—the entire TableLayoutPanel is made scrollable by setting AutoScroll to true.

TableLayoutPanel: Forms From a File

You can extend the technique shown in the previous example to create more a customizable user interface that's built out of a collection of TableLayoutPanel and FlowLayoutPanel objects. Doing so allows you to create more sophisticated, variable interfaces, like those that model business forms. The following example demonstrates one such example with a survey application.

In this application, the code reads XML tags that define the required interface. These tags are stored in a file, although you could easily modify the code so that it reads a block of XML from another source, like a database. The code then loops through the elements in the XML document, translating them into the appropriate controls. As the control objects are created, they're added to the form. This logic is fairly involved, but it's not nearly as messy as it would have been with .NET 1.x. That's because the code uses autosizing and layout panels to avoid dealing directly with control sizes and position. As long as the control is added to the right container, the entire form flows without a problem.

The basic structure of the form is made up of two pieces:

- A TableLayoutPanel with one column holds all the sections of the survey form. The TableLayoutPanel has a single column, with a width of 100 percent.

- Each section of the survey form is inserted as another panel (either a TableLayoutPanel or a FlowLayoutPanel depending on the type of content). This panel control is placed in a separate cell.

The top-level TableLayout is also placed into an ordinary Panel container. This extra step is one approach to add a border around the TableLayoutPanel without adding a border between cells. (Another approach would be to perform some custom drawing in response to the Form.Paint event.)

Figure 21-21 shows a sample survey form.

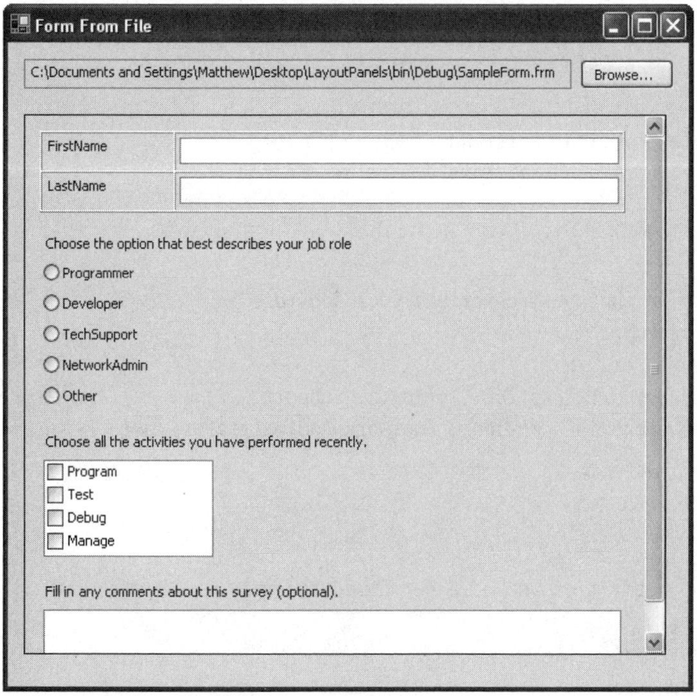

Figure 21-21. *Generating a data entry form from a .frm file*

The Form File

All forms are modeled as XML files with a root <Form> element. In the root element, you can add one of four different panels, depending on the type of survey content you need:

- **<TextBoxPanel>.** Rendered as a two-column table, with labels on the left and text boxes for data entry on the right. Each row requires a separate <TextItem> tag.

- **<GroupSelectionPanel>.** Rendered as a group of radio buttons, one for each item, with a caption at the top. Each radio button requires a separate <SelectionItem> tag.

- **<CheckBoxListPanel>.** Rendered as a CheckBoxList control, which shows multiple items in a list box, each of which can be checked or unchecked. Each item requires a separate <SelectionItem> tag.

- **<LargeTextBoxPanel>.** Rendered as one or more full-width multiple line text boxes, with a caption at the top. Each text box requires a separate <TextItem> tag.

The form code defines an enumeration that represents the four allowed types of panels:

```
enum PanelTypes
{
    TextBoxPanel, GroupSelectionPanel,
    CheckBoxListPanel, LargeTextBoxPanel
}
```

Here's the sample survey form used to create the user interface in Figure 21-21:

```xml
<?xml version="1.0"?>
<Form>
  <TextBoxPanel>
    <TextItem id="FirstName" caption="First Name" />
    <TextItem id="LastName" caption="Last Name" />
  </TextBoxPanel>

  <GroupSelectionPanel
   caption="Choose the option that best describes your job role">
    <SelectionItem id="Programmer" />
    <SelectionItem id="Developer" />
    <SelectionItem id="TechSupport" caption="Technical Support" />
    <SelectionItem id="NetworkAdmin" caption = "Network Administrator" />
    <SelectionItem id="Other" />
  </GroupSelectionPanel>

  <CheckBoxListPanel
   caption="Choose all the activities you have performed recently.">
    <SelectionItem id="Program" />
    <SelectionItem id="Test" />
    <SelectionItem id="Debug" />
    <SelectionItem id="Manage" />
  </CheckBoxListPanel>

  <LargeTextBoxPanel caption="Fill in any comments about this survey (optional).">
    <TextItem id="Comments" />
  </LargeTextBoxPanel>
</Form>
```

The caption attributes define text that's rendered in the user interface. The id attributes define the unique names that will be used for the automatically generated controls. The id also will be used when saving the filled-out survey data. Notice that you don't need to supply the caption attribute for the <SelectionItem> element—if you don't, the caption is set to match the id.

The Form Parsing Code

In the application, the first step is to choose a survey file by clicking the Browse button. At this point, a dialog box is shown with all the available survey files (which are given a .frm extension). Once a file is selected, the work is handed off to the SurveyDeserializer class:

```
private void cmdBrowse_Click(object sender, EventArgs e)
{
    if (openFileDialog.ShowDialog() == DialogResult.OK)
    {
        txtFileName.Text = openFileDialog.FileName;
        SurveyDeserializer surveyReader = new
          SurveyDeserializer(openFileDialog.FileName, tableLayoutPanel1);
        tableLayoutPanel1.SuspendLayout();
        surveyReader.LoadForm();
        tableLayoutPanel1.ResumeLayout();
    }
}
```

In its constructor, the SurveyDeserializer stores the file name and layout panel information for future reference:

```
private string fileName;
private Panel targetContainer;

public SurveyDeserializer(string fileName, Panel targetContainer)
{
    this.fileName = fileName;
    this.targetContainer = targetContainer;
}
```

Next, the SurveyDeserializer.LoadForm() method begins by disposing any controls that exist inside the survey panel.

```
public void LoadForm()
{
    // Clear the current table content.
    foreach (Control ctrl in targetContainer.Controls)
    {
        ctrl.Dispose();
    }
    ...
```

Note that it's not enough to call the Panel.Controls.Clear() method. This removes the control objects from the Controls collection, but it doesn't release them. As a result, you'll tie up control handles every time you generate a new form and reduce system performance.

■**Tip** In some layout situations, you may use a panel to show one of a small set of different views. In this scenario, the most efficient way to deal with your controls is to simply hide them (or their container), rather than dispose and re-create them.

The next step is to read the survey file into an in-memory XmlDocument object. The code then iterates over the panel elements, checking to make sure that the type matches one of the values defined in the enumeration.

```
...
try
{
    // Load the form into memory.
    XmlDocument doc = new XmlDocument();
    doc.Load(fileName);

    // Iterate over panel nodes.
    foreach (XmlNode nodePanel in doc.DocumentElement.ChildNodes)
    {
        // Convert the element name into the appropriate enum value.
        PanelTypes type =
        (PanelTypes)Enum.Parse(typeof(PanelTypes), nodePanel.LocalName);

        // Check for caption node.
        string caption = CheckForAttribute(nodePanel, "caption");
        ...
```

You'll notice that the code also makes use of a simple CheckForAttribute() method, which looks for an attribute with a specific name. If the attribute is found, CheckForAttribute() returns it value. If not, CheckForAttribute() returns an empty string.

The work of actually creating the corresponding container is handed off to another method, called CreateContainer(). It generates the container control that will hold the content for that survey element.

```
    ...
    // Create the container for this survey element.
    // It's placed into the next available cell.
    Control container = CreateContainer(type, caption);
    ...
```

Finally, the code loops through all the tags in the container. These are the <SelectionItem> and <TextItem> elements that define specific text boxes, check boxes, or radio buttons. Each time it finds a nested element, the code extracts the relevant id and caption information, and passes it to another private method—CreateContent(). CreateContent() creates the required child control and inserts it in the container.

```
    ...
    // Remember, when there is more than one level of container at work,
    // you need to call SuspendLayout() on each level to get the
    // performance benefits.
    container.SuspendLayout();
```

```
            // Iterate over the nested nodes.
            foreach (XmlNode nodeItem in nodePanel.ChildNodes)
            {
                // Get the node information.
                string id = CheckForAttribute(nodeItem, "id");
                caption = CheckForAttribute(nodeItem, "caption");
                if (caption.Length == 0) caption = id;

                // Create the content inside the survey element.
                CreateContent(type, nodeItem.LocalName,
                  caption, id, container);
            }
            container.ResumeLayout();
        }
    }
    catch (Exception err)
    {
        MessageBox.Show("Failure parsing file.\n" + err.Message);
    }
}
```

Essentially, the LoadForm() method takes care of parsing the XML document. The CreateContainer() and CreateContent() perform the real work—generating the controls and inserting them into the current position in the survey table.

Every survey element is stored inside a nested TableLayoutPanel or FlowLayoutPanel. This is referred to as the top-level container for the survey element. The rest of the survey content may be added to the top-level container, or it may be added to another control in the top-level container. For example, consider the <CheckBoxListPanel> survey element. For this element, a FlowLayoutPanel hosts the caption and a CheckBoxList. The FlowLayoutPanel is the top-level container, but the CheckBoxList is the container for survey elements. It's the control that's returned by the CreateContainer() method.

To make it easier to manipulate these ingredients, the CreateContainer() method defines them immediately, as shown here:

```
private Control CreateContainer(PanelTypes type, string caption)
{
    // Represents the top-level container
    // (a TableLayoutPanel or FlowLayoutPanel,
    // depending on the survey element).
    TableLayoutPanel pnlTable = null;
    FlowLayoutPanel pnlFlow = null;

    // Represents the control object that contains
    // the rest of the survey content.
    Control container = null;
```

```
// Represents a caption that can be inserted at
// the top of the panel.
Label lblCaption;
...
```

The next step is to identify the type of survey element, and create the appropriate container. For example, if a TextBoxPanel is required, a new nested TableLayoutPanel is generated with two columns, one for the label text and one for the text box:

```
...
switch (type)
{
    case PanelTypes.TextBoxPanel:
        pnlTable = new TableLayoutPanel();
        pnlTable.CellBorderStyle = TableLayoutPanelCellBorderStyle.Outset;
        pnlTable.ColumnCount = 2;

        // Make sure the full width of the form is used
        // for the text box.
        pnlTable.Anchor = AnchorStyles.Left | AnchorStyles.Right;

        // Set the container, which will be used to add more content.
        container = pnlTable;
        break;
        ...
```

Note that, when created programmatically, a TableLayoutPanel has no ColumnStyle objects. (When created at design time, the ColumnStyle objects are generated automatically.) You don't necessarily need to add these objects, if the default AutoSize behavior makes sense. In this example, the AutoSize behavior does make sense, because you want the first column (the label) to be only as wide as necessary. The second column (with the text box) is the last column, so it automatically fills the remaining space.

The code for creating a <GroupSelectionPanel> is similar, except it uses a FlowLayoutPanel as the top-level container that's inserted in the cell. The FlowLayoutPanel uses FlowDirection. TopDown so that the contained caption (a Label control) and each radio button inside it will take a full line.

```
    ...
    case PanelTypes.GroupSelectionPanel:
        pnlFlow = new FlowLayoutPanel();
        pnlFlow.FlowDirection = FlowDirection.TopDown;

        // Add a caption.
        lblCaption = new Label();
        lblCaption.Text = caption;
        lblCaption.AutoSize = true;
        pnlFlow.Controls.Add(lblCaption);
```

```
        container = pnlFlow;
        break;
    ...
```

The <CheckBoxListPanel> and <LargeTextBoxPanel> use the same approach. Here's the complete code:

```
    ...
    case PanelTypes.CheckBoxListPanel:
        pnlTable = new TableLayoutPanel();
        pnlTable.ColumnCount = 1;

        // Add a caption.
        lblCaption = new Label();
        lblCaption.Text = caption;
        lblCaption.AutoSize = true;
        pnlTable.Controls.Add(lblCaption);

        // Add the check-box list.
        CheckedListBox checks = new CheckedListBox();
        checks.AutoSize = true;
        pnlTable.Controls.Add(checks);

        container = checks;
        break;

    case PanelTypes.LargeTextBoxPanel:
        pnlTable = new TableLayoutPanel();
        pnlTable.ColumnCount = 1;
        pnlTable.Anchor = AnchorStyles.Left | AnchorStyles.Right;

        // Add a caption.
        lblCaption = new Label();
        lblCaption.Text = caption;
        lblCaption.AutoSize = true;
        pnlTable.Controls.Add(lblCaption);

        container = pnlTable;
        break;
}
...
```

The last step is to add the top-level container to the table, and return the control container so the rest of the content can be inserted into it:

```
...
Panel pnl = null;
if (pnlTable != null)
{
    pnl = pnlTable;
}
else
{
    pnl = pnlFlow;
}
// Ensure 7 pixels of spacing between each survey element.
pnl.Margin = new Padding(7);
pnl.AutoSize = true;

// Add the panel for this survey element to the top-level container
// for the whole survey.
targetContainer.Controls.Add(pnl);

// Return the container control, so more content can
// be inserted inside it.
return container;
}
```

The CreateContent() method is the last piece of the puzzle. It accepts several pieces of information, creates the corresponding input control, and adds it to the panel. It also performs basic validation by checking that the name of the element matches the expected content.

Here's the full code:

```
private void CreateContent(PanelTypes type, string elementName,
 string caption, string id, Control container)
{
    Control ctrl = null;
    switch (type)
    {
        case PanelTypes.TextBoxPanel:
            if (elementName != "TextItem")
              throw new XmlException("Element " + elementName + " not expected");

            // Generate a Label and TextBox pair for the row.
            ctrl = new Label();
            ctrl.Text = caption;
            container.Controls.Add(ctrl);
            ctrl = new TextBox();
            ctrl.Name = id;
            ctrl.Dock = DockStyle.Fill;
            container.Controls.Add(ctrl);
            break;
```

```
        case PanelTypes.GroupSelectionPanel:
            if (elementName != "SelectionItem")
              throw new XmlException("Element " + elementName + " not expected");

            ctrl = new RadioButton();
            ctrl.Name = id;
            ctrl.Text = caption;

            // Keep the adjacent radio buttons close together by shrinking
            // the top and bottom margins.
            ctrl.Margin = new Padding(3, 0, 3, 0);
            container.Controls.Add(ctrl);
            break;

        case PanelTypes.CheckBoxListPanel:
            if (elementName != "SelectionItem")
              throw new XmlException("Element " + elementName + " not expected");

            // Add items to the CheckedListBox.
            ((CheckedListBox)container).Items.Add(
              new CheckBoxListItem(caption, id));
            break;

        case PanelTypes.LargeTextBoxPanel:
            if (elementName != "TextItem")
              throw new XmlException("Element " + elementName + " not expected");

            ctrl = new TextBox();
            ctrl.Dock = DockStyle.Fill;
            ((TextBox)ctrl).WordWrap = true;
            ((TextBox)ctrl).AcceptsReturn = true;
            ((TextBox)ctrl).Multiline = true;

            // Set the text box to a line height of 3 lines.
            // This information could also be configurable through a
            // class property, or it could be read from the XML document.
            ctrl.Height *= 3;
            container.Controls.Add(ctrl);
            break;
    }
}
```

Storing the Form Data

This example leaves out one detail—how do you save the survey data once the form is complete?
Because the controls are created dynamically, you can't make use of any form-level references.
Instead, you need to iterate through the Controls collection, looking for input controls (in this

case, the TextBox, RadioButton, and CheckBoxList). Each time you find one of these controls, you can record the Name property (which reflects the id set in the survey file) and the user-supplied data.

FlowLayoutPanel: A Modular Interface

One interesting application of the FlowLayoutPanel is to lay out multiple modules in a portal-style application. For example, you might have an application that provides different features or data views to different users, depending on their roles or their preferences. You can implement each feature using a separate user control, and then show the appropriate group of user controls in a FlowLayoutPanel. (Depending on the way you want to arrange these controls, you might alternatively choose to use a TableLayoutPanel with defined columns.)

Figure 21-22 shows an example that puts several CollapsiblePanel controls (from Chapter 12) into a FlowLayoutPanel.

Figure 21-22. *A portal-style application with layout panels*

What's interesting about this example is the way it's modular: You can hide individual panels and the interface will reflow seamlessly. To help demonstrate this, the form presents a list of all the currently displayed modules. When the form first loads, it scans through the FlowLayoutPanel looking for panels and adds them to the list:

```
private void ModularPortal_Load(object sender, EventArgs e)
{
    foreach (Control ctrl in flowLayoutPanel1.Controls)
    {
        if (ctrl is Panel)
            lstModules.Items.Add(ctrl.Text, true);
    }
}
```

A single click in the list is all you need to hide or show a panel:

```
private void lstModules_ItemCheck(object sender, ItemCheckEventArgs e)
{
    foreach (Control ctrl in flowLayoutPanel1.Controls)
    {
        if (ctrl.Text == lstModules.Text)
        {
            if (e.NewValue == CheckState.Checked)
            {
                ctrl.Visible = true;
            }
            else
            {
                ctrl.Visible = false;
            }
            return;
        }
    }
}
```

Figure 21-23 shows the result after hiding two panels.

Microsoft has some interesting proof-of-concept application that demonstrates exactly this approach. This application works as an RSS viewer that displays news feeds from the Internet. Each module is a separate user control. You can find this more detailed example in the RSSReader project with the sample code for this chapter.

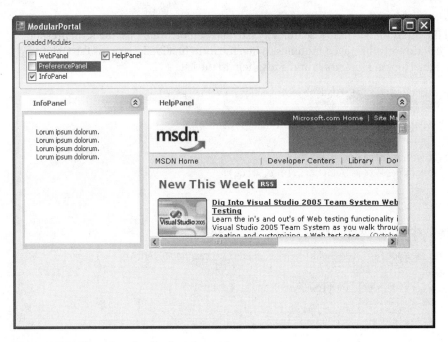

Figure 21-23. *Changing the displayed panels*

Markup-Based User Interface

The future of user interface is probably an entirely different approach to programmatic control creation. This approach, first popularized with the Web, is markup based. Rather than writing code to programmatically create and insert controls into a container, with markup-based user interface you write a template (typically in an XML-based format) that defines each control. The user interface framework parses this file and then creates the corresponding controls (typically one for each tag it finds).

One of the goals of markup-based user interface language is to allow a proper separation between user interface code (the event handlers) and the user interface itself (the graphical widgets). In an ideal world, this separation would let professional graphic designers perfect the user interface look –and feel without compromising the security or integrity of your code. Of course, it's also a great way to create flexible, extensible user interfaces. For example, you could build a tool for filling out forms (like the one shown earlier in this chapter) much more easily. Instead of writing the logic to interpret your own custom XML format, you could simply create a template for each form using a markup-based language like XAML or WFML.

■**Note** The idea of markup-based user interface is similar to the dynamic form generator shown in this chapter. There are two key differences. First, in the form generator you need to write the parsing, whereas XAML and WFML provide their own parsers that automate this low-level grunt work. The second difference is that the form generator uses a higher-level model that has elements map to logical survey elements. In the XAML and WFML standards, elements map directly to controls.

XAML

A significant example of markup-based user interface is XAML (Extensible Application Markup Language, but pronounced "Zamel"). XAML is an XML-based markup language for defining user interfaces that was created by Microsoft, and is the planned standard for the Avalon display technology in Windows Vista, Microsoft's next version of Windows. Although Windows Vista isn't likely to materialize anytime soon (2006 is a realistic estimate), you can start using XAML in .NET applications if you want to experiment with third-party products like Xamlon (see www.xamlon.com). You can start experimenting with Avalon through a downloadable tech preview or beta—see http://msdn.microsoft.com/windowsvista/experience for more information.

Using XAML, you can define your windows with tags and write the logic behind it using your favorite .NET language, giving you the ability to tweak either piece separately. Of course, you might not want to delve into the emerging XAML standard yet, because using a third-party product like XAML adds complexity and overhead to today's Windows Forms applications. If you're still interested in markup-based user interface, you might want to explore a lighter-weight option called WFML.

WFML

WFML (Windows Forms Markup Language) provides a more straightforward model for using markup with Windows Forms applications. Essentially, WFML consists of two pieces: the WFML markup standard (which dictates how you can build templates) and the WFML parser (which reads templates and creates the corresponding control objects).

■**Note** If you've programmed with ASP.NET before, the idea of WFML will seem surprisingly familiar. Like WFML, ASP.NET uses a parser to process a template (in this case, the .aspx file) and generate web page controls before your code executes.

WFML is described in detail on the Microsoft Windows Forms community site at http://windowsforms.net/articles/wfml.aspx. WFML isn't a standard—it's really a proof-of-concept demonstration of markup-based language, and it won't ever be incorporated into the .NET Framework. However, it's still usable in current Windows Forms applications.

The Last Word

This chapter considered dynamic user interfaces. Rather than limiting the discussion to questions about how to create controls at runtime and hook up their events (which, as you've seen, is relatively trivial once you know how to do it), the chapter examined some more radical approaches. These techniques allow you to dynamically build entire interfaces to suit localization needs, changing data, or user-specific customization.

Many of these applications have specific niches, and the techniques discussed here aren't suitable for all applications. On the other hand, if you need to create a data-driven or highly customizable application like the portal example in this chapter, you *need* to use a dynamic interface—without it you'll be trapped in an endless cycle of user interface tweaking and recompiling as the underlying data change. Perhaps best of all, dynamic user interfaces give developers a chance to write innovative code—and that's always fun.

■ ■ ■

Help Systems

Help: Is it the final polish on a professional application, or a time-consuming chore? It all depends on the audience, but most applications need a support center where users can seek assistance when they become confused or disoriented. Without this basic aid, you (or your organization's technical support department) are sure to be buried under an avalanche of support calls.

In this chapter, you learn the following:

- How to integrate Windows Help files into your applications. You look at launching Help manually and using the context-sensitive HelpProvider.

- When to design your own Help, and how you can weave it into an application using an extensible database-based or XML-based model.

- How to break down the limits of Help and design *application-embedded support*: user assistance that's integrated into the software it documents instead of slapped in a separate file as an afterthought. You explore some simple approaches such as affordances and a few advanced techniques such as animated agents.

Understanding Help

In recent years there has been a shift away from printed documentation. The occasional weighty manual (like the book you're holding now) is still required for learning advanced tools, but the average piece of office productivity or business software no longer assumes the user is willing to perform any additional reading. Instead, these programs are heavily dependent on natural, instinctive interfaces, and use online Help to patch the gaps and answer the occasional user question.

Online Help doesn't have to take the form of a second-rate user manual, however. The advantages of online Help are remarkable:

- **Increased control.** With a little effort, you can determine exactly what information users see when they click the F1 key. With a printed book, users might look for information using the index, table of contents, or even a third-party *For Dummies* guide, and you have no way of knowing what they will find.

- **Rich media.** With online Help you can use as many pictures as you want, in any combination, and even include sounds, movies, and animated demonstrations.

- **Searching tools and context-sensitivity.** Help systems can automate most of the drudgery associated with finding information. They can look for keywords with a full-text search (rather than relying on a human-compiled index), and programs can use context-sensitivity to make sure users see the appropriate topic immediately.

All Help standards provide these advantages in one form or another.

Classic "Bad Help"

Have you ever had this experience? You find an unusual option buried deep in an application, and it piques your curiosity. You hit F1, curious to find out what this option accomplishes. But your optimism dwindles when you read the description provided by the context-sensitive Help system: "To enable option X, click once on the option X check box. To disable option X, click the option X check box again to remove the check mark. Click OK to save your changes."

Clearly something is missing here. You want to know what option X does; the Help wants to explain, in oddly explicit detail, how to use a check box. The situation is ridiculous, as the function of option X is not at all obvious, but the way to use a check box is instinctive to every computer user. If you don't know how to use a check box, you probably wouldn't have guessed to press the F1 key for Help.

This is an example of classic bad Help. Some of the characteristics of bad Help include:

- **It describes the user interface.** Users don't need to know how the interface works—they can often discover that by trial and (occasionally) error. Instead, users need to know what tasks the application performs.

- **It's excessively long.** Help doesn't have the same bandwidth as a printed document, and endless scrolling is sure to frustrate users.

- **It uses visual clues.** Instructing the user to look at the "top left" or "middle right" may seem logical enough, but with the application running in another (potentially minimized) window, it can cause confusion.

- **It omits information.** Printed documents can afford to choose what they cover. However, Help documents are shipped with the software, and are expected to provide a matching reference. Thus, you can't ignore any option or setting that's in the interface.

To understand good Help, you need to recognize that most Help is designed to provide reference information. Help really shines compared to a printed book when it's able to use context sensitivity to automatically display a piece of information about a specific window or setting. This is the type of information that all users need occasionally while working with an application they mostly understand.

On the other hand, Help is relatively poor at providing tutorial-based learning, which explains tasks that incorporate many different parts. In this case, it's generally easier to use a printed book. Help that tries to provide descriptive task-based learning is generally frustrating for a number of reasons—users can't see the Help window at the same time they look at the program window, the Help window doesn't provide enough space for the long descriptions that are needed, and most users don't want to read a large amount of information from the computer screen anyway.

When creating Help, you should aim to divide it into discrete topics that describe individual windows, complete with all their details. This provides the most useful context-sensitive Help system.

■Tip Help can be used for tutorial-based learning… but not ordinary Help. Instead, applications and games that teach users as they work need to incorporate custom solutions, which are generally referred to as application-embedded support. You'll look at this technology later in the chapter. Application-embedded support supplements the standardized reference-based Help systems; it doesn't replace them.

In the next section, you explore the Help landscape.

Types of Help

Standardized Help has existed since the Windows platform was created, and even in the DOS world in little-known tools like QuickHelp. Throughout the years (and versions of Windows), Help has continued to evolve, passing through several distinct stages, which are described in the next few sections.

WinHelp

The WinHelp format used in Windows 3.0 still exists (see Figure 22-1), and can be used in the most modern Windows application. Unfortunately, it looks irredeemably garish. Help files from different authors tended to look—and act—differently.

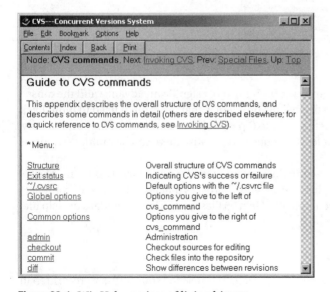

Figure 22-1. *WinHelp: a piece of living history*

WinHelp 95

When Windows 95 was introduced, a new standard (often referred to as WinHelp 95—see Figure 22-2) took over. WinHelp 95 files are familiar to almost any computer user, and they are still used in countless programs.

WinHelp 95 was a major improvement in the Help world. Whereas the original WinHelp forced developers to create their own contents pages with hyperlinks, WinHelp 95 files use a separate contents file (with the extension .cnt) to define the standardized multilevel table of contents. WinHelp 95 really has two parts: the .cnt contents page (which also provides a standardized index and full-text search), and the .hlp Help file, which provides the actual topics. When a user double-clicks a topic, the table of contents is replaced with the appropriate Help window.

Figure 22-2. *WinHelp 95: a facelift*

The standardized table of contents was both the most significant advance and the most obvious limitation of WinHelp 95. The obvious problem is that users often need to jump back and forth between the table of contents and the topic pages before they find the content they need. This process is tedious, and it feels complicated because there can be multiple windows scattered about the desktop.

To create a WinHelp 95 file, you write the content in one or more Rich Text Format (.rtf) files. These files are then put through a "compilation" process that creates a linked, compact binary format. The easiest way to generate WinHelp 95 files (or any other standard of Help file) is with a dedicated Help-authoring program.

HTML Help

The next version of WinHelp was named HTML Help, because the source files were written in HTML markup instead of Rich Text Format. HTML Help debuted with Windows 98 and also shipped with Internet Explorer 4. A common source of confusion about HTML Help is the idea that it is somehow supposed to provide help over the Web or browser-integrated Help. While

HTML Help depends on some components that are also used in Internet Explorer, it really has little to do with the Internet. Instead, HTML Help is an improvement to WinHelp that combines the table of contents and topic views in the same window (see Figure 22-3).

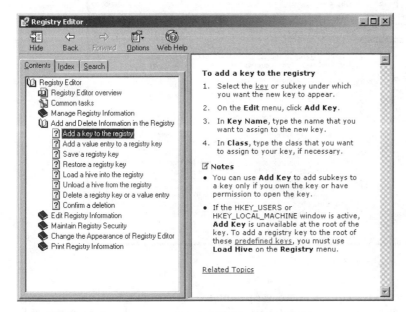

Figure 22-3. *HTML Help: the industrial revolution of Help*

The HTML Help view makes it dramatically easier to browse through a long, multilevel table of contents without losing your place. By dividing and subdividing information into its smallest bits, Help developers are able to put fairly lengthy, complex content in a Help file. With HTML Help, developers also started to use DHTML and JavaScript text directly in their Help to create collapsible headings and other neat tricks. In some cases (for example, the Visual Studio 6 documentation and the SQL Server documentation), Microsoft refers to these Help files as "books online." HTML Help files always use the .chm extension.

In the years since HTML Help first appeared, Microsoft has experimented with several other approaches, including proprietary Help windows in Microsoft Office and Windows XP. However, these other approaches have never been officially released to third parties, and the slightly shopworn HTML Help remains the official current standard.

MS Help 2

Microsoft originally planned to make MS Help 2, the Help engine that debuted in Visual Studio .NET 2002, the next Help revolution (see Figure 22-4). Help 2 promised some long-awaited improvements to HTML Help, like a redesigned user interface, and the ability to embed a Help window in an application interface with minimum fuss. However, it also had its idiosyncrasies. For example, every Help 2 file must be registered with the Windows operating system. You can't simply copy the appropriate .HxS file to another computer.

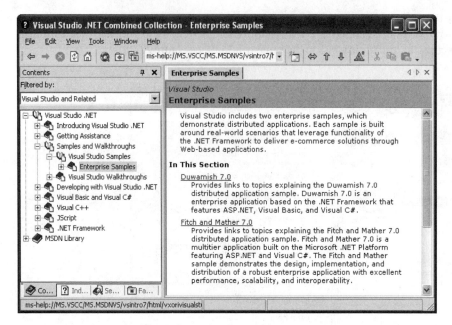

Figure 22-4. *Help 2.0: an aborted standard*

Sadly, the release of the Help 2 standard was postponed in December 2001, and ultimately canceled in January 2003. Instead, Microsoft is perfecting a new standard that will debut with the next version of Windows, called Windows Vista. The key issue with Help 2 is the lack of integration with the operating system. However, it's still widely used by third parties to distribute .NET developer documentation (as all .NET developers have the Help 2 engine installed, either through Visual Studio or the .NET SDK). To find out more information about Help 2, refer to the excellent community site `http://helpware.net`. You can also find a variety of tools for registering and compiling Help 2 collections.

Help-Authoring Tools

Microsoft provides only rudimentary tools for compiling source files to create Help systems. To have the full range of tools for designing, linking, and configuring your Help, you will probably need to turn to a third-party design tool. Creating Help is beyond the scope of this book, but there are a few starting points:

- The HTML Help SDK (`http://msdn.microsoft.com/library/en-us/htmlhelp/html/hwMicrosoftHTMLHelpDownloads.asp`) is available from Microsoft. It contains authoring information and a basic tool for compiling HTML pages into a .chm file with a table of contents. However, professional Help is almost always authored with more-powerful authoring tools (see the following two items).

- Professional Help-design systems tend to ship with countless tools—and intimidating prices. One leading example is RoboHelp (www.macromedia.com/software/robohelp), although numerous other mutually incompatible design tools are available. Some Help systems are designed from the ground up with single-sourcing in mind, with varied degrees of success. For example, WebWorks Publisher (www.quadralay.com) attempts to create HTML from FrameMaker files—at the cost of forcing you to learn a proprietary language.

- Numerous smaller-scale utilities assist with the compilation or some aspects of development (like creating a table of contents), but don't assume you'll use an HTML editor or other tool to write the actual content. An example of a program like this is FAR (www.helpware.net), which is unique in being one of the few third-party tools to support MS Help 2. Another example is the HTML Help to MS Help conversion utility at www.mvps.org/htmlhelpcenter/mshelp2/h2conv.html.

- Developer tools, like the open-source NDoc, allow you to generate impressive Help 2 references based on your source code and a set of XML comments. Visit http:// ndoc.sourceforge.net to download this tool and put it to work.

Basic Help with the HelpProvider

.NET supports several different types of Help. You can use the following:

- Simple strings that appear in pop-up windows

- HTML pages that launch in a stand-alone browser window

- Full-fledged compiled Help files, such as WinHelp (.hlp) or HTML Help (.chm) files, which appear in their own windows

---

■ Note Officially, Microsoft supports MS Help 2 only to provide Help for Visual Studio plug-ins and extensions. There is no support for MS Help 2 in the .NET Framework.

No matter which approach you use, it all works through the HelpProvider component. To begin, you add an instance of the HelpProvider to your form. It will appear in the component tray (Figure 22-5).

Figure 22-5. *The HelpProvider*

The HelpProvider is an extender provider—it works by plugging into other controls and adding additional properties. You first saw extender providers with the ToolTip component in Chapter 4. The HelpProvider gives each control the four properties shown in Table 22-1.

Table 22-1. *HelpProvider Extended Properties*

Property	Description
ShowHelp	Set this to true to bind a control to the HelpProvider. That HelpProvider will listen for the HelpRequested event, which fires when the F1 key is pressed. At this point, it will show the appropriate Help.
HelpString	Use this property if you want a simple Help pop-up (which is somewhat like a tooltip) instead of using a full-fledged Help file. Set this to the text you want to show in the pop-up.
HelpNavigator	Use this property if you're binding to a full-fledged Help file. You choose the part of your Help file that should be shown—the index, search page, table of contents, or a specific topic. Note that the name of the Help file itself isn't set on the control. Instead, it's global to all controls that use this HelpProvider and you set it through the HelpProvider.HelpNamespace property.
HelpKeyword	Used to provide context-sensitive Help with a full-fledged Help file, when HelpNavigator is set to Topic or TopicId. You set a keyword that identifies the topic for this control.

To bind a control to this HelpProvider, you simply need to set its extended ShowHelp property to true. At this point, the HelpProvider begins monitoring the control, and shows some type of Help (depending on how you've configured it) if the user presses the F1 key while this control has focus.

You can also connect or disconnect Help manually in code, using the HelpProvider. SetShowHelp() method. Just pass the control that you want to use as an argument.

```
// This turns on F1 help support for cmdAdd.
hlp.SetShowHelp(cmdAdd, true);

// This disables it.
hlp.SetShowHelp(cmdAdd, false);
```

In the following sections, you'll consider some common scenarios with the HelpProvider.

Simple Pop-Ups

For really simple Help, you don't need to use a Help file at all. Instead, you can display a pop-up window with a short message (formerly referred to as What's This Help). To do so, make sure that you do not set the HelpProvider.HelpNamespace property to anything other than an empty string.

Then, find the control you want to use, and supply the Help text by settings its HelpString property in the Properties window. Alternatively, you can do it programmatically by calling the SetHelpString() method, as shown here:

```
hlp.SetHelpString(cmdAdd, "Choose another item from the catalog.");
hlp.SetHelpString(cmdDelete, "Delete the selected item from your order.");
```

Note that when you set use the SetHelpString() method, you automatically enable Help for the control. That means that you don't need to call the SetShowHelp() method (unless you want to explicitly disable Help for the control).

■Tip If you set the HelpString property at design time (in the Properties window), you can employ Visual Studio's automatic localization support, as described in Chapter 5.

Now, if the user gives focus to this control and presses F1, a pop-up message appears, as shown in Figure 22-6. It remains until the user clicks or presses a key.

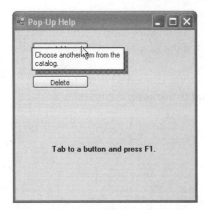

Figure 22-6. *What's This Help*

There are some quirks with this approach:

- The Help text is displayed by the mouse cursor, not the actual control. This can be confusing to the user.

- The Help text can't be formatted in any way (for example, you can't bold command names).

- It forces the user to understand the rather complicated model of changing focus to the correct control and then pressing F1.

In fact, if you're satisfied with simple pop-ups, you can achieve a more satisfying result by implementing it yourself. Just handle the Control.HelpRequested event to respond to the F1 key. The only limitation is that you're stuck hard-coding Help strings unless you store the strings in resources and write your own localization code.

External Web Pages

Some organizations use the same Help online and bundled with their products (or make only slight changes between the two). Rather than creating a dedicated Help file, they distribute a collection of HTML pages, which the client can browse for reference information.

To implement this model, set the HelpProvider.HelpNamespace property with a path that points to the first page on your site:

```
HelpProvider.HelpNamespace = Application.StartupPath + @"/Help/index.html";
```

Make sure the bound control doesn't set the HelpString property. However, it still must set ShowHelp to true.

Now when you give focus to a bound control and press F1, a browser window will open on this page. The only limitation with this approach is that it isn't control-specific. Each control uses the same path, and thereby sends the user to the same page.

For that reason, you probably don't need to waste time wiring up individual controls. Instead, set the ShowHelp property of the form to true. This way, the F1 key always launches the Help page, regardless of which control has focus and whether it has ShowHelp set to true. Later in this chapter, you'll consider different types of granularity for context-sensitive Help.

Compiled Help Files

You can use compiled WinHelp (.hlp) or HTML Help (.chm) files just as easily as you use an external Web site. The only difference is that you need to set the HelpProvider.HelpNamespace property so it points to the appropriate Help file. Each bound control sets ShowHelp to true, and leaves HelpString blank.

Of course, you also need to create the Help file, which is a feat considered later in this chapter. For now, test out this approach with a sample Help file from another product.

The HelpProvider gives you control over what part of your Help file is shown. You determine this using the HelpNavigator property of the linked control. Table 22-2 outlines your options. Note that while all these choices are supported by HTML Help, the support in WinHelp and WinHelp 95 is notoriously poor.

Table 22-2. *Values for the HelpNavigator Enumeration*

HelpNavigator	Description
TableOfContents	Shows the table of contents for the Help file. This is the most common option if you aren't linking to a specific topic.
Index	Shows the index for the Help file, if it exists.
KeywordIndex	Shows the index, and automatically highlights the first topic that matches the HelpKeyword property. For example, if HelpKeyword is "format" for this control, the most similar entry is highlighted in the index list.
AssociateIndex	Shows the index and automatically highlights the index entry for the first letter of the HelpKeyword.
Find	Shows the search page for the Help file, which allows the user to perform unguided text searches. This feature tends to provide poorer (and slower) results than the index or table of contents, and is best avoided if possible.
Topic	Shows the topic page that has the unique topic URL specified by the HelpKeyword property. For example, the HelpKeyword might be "welcome.htm" which instructs the HelpProvider to jump straight to the topic page named Welcome.
TopicId	Similar to Topic, but instead of matching the topic URL, matches a unique number (called the topic identifier).

Both the Topic and TopicID values are used to create context-sensitive Help in conjunction with the HelpKeyword property. You'll see it in action in the next section.

HTML Help with the HelpProvider

As you saw in the previous section, binding Help files to .NET controls is easy thanks to the HelpProvider. However, getting the result you want—a well-integrated Help system—is a little trickier, because it requires some knowledge of Help standards. In this section, you'll walk through creating a basic HTML Help file and using it to add context-sensitive Help to an application.

Creating a Basic HTML Help File

All Help files consist of *topics*. Each topic is a page with Help information that you view separately. In HTML Help (the standard used in this chapter), each topic is analogous to a Web page and can contain arbitrary HTML, pictures, links to other topics, CSS (Cascading Style Sheets) styles, JavaScript (which can be used to great effect), and even ActiveX controls (although this isn't recommended). You can also refer to topics by a unique topic name or numeric ID. This gives you the ability to launch a Help file and position it at a specific topic to give the user information that's relevant to the current window or task. This is the basic tool for incorporating context-sensitive Help.

Essentially, a Help file is nothing more than a collection of topics. However, Help files typi-cally have a few extras, such as a table of contents, index, and full-text search. The index and full-text search, if you choose to use it, is generated for you automatically when you compile your Help. You build the table of contents, and have each link in it lead to a specific topic (although you can have topics that aren't in the table of contents, and can be reached only by clicking a link in another topic).

As explained earlier, sophisticated Help is designed with professional tools (or a collection of shareware and freeware utilities). However, if you're completely new to Help, you can learn a fair bit by creating a basic, barebones Help file and using it in a Windows application. Along the way, you'll learn some of the basic concepts that you need to create Help files in any application.

Before you begin, you can download and install the HTML Help SDK from `http://msdn.microsoft.com/library/en-us/htmlhelp/html/hwMicrosoftHTMLHelpDownloads.asp`. However, because the HTML Help SDK doesn't provide much of an editor, it's easier to prepare your files before you use it.

■Tip For a detailed reference that includes advanced topics with HTML Help SDK, read the PDF tutorials at `www.mvps.org/htmlhelpcenter/htmlhelp/hhtutorials.html`.

You can start by planning your table of contents. In this example, the table of contents includes these topics:

```
Welcome
Introduction
    The Value of Help
    Bad Help
```

The indents represent different levels of hierarchy. In other words, the last two topics are contained inside the Introduction topic. Stand-alone topics are represented as pages, whereas topics that contain subtopics are usually shown as a folder or book (although technically you can customize both of these images). Each of these items is linked to a topic page, including the Introduction topic. Figure 22-7 shows the table of contents as it will appear in the Help window.

Figure 22-7. *A basic table of contents*

Creating the Topic Pages

Now that you've decided what topics to use, choose some reasonable file names. Note that each topic can be created as a stand-alone HTML file using whatever HTML editor you prefer (including FrontPage, Dreamweaver, or just Notepad).

```
Welcome.htm
Introduction.htm
ValueOfHelp.htm
BadHelp.htm
```

All of these files should be placed in the same directory.

In this example, we'll also use a style sheet named stylesheet.css to define the font for the document, the margins for all paragraphs, and a highlighted background for headings:

```
body {
  font-family: Verdana;
  font-size: x-small;
}

p {
  margin-bottom: 8px;
  margin-top: 8px;
}

h1 {
  font-size: medium;
  padding: 10px;
  background-color: lightblue;
}
```

Here's the content for the Welcome.html file:

```
<html>
  <head>
    <title>Welcome</title>
    <link rel="stylesheet" type="text/css" href="stylesheet.css">
  </head>
```

```
<body>
  <h1>Welcome</h1>
  <p>Welcome to the first page of this HTML Help file.</p>
  <p>Click on other topics to browse them, or go straight
  to the <a href="Introduction.htm">introduction</a> page.</p>
</body>
</html>
```

Figure 22-8 shows this page on its own. It includes a link that leads straight to the Introduction.htm file. It's a good idea to add these cross-topic links in addition to the table of contents.

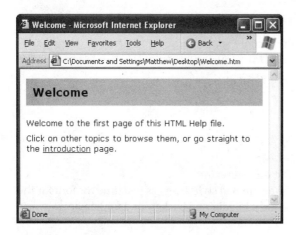

Figure 22-8. *One topic from a Help project (not compiled)*

Creating the HTML Help Project

Once you've completed all these HTML pages, you can add them to an HTML Help project. Follow these steps:

1. Launch the HTML Help Workshop (choose Programs ➤ HTML Help Workshop ➤ HTML Help Workshop from the Windows Start button.

2. Choose File ➤ New.

3. In the New dialog box, select Project and click OK. Click Next to start moving through the project.

4. Choose the location where you want to place your Help project, and add a name for the Help project file onto the end (like HelpTest). Click Next.

5. In the Existing Files list, select HTML files, because you've already created these outside of the HTML Help Workshop. Click Next.

6. Click Add, browse to the Help topic files, and click OK to add them. When you're finished adding all your HTML topic pages (and the style sheet, if you used one), click Next.

7. Click Finish to complete the process and generate your Help project.

You can play around with many options in the HTML Help Workshop. However, the key step you need to perform to get your Help up and running is to add a table of contents, with a topic for each of your pages.

Creating the Table of Contents

To get started with the table of contents, click the Contents tab, choose Create a New Contents File, and click OK. You can give the contents file any name you want.

Now you need to create the topics and organize them appropriately. You can do this using two buttons. Insert a Heading adds a topic that has subtopics, and Insert a Page inserts a topic that doesn't (see Figure 22-9).

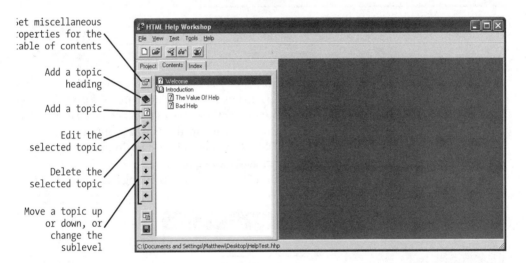

Figure 22-9. *Creating the table of contents*

For example, to create a topic for the Welcome.htm page, click the Insert a Page button. The Table of Contents Entry dialog box (Figure 22-10) appears.

Type in the topic heading (in this case, Welcome) in the Entry Title box. Then click Add and choose the correct page from the list of pages in your project. This list shows the title of each page, as defined in the HTML document. Finally, click OK to insert the topic.

Repeat this started process until you create all the links shown in Figure 22-9. That gives you a complete HTML Help project that's ready for compilation.

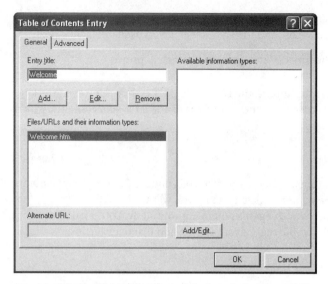

Figure 22-10. *Adding a new table of contents entry*

Compiling the Help File

Once you've started ~~perfected~~ your table of contents, you're ready to move on to the last stage and compile your project into a single HTML Help file. The compilation process isn't anything like the compilation of a programming language. In fact, your pages aren't changed in any way; they're simply compressed and combined into a single binary file using a proprietary standard.

To start the compilation process, select File ➤ Compile and click the Compile button. A log that lists the number of topics, links, and the final file size appears.

To try out your Help, double-click the .chm file. You'll see something like Figure 22-11.

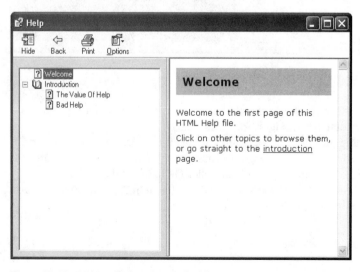

Figure 22-11. *A compiled HTML Help file*

Using Context-Sensitive Help

Now you're ready to use the Help file in a project. Just follow these steps:

1. Right-click on your project and choose Add ➤ Existing Item. Browse to the compiled Help file, and add it to the project. (This step is optional, but it makes it easier to keep track of the file and to make sure it's deployed along with the executable.)

2. Select the .chm file in the Solution Explorer. Using the Properties window, change the Copy to Output Directory setting to Copy Always or Copy If Newer.

3. Add a HelpProvider to your form and set the HelpProvider.HelpNamespace property to the file name of your .chm file (like HelpTest.chm). Don't worry about specifying a fully qualified path, because you'll be placing the .chm file in the same directory as the application executable.

4. Add a control that can receive focus (like a button or text box). Set the HelpNavigator property to Topic and set the HelpKeyword property to the original file name of the topic. For example, in the previous example you could use Introduction.htm, Welcome.htm, BadHelp.htm, and so on.

5. Repeat the previous step with a second control, but use a different HelpKeyword value.

6. Run the application. Switch to one of the controls and press F1. The HTML Help window will appear with the corresponding topic. If you switch back to the application, choose a different control, and press F1 again, the original Help window will return to the foreground with the new topic shown.

This is the preferred way to set up context-sensitive Help, but .NET 2.0 also adds support for the older system of topic numbers. To use these with HTML Help, you need to set up your project accordingly, and specifically map each topic to an ID. You can then use that number in your Windows application—simply set the HelpKeyword property to the number, and set HelpNavigator to TopicId. You can find more information about creating topic numbers at www.mvps.org/htmlhelpcenter/htmlhelp/hhtutorials.html.

Control-Based and Form-Based Help

Control-by-control context sensitivity is usually too much for an application. It's rare that a Help file is created with separate topics for every control in a window, and even if it were, most users simply click F1 as soon as they encounter a confusing setting. In other words, they don't explicitly tab to the setting they want to find out about to give it focus before invoking Help. For that reason, the control that is launching the Help is quite possibly not the control that the user is seeking information about.

One easy way around this is to define an individual context-sensitive Help topic for every form. For a settings dialog, this topic should contain a list of every option. Nicely designed Help might even use dynamic HTML to make this list collapsible (see Figure 22-12).

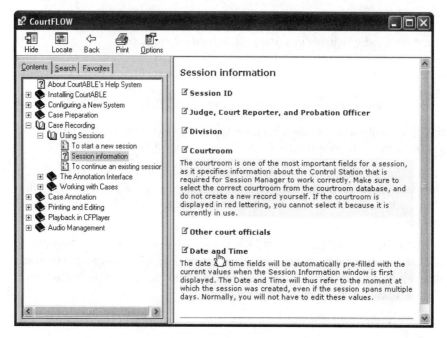

Figure 22-12. *Collapsible Help for one window*

You don't need any proprietary tricks to get this feature—it's all in the HTML you write for the Help topics. To implement the approach shown in Figure 22-12 you simply need a script that finds the corresponding section of the HTML document and tweaks its visibility.

The only subtlety to understand with form-based Help is that when you enable Help for the form, you also enable Help for every control it contains. If the user presses F1 while the focus is on a control that is specifically configured with different Help settings, these settings take precedence. If, however, the current control has ShowHelp set to false, the request will be forwarded to the containing form, which launches its own Help. This process works analogously with all container controls, and it allows you to define Help that's as specific as you need while being able to fall back on a generic form-wide topic for controls that aren't specifically configured.

■**Tip** The online samples for this chapter (in the Source Code area of www.apress.com) include a HelpTest project that shows a simple project with three windows. Each of three windows uses a different granularity of Help: form-based, frame-based, and control-based. You can run this application with the included Help file to get a better understanding of the options you have for linking context-sensitive Help to an application.

Invoking Help Programmatically

The examples so far require the user to press the F1 key. This automated approach doesn't work as well if you want to provide your own buttons that allow the user to trigger Help when needed. Sometimes, that sort of prominent reminder can reassure the user that Help is nearby.

To trigger Help programmatically, you need to use the static ShowHelp() method of the Help class (in the System.Windows.Forms namespace). The Help class works analogously to the HelpProvider—in fact, the HelpProvider uses the Help class behind the scenes when the user presses F1.

There are several overloaded versions of the ShowHelp() method. The simplest requires a Help file name (or URL) and the control that is the parent for the Help dialog (this second parameter is required for low-level Windows operating system reasons). Here's an example that shows the test.hlp file:

```
Help.ShowHelp(this, "test.hlp");
```

Additionally, you can use a version of the ShowHelp() method that requires a HelpNavigator, one that requires a keyword, or one that requires both a keyword and a HelpNavigator. Here's an example that could be used for context-sensitive Help:

```
Help.ShowHelp(this, "test.hlp", HelpNavigator.Topic, "about.htm");
```

To save yourself some work when using this technique with the HelpProvider, you would probably retrieve these values from the HelpProvider. For example, you might provide a button on your form that invokes the default form Help:

```
private void cmdHelp_Click(object sender, System.EventArgs e)
{
    Help.ShowHelp(this, hlp.HelpNamespace, hlp.GetHelpNavigator(this),
      hlp.GetHelpKeyword(this));
}
```

Similarly, you might use a right-click context menu for a control that provides the control's default Help:

```
private void mnuHelp_Click(object sender, System.EventArgs e)
{
    Control ctrl = mnuLabel.SourceControl;
    Help.ShowHelp(ctrl, hlp.HelpNamespace, hlp.GetHelpNavigator(ctrl),
      hlp.GetHelpKeyword(ctrl));
}
```

This menu event handler is written using the SourceControl property, which means it's generic enough to be used with any control. When the menu is clicked, it retrieves the control attached to the context menu, and gets its assigned Help keyword.

Now that you are this far, it's possible to unshackle yourself completely from the HelpProvider class. Just handle the HelpRequested event of any form or control. Then launch the appropriate Help programmatically with the Help class.

Now that you've seen how it can be done, why would you want to do it? You'll examine two of the most common reasons in the next two sections.

Using Database-Based Help

Help files, like any other external resource, change (or need to be localized). You don't want to embed information such as topic URLs all over your user interface, because they are difficult and time-consuming to update. Instead, you can use a basic form event handler that calls a method in a custom AppHelp class. It would look something like this:

```
private void form1_HelpRequested(object sender  HelpEventArgs e)
{
    Global.Help.ShowHelp(this);
}
```

The Global class simply provides the current AppHelp instance through a static Help member:

```
public static class Global
{
    public static AppHelp Help = new Help();
}
```

The AppHelp.ShowHelp() method examines the submitted form, compares it with a list of forms in a database, and thus determines the appropriate context topic, which it launches. Note that for performance reasons, this list of form-topic mappings would be read once when the application starts, and stored in a member variable.

The AppHelp class is shown in the following example. The database code to retrieve the FormHelpMappings table has been omitted.

```
public class AppHelp
{
    public DataTable FormHelpMappings = null;
    public string HelpFile = "";

    public void ShowHelp(Form helpForm)
    {
        foreach (DataRow row in FormHelpMappings.Rows)
        {
            if (helpForm.Name.CompareTo((string)row["FormName"]) == 0)
            {
                // A match was found. Launch the appropriate Help topic.
                Help.ShowHelp(helpForm, HelpFile, HelpNavigator.Topic,
                  row["Topic"].ToString());
                return;
            }
        }
    }
}
```

Using Task-Based Help

Another reason you might take control of the Help process is to get around the limitations of form-based Help. Form-specific Help works well in a dialog-based application, but falters when you create a document-based or workspace-based program where users perform a number of different tasks from the same window. Rather than try to write the code to modify

Help keywords dynamically, you can use the AppHelp class to track the current user's task. When Help is invoked, you can use this information to determine what topic should be shown.

Here's the remodeled AppHelp class. In this case, it doesn't decide what topic to show based on form name, but rather based on one of the preset task types. The logic that links tasks to topics is coded centrally in the AppHelp class (not in the user interface), and it could be moved into a database for even more control. An enumeration is used to ensure that the client code always sets a valid value.

```
public class AppHelp
{
    // These are the types of tasks that have associated Help topics.
    public enum Task
    {
        CreatingReport,
        CreatingReportWithWizard,
        ManagingReportFiles,
        ImportingReport
    }

    private string helpFile;
    public string HelpFile
    {
        get { return helpFile; }
        set { helpFile = value; }
    }

    private Task currentTask;
    public Task CurrentTask
    {
        get { return currentTask; }
        set { currentTask = value; }
    }

    // Show Help based on the current task.
    public void ShowHelp(Form helpForm)
    {
        string topic = "";
        switch (CurrentTask)
        {
            case Task.CreatingReport:
                topic = "Reports.htm";
                break;
            case Task.CreatingReportWithWizard:
                topic = "Wizard.htm";
                break;
            case Task.ManagingReportFiles:
                topic = "Reports.htm";
                break;
```

```
        case Task.ImportingReport:
            topic = "Importing.htm";
            break;
    default:
        return;
    }


    Help.ShowHelp(helpForm, HelpFile, HelpNavigator.Topic, topic);
    }
}
```

Now the code simply needs to "remember" to set the task at the appropriate times.

```
Global.Help.CurrentTask = AppHelp.Task.CreatingReport;
```

When Help is invoked, the form doesn't need to determine what task is underway—the AppHelp class simply uses the most recent task setting.

```
private void form1_HelpRequested(object sender  HelpEventArgs e)
{
    Global.Help.ShowHelp(this);
}
```

This system could be made much more complex by using a task list or tracking multiple different types of context information in the AppHelp class, which is conceptually similar to the way many advanced consumer applications (such as office productivity software) work.

Creating Your Own Help

Another advanced option you might want to pursue is to create your own Help from scratch rather than relying on one of the formats I've described. This technique has significant drawbacks: you surrender advanced features like text searching, a hierarchical table of contents, and an index. However, it also has significant advantages, the most important being that you can easily integrate Help content into your application. With the current HTML Help system, it is almost impossible to embed and control a Help window in your application. MS Help 2 promises some improvements, but the required tools have not yet appeared.

Creating your own Help generally follows two approaches:

- You store Help as long strings in a database record. This generally works best when you are using your custom Help for error messages, a "tip of the day: feature, or some other simple content.

- You store links to an HTML file that is contained in the program directory (or a Help subdirectory). This allows you to easily create files using any HTML design tool, take advantage of linking, and even provide the Help externally (possibly through an Internet browser). Hosting an HTML window in your application is much easier than trying to integrate a Help window. (In fact, you can handle this easily with the WebBrowser control described in Chapter 17.)

These designs allow you to provide a design like the one shown in Figure 22-13. It provides a slide-out window that can give a list of steps with information for the current task. The information itself is retrieved from a database and displayed in the application.

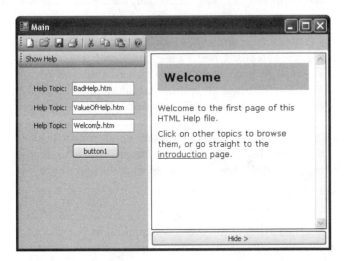

Figure 22-13. *Integrated custom Help*

This .NET example uses a WebBrowser control to display a formatted list of instructions. Thanks to the linking power of HTML, the user can browse to other topics of interest.

Application-Embedded Support

One of the crucial shortcomings with the Help systems you have looked at is that they are all designed to provide fine-grained reference information about specific windows and controls. As I described earlier, Help usually fails miserably when it tries to walk the user through a long, involved task. However, better Help is possible. What's needed is a change to how Help is designed and integrated in applications.

Application-embedded support represents that change. Quite simply, embedded Help is user assistance that is a first-class member of an application. It's designed as part of the software, not added to the software after it's complete. Embedded Help provides far greater user assistance, but also requires far more development work.

Some examples of embedded Help include the following:

- **Process-oriented.** Some applications reserve a portion of their interface for continuous tip messages, or use a tiny information icon that a user can click for more information about the current task. This type of Help trains users as they work, and is used to great effect in fairly complex computer games (like the popular hit *The Sims*). Wizards are another example of process-oriented Help.

- **Stationary embedded.** This is the most common form of embedded Help, and it refers to the content added to dialog boxes to explain options (affordances) and actual embedded Help windows.

- **Agents.** This is one of the most advanced and time-consuming types of embedded Help. It was pioneered largely by Microsoft in Microsoft Office (and later abandoned). Microsoft's attitude toward agents is extremely schizophrenic—it provides tools to make it easy for all developers to use this level of support, but it only occasionally devotes the intense coding time needed to integrate it into its flagship applications.

- **Bidirectional.** To some, this is a holy grail of embedded Help, but it's rarely achieved, and usually only in a primitive form. Essentially, one of the critical drawbacks with Help is that it's cut off from the applications in two ways. Not only does the user have to leave the application to read most Help files, but once the appropriate information is found in the Help file, the user has to perform the actual work. There's no way for the Help file to act on the user's behalf, and actually show the user how to do what is needed. Some Help files do provide rudimentary Show Me links that can prompt the application to display the appropriate window, but this communication is difficult and fragile. With bidirectional Help, Help can perform the necessary task once it determines what the user needs.

Affordances

Affordances are the visual "clues" designed to demystify a complex application. For example, Windows uses brief descriptions to provide a little information about your computer's Internet settings, as shown in Figure 22-14.

Figure 22-14. *A dialog with affordances*

Help and affordances represent a bit of a paradox. Nothing can clarify a confusing dialog box more than a couple of well-placed words or icons. On the other hand, users often ignore descriptions, error messages, or anything else that requires reading. They either try to figure out the task on their own or, in the case of an error, repeat the task a few times and then give up.

Given this problem, what is the role of Help in an application? It's hard to believe that Help is useless, as you can routinely see innovative games and Web sites that have no problem guiding users through new and unusual interfaces with a few carefully integrated explanations. Unfortunately, the customary current stand-alone Help is designed to provide reference information. It's very poor at the task-based explanations that most beginning users require—in fact, it's really little more than a limited electronic book.

Agents

Agents are the animated characters that appear in applications to guide users through a task. The most infamous example of an agent is the (now defunct) Clippy character included with Microsoft Office. Most developers don't consider agents for their applications because of several factors:

- Agents require first-rate design work. An ugly agent is worse than no agent at all.

- Agents require tedious programming. Every action or tip the agent gives must be individually triggered by the application code. If not handled properly, this can lead to Help code that is tangled up with the application's core functionality.

- Agents are "silly," and appeal more for novelty than for any actual assistance they provide.

These are legitimate concerns. However, in a consumer application, an agent can act as an appealing and distinctive feature that attracts the user's attention. Agents also perform the remarkable trick of turning tedium into fun. Quite simply, users often enjoy using programs with agents. (Of course, it helps to know your user. Relatively inexperienced users may enjoy agents while power users might find they slow them down or interfere with their workflow.)

Creating a program with agent support is not as difficult as most developers believe, because Microsoft provides some remarkable tools, and a set of four standard characters that can be freely distributed with your applications. To download the agent libraries, refer to `http://msdn.microsoft.com/library/en-us/msagent/userinterface_3y2a.asp`. The Microsoft Agent Control is available only as a COM component, but it can be easily consumed in a .NET program by creating a runtime-callable wrapper (RCW), a task Visual Studio carries out automatically when you add a reference to a COM component in your project. To use the Microsoft Agent control, right-click the Toolbox and select Choose Items. Then click on the COM Components tab and add a check mark next to Microsoft Agent Control 2.0 (see Figure 22-15), and click OK. This adds the agent control to the Toolbox—you can then drag it onto any form and Visual Studio will automatically create the RCW.

The Microsoft Agent control allows you to use Merlin (a genie), Peedy (a bird), or Robbie (a robot), or all of them at once. All components are complete with rotoscoped animations, can perform various actions as you direct them, can move about the screen, can think or "speak" text (either using a poor voice synthesizer that's included, or a wave file you specify). When speaking with a voice file, the characters' mouths even move to synchronize closely with the words, creating a lifelike illusion. Best of all, Microsoft gives these features away for free. You can purchase other agent characters from third-party sites online, or create them independently, although the tools provided won't help you create lifelike animations.

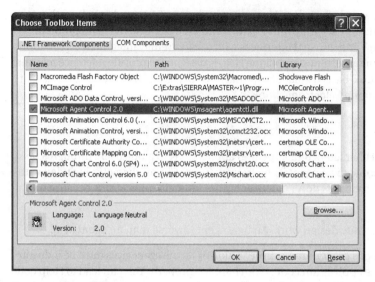

Figure 22-15. *Adding the Microsoft Agent control*

The online samples include an AgentTryout application that allows you to put an agent character through its paces, speaking and thinking the text you specify, moving about the screen, and performing various animations (see Figure 22-16).

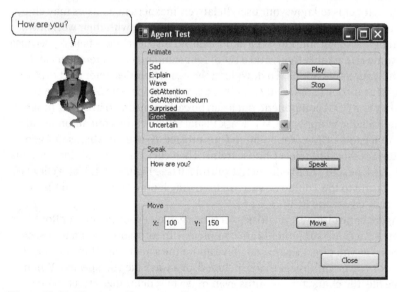

Figure 22-16. *The AgentTryout application*

The AgentTryout application interacts with any of the three agent characters through a special AgentController class, which encapsulates all the functionality for controlling movements, speech, and action. This class code can be reused in any application.

The class AgentController class begins by defining some constants used when setting agent properties:

```
public class AgentController : IDisposable
{
    // Balloon constants
    private const short BalloonOn = 1;
    private const short SizeToText = 2;
    private const short AutoHide = 4;
    private const short AutoPace = 8;
    ...
```

To use the AgentController class, you need to create an instance of the Microsoft Agent control on your form. You then pass that instance to the AgentController class constructor, along with the name of the character you want to show. The constructor loads up the agent character and stores it in a member variable for future use.

```
    ...
    // Name of the initialized character.
    private string characterName;

    // Agent variable.
    private AgentObjects.IAgentCtlCharacterEx agentChar;

    public AgentController(AxAgentObjects.AxAgent agentHost,
     string character)
    {
        agentHost.Characters.Load(character, null);
        agentChar = agentHost.Characters[character];

        characterName = character;

        // You could put your own options in this menu, if desired.
        agentChar.AutoPopupMenu = false;

        // Set balloon style.
        agentChar.Balloon.Style = agentChar.Balloon.Style | BalloonOn;
        agentChar.Balloon.Style = agentChar.Balloon.Style | SizeToText;
        agentChar.Balloon.Style = agentChar.Balloon.Style | AutoHide;
    }
    ...
```

The AgentController wraps all the functionality you will need. Simply call the appropriate method to trigger the corresponding animation. Call Show() to reveal the character; Hide() to make it disappear; and use methods like Speak(), Think(),GestureAt(), and MoveTo() to interact with the user.

```
...
public void Show()
{
    agentChar.Show(null);
}

public void Hide()
{
    agentChar.Hide(null);
}

public void Speak(string text)
{
    agentChar.StopAll(null);
    agentChar.Speak(text, "");
}

public void Think(string text)
{
    agentChar.StopAll(null);
    agentChar.Think(text);
}

public void MoveTo(short x, short y)
{
    agentChar.MoveTo(x, y, null);
}

public void GestureAt(short x, short y)
{
    agentChar.GestureAt(x, y);
}

public void StopAll()
{
    agentChar.StopAll(null);
}
...
```

For more-exotic effects, you can use one of the custom animations that the agent supports. You can retrieve the full list from the GetAnimations() method, and you can trigger an animation by name by calling Animate().

```
...
public List<string> GetAnimations()
{
    List<string> list = new List<string>();
    foreach (string animation in agentChar.AnimationNames)
    {
        list.Add(animation);
    }
    return list;
}

public void Animate(string animation)
{
    agentChar.StopAll(null);
    agentChar.Play(animation);
}
...
```

■Tip Beware of animations that have the word "left" or "right" in them. These refer to the character's left and right, not *your* right and left. For example, if you use the GestureLeft animation, the agent will point to its right.

Finally, the Dispose() method makes sure the agent is properly cleaned up:

```
...
public void Dispose()
{
    if (agentChar.Visible)
    {
        agentChar.StopAll(null);
        agentChar.Hide(null);
    }
}
}
```

To try this out, create a form, add the Microsoft Agent control, and then create an instance of the AgentController. For example, the AgentTryout project uses the following code to create the agent and fill a list control with a list of supported animations:

```
private AgentController controller;

private void Form1_Load(object sender, System.EventArgs e)
{
    // Create the agent.
    controller = new AgentController(axAgent1, "Genie");

    // List the supported animations.
    lstAnimations.DataSource = controller.GetAnimations();

    // Show the agent.
    controller.Show();
}
```

The animation is played with a single line of code in response to a button click:

```
private void cmdPlay_Click(object sender, System.EventArgs e)
{
    controller.Animate(lstAnimations.Text);
}
```

Moving, thinking, and speaking (shown below) are similarly easy:

```
private void cmdSpeak_Click(object sender, System.EventArgs e)
{
    controller.Speak(txtSpeak.Text);
}
```

Even if you don't like the idea of animated characters, it's hard to complain about the agent control. Similar functionality from a third-party developer comes at quite a price.

■**Note** To use the agent control successfully, you need to use the RCW for the ActiveX control (which shows up in the AxInterop.AgentObjects library). In the past, Microsoft has recommended that you use this version only in Web pages and rely instead on the nonvisual COM components in Windows applications (which are exposed through the AgentObjects library). This way you don't need to create an instance of the ActiveX control on each form. However, in a .NET application the AgentObjects library doesn't work successfully on its own, so you *must* use the ActiveX control. Luckily, both the ActiveX control and the COM component provide the same interface to interact with the agent character.

The Last Word

Help strategies and systems vary widely depending on the intended audience and the application design. In this chapter we toured the wide and diverse world of Help programming. None of the solutions examined here can be used in every scenario. Instead, it helps to keep some basic principles in mind:

- A Help file should describe the purpose of various settings, not how to use common controls. No one needs an explanation of how to click a check box. Instead, users need to know why they should.

- The best affordances are descriptive labels, not instructions. No dialog box has the space or formatting power of a printed document.

- The best error is one that doesn't happen. It may take more effort in your code to disable or hide invalid options, but it will prevent dozens of common mistakes in the input fields.

- Help must be context-sensitive. A confused user won't search through a Help file to find a relevant topic—a printed document is better at that.

- Perform usability tests. When writing a program, you design based on who you *believe* the audience is. At some point, you need to bring in some new users and find out what their capabilities really are.

PART 5

Advanced Custom Controls

■ ■ ■

CHAPTER 23

Skinned Forms and Animated Buttons

There's a whole class of Windows applications that don't resemble the examples you've seen so far. They use highly stylized interfaces with shaped windows and animated buttons, and often look more like a Flash-animated Web page or futuristic dashboard than a typical Windows Forms user interface.

However, these interfaces aren't beyond the capabilities of the Windows Forms toolkit. In fact, with a few basic tricks (and more than a dash of artistic resources), you can create your own skinned interfaces. In this chapter, you'll consider a few ingredients that will help you build skinned interfaces:

- Nonrectangular *shaped* forms that contour themselves according to a complex shape or a background image.

- Animated buttons that change their appearance when the user moves the mouse over them or clicks them, similar to a Web rollover button.

- Optimizations you can use to improve rendering speed and reduce memory usage when creating a large number of custom-drawn controls.

These tricks of the trade are enough to get you started creating a truly unique, modern interface.

Shaped Forms and Controls

Irregularly shaped forms are often the trademark of cutting-edge consumer applications like photo editors, movie makers, and MP3 players. In the past, creating them required a bit of API wizardry. With .NET, creating a shaped form is almost effortless, thanks to GDI+.

To create a simple shaped control in .NET, all you need to do is assign a new shape (represented by an instance of the System.Drawing.Region class) to the Control.Region property. There is more than one way to create a Region object, but one of the easiest is by using the GraphicsPath class, which allows you to build a complex shape out of as many sub-shapes as you need (as described in Chapter 7). You can then pass the GraphicsPath to the Region class constructor.

A Simple Shaped Form

The following example code creates a shaped form. It defines an ellipse with the same bounds of the form and adds it to a GraphicsPath. Once the GraphicsPath is assigned to the Region property of the form, only the part of the form that fits inside the ellipse is shown.

```
private void SimpleShapedForm_Load(object sender, System.EventArgs e)
{
    GraphicsPath path = new GraphicsPath();
    path.AddEllipse(0, 0, this.Width, this.Height);
    this.Region = new Region(path);
}
```

Figure 23-1 shows this unusual form, displayed over an ordinary Notepad window so you can see how content underneath is displayed.

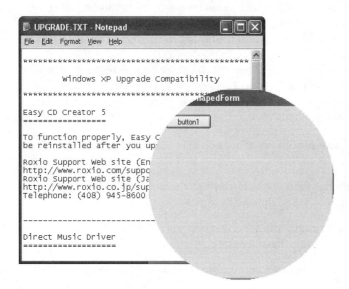

Figure 23-1. *A shaped form*

You can see part of the original window border at the top and bottom of the shaped form, and the single contained button in the middle. However, the form acts completely like an ellipse. For example, if you click in the cutout portion that the original rectangular form occupied (that is, just above the left edge of the ellipse), your click won't activate the form. Instead, you'll activate whatever application is currently underneath the form.

You also can create a shaped form made up of a combination of shapes. In fact, these shapes don't even need to overlap. The following example creates the more unusual shaped form shown in Figure 23-2:

```
private void CompoundShapedForm_Load(object sender, System.EventArgs e)
{
    GraphicsPath path = new GraphicsPath();

    path.AddEllipse(0, 0, this.Width / 2, this.Height / 2);
    path.AddRectangle(new Rectangle(this.Width / 2, this.Height / 4,
        this.Width / 2, this.Height / 4));
    path.AddEllipse(this.Width / 2, this.Height / 2, this.Width / 2,
        this.Height / 2);

    this.Region = new Region(path);
}
```

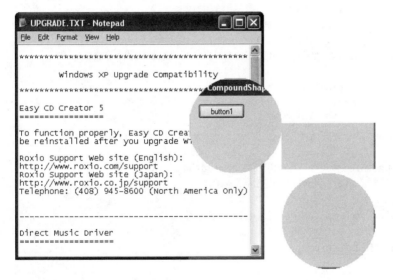

Figure 23-2. *A noncontiguous shaped form*

Creating a Background for Shaped Forms

You'll quickly notice a few problems with shaped forms:

- The Region defines a shape, but this shape does not provide any borders. Instead, a shaped form is just a geometric figure that reveals a portion of the underlying form.

- If you use a curved shape, the edges are somewhat jagged. To smoothen these edges, Windows would need to perform antialiasing between the foreground (the form) and the background (the other applications or the desktop), which it can't do.

- If you cut off the nonclient area of the form (the title bar), the user won't have any way to drag it around the desktop or close it.

- Ordinary controls (like standard windows buttons) aren't well suited for a shaped form—the styles seem to clash.

To handle these problems, you need to create the content for your shaped form from scratch. One approach is to use GDI+ to perform all your drawing. For example, you could revise the earlier example so that it draws the form border.

Begin by setting Form.FormBorderStyle to FormBorderStyle.None, to remove all the nonclient areas (like the title bar), which makes drawing calculations easier. Then, use the same region for drawing that you use to define the shape of the form:

```
public partial class CompoundShapedForm : Form
{
    private GraphicsPath path = new GraphicsPath();

    private void CompoundShapedForm_Load(object sender, EventArgs e)
    {
        path.AddEllipse(0, 0, this.Width / 2, this.Height / 2);
        path.AddRectangle(new Rectangle(this.Width / 2, this.Height / 4,
          this.Width / 2, this.Height / 4));
        path.AddEllipse(this.Width / 2, this.Height / 2, this.Width / 2,
          this.Height / 2);
        this.Region = new Region(path);
    }

    private void CompoundShapedForm_Paint(object sender, PaintEventArgs e)
    {
        e.Graphics.SmoothingMode = SmoothingMode.HighQuality;
        e.Graphics.FillPath(Brushes.LightBlue, path);

        using (Pen pen = new Pen(Color.SlateBlue, 8))
        {
            e.Graphics.DrawPath(pen, path);
        }
    }
}
```

Now the edging of the form is drawn, and the only part that looks out of place is the single ordinary button (see Figure 23-3). Note that all the labels use a BackColor of Color.Transparent so that the blue painted background shows through.

Of course, designing this form in Visual Studio isn't quite as easy, because you won't see the shaped regions at design time. As a result, you may have trouble aligning the content appropriately.

Although this approach works, a more typical approach in a professional application is to design the appropriate images in a dedicated graphics program and import them into your .NET application as embedded resources. For example, you can set the Form.BackgroundImage property to a picture that has the same shape you want to use, and includes a border. Best of all, you'll see the background shape at design time.

Figure 23-4 shows an example with a background graphic. The text and button have been added to the form using controls. The background texture and title section are part of the background image.

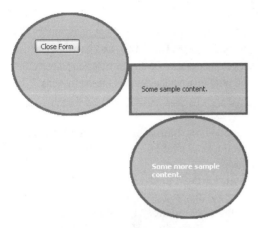

Figure 23-3. *Painting a form border*

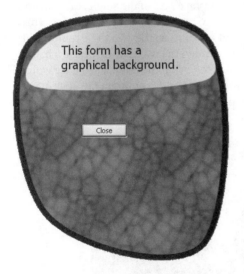

Figure 23-4. *Shaping a form to match a bitmap*

To design the application shown in Figure 23-4, a custom bitmap is assigned to the background, which "skins" the application. However, there's still the problem of getting the form background to match the picture background. You can handle this by constructing a Region object with the same dimensions, but there's actually a far easier approach, which works through the Form.TransparencyKey property.

Here's how it works: You can define a special color for the form that will automatically be cut out by setting the TransparencyKey property. For example, if you choose dark blue, all occurrences of dark blue in your form become invisible. To use this technique with a background image like the one in Figure 23-4, all you need to do is make sure the outside of your picture is filled with a color that is clearly distinguishable from all the colors on the form (often, a near-fluorescent pink is used). Then you can show the picture on the form by setting the Form.BackgroundImage property, and the portion outside the edges will be chopped out automatically.

Note The TransparencyKey property is supported only on Windows 2000 or later. Plus, transparency can fail to work on certain video cards if your color depth is greater than 24-bit, and it can also fail when you use double buffering. As a result, when using TransparencyKey you should also use the Form.Region property. Set the region to be at least an approximation of the shape you want to avoid the worst of these problems.

When designing a background image, you may need to experiment to get the best result. Ideally, you want a clean, shaped border around all edges. To avoid problems, you may want to minimize curves altogether and use mostly straight lines.

When adding the region behind your picture, you also need to make sure that your drawing program doesn't use antialiasing. For example, to create the background picture for the form shown in Figure 23-4, a bright yellow background was used behind the shaped image (Figure 23-5). This yellow color exactly matches the Form.TransparencyKey yellow. However, if the drawing program uses antialiasing to blend the background edges with the yellow color underneath (as most drawing programs do), you'll have a problem. Near the edges of the shape, the drawing program will use other, subtly different shades of yellow to create a softer blended edge. These shades of yellow won't match the Form.TransparencyKey value, so they won't be removed. To avoid this problem, you need to prevent antialiasing between the two shapes, or use a background color that's similar enough to the image border color that the antialiased edge won't stand out. To get a really professional look, you may need to hand-smoothen the edge of your shape before you apply the background. Artistic techniques like this could improve the edging you see in Figure 23-4.

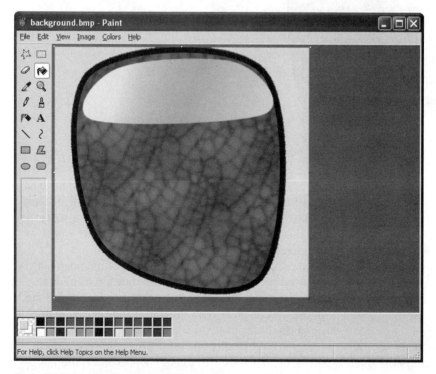

Figure 23-5. *The background picture*

There's one other side effect of the TransparencyKey property that you might not appreciate immediately. When you set a transparent color, *all* occurrences of that color are affected. This includes occurrences of the color in an image, a control, or even the form's background.

For example, Figure 23-6 shows an example that contains several picture box controls, each of which has the TransparencyKey color as its background. At runtime, these picture boxes disappear. Using this technique, you can create imaginative effects, like removing any portion of a form.

Figure 23-6. *A form (with the desktop showing through)*

Moving Shaped Forms

As you've seen, one limitation of shaped forms is that they usually omit the nonclient title bar portion, which allows the user to easily drag the form around the desktop. There are several ways to remedy this problem. You could react to mouse events like MouseDown, MouseUp, and MouseMove, and move the form manually when the user clicks and drags (as demonstrated in Chapter 4). However, there's an even easier approach if you're willing to step outside of the .NET Framework by overriding the WndProc() method of the form.

The WndProc() method fires every time the form receives a Windows message. The trick is to override this method and check for the WM_NCHITTEST message. This WM_NCHITTEST message is sent when the mouse is moved over your form, at which point you are supposed to tell Windows which part of the form the mouse is positioned above. This message is used by Windows to determine what shape it should give the cursor (such as the diagonal arrow when on the resizable bottom-right area). But more interestingly, you can return the code corresponding to the caption area, to instruct Windows to treat clicks on the client area in the same way as caption clicks—in other words, the user can click and drag anywhere on the form to move it. You could add additional tests if you want to make only part of the window draggable in this way, but that's entirely up to you.

The code you need isn't obvious, but it's quite short:

```
protected override void WndProc(ref Message m)
{
    // Allow the base class to handle all messages first.
    base.WndProc(ref m);
```

```
    // Look for the WM_NCHITTEST message.
    int WM_NCHITTEST = 0x84;
    if (m.Msg == WM_NCHITTEST)
    {
        // Treat this click as a click on the caption.
        int HTCLIENT = 1;
        int HTCAPTION = 2;
        if (m.Result.ToInt32() == HTCLIENT)
          m.Result = (IntPtr)HTCAPTION;
    }
}
```

Now the user can click anywhere on the form and drag it around. However, the WndProc() method isn't called when you move over other controls, because they provide their own WndProc() implementation to handle this message. (Of course, workarounds are possible. For example, you could create a custom control that overrides WndProc() and returns a value of HTTRANS-PARENT. This allows the form to receive the click.)

Shaped Controls

You don't need to stop at shaped forms. You can apply similar techniques to create irregularly shaped controls. Most controls will let the background of the parent show through if you set a transparent BackColor. More powerfully, you can use the Control.Region property, which works the same as the Form.Region property, to assign a nonrectangular region to a form. Control mouse handling and control painting is performed only in the control's region. You'll see an example of irregularly shaped controls with the vector-based drawing application in Chapter 24.

Controls don't provide a TransparencyKey property, although they are affected by the TransparencyKey of the form. If a control has any of the transparent color, this region of the control is made completely transparent—both the control *and* the underlying form become invisible.

■**Tip** For more examples of shaped controls, check out the curved panel in the RegionMaster control sample provided by Microsoft at `http://windowsforms.net/articles/` `usingregionmastercontrols.aspx`.

Animated Buttons

One problem that remains with shaped and skinned forms is that many of the ordinary Windows controls (like buttons) look out of place on a rich, graphical background. The easiest solution to this problem is to build owner-drawn controls. In this section, you'll take a look at how you can build animated buttons.

Basic Animated Buttons

When building an animated buttons, there are two chief goals. First, you want to create a distinct, modern look with hand-tooled graphics. Second, you want to use some sort of visual effect to alert the user when the mouse is over the button. This allows the user to spot buttons more easily, even though they don't have the standard Windows look. It also gives the application a more dynamic feel. Commonly used visual effects include the following:

- Adding a raised border when the mouse is over the button.

- Highlighting button text, outlines, or a small glyph (like a bullet).

- Enlarging the button picture.

- Making the button "bounce" (grow and shrink in rapid succession until the user moves the mouse off the button).

Based on this discussion, a couple of points should be immediately clear. First, developers are likely to create a wide range of custom controls to implement different effects. Second, all of these buttons use the same basic pattern of interaction (they change their appearance in response to a mouse-over). Thus, to simplify your life, you can start designing a custom button by creating a base class that implements this pattern. You can then derive from that base class to create specific types of animated buttons. This is a worthwhile design, because button controls require a considerable amount of boilerplate for managing focus, state, click events, and so on.

A Base Class for Animated Buttons

To create any button control class, it makes most sense to derive directly from Control, because you need to implement all the drawing on your own.

```
public abstract class AnimatedButtonBase : Control
{ ... }
```

The AnimatedButtonBase control is declared as an abstract class, which means it can't be instantiated directly. Although this design is conceptually good, it does mean you'll receive a design-time warning if you try to switch to design view while creating a class that derives from AnimatedButtonBase. (The specific problem is that the designer can't create abstract classes, as discussed in Chapter 11 with visual inheritance.) If this bothers you, you can choose to implement AnimatedButtonBase as a normal class, but add the ToolboxItem attribute to hide it so it won't appear in the Visual Studio toolbox.

In the following sections, you'll see how to build each piece of the AnimatedButtonBase class.

The IButtonControl Interface

All buttons should implement the IButtonControl interface, which allows other programs to recognize them as being inherently button-like. By implementing IButtonControl, your button control gains the following features:

- Other classes can programmatically trigger a button click in your control.

- Your control can be used as a default button for a form (if you set the Form.AcceptButton or Form.CancelButton properties).

- Your control can be used to close a modal form and return a value from the DialogResult enumeration.

The most important part of the IButtonControl interface is the PerformClick() method. Other classes can call this method to trigger a click programmatically. This is the basic requirement for all the features described previously. For example, if you want your button to be an AcceptButton for a form, the form simply needs a way to trigger a click when the Enter key is pressed. It does this by calling IButtonControl.PerformClick(). Additionally, the IButtonControl interface requires a DialogResult property that stores the result associated with your button (like OK, Cancel, and so on), and a NotifyDefault() method that alerts your control that it has become the default button, in which case it can adjust its rendering if desired.

Here's the definition of the AnimatedButtonBase class, with the members that are required to implement IButtonControl

```
public abstract class AnimatedButtonBase : Control, IButtonControl
{
    public void PerformClick()
    {
        OnClick(EventArgs.Empty);
    }

    private DialogResult dialogResult;
    public DialogResult DialogResult
    {
        get { return dialogResult; }
        set { dialogResult = value; }
    }

    public void NotifyDefault(bool value)
    {
        // Fires when the button is made into a default.
        // You could set properties to adjust the rendering,
        // but that's not necessary.
        OnNotifyDefault(value);
    }

    public virtual void OnNotifyDefault(bool value)
    {
        // This method can be overriden in derived classes
        // if they wish to apply rendering customizations.
    }
}
```

Button States

The AnimatedButtonBase distinguishes among four states. An ordinary button appears in Normal state. MouseOver state occurs when the mouse is moved over the button, and Pushed occurs when the button is clicked (the mouse button is currently pressed down). Additionally, the button can be placed into a Disabled state, at which point it is essentially inactive and does not respond to user actions.

```
public enum States
{
    Normal,
    MouseOver,
    Pushed,
    Disabled
}
```

Clearly, the whole idea of the AnimatedButtonBase control is that it changes its rendering when it moves from one state to another. However, it's possible that the button might be repeatedly placed into the same state. This may occur in the design environment or if some code is reapplying a default. In this case, a refresh should not be triggered.

To facilitate this pattern, the AnimatedButtonBase has a State property. When this property is set, it checks it the value has changed, and triggers a refresh if it has. All the other code in the AnimatedButtonBase control must then work through the State property to ensure that this automatic refresh happens appropriately.

```
// Begin in normal state.
private States state = States.Normal;

// This property procedure ensures the control is
// invalidated only when the state changes.
private States State
{
    get { return state; }
    set
    {
        if (state != value)
        {
            state = value;
            Invalidate();
        }
    }
}
```

You can bridge the gap between the Enabled property and the Disabled state like this:

```
protected override void OnEnabledChanged(EventArgs e)
{
    if (!Enabled)
    {
        State = States.Disabled;
    }
    else if (Enabled && State == States.Disabled)
    {
        State = States.Normal;
    }
    base.OnEnabledChanged(e);
}
```

It also makes sense to trigger a refresh when other details change that affect the button display. Currently, the AnimatedButtonBase control uses this technique only when the button text is changed.

```
public override string Text
{
    get { return base.Text; }
    set
    {
        if (value != base.Text)
        {
            base.Text = value;
            Invalidate();
        }
    }
}
```

Mouse Movements

To update the state of the button, the AnimatedButtonBase needs to handle several mouse events. You do this by overriding the OnMouseMove() and OnMouseLeave() methods.

However, before implementing either of those methods, it's important to create one additional ingredient—the HitTest() method. The HitTest() method allows you to create buttons that include clickable button content and nonclickable content on the same surface. Essentially, the HitTest() method returns true if the mouse cursor is positioned over a clickable area. In the simple implementation of AnimatedButtonBase, the entire control region is treated as clickable, and so HitTest() always returns true. However, derived controls can override this method to implement their own logic.

```
// If you want to make only a portion of the button
// clickable, this is the method to override.
protected virtual bool HitTest(int X, int Y)
{
    return true;
}
```

Now, when the OnMouseMove() method is triggered, you need to call HitTest() to determine whether the mouse is over a clickable area. If so, the state is changed to MouseOver; if not, the state is set to Normal. If the button has been placed in a disabled state, this logic is bypassed altogether.

```
protected override void OnMouseMove(System.Windows.Forms.MouseEventArgs e)
{
    base.OnMouseMove(e);

    // Do nothing if the button is disabled.
    if (State == States.Disabled) return;

    if (HitTest(e.X, e.Y))
    {
        if (State != States.Pushed) State = States.MouseOver;
    }
    else
    {
        State = States.Normal;
    }
}
```

Remember, as long as you change the state through the State property, you ensure a refresh is performed only if necessary.

Similar logic is used when the mouse leaves the control altogether. However, there's no longer a need to call HitTest() on the control, because it's obvious the mouse pointer is no longer over a clickable region.

```
protected override void OnMouseLeave(System.EventArgs e)
{
    if (State != States.Disabled) State = States.Normal;
}
```

Finally, the OnMouseDown() and OnMouseUp() events change the state to Pushed and back to MouseOver:

```
protected override void OnMouseDown(System.Windows.Forms.MouseEventArgs e)
{
    // Do nothing if the button is disabled.
    if (State == States.Disabled) return;

    if (HitTest(e.X, e.Y))
    {
        if ((e.Button & MouseButtons.Left) == MouseButtons.Left)
        {
            State = States.Pushed;
            Focus();
        }
    }
}
```

```
protected override void OnMouseUp(System.Windows.Forms.MouseEventArgs e)
{
    // Do nothing if the button is disabled.
    if (State == States.Disabled) return;

    if ((e.Button & MouseButtons.Left) == MouseButtons.Left)
    {
        if (HitTest(e.X, e.Y))
        {
            State = States.MouseOver;
        }
        else
        {
            State = States.Normal;
        }
    }
}
```

The last detail is to make sure the clicks are propagated into Click events only if they are on a clickable area. Unfortunately, the mouse coordinates aren't available in the EventArgs parameter, but you can check the current state of the button to determine whether it's changed to Pushed in OnMouseDown to indicate a valid click.

```
protected override void OnClick(System.EventArgs e)
{
    if (State == States.Pushed)
    {
        base.OnClick(e);
    }
}
```

Painting

Now that you have the infrastructure in place for changing the state at the right moment and refreshing the control as needed, the painting logic is quite straightforward. However, the AnimatedButtonBase class isn't intended to perform the painting on its own. Instead, this task is handled by the deriving class, which knows best what effect to apply in the MouseOver and Pushed states.

To make this design clear, the OnPaint() method actually triggers several other methods to perform the painting work, depending on the state of the button. For example, if the button is disabled, it calls PaintDisabled(). Here's the full code:

```
protected override void OnPaint(System.Windows.Forms.PaintEventArgs e)
{
    switch (State)
    {
        case States.Normal:
            PaintNormal(e.Graphics);
            break;
```

```
        case States.MouseOver:
            PaintMouseOver(e.Graphics);
            break;
        case States.Pushed:
            PaintPushed(e.Graphics);
            break;
        case States.Disabled:
            PaintDisabled(e.Graphics);
            break;
    }
    if (this.Focused && State != States.Disabled) PaintFocusRectangle(e.Graphics);
}
```

The trick is that each of these methods is abstract, so the deriving class is forced to implement them appropriately. The painting methods receive the Graphics object, which they use to render their output.

```
protected abstract void PaintNormal(Graphics g);
protected abstract void PaintMouseOver(Graphics g);
protected abstract void PaintPushed(Graphics g);
protected abstract void PaintDisabled(Graphics g);
```

Focus

The final step of the OnPaint() drawing method is to call a method named PaintFocusRectangle(), provided the button is focused and not disabled. At this point, the focus cue is drawn around the borders of the control, provided the PaintFocusCue property is true. (If it's false, the PaintFocusRectangle() method isn't called at all.)

```
private bool paintFocusCue = true;
public bool PaintFocusCue
{
    get { return paintFocusCue; }
    set
    {
        if (value != paintFocusCue)
        {
            paintFocusCue = value;
            Invalidate();
        }
    }
}

protected virtual void PaintFocusRectangle(Graphics g)
{
    ControlPaint.DrawFocusRectangle(g, this.ClientRectangle);
}
```

Notice that the PaintFocusRectangle() is marked virtual, which means the deriving class can override it with a different implementation if the ordinary dotted square isn't enough.

Finally, the control needs to listen for focus events and update itself accordingly:

```
protected override void OnGotFocus(EventArgs e)
{
    if (paintFocusCue) Invalidate();
}

protected override void OnLostFocus(EventArgs e)
{
    if (paintFocusCue) Invalidate();
}
```

These methods simply trigger a refresh of the complete button, but in most cases you could create a Graphics object for the control using Control.CreateGraphics(), and then call PaintFocusRectangle() to add this detail on top of the current drawing.

This completes all the code you need to build the AnimatedButtonBase. In the next sections, you'll see how easy it is to build on this model to design your own animated buttons. You'll see three examples:

- A simple button that glows when it's highlighted.

- A more advanced button that includes a clickable picture region, which becomes raised when the mouse moves over it.

- A rollover button that swaps pictures when the mouse hovers over it.

A Simple Glow Button

The first example you'll see demonstrates how easy it is to extend the AnimatedButtonBase class. The SimpleGlowButton creates a couple of drawing objects in its constructor, and simply overrides the four paint methods to paint a button with a different background color.

Here's the complete code:

```
public class SimpleGlowButton : AnimatedButtonBase
{
    private Pen penOutline;
    private StringFormat textFormat;

    public SimpleGlowButton()
    {
        // In a more sophisticated details, these hard-coded
        // details would be mapped to properties.
        penOutline = new Pen(Color.Black, 2);
        penOutline.Alignment = PenAlignment.Inset;

        textFormat = new StringFormat();
        textFormat.Alignment = StringAlignment.Center;
        textFormat.LineAlignment = StringAlignment.Center;
    }
```

```
protected override void PaintNormal(Graphics g)
{
    g.FillRectangle(Brushes.LightGray, ClientRectangle);
    g.DrawRectangle(penOutline, ClientRectangle);
    g.DrawString(Text, Font, Brushes.Black, ClientRectangle, textFormat);
}

protected override void PaintMouseOver(Graphics g)
{
    g.FillRectangle(Brushes.LimeGreen, ClientRectangle);
    g.DrawRectangle(penOutline, ClientRectangle);
    g.DrawString(Text, Font, Brushes.White, ClientRectangle, textFormat);
}

protected override void PaintPushed(Graphics g)
{
    g.FillRectangle(Brushes.Lime, ClientRectangle);
    g.DrawRectangle(penOutline, ClientRectangle);
    g.DrawString(Text, Font, Brushes.White, ClientRectangle, textFormat);
}

protected override void PaintDisabled(Graphics g)
{
    g.FillRectangle(Brushes.LightSlateGray, ClientRectangle);
    g.DrawRectangle(penOutline, ClientRectangle);
    g.DrawString(Text, Font, Brushes.White, ClientRectangle, textFormat);
}
}
```

Figure 23-7 shows the result.

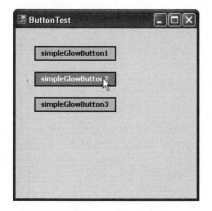

Figure 23-7. *The SimpleGlowButton*

A Raised Image Button

The next example is a little more interesting, because it overrides the HitTest() method to create a button where only a portion is clickable. This portion is an image icon that is displayed just to the left of the text. When the mouse is positioned over the image, the image appears with a raised border (see Figure 23-8).

Figure 23-8. *The PopImageButton*

This control project raises some unique, subtle challenges:

- The clickable portion of the button should include only the image. Thus, the control needs to use hit testing when a click is detected, and suppress click events if the text portion is clicked.

- The button must be able to deal with any valid image size.

When designing this control, you need to add an Image property to store the picture it will display. Here's the first part of the code for the PopImageButton:

```
public class PopImageButton : AnimatedButtonBase
{
    private Image image;
    private Rectangle bounds;

    public Image Image
    {
        get { return image; }
        set
        {
            image = value;
            if (image != null)
            {
                bounds = new Rectangle(0, 0, image.Width + 5, image.Height + 5);
            }
```

```
        Invalidate();
    }
}
...
```

Notice that a private member variable called bounds is used to track the drawing area of the control. This rectangle is slightly larger than the image itself because it needs to accommodate the focus rectangle.

The HitTest() method uses the bounds to test the placement of the mouse cursor:

```
...
protected override bool HitTest(int X, int Y)
{
    // Check if the mouse pointer is over the button.
    if (image == null)
        return false;
    else
        return bounds.Contains(X, Y);
}
...
```

The drawing code uses the same paint methods you saw earlier. It uses a raised three-dimensional border when the mouse is positioned over the button, and a sunken border when it is clicked, which is similar to the image bar style used in Microsoft Outlook. The text is placed to the right of the picture, and is vertically centered with the midpoint of the image by measuring the image and font sizes.

```
...
protected override void PaintNormal(Graphics g)
{
    if (image != null) g.DrawImage(image, 2, 2);
    PaintText(g);
}

protected override void PaintMouseOver(Graphics g)
{
    if (image != null)
    {
        ControlPaint.DrawBorder3D(g, bounds,
            Border3DStyle.Raised, Border3DSide.All);
        g.DrawImage(image, 2, 2);
    }
    PaintText(g);
}
```

```
protected override void PaintPushed(Graphics g)
{
    if (image != null)
    {
        ControlPaint.DrawBorder3D(g, bounds,
            Border3DStyle.Sunken, Border3DSide.All);
        g.DrawImage(image, 3, 3);
    }
    PaintText(g);
}

protected override void PaintDisabled(Graphics g)
{
    if (image != null)
    {
        ControlPaint.DrawImageDisabled(g, image, 2, 2,
            BackColor);
    }
    PaintText(g);
}
...
```

The drawing logic benefits from the ControlPaint class, which provides the DrawBorder3D()
and the DrawImageDisabled() methods. This class was described in Chapter 7.

Additionally, a private PaintText() method draws the text, because it's rendered the same
for all states:

```
...
private void PaintText(Graphics g)
{
    // If there is no image, center the text (vertically) between
    // the borders of the control.
    // If there is an image, center the text to the midline of the image.
    int y = 0;
    if (image == null)
        y = Height;
    else
        y = bounds.Height;

    SolidBrush brush = new SolidBrush(ForeColor);
    g.DrawString(Text, Font,
      brush, bounds.Width + 3, (y - Font.Height) / 2);
    brush.Dispose();
}
}
```

There's clearly a lot more you could add to this button control. For example, you could allow the user to change the orientation, place the text under the image, add support for text wrapping, or even create a compound control that contains a collection of images.

Rollover Button

The last button control you'll consider here is an all-purpose rollover button. With the rollover button, very little work is performed with GDI+. Instead, button images for all the four states are prepared in a separate program, and imported into the application as resources. These images are then assigned to the control, which switches between them seamlessly.

To implement the rollover button, you need to begin by defining the image properties. To save space, the following code shows only the image property for the initial, normal-state image. (The other image properties are almost identical.)

```
public class RolloverButton : AnimatedButtonBase
{
    private Image normalImage;
    private Image mouseOverImage;
    private Image pushedImage;
    private Image disabledImage;

    public Image NormalImage
    {
        get { return normalImage; }
        set
        {
            normalImage = value;
            // Just perform this tweak the first time the image is set
            // at design time.
            if (normalImage != null && DesignMode)
            {
                Size = new Size(
                    normalImage.Size.Width + 10, normalImage.Size.Height + 2);
            }
            Invalidate();
        }
    }
}
...
```

One interesting detail is that the button automatically adjusts its size when you set the NormalImage property, which saves the hassle of resizing each button in the design environment. You also may want to set the background to transparent, so that any region that extends beyond the dimensions of the button picture shows the form background.

Now, all the RolloverButton needs to do is to copy its images to the drawing surface in the appropriate paint methods. Here's an example that draws the normal state image:

```
...
protected override void PaintNormal(Graphics g)
{
    if (normalImage != null)
        g.DrawImageUnscaled(normalImage, new Point(0,0));
}
...
```

However, a good rollover button doesn't force you to supply every picture. Instead, it's clever enough to substitute one picture for another if needed, or possibly even create a selected or disabled image by manipulating the color of the normal image. The RolloverButton is relatively simple in this regard—it paints disabled images using the ControlPaint class if no disabled image is supplied, tries to substitute the mouse-over image if the pressed image is missing, and so on.

```
...
protected override void PaintMouseOver(Graphics g)
{
    if (mouseOverImage != null)
    {
        g.DrawImageUnscaled(mouseOverImage, new Point(0,0));
    }
    else if (normalImage != null)
    {
        // If there is no mouse-over image, fall back on the
        // normal image (if it exists).
        g.DrawImageUnscaled(normalImage, new Point(0,0));
    }
}

protected override void PaintPushed(Graphics g)
{
    // Try pushed, mouse-over, and normal images, in
    // that order of preference.
    if (pushedImage != null)
    {
        g.DrawImageUnscaled(pushedImage, new Point(0,0));
    }
    else if (mouseOverImage != null)
    {
        g.DrawImageUnscaled(mouseOverImage, new Point(0,0));
    }
    else if (normalImage != null)
    {
        g.DrawImageUnscaled(normalImage, new Point(0,0));
    }
}
```

```
protected override void PaintDisabled(Graphics g)
{
    if (disabledImage != null)
    {
        g.DrawImageUnscaled(disabledImage, new Point(0,0));
    }
    else
    {
        if (normalImage != null)
        {
            // Fake a disabled image.
            // Serveral techniques are possible, but this is the easiest.
            ControlPaint.DrawImageDisabled(g, normalImage, 0, 0, BackColor);
        }
    }
}
```

Figure 23-9 shows a skinned form with several rollover buttons.

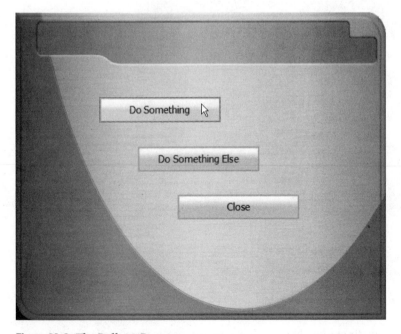

Figure 23-9. *The RolloverButton*

■Note To see some more examples of controls with images, check out the Visual Basic Power Pack, which has its own image button control (http://msdn.microsoft.com/vbasic/default.aspx?pull=/library/en-us/dv_vstechart/html/vbpowerpack.asp) and the **RegionMaster** controls http://windowsforms.net/articles/usingregionmastercontrols.aspx), which use a timer to make a moused-over button "bounce" repeatedly.

Transparency

Currently, the PopImageButton (like all Control-derived classes) doesn't support transparency. If you're using ordinary forms, you won't notice the problem. That's because the default implementation on Control.OnPaintBackground() fills the background color of the form behind your custom control. However, if you place your control on a form that uses a background image, and size your control so that its bounds are larger than its content, you'll see the incorrect background (see Figure 23-10).

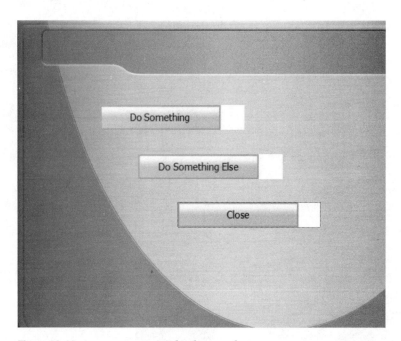

Figure 23-10. *A nontransparent background*

This is an unnecessary limitation. In fact, it's useful to have the form background show through behind the text if you want to combine your button with the skinned form techniques shown earlier. Fortunately, it's not hard to make a transparent control.

The key step is to use the Control.SetStyle() method to specifically indicate that your control supports a BackgroundColor value of Color.Transparent. Without this step, you'll receive an exception if you attempt to set a transparent background color. In this example, the support for transparency is implemented in the AnimatedButtonBase class, from which RolloverButton derives:

```
public AnimatedButtonBase()
{
    SetStyle(ControlStyles.SupportsTransparentBackColor, true);
}
```

Next, you need to set the BackColor of your control to Color.Transparent. It's that easy! Now the OnPaintBackground() method will copy the form's background image, so that all your button painting is performed on top of that surface.

Improving the Performance of Owner-Drawn Controls

The simple controls developed in this chapter work by drawing their content on the fly. In many cases, this approach is completely acceptable. However, in some situations, it can slow down the responsiveness of your application's user interface.

Problems are most likely to occur when you have a large number of controls that render themselves with complex painting logic. For example, if your buttons incorporate gradients, multiple images, alpha blending, and other effects, refreshes may perform sluggishly. Although there are no hard and fast rules, refreshes are typically considered to take an unreasonable amount of time if they include a delay that's noticeable to the user.

■**Note** Unfortunately, double buffering can't solve this problem. First of all, double buffering is implemented on a class-specific basis. This means you can buffer the painting in a form's OnPaint() method or a single control's OnPaint() method, but you can't put several controls into the same buffer. Another problem is that double buffering simply reduces flicker, it doesn't improve refresh speed. If your drawing is time consuming, it could take an unreasonable amount of time to redraw on-screen elements.

Caching Images

One solution to this problem is to implement caching in your control. The basic idea is for your control to create in-memory buffers of the different button states. Then, when a button changes from one state to another, you simply need to copy the buffer to the control surface (rather than rerender it from scratch). This approach increases memory usage, but reduces redraw times.

In the examples shown earlier, the AnimatedButtonBase class is an ideal place to implement the caching logic, because then any derived class can take advantage of it. Classes like the RolloverButton, which simply write out images that are embedded in the assembly as resources, probably don't benefit from caching. Complex gel buttons that are rendered dynamically quite possibly will benefit.

The first step to implement caching is to create a property that allows you to switch caching on or off:

```
private bool cacheImages = true;
public bool CacheImages
{
    get { return cacheImages; }
    set { cacheImages = value; }
}
```

> **Note** In the implementation you'll see in this example, the CacheImages property only has an effect if set *before* other properties. You could use ISupportInitialize to ensure that this is the case, but in this example it's not needed because the CacheImages property is serialized before the other image properties (because Visual Studio serializes properties in alphabetical order by default).

The cached images are stored in several private member variables:

```
private Image normalImage;
private Image mouseOverImage;
private Image pushedImage;
private Image disabledImage;
```

Additionally, a FlushCache() method is included so that cached images can be removed when other properties change:

```
protected void FlushCache()
{
    normalImage = null;
    mouseOverImage = null;
    pushedImage = null;
    disabledImage = null;
}
```

For example, you should use this when the text is modified:

```
public override string Text
{
    get { return base.Text; }
    set
    {
        if (value != base.Text)
        {
            base.Text = value;
            FlushCache();
            Invalidate();
        }
    }
}
```

To complete this example, you'd probably want to override other properties (or react to their change events), so that the cache is cleared when other details that affect the images are modified, like text font, foreground and background colors, and so on.

The painting logic is where the caching logic actually takes place. Essentially, the painting code needs to check the state of the button first. Then, it needs to look for the matching image. If it doesn't exist, it's time to call the derived class implementation of the painting method, and store the result. If the image does exist, it can be simply copied to the design surface.

The most compact way to encapsulate this behavior is to create a generic method that performs this task. This method requires three details—a reference to the cached image, a reference to the method that renders the image, and a reference to the final drawing surface where the image should be painted.

Here's the code:

```
private delegate void ClientPaintMethod(Graphics g);

private void CreateAndPaintCachedImage(Image image,
  ClientPaintMethod paintMethod, Graphics g)
{
    // Check if the image needs to be created.
    if (image == null)
    {
        // Create the in-memory buffer.
        image = new Bitmap(Width, Height);
        Graphics bufferedGraphics = Graphics.FromImage(image);

        // Call the derive painting method, but pass in a Graphics object
        // that refers to the in-memory bitmap, not the actual control surface.
        paintMethod(bufferedGraphics);

        // Release the drawing surface (but keep the Bitmap object).
        bufferedGraphics.Dispose();
    }
    // Copy the buffer to the real drawing surface.
    g.DrawImageUnscaled(image, new Point(0, 0));
}
```

With this building block, you can revise the OnPaint() method to take advantage of caching:

```
protected override void OnPaint(System.Windows.Forms.PaintEventArgs e)
{
    if (!cacheImages)
    { ... }
    else
    {
```

```
            switch (State)
            {
                case States.Normal:
                    CreateAndPaintCachedImage(normalImage,
                       new ClientPaintMethod(PaintNormal), e.Graphics);
                    break;
                case States.MouseOver:
                    CreateAndPaintCachedImage(mouseOverImage,
                       new ClientPaintMethod(PaintMouseOver), e.Graphics);
                    break;
                case States.Pushed:
                    CreateAndPaintCachedImage(pushedImage,
                       new ClientPaintMethod(PaintPushed), e.Graphics);
                    break;
                case States.Disabled:
                    CreateAndPaintCachedImage(disabledImage,
                       new ClientPaintMethod(PaintDisabled), e.Graphics);
                    break;
            }
            // Always paint the focus rectangle last, because this is
            // independent of the current button state.
            if (this.Focused) PaintFocusRectangle(e.Graphics);
        }
}
```

The best part of this example is the fact that the derived classes you created earlier continue to work. They can choose whether or not to opt into the caching model.

Reusing Images

Before you implement the caching approach, you need to give some thought to the additional overhead incurred by tying up extra memory with the Bitmap. You might want to store a cached copy only if the panel isn't extremely large, at which point the caching benefit won't be worth the memory overhead.

Tip Another option is to use the System.WeakReference class to wrap the bitmap, which allows the bitmap to be garbage-collected if system resources become scarce. It's fairly easy to wrap another object with a WeakReference instance—just pass the object as an argument in the constructor. You can retrieve or set the wrapped object at any time through the WeakReference.Target property, but before you try to access it check WeakReference.IsAlive to make sure it wasn't garbage-collected because of memory pressure,

---

If you are creating an application that has dozens of identical buttons, you may be able to use a different technique to cut down on the memory usage. For example, if you have relatively large OK and Cancel buttons that you use on forms throughout your application, it makes little sense to cache each instance of the button separately. Instead, you should cache one copy in memory, and use it for every button. There are several possibilities for implementing this design. All of them rely on static members.

First of all, you should start with a class that encapsulates the details you want to cache, as shown here:

```
public class AnimatedButtonCachedImages
{
    private Image normalImage;
    private Image mouseOverImage;
    private Image pushedImage;
    private Image disabledImage;

    // (Public properties omitted.)
}
```

Then you could create a class that caches a group of these objects. Here's how you could keep a collection of AnimatedButtonCachedImages, indexed by name and available to your entire application:

```
public static Dictionary<string, AnimatedButtonCachedImages> CachedImages;
```

Now you can add a StyleName property to the AnimatedButtonBase class, and rewrite the code in CreateAndPaintCachedImage(). Before rendering a button, the control can check if an AnimatedButtonCachedImages object with the same style name exists in the static cache. If it does, it can be reused—if not, you can create the images, and then cache them in the collection for future use.

Of course, it's possible to get much fancier. Rather than simply create a class that caches the images, why not create a class that encapsulates all the style-related details? You could then apply a style to an instance of your control by setting the style name, and define your styles using another tool (or by writing code). This approach of factoring out style details to ensure good performance for more objects is used in other .NET controls. For example, the DataGrid-View uses a style model that shares style objects wherever possible, thereby avoiding the need to create a separate style object for each cell that shares the same formatting. Implementing a design like this is a fair bit of work (and can be prone to minor errors), but will ensure good performance if you plan many instances of an owner-drawn control in a large application.

The Last Word

In this chapter, you learned how to design one of the most practical types of owner-drawn controls—buttons. You also learned how you can place these customized buttons on a shaped form, thereby giving your application a modern facelift.

Now that you understand the basic model, there's much more you can do with a little creativity, a dash of artistic insight, and a generous helping of GDI+ drawing code. The best inspiration is to check out what other developers have designed. Community sites like www.windows.net and www.gotdotnet.com are filled with examples you can explore.

■ ■ ■

CHAPTER 24

Dynamic Drawing with a Design Surface

Drawing programs exist in two basic flavors. The first type is painting programs, like Microsoft Paint, which allow users to create bitmaps with static content. In these programs, once the user draws a shape or types some text onto the drawing area, it can't be modified or rearranged. But in more-sophisticated *vector-based* drawing programs (everything from Adobe Illustrator to Microsoft Visio), the user's drawing is actually a collection of objects. The user can click and change any object at any time or remove it entirely.

It's relatively easy to create a bitmap-based drawing program once you learn GDI+. However, a vector-based drawing or diagramming program can be a little more complex, because you need to keep track of every object and its location individually. When the user clicks on the drawing surface, you may need to use some fairly intricate logic to find out which object the user is trying to select, and handle the overlapping painting.

You might use two approaches to tackle this problem:

- **Use child controls for each drawing element.** This is the simplest approach to solve the problem, but it isn't flexible enough for a professional drawing application.

- **Draw and track each element manually.** This approach gives you the greatest flexibility and power, but it will force you to step up with a fair bit of extra code.

In this chapter, you'll learn how create an application that lets you draw, configure, and move shapes around a form surface using both techniques. This application is a great starting point if you need to build some sort of dynamic drawing or diagramming tool, and it's a good example of owner-drawn controls and GDI+ drawing.

A Drawing Program with Controls

The basic application (shown in Figure 24-1) allows the user to create rectangles, ellipses, or triangles of any color, and then resize them or drag them around the form to a new location. Rather than coding all the logic to manage the hit testing, selection, and layering, you can make use of a convenient shortcut by turning each shape into a custom control. Because each control has its own built-in smarts for handling user interaction like mouse clicks and key presses, this approach simplifies your life considerably.

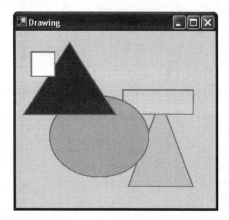

Figure 24-1. *A vector-based drawing application*

The basic concept in this application is to let the shapes draw themselves. Essentially, each shape is an owner-drawn control that paints its surface. The support for dragging, resizing, and changing shape colors is built into the form code, but it's not terribly difficult to implement. Really, all the form needs to do is react to the user's mouse actions, and set properties like Location and Size accordingly. It's easy to react to an event when a specific shape is clicked, because the shape controls inherit all the basic mouse notification events from the Control class.

Using this application, you could easily add more shape types and enhance the drawing functionality with additional features. You'll see some of these enhancements in the revised, non–control-based version of this application.

The Shape Control

The drawing program works by dynamically creating an instance of a custom Shape control. It supports rectangles, circles, and triangles, but it could easily support any arbitrary or unusual shape.

Before you consider the Shape control, you need to understand one possible problem. If the user draws a circle, you want the circle shape to act like a circle for all mouse operations. In other words, the user shouldn't be able to click on a part of the control outside the circle and use that to move the control. Similarly, this "invisible" portion of the control shouldn't over-write other controls on the drawing surface.

Figure 24-2 shows a drawing program with shapes that doesn't take this into account.

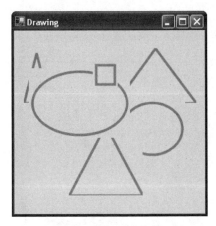

Figure 24-2. *A flawed drawing program*

Luckily, .NET makes it easy to create a control that has a nonrectangular bounding area. (In fact, you saw this technique in Chapter 23 with irregularly shaped forms.) All that's required is to set the Control.Region property, which defines a new clipping region. Note that this does have a minor side effect: The control cannot be as effectively antialiased (or blended with the background). As a result, the border appears more jagged.

Overall, the Shape control needs to have the following key features:

- It provides a ShapeType enumeration that defines the shapes it can represent. The programmer chooses a shape by setting the Shape property. (Another option would be to create a separate class for each shape type. However, in this example the shape drawing is quite simple, so encapsulating it in a single class is still practical.)

- The Shape control uses a private path member variable that references a GraphicsPath object with the associated shape. Whenever the Shape property is modified, the control creates a new GraphicsPath, and adds the appropriate shape to it. It then sets the control's Region property, effectively setting its clipping bounds to match the shape.

- The painting logic is the easiest part. It simply uses the FillPath() method to draw the shape, and the DrawPath() method to outline it.

Here's the complete Shape class code:

```
public class Shape : System.Windows.Forms.Control
{
    // The types of shapes supported by this control.
    public enum ShapeType
    {
        Rectangle, Ellipse, Triangle
    }
}
```

```
// The current shape.
private ShapeType shape = ShapeType.Rectangle;
private GraphicsPath path = null;
public ShapeType Type
{
    get { return shape; }
    set
    {
        shape = value;
        RefreshPath();
        this.Invalidate();
    }
}

// Create the corresponding GraphicsPath for the shape, and apply
// it to the control by setting the Region property.
private void RefreshPath()
{
    if (path != null) path.Dispose();
    path = new GraphicsPath();
    switch (shape)
    {
        case ShapeType.Rectangle:
            path.AddRectangle(this.ClientRectangle);
            break;
        case ShapeType.Ellipse:
            path.AddEllipse(this.ClientRectangle);
            break;
        case ShapeType.Triangle:
            Point pt1 = new Point(this.Width / 2, 0);
            Point pt2 = new Point(0, this.Height);
            Point pt3 = new Point(this.Width, this.Height);
            path.AddPolygon(new Point[] {pt1, pt2, pt3});
            break;
    }
    this.Region = new Region(path);
}

protected override void OnPaint(System.Windows.Forms.PaintEventArgs e)
{
    base.OnPaint(e);
    if (path != null)
    {
        SolidBrush shapeBrush = new SolidBrush(this.BackColor);
        Pen shapePen = new Pen(this.ForeColor, 5);
```

```
            e.Graphics.SmoothingMode = SmoothingMode.AntiAlias;
            e.Graphics.FillPath(shapeBrush, path);
            e.Graphics.DrawPath(shapePen, path);

            shapePen.Dispose();
            shapeBrush.Dispose();
        }
    }

    protected override void OnResize(System.EventArgs e)
    {
        base.OnResize(e);
        RefreshPath();
        this.Invalidate();
    }
}
```

As you can see, there's no need to code properties like BackColor, ForeColor, Location, or Size because these members are all built into the base Control class. The code emphasizes that it's using built-in members by using the this keyword (as in this.BackColor rather than just BackColor).

■**Tip** To avoid re-creating the brushes and pens each time the shape is drawn, you could create the brush and pen once, and store them in member variables. You would then need to check to make sure the color hasn't changed before you reuse the pen and brush (or react to the ForeColorChanged and BackColorChanged events).

The Drawing Surface

The drawing application begins with an empty canvas. To create a shape, the user right-clicks the form drawing area, and chooses one of the three menu options. These menu options (New Rectangle, New Ellipse, and New Triangle) are represented by three menu items (mnuRectangle, mnuEllipse, and mnuTriangle). However, the click event for each of these objects triggers the same event handler, which just sets the ShapeType property accordingly.

```
private void mnuNewShape_Click(object sender, System.EventArgs e)
{
    // Create and configure the shape with some defaults.
    Shape newShape = new Shape();
    newShape.Size = new Size(40, 40);
    newShape.ForeColor = Color.Coral;
```

```
    // Configure the appropriate shape depending on the menu option selected.
    if (sender == mnuRectangle)
    {
        newShape.Type = Shape.ShapeType.Rectangle;
    }
    else if (sender == mnuEllipse)
    {
        newShape.Type = Shape.ShapeType.Ellipse;
    }
    else if (sender == mnuTriangle)
    {
        newShape.Type = Shape.ShapeType.Triangle;
    }

    // To determine where to place the shape, you need to convert the
    // current screen-based mouse coordinates into relative form coordinates.
    newShape.Location = this.PointToClient(Control.MousePosition);

    // Attach a context menu to the shape.
    newShape.ContextMenuStrip = mnuSelectShape;

    // Connect the shape to all its event handlers.
    newShape.MouseDown += new MouseEventHandler(ctrl_MouseDown);
    newShape.MouseMove += new MouseEventHandler(ctrl_MouseMove);
    newShape.MouseUp += new MouseEventHandler(ctrl_MouseUp);

    // Add the shape to the form.
    this.Controls.Add(newShape);
}
```

Once this code runs, the shape appears (with the default size) at the current mouse location.

There are three things the user can do with a shape once it is created:

- Click and drag it to a new location.

- Click its bottom-right corner and resize it.

- Right-click to show its context menu, which provides an option for changing the color or deleting the object.

All these actions happen in response to the MouseDown event. At this point, the code retrieves a reference that points to the control that fired the event, and then examines whether the right mouse button was clicked (in which case the menu is shown). If the left mouse button has been clicked, the form switches into resize or drag mode (using one of two Boolean form-level variables), depending on the location of the cursor. Resizing can be performed only from the bottom-right corner, the bottom side, and the right side.

```
// Keep track of when drag or resize mode is enabled.
private bool isDragging = false;
private bool isResizing = false;

// Store the location where the user clicked on the control.
private int clickOffsetX, clickOffsetY;

private void ctrl_MouseDown(object sender,
 System.Windows.Forms.MouseEventArgs e)
{
    // Retrieve a reference to the active label.
    Control currentCtrl;
    currentCtrl = (Control)sender;

    if (e.Button == MouseButtons.Right)
    {
        // Show the context menu.
        mnuForm.Show(currentCtrl, new Point(e.X, e.Y));
    }
    else if (e.Button == MouseButtons.Left)
    {
        clickOffsetX = e.X;
        clickOffsetY = e.Y;

        if (currentCtrl.Cursor == Cursors.SizeNWSE ||
          currentCtrl.Cursor == Cursors.SizeNS ||
          currentCtrl.Cursor == Cursors.SizeWE)
        {
            // The mouse pointer is at one of the sides,
            // so resizing mode is appropriate.
            isResizing = true;
        }
        else
        {
            // The mouse is somewhere else, so dragging mode is
            // appropriate.
            isDragging = true;
        }
    }
}
```

The MouseMove event changes the position or size of the shape if it is in drag or resize mode. It also changes the cursor to the resize icon to alert the user when the mouse pointer is aligned on one of the sides of the shape.

```
private void ctrl_MouseMove(object sender, System.Windows.Forms.MouseEventArgs e)
{
    // Retrieve a reference to the active shape.
    Control currentCtrl;
    currentCtrl = (Control)sender;

    if (isDragging)
    {
        // Move the control.
        currentCtrl.Left = e.X + currentCtrl.Left - clickOffsetX;
        currentCtrl.Top = e.Y + currentCtrl.Top - clickOffsetY;
    }
    else if (isResizing)
    {
        // Resize the control, according to the resize mode.
        if (currentCtrl.Cursor == Cursors.SizeNWSE)
        {
            currentCtrl.Width = e.X;
            currentCtrl.Height = e.Y;
        }
        else if (currentCtrl.Cursor == Cursors.SizeNS)
        {
            currentCtrl.Height = e.Y;
        }
        else if (currentCtrl.Cursor == Cursors.SizeWE)
        {
            currentCtrl.Width = e.X;
        }
    }
    else
    {
        // Change the cursor if the mouse pointer is on one of the right
        // and lower edges of the control.
        if (((e.X + 5) > currentCtrl.Width) &&
            ((e.Y + 5) > currentCtrl.Height))
        {
            currentCtrl.Cursor = Cursors.SizeNWSE;
        }
        else if ((e.X + 5) > currentCtrl.Width)
        {
            currentCtrl.Cursor = Cursors.SizeWE;
        }
```

```
        else if ((e.Y + 5) > currentCtrl.Height)
        {
            currentCtrl.Cursor = Cursors.SizeNS;
        }
        else
        {
            // This misleadingly named cursor is the four-way
            // mouse pointer often used for moving objects.
            currentCtrl.Cursor = Cursors.SizeAll;
        }
    }
}
```

Figure 24-3 shows the process of resizing a shape.

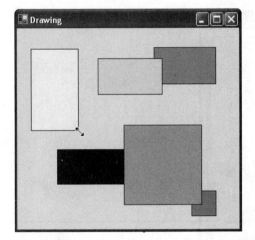

Figure 24-3. *Resizing a shape*

The MouseUp event ends the dragging or resizing operation.

```
private void ctrl_MouseUp(object sender, System.Windows.Forms.MouseEventArgs e)
{
    isDragging = false;
    isResizing = false;
}
```

Finally, the context menu provides two options. The first, when clicked, allows the user to change the shape's fill color using a common color dialog box. Note that the code retrieves the active control through the SourceControl property of the ContextMenuStrip, as shown here:

```
private void mnuColorChange_Click(object sender, System.EventArgs e)
{
    // Show color dialog.
    ColorDialog dlgColor = new ColorDialog();
    if (dlgColor.ShowDialog() == DialogResult.OK)
    {
        // Change shape background.
        Control ctrl = (Control)sender;
        mnuSelectShape.SourceControl.BackColor = dlgColor.Color;
    }
}
```

Figure 24-4 shows how a shape's background color can be modified using this color dialog box.

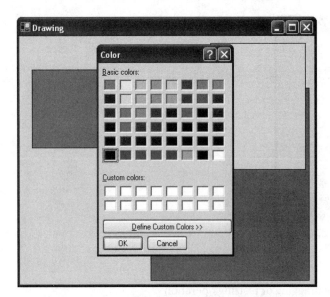

Figure 24-4. *Changing a shape's background color*

The second option allows the user to remove the currently selected shape:

```
private void mnuRemoveShape_Click(object sender, System.EventArgs e)
{
    Control ctrlShape = mnuSelectShape.SourceControl;
    this.Controls.Remove(ctrlShape);
}
```

You could add a number of additional frills to this simple application. For example, you could extent the Shape control to support drawing-contained text or a custom border. You could also use methods like Control.BringToFront() and Control.SendToBack() to allow shapes be layered in various ways, according to the user's selections ((demonstrated with the download-able code for this chapter).. You could even use different controls. Currently, all the event handlers assume they are dealing with generic control events, and thus work with buttons, text boxes, picture boxes, and just about any other control, whether it is owner-drawn or not.

A Drawing Program with Shape Objects

Although the first drawing program was refreshingly easy to create, if you extend it you'll eventually run into a few inherent limitations. Some of the problems include the following:

- **Rendering quality.** Unfortunately, .NET doesn't deal all that well with overlapped controls. The edges are never as smooth as they are with the overlapped elements of a single image drawn through GDI+.

- **Focus cues.** If you want to support shape manipulation, you probably want to highlight the currently selected object with some sort of dotted outline or sizing grips. Unfortunately, there's no easy way to add these details. You can't make it a part of the shape, because it extends beyond the bounds of the clipping region. (For example, even an ellipse should have a large square focus cue around it.) If you draw it through the form, all the other shapes will appear on top of it, because child controls are always drawn after the form content you render in the OnPaint() method. (The online code for the previous example uses one such naive implementation of focus cues.)

- **Advanced features.** Plan to add a feature that allows the user to group multiple shapes into one? Or how about one that lets you skew and rotate the image to your heart's content, or save a completed drawing? All of these techniques are easier to implement when you paint the whole image by hand.

An alternate approach to the control-based solution is to use GDI+ to draw the shapes by hand, and track them in a collection. You then need to rely on hit testing for shape selection and manipulation, which can become a little messy. However, this approach ultimately gives you much more flexibility. You'll now see this technique developed to create the richer drawing program shown in Figure 24-5.

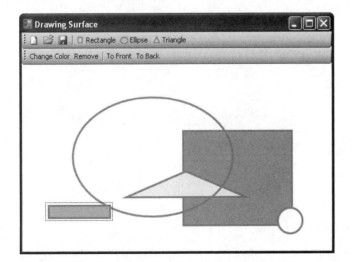

Figure 24-5. *A more advanced drawing program*

■**Note** One change you'll notice right away in the revised application is the smoother drawing that results from the improved antialiasing that happens when you draw the complete image with GDI+.

The Shape Class

The new Shape class borrows from the Shape control in the previous example. However, it's now rendered painstakingly from scratch. Additionally, the Shape is an abstract class, from which other types of shapes derive.

```
public abstract class Shape
{ ... }
```

Because the Shape class draws itself from scratch and doesn't derive from Control, properties like ForeColor, BackColor, Location, and Size need to be added by hand:

```
private Color foreColor;
public Color ForeColor
{
    get { return foreColor; }
    set { foreColor = value; }
}

private Color backColor;
public Color BackColor
{
    get { return backColor; }
    set { backColor = value; }
}

private Size size;
public Size Size
{
    get { return size; }
    set
    {
        size = value;
        path = null;
    }
}

private Point location;
public Point Location
{
    get { return location; }
```

```
    set
    {
        location = value;
        path = null;
    }
}
```

Notice that the Location and Size properties, when set, clear the current GraphicsPath that represents the shape. The same lazy creation pattern is used when setting the shape type. The GraphicsPath for the shape is no longer regenerated every time a property is modified. Instead, it's created when needed—which is whenever a piece of code requests the Path property.

```
// Even internally, all access to the path should
// go through the Path property, so that the path
// is regenerated if null.
private GraphicsPath path = null;
public GraphicsPath Path
{
    get
    {
        // The path is refreshed automatically
        // as needed.
        if (path == null)
        {
            RefreshPath();
        }
        return path;
    }
}
```

The RefreshPath() method doesn't actually perform any work. It delegates the task to the deriving class, through an abstract GeneratePath() method:

```
// Create the corresponding GraphicsPath for the shape.
private void RefreshPath()
{
    path = GeneratePath();
}
protected abstract GraphicsPath GeneratePath();
```

One of the major new features in the Shape class is the ability to draw a focus rectangle. To keep track of when this is needed, each shape has a Selected property:

```
private bool selected;
public bool Selected
{
    get { return selected; }
    set { selected = value; }
}
```

The Derived Shape Classes

The derived shape classes (RectangleShape, EllipseShape, and TriangleShape) require very little code, because all the hit-testing smarts and drawing logic are encapsulated by the base Shape class. In fact, the only code they contain is the GeneratePath() method that identifies the control region.

Here's the code for all three shape classes:

```
public class RectangleShape : Shape
{
    protected override GraphicsPath GeneratePath()
    {
        GraphicsPath path = new GraphicsPath();
        path.AddRectangle(new Rectangle(
          Location.X, Location.Y, Size.Width, Size.Height));
        return path;
    }
}

public class EllipseShape : Shape
{
    protected override GraphicsPath GeneratePath()
    {
        GraphicsPath path = new GraphicsPath();
        path.AddEllipse(Location.X, Location.Y, Size.Width, Size.Height);
        return path;
    }
}

public class TriangleShape : Shape
{
    protected override GraphicsPath GeneratePath()
    {
        GraphicsPath path = new GraphicsPath();
        Point pt1 = new Point(Location.X + Size.Width / 2, Location.Y);
        Point pt2 = new Point(Location.X, Location.Y + Size.Height);
        Point pt3 = new Point(Location.X + Size.Width, Location.Y + Size.Height);
        path.AddPolygon(new Point[] { pt1, pt2, pt3 });
        return path;
    }
}
```

The code for calculating the path is quite similar to the drawing code used with the control-based example you considered earlier. However, the coordinates change. Because the shape is passed a reference to the entire drawing surface, it needs to take its location into account when creating the region. (Otherwise, the shape will always appear at the top-left corner of the drawing.) The calculations with the Shape control (shown earlier) are slightly easier because the coordinates that the Shape control sees are always relative to its current position.

Tip In some cases, taking the location into account may result in excessively complex calculations. In this case, you can use a coordinate transformation to move the origin to the top-left corner of the shape. Transformations are discussed in Chapter 7.

The Drawing Code

Although the Shape class can't paint itself directly, it still makes sense to centralize the painting logic inside the Shape class. In this case, the containing form can ask the shape to paint itself by calling Render() and passing in a suitable drawing surface (represented by the Graphics object). Note that the drawing logic doesn't set the rendering quality, because it's the form that takes control of these details.

```
// These details could be wrapped in properties
// to provide more customization for line thickness
// and border patterns.
private int penThickness = 5;
private int focusBorderSpace = 5;
Pen outlinePen;

public void Render(Graphics g)
{
    if (outlinePen != null) outlinePen.Dispose();
    outlinePen = new Pen(foreColor, penThickness);
    Brush surfaceBrush = new SolidBrush(backColor);

    // Paint the shape.
    g.FillPath(surfaceBrush, Path);
    g.DrawPath(outlinePen, Path);

    // If required, paint the focus box.
    if (Selected)
    {
        Rectangle rect = Rectangle.Round(Path.GetBounds());
        rect.Inflate(new Size(focusBorderSpace, focusBorderSpace));
        ControlPaint.DrawFocusRectangle(g, rect);
    }
    surfaceBrush.Dispose();
}
```

There's one unusual detail here. The outline pen isn't disposed at the end of the drawing routine, because you need it to perform property hit testing (namely, you need the thickness and edge settings of the pen to distinguish between clicks on the surface and clicks on the outline). However, the code does dispose of the current pen at the beginning of the drawing code, before it creates a new one.

Hit Testing

To be self-sufficient, the shape now needs the ability to hit-test arbitrary points, and see if they fall inside the bounds of the path. There are three types of hit test you might want to perform:

- Checking if a point falls inside the shape.

- Checking if a point falls on the edge of a shape. In the sample project we're building right now, this is treated the same as clicking inside the shape.

- Checking if a point falls on the focus cue (dotted rectangle) drawn around a shape. This is relevant only if the shape is currently selected.

In this application, the first two actions are used to select or drag a shape. The third action (selecting the focus square) is employed when the user wants to resize the shape.

The code for hit-testing points in the shape and border is easy, thanks to the IsVisible() and IsOutlineVisible() methods of the GraphicsPath:

```
// Check if the point is in the shape.
public virtual bool HitTest(Point point)
{
    return Path.IsVisible(point);
}

// Check if the point is in the outline of the shape.
public virtual bool HitTestBorder(Point point)
{
    return Path.IsOutlineVisible(point, outlinePen);
}
```

Notice that both these methods are virtual, so the derived shape class can override them if necessary.

■**Note** Handling clicks that fall on the edge of the shape are particularly important if the shape has a thick border. Otherwise, these clicks will be ignored.

Hit-testing the focus border is much more work. The problem is that the routine needs to distinguish where the hit occurred. Here's an enumeration that represents the different possibilities:

```
public enum HitSpot
{
    Top, Bottom, Left, Right,
    TopLeftCorner, BottomLeftCorner,
    TopRightCorner, BottomRightCorner,
    None
}
```

You can perform a simple test for the focus border by hit-testing two rectangles—the outer rectangle (where the focus border is drawn) and the inner rectangle (where the control is drawn). If the point falls inside the outer rectangle but not inside the inner rectangle, the focus border was hit. The Rectangle.Contains() method makes this approach easy:

```
public bool HitTestFocusBorder(Point point, out HitSpot hitSpot)
{
    hitSpot = HitSpot.None;

    // Ignore controls that don't have a focus square.
    if (!selected)
    {
        return false;
    }
    else
    {
        Rectangle rectInner = Rectangle.Round(Path.GetBounds());
        Rectangle rectOuter = rectInner;
        rectOuter.Inflate(new Size(focusBorderSpace, focusBorderSpace));
        if (rectOuter.Contains(point) && !rectInner.Contains(point))
        {
            // Point is on (or close enough) to the focus square.
        }
        else
        {
            return false;
        }
        ...
```

Unfortunately, the Rectangle.Contains() method can't give you any information about where the hit occurred. To get these details, you need to go to the extra work of comparing the space between the clicked point and the appropriate edge. You need to perform *all* these tests for every point, in case it's close to two edges, in which case it's interpreted as a corner hit.

Here's the complete code:

```
    ...
    bool top = false;
    bool bottom = false;
    bool left = false;
    bool right = false;

    // Check the point against all edges.
    if (Math.Abs(point.X - location.X) < focusBorderSpace)
        left = true;
    if (Math.Abs(point.X - (location.X + size.Width)) < focusBorderSpace)
        right = true;
    if (Math.Abs(point.Y - location.Y) < focusBorderSpace)
        top = true;
```

```
        if (Math.Abs(point.Y - (location.Y + size.Height)) < focusBorderSpace)
          bottom = true;

        // Determine the hit spot based on the edges that are close.
        if (top && left) hitSpot = HitSpot.TopLeftCorner;
        else if (top && right) hitSpot = HitSpot.TopRightCorner;
        else if (bottom && left) hitSpot = HitSpot.BottomLeftCorner;
        else if (bottom && right) hitSpot = HitSpot.BottomRightCorner;
        else if (top) hitSpot = HitSpot.Top;
        else if (bottom) hitSpot = HitSpot.Bottom;
        else if (left) hitSpot = HitSpot.Left;
        else if (right) hitSpot = HitSpot.Right;

        if (hitSpot == HitSpot.None)
        {
            return false;
        }
        else
        {
            return true;
        }
    }
}
```

There's one more method related to hit testing in the Shape class—the GetLargestPossibleRegion() method. This method returns a Region object that represents the maximum space that the shape can occupy, which occurs when the focus rectangle is drawn. The code for making this calculation is the same as the code to determine the size of the focus rectangle when the shape is rendered:

```
public virtual Rectangle GetLargestPossibleRegion()
{
    Rectangle rect = Rectangle.Round(Path.GetBounds());
    rect.Inflate(new Size(focusBorderSpace, focusBorderSpace));
    return rect;
}
```

The GetLargestPossibleRegion() method is useful when refreshing the form. When the user is interacting with a single shape, the form code can invalidate just that portion of the window, ensuring a speedy refresh.

Z-Order

Controls have built-in support for layering. You can use methods like BringToFront() and SendToBack() to change how controls overlap, and you can use the ControlCollection. SetChildIndex() and ControlCollection.GetChildIndex() to explicitly change the z-index.

■**Tip** Remember, the z-index is a number that represents the layer on which a control is placed. (Each control is on a separate layer.) A control with a smaller z-index is superimposed on a control with a larger z-index when they overlap. See Chapter 2 for more information about z-index.

You need to explicitly build this functionality into the Shape class. The first step is to define a property that stores the numeric z-index value:

```
private int zOrder;
public int ZOrder
{
    get { return zOrder; }
    set { zOrder = value; }
}
```

As with controls, the actual reordering is performed by the container, because it involves comparing the z-index of each item. In this case, it's the ShapeCollection class (described in the next section) that plays this role. To make the sorting process even easier, the Shape class implements the IComparable interface:

```
public abstract class Shape : IComparable
{ ... }
```

Now the Shape class needs to implement the CompareTo() method, which compares two shape objects and determines which one should occur "first," which is important when hit-testing and drawing multiple shapes. The goal in this example is to make sure the shapes with the highest z-index occur first in the list.

When implementing CompareTo(), you can return one of three values—0 to indicate two values are equal, -1 to indicate that the current instance is less than the instance supplied through the parameter, and 1 to indicate that the object supplied through the parameter is larger than the current instance. However, to make the code even shorter, you can implement it by invoking the CompareTo() method of the ZOrder property, because a basic implementation of CompareTo() is built into all integers. Here's the code to implement this behavior:

```
public int CompareTo(object shape)
{
    return ZOrder.CompareTo(((Shape)shape).ZOrder);
}
```

None of the code you've seen so far actually calls the CompareTo() method. To fill in that detail, you need to build the ShapeCollection class that holds shape objects.

The Shape Collection

You could use the generic List<Type> class to create a collection for storing shapes without needing to create a new class. However, in this case creating a custom collection class makes sense because it gives you a good place to put code that works on groups of shapes (like hit-testing and reordering).

There are several options for creating the custom shape collection. You could derive from List<Shape> to add your logic to the strongly typed List<Type> class, or you could derive from CollectionBase, which wraps an ArrayList and exposes it through your own strongly typed methods. The following example uses the ArrayList approach.

```
public class ShapeCollection : CollectionBase
{ ... }
```

The actual collection is stored internally as an ArrayList, but you need to add the strongly typed Add() and Remove() methods. When these methods are called, you access the internal ArrayList through one of two properties: List (which provides access to the collection through the IList interface) or InnerList (which provides the full ArrayList).

Here are the strongly typed Remove() method and collection indexer:

```
public void Remove(Shape shapeToRemove)
{
    List.Remove(shapeToRemove);
}

public Shape this[int index]
{
    get { return (Shape)this.List[index]; }
}
```

The Add() method is a little more interesting. It has the additional responsibility of making sure the new item has the lowest z-index so that it appears on top of all other shapes.

```
public void Add(Shape shapeToAdd)
{
    // Reorder the shapes so the new shape is on top.
    foreach (Shape shape in List)
    {
        shape.ZOrder++;
    }
    shapeToAdd.ZOrder = 0;
    List.Add(shapeToAdd);
}
```

The ShapeCollection class also provides BringShapeToFront() and SendShapeToBack() methods that allow the z-order of a shape to be changed relative to the rest of the collection:

```
public void BringShapeToFront(Shape frontShape)
{
    foreach (Shape shape in List)
    {
        shape.ZOrder++;
    }
    frontShape.ZOrder = 0;
}
```

```
public void SendShapeToBack(Shape backShape)
{
    int maxZOrder = 0;
    foreach (Shape shape in List)
    {
        if (shape.ZOrder > maxZOrder) maxZOrder = shape.ZOrder;
    }
    maxZOrder++;
    backShape.ZOrder = maxZOrder;
}
```

But the most useful method of the ShapeCollection is HitTest(), which loops through all the shapes and calls their HitTest() and HitTestBorder() methods, looking for a hit. The important part of this method is that before it starts checking, it sorts the collection so that the lowest z-index elements are first. This ensures that if one image is layered on top of another, the image on top has the first chance to receive the mouse click.

```
public Shape HitTest(Point point)
{
    Sort();
    foreach (Shape shape in List)
    {
        if (shape.HitTest(point) || shape.HitTestBorder(point))
        {
            return shape;
        }
    }
    return null;
}

public void Sort()
{
    InnerList.Sort();
}
```

However, this sorting method won't suit all tasks. The problem occurs when painting a series of shapes. In this case, you need higher z-indexes first and smaller values at the end of the list, which is the reverse of usual numeric ordering. That way, objects that are at the back are drawn first, and shape objects that are on subsequent layers are drawn over them.

To support this design, you need to add a ReverseSort() method that performs the reverse ordering. The IComparable implementation that's provided in the Shape class is no longer of any help, because it uses the lowest-to-highest sort. Instead, you need to perform the sorting on your own. A more elegant option is to create a dedicated class that implements IComparer and encapsulates your ordering logic. This way, you don't need to code a sorting algorithm— instead, you simply define how a set of two shapes should be compared to one another.

The IComparer interface defines a single Compare() method, which takes two objects and performs the comparison. The trick is to reverse the usual order by calling CompareTo() on the second object instead of the first.

```
public class ReverseZOrderComparer : IComparer
{
    public int Compare(object shapeA, object shapeB)
    {
        // Call the CompareTo() method in the reverse order.
        // This gives a highest-to-lowest sort.
        return ((Shape)shapeB).CompareTo((Shape)shapeA);
    }
}
```

Now you can add the ReverseSort() method that uses it:

```
private IComparer ReverseComparer = new ReverseZOrderComparer();
public void ReverseSort()
{
    InnerList.Sort(ReverseComparer);
}
```

The Drawing Surface

The drawing surface (the form) has the responsibility of tracking all the shapes that are added to it. It accomplishes this with a form-level reference to a ShapeCollection object:

```
private ShapeCollection shapes = new ShapeCollection();
```

Adding a shape works in almost the same way that it did in the previous example. You still set the same ForeColor, BackColor, Type, Size, and Location properties. The only real change is that the shape is inserted into the shapes collection (at which point the z-index is set), and special care is taken to invalidate just the portion of the form where the new shape has been added:

```
shapes.Add(newShape);
Invalidate(newShape.GetLargestPossibleRegion());
```

When the form is asked to paint itself, it loops through these shapes (in the reverse z-order), and paints each one in turn by calling the Shape.Render() method and passing the current Graphics object:

```
private void Form1_Paint(object sender, PaintEventArgs e)
{
    e.Graphics.SmoothingMode = SmoothingMode.AntiAlias;

    // Erase the current image (necessary because of the way
    // OnPaintBackground() is overriden).
    e.Graphics.Clear(Color.White);

    // Ensure shapes on the top obscure shapes on the bottom.
    shapes.ReverseSort();
```

```
    // Ask all the shapes to paint themselves.
    foreach (Shape shape in shapes)
    {
        shape.Render(e.Graphics);
    }
}
```

Remember—when you pass a region to the Form.Invalidate() method, your complete drawing code (in the OnPaint() method or a Paint event handler) still runs. The difference is that as you render the image, .NET ignores any portions that fall outside of the specified region. This increases the painting speed and reduces flicker, but it still doesn't change the time taken to execute your drawing logic. To optimize this process, you can specifically check if the invalidated region overlaps with a given shape. If it doesn't, there's no reason to draw it, as that part of the form isn't being updated. You can get the invalidated region from the PaintEventArgs.ClipRectangle property.

Here's the change you need:

```
foreach (Shape shape in shapes)
{
    if (e.ClipRectangle.IntersectsWith(shape.GetLargestPossibleRegion()))
    {
        shape.Render(e.Graphics);
    }
}
```

Finally, you can make the rendering dramatically smoother by turning on double-buffering (set the Form.DoubleBuffered property to true).

Without these steps, there is a significant amount of flicker when shapes are moved. With these steps, there is virtually no flicker. In other words, properly handling this detail is a key to distinguishing your application and making it look professional.

Detecting Mouse Clicks

Dealing with mouse clicks is an intricate issue. To determine what should happen, the application needs to determine which shape was clicked. The best approach is to follow these steps:

1. Check if there is a currently selected shape. If there is, test for a hit on the focus square. This has highest precedence.

2. If there's no hit on the focus square, loop through all the shapes and perform a hit test on each one (checking both the surface and the border). This technique is easy thanks to the ShapeCollection.HitTest() method, which respects the proper z-order.

3. If there's no hit on any shape, clear the last selected shape and (depending on the mouse button that was clicked) show a menu.

To make this series of steps run smoothly, you need two new details. First of all, you need a form-level variable to track the currently selected shape:

```
private Shape currentShape;
```

You also need a helper method to remove the currently selected shape, making sure the Selected property is set to false so the focus square will disappear:

```
private void ClearSelectedShape()
{
    if (currentShape != null)
    {
        currentShape.Selected = false;
    }
    currentShape = null;
}
```

Now you can put together the event handler for the MouseDown event. The first step is to check for a click on a focus square. If that's what happened, turn on resize mode (as in the control-based example).

```
private void Form_MouseDown(object sender, System.Windows.Forms.MouseEventArgs e)
{
    // Check for a hit on a focus square.
    Shape.HitSpot hitSpot;
    if ((currentShape != null) && (currentShape.Selected) &&
      (currentShape.HitTestFocusBorder(new Point(e.X, e.Y), out hitSpot)))
    {
        // The border was clicked. Turn on resize mode.
        clickOffsetX = e.X - currentShape.Location.X;
        clickOffsetY = e.Y - currentShape.Location.Y;
        isResizing = true;
    }
    ...
```

Otherwise, remove the current selection and perform a new hit test to see what shape (if any) was clicked.

```
    ...
    else
    {
        // Remove the last selected shape.
        ClearSelectedShape();

        // Retrieve a reference to the selected shape
        // using hit testing.
        currentShape = shapes.HitTest(new Point(e.X, e.Y));
        ...
```

If you don't find a shape, and the right mouse button was clicked, show the general form context menu. This allows the user to insert a new shape.

```
...
if (currentShape == null)
{
    // No shape was clicked.
    // Depending on the mouse button, show a menu.
    if (e.Button == MouseButtons.Right)
    {
        mnuForm.Show(this, new Point(e.X, e.Y));
    }
}
...
```

Otherwise, select the new shape and store it for future reference. Then, depending on the mouse button that was clicked, either show the context menu with shape-specific options (if the right button was clicked), or turn on dragging mode (if the left button was clicked).

```
...
else
{
    // Select the new shape.
    currentShape.Selected = true;

    // Make sure the display is updated to reflect
    // newly selected or deselected shapes.
    Invalidate(currentShape.GetLargestPossibleRegion());

    // Check what action should be performed with the
    // shape, depending on the mouse button that was clicked.
    if (e.Button == MouseButtons.Right)
    {
        // Show the context menu.
        mnuShape.Show(this, new Point(e.X, e.Y));
    }
    else if (e.Button == MouseButtons.Left)
    {
        // Start dragging mode.
        clickOffsetX = e.X - currentShape.Location.X;
        clickOffsetY = e.Y - currentShape.Location.Y;
        isDragging = true;
    }
}
...
    }
}
```

As with the control-based example, the dragging and resizing mode variables are cleared when the mouse button is released.

Manipulating Shapes

Once a shape is selected, it's easy to perform additional tasks with it. The code for changing the background color and removing the shape is very similar to the control-based version. The key difference is that rather than looking for a linked control, the event handlers use the shape object that's stored in the form-level currentShape variable. They are also fine-tuned to invalidate just the affected region where the shape is.

```
private void mnuColorChange_Click(object sender, System.EventArgs e)
{
    // Show color dialog.
    ColorDialog dlgColor = new ColorDialog();
    if (dlgColor.ShowDialog() == DialogResult.OK)
    {
        // Change shape background.
        currentShape.BackColor = dlgColor.Color;
        Invalidate(currentShape.Region);
    }
}

private void mnuRemoveShape_Click(object sender, System.EventArgs e)
{
    shapes.Remove(currentShape);
    ClearSelectedShape();
}
```

Two new menu commands allow the shapes to be reordered by sending them to different layers. Coding this functionality is easy, because it's already available through the BringShapeToFront() and SendShapeToBack() methods of the ShapeCollection class.

```
private void mnuToFront_Click(object sender, EventArgs e)
{
    shapes.BringShapeToFront(currentShape);
    Invalidate(currentShape.GetLargestPossibleRegion());
}

private void mnuToBack_Click(object sender, EventArgs e)
{
    shapes.SendShapeToBack(currentShape);
    Invalidate(currentShape.GetLargestPossibleRegion());
}
```

Watching the Mouse

The longest and most involved event handler in this application is the one that handles mouse movement. That's because there are three different tasks that you might perform at this point:

- If dragging mode is enabled, move the control.

- If resizing mode is enabled, resize the control.

- If neither mode is enabled, check if the mouse pointer is near one of the borders of the focus square, and then update the mouse pointer accordingly.

The first of these tasks is easy to accomplish and takes only a few lines of code:

```
private void Form_MouseMove(object sender, MouseEventArgs e)
{
    if (isDragging)
    {
        Rectangle oldPosition = currentShape.GetLargestPossibleRegion();
        currentShape.Location = new Point(e.X - clickOffsetX,
          e.Y - clickOffsetY);

        // Invalidate a section of the form that includes the old and new
        // positions.
        Rectangle newPosition = currentShape.GetLargestPossibleRegion();
        Invalidate(Rectangle.Union(oldPosition, newPosition));
    }
    ...
```

The resizing process is much more complicated. That's because the application supports resizing from several different locations, and in each case the resize behavior differs slightly. For example, if the user clicked on the top or top-right of the control, then horizontal resizing is allowed. That means the control can grow taller or shorter, but its width can't change. The current resize mode is stored in a form-level variable named resizingMode (not shown).

In addition, not only do you need to resize the shape correctly, you also need to check to make sure that the user hasn't tried to drag the shape to be less than the minimum bounds that are allowed. Here's how the process unfolds when the user is dragging the top edge:

```
    ...
    else if (isResizing)
    {
        int minSize = 5;
        Rectangle oldPosition = currentShape.GetLargestPossibleRegion();

        // Resize the control, according to the resize mode.
        switch (resizingMode)
        {
            // Clicks on the top and top-right corner are treated in the same
            // way. The top edge of the control is selected, and can be dragged
            // up or down.
```

```
case Shape.HitSpot.Top:
case Shape.HitSpot.TopRightCorner:
    // Before resizing the control, make sure the top edge hasn't
    // been dragged below the bottom edge.
    // The minimum size forces the shape to be a 5-pixel sliver.
    if (e.Y <
      (currentShape.Location.Y + currentShape.Size.Height - minSize ))
    {
        // When the top edge is dragged, you need to change both the
        // position of the control and the size to reflect the new
        // top edge.
        currentShape.Size = new Size(currentShape.Size.Width,
          currentShape.Location.Y + currentShape.Size.Height -
          (e.Y - clickOffsetY));
        currentShape.Location = new Point(currentShape.Location.X,
          e.Y - clickOffsetY);
    }
    break;
...
```

The calculation becomes a little bit simpler for the bottom edge, because the position doesn't need to be changed. Only the size is tweaked.

```
...
case Shape.HitSpot.Bottom:
    if (e.Y > (currentShape.Location.Y + minSize))
    {
        currentShape.Size = new Size(currentShape.Size.Width,
          e.Y - currentShape.Location.Y);
    }
    break;
...
```

The code for dealing with the left and right edges performs similar calculations:

```
...
case Shape.HitSpot.Left:
case Shape.HitSpot.BottomLeftCorner:
case Shape.HitSpot.TopLeftCorner:
    if (e.X <
      (currentShape.Location.X + currentShape.Size.Width - minSize))
    {
        currentShape.Size = new Size(
          (currentShape.Location.X + currentShape.Size.Width) -
          (e.X - clickOffsetX), currentShape.Size.Height);
        currentShape.Location = new Point(e.X - clickOffsetX,
          currentShape.Location.Y);
    }
    break;
```

```
      case Shape.HitSpot.Right:
          if (e.X > (currentShape.Location.X + minSize))
          {
              currentShape.Size = new Size(e.X - currentShape.Location.X,
                  currentShape.Size.Height);
          }
          break;
      ...
```

The bottom-right corner is a special exception. It allows free resizing in either direction (so long as the resized shape isn't less that the minimum bounds). Here's the logic that implements this behavior:

```
      ...
      case Shape.HitSpot.BottomRightCorner:
          if (e.Y > (currentShape.Location.Y + minSize))
          {
              currentShape.Size = new Size(currentShape.Size.Width,
                  e.Y - currentShape.Location.Y);
          }
          if (e.X > (currentShape.Location.X + minSize))
          {
              currentShape.Size = new Size(e.X - currentShape.Location.X,
                  currentShape.Size.Height);
          }
          break;
  }
  ...
```

You could use a similar approach for the other corners, but for the sake of simplicity, clicks on these corners are treated the same as a click on the nearest edge. No matter what type of resize was performed, the form is invalidated so it can be refreshed:

```
  ...
  Rectangle newPosition = currentShape.GetLargestPossibleRegion();
  Invalidate(Rectangle.Union(oldPosition, newPosition));
}
...
```

Assuming the form isn't in dragging or resizing mode, the final test is performed. The code checks if there is a currently selected shape. If there is, the code checks if the mouse has moved over one of the edges by calling the Shape.HitTestFocusBorder() method.

The HitTestFocusBorder() method returns the exact spot where the hit occurs, and it's up to the form to decide how to deal with different hits. In this case, the hit-spot information is simplified slightly. If the hit occurs in any corner except the bottom-right corner, it's treated as a hit on the adjoining side. Depending on where the mouse pointer is, the pointer is changed to a different resize arrow.

```
    ...
    else
    {
        if ((currentShape != null) && (currentShape.Selected)
         && (currentShape.HitTestFocusBorder(new Point(e.X, e.Y),
            out resizingMode)))
        {
            switch (resizingMode)
            {
                case Shape.HitSpot.Top:
                case Shape.HitSpot.Bottom:
                case Shape.HitSpot.TopRightCorner:
                    Cursor = Cursors.SizeNS;
                    break;
                case Shape.HitSpot.Left:
                case Shape.HitSpot.Right:
                case Shape.HitSpot.BottomLeftCorner:
                case Shape.HitSpot.TopLeftCorner:
                    Cursor = Cursors.SizeWE;
                    break;
                case Shape.HitSpot.BottomRightCorner:
                    Cursor = Cursors.SizeNWSE;
                    break;
                default:
                    Cursor = Cursors.Arrow;
                    break;
            }
        ...
```

If all of these tests turn up nothing, the last step is to return the mouse pointer to the default arrow, just in case the user moves over the edge of a focus square and then moves off the focus square and back over the rest of the form.

```
    ...
    }
    else
    {
        Cursor = Cursors.Arrow;
    }
  }
}
```

Saving and Loading Images

One of the frills that you can implement quite easily is the ability to save all the shapes that are currently displayed into a file, and then retrieve and redisplay them later. This feature would have been more difficult to create with the control-based example, because controls can't be serialized directly. However, because you control the code for the Shape and ShapeCollection classes, you can ensure that both of them are serializable. .NET has great built-in smarts for dealing with serializable classes. It can take live objects, convert them to a stream of bytes, and perform the reverse magic to reconstitute an object from its serialization information.

To make the Shape and ShapeCollection classes serializable, simply add the [Serializable] attribute to the class declaration, as shown here:

```
[Serializable]
public class Shape : IComparable
{ ... }
```

```
[Serializable]
public class ShapeCollection : CollectionBase
{ ... }
```

For a class to be serializable, all of its private member variables (and those in any parent classes that it inherits from) must also be serializable. The ShapeCollection class meets this requirement, but the Shape class falls short. It includes four offending members: graphicsPath, region, outlinePen, and surfaceBrush. Fortunately, you don't need to store any of these details. The graphicsPath and region objects are created transparently based on the shape type, location, and size when you access the GraphicsPath property. The outlinePen and surfaceBrush are created in the Render() method using the current ForeColor and BackColor. Thus, all you need to do is add the [NonSerialized] attribute in front of each of these members. This tells .NET to ignore this variable while serializing the containing object. As a result, when you deserialize the object, this information will revert to the default value (for example, null).

Here's an example with the graphicsPath member:

```
[NonSerialized] private GraphicsPath path = null;
```

Once you have the serialization attributes in place, it's easy to write the serialization code. First, import the following two namespaces, which have the file and serialization classes, respectively:

```
using System.IO;
using System.Runtime.Serialization.Formatters.Binary;
```

Rather than serialize individual shape objects, you can serialize the entire ShapeCollection and all its contents in one step. All you need to do is create a BinaryFormatter object to perform the serialization work, and call its Serialize() method. When you call serialize, you supply both the object you want to serialize and the stream where you want the serialized data to be placed. In this case, it makes sense to store them in a FileStream.

Here's the complete code that prompts the user for a file with the help of the SaveFileDialog, and then serializes the current shape collection to that file:

```
private void mnuSave_Click(object sender, EventArgs e)
{
    if (saveFileDialog.ShowDialog() == DialogResult.OK)
    {
        try
        {
            using (FileStream fs = File.Create(saveFileDialog.FileName))
            {
                BinaryFormatter f = new BinaryFormatter();
                f.Serialize(fs, shapes);
            }
        }
        catch (Exception err)
        {
            MessageBox.Show("Error while saving. " + err.Message);
        }
    }
}
```

Deserializing is just as easy. Instead of using the Serialize() method, you use the Deserialize() method of the BinaryFormatter. You pass the stream you want to deserialize, and cast the returned object to the appropriate data type (in this case, ShapeCollection). Finally, you need to invalidate the form to trigger a refresh.

```
private void mnuLoad_Click(object sender, EventArgs e)
{
    if (openFileDialog.ShowDialog() == DialogResult.OK)
    {
        ShapeCollection newShapes = null;
        try
        {
            using (FileStream fs =
                File.Open(openFileDialog.FileName, FileMode.Open))
            {
                BinaryFormatter f = new BinaryFormatter();
                newShapes = (ShapeCollection)f.Deserialize(fs, null);
            }
        }
        catch (Exception err)
        {
            MessageBox.Show("Error while loading. " + err.Message);
            return;
        }

        // Trigger a refresh.
        shapes = newShapes;
        Invalidate();
    }
}
```

The Last Word

This chapter worked through a useful example that demonstrates how you make a dynamic drawing surface where objects can be dragged, deleted, and manipulated. We considered two approaches: building the program using .NET's support for controls, and building it by hand using only the features of GDI+. The control-based approach is a great shortcut if you want to add drawing or diagramming features to a business application in the easiest and most convenient way possible. On the other hand, the lower-level approach is the right road to take if you are planning to build a sophisticated drawing application.

CHAPTER 25

■ ■ ■

Custom Extender Providers

Extender providers are a specialized type of component that can enhance other controls. Essentially, an extender provider works by adding "virtual properties" to existing controls. For example, the ErrorProvider adds an Error property that you can set to display a flashing error icon next to input controls that contain invalid information. Other examples include the ToolTip, which displays a tooltip next to other controls, and the HelpProvider, which invokes context-sensitive Help on a control's behalf when the F1 key is pressed. Chapter 4 introduced the basic extender providers included with Windows Forms. These are prebuilt components, but you can also build your own.

The beauty of extender providers is that they give you another route to enhance controls. Throughout this book, you've seen examples that have used inheritance to create customized controls. Extender providers give you another option—rather than derive a custom control, you can build a lightweight component that adds just the features you need.

Understanding Extender Providers

Extender providers work by hooking into control events. Essentially, every provider tracks specific events that occur in a group of one or more controls.

It's up to you to register a control with an extender provider to set up this link. When you do, the provider attaches its event handlers. For example, the HelpProvider monitors key presses for the F1 key. When you register a control with the HelpProvider, it attaches an event handler to that control's KeyPress event. When the F1 key is pressed, it springs into action.

Extender providers have both advantages and drawbacks. The key advantage is that the model is much more loosely coupled than custom controls. For example, imagine you derive a custom control from the ComboBox class and override several protected members. A future version of the ComboBox class could change its internal logic enough to break your derived class. This problem is much less likely if you create an extender provider for the ComboBox. An extender provider reacts only to events, and event definitions are unlikely to change because they are a part of the control's public interface. Figure 25-1 compares the two approaches.

Additionally, because your extender provider supports the ComboBox, it also supports any custom control that derives from ComboBox. If you created your own custom ComboBox control, this type of integration wouldn't be possible. The loosely coupled provider model also allows you to extend controls that have sophisticated design-time features, without forcing you to re-implement details like control builders. That's because you're not changing the original control—you're just adding to the existing model.

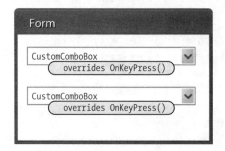 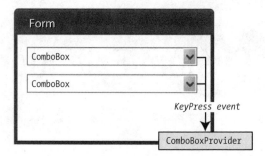

Figure 25-1. *Custom controls (left) versus extender providers (right)*

Another advantage of this loosely coupled design is the fact that your extender provider doesn't need to be coded to a single specific control class. It's quite easy to create an extender provider that extends multiple types of controls, or even one that extends *every* control. In this chapter you'll see a provider that extends all classes derived from ToolStripItem. Not only does this support all the ToolStripItem controls in the .NET class library; it also works equally well with custom ToolStripItem classes that other developers may create in the future.

The key limitation of extender providers is that they really have only one point of extensibility: control events. If you want to react to a certain action but a control doesn't define an event for that action, you're out of luck. Custom controls suffer from this limitation, but to a lesser extent. That's because a custom control can override protected methods, which often provide access to some of the internal workings of a control. A typical control will provide many more protected methods than public events, and so it has more extensibility points when you create a custom control.

It would be difficult to implement a derived control like the DirectoryTree (shown in Chapter 11) using an extender provider, because it changes the control too much. Even if you could, the result wouldn't be as intuitive, because extender providers don't give you the freedom to hide unnecessary members and add design-time frills to the control you're extending.

Overall, extender providers tend to be specialized solutions, and you may design dozens of custom controls before even contemplating a custom provider. Nonetheless, custom providers can achieve some remarkable tricks. This chapter demonstrates two extender providers. The first provider brings back an old-fashioned MFC trick—Help text that automatically appears in the status bar when you hover over a toolbar button or menu item. The second provider displays a clickable icon that launches context-sensitive Help.

Tip To create an extender provider, it's easiest to create the custom provider class in a class library project, and compile it into a DLL file. Visual Studio will automatically add it to a temporary tab in the Toolbox, as described in Chapter 9, so you can drag it onto a form in the project, or forms in other projects in the same solution.

The StatusStripHelpLabel Provider

The goal of the first provider is to extend an ordinary toolbar or menu by associating each item in it with a unique Help string. Then, when the user hovers over an item, the extender provider will retrieve the matching Help string and display it in a status bar. This is a common (albeit slightly outdated) user-interface convention, and while it's not terribly useful for the average user, it does provide a good example of an extender provider at work.

Choosing a Base Class

The first step when creating an extender provider is to create a class that implements the IExtenderProvider interface and uses the ProvideProperty attribute (both of these types are found in the System.ComponentModel namespace). This can be any type of class, including a user control, inherited control, or just a basic Component class that doesn't derive from any control. The type of class depends on the type of provider you are creating.

A control-based provider, like the StatusStripHelpLabel provider, uses a dedicated control to display information in a specific location on a form. In this example, the StatusStripHelpLabel inherits from the ToolStripStatusLabel class, which is used to display static text in a status bar. Thanks to this design, you can add the StatusStripHelpLabel to any StatusStrip, and it will update its display to provide the appropriate text automatically. Figure 25-2 diagrams this relationship.

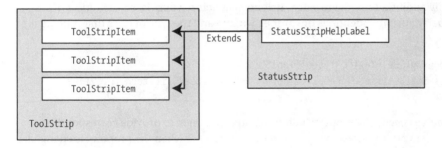

Figure 25-2. *The StatusStripHelpLabel extender*

Here's the bare skeleton of the extender provider:

```
public class StatusStripHelpLabel : ToolStripStatusLabel, IExtenderProvider
{ ... }
```

By inheriting from ToolStripStatusLabel, the provider gets the ability to appear in a StatusStrip and display text. None of this functionality needs to be coded. The real task is to implement the required members of the IExtenderProvider.

Choosing the Control to Extend

Once you've decided what type of provider you are creating, your next decision is to determine the type of object that you are extending. Many providers extend any type of Windows control, while some are limited to specific classes. To specify the appropriate type of object, you need to implement the IExtenderProvider.CanExtend() method, which is the only method in the IExtenderProvider interface.

In the CanExtend() method, your code examines the supplied type of object, and then makes a decision about whether your provider can extend it. To make this decision you can evaluate any information about the target, including the type (the most common criteria), whether it is hosted in another control or placed directly on a form, and even its name. You return true if the object can be extended.

The ToolStripStatusLabel provider extends only ToolStripItem objects. Here's the code that enforces this restriction:

```
public bool CanExtend(object extendee)
{
    return (extendee is ToolStripItem);
}
```

If you wanted to be stricter, you could limit the provider to ToolStripMenuItem objects, which represent items in a ToolStrip menu. However, this approach gives more flexibility—you can use the provider to extend menus or any other type of ToolStripItem, including ordinary ToolStripButton items.

Providing the Extended Property

The next step is to identify the virtual property that will be assigned to all extended controls. You do this by adding a ProvideProperty attribute just before your class declaration. The ProvideProperty attribute identifies the property name and the type of class that is being extended.

```
[ProvideProperty("HelpText", typeof(ToolStripItem))]
public class StatusStripHelpLabel : ToolStripStatusLabel, IExtenderProvider
{ ... }
```

Once you've specified a property in this fashion, you need to provide corresponding Get*Xxx*() and Set*Xxx*() methods that perform the actual work when the property is changed. These members are preceded with "Get" or "Set" and use the same name you identified in the ProvideProperty attribute. These methods must be public.

```
public void SetHelpText(object extendee, string value)
{ ... }
```

```
public string GetHelpText(object extendee)
{ ... }
```

Remember, neither of these methods is explicitly defined in the IExtenderProvider interface. When the Windows Forms infrastructure hooks up an extender provider, it uses reflection. Interestingly, it does so in a way that works even if you change the parameter types. That means you're free to use this strongly typed code and avoid an extra cast:

```
public void SetHelpText(ToolStripItem extendee, string value)
{ ... }

public string GetHelpText(ToolStripItem extendee)
{ ... }
```

Tip In this example, the extender provider provides a single property. However, there's no reason why you can't create an extender provider that provides multiple properties—you simply need to apply the ProvideProperty attribute once for each property, and include the corresponding SetXxx() and GetXxx() methods for each one.

You'll notice that the GetProperty() and SetProperty() methods accept a reference to the target control. That's because a single instance of your extender can be reused to extend dozens of controls (and, conversely, two similar providers can extend the same control). To support this sort of scenario, it's up to you to keep track of all the extended controls in your extender provider. The usual technique is to use a collection. In the StatusStripHelpLabel, a type-safe dictionary collection allows the provider to keep track of registered controls, and the supplied Help text for each one:

```
// The collection for tracking the Help text information.
private Dictionary<ToolStripItem, string> helpText =
  new Dictionary<ToolStripItem, string>();
```

Implementing the SetXxx() and GetXxx() Methods

To complete the StatusStripHelpLabel, you need to add the implementation logic for the SetHelpText() and GetHelpText() methods. The first step is to fill in the SetHelpText() method, which requires the most coding. When the Help text is set, the provider needs to add the supplied ToolStrip to the internal collection for tracking, and then dynamically attach event handlers to receive the MouseEnter and MouseLeave events. Additionally, your code needs to politely detach the event handlers when a blank Help string is supplied. Finally, the code needs to avoid hooking itself up more than once. The Visual Studio designer is prone to calling the SetXxx() method multiple times in a row, and you don't want the overhead of detaching and reattaching the event handlers with each call.

Here's the complete SetHelpText() code:

```
public void SetHelpText(ToolStripItem extendee, string value)
{
    // A blank value string indicates the control is trying to unregister.
    if (value.Length == 0)
    {
        // Check if the item is registered.
        if (!helpText.ContainsKey(extendee) && !DesignMode)
        {
```

```
                // Unregister.
                extendee.MouseEnter -= new EventHandler(MenuSelect);
                extendee.MouseLeave -= new EventHandler(MenuClear);
            }
            helpText.Remove(extendee);
        }
        else
        {
            // The user has supplied Help text.
            // Check if the item is registered.
            if (!helpText.ContainsKey(extendee) && !DesignMode)
            {
                // It hasn't been registered yet. Register it now.
                extendee.MouseEnter += new EventHandler(MenuSelect);
                extendee.MouseLeave += new EventHandler(MenuClear);
            }
            // Either way, update the Help text.
            helpText[extendee] = value;
        }
    }
```

Note With extender providers, calling a SetXxx() method with an empty string is assumed to mean removing the extension. This is a common convention.

When the MouseEnter event occurs, the Help text is retrieved and displayed in the StatusStrip label. When the MouseLeave event occurs, the text is cleared. You could just as easily monitor different events (like key presses, focus changes, and so on).

```
private void MenuSelect(object sender, System.EventArgs e)
{
    base.Text = helpText[(ToolStripMenuItem)sender];
}

private void MenuClear(object sender, System.EventArgs e)
{
    base.Text = string.Empty;
}
```

Implementing the GetHelpText() method is much quicker. It simply returns the Help text from the dictionary:

```
public string GetHelpText(ToolStripItem extendee)
{
    if (helpText.ContainsKey(extendee))
    {
        return helpText[extendee];
    }
    else
    {
        return string.Empty;
    }
}
```

Testing the Provider

To try out this example, create a new test form and add a ToolStrip and a StatusStrip. Inside the StatusStrip, add the StatusStripHelpLabel provider. Remember, the automatic designer support means that this class will appear in the Items Collection Editor dialog box as one of the possible choices (as discussed in Chapter 14). The only requirement is that the project must have a reference to the StatusStripHelpLabel assembly.

Now, add some sample items to the ToolStrip. For each item, you'll see a property like "HelpText on statusStripHelpLabel1." When you set this property, Visual Studio adds the code to call the SetHelpText() method, like this:

```
statusStripHelpLabel1.SetHelpText(mnuNew,
    "Create a new document and abandon the current one.");
```

You can also call the SetHelpText() method directly if you want to set the Help text programmatically.

Figure 25-3 shows the help text that appears automatically when you hover over a menu item that has been extended.

Figure 25-3. *The StatusStripHelpLabel provider in action*

Changing How Extended Properties Appear

By default, extended properties appear differently in the Properties window, because they always incorporate both the property name and the name of the extender object reference. For example, instead of just HelpText, you'll see the extended property HelpText on statusStripHelpLabel1. This has the benefit of making sure developers realize what properties are built into the control, and what ones come courtesy of an extender provider. However, if it's too cumbersome you can change this using the DisplayName attribute on the GetXxx() method to set a different name, as shown here:

```
[DisplayName("HelpText")]
public string GetHelpText(ToolStripItem extendee)
{ ... }
```

And while you're at it, why not add some of the usual attributes for configuring the description and category in the Properties window (as described in Chapter 13):

```
[DisplayName("HelpText")]
[Category("Behavior")]
[Description("This text appears in the linked StatusStripHelpLabel.")]
public string GetHelpText(ToolStripItem extendee)
{ ... }
```

The HelpIconProvider

The HelpIconProvider is an extender provider that gives users quick access to context-sensitive Help. It plays the same role as the HelpProvider discussed in Chapter 23, except it doesn't wait for the F1 key to be pressed. Instead, it adds a help icon next to the control that provides the Help. The user can click this icon to launch the Help. This model is much more intuitive because each control that provides worthwhile Help clearly advertises that fact, and the user can spot this information at a glance (rather than check for it by trial and error).

Choosing a Base Class

In many ways, the HelpIconProvider is a more typical provider because it extends other controls without being a control itself. Instead, it derives from the System.ComponentModel.Component class, as shown here:

```
[ProvideProperty("HelpID", typeof(Control))]
public class HelpIconProvider : Component, IExtenderProvider
{
    public bool CanExtend(object extendee)
    {
        return (extendee is Control);
    }
    ...
}
```

As you can tell from the ProvideProperty attribute, the HelpIconProvider supports any control, and it adds a property named HelpID. The HelpID tracks a context-sensitive ID that's used to find the appropriate Help topic.

As for the Help file, the HelpIconProvider code assumes that all controls are using topics from the same file. Thus, the HelpIconProvider includes an overall HelpFile property (rather than a control-specific extended property):

```
private string helpFile;
public string HelpFile
{
    get { return helpFile; }
    set { helpFile = value; }
}
```

Providing the Extended Property

Even though the HelpIconProvider isn't a dedicated control, it still has a graphical representation. It creates this representation dynamically when you attach it to other controls. To do this, the HelpIconProvider retrieves a reference to the form that contains the extended control and adds a small PictureBox control with a question mark icon in it.

This approach complicates the code. First of all, the HelpIconProvider now needs to include two collections. The first collection, named contextIDs, keeps track of each extended control and the associated Help context ID. The second collection, named pictures, stores the dynamically generated PictureBox control:

```
// Store the context-senstive ID for each control.
private Dictionary<Control, string> contextIDs =
  new Dictionary<Control, string>();

// Store the dynamically inserted PictureBox controls.
private Dictionary<Control, PictureBox> pictures =
  new Dictionary<Control, PictureBox>();
```

The next challenge is in adding the PictureBox. You could do this when the SetHelpText() method is called. Unfortunately, if the developer configures the form at design time, the SetHelpText() method will be called before the extended control has been added to the form. As a result, the HelpIconProvider won't be able to find the form and add the required PictureBox.

The solution to this challenge is the use the ISupportInitialize interface introduced in Chapter 13. That way, the SetHelpText() method can register itself with the appropriate context ID, and the HelpIconProvider can add the associated PictureBox when the ISupportInitialize. EndInit() method is called, when all the controls are sited on the form.

```
[ProvideProperty("HelpID", typeof(Control))]
public class HelpIconProvider : Component, IExtenderProvider, ISupportInitialize
{ ... }
```

However, the ISupportInitialize approach adds its own stumbling block—namely, it works *only* for controls added at design time. If you call SetHelpText() programmatically, the PictureBox won't be added because the EndInit() method has already been invoked.

The solution is to consider the state of the extended control, and add the PictureBox at the most appropriate time. The SetHelpID() method accomplishes this by testing the Control.Parent for a null reference. If no parent is found, the control isn't registered. Either way, it's still appropriate to add the control to the contextIDs collection.

Here's the complete code for the SetHelpID() method:

```
public void SetHelpID(Control extendee, string value)
{
    // A blank value string indicates the control is trying to unregister.
    if (value.Length == 0)
    {
        // Check if the item is registered.
        if (pictures.ContainsKey(extendee) && !DesignMode)
        {
            // Perform this step only if the form is created.
            if (extendee.Parent != null)
                UnRegister(extendee);
        }
        // Stop maintaining the help ID.
        contextIDs.Remove(extendee);
    }
    else
    {
        // The user has supplied a value.
        // Check if the item is registered.
        if (!pictures.ContainsKey(extendee) && !DesignMode)
        {
            if (extendee.Parent != null)
                Register(extendee);
        }
        // Update or store the help ID.
        contextIDs[extendee] = value;
    }
}
```

You'll notice that the SetHelpID() method actually relies on two private methods—Register() and Unregister()—to create the PictureBox. This way, you can call the same methods from the EndInit() method, rather than coding the same code in two places. Here's the code you need:

```
public void BeginInit()
{}

public void EndInit()
{
    // No design-time PictureBox controls are created.
    // Add them now.
```

```
        foreach (KeyValuePair<Control, string> item in contextIDs)
        {
            Register(item.Key);
        }
    }
}
```

As you can see, the EndInit() method simply steps through the collection of controls and registers everything it finds. This makes sense—if there's a control in the collection at this time, it must have been added at design time, and the PictureBox hasn't been set up yet.

The heavy lifting is performed in the Register() method. It creates the PictureBox, adds it to the form, and registers for the PictureBox.DoubleClick event. Notice that the PictureBox image is drawn from a resource in the assembly that contains the HelpIconProvider. To further refine the provider, you could handle more events from the dynamically generated picture box, perhaps tailoring the mouse cursor when it is positioned over the picture box.

```
private void Register(Control control)
{
    // Create new PictureBox.
    PictureBox pic = new PictureBox();
    pic.Image = Properties.Resources.help;
    pic.Size = new Size(16, 16);
    pic.Location = new Point(control.Right + 10, control.Top);

    // Register for DoubleClick event.
    pic.DoubleClick += new EventHandler(PicDoubleClick);

    // Store a reference to the help icon
    // So you can remove it later.
    pictures[control] = pic;

    // Add it to the form.
    control.Parent.Controls.Add(pic);
}
```

■**Tip** This extender works by adding another control to the form. Instead of taking this approach, you could draw the icon by hand. In order to do this correctly, your extender would need to hook into two events: the Form.Paint event (to repaint the help icon) and the Form.DoubleClick event (to hit-test and see if the help icon was double-clicked).

The UnRegister() method, which is called when an empty string is passed to the SetHelpID() method, detaches the event handler and disposes the PictureBox.

```
private void UnRegister(Control control)
{
    // Detach event handler.
    pictures[control].DoubleClick -= new EventHandler(PicDoubleClick);

    // Remove the picture from the form.
    pictures[control].Dispose();
    control.Parent.Controls.Remove(pictures[control]);

    pictures.Remove(control);
}
```

For good form, you should remove all PictureBox references when the provider is disposed. Of course, you could still get a fair bit more paranoid and perform even more cleanup work, but this is sufficient to keep the HelpIconProvider well-behaved.

```
protected override void Dispose(bool disposing)
{
    if (disposing)
    {
        // Dispose all the PictureBox controls.
        foreach (KeyValuePair<Control, PictureBox> item in pictures)
        {
            item.Key.Dispose();
        }
    }
}
```

Lastly, the GetHelpID() method is as simple as ever—it simply retrieves the relevant Help context ID:

```
public string GetHelpID(Control extendee)
{
    if (contextIDs.ContainsKey(extendee))
    {
        return contextIDs[extendee];
    }
    else
    {
        return String.Empty;
    }
}
```

When the PictureBox.DoubleClick event occurs, the HelpIcon provider searches for the matching control. Then it launches the Help file with the appropriate context identifier.

```
public void PicDoubleClick(object sender, EventArgs e)
{
    // Find the related control.
    Control ctrl = null;
    foreach (KeyValuePair<Control, PictureBox> item in pictures)
    {
        if (item.Value == sender)
        {
            ctrl = item.Key;
            break;
        }
    }

    // Show the help.
    if (ctrl != null)
    {
        Help.ShowHelp(ctrl, helpFile, HelpNavigator.Topic,
            contextIDs[ctrl]);
    }
}
```

It's important to note that if you don't have a valid Help file and context identifier, nothing will happen when you double-click the help icon. For this reason, the version of this example included with the code download at www.apress.com uses a message box to let you know the event has been detected. You can find out much more about the Help class this control uses to invoke the Help engine in Chapter 23.

To invoke this control, just specify a global Help file for the provider and set a Help context ID for a specific control, using either the Properties window or code like this:

```
helpIconProvider1.HelpFile = "myhelp.hlp";
helpIconProvider1.SetHelpID(TextBox1, "10001");
helpIconProvider1.SetHelpID(TextBox2, "10002");
```

Figure 25-4 shows the HelpIconProvider in action.

Figure 25-4. *A HelpIconProvider extending two text boxes*

■**Tip** By now, you've probably recognized that a lot of infrastructure is shared in almost every extender provider. To deal with this in a more elegant way, you could create a base class for extender providers that implements the registration pattern shown in the HelpIconProvider. Then to create a custom provider you would simply need to override the Register() and UnRegister() methods to hook into your desired event, and the CanExtend() method to choose the controls you support. The process of tracking controls and adding them to the collection can be abstracted away, simplifying the model.

The Last Word

In this chapter, you've taken a look at two extender providers that can add new features to existing controls. The StatusStripHelpLabel allows you to synchronize menu Help text with a status bar, and the HelpIconProvider helps you link to context-sensitive Help with a graphical icon. The important part about both of these controls is that they give you a whole new way to extend the Windows Forms framework. Instead of deriving classes that extend specific controls, you can generically apply a new feature to a range of controls by building a new provider. Best of all, this provider can be dropped into existing projects and will start working immediately, with no control customization required.

CHAPTER 26

■■■

Advanced Design-Time Support

In Chapter 13 you explored how you could add a respectable level of design-time support to your control. You saw how attributes, type converters, and type editors could improve the Properties-window support for your control and ensure proper code serialization. In this chapter, you'll continue to add to your design-time skills by considering a few more topics.

- **Control designers.** Control designers allow you to manage the design-time behavior and the design-time interface (properties and events) exposed by your control. Although control designers are quite complex pieces of the Windows Forms infrastructure (and creating one from scratch is far beyond the scope of this book), it's not difficult to customize an existing control designer to add new features.

- **Smart tags.** The new .NET 2.0 controls provide them, so why can't your controls? As you'll see, it's quite easy.

- **Collection controls.** You've already learned the basics about type converters and type editors. In this section, you'll learn how to apply these to more complex controls that model collections of items, and add some extra features with a control designer.

- **Licensing.** If you want to restrict how your control can be used (either at runtime or at design time), you'll need to implement some sort of licensing policy.

Control Designers

A control designer influences the design-time behavior and design-time appearance for a control. Technically a designer is a class that implements the System.ComponentModel.Design. IDesigner interface (see Table 26-1). Designers often implement the IDesignerFilter interface (which is covered in the next section) to change the design-time interface of their control.

Table 26-1. *IDesigner Members*

Property	Description
Component	Gets the component (in this case, the custom control) that this designer is designing.
Verbs	Gets the design-time verbs (commands that are exposed through a context menu) when you right-click on the control. You can override this method to supply custom commands.
DoDefaultAction()	Performs the default action for this designer. This is called when the control is double-clicked on the design surface, and you can override this method to customize this behavior.
Initialize()	Initializes the designer for the appropriate component. You can override this method to perform your own custom design-time initialization for the control. This initialization takes place immediately after the component is created and its constructor code has executed.

Fortunately, you'll rarely be forced to create your own from scratch. The .NET Framework provides a basic component designer in the System.ComponentModel.Design. ComponentDesigner class that is provided to all IComponent classes, and a control designer with the System.Windows.Forms.Design.ControlDesigner class that applies to all controls. These classes contain a great deal of functionality and provide many more methods that you can override to plug into different parts of the designer behavior. In addition, there are derived control designers that add support for child control containment and scrolling. Figure 26-1 shows the hierarchy.

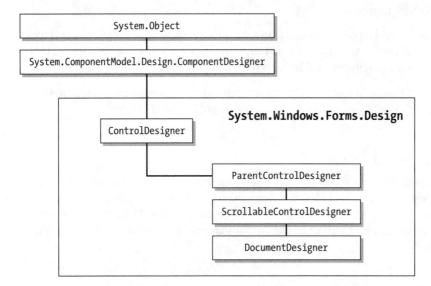

Figure 26-1. *Control designer classes*

You can also derive a custom control designer to use with your custom controls. Why would you create your own designer?

- To add design-time conveniences, like context menu options and smart tags.

- To remove inappropriate events or properties from view (or add design-time-only events or properties).

- To tailor the design-time appearance of the control so that it differs from the runtime appearance (for example, adding a border around an empty panel).

- To add support for controls that contain other controls (like the toolbar) or controls with special design-time needs (like menus).

At design time, the designer infrastructure attaches a designer to each component as it is sited on a form. (If more than one instance of the same component is added to a form, Visual Studio will reuse the same designer for all instances.) Once this connection is established, the control designer has the ability to take part in the interaction between the developer and the control.

To create a basic control designer, begin by deriving a class from ControlDesigner (or ParentControlDesigner, if you want to create a container control that can hold child controls). Here's an example that creates a designer for the DirectoryTree control from Chapter 11:

```
public class DirectoryTreeDesigner : ControlDesigner
{ ... }
```

You can then add functionality to your control designer by overriding the built-in methods. When you're finished, you need to link the custom control designer to the appropriate control. To do this, you apply the Designer attribute to the control declaration and specify the appropriate designer type. Here's an example that links the DirectoryTreeDesigner to the DirectoryTree control:

```
[Designer(typeof(DirectoryTreeDesigner))]
public class DirectoryTree : TreeView
{ ... }
```

■Tip Instead of supplying a type, you can use a different constructor overload that accepts a string with a full assembly name. This is handy, because it allows you to separate the runtime and design-time code for your custom control. If you develop extensive design-time support, this ensures that the runtime version of your control remains as small as possible.

A designer can be as complex or as simple as you want. In the following sections, you'll see a number of techniques you can use with control designers. Although these topics are by no means comprehensive, they provide a good overview of what you can accomplish.

■Note When you derive a custom control from an existing .NET control, you automatically acquire the same control designer as the base class. This is significant, because many controls (including the TreeView) have custom designers. However, you can reapply the Designer attribute to choose a different designer for your custom control.

Filtering Properties and Events

Sometimes, an event or property needs to be hidden from a control, but not removed entirely. For example, the ProgressBar control provides a Text property, which it inherits from the base Control class. This property can be used at the programmer's discretion, but it does not have any visible text because the ProgressBar doesn't provide a caption. For this reason, the Text property should be hidden from the Properties window.

If you are defining or overriding a property, you can use the Browsable attribute to keep it from appearing in the Properties window. However, consider the TreeView control, which provides a Nodes collection. You may have noticed that the custom DirectoryTree control (first presented in Chapter 11) displays the Nodes property in the designer and allows it to be modified, although the display is built automatically at runtime based on the Drive property. The TreeView.Nodes property is not overridable, so you can't use the Browsable attribute. However, you can create a custom designer that ensures it won't appear at design time.

Designers provide six methods from the IDesignerFilter interface that you can override to filter properties, events, and attributes. These methods are listed in Table 26-2.

Table 26-2. *IDesignerFilter Methods*

Method	Description
PostFilterAttributes	Override this method to remove unused or inappropriate attributes.
PostFilterEvents	Override this method to remove unused or inappropriate events.
PostFilterProperties	Override this method to remove unused or inappropriate properties.
PreFilterAttributes	Override this method to add attributes.
PreFilterEvents	Override this method to add events.
PreFilterProperties	Override this method to add properties.

Technically, the filtering methods allow you to modify a System.ComponentModel.TypeDescriptor object that stores the property, attribute, and event information for your custom control. Visual Studio uses the information from this TypeDescriptor to determine what it makes available in the design-time environment.

Removing Members

To filter the Nodes property so it doesn't appear in the DirectoryTree control, you need a control designer that overrides the PostFilterProperties() method. Here's the complete control designer code:

```
public class DirectoryTreeDesigner : ControlDesigner
{
    protected override void PostFilterProperties(System.Collections.IDictionary
     properties)
    {
        properties.Remove("Nodes");
        base.PostFilterProperties(properties);
    }
}
```

Now, when you recompile the control and test it in the client, you'll notice that the Nodes property does not appear in the Properties window. However, the Nodes property is still accessible in code. This allows clients to perform other useful tasks (like enumerating through the collection of nodes) at their discretion. This code also ensures that the Nodes collection is not serialized at design time, effectively sidestepping the problem where the same set of drive nodes is added more than once to an instance of the DirectoryTree control.

You can extend this example to get rid of other details you don't need. For example, you might want to remove the AfterSelect event from view because you've added a more useful DirectorySelected event. Here's how you'd do that:

```
protected override void PostFilterEvents(System.Collections.IDictionary events)
{
    events.Remove("AfterSelect");
    base.PostFilterEvents(events);
}
```

Adding Design-Time Members

Just as you can remove properties and events in the PostFilterXxx() methods, you can also add properties events in the PreFilterXxx() methods. This technique is most commonly used with properties in the PreFilterProperties() method.

It's important to realize that when you add a property in the PreFilterProperties() method, you aren't adding it to the underlying control. Instead, you're adding a design-time-only property that your designer is responsible for tracking. It's also your designer that reacts if the property is changed to alter some aspect of the design-time experience.

For example, consider the MarqueeLabel first shown in Chapter 12. In this control, it makes sense not to fire the timer events at design time, and for that reason, the timer isn't enabled when the control is in design mode. But what would it take to give the developer the choice as to whether the label should scroll or stay fixed? It turns out this design is quite easy to implement with a design-time property.

The first step is to create a control designer for the MarqueeLabel and attach it to the MarqueeLabel with the Designer attribute. Next, you need to add the virtual property to the control designer, *not* the control. Notice that this property finds the associated control (through the ControlDesigner.Control or the ComponentDesigner.Component property), and then uses the Scroll() method to turn scrolling on or off.

```
private bool allowDesignTimeScroll;
public bool AllowDesignTimeScroll
{
    get { return allowDesignTimeScroll; }
    set
    {
        ((MarqueeLabel)Control).Scroll(value);
        allowDesignTimeScroll = value;
    }
}
```

■Tip In this case, the control already contains a Scroll() method that you can call to get the desired effect. However, it's possible in other situations that you might want to trigger a change in a control and there won't be a suitable public method or property. In this case, consider creating an internal method, which is accessible only to classes that are compiled in the same assembly.

The next part is more interesting. In the PreFilterProperties() method, you need to create a PropertyDescriptor that represents the AllowDesignTimeScroll property. You can accomplish this with the static TypeDescriptor.CreateProperty() method. You simply need to specify the type where the property is defined, the property name (as a string), and the property data type, as shown here:

```
PropertyDescriptor prop = TypeDescriptor.CreateProperty(
    typeof(MarqueeLabelDesigner), "AllowDesignTimeScroll", typeof(bool),
    CategoryAttribute.Design, DesignOnlyAttribute.Yes);
```

In addition, the last two parameters of the CreateProperty() method specify the category where the attribute should appear in the Properties window, and whether or not it should be considered a design-time-only property. If you specify that it is, the property setting will be persisted in the .resx resources file for the form (ensuring that Visual Studio remembers the value if you close the project and open it later).

If you don't specify that the property is a design-time-only value, Visual Studio will generate the code to set this property and add it to the InitializeComponent() section of the form. This will cause an error when you run the application, because the control designer won't exist at that point, and the AllowDesignTimeScroll property isn't really a part of the MarqueeLabel.

Once you've created the PropertyDescriptor that defines your property, you can add it to the properties collection. Here's the complete code:

```
protected override void PreFilterProperties(IDictionary properties)
{
    base.PreFilterProperties(properties);

    // Add a new property.
    properties["AllowDesignTimeScroll"] = TypeDescriptor.CreateProperty(
      typeof(MarqueeLabelDesigner), "AllowDesignTimeScroll", typeof(bool),
      CategoryAttribute.Design, DesignOnlyAttribute.Yes);
}
```

■**Note** As a general rule, always call the base method first in the PreFilterXxx() methods and last in the PostFilterXxx() methods. This way, all designer classes are given the proper opportunity to apply their changes. The ControlDesigner and ComponentDesigner use these methods to add properties like Visible, Enabled, Name, and Locked.

When you recompile your code, the AllowDesignTimeScroll property will appear in the design-time window. If you set it to true, the label will begin scrolling in the design-time environment.

Shadowing Members

Another trick you might want to use with filtering is to *shadow* a member. Shadowing a member is a technique in which you replace a control property with a duplicate control-designer property that has the same name. This allows your designer to intercept when the property is set, and decide whether it should pass a value to the underlying control at design time. This technique ensures that properties like Visible or Enabled don't have any effect at design time.

■**Note** Another way to achieve this result is to explicitly check the DesignMode attribute in your control code. However, the shadowing approach is preferable. Not only does it enforce better separation between the design-time and runtime logic of your control, it also prevents the control code from becoming unnecessarily tangled with conditional statements.

To see a shadowed member at work, it's worth considering a more realistic version of the MarqueeLabel control. A more typical design would add a property to MarqueeLabel that determines whether scrolling should be performed. This allows the application to stop and start the label at will:

```
public bool EnableScrolling
{
    get { return tmrScroll.Enabled; }
    set { tmrScroll.Enabled = value; }
}
```

In this case, the developer will probably want to be able to set the EnableScrolling property at design time. However, you still want to prevent the label from scrolling until the application is launched. You can solve this by shadowing the property.

Here's the duplicate EnableScrolling property that you need to add to the control designer:

```
public bool EnableScrolling
{
    get { return (bool)ShadowProperties["EnableScrolling"]; }
    set { ShadowProperties["EnableScrolling"] = value; }
}
```

Notice that the value for the EnableScrolling property isn't stored in a member variable. Instead, the ControlDesigner class provides a collection named ShadowProperties that you can use for this purpose.

When the control designer is first created, you need to make sure its EnableScrolling property is set to match the underlying control. At the same time, you should switch off scrolling, no matter what the property value is. To do this, you need to override the Initialize() method. The Initialize() method is called before any other tasks happen with the designer.

```
public override void Initialize(IComponent c)
{
    base.Initialize(c);

    // Shadow the EnableScrolling property.
    EnableScrolling = ((MarqueeLabel)Control).EnableScrolling;

    // Now turn off scrolling in the underlying control.
    ((MarqueeLabel)Control).EnableScrolling = false;
}
```

The last step is to use the PreFilterProperties() method to replace the MarqueeLabel. EnableScrolling property with the shadowed MarqueeLabelDesigner.EnableScrolling property:

```
protected override void PreFilterProperties(IDictionary properties)
{
    base.PreFilterProperties(properties);

    properties["EnableScrolling"] = TypeDescriptor.CreateProperty(
        typeof(MarqueeLabelDesigner),
        (PropertyDescriptor)properties["EnableScrolling"],
        new Attribute[0]);
}
```

This completes the example. You might expect that you need to add more code to copy the value of the shadowed property from the designer back to the control. However, this isn't the case. That's because a shadowed version of the EnableScrolling property doesn't have the design-time-only flag. As a result, when the developer sets this property in the Properties window, Visual Studio generates the code and adds it to the InitializeComponent() method:

```
marqueeLabel1.EnableScrolling = true;
```

At runtime, the control designer no longer exists, and this statement acts directly on the control, switching on scrolling.

Interacting with the Mouse

One dramatic difference between how controls work at runtime and how they work at design time is the handling of the mouse. In the design-time environment, mouse actions are ignored, and never passed on to the control. You can click a control to select it, but that won't fire the underlying control events.

You have several options for extending how a control designer works with mouse actions, or changing this behavior entirely. For example, you can override the OnMouseEnter(), OnMouseHover(), and OnMouseLeave() methods of the ControlDesigner class to react to these actions. (A similar set of methods is available for responding to drag-and-drop operations.)

The following example shows a control designer that reacts to the mouse movement, and sets a member variable in the designer to indicate if the mouse pointer is currently over the control. If it is, it adds a red dashed outline around the control (see Figure 26-2).

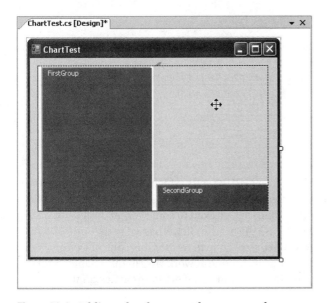

Figure 26-2. *Adding a border around your control*

The trick to enabling this is using the OnPaintAdornments() method. The OnPaintAdornments() method allows you to paint some elements that appear only at design time, and it's called immediately after your control finishes its own painting. This technique is commonly used to add helpful cues (like a border around an empty panel). You might also want to use OnPaintAdornments() to substitute a generic representation for a complex control that isn't rendered at design time.

Here's the complete code:

```
bool mouseOver;
protected override void OnMouseEnter()
{
    base.OnMouseEnter();
    mouseOver = true;
    Control.Invalidate();
}

protected override void OnMouseLeave()
{
    base.OnMouseLeave();
    mouseOver = false;
    Control.Invalidate();
}

protected override void OnPaintAdornments(PaintEventArgs pe)
{
    base.OnPaintAdornments(pe);

    if (mouseOver)
    {
        // Draw the rectangle adornment.
        Pen pen = new Pen(Color.Red);
        pen.DashStyle = System.Drawing.Drawing2D.DashStyle.Dash;
        pe.Graphics.DrawRectangle(pen, 0, 0, Control.Width - 1,
          Control.Height - 1);
        pen.Dispose();
    }
}
```

Another related method is ControlDesigner.GetHitTest(), which allows you to pass mouse clicks on to the underlying control. Typically, you'll use the code in this method to test if the click occurred in a specific region of the control (one that's linked to some sort of design-time feature). You can then return true, in which case the mouse click is passed to the control, which then fires its Click event. It's then up to your control code to test for the Control.DesignMode property, and react accordingly. You'll see this technique at work later in this chapter with the SimpleChart example, where it allows you to select individual bar items at design time.

Selection and Resize Rules

Sometimes you'll come across controls that don't allow all the normal resizing operations. For example, when you add a TextBox that has the MultiLine property set to false, you can't resize it vertically. Similar restrictions can exist for moving or resizing child controls in a special container (think of a custom toolbar).

Control designers make it easy to implement these restrictions with the help of the ControlDesigner.SelectionRules property. You can override this property and return a combination of values from the SelectionRules enumeration to specify what the control can do. For example, the following set of selection rules allows moving a control, but prevents it from being resized vertically (like the TextBox):

```
public override System.Windows.Forms.Design.SelectionRules SelectionRules
{
    get
    {
        return SelectionRules.LeftSizeable | SelectionRules.RightSizeable |
            SelectionRules.Visible | SelectionRules.Moveable;
    }
}
```

Table 26-3 lists the values you can return.

Table 26-3. *Values for the SelectionRules Enumeration*

Value	Description
AllSizeable	The control supports sizing in all directions.
BottomSizeable, LeftSizeable, RightSizeable, and TopSizeable	The control supports sizing in the specified directions. It doesn't support sizing in any direction you omit.
Locked	The control is locked to its container. This prevents moving and sizing, even if you've specified those flags.
Moveable	The control supports moving to different locations in its container.
Visible	The control has some form of visible user interface. When selected, the selection service will draw a selection border around it.

Designer Verbs

So far, you've seen how a control designer can change the way a control works. But another reason to use designers is to add frills, like fancy wizards that make it easier to set complex properties. For example, you can use a custom designer to add to the context menu that is displayed when a programmer right-clicks your control in the design environment. This menu always contains some standard options provided by Visual Studio, but it can also contain your commands (technically known as *verbs*).

To add verbs, you need to override the Verbs property in your custom designer, create a new DesignerVerbCollection, and add the appropriate DesignerVerb object entries. Your control designer handles the verb click event, generally by updating the associated control.

The following example retrieves a list of all the drives on the current computer, and adds a context menu entry for each one. The user can click the appropriate entry to set the Drive property of the control.

```
public class DirectoryTreeDesigner : ControlDesigner
{
    private DesignerVerbCollection verbs = new DesignerVerbCollection();

    public DirectoryTreeDesigner()
    {
        // Configure the designer verb collection.
        string[] drives = System.IO.Directory.GetLogicalDrives();

        foreach (string drive in drives)
        {
            verbs.Add(new DesignerVerb("Set Drive " + drive,
                new EventHandler(OnVerb)));
        }
    }

    public override DesignerVerbCollection Verbs
    {
        get { return verbs; }
    }

    protected void OnVerb(object sender, EventArgs e)
    {
        // Retrieve the selected drive.
        char driveLetter = ((DesignerVerb)sender).Text[10];

        // Adjust the associated control.
        ((DirectoryTree)this.Control).Drive = driveLetter;
    }

}
```

Note This example shows the naïve approach that modifies the control directly. The problem is that this doesn't inform Visual Studio that a change has taken place, and the user interface won't be refreshed properly. To deal with this issue, you need to take additional steps to notify Visual Studio, as described at the end of this section.

The resulting context menu for the DirectoryTree control is shown in Figure 26-3.

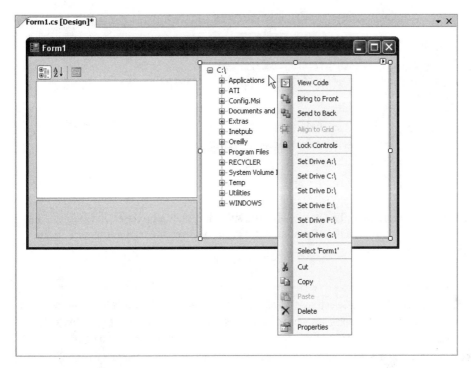

Figure 26-3. *Designer verbs*

Generally, you won't use your designer verbs to provide settings for a simple property. A more interesting technique is to provide higher-level configuration operations that adjust several properties at once.

Implementing this design is refreshingly easy. Just add a Windows Form to your project and display it when the appropriate designer verb is selected. Here's another simple example using the DirectoryTree. This time, only a single verb is available, which displays a window that allows the user to choose a drive. When a drive is chosen, a public form-level variable is set, and the designer retrieves it and applies the change. This approach is more manageable than the previous design, and doesn't clutter the context menu with drive letters.

```
public class DirectoryTreeDesigner : ControlDesigner
{
    private DesignerVerbCollection verbs = new DesignerVerbCollection();

    public DirectoryTreeDesigner()
    {
        verbs.Add(new DesignerVerb("Set Drive",
          new EventHandler(OnVerb)));
    }

    public override DesignerVerbCollection Verbs
    {
        get { return verbs; }
    }
```

```
protected void OnVerb(object sender, EventArgs e)
{
    // Show the form.
    SelectDrive frm = new SelectDrive();
    frm.DriveSelection = ((DirectoryTree)this.Control).Drive;
    frm.ShowDialog();

    // Adjust the associated control.
    ((DirectoryTree)this.Control).Drive = frm.DriveSelection;
}

}
```

The SelectDrive form is quite simple—it's the selection dialog box used in Chapter 13 as a modal type editor. It shows a list of available drives, and stores the user's selection in the SelectDrive.Drive property.

■**Note** When you add a form like SelectDrive to a control project, the client will be able to see the form class in your designer and create and display instances of it. If this isn't the behavior you want, you need to declare your form class as internal. (Another alternative is to nest it inside your control class, and declare it as private or protected, but if you do this you have to forego Visual Studio's design-time support for the form).

One quirk remains in the control designer. When the designer modifies the DirectoryTree.c, the Properties window is not updated until the control is deselected and then reselected. To correct this defect, you need to explicitly notify the IDE that a change has been made by using the PropertyDescriptor for the property.

The rewritten OnVerb() method handles this detail:

```
protected sub OnVerb(object sender, EventArgs e)
{
    // Show the form.
    SelectDrive frm = new SelectDrive();
    frm.DriveSelection = ((DirectoryTree)this.Control).Drive;
    frm.ShowDialog();

    // Adjust the associated control.
    ((DirectoryTree)this.Control).Drive = frm.DriveSelection;

    // Notify the IDE that the Drive property has changed.
    PropertyDescriptorCollection properties;
    properties = TypeDescriptor.GetProperties(typeof(DirectoryTree));
    PropertyDescriptor changedProperty = properties.Find("Drive", false);
    RaiseComponentChanged(changedProperty, "", frm.DriveSelection);
}
```

Rather than use the RaiseComponent method, you could set the property through the PropertyDescriptor by using the PropertyDescriptor.SetValue() method:

```
PropertyDescriptorCollection properties;
properties = TypeDescriptor.GetProperties(typeof(DirectoryTree));
PropertyDescriptor property = properties.Find("Drive", false);
property.SetValue(Control, frm.DriveSelection);
```

Although these two approaches are equivalent in this case, it's better to use the latter approach. When you start using smart tags, you need to use the SetValue() method to ensure that the Undo feature works correctly.

■**Note** Technically, there is another option—you can start and commit a *designer transaction* manually. You'll learn about designer services in the next section, but the PropertyDescriptor.SetValue() approach is much simpler in this scenario.

Designer Services

If you're planning to create sophisticated designers, you'll soon encounter the concept of *designer services*. These services allow you to interact with the Windows Forms design-time infrastructure in some powerful ways.

The method you use to access a service is named GetService(), and it's part of the IServiceProvider interface. It turns out that a number of different ingredients implement IServiceProvider, so you have several choices for getting access to a service. For example, every component implements it and provides a Component.GetService() method. Seeing as all controls derive from Component, this means you can call GetService() on any control. Similarly, the ComponentDesigner implements IServiceProvider. Seeing as ControlDesigner derives from ComponentDesigner, and all the designers you use derive from ControlDesigner, you can also rely on ComponentDesigner.GetService() to get access to a service. In other words, whether you have access to a control or to a designer, the service you need is never far off.

So what services can you use? There is a dizzying array of choices (see Table 26-4), and you can even add your own.

Table 26-4. *Designer Services*

Service Interface	Description
IComponentChangeService	Allows a designer to receive notifications of when components are changed, added, or removed from the design-time environment.
IDesignerEventService	Allows a designer to receive notifications when other designers are added or removed from the design-time environment.
IDesignerFilter	Allows a designer to add to and filter the set of properties displayed in a property browser for its component. (You've already seen this service at work with the DirectoryTree example.)

Table 26-4. *Designer Services (Continued)*

Service Interface	Description
IDesignerHost	Allows a designer to react when components are created or destroyed and manage designer transactions.
IDesignerOptionService	Allows a designer to get and set the values of properties in the Properties window.
IDictionaryService	Allows a designer to store miscellaneous information in a key-based collection.
IEventBindingService	Allows a designer to register event handlers to component events.
IExtenderListService	Allows a designer to obtain the currently active extender providers, and add or remove them.
IHelpService	Allows a designer to create and remove help service contexts, create and remove help context attributes, and display help topics by keyword or URL.
IInheritanceService	Allows a designer to search for components of derived classes and identify any inheritance attributes of each.
IMenuCommandService	Allows a designer to search for, add, remove, or invoke menu commands in the design-time environment.
IReferenceService	Allows a designer to obtain the name of an object by reference, or a reference to an object based on its name. You can also get a reference to the parent of a specified component, or references to all objects of a specified type.
IResourceService	Allows a designer to obtain a resource reader or resource writer for a specified CultureInfo.
IRootDesigner	Allows a designer to provide the background design surface when it's the top-level designer.
ISelectionService	Allows a designer to determine what components are selected, set the selection programmatically, or react when the selection changes.
IServiceContainer	Allows a designer to add or remove services that can be used by other components or designers.
ITypeDescriptorFilterService	Allows a component or designer to filter the attributes, events, and properties exposed by any component at design time.
ITypeResolutionService	Allows a designer to add a reference to an assembly to the project, obtain a type or assembly by name, and obtain the path of a specified assembly.

The most common pattern for using a designer service is through a control designer. If your goal is to receive events from a service, you'll override the Initialize() method of your designer. There, you'll call GetService() and attach your event handlers. You can then detach your event handlers by overriding the Dispose() method. If you simply need to perform an action through a designer, you'll probably just retrieve it when you need it using GetService() and call the appropriate method.

In the following sections, you'll see two of the most common services at work in custom control designers.

Designer Notifications

One common reason to use a designer service is to receive notifications whenever controls are added, removed, or changed. This works through the IComponentChangeService, which exposes the methods shown in Table 26-5.

Table 26-5. *IComponentChangeService Methods*

Event	Description
ComponentAdding	Triggered when a component is in the process of being added to the control at design time
ComponentAdded	Triggered when a component is added to the control at design time
ComponentChanging	Triggered when a component is in the process of changing at design time
ComponentChanged	Triggered when a contained component has changed at design time
ComponentRemoving	Triggered when a component is in the process of being removed
ComponentRemoved	Triggered when a component is removed at design time
ComponentRename	Triggered when a component is renamed

■**Note** The IComponentChangeService also provides two methods, OnComponentChanging() and OnComponentChanged(), which you can call to notify the designer about changes you're making to a control.

The following example modifies the DirectoryTreeDesigner to use this service. Here's the basic idea—rather than providing a designer verb for every possible drive, the context menu should show every drive *except* the currently selected one. For example, if the DirectoryTree.Drive property is currently set to C, the control's context menu should either hide (set DesignerVerb.Visible to false) or disable (set DesignerVerb.Enabled to false) the Set Drive C:\ command.

The problem is that there are several possible ways to change the Drive property: through a designer verb, through the Properties window, through a type editor, and so on. Your designer needs to be notified of property changes no matter how they take place, and adjust the corresponding DesignerVerb object. The only way to do this is to react to the IComponentChangeService.ComponentChanged event.

You can hook up the service by overriding the designer's Initialize() method:

```
private IComponentChangeService changeService;

public override void Initialize(IComponent component)
{
    base.Initialize(component);
```

```
    // Get the service.
    changeService =
        (IComponentChangeService)GetService(typeof(IComponentChangeService));

    // Connect the event handler.
    if (changeService != null)
    {
      changeService.ComponentChanged +=
        new ComponentChangedEventHandler(ComponentChanged);
    }
}
```

Notice how the designer tests for a null reference before hooking up the event handler. This is a best practice, because a control can potentially be designed in different editors, and not all will necessarily provide the same set of design-time services. If a service isn't available, your control should still function, albeit with fewer frills.

Now all you need to do is react accordingly, find the corresponding verb, and modify it:

```
private void ComponentChanged(object sender, ComponentChangedEventArgs e)
{
    DirectoryTree tree = (DirectoryTree)this.Control;

    if (tree != null)
    {
        foreach (DesignerVerb verb in verbs)
        {
            if (verb.Text[10] == tree.Drive)
                verb.Enabled = false;
            else
                verb.Enabled = true;
        }
    }
}
```

And just to behave properly, you should remove the event handler when the designer is disposed:

```
protected override void Dispose(bool disposing)
{
    if (changeService != null)
    {
        changeService.ComponentChanged -=
            new ComponentChangedEventHandler(ComponentChanged);
    }
}
```

The IComponentChangeService can facilitate many more complex scenarios that involve linked controls. However, the basic technique of connecting event handlers remains exactly the same.

Designer Transactions

Designer transactions ensure that when several small changes are made at design time as part of a logical operation, they can be reversed using the Undo command. Not only do designer transactions support the Undo feature, they also improve performance because the design surface isn't refreshed until the transaction is complete.

For example, consider the DirectoryTreeDesigner. When you select an option from its context menu, the Drive property is changed. This is a single action, which means you can accomplish it easily through the PropertyDescriptor without starting a transaction. (The PropertyDescriptor.SetValue() method implicitly starts and commits a designer transaction.)

However, life isn't as easy if you need to provide a command that implements a series of changes. For example, consider this method, which applies a series of changes to the MarqueeLabel control:

```
protected void OnVerbFunky(object sender, EventArgs e)
{
    // Get the associated control.
    MarqueeLabel lbl = (MarqueeLabel)Control;

    lbl.ForeColor = Color.LimeGreen;
    lbl.BackColor = Color.Yellow;
    lbl.Font = new Font(lbl.Font.Name, 48, FontStyle.Bold);
}
```

It's attached to a designer verb:

```
private DesignerVerbCollection verbs = new DesignerVerbCollection();

public MarqueeLabelDesigner()
{
    verbs.Add(new DesignerVerb("Apply Funky Theme",
      new EventHandler(OnVerbFunky)));
}

public override DesignerVerbCollection Verbs
{
    get { return verbs; }
}
```

The problem right now is that this set of changes doesn't use the designer transaction features. If you trigger this command and then select Edit ➤ Undo, you're likely to have that operation and several more rolled back at the same time.

To create a designer transaction, you need a reference to the IDesignerHost service, which provides a CreateTransaction() method. This returns a DesignerTransaction object, which has a Commit() method you use to finalize the transaction.

However, there's another consideration when using a designer transaction. To make sure other designers and other parts of the design-time infrastructure (like the Properties window) are notified about the changes that are taking place, you need to use the IComponentChangeService. You must call IComponentChangeService.OnComponentChanging() before you make a change, and IComponentChangeService.OnComponentChanged() afterward. The methods take several parameters, which allow you to identify exactly which property is being changed.

If you are performing a change that affects multiple properties and you don't want to call the OnComponentChanging() and OnComponentChanged() methods multiple times, you can simply pass null references instead of property names and values.

Here's how you can revise the previous example to use a transaction:

```
protected void OnVerbFunky(object sender, EventArgs e)
{
    // Get the associated control.
    MarqueeLabel lbl = (MarqueeLabel)Control;

    // Get the IComponentChangeService.
    IDesignerHost host = (IDesignerHost)GetService(typeof(IDesignerHost));
    IComponentChangeService changeService =
     (IComponentChangeService)GetService(typeof(IComponentChangeService));

    // Start the transaction.
    DesignerTransaction tran = host.CreateTransaction("Apply Funky Theme");

    changeService.OnComponentChanging(lbl, null);
    lbl.ForeColor = Color.LimeGreen;
    lbl.BackColor = Color.Yellow;
    lbl.Font = new Font(lbl.Font.Name, 48, FontStyle.Bold);
    changeService.OnComponentChanged(lbl, null, null, null);

    // Commit the transaction.
    tran.Commit();
}
```

■**Note** You are not quite finished with designer services. You'll see an example of the component-selection service (ISelectionService) later in this chapter when we consider collection controls.

Smart Tags

Visual Studio 2005 includes a new feature for creating a rich design-time experience—smart tags. Smart tags are the pop-up windows that appear next to a control when you click the tiny arrow in the corner.

Smart tags are similar to menus in that they have a list of items. However, these items can be commands (which are rendered like hyperlinks), or other controls like check boxes, drop-down lists, and more. They can also include static descriptive text. In this way, a smart tag can act like a mini Properties window.

Figure 26-4 shows an example of the custom smart tag that's created in the next example. It allows the developer to set a combination of GradientPanel properties. It includes three drop-down lists that let you change the gradient colors and fill style, a Randomize Colors link that chooses random gradient colors, and some static information that indicates the control's current size and location. Additionally, there's a link for docking the control at the very bottom of the smart tag, which is thrown in for free because we're using the ParentControlDesigner (the natural control designer for control containers like Panel).

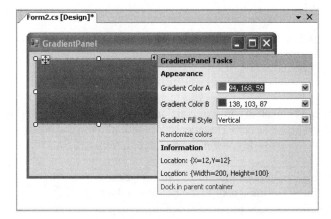

Figure 26-4. *A custom smart tag*

To create this smart tag, you need the following ingredients:

- **A collection of DesignerActionItem objects.** Each DesignerActionItem represents a single item in the smart tag.

- **An action list class.** This class has two roles—it configures the collection of DesignerActionItem instances for the smart tag and, when a command or change is made, it performs the corresponding operation on the linked control.

- **A control designer.** This hooks your action list up to the control so the smart tag appears at design time.

In the following sections, you'll build this solution piece-by-piece.

The Action List

Creating a smart tag is conceptually similar to adding designer verbs—you override a method in your control designer, and return a collection of commands you want to support. (This list of commands is called an *action list*.)

However, smart tags allow many more options than designer verbs, and so the associated code is likely to be more complex. To keep it all under control, it's a good idea to separate your code by creating a custom class that encapsulates your action list. This custom class should derive from DesignerActionList (in the System.ComponentModel.Design namespace).

Here's an example that creates an action list that's intended for use with the GradientPanel:

```
public class GradientPanelActionList : DesignerActionList
{ ... }
```

You should add a single constructor to the action list that requires the matching control type. You can then store the reference to the control in a member variable. This isn't required, because the base ActionList class does provide a Component property that provides access to your control. However, by using this approach, you gain the convenience of strongly typed access to your control.

```
private GradientPanel linkedControl;

public GradientPanelActionList(GradientPanel ctrl) : base(ctrl)
{
    linkedControl = ctrl;
}
```

Before you can build the smart tag, you need to equip your action-list class with the required members. For every link you want to add to the tag (via a DesignerActionMethodItem), you need to create a method. For every property you want to add (via the DesignerActionPropertyItem), you need to create a property procedure.

The smart tag in Figure 26-4 includes eight custom items: two category headers, three properties, one action link, and two pieces of static text (at the bottom of the tag).

The first step is to add the properties. The get property procedure needs to retrieve the value of the property from the linked control. The set property procedure needs to apply the new value to the linked control. However, there's a catch—you can't set the new value directly. If you do, other parts of the designer infrastructure won't be notified about the change. Instead, you need to work through the PropertyDescriptor.SetValue() method, as described in the previous section. To make this easier, you can define a private helper method in your action-list class that retrieves the PropertyDescriptor for a given property by name:

```
private PropertyDescriptor GetPropertyByName(string propName)
{
    PropertyDescriptor prop;
    prop = TypeDescriptor.GetProperties(linkedControl)[propName];

    if (null == prop)
    {
        throw new ArgumentException("Matching property not found.", propName);
    }
    else
    {
        return prop;
    }
}
```

Now you can create the three properties that wrap the properties in the GradientPanel control:

```
public Color ColorA
{

    get { return linkedControl.ColorA; }
    set { GetPropertyByName("ColorA").SetValue(linkedControl, value); }
}

public Color ColorB
{

    get { return linkedControl.ColorB; }
    set { GetPropertyByName("ColorB").SetValue(linkedControl, value); }
}

public LinearGradientMode GradientFillStyle
{

    get { return linkedControl.GradientFillStyle; }
    set { GetPropertyByName("GradientFillStyle").SetValue(linkedControl, value);
}
```

Note Not all properties can be edited natively in a smart tag—it all depends on the data type. If the data type has an associated UITypeEditor (for editing the property graphically) or a TypeConverter (for converting the data type to and from a string representation), editing will work. Most common data types have these ingredients, but your custom objects won't - as a result, all you'll see is a read-only string generated by calling ToString() on the object..

The next step is to build the functionality for the Randomize Colors command. To do this, all you need to do is create a method in the action-list class. Here's an example:

```
public void ChooseRandomColors()
{

    Random rand = new Random();

    // Set the colors through the property procedures
    // in this class.
    ColorA = Color.FromArgb(rand.Next(255), rand.Next(255), rand.Next(255));
    ColorB = Color.FromArgb(rand.Next(255), rand.Next(255), rand.Next(255));
}
```

The DesignerActionItem Collection

The DesignerActionItem class represents the individual items in a smart tag. The .NET Framework provides four basic classes that derive from DesignerActionItem, as described in Table 26-6.

Table 26-6. *Classes Derived from DesignerActionItem*

Method	Description
DesignerActionMethodItem	This item is rendered as a link. When you click it, it triggers an action by calling a method in your DesignerActionList class.
DesignerActionPropertyItem	This item is rendered as an edit control, using logic that's very similar to the Properties window. Strings are given edit boxes, enumerated values become drop-down lists, and Boolean values are turned into check boxes. When you change the value, the underlying property is modified.
DesignerActionTextItem	This item is rendered as a static piece of text. Usually, it provides additional information about the control. It's not clickable.
DesignerActionHeaderItem	This item derives from DesignerActionTextItem. It's a static piece of text that's styled as a heading. Using one or more header items, you can divide the smart tag into separate categories, and group your other properties accordingly. It's not clickable.

To create your smart tag, you need to build a DesignerActionItemCollection that combines your group of DesignerActionItem objects. Order is important in this collection, because Visual Studio will add the DesignerActionItem objects to the smart tag from top to bottom in the order they appear.

To build your action list, you override the DesignerActionList.GetSortedActionItems() method, create the DesignerActionItemCollection, add each DesignerActionItem to it, and then return the collection. Depending on the complexity of your smart tag, this may take several steps.

The first step is to create the headers that divide the smart tag into separate regions. You can then add other items into these categories. This example uses two headers:

```
public override DesignerActionItemCollection GetSortedActionItems()
{
    // Create eight items.
    DesignerActionItemCollection items = new DesignerActionItemCollection();

    // Begin by creating the headers.
    items.Add(new DesignerActionHeaderItem("Appearance"));
    items.Add(new DesignerActionHeaderItem("Information"));
    ...
```

Next, you can add the properties. You specify the name of the property and the class, followed by the name that should appear in the smart tag. The last two items include the category where the item should be placed (corresponding to one of the DesignerActionHeaderItems you just created), and a description (which appears as a tooltip when you hover over that item).

```
    ...
    // Add items that wrap the properties.
    items.Add(new DesignerActionPropertyItem("ColorA",
      "Gradient Color A", "Appearance",
      "Sets the first color in the gradient."));
```

```
items.Add(new DesignerActionPropertyItem("ColorB",
    "Gradient Color B", "Appearance",
    "Sets the second color in the gradient."));

items.Add(new DesignerActionPropertyItem("GradientFillStyle",
    "Gradient Fill Style", "Appearance",
    "Sets the blend direction for the gradient."));
...
```

Visual Studio connects the action item to the property in the action-item class by using reflection with the property name you supply. If you add more than one property to the same category, they're ordered based on the order in which you add them. If you add more than one category header, the categories are ordered the same way.

The next step is to create a DesignerActionMethodItem(), which binds a smart tag item to a method. In this case, you specify the object where the callback method is implemented, the name of the method, the name that should appear in the smart tag display, the category where it will appear, and the tooltip description. The last parameter is a Boolean value. If true, the item will be added to the context menu for the control, as well as to the smart tag.

```
...
items.Add(new DesignerActionMethodItem(this,
    "ChooseRandomColors", "Randomize colors",
    "Appearance", "Chooses random colors for the gradient.",
    true));
...
```

Finally, you can create new DesignerActionTextItem objects with the static text you want to show, and return the complete array of items:

```
...
items.Add(new DesignerActionTextItem(
    "Location: " + linkedControl.Location.ToString(),
    "Information"));

items.Add(new DesignerActionTextItem(
    "Dimension: " + linkedControl.Size.ToString(),
    "Information"));

    return items;
}
```

The Control Designer

Once you've perfected your smart tag action list, you still need to connect it to your control. You accomplish this by creating a custom designer and overriding the ActionList property so that it returns an instance of your custom action-list class, as the following control designer demonstrates. Notice that the action list isn't created each time ActionList is called—instead, it's cached it as private member variable to optimize performance.

```
public class GradientPanelDesigner : ParentControlDesigner
{
    private DesignerActionListCollection actionLists;

    public override DesignerActionListCollection ActionLists
    {
        get
        {
            if (actionLists == null)
            {
                actionLists = new DesignerActionListCollection();
                actionLists.Add(
                    new GradientPanelActionList((GradientPanel)Control));
            }
            return actionLists;
        }
    }
}
```

Container and Collection Controls

Some of the most complex control types are controls that contain child items. These controls can range from simple containers to custom toolbars, trees, and graphical charts. A host of design-time issues come into play specifically with these control types.

Although there's no formal definition for container controls or collection controls, it's helpful to make a distinction between two related but different types. *Container controls* are simply controls that can hold other controls. These child controls are added directly to the Control.Controls collection—one example is the Panel control. Depending on the result you want, you might use design-time features to restrict containers to specific types of children, or you might put the container control completely in charge of layout, in such a way that it disregards the Size and Location properties of its children.

Collection controls are generally a more flexible and common design. They represent a similar concept, but use a more carefully focused object model. The idea with a collection control is that it exposes some collection that accepts child objects—but these objects are not controls. The collection control then performs its drawing from scratch, based on the current collection of children. One example of a collection control is the ListView.

In the following sections, you'll consider some of the design-time basics for both these scenarios, and you'll add design-time support to the SimpleChart custom control.

Collection Controls

The term *collection controls* is commonly used to describe controls that expose a collection of items and then render each item graphically. For example, the TreeNode is a collection control, because it exposes a collection of TreeNode objects and uses them to build a tree. Similarly, the ToolStrip is a collection control that shows ToolStripItem instances (commands, labels, and so on) in a toolbar. Unlike container controls, the child items in a collection controls aren't necessarily controls in their own right. For example, a TreeNode isn't a control—it's just a programming abstraction, and it's up to the TreeView to handle mouse selection, keyboard handling, and painting for all the nodes it shows. The same is true of the ToolStripItem. Unlike the TreeNode, it's a component (which gives it some design-time support) but it isn't a control.

Collection controls pose a few challenges with design-time support. Notably, you need a way to let the developer add child items at design time. You might also want to handle other designer services to provide additional features, like the ability for the developer to select individual child items and configure them in the Properties window (which is possible in the ToolStrip but not the TreeView). Fortunately, the skills you learned in Chapter 13 are enough for you to outfit a collection control with a basic level of support using a type editor and a type converter. This takes care of control serialization and property editing. Additionally, you can use a control designer to provide other services.

To try this out, consider the SimpleChart custom control presented in Chapter 12. The SimpleChart accepts a collection of BarItem objects and uses them to draw a bar chart. The SimpleChart's drawing logic simply loops through the Bars collection, calculates the appropriate bounds, and draws a rectangle representing each BarItem using GDI+.

However, at design time the control doesn't perform as well. When you look at the SimpleChart.Bars property in the Properties window, you'll see the familiar ellipsis (...) button. If you click on it, it calls up the standard CollectionEditor type editor (from the System.ComponentModel.Design namespace). However, if you try to use this dialog box to add BarItem objects, you'll receive an error because the BarItem collection doesn't provide a default constructor. And even if you add a default constructor, the quirks won't go away. Even though you'll be able to create BarItem objects, they won't be serialized into your form-designer code.

The proper solution to this problem is to develop your own type editor and type converter.

The BarItem Type Converter

First of all, you need a way to tell Visual Studio how to create BarItem objects, using the correct constructor. As you learned in Chapter 13, the way to use a nondefault constructor is to support conversion to an InstanceDescriptor.

Let's dissect the code piece-by-piece. First of all, the BarItemConverter derives from ExpandableObjectConverter, giving it the ability to expand and show subproperties in the Properties window:

```
public class BarItemConverter : ExpandableObjectConverter
{ ... }
```

The CanConvertFrom() method indicates that it supports conversions from a string representation:

```
public override bool CanConvertFrom(ITypeDescriptorContext context, Type t)
{
    if (t == typeof(string))
        return true;
    else
        return base.CanConvertFrom(context, t);
}
```

The string representation used in this example is a simple comma delimited format like this: BarItem.ShortForm, BarItem.Value. The ConvertFrom() method builds this string from a live BarItem object.

```
public override object ConvertFrom(ITypeDescriptorContext context,
 CultureInfo info, object value)
{
    if (value is string)
    {
        try
        {
            string[] elements = ((string)value).Split(',');
            return new BarItem(elements[0], float.Parse(elements[1]));
        }
        catch
        {
            throw new ArgumentException("Could not convert the value");
        }
    }
    return base.ConvertFrom(context, info, value);
}
```

Life gets a little more interesting with CanConvertTo(), because it supports two conversion paths—to a string (used for display in the Properties window), or to an InstanceDescriptor (used for code serialization).

```
public override bool CanConvertTo(ITypeDescriptorContext context, Type destType)
{
    if (destType == typeof(InstanceDescriptor) || destType == typeof(string))
        return true;
    else
        return base.CanConvertTo(context, destType);
}
```

The ConvertTo() method implements the conversion. The conversion to string is straightforward. The conversion to an InstanceDescriptor needs to get the matching constructor, which takes two parameters (string and float).

```
public override object ConvertTo(ITypeDescriptorContext context, CultureInfo info,
  object value, Type destType)
{
    if (destType == typeof(string))
    {
        BarItem item = (BarItem)value;
        return String.Format("{0}, {1}", item.ShortForm, item.Value);
    }
```

```
    else if (destType == typeof(InstanceDescriptor))
    {
        BarItem item = (BarItem)value;
        ConstructorInfo ctor =
          typeof(BarItem).GetConstructor(
          new Type[] { typeof(string), typeof(float) });

        return new InstanceDescriptor(ctor,
          new object[] { item.ShortForm, item.Value });
    }
    else
    {
        return base.ConvertTo(context, info, value, destType);
    }
}
```

This is the first step in adding design-time support to the SimpleChart. Now you'll be able to edit the BarItem collection at design time using the familiar CollectionEditor, and it will successfully create BarItem objects. However, the CollectionEditor has a significant limitation— it serializes collection items only if they implement IComponent. That means you need to either modify the BarItem class so that it derives from Component (which is unnecessarily clunky), or create your own type editor, as demonstrated in the next section.

The BarItemCollectionEditor

Now that you've added serialization support to the BarItem class, you need to consider how the developer edits the Bars collection. It's not attaching a type editor to the BarItem class, because the developer doesn't edit the BarItem objects individually. Instead, you need a way to control the editing for the entire *collection*.

This task is actually easier than it seems. The first step is to create a custom collection class. In the current version of the SimpleChart control, a generic collection provides access to BarItem instances:

```
private List<BarItem> bars = new List<BarItem>();
```

The problem here is that there's no way to control what type editor is used to edit the bars collection. To solve this problem, you need to use a custom collection.

```
private BarItemCollection bars = new BarItemCollection();
```

It's easy to create the BarItemCollection. Here's a basic example that makes the BarItemCollection more or less the same as an ArrayList, with support for each iteration and Add() and Remove() methods. Only BarItem objects are allowed in the BarItemCollection.

```
public class BarItemCollection : CollectionBase
{
    public void Add(BarItem item)
    {
        this.List.Add(item);
    }

    public void Remove(int index)
    {
        // Check to see if there is an item at the supplied index.
        if ((index > Count - 1) || (index < 0))
        {
            throw new System.IndexOutOfRangeException();
        }
        else
        {
            this.List.RemoveAt(index);
        }
    }

    public BarItem this[int i]
    {
        get {return (BarItem)this.List[i]; }
        set {this.List[i] = value;}
    }
}
```

Now you can create a custom collection editor. Although you can implement your own functionality from scratch, the easiest approach is to just derive a class from CollectionEditor, which gives you the familiar collection-editing dialog box with a list of items in the collection and a property grid for changing the settings of the currently selected item. Figure 26-5 shows the final result.

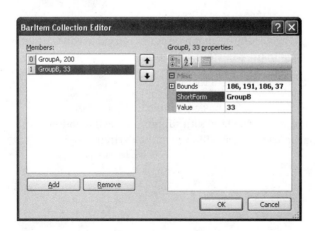

Figure 26-5. *A custom type editor for the BarItemCollection*

When building your custom collection editor, you can add functionality by overriding one of several methods. Table 26-7 lists some of your options.

Table 26-7. *Overridable CollectionEditor Methods*

Method	Description
CreateInstance()	Creates a new collection item, which is added to the collection (occurs when the Add button is clicked). Override this method to customize the default values of new items.
DestroyInstance()	Destroys the specified collection item (occurs when the Remove button is clicked).
EditValue()	Modifies an item in the collection (occurs when changes are made in the property grid).
CancelChanges()	Reverts the changes that have been made so far (triggered when the Cancel button is clicked).
CreateNewItemTypes()	Returns the types of all items in the collection. Override this method if you want the collection editor to allow several different item types. Once you do, the Add button will show a drop-down arrow giving you the choice of supported items.
CanRemoveInstance()	Returns true (the default) if existing members of the collection can be removed with the Remove button.
CanSelectMultipleInstances()	Returns true (the default) to indicate that multiple collection items can be selected and modified at once in the property grid.
GetDisplayText()	Retrieves the display text for the given list item.
ShowHelp()	Displays the default Help topic for the collection editor.

In this example, it makes sense to override two methods. By overriding EditValue(), you can make sure the chart is refreshed to show the new set of bars when any item is changed. By overriding CreateInstance() , you can supply default values for each new BarItem that's created when the developer clicks the Add button.

Here's the complete code:

```
public class BarItemCollectionEditor : CollectionEditor
{
    public BarItemCollectionEditor(Type type) : base(type)
    { }

    public override object EditValue(ITypeDescriptorContext context,
      IServiceProvider provider, object value)
    {
        object returnObject = base.EditValue(context, provider, value);
((SimpleChart)Context.Instance).RebuildChart();
        return returnObject;
    }
```

```
protected override object CreateInstance(Type itemType)
{
    BarItem item = new BarItem("Enter Title Here", 0);
    return item;
}
}
```

Finally, you need to attach the type editor to the Bars property of the BarItemCollection class:

```
[Editor(typeof(BarItemCollectionEditor), typeof(UITypeEditor))]
public class BarItemCollection : CollectionBase
{...}
```

This completes the example, and gives you the ability to add and modify the collection BarItem objects used for the SimpleChart at design time.

Selecting BarItem Objects at Design Time

There's one more frill you can add to the SimpleChart example. Now that you have the ability to create and configure BarItem objects at design time, you might also want to allow the developer to select individual BarItem objects from the form-design surface, and configure them directly in the Properties window. In the case of the SimpleChart control, this doesn't add a lot to the overall picture, but it's still a useful technique. It also demonstrates how to use the ISelectionService.

The first step is to override the ControlDesigner.GetHitTest() method. In this method, you need to convert the mouse coordinates from screen to form coordinates. Then you can use the Rectangle.Contains() method to find out if this point falls into any bar.

```
protected override bool GetHitTest(System.Drawing.Point point)
{
    point = Control.PointToClient(point);

    SimpleChart chart = (SimpleChart)Component;
    foreach (BarItem item in chart.Bars)
    {
        Rectangle rect = item.Bounds;
        if (rect.Contains(point)) return true;
    }
    return false;
}
```

In this example, the designer returns true to pass the click to the SimpleChart control if it falls on a bar. The SimpleChart control can then handle the MouseDown event and select the corresponding BarItem object. This step requires the ISelectionService, which is described in Table 26-8.

Table 26-8. *ISelectionService Members*

Member	Description
PrimarySelection	Gets the object that is currently the primary selected object. If more than one object is selected, PrimarySelection gets the object that was selected most recently.
SelectionCount	Gets the total number of selected objects.
GetComponentSelected()	Tests if a specific component is currently selected.
GetSelectedComponents()	Gets a collection with all the components that are currently selected.
SetSelectedComponents()	Selects the components you specify. You must supply a collection object with the components you want to select, even if you want to select only a single component.
SelectionChanging event	Occurs when the current selection is about to change.
SelectionChanged event	Occurs once the current selection has changed.

Here's the code you need:

```
protected override void OnMouseDown(System.Windows.Forms.MouseEventArgs e)
{
    base.OnMouseDown(e);
    if (DesignMode)
    {
        foreach (BarItem bar in Bars)
        {
            Rectangle rect = bar.Bounds;
            if (rect.Contains(e.X, e.Y))
            {
                ISelectionService selectService =
                    (ISelectionService)GetService(typeof(ISelectionService));
                ArrayList selection = new ArrayList();
                selection.Add(bar);
                selectService.SetSelectedComponent(a);
                break;
            }
        }
    }
}
```

In this case, you don't really need the GetHitTest() method—in fact, you could improve this design by performing all the logic in the ControlDesigner.MouseDown() method. Because the bounds of each bar are publicly accessible, the ControlDesigner can perform all the hit testing and use the ISelectionService. However, the GetHitTest() method is important if the control needs to perform more work or change its internal state (for example, rearranging an internal collection or adjusting several child items).

Container Controls

A container control is a control that can contain other controls. Technically, any control has this ability by virtue of its Controls collection. However, only some controls provide this functionality in the design-time environment.

You can create a container control by inheriting from ContainerControl or a derived class (like Panel). This works because these controls use the ParentControlDesigner (or one of its derived classes), which has the design-time ability to host other controls. However, even if you decide to create your own control that doesn't derive from ContainerControl, you can still get this functionality—all you need to do is attach the ParentControlDesigner by hand.

■**Note** One ContainerControl that doesn't use ParentControlDesigner is the UserControl. If you want the (potentially confusing) ability to create a user control that allows the developers to add additional child controls, you'll need to attach the ParentControlDesigner with the Designer attribute.

For example, consider the following exceedingly simple control, which paints a large blue border:

```
[Designer(typeof(ParentControlDesigner))]
public class Container : Control
{
    protected override void OnPaint(PaintEventArgs e)
    {
        Pen p = new Pen(Color.Blue, 10);
        e.Graphics.DrawRectangle(p, this.ClientRectangle);
        p.Dispose();
    }
}
```

Because this control attaches the ParentControlDesigner, you can drag and drop other controls inside it at design time (see Figure 26-6). When you move the container, these child controls will move with it.

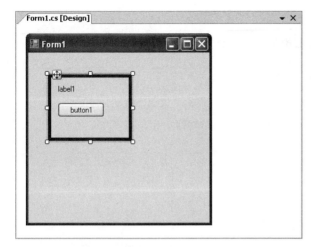

Figure 26-6. *A custom container control*

When creating a container control, you might want the ability to restrict what types of controls can be placed inside. You have two options, and both involve creating a custom control designer. To restrict the container control from hosting other types of controls, you need to override the ParentControlDesigner.CanParent() method so that it returns true only for supported controls (in this case, the ContainerChild control).

```
public class ContainerDesigner : ParentControlDesigner
{
    public override bool CanParent(Control control)
    {
        // Children can only be of type ContainerChild.
        if (control is Panel)
        {
            return(base.CanParent(control));
        }
        else
        {
            return(false);
        }
    }
}
```

To restrict a control from being added to certain containers, you need to override the ControlDesigner.CanBeParentedTo() method so that it returns true only for supported containers:

```
public class ContainerChildDesigner : ControlDesigner
{
    public override bool CanBeParentedTo(IDesigner parentDesigner)
    {
        // Control can be parent only by Container
        if (parentDesigner is ContainerDesigner)
        {
            return(base.CanBeParentedTo(parentDesigner));
        }
        else
        {
            return(false);
        }
    }
}
```

There's still a problem with this example. Right now the control designers prevent you from moving the wrong type of child into the Container, or taking a ContainerChild outside. However, you won't be prevented from breaking these rules if you add a control from the toolbox.

■**Tip** If you want to create a set of child and parent controls that are used together exclusively (like the TabControl and TabPage controls), there are a few steps you can take. First of all, add the ToolboxItem attribute to your child control and use the constructor argument false so it doesn't appear in the toolbox at all. Then, allow instances to be created exclusively through designer verbs and smart tags that are provided on the container. You can use the techniques demonstrated in this chapter to implement this design.

Licensing Custom Controls

Licensing in the .NET world is far more customizable and far less painful than it is with older component technologies like COM. The .NET Framework provides several licensing classes in the System.ComponentModel namespace. By using and extending these classes, you can grant or allow access to your control, using ordinary .NET code to check external resources like the Windows registry, an XML file, or even a remote Web service for registration information.

There are four basic ingredients for .NET licensing:

- **The license.** This is an object that contains the licensing information. You might create it based on the information in a license file, a registry key, a piece of hardware, or something entirely different. However, this is the programming abstraction that your licensing code will evaluate. You can create a custom license class by deriving from System.ComponentModel.License.

- **The license provider.** This is where you write the code to implement your licensing policy. The license provider creates the license object. To build a custom license provider, you derive from System.ComponentModel.LicenseProvider and override IsKeyValid() and GetLicense().

- **The LicenseProvider attribute.** This connects a component to a license provider.

- **The LicenseManager.** This is a part of the .NET infrastructure. Once you've attached your license provider with the LicenseProvider attribute, it's up to you to call the LicenseManager.Validate() method when your class is instantiated to verify that the license is in order. In turn, the LicenseManager communicates with your license provider, and then provides your component with the license object. Your component holds on to its license for the duration of its lifetime.

Figure 26-7 shows how these classes interact.

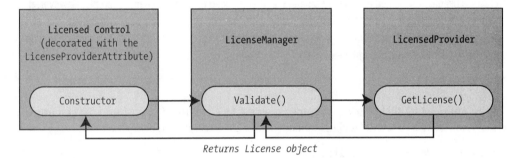

Figure 26-7. *The licensing classes*

The .NET licensing model allows you to distinguish between application and control licensing. *Application licensing* is concerned mainly with the runtime requirements of an application. *Control licensing* distinguishes between runtime use (which is often unrestricted) and design-time use. The goal is to allow free distribution of the control, but make money selling the control assembly to developers. Making this distinction in your licensing classes is easy, because the GetLicense() method that's a part of all license providers includes the information about whether the component is in runtime or design-time mode.

■**Note** Technically, licensing can be applied to any class. However, in this discussion we're primarily interested in licensing control classes.

Simple LIC File Licensing

To best understand .NET licensing, it helps to start with a simple example using the LicFileLicenseProvider class. The LicFileLicenseProvider is a simple file-based licensing implementation that derives from LicenseProvider. This class doesn't provide any real protection, but it's a stepping-stone to the more-advanced licensing strategies you'll look at next.

The LicFileLicenseProvider searches for a text file in the same directory as the control assembly. This LIC file uses the control's fully qualified class name for a file name, so a control named SimpleControl in a project named LicensedControl requires a license file named LicensedControl.SimpleControl.LIC. The file starts with a simple predefined text string in the format "[Component] is a licensed component."

Thus, the contents of the LicensedControl.SimpleControl.LIC file would be as follows:

```
LicensedControl.SimpleControl is a licensed component.
```

This file must be placed in the client project's Bin\Debug directory (where Visual Studio compiles the final EXE application just prior to launching it).

■**Note** It's worth noting that these LIC files don't need to be distributed with a client application. When you compile a Windows program, a license.licx file is created with all the licensing information for all license controls. This file is compiled as a binary resource and embedded in the final client assembly. However, if another developer wants to create a client application with your control, a LIC source file *is* needed. This gives you a separate licensing path for design-time use (in which case you need the LIC file) and runtime use (in which case you need only the embedded resource) with a control.

To enforce LIC file licensing, you need to add a LicenseProvider attribute to your control class to tell .NET to use the LicFileLicenceProvider class to validate licenses.

```
[LicenseProvider(typeof(LicFileLicenseProvider))]
public class SimpleControl : Control
```

Additionally, you need to create the license when the control is created, using the static Validate() method of the LicenseManager class:

```
private License license;

public SimpleControl()
{
    license = LicenseManager.Validate(this.GetType(), this);
}
```

The Validate() method throws a LicenseException if it doesn't find the correct string in the LIC file, and refuses to create your control.

Finally, you need to dispose of the license when the control is disposed.

```
protected override void Dispose(bool disposing)
{
    if (license != null)
    {
        license.Dispose();
    }
    base.Dispose(disposing);
}
```

Now if you try to add this control to a form and you haven't created the correct LIC file, you'll be refused with an error message. If you create the LIC file, you'll be able to add instances of the control to the form.

Custom LIC File Licensing

Clearly, simple LIC file licensing doesn't offer much in the way of protection. Any user who knows a little about the .NET Framework will realize the generic format that must be created for a LIC file. However, you can add more-stringent requirements by creating a custom license provider based on the LicFileLicenseProvider.

All you need to do is inherit from the class and override the IsValid() method to change the validation routine. The IsValid() method receives the contents of the LIC file, and returns true or false to indicate if the contents are correct. Thus, you could use the IsValid() method to check a license number against a company-specific algorithm. (You can also override the GetLicense() method if you want to retrieve the license file from another location. You'll see an example of how to override GetLicense() a little later on.)

The example below extracts the first three characters from the license file, and verifies that they correspond to a number that is divisible by 7.

```
public class FileLicenseProvider : LicFileLicenseProvider
{
    protected override bool IsKeyValid(string key, System.Type type)
    {
        int code = int.Parse(key.Substring(0, 3));
        if (code != 0)
        {
            if (Math.IEEERemainder(code, 7) == 0)
            {
                return true;
            }
            else
            {
                return false;
            }
        }
        else
        {
            return false;
        }
    }
}
```

More-Advanced License Providers

Control licensing doesn't need to be based on LIC files. In fact, you can create any type of licensing scheme imaginable. You can even perform tremendously annoying tricks like allowing controls to be registered only to specific computers. To implement a custom licensing scheme, you need to create two classes: a custom license provider and a custom license.

The custom license is the easiest ingredient. It simply derives from the base License class, overrides the LicenseKey property and the Dispose() method, and adds properties for any required pieces of information. You also need to add a constructor that configures the license, as the LicenseKey property is read-only.

```
public class CustomLicense : License
{
    private string key;

    public override string LicenseKey
    {
        get { return key; }
    }

    public CustomLicense(string key)
    {
        this.key = key;
    }

    public override void Dispose()
    {
        // This method must be overriden.
    }
}
```

The custom LicenseProvider plays the same role as the LicFileLicenseProvider. It provides a GetLicense() method, which the .NET Framework calls to validate the control. For example, when you use the LicenseManager.Validate() method in the constructor for the DirectoryTree control, .NET uses the LicenseProvider.GetLicense() method to retrieve the license.

In the GetLicense() method, you may want to examine whether the component is in design-time or runtime mode, look for license information from another source than a simple LIC file, and apply different rules. Additionally, you may want to return a valid license object, return nothing at all, or throw a LicenseException to indicate that the control should not be created. The LicFileProvider throws a LicenseException to indicate when a LIC file is not valid.

The example that follows looks for a predefined registry entry at design time. At runtime, it first examines the current context, and then defaults to the registry if a compiled license key can't be found. The registry value is stored under a predefined company name, followed by the fully qualified name of the control. The key is validated as long as it matches the string "1234567890" and a CustomLicense object encapsulating this key is returned.

```
public class RegistryLicenseProvider : LicenseProvider
{
    public override System.ComponentModel.License GetLicense(
      System.ComponentModel.LicenseContext context,
      System.Type type, object instance, bool allowExceptions)
    {
        string key = string.Empty;

        if (context.UsageMode == LicenseUsageMode.Runtime)
        {
            // Try to find key in current context.
            key = context.GetSavedLicenseKey(type, null);
        }
```

```
        // Always look in the registry at design time.
        // If the key wasn't found in the current context at runtime,
        // we can also look in the registry.
        // Another option might be to always allow the control at runtime,
        // and restrict it just at design time.
        if (key.Length == 0)
        {
            // A debugging hint (remove when you perfect the licensing scheme):
            MessageBox.Show("Performing registry lookup.",
                            "RegistryLicenseProvider");

            RegistryKey rk;
            rk = Registry.LocalMachine.OpenSubKey(@"Software\MyCompany\" +
                type.ToString());
            if (rk != null)
            {
                key = rk.GetValue("LicenseKey", "") as string;
            }

            // Save key in current context.
            if ((key != null) && (key.Length != 0))
            {
                context.SetSavedLicenseKey(type, key);
            }
        }

        // Check if key is valid.
        if (!IsValid(key))
        {
            if (allowExceptions)
            {
                throw new LicenseException(type);
            }
            return null;
        }

        // Return the license object.
        return new CustomLicense(key);
    }

    private bool IsValid(string key)
    {
        return (key.CompareTo("1234567890") == 0);
    }
}
```

The GetLicense() method is provided with a fair bit of information, including the current LicenseContext, the type of the component that is requesting the license, and a reference to an instance of the component. The LicenseContext object is particularly useful—it allows you to tell if the component is being used at design time or runtime by evaluating the LicenseContext.UsageMode property.

Using the information supplied to the GetLicense() method, you can easily create a single LicenseProvider that could handle the licensing for all different types of controls. Custom licensing schemes are limited only by your imagination, and can become quite complex. The material presented here is only a basic introduction for what a component vendor might do.

The Last Word

In this chapter, you've considered a wide range of techniques for implementing better design-time support. You began by creating custom designers and using them to filter properties, interact with the mouse, and add frills like designer verbs. You then considered how to access designer services, create custom smart tags, and build your own collection controls. Finally, the chapter wrapped up with an introduction to licensing.

There's still a lot to learn before you're a master of control development. If you want to learn more, start by exploring the other designer services, which allow you to plug in to other important areas of IDE functionality. You can also look at the other methods that the ComponentDesigner and ControlDesigner base classes provide. By overriding these, you can configure even more details about your control's design-time behavior, including how it participates with snap lines, whether it supports drag-and-drop operations, and how it tracks linked controls. The MSDN class reference is your best bet for exploring these details. You may also want to consider the sample code for more-elaborate sample controls—some of which you can find at www.windowsforms.net.

■■■

Creating Usable Interfaces

Sometimes it seems that no one can agree about what user interface design really is. Is it the painstaking process an artist goes through to create shaded icons that light up when the mouse approaches? Is it the hours spent in a usability lab subjecting users to a complicated new application? Is it the series of decisions that determine how to model information using common controls and metaphors?

In fact, user interface design is a collection of several different tasks:

- **User interface modeling.** This is the process in which you look at the tasks a program needs to accomplish, and decide how to break these tasks into windows and controls. To emerge with an elegant design, you need to combine instinct, convention, a dash of psychology, and painstaking usability testing.

- **User interface architecture.** This is the logical design you use to divide the functionality in your application into separate objects. Creating a consistent, well-planned design makes it easy to extend, alter, and reuse portions of the user interface framework.

- **User interface coding.** This is the process in which you write the code for managing the user interface with the appropriate classes and objects. Ideally, you follow the first two steps to lay out a specific user interface model and architecture before you begin this stage.

This book concentrates on the second and third steps, where user interfaces designs are translated into code using the tools and techniques of .NET. This appendix, however, focuses on the first task of user interface design. Here you'll examine the essential guidelines that no programmer can afford to ignore. You learn basic tips for organizing information, handling complexity, and entering into the mind of that often-feared final judge—the end user.

You could ignore these topics completely. However, the greatest programming framework in the world won't solve some common, critical user interface mistakes. Learning how to design an interface is no less important than learning how to work with it in code.

Why Worry About the Interface?

The user interface is the thin outer shell that wraps a program's logic and provides a way for ordinary users to interact with it. Usually, user interfaces have three responsibilities:

- Interpreting what a user wants and translating it into the corresponding operations

- Retrieving information and displaying it in different ways

- Guiding users through a task (and steering them away from common mistakes)

User interfaces bear the weight of a program, because they are the only part the user interacts with. It doesn't matter what your program can do if it's trapped behind a limited, frustrating interface—it's a little like locking a concert pianist in a prison cell. As with anything else, people judge and identify programs based on what they can see from the outside. Friendly, enjoyable interfaces are able to attract users just because of the way of they look. Ugly and confusing interfaces, on the other hand, lead to a legacy of headaches for developers and end users.

In programming circles, user interfaces are often the subject of heated debate. Some developers resent the whole topic of user interface design because they feel it detracts from "real" programming. They dread the vaguely defined requirements, the hard-to-please end users, and the perception that they have to simplify the product of their perfectly natural first instincts. Another group is made up of developers who love to experiment with the latest user interface fad. They aim to discover the newest and most avant-garde user interface controls before they have been adopted as standards, even when they lead to somewhat bizarre applications.

Ultimately, both approaches are bad news for end users, who just want a simple, unobtrusive interface that works exactly the way they expect it to. To create a good user interface—one that satisfies the average user—you need to know the unwritten rules of user interface design.

■**Tip** It's sometimes suggested that there is no such as thing as bad interfaces—just interfaces that are suited for different types of users. Allow me to put this myth to rest. There are definitely bad (and even atrocious) interfaces. Although it's certainly true that you need to tailor the interface to the audience, user confusion is usually the result of violating conventions.

A Brief History of User Interfaces

You might think that user interface design is a history of continuous innovation. In fact, user interface design is marked by a series of distinct eras. Typically, in each era one predominant approach develops. Then, at some unpredictable time, a lone programmer or innovative programming team creates a truly new user interface model that dazzles the world. In the months that follow, hundreds of developers rush to create similar but mutually incompatible versions. This process of imitation continues until the next revolution.

So what are these eras of user interface development? It all began very simply....

The Command-Line Era

Almost everyone who has any experience with computers has at least glimpsed the fabled command line. Today's novice users instinctively think of it as some back-door way of accessing features that are forbidden and hidden from most people. Even advanced computer users are sometimes bound by the superstition that a command line lurks behind the scenes in the latest Windows operating system, secretly controlling things.

A command-line interface is the power user's dream. Of course, even power users have to learn somewhere, and although modern-day command-line interfaces are usually fairly friendly because they include an autocompletion feature to help you fill in hard-to-remember commands, the command line was not always an easy tool to master.

The command line is, in many respects, the original way of doing things, and it's arguable that it's not so much an interface design as a lack of any user interface, at least in the sense we use the term today. Command lines began as the basis for operating systems like DOS (see Figure A-1) and UNIX, were the basis for early database applications like dBase, and continue to proliferate in unusual places.

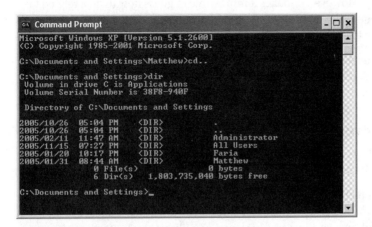

Figure A-1. *The archetypal command-line interface*

For example, the Visual Studio interface provides a Command Window that lets you interact with the IDE or execute code statements against the currently running application. Besides a few rudimentary enhancements (like autocomplete), it's still a basic command-line interface (see Figure A-2).

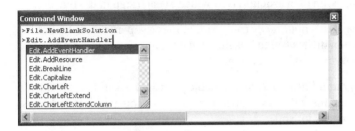

Figure A-2. *The command line in Visual Studio*

Command-line interfaces are characterized by the following traits:

- **Ultimate control.** Users can do anything in any order, so long as they remember the "secret codes."

- **Ultimate lack of structure.** Users not only have to remember what to do, but what order to do it in. In DOS, just moving a file to a new directory can be an agonizing multistep operation. By default, the command line assumes that each operation is atomic, and it doesn't associate one task with another.

- **A "hands-off" treatment of the user.** With a few minor exceptions, there are no helpful prompts, tips, or guidance.

- **No metaphors.** This makes it easy to grasp the basic process (type in words, press Enter), which never changes. However, it makes it impossible to guess how to do a related task based on a previous one. (For example, if you know how to copy a file in UNIX, that doesn't mean you know how to delete it.)

Today, a command-line model could still turn up in one of your user interfaces, but it's unlikely. On the other hand, it's still a familiar tool in the developer world, particularly with formula-based languages and SQL.

The Question-Answer Model

The question-answer model is one of the oldest user interface models, and it's still alive and well in the modern world. Its principles are the polar opposite of a command-line interface:

- **Prompts at every step of the way.** Thus, you don't need to remember what the program requires. However, you are also immediately stuck if you are missing a piece of information, as question-and-answer programs are usually unidirectional—if you can't move forward, you can't go anywhere.

- **No control.** This can be either a blessing or a curse. If the program has an accurate idea of your needs, you are in a "benevolent dictator" scenario, which makes your life considerably less complicated. But if the program makes the wrong assumptions, you have no way to fight it.

- **Ultimate guidance.** Some kind of instruction is provided at each step in the process.

- **Still no metaphors.** Well, that's not exactly true—sometimes a superficial metaphor is used, in which the program invites you to imagine that a friendly guide is asking you a series of questions, and trying to do what you need.

The question-answer programming model has a valuable place in the world today, and it's seen commonly in Windows programs with *wizards*. Wizards lead you through a set of questions, and then perform a complicated task for you.

As you've no doubt discovered, there are useful wizards (like those that set up hardware on your computer). There are also less-useful wizards that seem to be more complicated, demanding, and restrictive than the program itself (like those that create documents for you in some popular graphics programs). Figure A-3 shows the wizard Windows uses for adding a shortcut.

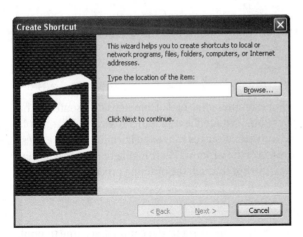

Figure A-3. *A genuinely useful wizard*

■**Tip** One good habit is to implement a wizard in your application only *after* you have created a standard Windows interface. This ensures that you don't end up inadvertently coding the application functionality inside the wizard itself, which would limit flexibility.

Question-answer programs are double-edged swords that can frustrate as much as they please. The next few sections outline a few key principles that can help you use this model.

Ask What the User Can Tell You

It makes sense to ask a user to tell you what company made his or her printer. However, it doesn't make sense to ask a user whether you should convert tabs to spaces for DOS print operations. Instead, just pick a suitable default. Remember, no one likes to be asked a question they can't answer. Novice computer users might just give up altogether, or stop reading other prompts.

Restrict It to a Single Task

A wizard works well for a single task that can be accomplished in only one way (like adding a printer driver). As soon as you start adding an element of variety or creativity, the wizard can't keep up. Don't think that you should be proud of a complex wizard that branches out conditionally to use different windows depending on previous user selections. All you've done is created a traditional single-screen DOS program wherein tasks must be completed in separate windows and in a set order.

Beware of Forcing Your Preferences

Every wizard has its own hard-coded patterns. The user never has a choice of what order to answer questions or supply information, and that lack of control can frustrate anyone who wants to approach the task differently. Be forewarned, especially if you are using a wizard for a complex task: you are enforcing a single way of working according to your assumptions and biases. If those don't match the way the majority of users want to work, your wizard will only make them miserable.

Use Signposts

Let the user know what step is coming next. For example, at the end of one step add a sentence that helps prepare for the next. Give a general overview of where the user is in the wizard (for example, "Step 3/5"). Even better, separate the wizard into logical stages (Choose a Location, Choose Files, Copy Files, and so on), and list these all at the top of the window. Then, highlight the current stage. This is similar to the way Amazon.com guides a visitor through the ordering process.

The Menu-Driven Model

The menu-driven model is the most easily recognizable user interface model. It came to popularity with document-based programs like DOS word processors, and then took over nearly every application with the Windows operating system. It's easy to see why: menus represent an attractive compromise, allowing you to prompt users without restricting the way they work.

- **Commands performable in any order.** You have the same freedom you have with the command-line interface, and the same ability to use keyboard shortcuts.

- **On-screen prompts.** You are never left on your own, and the very grouping of elements can sometimes help you remember what you want to do. For example, if you want to change spacing in Microsoft Word you might not know it has anything to do with paragraphs, but you would be able to decide that the Format menu is probably the best place to start your exploration.

Menus are one of the dominant interface elements in Windows programming, and they allow absolutely no room for experimentation or innovation (unless, of course, you're Microsoft, in which case you can roll out a new menu "standard" with each new version of Office). To create a menu, you copy Microsoft Office as closely as possible, even adding a vestigial File menu when your program has nothing to do with files or documents. Similarly, you would do best to emulate basic options like Edit, View, Window, and even Tools before you start adding menus organized around program-specific concepts. You'll learn more about Microsoft's role in your user interface design a little later in this appendix.

The GUI Era

Shortly after the menu excitement subsided, everyone fell in love with pictures and buttons with the Macintosh OS and Microsoft Windows. The GUI era introduced an avalanche of concepts and user interface elements, several of which are often summarized with the acronym WIMP (windows, icons, mouse, and pointers). One key innovation in the GUI era was the introduction of the mouse, which provides more points of entry for interacting with an application (as in, "I want to click *here*"). Another change was the shift to realistic representation—for example, word processors that show a close approximation of how a printed document will look. A central idea in the GUI era was to base user interfaces on real-world metaphors. For example, if you want to delete a file, drag it to an icon that looks like a trash can because that's what you use to dispose of rubbish in the real world.

Of course, some things are much harder to convey with pictures than others are (for example, no application provides an icon that accurately suggests "synchronize my e-mail"). Metaphors are also notoriously difficult to *localize*, or adapt for other languages and cultures.

The following are some of the hallmarks of the GUI era:

- **Visual clues.** A button with a grey border seems to pop off the window—it just looks pushable. Web-like buttons that glow when the mouse moves over them also give valuable feedback, and future versions of Windows (like Vista) will add similar feedback mechanisms.

- **Real-world analogies.** A tabbed dialog box looks like a set of tabbed pages in a binder; sticky notes in Microsoft Outlook look like real-life sticky notes. Most contact-management software tries to look like a wall calendar and an address book (see Figure A-4 for an example). The idea is that the user already knows how to use these things in the real world.

- **Transferable knowledge.** For example, if you learned how to delete a file, a program can provide a trash can that lets you delete a product record, and you might be able to guess how to use it based on the similarity. (Of course, metaphors enforce their own biases— knowing how to format a paragraph won't help you format a floppy disk.)

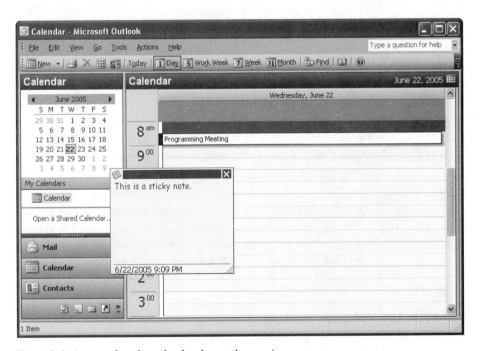

Figure A-4. *A metaphor-based calendar and organizer*

All these points are essentially an effort to make a program so logical it's almost instinctual. The goal is for a user to require no special training, and just be able to apply assumptions garnered from other programs and the real world when learning a new application. Of course, because the focus is on the user, you need to know quite a bit about how an average user thinks before you can create the interface.

The GUI model provides a great deal of freedom for the developer (some might say too much freedom). In the Windows world, designing a first-rate user interface has less to do with inventing metaphors, and more to do with following established conventions.

Creativity vs. Convention

Many user interface projects are sidetracked when they meet up with the developer's need for creativity. Unfortunately, an application's user interface doesn't just determine how a program looks; it also determines how it acts (or from the user's point of view, how it works).

Ask yourself this question: Would car manufacturers allow the same degree of creativity that some developers take in application design? The world's reliance on vehicles (and the seriousness of any mistake) makes it almost impossible to imagine a car manufacturer taking such liberties. Every year, new car models appear that have been tweaked by entire design teams of engineers with bold promises that they are entirely new and modern. But it doesn't take much inspection to see that the air conditioners and radios always work almost exactly the same as before, down to the last button; the steering wheel looks and works exactly the same way; the seat configuration is generally unchanged; and the controls for starting, stopping, and slowing the car down are indistinguishable. The average driver could close his or her eyes and still locate the ignition in most cars.

Even in some of today's better applications, this level of consistency is rare. If you install a new program on your computer, are you confident that Ctrl+S is the Save command? Will File ➤ Print send your document straight to the printer, or give you a chance to tweak some settings first? And exactly where do you find the menu command for that all-important Preferences or Options window... under Tools, Edit, or File?

■**Tip** Some conventions are well-followed (like using Esc to exit a dialog box). Other conventions have taken over just because Microsoft enforces them (like the way you resize or move a window).

Convention is the way that users learn to work with a variety of software. Violating convention because convention is somehow inferior to your highly idiosyncratic vision is a poor idea. It just multiplies the amount of information a user needs to know to use computer software. Users aren't interested in spending long hours to learn new user interface idioms for business software—and companies aren't interested in paying to train them for it.

Consistency in .NET

Microsoft has made no secret of its goal to use the .NET platform to make the programming model more consistent for different programmers. You can see evidence of this in the different .NET languages, which share a consistent set of data types and functionality drawn from a shared class library. You can see it in the lavish use of interfaces and inheritance, which defines how specialized classes should work so they resemble other, similar classes. You can even see it in the way Visual Studio allows you to use its powerful debugging tools, regardless of whether you're working with code for a Windows project, an ASP.NET page, or even a database stored procedure.

In short, if cutting-edge software developers prize consistency, why would anyone assume it's not just as important to the beginning computer user?

The "Act Like Microsoft Office" Principle

Windows developers have it rather easy. The secret to making a program that the average user can understand, and even enjoy, is usually just to copy Microsoft as closely as possible. That isn't to say that Microsoft has made the best choices in its applications—but for the most part, that isn't important. If the users of your application have ever used another application, chances are that it's been Microsoft Office or Internet Explorer. In fact, if your users are regular computer users, they probably spend the majority of their computing time with Word and Excel.

There's rarely a good reason for deviating from Microsoft standards. If average users have learned anything, it's the common keystrokes and menu organizations in an Office application. Not only that, but Microsoft is known to pour ridiculous amounts of money into extensive usability tests, suggesting that their designs might not only be more recognizable than yours, but they could very well be *better*.

If you aren't creating an office-productivity or document-based application, you should still pay careful attention to Microsoft's designs. In almost every field, Microsoft has a well-worn example (including utilities for playing music, browsing the Internet, and reading e-mail). In some cases, you might need to investigate another application (like Adobe Photoshop in the graphics arena), but Microsoft is generally the standard.

■**Tip** Remember, when you follow expected conventions, you don't just make it easier for users to learn your application. You also help train those users for the next programmer's software.

Administrative Utilities

One good example of a Windows convention is found in Microsoft's design of system and management utilities. These utilities almost always use a paired TreeView and ListView control, loosely resembling Windows Explorer. In Windows 2000 and later operating systems, Microsoft uses this design everywhere it can, even stretching the convention to apply it to computer hardware configuration and user management (see Figure A-5).

This type of design has significant merits. First, it's easy to see how items are related. The TreeView suggests the basic levels of grouping and subgrouping. You can often add multiple TreeView levels to combine features that would otherwise be scattered across several different windows. Additionally, you can gather a great deal of information without leaving the window. The ListView pane can be adapted to show a variety of data types without obscuring the navigational controls (the TreeView). This allows users to be at ease. Furthermore, the TreeView/ListView design doesn't enforce any required order for performing tasks, and it employs graphical icons to help break up the monotony of a great deal of information displayed at once.

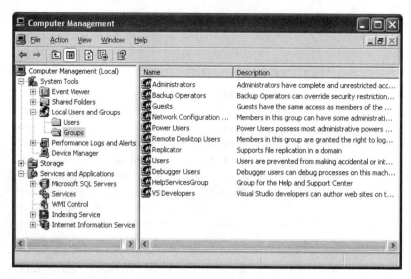

Figure A-5. *An Explorer-like user interface*

This design also has some idiosyncrasies. For example, the menu conventions favor a streamlined Action menu instead of File and Tools menus. Sometimes records are edited in a special window that appears in place of the ListView, and in other cases a separate window pops up to allow the changes. It's also extremely ambitious. It could quickly confuse basic users, who tend to have trouble understanding the relationship between the TreeView and the ListView control. Thus, your decision to use this interface style should depend on your target audience.

In an impressive attempt to achieve standardization, this design is found in almost all of Microsoft's current programs, from SQL Server to Visual Studio. It's an example of a lesser-known yet keenly important Microsoft standard: the Microsoft Management Console (MMC) framework. Currently, you can't create MMC applications in .NET, but you can (and should) follow the organization and conventions for common utility and management tasks like configuring users or browsing a database.

Ultimately, you need to know both your application type and your audience. For example, while the MMC design is ideal for advanced tasks, Microsoft Office provides the canonical rules for document-based applications geared to less-experienced users.

Know Your Application Type

If you can't identify the type of application you are creating, you are in for a rough time. Here are some common types (which are detailed in other chapters of this book):

- **Configuration utility.** This may be based on a single control panel, an MMC or Explorer-like interface, or a sophisticated wizard.

- **Workspace.** The workspace is an "application desktop" that combines a set of features into a common environment that may add some kind of status display. This application type is best suited to sophisticated applications, particularly for proprietary software that may be the only application used on certain workstations.

- **Document editor.** This is one of the most common Windows application types that we're all very familiar with; I mention it here for completeness of common application types.

- **Monitor.** Generally, this is a system tray program that lurks in the background, automatically performing certain tasks when it's directed by the user or when it receives notification from the operating system. For example, a monitor might wait for a file and copy or import it automatically. If you need to interact with this program, you'll typically do so through a context menu for its system tray icon.

- **Data browser.** This is generally organized as an Explorer–type application that lists records and allows you to view and update them.

Know Your User

Different audiences require different degrees of assistance. The user browsing quickly and effortlessly through the intricacies of the Windows registry with regedit.exe is not the same user who turns to Microsoft Agent for help creating a graph. If you are designing a professional application for a specific audience, it may help you to begin by creating a profile that clearly identifies the abilities, expectations, and computer comfort level of the end user.

However, the "know your user" principle is often used as a crutch to excuse complicated interfaces based on the imagined requirements of professional users. As a rule, it is possible to design an interface that combines power-user shortcuts *and* first-time-user guidance. In fact, it's essential. The users of your application will have different requirements when they first use the software (or evaluate it for a potential purchase) than when they master it as part of their daily routine. A good interface recognizes these challenges, and helps guide users as much as necessary without obstructing functionality. For example, consider Microsoft Word, in which novice users find their way around using the menus for clues, intermediate users save clicks with the toolbar icons, and power users can work speedily with shortcut keys and drag and drop. Not only does this interface handle multiple user levels, but it helps users *graduate* from one level to another, because toolbar buttons match menu commands, and menu text includes the relevant shortcut keys.

Warning Be careful not to overestimate the user. The typical programmer spends an incredible amount of time planning and working with an application, and can't really imagine what it would be like to see the application for the first time.

The greatest art of user interface design is creating applications that can be used efficiently by different levels of users. To master this art, you need to know where to impose restrictions and how to handle complexity.

Handling Complexity

Some programmers (and many management types) believe the myth that when users complain that an application is too complicated, it's because a specific feature is not prominently available.

The immediate solution is often just to slap a new button somewhere that will supposedly make it quicker to access features and thus render the program easier to use. Unfortunately, life (and user interface programming) isn't that easy.

For example, consider the sample audio recorder and its "improved" version, both shown in Figure A-6. It may be a little quicker to open and save files in the second version, but is the interface actually easier to use?

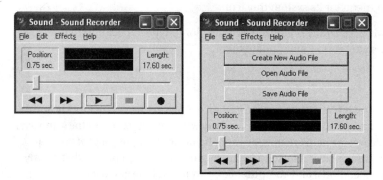

Figure A-6. *Two approaches to an audio recorder*

In reality, when a user complains that an interface is confusing, it's rarely because it lacks a few quick shortcut controls or time-saving features. Rather, it's almost always a sign that the user interface is not logically organized. Adding more buttons to the audio recorder doesn't just make the interface look ugly; it also makes it seem impossibly complicated.

Segmenting Information

Deciding how to divide a product's functionality into separate applications, windows, and controls is the most important user interface decision you will make. One common pattern is to group different types of information into similar management windows. For example, a database application might have an add/remove/configure window for configuring customer records or product records. Other applications use a task-based approach, with a wizard that presents multiple steps leading to a single goal. Before beginning an application, you should identify the most obvious logical divisions, and build your application along those lines.

Some other design principles are outlined here:

- **Use the common Windows analogies.** These are "obvious" metaphors (for example, document icons represent files) and shouldn't require any imagination.

- **Don't let metaphors take over your program.** You shouldn't find a cute way to reuse a metaphor when it will just make a program more confusing. (An example of this problem is the Mac OS's use of a trash can both to delete files and to eject discs.)

- **Use the right controls to offload the work.** Controls like the TreeView, ListView, and DataGrid can handle the basic user interface infrastructure.

- **Hide unnecessary information.**

- **Keep it simple to use.** A program appears logical when it does what the user expects. Keep this in mind, and you can create the illusion of an intuitive program.

Inductive User Interface

Microsoft has a new methodology designed to make user interfaces simpler by breaking features into individual self-explanatory windows. Each window is used for one task, rather than the common combined window that incorporates a set of tasks related to a single type of information. This type of interface, geared toward the lowest (and most common) level of computer user, often combines Web-style forms and requires more windows than usual. At best, it's refreshingly easy to understand; at worst, it's awkward (because it takes multiple clicks to move from page to page and complete a simple operation). Inductive user interface (IUI) design is present, for example, in recent versions of Microsoft Money.

IUI is in its infancy. No clear conventions exist, and it's fairly labor-intensive to design. For most programmers it makes sense to ignore IUI until it is better-established and more conventionalized. You can read the initial IUI guidelines online at `www.msdn.microsoft.com/library/en-us/dnwui/html/iuiguidelines.asp`.

The next generation of the Windows operating system (called Vista) will incorporate an entirely new user interface framework (called Avalon), which will introduce new GUI elements that make it easier to design an IUI. You can get early preview information (and even download beta bits usable on Windows XP and Windows Server 2003) from `www.msdn.microsoft.com/windowsvista/building/presentation`.

Helpful Restrictions

Most programmers fall into the category of "power users" of computer systems. Therefore, it sometimes comes as a surprise when programmers learn that one of the kindest things they can do for a user is to impose restrictions. To a developer, restrictions often seem contrary to the goal of application programming—they make a program less able to do things. However, when you use intelligent restrictions you may curb the overall abilities of your program while increasing the average user's efficiency and confidence.

Restricting the User's Ability to Make a Mistake

If you aren't careful, a great deal of code can be wasted attempting to detect and deal with errors. The problem is that once a user error has occurred, there is no elegant way to report it to the user and help the user continue. No matter how carefully worded or helpful the error message attempts to be, it's likely to make the user feel foolish, guilty, and frustrated. (In fact, usability studies show us that users will probably just click OK or Cancel as soon as the message appears to clear it from the screen, and then try the same thing again.)

It doesn't matter whether you display this message after the user clicks the OK button or (worse yet) as soon as a field loses focus. Mentally, the user has moved on to the next task, and the error message is an interruption.

A better approach is to spend your energy preventing errors from happening in the first place. Here are some examples of how to do this:

- Limit the number of characters a text box can accept, and use the key-press event to make sure invalid characters are ignored.

- Use drop-down lists when the user is selecting one of several predefined choices.

- Disable invalid options. In the case of a complex application with many menu options and toolbars, you may need to centralize this task in some sort of state function or link different user interface elements.

If you must show error messages, don't interrupt the user. Instead, use a polite notification technique (like tooltips). The .NET ErrorProvider makes this easy (see Chapter 25).

■**Tip** Many of these options represent a trade-off between usability and maintainability. For example, enforcing field-length restrictions in a text box can cause quite a headache if the allowed length of the underlying database field changes. A better approach may be to dynamically determine the length of the field from the database when the form first loads. This ensures that you won't need to recompile your code when the database changes, but it also forces you to write (and test) additional code.

Restricting the User's Choices

Another common myth in user interface programming is that the more advanced an application is, the more options it should provide. Some developers even believe that if you can't decide between two different ways to provide a feature, you should do both and allow the user to choose. Unfortunately, this type of logic (deciding not to decide) is shirking your duty as a user interface designer. The end user will not have your in-depth understanding of the application, and may not even know that a configuration option is available or how it works. Adding more options dramatically raises the number of possible problems, and guarantees a lack of consistency across different installations.

The basic rule is that if something appears more complicated, it *is* more complicated. Adding gratuitous options can make simple operations complicated (and intimidating). Think of the incredible complexity of nonconfigurable devices like a car or a microwave. If microwave users had to navigate through a series of menus that gave options about the pitch of the "food ready" beep, the intensity of the interior light, and the time-display mode, the common household appliance would be much more intimidating. Even more-practical enhancements, like allowing the user to fine-tune power levels, preset cooking time a day in advance, or set the platter rotation speed probably aren't worth the added complexity.

Heavily customizable applications also bury genuinely useful options in a slew of miscellaneous, less-important properties. Few users dig through the whole list to find the important options—therefore you actually reduce the usable features of an application as you add extraneous elements. Most options either can be eliminated and handled by a reasonable default, or should graduate to a prominent place where the average user can configure them. Remember that every time you give a user an option, you are forcing the user to make a decision. Many users become increasingly unsettled and less confident as they pass by options they don't understand.

Restricting the User's Imagination

If you've ever worked at a help desk, you probably understand that the human mind thinks in terms of cause and effect. The human desire to identify underlying reasons for events is so strong that users actually invent explanations for mysterious problems or unexpected behavior with their applications, even if these explanations seem wildly fantastical to a more experienced user.

When designing a program, there are various ways to restrict this natural tendency:

- **Give feedback for long tasks.** Some possibilities include a continuously updating dialog-box message, progress bar, or status-bar text. When feedback isn't arriving, most users assume the program isn't working.

- **Show—don't tell.** The average user mistrusts long-winded dialog boxes that explain what will happen next. It's far better to avoid written explanations, and find another way to convey the information (or just direct the user to an important area of the screen). For example, many drawing programs now use thumbnail previews that allow users to see the result of an action before it begins.

- **Avoid the superintelligent interface.** People love to see the demon in the machine. Even in a painstakingly designed application like Microsoft Word, automatic features for capitalizing text and applying formatting often confound users of all levels. Don't assume your application can determine what the user intends to do. Automatic fixes and modifications are not only likely to frustrate users by removing control, but they can also insult users.

- **Always include a print preview.** Just about every user wants to see what the finished product will look like, even when all the information is already on-screen. With .NET, it's easier than ever to create a preview that matches the pagination and formatting of the final copy.

These tips can't redeem a terrible interface. However, if used when needed, they can bridge the gap between an attractive application and one that's truly *usable*.

The Last Word

Creating a user interface requires a blend of common sense, bitter experience, and a little luck. Many other books treat the subject in more detail, and can provide some fascinating reading. One interesting resource is *User Interface Design for Programmers* by Joel Spolsky (Apress, 2001), a short and insightful book. There are also seminal works from Microsoft on Windows conventions, although the most well-known, *Microsoft Windows User Experience* (Microsoft, 1999), is starting to show its age and no longer reflects modern controls and Microsoft's latest trends. Parts of *Microsoft Windows User Experience* can be read online at `www.msdn.microsoft.com/library/en-us/dnwue/html/welcome.asp`.

A large part of this appendix has focused on a back-to-basics approach that stresses organization and logic instead of graphic artistry. However, sometimes it's OK to be cool. The dividing line is usually drawn between productivity applications and entertainment. For example, Winamp can get away with a highly proprietary interface, but you might find that the market for skinnable word processors isn't nearly as large.

APPENDIX B

■ ■ ■

ClickOnce

.**N**ET has dramatically changed the way rich client applications are deployed. In .NET 1.x the central story was *no-touch deployment*—the ability to deploy a Windows Forms application by simply copying its assemblies to the target computer (or placing them in a shared network drive), with no component registration required. In .NET 2.0 the same no-touch deployment model remains. However, .NET 2.0 also builds on this model with a new setup technology called ClickOnce.

ClickOnce has the same key benefit as no-touch deployment: there's no component registration required. It also has the same stumbling block—namely, it works only if the target computer already has the .NET Framework installed. However, the ClickOnce bootstrapper can install .NET and other prerequisites more-or-less seamlessly, provided the user who's performing the installation is an administrator.

ClickOnce adds a few new features to the no-touch deployment model:

- **It generates setup UI automatically.** In other words, you publish a ClickOnce application, and the .NET Framework creates the setup wizard that guides the user through the installation process. The setup wizard not only copies the application; it also handles other niceties like creating a shortcut in the Start menu.

- **It manages the update process as well as the installation process.** Here you have a variety of options as to when updates are made and whether they are mandatory. For example, you can configure an application so that every time it's launched, it checks the original site where it was published for a new version.

- **It's integrated with code access security.** ClickOnce makes it possible to deploy applications in partial trust scenarios. That means a nonadministrator user can install an application from a third-party site, and be secure in the knowledge that the application is prevented from undertaking potentially dangerous actions like reading and writing local files.

Although this book is primarily concerned with creating user interfaces, not deploying them, ClickOnce is still worth a quick look. Fortunately, you can learn all the basics with a quick tour. In this chapter, you'll use ClickOnce to deploy applications and handle several common setup scenarios.

The Ground Rules

Although ClickOnce allows for a fair bit of customization, some details never change. Before you start using ClickOnce, it's important to get an understanding of the basic model and its limitations.

ClickOnce is designed with a specific type of application in mind—line-of-business applications and internal company software. Typically, these applications perform their work with the data and services on middle-tier server computers. As a result, they don't need privileged access to the local computer. These applications are also deployed in enterprise environments that may include thousands of workstations. In these environments, the cost of application deployment and updating isn't trivial, especially if it needs to be handled by an administrator. As you'll see, this reality has shaped the ClickOnce technology into a simple, straightforward enterprise software deployment system for .NET applications. However, ClickOnce technology isn't designed to replace the more-sophisticated setup applications you can create using MSI (Microsoft Installer).

ClickOnce may also make sense for consumer applications that are deployed over the Web, particularly if these applications are updated frequently and don't have extensive installation requirements. However, the limitations of ClickOnce (such as the lack of flexibility for customizing the setup wizard) don't make it practical for sophisticated consumer applications that have detailed setup requirements or need to guide the user through a set of proprietary configuration steps.

The ClickOnce Installation Model

Although ClickOnce supports several types of deployment, the overall model is designed to make Web deployment practical and easy. Here's how it works. You use Visual Studio to publish your ClickOnce application to a Web server. Then, the user surfs to an automatically generated Web page (named publish.htm) that provides a link to install the application. When the user clicks that link, the application is downloaded, installed, and added to the Start menu. Figure B-1 shows this process.

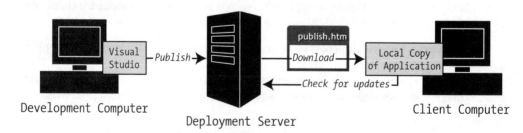

Figure B-1. *Installing a ClickOnce application*

Although ClickOnce is ideal for Web deployment, the same basic model lends itself to other scenarios, including the following:

- Deploying your application from a network file share.

- Deploying your application from a CD or DVD.

- Deploying your application to a Web server or network file share, and then sending a link to the setup program via e-mail.

When deploying to network file share or a CD or DVD, the installation Web page isn't created. Instead, users install the application by running the setup.exe program directly.

The most interesting part of a ClickOnce deployment is the way it supports updating. Essentially, you (the developer) have control over several update settings. For example, you can configure the application to check for updates automatically or periodically at certain intervals. You can even configure your application to use a Web-like online-only mode. In this situation, the application *must* be launched from the ClickOnce Web page. The application is still cached locally for optimum performance, but users won't be able to run the application unless they're able to connect to the site where the application was published. This ensures that users always run the latest, most up-to-date version of your application.

ClickOnce Requirements

To successfully install an application with ClickOnce, the target computer must meet these minimum requirements:

- Windows 98 or later, excluding Windows NT 4

- .NET Framework 2.0 runtime

The second requirement isn't as limiting as it might seem. The .NET Framework can be installed in a variety of ways, including via the Windows Update feature, and with enterprise distribution systems like Microsoft Systems Management Server (SMS). However, the most attractive option is to use the *bootstrapping* functionality that's part of all ClickOnce applications.

Essentially, it works like this: When you launch the setup.exe program for an application, the bootstrapper runs first. It checks to see if the system requirements are met. If the .NET Framework runtime isn't installed, the bootstrapper launches that installation, either from Microsoft's Web site or from an installation file that you've chosen to include with the setup. The only limitation is that the .NET Framework setup requires administrator privileges, unlike most ClickOnce applications. Once the prerequisites are installed, the application setup is launched automatically.

Note In this chapter, you'll frequently see the term *ClickOnce application*. However, this is just shorthand to indicate an application that's deployed through ClickOnce. The application itself doesn't require any change in code or configuration.

ClickOnce Limitations

ClickOnce is designed to be a lighter setup option than MSI-based setups. As a result, ClickOnce deployment doesn't allow for much configuration. Many aspects of its behavior are completely fixed, either to guarantee a consistent user experience or to encourage enterprise-friendly security policies.

The limitations of ClickOnce include the following:

- ClickOnce applications are installed for a single user. You cannot install an application for all users on a workstation.

- ClickOnce applications are always installed in a system-managed user-specific folder. You cannot change or influence the folder where the application is installed.

- If ClickOnce applications are installed in the Start menu, they show up as a single shortcut in the form [Publisher Name] ➤ [Product Name]. You can't change this, nor can you add additional shortcuts, like a shortcut for a help file, related Web site, or an uninstall feature. Similarly, you can't add a ClickOnce application to the Startup group, the Favorites menu, and so on.

- You can't change the user interface of the setup wizard. That means you can't add new dialogs, change the wording of existing ones, and so on.

- You can't change the installation page that ClickOnce applications generate. However, you can edit the HTML by hand after it's generated.

- A ClickOnce setup can't install shared components in the GAC (global assembly cache).

- A ClickOnce setup can't perform custom actions (like creating a database, registering file types, or configuring registry settings).

You can work around some of these issues. For example, you could configure your application to register custom file types or set registry defaults the first time it's launched on a new computer. However, if you have complex setup requirements, you're much better off creating a full-fledged MSI (Microsoft Installer) setup program. You can use a third-party tool, or you can create a Setup Project in Visual Studio. Both of these options are beyond the scope of this book.

A Simple ClickOnce Deployment

The easiest way to publish an application through ClickOnce is to choose Build ➤ Publish [ProjectName] from the Visual Studio menu, which walks you through a short wizard. This wizard doesn't give you access to all the ClickOnce features you'll learn about in this appendix, but it's a quick way to get started.

The first choice you're faced with in the publishing wizard is choosing the location where you want to publish the application (see Figure B-2).

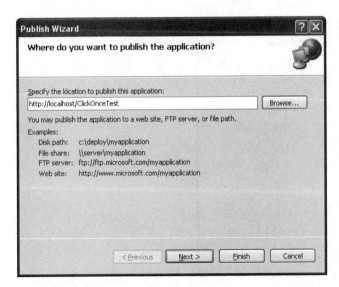

Figure B-2. *Choosing a publish location*

There's nothing particularly important about the location where you first publish your application, because this isn't necessarily the same location you'll use to host the setup files later on. In other words, you could publish to a local directory, and then transfer the files to a Web server. The only caveat is that you need to know the ultimate destination of your files when you run the publishing wizard, because you need to supply this information. Without it, the automatic update feature won't work.

Of course, you could choose to publish the application directly to its final destination, but it's not necessary. In fact, building the installation locally is often the easiest option.

Choosing a Location

To get a better sense for how this works, start by choosing a local file path location (like c:\Temp\ClickOnceApp). Then click Next. You're now faced with the real question—where users will go to install this application (see Figure B-3).

This bit is very important, because it influences your update strategy. The choices you make are stored in a manifest file that's deployed with your application.

■Note There is one case in which you won't see the dialog in Figure B-3. If you enter a virtual directory to a Web server for the publish location (in other words, a URL starting with http://), the wizard assumes this is the final installation location.

In Figure B-3, you have essentially three choices. You can create an installation for a network file share, a Web server, or CD or DVD media. The following sections explain each approach.

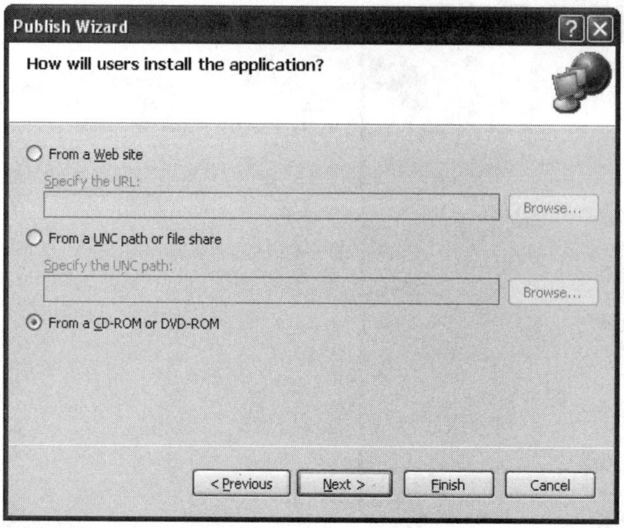

Figure B-3. *Choosing the installation type*

Publishing for a Network File Share

In this case, all the users in your network will access the installation by browsing to a specific UNC path and running a file named setup.exe at that location.

A UNC path is a network path in the form \\ComputerName\ShareName. You can't use a networked drive, because networked drives depend on system settings (so different users might have their drives mapped differently). To provide automatic updates, the ClickOnce infrastructure needs to know *exactly* where it can find the installation files, because this is also the location where you'll deploy updates.

Publishing for a Web Server

You can create an installation for a Web server on a local intranet or the Internet. Visual Studio will generate an HTML file named publish.htm that simplifies the process. Users request this page in a browser, and click a link to download and install the application.

You have several options for transferring your files to a Web server. If you want to take a two-step approach (publish the files locally and then transfer them to the right location), you simply need to copy the files from the local directory to your Web server using the appropriate mechanism (like FTP). Make sure you preserve the directory structure.

If you want to publish your files straight to the Web server without any advance testing, you have two choices. If you are using IIS (Internet Information Services), and the current account you're running has the necessary permissions to create a new virtual directory on the Web server (or upload files to an existing one), you can publish files straight to your Web server. Just supply the virtual directory path in the first step of the wizard. For example, you could use the publish location http://ComputerName/VirtualDirectoryName (in the case of an intranet) or http://DomainName/VirtualDirectoryName (for a server on the Internet).

You can also publish straight to a Web server using FTP. This is often required in Internet (rather than intranet) scenarios. In this case, Visual Studio will contact your Web server and transfer the ClickOnce files over FTP. You'll be prompted for user and password information when you connect.

Note FTP is used to transfer files—it's not used for the actual installation process. Instead, the idea is that the files you upload become visible on some Web server, and users install the application from the publish.htm file on that Web server. As a result, when you use an FTP path in the first step of the wizard (Figure B-1), you'll still need to supply the corresponding Web URL in the second step (Figure B-2). This is important, because the ClickOnce publication needs to return to this location to perform its automatic update checks.

Publishing for a CD or DVD

If you choose to publish to setup media like a CD or DVD, you still need to decide whether you plan to support the automatic update feature. Some organizations will use CD-based deployment exclusively, while others will use it to supplement their existing Web-based or networked-based deployment. You choose which option applies for use in the third step of the wizard (see Figure B-4).

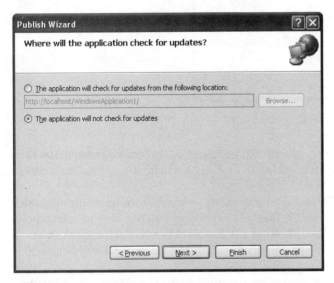

Figure B-4. *Support for automatic updates*

Here, you have a choice. You can supply a URL or UNC path that the application will check for updates. This assumes that you plan to publish the application to that location. Alternatively, you can leave out this information and bypass the automatic update feature altogether.

Note The publishing wizard doesn't give you an option for how often to check for updates. By default, ClickOnce applications check for an update whenever they're launched. If a new version is found, they prompt the user to install it before launching the application. You'll learn how to change these settings later in this appendix.

Online or Offline

If you're creating a deployment for a Web server or network share, you'll get one additional option, as shown in Figure B-5.

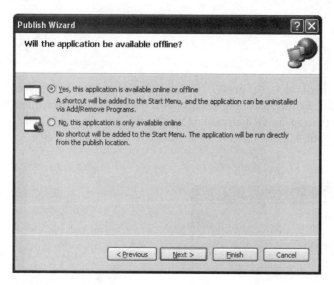

Figure B-5. *Support for offline use*

The default choice is to create an online/offline application that runs whether or not the user can connect to the published location. In this case, a shortcut for the application is added to the start menu.

If you choose to create an online-only application, the user needs to return to the published location to run the application. (To help make this clear, the publish.htm Web page will show a button labeled Run instead of Install.) This ensures that an old version of the application can't be used after you roll out an update. This part of the deployment model is analogous to a Web application.

When you create an online-only application, the application will still be downloaded (into a locally cached location) the first time it's launched. Thus, while startup times may be longer (because of the initial download), the application will still run as quickly as any other installed Windows application. However, the application can't be launched when the user isn't connected to the network or Internet, which makes it unsuitable for mobile users (such as laptop users who don't always have an Internet connection available).

If you choose to create an application that supports offline use, the setup program will add a Start menu shortcut. The user can launch the application from this shortcut, regardless of whether the computer is online or offline. If the computer is online, the application will check for new versions in the location where the application was published. If an update exists, the application will prompt the user to install it. You'll learn how to configure this policy later on.

Note If you choose to publish for a CD installation, you don't have the option of creating an online-only application.

This is the final choice in the publishing wizard. Click Next to see the final summary, and Finish to generate the deployment files and copy them to the location you chose in step 1.

Deployed Files

ClickOnce uses a fairly straightforward directory structure. It creates a setup.exe file in the location you chose, and a subdirectory for the application.

For example, if you deployed an application named ClickOnceTest to the location c:\ClickOnceTest, you'll end up with files like these:

c:\ClickOnceTest\setup.exe

c:\ClickOnceTest\publish.htm

c:\ClickOnceTest\ClickOnceTest.application

c:\ClickOnceTest\ClickOnceTest_1_0_0_0.application

c:\ClickOnceTest\ClickOnceTest_1_0_0_0\ClickOnceTest.exe.deploy

c:\ClickOnceTest\ClickOnceTest_1_0_0_0\ClickOnceTest.exe.manifest

The publish.htm file is present only if you're deploying to a Web server. The .manifest and .application files store information about required files, update settings, and other details. (You can get a low-level look at these files and their XML file in the MSDN Help.) The .manifest and .application files are digitally signed at the time of publication, so these files can't be modified by hand. If you do make a change, ClickOnce will notice the discrepancy and refuse to install the application.

As you publish newer versions of your application, ClickOnce adds new subdirectories for each new version. For example, if you change the publish version of your application to 1.0.0.1, you'll get a new directory like this:

c:\ClickOnceTest\ClickOnceTest_1_0_0_1\ClickOnceTest.exe.deploy

c:\ClickOnceTest\ClickOnceTest_1_0_0_1\ClickOnceTest.exe.manifest

When you run the setup.exe program, it handles the process of installing any prerequisites (like the .NET Framework) and then installs the most recent version of your application.

Installing a ClickOnce Application

To see ClickOnce in action with a Web deployment, follow these steps:

1. Make sure you have the optional IIS Web server component installed. Choose Settings ➤ Control Panel ➤ Add or Remove Programs from the Start menu, choose the Add/Remove Windows Components section, and scroll through the list until you find Internet Information Services (IIS). This option must be checked.

2. Using Visual Studio, create a basic Windows application and compile it.

3. Launch the publishing wizard (by choosing Build ➤ Publish), and select http:// localhost/ClickOnceTest for the publish location. The localhost portion of the URL points to the current computer. As long as IIS is installed and you are running with sufficient privileges, Visual Studio will be able to create this virtual directory.

4. Choose to create an online and offline application, and then click Finish to end the wizard. The files will be deployed to a folder named ClickOnceTest in the IIS Web server root (by default, the directory c:\Inetpub\wwwroot).

5. Run the setup.exe program directly, or load up the publish.htm page (shown in Figure B-6) and click Install. You'll receive a security message asking if you want to trust the application (similar to when you download an ActiveX control in a Web browser).

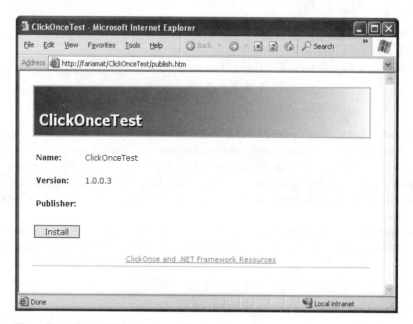

Figure B-6. *The publish.htm installation page*

6. If you choose to continue, the application will be downloaded and you'll be asked to verify that you want to install it.

7. Once the application is installed, you can run it from the Start menu shortcut or uninstall it using the Add/Remove Programs window.

The shortcut for ClickOnce applications isn't the standard shortcut you're probably accustomed to. Instead, it's an *application reference*—a text file with information about the application name and the location of the deployment files. The actual program files for your application are stored in a location that's difficult to find and impossible to control. The location follows this pattern:

```
c:\Documents and Settings\[UserName]\Local Settings\Apps\2.0\[...]\[...]\[...]
```

The final three portions of this path are opaque, automatically generated strings like C6VLXKCE.828. Clearly, you aren't expected to access this directory directly.

Updating a ClickOnce Application

To see how a ClickOnce application can update itself automatically, follow these steps with the installation from the previous example:

1. Make a minor but noticeable change in the application (for example, adding a button).

2. Recompile the application and republish it to the same location.

3. Run the application from the Start menu. The application will detect the new version, and ask you if you'd like to install it (see Figure B-7).

4. Once you accept the update, the new version of the application will install and start.

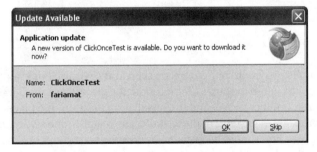

Figure B-7. *Detecting a newer version of a ClickOnce application*

In the following sections, you'll learn how to customize some additional ClickOnce options.

■**Note** The ClickOnce engine, dfsvc.exe, handles updates and downloads.

ClickOnce Options

The publishing wizard is a quick way to create a ClickOnce deployment, but it doesn't allow you to adjust all the possible options. To get access to more ClickOnce settings, double-click the Properties node in the Solution Explorer, and then click the Publish tab. You'll see the settings shown in Figure B-8.

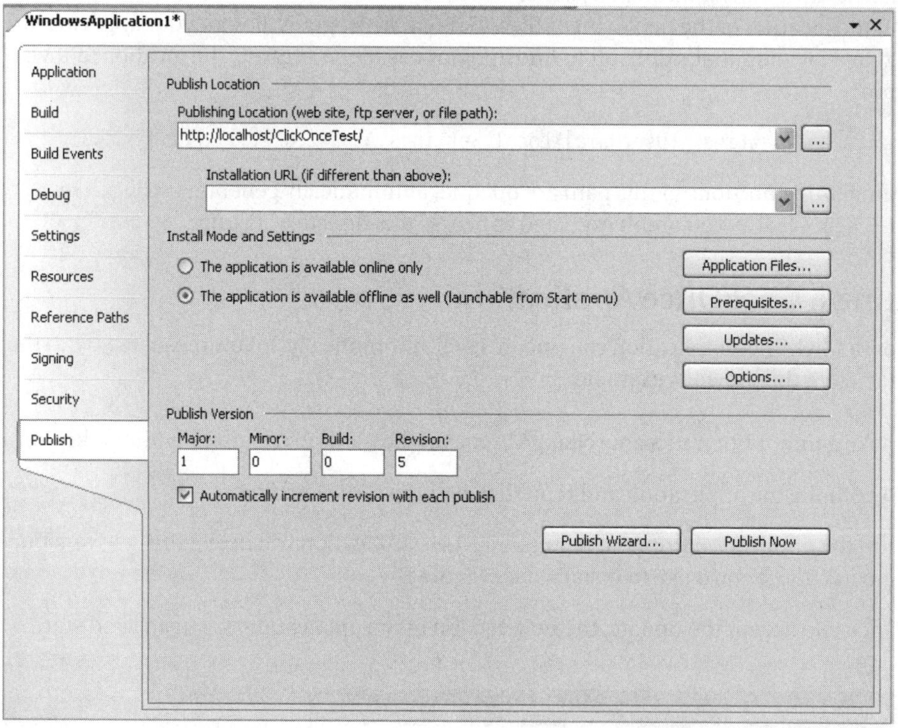

Figure B-8. *ClickOnce project settings*

Some of these settings duplicate details you've already seen in the wizard. For example, the first two text boxes allow you to choose the publishing location (the place where the ClickOnce files will be placed, as set in step 1 of the wizard) and the installation location (the place from which the user will run the setup, as set in step 2 of the wizard). The Install Mode setting allows you to choose whether the application should be installed on the local computer or run in an online-only mode, as described earlier in this appendix. At the bottom of the window, the Publish Wizard... button launches the wizard you saw earlier, and the Publish Now button publishes the project using the previous settings.

The following sections discuss the settings that you haven't already seen.

Publish Version

The Publish Version section sets the version of your application that's stored in the ClickOnce manifest file. This isn't the same as the assembly version, which you can set in the Application tab, although you might set both to match.

The key difference is that the publish version is the criteria that's used to determine whether a new update is available. If a user launches version 1.5.0.0 of an application and version 1.5.0.1 is available, the ClickOnce infrastructure will show the update dialog box (Figure B-7).

By default, the Automatically Increment Revision with Each Publish check box is set, in which case the final part of the publish version (the revision number) is incremented by 1 after each publication, so 1.0.0.0 becomes 1.0.0.1, then 1.0.0.2, and so on. If you want to publish the same version of your application to multiple locations using Visual Studio, you should switch off this option. However, keep in mind that the automatic update feature springs into action only if it finds a higher version number. The date stamp on the deployed files has no effect (and isn't reliable).

It may seem horribly inelegant to track separate assembly and publication version numbers. However, there are cases where it makes sense. For example, while testing an application you may want to keep the assembly version number fixed without preventing testers from getting the latest version. In this case, you can use the same assembly version number but keep the autoincrementing publish version number. When you're ready to release an official update, you can set the assembly version and the publish version to match. Also, a published application might contain multiple assemblies with different version numbers. In this case, it wouldn't be realistic to use the assembly version number—instead, the ClickOnce infrastructure needs to consider a single version number to determine whether an update is warranted.

Updates

Click the Updates button to show the Application Updates dialog box (Figure B-9), where you can choose your update strategy.

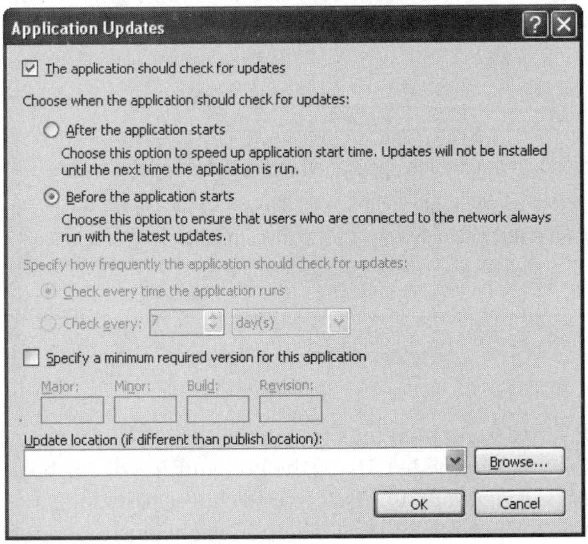

Figure B-9. *Setting update options*

Note The Updates button isn't available if you're creating an online-only application. An online-only application always runs from its published location on a Web site or network share.

You first choose whether the application performs update checking. If it does, you can choose *when* updates are performed. You have two options:

- **Before the application starts.** If you use this model, the ClickOnce infrastructure checks for an application update (on the Web site or network share) every time the user runs the application. If an update is detected, it's installed and *then* the application is launched. This option is a good choice if you want to make sure the user gets an update as soon as it's available.

- **After the application starts.** If you use this model, the ClickOnce infrastructure checks for a new update after the application is launched. If an updated version is detected, this version is installed the *next* time the user starts the application. This is the recommended option for most applications, because it improves load times.

If you choose to perform checks after the application starts, the check is performed in the background. You can choose to perform it every time the application is run (the default option), or in less-frequent intervals. For example, you can limit checks to once per number of hours, days, or weeks.

You can also specify a minimum required version. You can use this to make updates mandatory. For example, if you set the publish version to 1.5.0.1 and the minimum version to 1.5.0.0 and then publish your application, any user who has a version older than 1.5.0.0 will be forced to update before being allowed to run the application. (By default there is no minimum version and all updates are optional.)

Note Even if you specify a minimum version and require the application to check for updates before starting, a user could end up running an old version of your application. This happens if the user is offline, in which case the update check will fail without an error. The only way around this limitation is to create an online-only application.

Prerequisites

By default, every ClickOnce setup checks for certain prerequisites (namely, the .NET Framework), and then directs the user to install them as needed. Using the Prerequisites dialog box, you can choose additional prerequisites (see Figure B-10). You can also choose to include prerequisites along with your setup files in the publish location. This option obviously requires more space, but it make sense in some scenarios—for example, if you want to create a CD setup that can be installed even if the target computer isn't online.

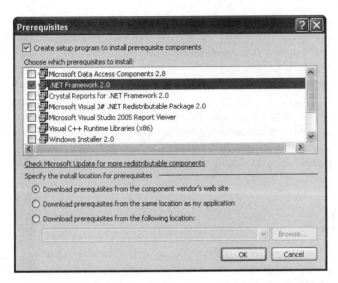

Figure B-10. *Possible prerequisites for a ClickOnce application*

Options

The Options dialog box has a slew of miscellaneous options (see Figure B-11).

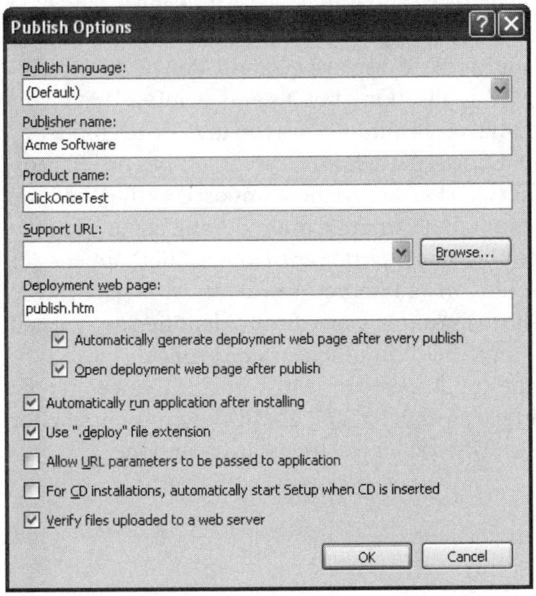

Figure B-11. *Miscellaneous ClickOnce options*

The publisher and product names are used to create the Start menu hierarchy. In the example shown in B-12, the shortcut will be generated as Start ➤ Acme Software ➤ ClickOnceTest. This information also turns up with the application information in the Add/Remove Programs dialog box, along with the support URL.

You can also use the Options dialog box to change the name of the installation page in Web deployments (which is publish.htm by default), and you can choose whether you want Visual Studio to launch this page automatically after a successful publication (presumably so you can test it). Two more options give you control over how the setup works—allowing you to set whether the application is launched automatically once it's installed, and whether an autorun.inf file should be generated to tell CD players to launch the setup program immediately when the CD is inserted into the CD drive.

ClickOnce Security

ClickOnce security is based on the *code access security* system in .NET. Code access security acts like a configurable sandbox that restricts the abilities of a .NET application based on certain details, such as where it came from, who created it, and so on. Taken together, these details are called *evidence*.

When you run a .NET application, the code access security system compares the evidence of an application to the current security policy to determine what permissions it should have. For example, if an application is signed as being created by Microsoft, the security policy may grant a wide range of permissions on it. Although there may be a multitude of different rules applied to different evidence, the most-restrictive security settings come into effect, which means an application ends up with the smallest possible permission set. Permissions are fine-grained—they can restrict everything from reading a file to displaying information on the screen.

Code access security is in effect for all .NET applications, but it's easy to miss. That's because applications that are launched from the local computer are run in *full trust* mode, which means they can do anything they want. Code access security essentially has no effect on applications in full trust mode. Of course, other checks (such as those imposed by the Windows operating system based on the Windows account that's running the code) still come into play.

In some situations, an application can be placed into *partial trust* mode. This happens, for example, if you launch an executable that resides on an Internet Web server without saving it to the local hard drive first (unless the Web site in question is specifically identified as a trusted site according to the current security policy), or if the computer has been explicitly locked down with policy rules. In these situations, the application runs with a greatly reduced set of permissions. If the application tries to undertake an action that it doesn't have permission for (like writing to a local file), the code access security system will throw an exception.

ClickOnce Security Prompts

Partial trust mode comes into play with a ClickOnce application, depending on how you deploy the application. If the ClickOnce installation is launched from a CD drive, it's always launched with full trust. But if it's launched from an intranet site, the permissions are scaled down. If it's launched from an Internet site, the permissions are ratcheted down even more.

This has the potential to significantly complicate deployment. For example, it could make Web-based installations impractical by restricting their abilities so significantly that they can't perform anything practical. Microsoft's solution is to give the user the ability to escalate the permission level of a ClickOnce application when it's installed. Essentially, ClickOnce combines the evidence about your application with the security policy and compares it to the permissions you require (which are full trust, by default). If the permissions you require are within the permission set that's already been granted, the user won't see any message. However, if your application needs more permissions than it already has (for example, it's being installed from an untrusted Web server and it needs the ability to read and write to files), users will see a security prompt informing them and asking them if they want to grant the full set of permissions (assuming they're not restricted from doing so by the security policy on the machine). In this way, ClickOnce is reasonably secure—it restricts what an application can do unless it's being installed from a trusted location or the user explicitly accepts the risk.

Partial Trust and ClickOnce

As explained earlier, ClickOnce applications are set to require full trust by default. This introduces a couple of problems.

First, it guarantees that users will see the security message unless they're running the installation from a CD or local file path. More significantly, it violates the principle of *least privilege*, which states that your application should only be able to do what it needs to do. This is an excellent security guideline, particularly for enterprise applications (although it's often complex to implement in practice). If you follow the principle of least privilege, it greatly reduces the possibility that your application will be used or abused (deliberately or inadvertently) in a way you didn't intend that may harm the system.

To deal with these problems, you can explicitly configure the permission set that your application should have, as described in the next section.

Configuring for Partial Trust

You may want to follow the principle of least privilege and configure your application to run with the minimum permission set it needs. You can configure the required permissions in Visual Studio as part of the project properties. Here's how it works:

1. Double-click the Properties node in the Solution Explorer and choose the Security tab (see Figure B-12).

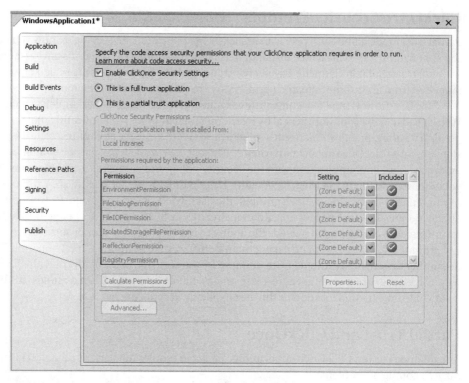

Figure B-12. *The default ClickOnce security settings*

2. Select the This Is a Partial Trust Application radio button and choose a security zone from the Zone list. This is the starting point for your security configuration, and you should choose the zone based on where you plan to publish your application. If you plan to use more than one zone (for example, an Internet Web server and a CD), choose the zone with the least permissions (Internet). If you want to start with a blank slate and add each permission you need, choose Custom.

3. Once you choose a zone, the Permissions list is updated with the default permissions for that zone. If the permission is included, it's shown with a green check mark.

4. Now you can adjust individual permissions by excluding those you don't need or configuring them in more detail (by clicking the Properties button). For example, if you need file access to a specific path only, you can configure the FileIOPermission to allow just this location. You can also add the permissions that you do need but that aren't included in your zone. This will lead to a security prompt that the user must accept when the application is installed.

■Tip You can use the Permissions Calculator tool to quickly assess all the permissions your application needs. Just click the Calculate Permissions button. Once the Permission Calculator has analyzed your application, it will adjust your permission settings accordingly. However, you should review the permissions that are determined by the Permission Calculator, because they may be broader than required. For example, the Permission Calculator may determine that you need FileIOPermission for the local hard drive, when really you need this permission only for a single, specific directory.

5. Once you're finished, publish the application.

Remember, the default level of trust given to an application depends on the location from which it's being installed. When an application is deployed from the Internet it receives a highly restrictive set of permissions, when it's deployed from a local intranet it receives greater permissions, and when it's deployed from a CD-ROM it receives full trust permissions. If an application needs more permissions than its zone allows, the user will be prompted to grant these permissions at install time.

■Tip To reduce the permissions you require, you may want to store user-specific files in the dedicated ClickOnce data directory. Each ClickOnce application has an isolated data directory, and you can retrieve it at runtime by calling AppDomain.GetData(). As with the ClickOnce application itself, the data directory is user-specific.

The Last Word

This chapter offered a quick tour of the new ClickOnce deployment model. It's provided you enough information to evaluate whether ClickOnce will work in your environment, and it's given you a taste of how ClickOnce deals with code access security. If you want to build a partial trust ClickOnce application, you'll find that the model takes some getting used to. You'll need to aggressively review the permission requirements of your application, and accept compromises about certain client-configuration details you can't control. To learn more about ClickOnce, refer to the MSDN Help or to the FAQ on the subject at http://www.windowsforms.net/FAQs.

Index

forums.apress.com

JOIN THE APRESS FORUMS AND BE PART OF OUR COMMUNITY. You'll find discussions that cover topics of interest to IT professionals, programmers, and enthusiasts just like you. If you post a query to one of our forums, you can expect that some of the best minds in the business—especially Apress authors, who all write with *The Expert's Voice*™—will chime in to help you. Why not aim to become one of our most valuable participants (MVPs) and win cool stuff? Here's a sampling of what you'll find:

DATABASES
Data drives everything.

Share information, exchange ideas, and discuss any database programming or administration issues.

PROGRAMMING/BUSINESS
Unfortunately, it is.

Talk about the Apress line of books that cover software methodology, best practices, and how programmers interact with the "suits."

INTERNET TECHNOLOGIES AND NETWORKING
Try living without plumbing (and eventually IPv6).

Talk about networking topics including protocols, design, administration, wireless, wired, storage, backup, certifications, trends, and new technologies.

WEB DEVELOPMENT/DESIGN
Ugly doesn't cut it anymore, and CGI is absurd.

Help is in sight for your site. Find design solutions for your projects and get ideas for building an interactive Web site.

JAVA
We've come a long way from the old Oak tree.

Hang out and discuss Java in whatever flavor you choose: J2SE, J2EE, J2ME, Jakarta, and so on.

SECURITY
Lots of bad guys out there—the good guys need help.

Discuss computer and network security issues here. Just don't let anyone else know the answers!

MAC OS X
All about the Zen of OS X.

OS X is both the present and the future for Mac apps. Make suggestions, offer up ideas, or boast about your new hardware.

TECHNOLOGY IN ACTION
Cool things. Fun things.

It's after hours. It's time to play. Whether you're into LEGO® MINDSTORMS™ or turning an old PC into a DVR, this is where technology turns into fun.

OPEN SOURCE
Source code is good; understanding (open) source is better.

Discuss open source technologies and related topics such as PHP, MySQL, Linux, Perl, Apache, Python, and more.

WINDOWS
No defenestration here.

Ask questions about all aspects of Windows programming, get help on Microsoft technologies covered in Apress books, or provide feedback on any Apress Windows book.

HOW TO PARTICIPATE:
Go to the Apress Forums site at **http://forums.apress.com/**.
Click the New User link.